STREET ATLAS
Nottinghamshire

www.philips-maps.co.uk
First published in 1994 by
Philip's, a division of
Octopus Publishing Group Ltd
www.octopusbooks.co.uk
Endeavour House, 189 Shaftesbury Avenue
London WC2H 8JY
An Hachette UK Company
www.hachette.co.uk

Third colour edition 2006
Third impression 2011
NOTCB

ISBN 978-0-540-08840-9 (spiral)

© Philip's 2008

Ordnance Survey®

This product includes mapping data licensed
from Ordnance Survey® with the permission
of the Controller of Her Majesty's Stationery
Office. © Crown copyright 2008. All rights
reserved. Licence number 100011710.

Contents

III	**Key to map symbols**
IV	**Key to map pages**
VI	**Route planning**
X	Administrative and Postcode boundaries

1	**Street maps** at 3½ inches to 1 mile
221	**Approach map of Nottingham**
222	**Street map of Nottingham city centre** at 7 inches to 1 mile

| 224 | **Index** of towns and villages |
| 225 | **Index** of towns, villages, streets, hospitals, industrial estates, railway stations, schools, shopping centres, universities and places of interest |

Digital Data

The exceptionally high-quality mapping found in this atlas is available as digital data in TIFF format, which is easily convertible to other bitmapped (raster) image formats.

The index is also available in digital form as a standard database table. It contains all the details found in the printed index together with the National Grid reference for the map square in which each entry is named.

For further information and to discuss your requirements, please contact philips@mapsinternational.co.uk

D1475968

(22a)	**Motorway** with junction number
	Primary route – dual/single carriageway
	A road – dual/single carriageway
	B road – dual/single carriageway
	Minor road – dual/single carriageway
	Other minor road – dual/single carriageway
	Road under construction
	Tunnel, covered road
	Rural track, private road or narrow road in urban area
	Gate or obstruction to traffic (restrictions may not apply at all times or to all vehicles)
	Path, bridleway, byway open to all traffic, road used as a public path
	Pedestrianised area
DY7	**Postcode boundaries**
	County and unitary authority boundaries
	Railway, tunnel, railway under construction
	Tramway, tramway under construction
	Miniature railway
Walsall	**Railway station**
	Private railway station
South Shields	**Metro station**
	Tram stop, tram stop under construction
	Bus, coach station

◆	**Ambulance station**
◆	**Coastguard station**
◆	**Fire station**
◆	**Police station**
✚	**Accident and Emergency entrance to hospital**
H	**Hospital**
✚	**Place of worship**
i	**Information Centre** (open all year)
⛬	**Shopping Centre**
P P&R	**Parking, Park and Ride**
PO	**Post Office**
⛺ 🚐	**Camping site, caravan site**
▶	**Golf course**
✕	**Picnic site**
Prim Sch	**Important buildings, schools, colleges, universities and hospitals**
	Built up area
	Woods
River Ouse	**Tidal water, water name**
	Non-tidal water – lake, river, canal or stream
⟨ I ⟩⊂⊏	**Lock, weir, tunnel**
Church	**Non-Roman antiquity**
ROMAN FORT	**Roman antiquity**
◀87	**Adjoining page indicators and overlap bands** The colour of the arrow and the band indicates the scale of the adjoining or overlapping page (see scales below)
246	

Enlarged mapping only

	Railway or bus station building
	Place of interest
	Parkland

Abbrev	Full	Abbrev	Full	Abbrev	Full
Acad	**Academy**	Inst	**Institute**	Recn Gd	**Recreation Ground**
Allot Gdns	**Allotments**	Ct	**Law Court**		
Cemy	**Cemetery**	L Ctr	**Leisure Centre**	Resr	**Reservoir**
C Ctr	**Civic Centre**	LC	**Level Crossing**	Ret Pk	**Retail Park**
CH	**Club House**	Liby	**Library**	Sch	**School**
Coll	**College**	Mkt	**Market**	Sh Ctr	**Shopping Centre**
Crem	**Crematorium**	Meml	**Memorial**	TH	**Town Hall/House**
Ent	**Enterprise**	Mon	**Monument**	Trad Est	**Trading Estate**
Ex H	**Exhibition Hall**	Mus	**Museum**	Univ	**University**
Ind Est	**Industrial Estate**	Obsy	**Observatory**	W Twr	**Water Tower**
IRB Sta	**Inshore Rescue Boat Station**	Pal	**Royal Palace**	Wks	**Works**
		PH	**Public House**	YH	**Youth Hostel**

■ The small numbers around the edges of the maps identify the 1 kilometre National Grid lines
■ The dark grey border on the inside edge of some pages indicates that the mapping does not continue onto the adjacent page

The scale of the maps on the pages numbered in blue is 5.52 cm to 1 km • 3½ inches to 1 mile • 1: 18103	0 ¼ ½ ¾ 1 mile 0 250m 500m 750m 1 kilometre
The scale of the maps on pages numbered in red is 11.04 cm to 1 km • 7 inches to 1 mile • 1: 9051	0 220 yards 440 yards 660 yards ½ mile 0 125m 250m 375m ½ kilometre

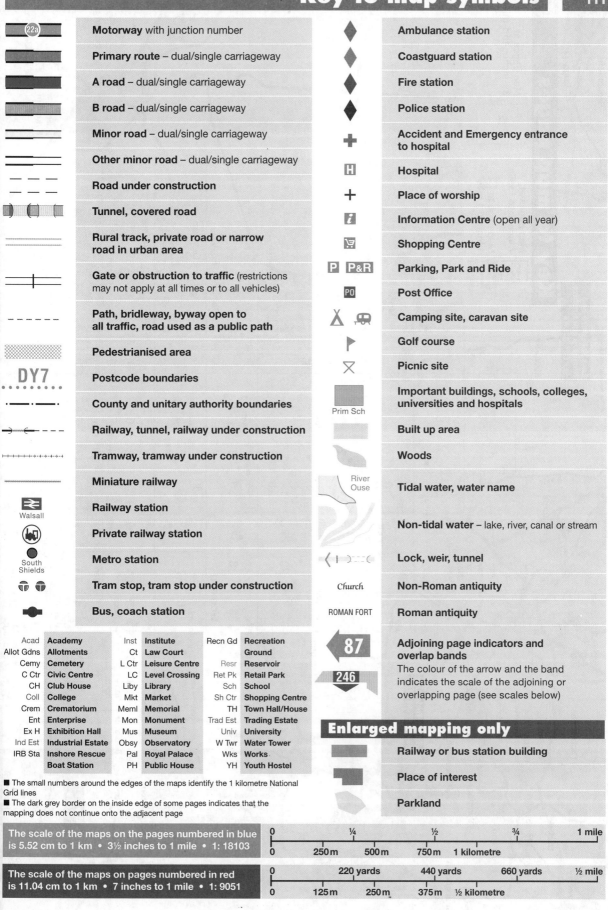

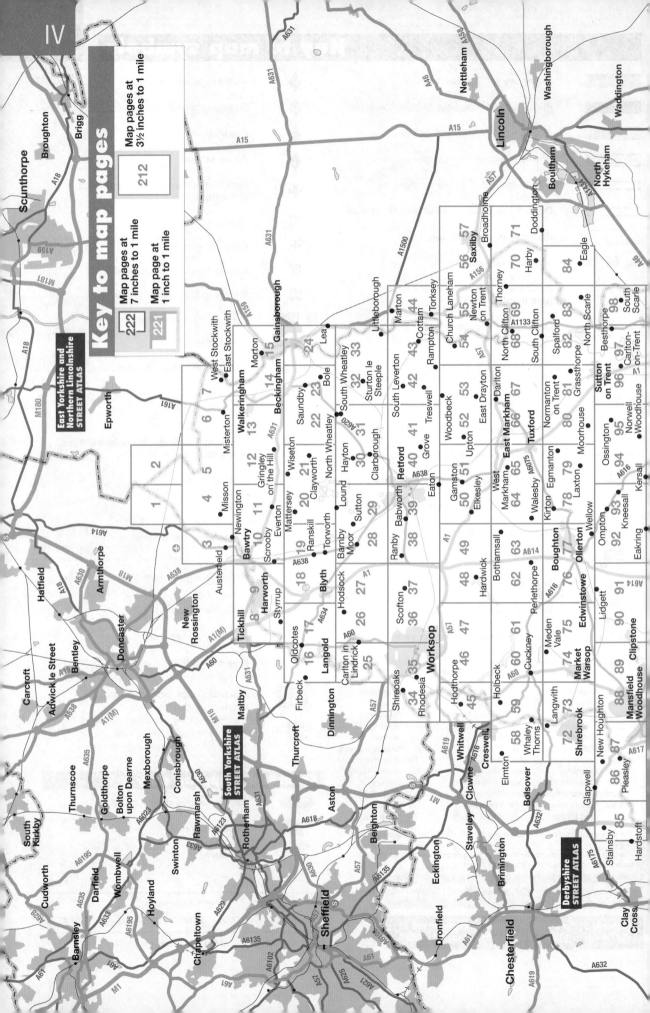

Key to map pages

Map pages at 3½ inches to 1 mile 212

Map pages at 7 inches to 1 mile 222

Map page at 1 inch to 1 mile 221

East Yorkshire and Northern Lincolnshire STREET ATLAS

South Yorkshire STREET ATLAS

Derbyshire STREET ATLAS

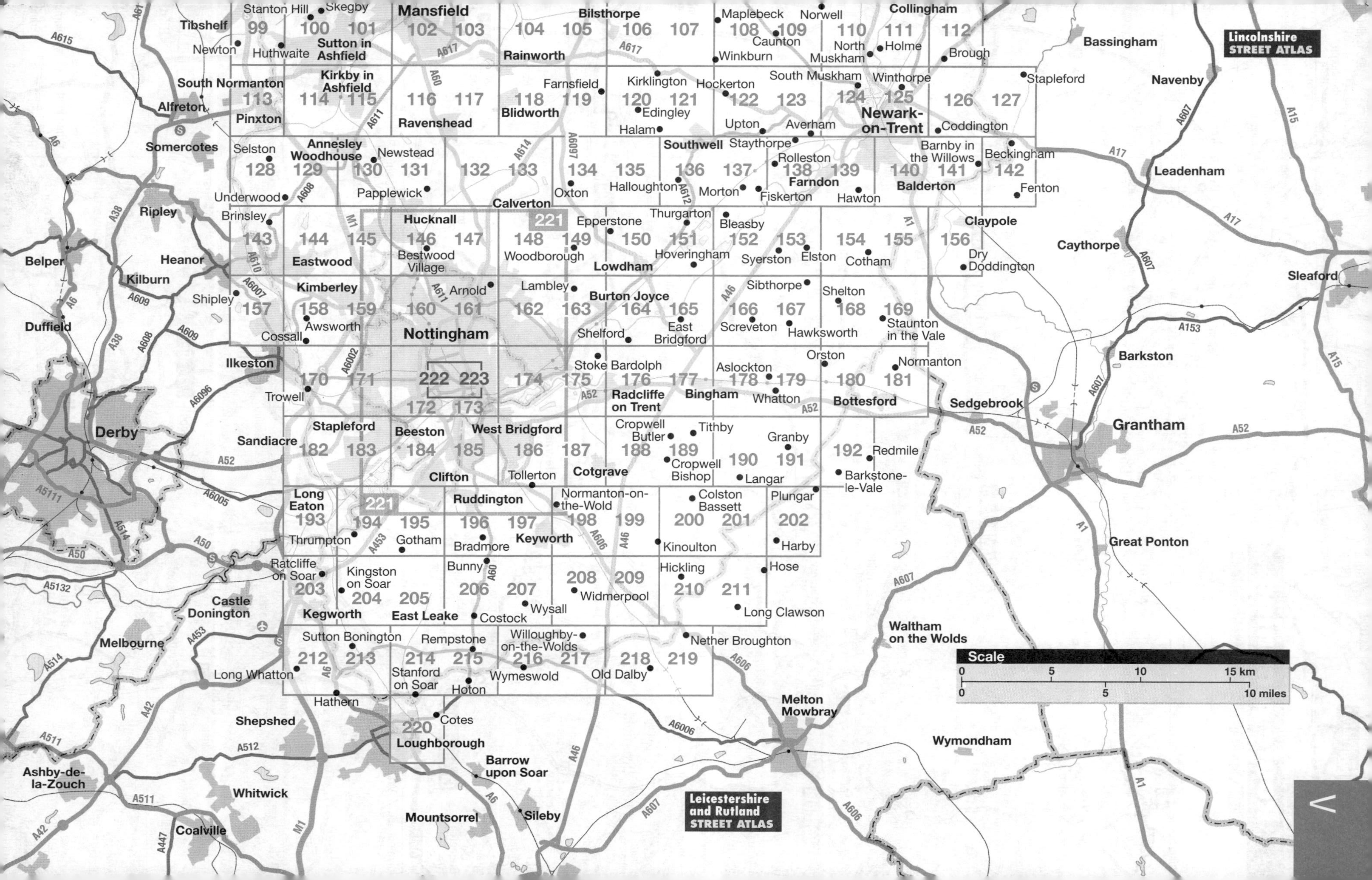
Lincolnshire STREET ATLAS
Leicestershire and Rutland STREET ATLAS
Scale
0 5 10 15 km
0 5 10 miles
Mansfield
Sutton in Ashfield
Kirkby in Ashfield
Rainworth
Bilsthorpe
Blidworth
Ravenshead
Farnsfield
Collingham
Newark-on-Trent
Southwell
Calverton
Hucknall
Eastwood
Kimberley
Nottingham
Lowdham
Burton Joyce
Radcliffe on Trent
Bingham
Bottesford
West Bridgford
Beeston
Stapleford
Clifton
Cotgrave
Ruddington
Keyworth
Long Eaton
Kegworth
East Leake
Loughborough
Farndon
Balderton
Claypole
Annesley Woodhouse
Pinxton
South Normanton
Tibshelf
Alfreton
Somercotes
Ripley
Heanor
Kilburn
Belper
Duffield
Derby
Ilkeston
Sandiacre
Castle Donington
Melbourne
Shepshed
Whitwick
Coalville
Ashby-de-la-Zouch
Mountsorrel
Sileby
Barrow upon Soar
Melton Mowbray
Wymondham
Waltham on the Wolds
Great Ponton
Grantham
Sedgebrook
Barkston
Caythorpe
Sleaford
Leadenham
Navenby
Bassingham
Stanton Hill
Skegby
Newton
Huthwaite
Selston
Newstead
Underwood
Papplewick
Brinsley
Bestwood Village
Arnold
Shipley
Awsworth
Cossall
Trowell
Stapleford
Thrumpton
Gotham
Bradmore
Bunny
Ratcliffe on Soar
Kingston on Soar
Costock
Wysall
Widmerpool
Sutton Bonington
Rempstone
Willoughby-on-the-Wolds
Wymeswold
Stanford on Soar
Hoton
Hathern
Cotes
Long Whatton
Old Dalby
Nether Broughton
Long Clawson
Hickling
Hose
Kinoulton
Harby
Plungar
Colston Bassett
Normanton-on-the-Wold
Tollerton
Cropwell Butler
Cropwell Bishop
Tithby
Langar
Granby
Redmile
Barkstone-le-Vale
Normanton
Orston
Whatton
Aslockton
Stoke Bardolph
Shelford
East Bridgford
Screveton
Hawksworth
Staunton in the Vale
Shelton
Sibthorpe
Lambley
Woodborough
Epperstone
Thurgarton
Hoveringham
Bleasby
Syerston
Elston
Cotham
Dry Doddington
Oxton
Halloughton
Morton
Fiskerton
Rolleston
Hawton
Staythorpe
Averham
Upton
Halam
Edingley
Kirklington
Hockerton
South Muskham
North Muskham
Winthorpe
Holme
Brough
Coddington
Barnby in the Willows
Beckingham
Fenton
Stapleford
Maplebeck
Caunton
Winkburn
Norwell
99 100 101 102 103 104 105 106 107 108 109 110 111 112
113 114 115 116 117 118 119 120 121 122 123 124 125 126 127
128 129 130 131 132 133 134 135 136 137 138 139 140 141 142
143 144 145 146 147 148 149 150 151 152 153 154 155 156
157 158 159 160 161 162 163 164 165 166 167 168 169
170 171 222 223 172 173 174 175 176 177 178 179 180 181
182 183 184 185 186 187 188 189 190 191 192
193 194 195 196 197 198 199 200 201 202
203 204 205 206 207 208 209 210 211
212 213 214 215 216 217 218 219
220
221
A1 A6 A15 A17 A38 A42 A46 A50 A52 A60 A61 A153 A447 A453 A511 A512 A514 A606 A607 A608 A609 A610 A611 A612 A614 A615 A617 A5111 A5132 A6002 A6005 A6006 A6007 A6096 A6097 M1

Route planning

Scale

0   5   10 km

0   2   4   6 miles

X

Administrative and Postcode boundaries

County and unitary authority boundaries
District boundaries
Postcode boundaries
Area covered by this atlas

North Lincolnshire

SE
SK

Doncaster

DN9

Misson
Misterton

DN10
Walkeringham

DN11
Harworth
Bawtry
Everton
Beckingham
DN21
Gainsborough

Sheffield

Rotherham

Langold
Ranskill
North Wheatley
Lea

Carlton in Lindrick
Blyth
Lound
Hayton
Sturton le Steeple
Marton

S81
Bassetlaw
Ranby
Retford

Worksop
Eaton
Rampton
Fenton
Saxilby

Hodthorpe
S80
Hardwick
Elkesley
DN22
East Drayton
LN1

Carburton
East Markham
South Clifton
Harby
LN6
Doddington

Whaley Thorns
Walesby
Tuxford
Weston
LN6
Eagle
North Scarle

NG20
Market Warsop
Boughton
Laxton

Shirebrook
Edwinstowe
Ollerton
Sutton on Trent
Besthorpe

Stainsby
S44
NG19
Mansfield Woodhouse
Nottinghamshire
Collingham

Teversal
Clipstone
Eakring
NG23

Mansfield
Mansfield
Bilsthorpe
Norwell

Tibshelf
Sutton in Ashfield
NG18
Holme
Stapleford

Newton
NG21
Newark and Sherwood
LN6

DE55
NG17
Rainworth
Blidworth
Farnsfield
Beckingham

South Normanton
Kirkby in Ashfield
Ravenshead
Southwell
Upton
Newark-on-Trent
LN5

Pinxton
Newstead
Oxton
NG25
Morton
Balderton
Fenton

Jacksdale
Ashfield
NG15
Calverton
NG14
Farndon
Claypole

Eastwood
NG16
Hucknall
Gedling
NG5
Lowdham
Elston
NG23
Dry Doddington

Shipley
NG6
Arnold
Lambley
Burton Joyce
Sibthorpe
NG23
Lincolnshire

DE75
Kimberley
Bulwell
East Bridgford

DE7
Ilkeston
2
NG8
1
NG3
Carlton
Bingham
Orston
Normanton
Bottesford

NG1
Nottingham
Radcliffe on Trent
Whatton
NG13

NG7
NG2
Cotgrave
Langar
Plungar

City of Derby
Stapleford
NG9
Beeston
Toton
Rushcliffe
NG12
Kinoulton
Harby

Long Eaton
Clifton
Ruddington
Keyworth
Hose

Sawley
NG10
Gotham
Bunny
Hickling
Long Clawson

Ratcliffe on Soar
NG11
Willoughby-on-the-Wolds
LE14

DE74
East Leake
Long Whatton
Kegworth
LE12
Hoton
Wymeswold
Old Dalby

Hathern

Loughborough
Cotes

LE11

Leicestershire

Rutland

1 City of Nottingham
2 Broxtowe

Derbyshire

Scale				
0	5	10	15	20 km
0		5		10 miles

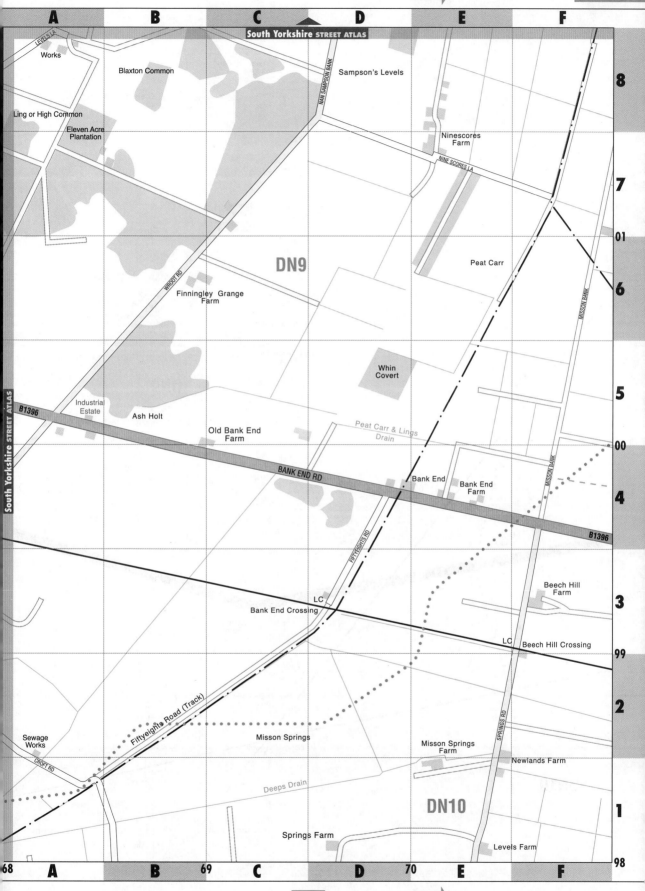

2

A B C D E F

South Yorkshire STREET ATLAS

South Yorkshire STREET ATLAS

Works

Blaxton Common

Sampson's Levels

Ling or High Common

Eleven Acre Plantation

Ninescores Farm

NINE SCORES LA

NAN SAMPSON BANK

DN9

Peat Carr

MISSON BANK

WROOT RD

Finningley Grange Farm

Whin Covert

B1396

Industrial Estate

Ash Holt

Old Bank End Farm

Peat Carr & Lings Drain

MISSON BANK

BANK END RD

Bank End

Bank End Farm

B1396

FIFTYEIGHTS RD

Beech Hill Farm

LC

Bank End Crossing

LC Beech Hill Crossing

Fiftyeights Road (Track)

SPRINGS RD

Sewage Works

Misson Springs

Misson Springs Farm

Newlands Farm

CROFT RD

Deeps Drain

DN10

Springs Farm

Levels Farm

68 A B 69 C D 70 E F 98

8
01
7
6
5
00
4
3
99
2
1

4 2

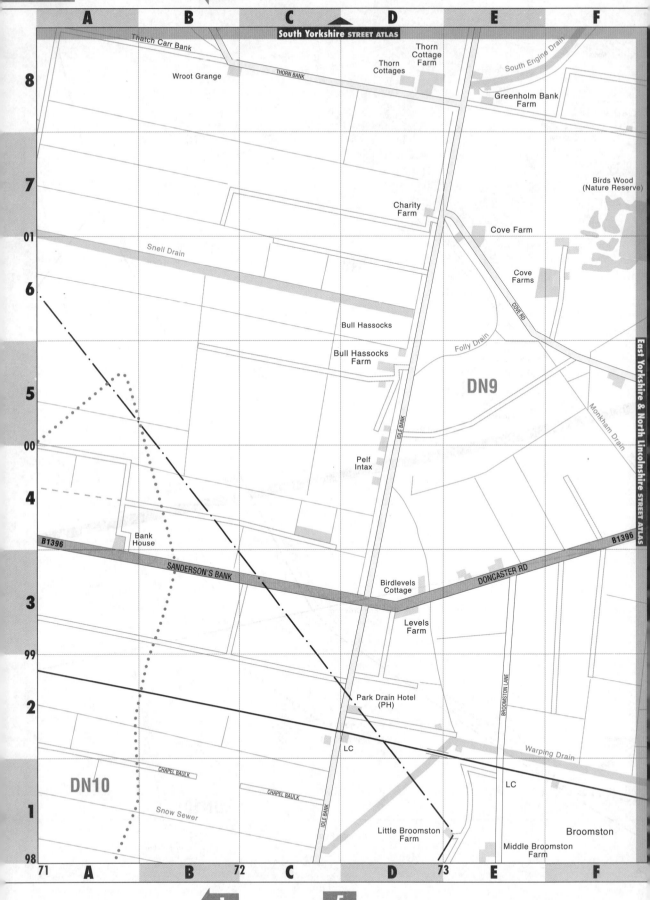

South Yorkshire STREET ATLAS

East Yorkshire & North Lincolnshire STREET ATLAS

Thatch Carr Bank

Wroot Grange

THORN BANK

Thorn Cottages

Thorn Cottage Farm

South Engine Drain

Greenholm Bank Farm

Birds Wood (Nature Reserve)

Charity Farm

Cove Farm

Cove Farms

COVE RD

Snell Drain

Bull Hassocks

Bull Hassocks Farm

Folly Drain

DN9

Monkham Drain

IDLE BANK

Pelf Intax

Bank House

B1396

B1396

SANDERSON'S BANK

Birdlevels Cottage

DONCASTER RD

Levels Farm

BROOMSTON LANE

Park Drain Hotel (PH)

LC

Warping Drain

LC

DN10

CHAPEL BAULK

CHAPEL BAULK

Snow Sewer

IDLE BANK

Little Broomston Farm

Broomston

Middle Broomston Farm

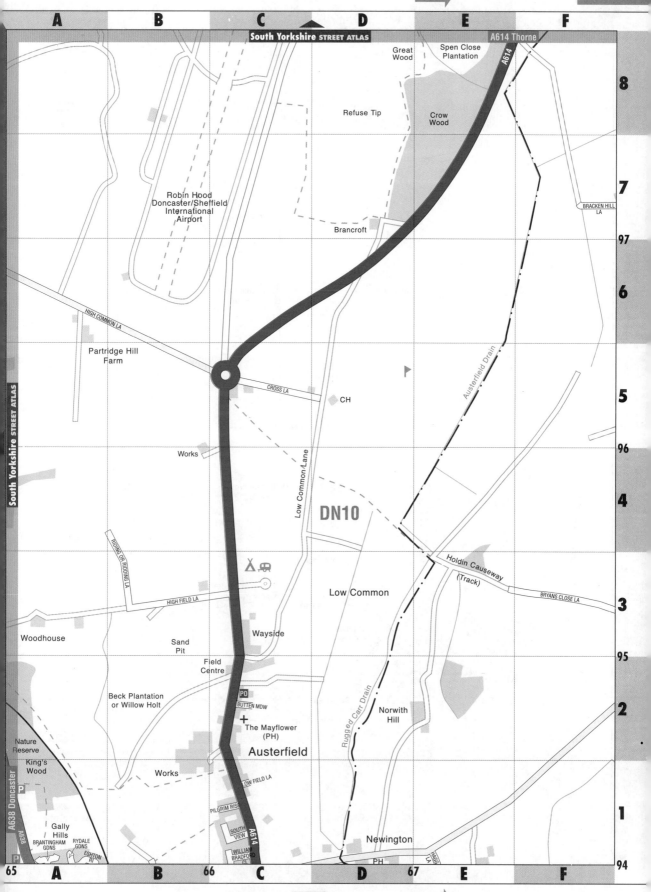

South Yorkshire STREET ATLAS

A614 Thorne

Great Wood

Spen Close Plantation

Refuse Tip

Crow Wood

Robin Hood Doncaster/Sheffield International Airport

Brancroft

BRACKEN HILL LA

HIGH COMMON LA

Partridge Hill Farm

Austerfield Drain

CROSS LA

CH

Low Common Lane

Works

DN10

RIDING OR RIDDING LA

Holdin Causeway

(Track)

HIGH FIELD LA

BRYANS CLOSE LA

Low Common

Woodhouse

Sand Pit

Wayside

Field Centre

Rugged Carr Drain

PO

BUTTEN MDW

Beck Plantation or Willow Holt

+ The Mayflower (PH)

Norwith Hill

Austerfield

Nature Reserve

King's Wood

Works

LOW FIELD LA

A638 Doncaster

P

Gally Hills

BRANTINGHAM GDNS

RYDALE GDNS

ESHTON RI

PILGRIM RISE

SOUTH VIEW

WILLIAM BRADFORD CL

A614

Newington

HIGG LA

PH

P

A638

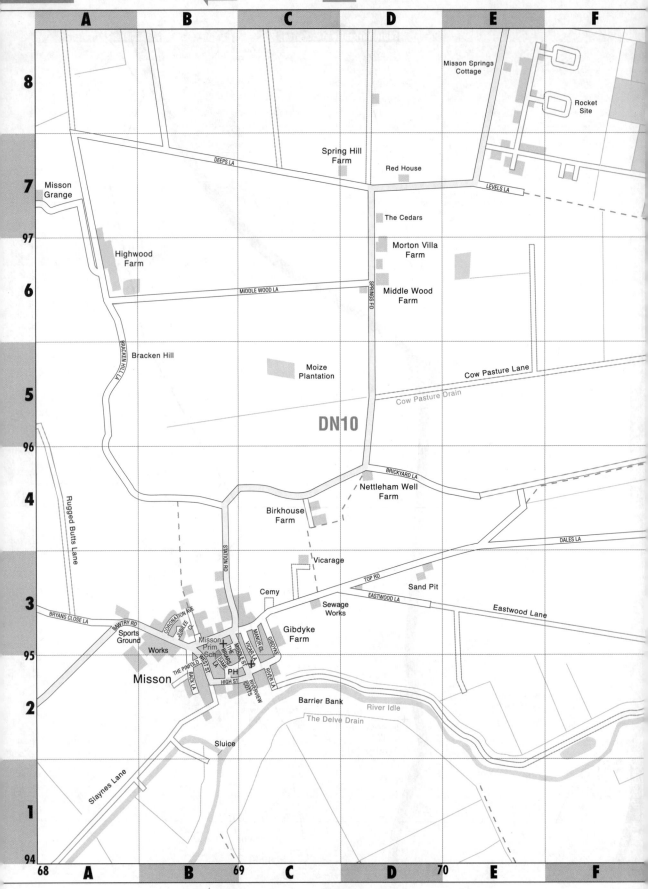

A B C D E F

8

DEEPS LA

Spring Hill
Farm

Red House

Misson Springs
Cottage

Rocket
Site

7

Misson
Grange

LEVELS LA

97

The Cedars

Highwood
Farm

Morton Villa
Farm

6

MIDDLE WOOD LA

SPRINGS FD

Middle Wood
Farm

Bracken Hill

BRACKEN HILL LA

Moize
Plantation

Cow Pasture Lane

5

Cow Pasture Drain

DN10

96

Rugged Butts Lane

BRICKYARD LA

4

Nettleham Well
Farm

Birkhouse
Farm

DALES LA

STATION RD

Vicarage

3

BRYANS CLOSE LA

Cemy

Sewage
Works

TOP RD

Sand Pit

EASTWOOD LA

Eastwood Lane

BAWTRY RD

CORONATION AVE

JUBILEE CL

Sports
Ground

Works

Misson
Prim Sch

THE BRAINS

MANOR CL

VICAR LA

GIBDYKE

Gibdyke
Farm

95

THE PINFOLD

WEST ST

DAME LA

MIDDLE ST

BACK LA

HIGH ST

PH

COTTS

RIVERVIEW

RIVER LA

Misson

Barrier Bank

River Idle

2

The Delve Drain

Sluice

Slaynes Lane

1

94

68 A B 69 C D 70 E F

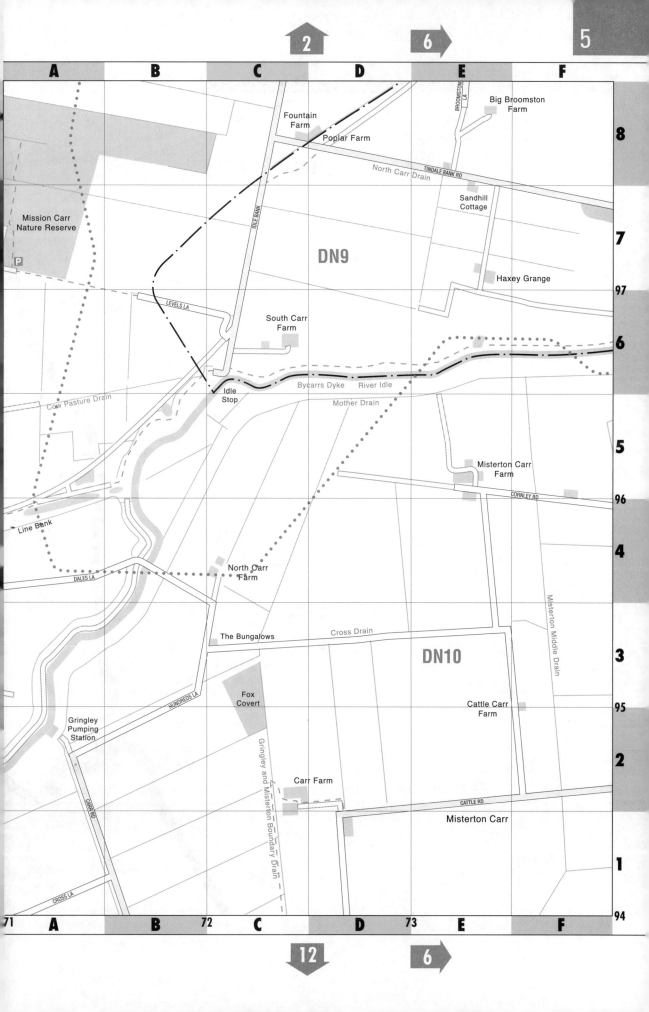

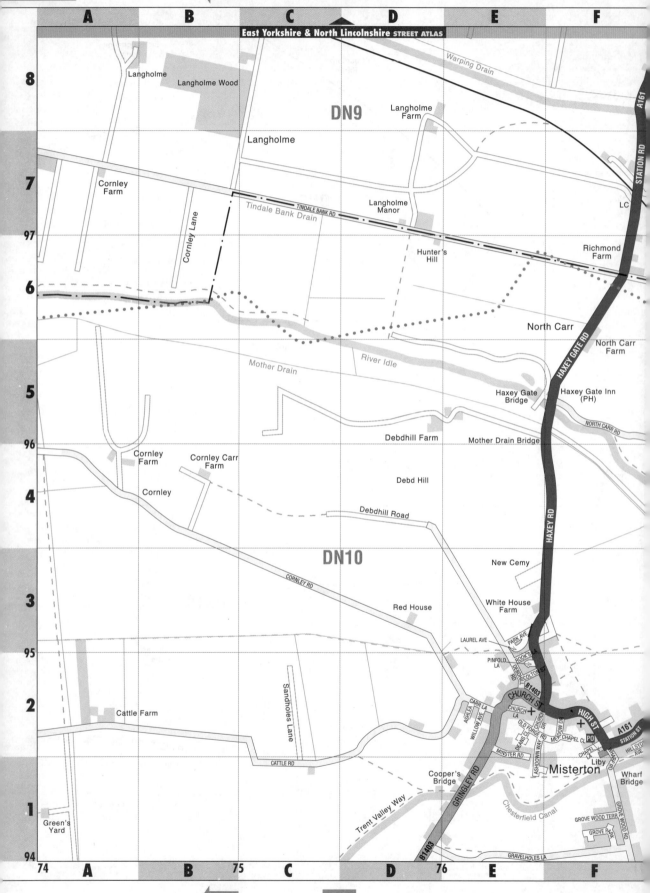

A   B   C   D   E   F

8

Langholme

Langholme Wood

DN9

Langholme Farm

Langholme

7

Cornley Farm

Cornley Lane

Langholme Manor

Warping Drain

A161

STATION RD

LC

97

TINDALE BANK RD

Tindale Bank Drain

Hunter's Hill

Richmond Farm

6

North Carr

North Carr Farm

Mother Drain

River Idle

HAXEY GATE RD

5

Haxey Gate Bridge

Haxey Gate Inn (PH)

96

Cornley Farm

Cornley Carr Farm

Debdhill Farm

Mother Drain Bridge

NORTH CARR RD

4

Cornley

Debd Hill

HAXEY RD

Debdhill Road

DN10

New Cemy

3

CORNLEY RD

Red House

White House Farm

LAUREL AVE

PARK AVE

95

PINFOLD LA

ROOK'S LA

COLTON ST

B1403

CHURCH ST

HIGH ST

2

Cattle Farm

Sandholes Lane

CARR LA

ASH LA

WILLOW AVE

CHURCH LA

OLD FORGE RD

MILL DR

CHURCH DR

MC CROWN DR

CHAPEL CL

A161

STATION ST

PO

MINSTER RD

ASHDOWN WAY

DEANS CL

CHAPEL LA

HILLSIDE AVE

CATTLE RD

Liby

Misterton

1

Green's Yard

Cooper's Bridge

GRINGLEY RD

Trent Valley Way

Chesterfield Canal

GROVE WOOD TERR

GROVE WOOD RD

GROVE PARK

Wharf Bridge

94

B1403

GRAVELHOLES LA

74   A   B   75   C   D   76   E   F

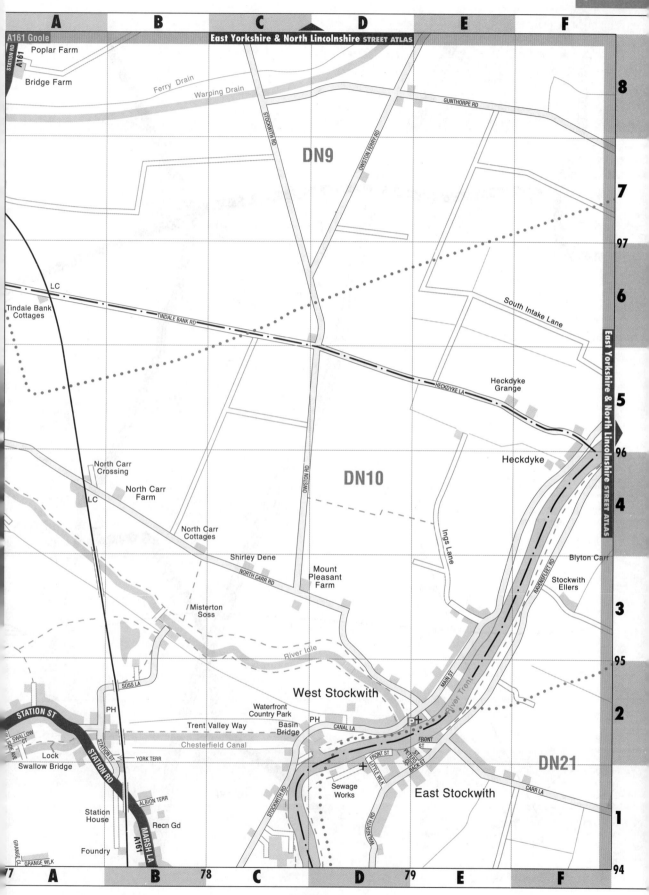

A161 Goole

Poplar Farm

Bridge Farm

STATION RD

A161

Ferry Drain

Warping Drain

STOCKWITH RD

OWSTON FERRY RD

GUNTHORPE RD

DN9

8

7

97

LC

Tindale Bank Cottages

TINDALE BANK RD

South Intake Lane

6

Heckdyke Grange

HECKDYKE LA

5

96

Heckdyke

North Carr Crossing

LC

North Carr Farm

OWSTON RD

DN10

Blyton Carr

RAVENSFLEET RD

Stockwith Ellers

North Carr Cottages

Shirley Dene

NORTH CARR RD

Mount Pleasant Farm

Ings Lane

4

3

Misterton Soss

River Idle

95

SOSS LA

West Stockwith

Waterfront Country Park

Trent Valley Way

Basin Bridge

PH

CANAL LA

MAIN ST

River Trent

PH

P

FRONT ST

2

STATION ST

SWALLOW CT

INGS IDE AVE

Lock

Swallow Bridge

STATION RD

York Terr

Chesterfield Canal

STOCKWITH RD

FRONT ST

PETER ST

BACK ST

LITTLE WLK

DN21

East Stockwith

CARR LA

Station House

ALBION TERR

Recn Gd

A161

MARSH LA

Sewage Works

WALKERITH RD

1

GRANGE CL

GRANGE WLK

Foundry

94

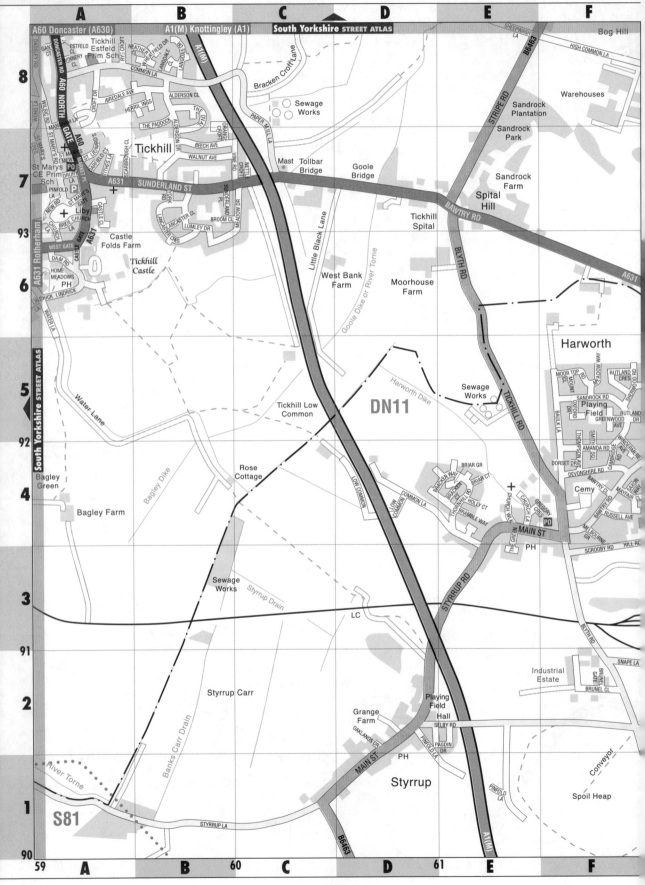

South Yorkshire STREET ATLAS

A B C D E F

8

7

93

6

5

92

4

3

91

2

1

90

DN11

A631

BAWTRY RD

Swinnow Wood

Tickhill Grange
Cottages

High Common
Farm

HIGH COMMON LA

Tickhill Grange

Warehouses

Martin Beck
Lane

Plumtree Farm
Ind Est

PLUMTREE RD

Caravan
Park

Playing
Field

Plumtree Farm

Bircotes &
Harworth
Comm Sch

GALWAY AVE

GALWAY DR

Recn
Gd

WELBECK RD

LINDSEY RD

GRANGE VIEW

GRANGE DR

BAWTRY RD

THORESBY

DORCHESTER CT

1 BALMORAL CT
2 SANDRINGHAM CT
3 STRATHMORE CT
4 WINDSOR CT
5 HARDWICK CT
6 BROOKSIDE WLK
7 HAREWOOD CT
8 CHATSWORTH CT
9 ARUNDEL WLK

WHITBY RD

BEECH RD

EAST ST

WEST ST

FESTIVAL AVE

YORK

BEVERLEY RD

HOLDERNESS CL

SANDYMOUNT WEST

SANDYMOUNT YORK

SANDYMOUNT EAST

GROSVENOR RD

WOODSIDE

RAYTON CL

ALEXANDRA RD

GILBERT RD

SNIPE PARK RD

CREWE RD

SHREWSBURY RD

SWINNOW RD

NORFOLK DR

WHITE HOUSE RD

WHITE HOUSE DR

DROVERSDALE RD

NORFOLK RD

ESSEX RD

ESSEX DR

SUFFOLK RD

SUFFOLK AVE

CUMBERLAND CL

WESTMORLAND CT

MILNE DR

Bircotes
L Ctr

St Patrick's
RC Prim Sch

Bircotes
L Ctr

North Border Inf
& Jun Schs

Harworth CE
Prim Sch

Liby
PO

TALBOT RD

HOWARD RD

WHITESLACK RD

THE CRESCENT

CHURCH RD

MONCKTON RD

MILNE AVE

NORFOLK RD

MILNE RD

Bircotes

SCROOBY RD

HILL TOP

COURT

HILL RD

COLLIERY RD

Sports
Ground

Droversdale
Wood

Spoil Heap

Ruins
Plantation

South
Carr

Sowcarr

Gibbet
Hill

White House
Plantation

Lady Holt Lane

Hawk's
Nest

A638

GREAT NORTH RD

A614

GIBBET HILL LA

MILE LA

South Carr
Farm

Riverside
Farm

Colliery

SNAPE LA

Works

Lords
Wood

Layland
Plantation

Coronation
Clump

Penny
Acre

River Ryton

Bawtry Lodge

Broom
Hill

The
Holt

GREAT NORTH RD

A638

SARACEN LA

Neale's
Covert

Playing
Field

BLYTH RD

Triangle

Steer Bank
Farm

A614 BAWTRY RD

Harworth
Lodge

Round
Holt

Roman Bank
Earthwork

DN10

Fish Pond
Wood

WEST WOOD
ESTATE

WESTWOOD RD

Menagerie
Wood

TICKHILL RD

A631

BELGRAVE CT 1
PORTMAN CT 2

BLENHEIM RISE 3
CARLTON DR 4
RICHMOND LA 5

BINBROOK CT

BEAUFORT GDNS

CHEYNE WLK

MADISON DR

CAVENDISH CL

YORK RD

BEDFORD RD

SALCOMBE GR

MALHAM

NEWLINGTON

LANDSEER

GRANGE AVE

INGHAM RD

SHINING
CLIFF CT

HERMES CL

ARGOSY CL

MARTIN LA

ST MARTIN'S
AVE

MARTIN LA

MAPLE GR

YEW TREE DR

LILAC GR

ASH TREE
AVE

SYCAMORE
CRES

CHESTNUT DR

ELM TREE
DR

OAK TREE RD

LIME TREE CRES

HIGH
MEADOW

62 63 64

A B C D E F

Newington

GRANGE AVE
INGHAM RD
WESTERN WLK
ST MARTINS AVE
HAREWOOD DR
BREWSTERS WALK
RYDALE GDNS
SANDBECK CT
Works
EAST DR
CENTRAL DR
KINGS WOOD CL
SOUTH AVE
MAYFLOWER CL
GRESLEY AVE
STIRLING AVE
WATT CL
SPRING GDNS
WILLIAM BRADFORD CL
HIGHFIELD RD
NICHOLL LA
NORTH AVE

A638
DONCASTER RD
THORNE RD
A614
BAWTRY RD
NEWINGTON RD

River Idle

Bawtry Carr
Bawtry Mayflower Jun & Inf Sch

Barrier Bank
Sluice
Slaynes La
HAGG LA
Mother Drain

Cemy
MARTIN LA
MAYFLOWER CL
RUSSET GR
IDLE LA
Bawtry
DUKE'S TERR
QUEEN'S CRES

8

Liby
TOWNGATE
TOP ST
SCOT LA
PEAKE'S CROFT
HIGH ST
SWAN ST
STATION RD
A614
PO
SCHOOL WLK

7

TICKHILL RD
A631
PH
WHARF ST
CHURCH WLK
Sewage Works

93

SOUTH PAR
A638
A631
THE PASTURES
COCKHILL CL
GOCK HILL LA
Bawtry Viaduct
GAINSBOROUGH RD
Bawtry Bridge

6

Sports Ground
P

Holly House Farm

Scaftworth Grange

Grange Cottages

Pasture La
Theaker La

DN10

5

Barrow Hills

92

River Ryton

Theaker La

Scaftworth

4

Theaker La
PH
Scaftworth Hall

BAWTRY RD
A631

Manor Farm

Cobblety Row

Cut Throat La

3

Stone Hill La

MILL LA

91

HOMEFIELD CROFT

Ling's Wood

Stone Hill
Stone Hill Farm

Youldholes La

CHAPEL LA
DOG LA
Scrooby
MANOR RD
LOW RD

2

PH
CHURCH LA
CHURCH VIEW
STATION RD
MAYFLOWER AVE
Home Farm

Warren Plantation

River Idle

A638
GREAT NORTH RD

Sheepcote House

Plantation Drive Farm

Sewage Works

1

BROOMFIELD LA

Mattersey Wood House

Sandhill Farm
PLANTATION DR

90

A638

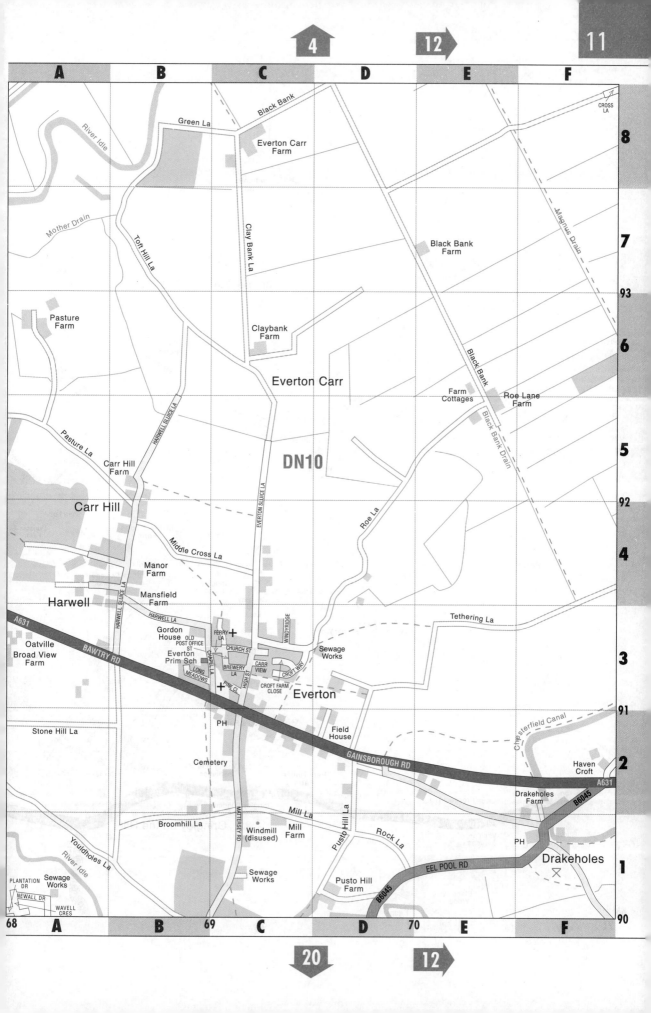

A   B   C   D   E   F

CROSS LA

River Idle

Black Bank

Green La

Everton Carr Farm

8

Mother Drain

Toft Hill La

Clay Bank La

Black Bank Farm

Magnus Drain

7

93

Pasture Farm

Claybank Farm

6

Everton Carr

Black Bank

Farm Cottages

Roe Lane Farm

Black Bank Drain

5

Pasture La

Harwell Sluice La

Carr Hill Farm

DN10

Everton Sluice La

Roe La

92

Carr Hill

Middle Cross La

4

Manor Farm

Harwell

Mansfield Farm

Tethering La

A631

Harwell La

Harwell Sluice La

Gordon House

OLD POST OFFICE ST

FERRY LA

CHURCH ST

WINDYRIDGE

Sewage Works

3

Oatville Broad View Farm

BAWTRY RD

Everton Prim Sch

LONG MEADOWS

CHAPEL LA

BREWERY LA

HIGH ST

CARR VIEW

CROFT WAY

PINE CL

CROFT FARM CLOSE

Everton

91

Stone Hill La

PH

Field House

GAINSBOROUGH RD

Chesterfield Canal

Haven Croft

A631

2

Cemetery

MATTERSEY RD

Mill La

Pusto Hill La

Rock La

Drakeholes Farm

B6045

Broomhill La

Windmill (disused)

Mill Farm

PH

Drakeholes

1

Youldholes La

River Idle

Sewage Works

EEL POOL RD

B6045

Pusto Hill Farm

PLANTATION DR

Sewage Works

NEWALL DR

WAVELL CRES

68   A   B   69   C   D   70   E   F   90

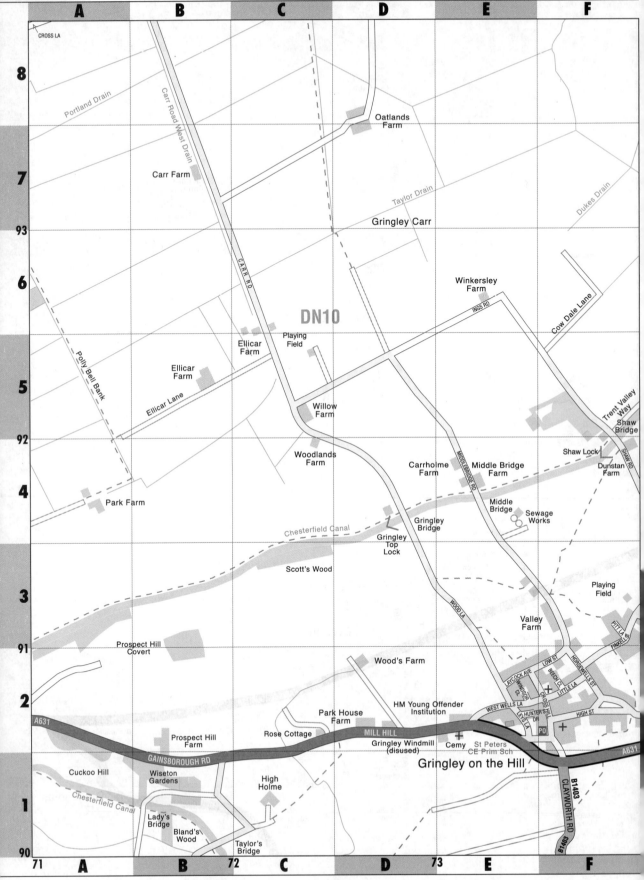

CROSS LA

Portland Drain

Carr Road West Drain

Carr Farm

Oatlands Farm

Taylor Drain

Gringley Carr

Dukes Drain

CARR RD

Winkersley Farm

INGS RD

Cow Dale Lane

DN10

Polly Bell Bank

Ellicar Farm

Playing Field

Ellicar Farm

Ellicar Lane

Willow Farm

Trent Valley Way

Shaw Bridge

Woodlands Farm

Carrholme Farm

Middle Bridge Farm

Shaw Lock

Dunstan Farm

SHAW RD

MIDDLEBRIDGE RD

Middle Bridge

Sewage Works

Park Farm

Chesterfield Canal

Gringley Bridge

Gringley Top Lock

Scott's Wood

Gringley Bridge

Playing Field

WOOD LA

Valley Farm

PITT LA

FINKELL ST

Prospect Hill Covert

Wood's Farm

LOW ST

LAYCOCK AVE

BEECH CL

HORSEWELLS ST

A631

Park House Farm

HM Young Offender Institution

WINDSOR DR

LITTLE LA

HIGH ST

CROSS HILL

WEST WELLS LA

HUNTER'S CL

Prospect Hill Farm

Rose Cottage

MILL HILL

Gringley Windmill (disused)

Cemy

St Peters CE Prim Sch

PO

GAINSBOROUGH RD

Gringley on the Hill

B1403

Cuckoo Hill

Wiseton Gardens

High Holme

CLAYWORTH RD

Chesterfield Canal

Lady's Bridge

Bland's Wood

Taylor's Bridge

A631

B1403

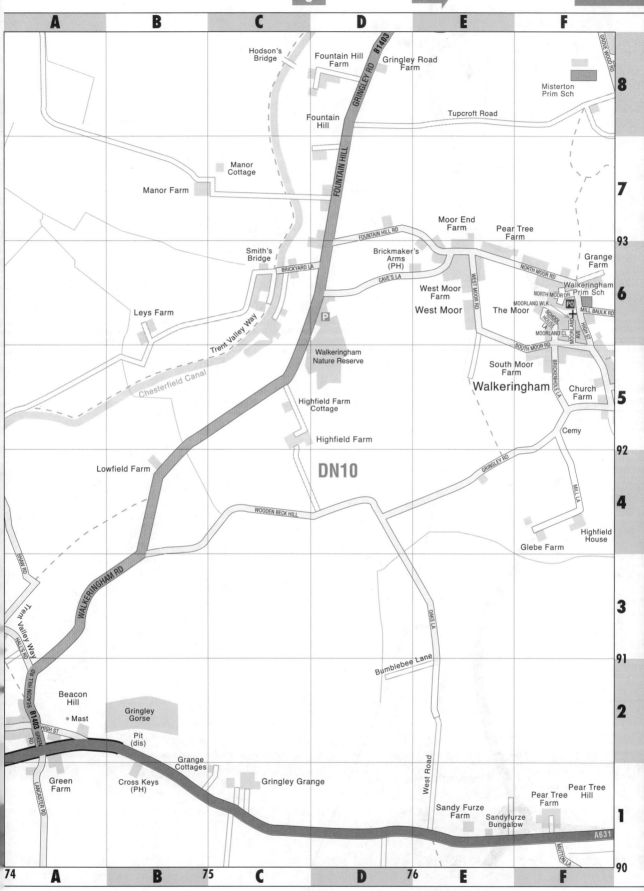

6 14

A B C D E F

8

Misterton
Prim Sch

GROVE WOOD RD

Hodson's
Bridge

Fountain Hill
Farm

Gringley Road
Farm

GRINGLEY RD B1403

Fountain
Hill

Tupcroft Road

7

Manor
Cottage

Manor Farm

FOUNTAIN HILL

93

Moor End
Farm

Pear Tree
Farm

Grange
Farm

Smith's
Bridge

Fountain Hill Rd

Brickmaker's
Arms
(PH)

NORTH MOOR RD

Walkeringham
Prim Sch

BRICKYARD LA

CAVE'S LA

West Moor
Farm

NORTH MOOR DR

MOORLAND WLK

PO

MILL BAULK RD

6

Leys Farm

West Moor

WEST MOOR RD

The Moor

SCHOOL
HOUSE
LA

MOORLAND CL

AVE

HIGH ST

P

MOORLAND

Trent Valley Way

Walkeringham
Nature Reserve

SOUTH MOOR RD

South Moor
Farm

Walkeringham

BRICKENHOLE LA

Church
Farm

5

Chesterfield Canal

Highfield Farm
Cottage

Cemy

92

Highfield Farm

DN10

GRINGLEY RD

MILL LA

Lowfield Farm

4

WOODEN BECK HILL

Highfield
House

Glebe Farm

3

SHAW RD

91

OAKS LA

Bumblebee Lane

Trent Valley Way

HALL'S RD

Beacon
Hill

GREEN HILL RD

Gringley
Gorse

2

Mast

B1403 HIGH ST

Pit
(dis)

WEST ROAD

Grange
Cottages

Green
Farm

LANCASTER RD

Cross Keys
(PH)

Gringley Grange

Sandy Furze
Farm

Pear Tree
Hill

Pear Tree
Farm

Sandyfurze
Bungalow

1

A631

MUTTON LA

90

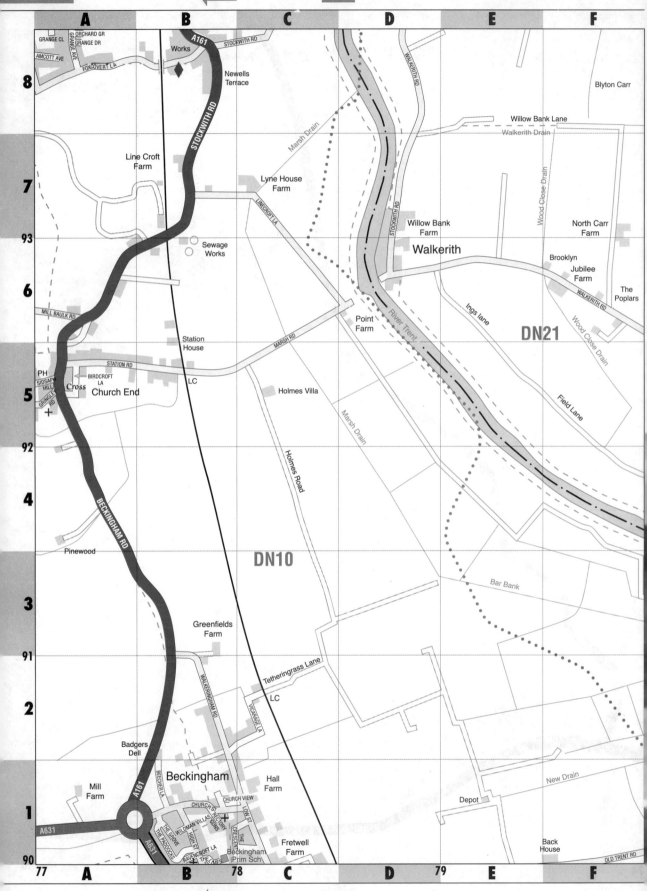

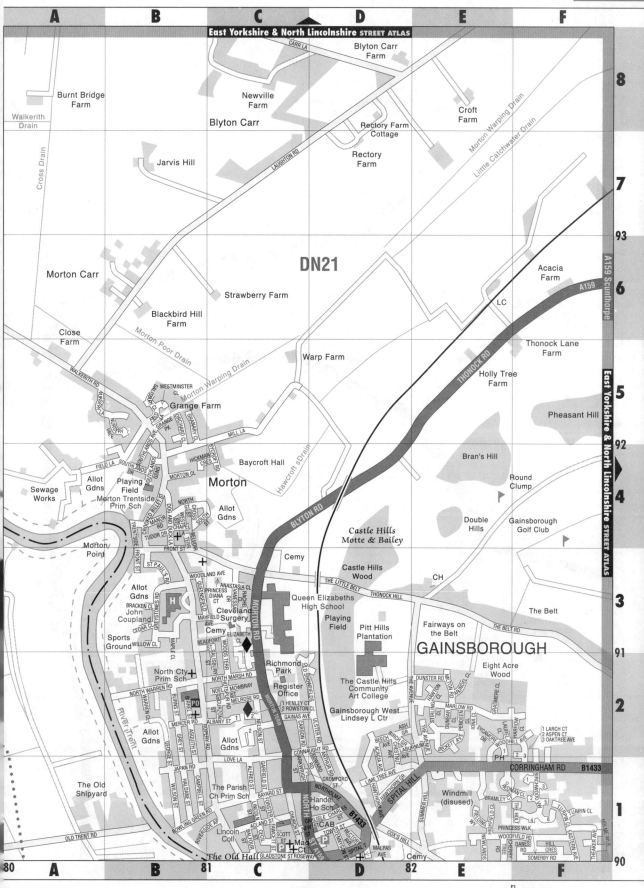

8

93

DN21

7

6

92

5

4

91

3

2

1

90

80   81   82   90

A   B   C   D   E   F

Walkerith Drain
Burnt Bridge Farm
Cross Drain
Blyton Carr
Newville Farm
Blyton Carr Farm
CARR LA
LAUGHTON RD
Rectory Farm Cottage
Croft Farm
Morton Warping Drain
Little Catchwater Drain
Jarvis Hill
Rectory Farm
A159 Scunthorpe
Morton Carr
Strawberry Farm
Acacia Farm
A159
LC
Close Farm
Blackbird Hill Farm
Morton Poor Drain
Warp Farm
Thonock Lane Farm
WALKERITH RD
Morton Warping Drain
THONOCK RD
Holly Tree Farm
Grange Farm
WESTMINSTER CL
Pheasant Hill
Hawcroft s Drain
GRANGE PK
ORCHARD CL
GRANARY CL
MILL LA
Baycroft Hall
Bran's Hill
Round Clump
Sewage Works
FIELD LA
SOUTHLANDS DR
SOUTHLANDS RD
HICKMAN CRES
MORTON CL
Morton
Allot Gdns
BLYTON RD
Castle Hills Motte & Bailey
Double Hills
Gainsborough Golf Club
Allot Gdns
Playing Field
Morton Trentside Prim Sch
NORTH ST
CROSS ST
BELVOIR TERR
Allot Gdns
Cemy
Morton Point
MANOR RD
TUDOR DR
CHAPEL LA
FRONT ST
DOG AND DUCK LA
Castle Hills Wood
CH
The Belt
ST PAUL'S RD
TRENTSIDE RD
FRONT ST
WOODLAND AVE
THE LITTLE BELT
THONOCK HILL
Allot Gdns
QUEENSFIELD
ANASTASIA CL
PRINCESS DIANA CT
Queen Elizabeths High School
THE AVENUE
THE BELT RD
John Coupland Hospital
BRACKEN CL
GREYSTONES RD
CEDAR CL
MAYFIELD AVE
Cleveland Surgery
Richmond Park
Playing Field
Pitt Hills Plantation
Fairways on the Belt
Sports Ground
BEAUFORT
SALISBURY
WILLOW CL
MAPLE CL
ELIZABETH CL
DUNSTER RD
GAINSBOROUGH
Eight Acre Wood
North Cty Prim Sch
North WARREN RD
BURNS ST
NORTH MARSH RD
MOWBRAY
NOEL ST
SPUR RD
CURZON
Register Office
MELROSE ST
GAINAS AVE
1 HENLEY CT
2 ROWSTON CL
The Castle Hills Community Art College
STIRLING CL
DUNBAR CL
MARLOW RD
PENDEEN
GRASMERE CL
MORLEY
1 LARCH CT
2 ASPEN CT
3 OAKTREE AVE
River Trent
Allot Gdns
MERCER ST
GREY ST
ASQUITH ST
ALBANY ST
NELSON ST
CARSON RD
ULSTER RD
CONNAUGHT RD
Gainsborough West Lindsey L Ctr
BEECH AVE
BIRCH RD
ACACIA AVE
ASH
LABURNUM AVE
THE AVENUE
PECKETT AVE
LAUREL CL
SYCAMORE DR
WOODHILL AVE
GEORGE ST
JAPAN RD
LOVE LA
LIME TREE AVE
CORRINGHAM RD
B1433
WILSON ST
CAMPBELL ST
The Parish Ch Prim Sch
BAYARD ST
FORSTER ST
GARFIELD ST
ALFRED ST
EDWARD
ARTHUR RD
CROMFORD ST
ARKWRIGHT
NORTHOLME
SPITAL HILL
SUMMER HILL
Windmill (disused)
BLACKTHORN CL
BIRCHWOOD RD
REDMAN CL
BRAMLEY CT
FIELDING WY
HIGHFIELD CL
THE HOLT
TURPIN CL
The Old Shipyard
LINCOLN ST
ACLAND ST
BACON ST
FAWCETT ST
CHURCH ST
Handel Ho Sch
NORTH TERR
Lincoln Coll
BOWLING GREEN RD
OLD TRENT RD
RIVERSIDE AP
The Old Hall
GLADSTONE ST
ROSEWAY
CARLISLE
CAB
MARKET
TOWER ST
MALPAS AVE
Cemy
COX'S HILL
PRINCESS WLK
WOODFIELD RD
NEWLANDS
DANES
HILL CRES
SOMERBY RD
HOLME WLK
THACKER AVE

F1
1 BLACKTHORN CL
2 THE ROWANS
3 FOSSEWAY
4 MAPLE CT
5 THE ALDERS
6 COUPLAND CL

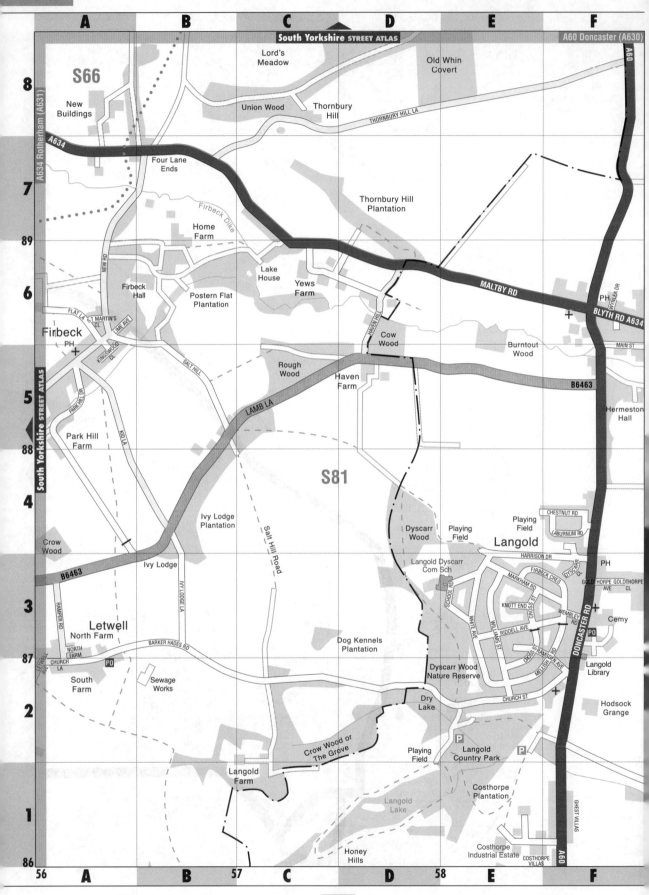

S66

S81

Firbeck

Letwell

Langold

Lord's Meadow

Old Whin Covert

Union Wood

Thornbury Hill

THORNBURY HILL LA

New Buildings

A634 Rotherham (A631)

A634

Four Lane Ends

Thornbury Hill Plantation

Firbeck Dike

Home Farm

Lake House

Yews Farm

MALTBY RD

PH

WYNLEA DR

BLYTH RD A634

Firbeck Hall

Postern Flat Plantation

HAVEN HILL

Cow Wood

Burntout Wood

MAIN ST

FLAT LA

ST MARTIN'S CL

LIME AVE

Rough Wood

Haven Farm

B6463

Hermeston Hall

PH

KINGSWOOD CL

SALT HILL

LAMB LA

PARK HILL DR

Park Hill Farm

KID LA

Crow Wood

Ivy Lodge Plantation

Salt Hill Road

Dyscarr Wood

Playing Field

Playing Field

CHESTNUT RD

LABURNUM RD

Langold

HARRISON DR

B6463

Ivy Lodge

IVY LODGE LA

Langold Dyscarr Com Sch

FIRBECK CRES

DYSCARR CL

PH

GOLDTHORPE GOLDTHORPE AVE CL

Letwell

North Farm

MARKHAM RD

SCHOOL RD

KNOTT END

CROSS RD

WEMBLEY RD

Cemy

RAMPER RD

BARKER HADES RD

WHITE AVE

WILLIAMS ST

RIDDELL AVE

PO

DONCASTER RD

NORTH FARM

CHURCH LA

PO

Dog Kennels Plantation

Langold Library

Dyscarr Wood Nature Reserve

RAMSDEN AVE

MELLISH RD

LETWELL AVE

South Farm

Sewage Works

CHURCH ST

Dry Lake

Hodsock Grange

Crow Wood or The Grove

Playing Field

P

Langold Country Park

P

Costhorpe Plantation

Langold Farm

Langold Lake

GHEST VILLAS

Honey Hills

Costhorpe Industrial Estate

COSTHORPE VILLAS

A60

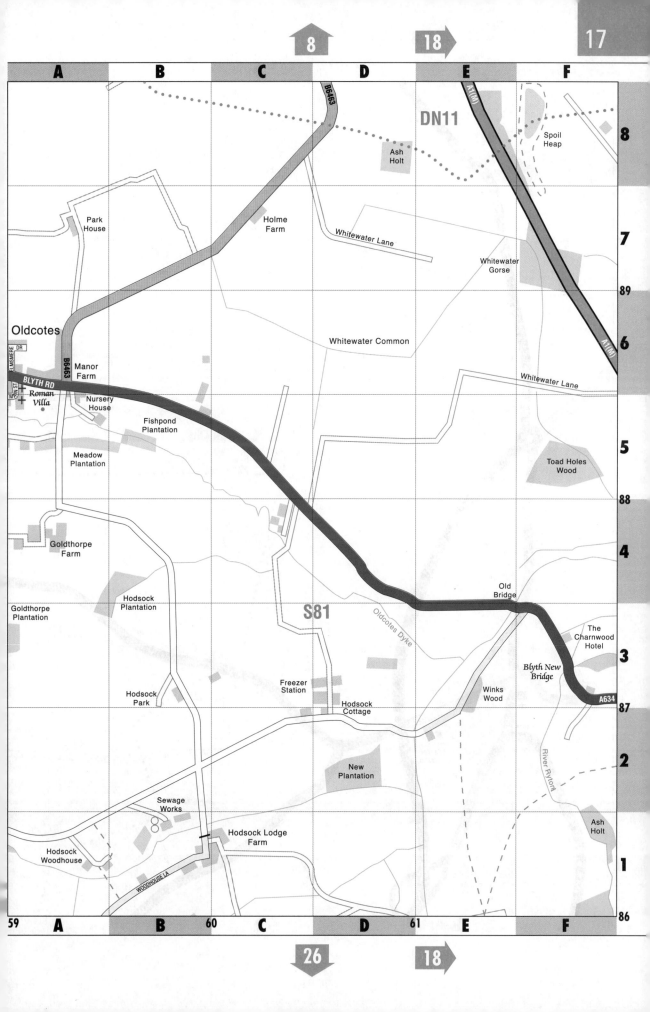

A   B   C   D   E   F

DN11

Spoil
Heap

8

Ash
Holt

Park
House

Holme
Farm

Whitewater Lane

7

Whitewater
Gorse

89

Oldcotes

Whitewater Common

6

ELMSMERE DR

Manor
Farm

BLYTH RD

Whitewater Lane

B6463

Roman
Villa

MTN ST

Nursery
House

Fishpond
Plantation

Toad Holes
Wood

5

Meadow
Plantation

88

Goldthorpe
Farm

4

Goldthorpe
Plantation

Hodsock
Plantation

Old
Bridge

The
Charnwood
Hotel

S81

Oldcotes Dyke

Blyth New
Bridge

3

Hodsock
Park

Freezer
Station

Hodsock
Cottage

Winks
Wood

A634

87

New
Plantation

River Ryton

2

Sewage
Works

Ash
Holt

Hodsock
Woodhouse

Hodsock Lodge
Farm

1

WOODHOUSE LA

86

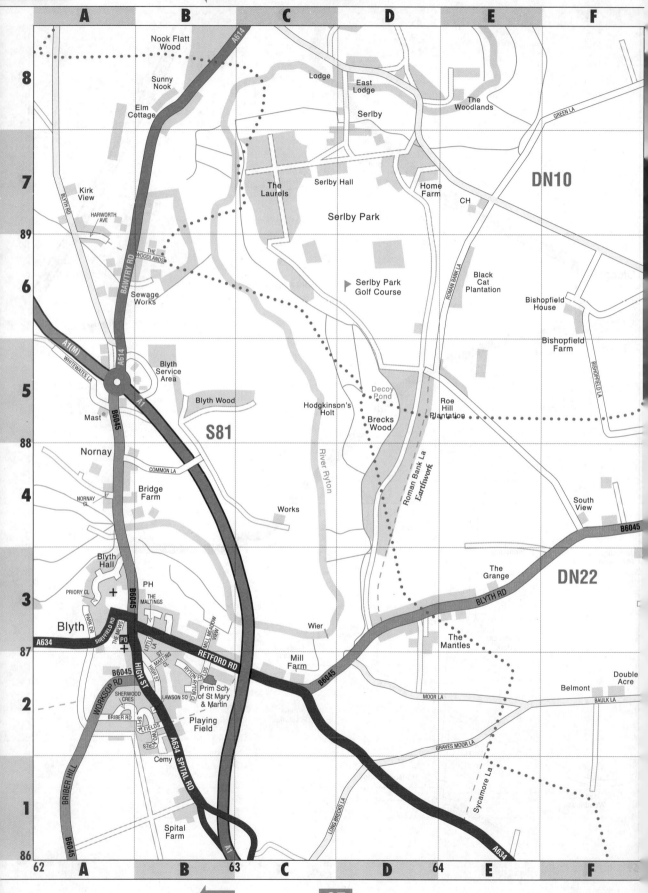

Nook Flatt Wood

Sunny Nook

Elm Cottage

Lodge

East Lodge

Serlby

The Woodlands

DN10

8

Kirk View

HARWORTH AVE

BLYTH RD

BAWTRY RD

THE WOODLANDS

The Laurels

Serlby Hall

Serlby Park

Home Farm

CH

GREEN LA

7

89

Sewage Works

Serlby Park Golf Course

ROMAN BANK LA

Black Cat Plantation

Bishopfield House

6

A1(M)

WHITEWATES LA

A614

A1

B6045

Blyth Service Area

Blyth Wood

Hodgkinson's Holt

Decoy Pond

Brecks Wood

Roe Hill Plantation

Bishopfield Farm

BISHOPFIELD LA

5

Mast

S81

88

Nornay

NORNAY CL

COMMON LA

Bridge Farm

Works

River Ryton

Roman Bank La Earthwork

South View

B6045

4

Blyth Hall

PRIORY CL

B6045

PARK DR

PH

THE MALTINGS

MILL MEADOW VIEW

Wier

The Grange

BLYTH RD

DN22

3

Blyth

A634

SHEFFIELD RD

THE MEWS

PO

RETFORD RD

LITTLE HIGH ST

ST MARTINS LA

RYTON FIELDS

Mill Farm

B6045

The Mantles

87

WORKSOP RD

HIGH ST

B6045

SHERWOOD CRES

BRIBER RD

SPITAL

LAWSON SQ

Prim Sch of St Mary & Martin

Playing Field

MOOR LA

BAULK LA

Belmont

Double Acre

2

BRIBER HILL

B6045

A634 SPITAL RD

TWO... CRES

Cemy

A1

LONG BRECKS LA

GRAVES MOOR LA

Sycamore La

A634

1

Spital Farm

86

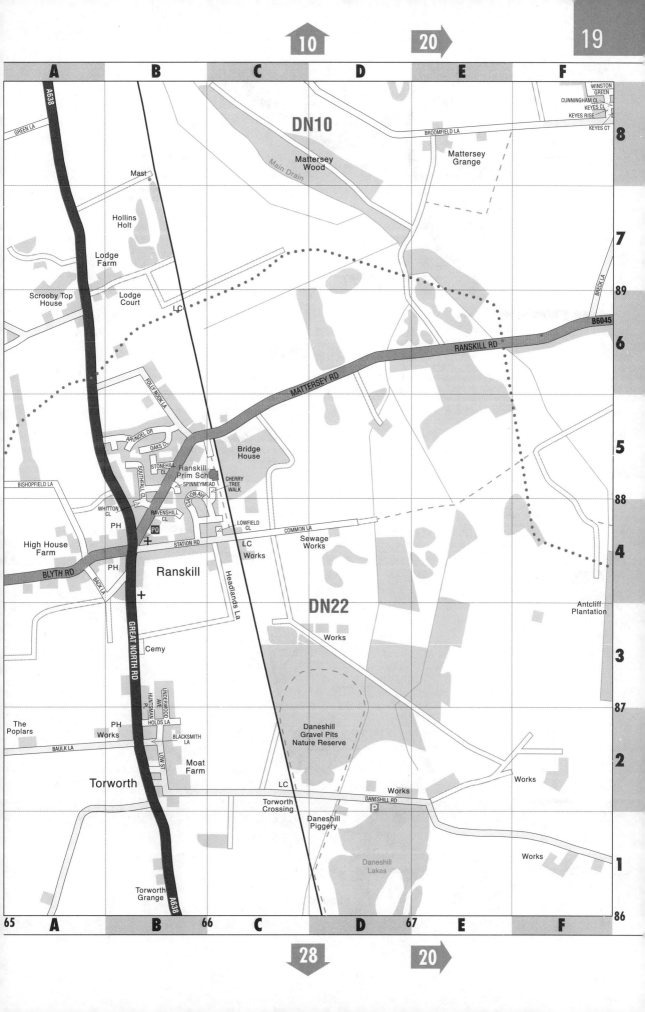

A   B   C   D   E   F

DN10

WINSTON GREEN
CUNNINGHAM CL
KEYES CL
KEYES RISE
KEYES CT

BROOMFIELD LA

8

GREEN LA

Mattersey Wood

Mattersey Grange

Main Drain

Mast

7

Hollins Holt

Lodge Farm

BRECK LA

89

Scrooby Top House

Lodge Court

LC

B6045

6

FOLLY NOOK LA

RANSKILL RD

MATTERSEY RD

ARUNDEL DR

OAKS CL

Bridge House

5

SOUTHFALL CL

STONEHILL CL

Ranskill Prim Sch

SPINNEYMEAD

CHERRY TREE WALK

BISHOPFIELD LA

88

WHITTON CL

RAVENSHILL CL

STATION AVE

LOWFIELD CL

COMMON LA

PH

PO

Sewage Works

High House Farm

+

STATION RD

LC

Works

4

PH

BLYTH RD

BACK LA

Ranskill

+

Headlands La

DN22

Antcliff Plantation

Works

GREAT NORTH RD

3

Cemy

UNDERWOOD AVE

HUNTSMAN PL

HOLDS LA

87

The Poplars

PH
Works

BLACKSMITH LA

Daneshill Gravel Pits Nature Reserve

Works

BAULK LA

2

LOW ST

Moat Farm

Torworth

LC

Torworth Crossing

Works

DANESHILL RD

P

Daneshill Piggery

Works

1

Daneshill Lakes

Torworth Grange

A638

65   A   B   66   C   D   67   E   F   86

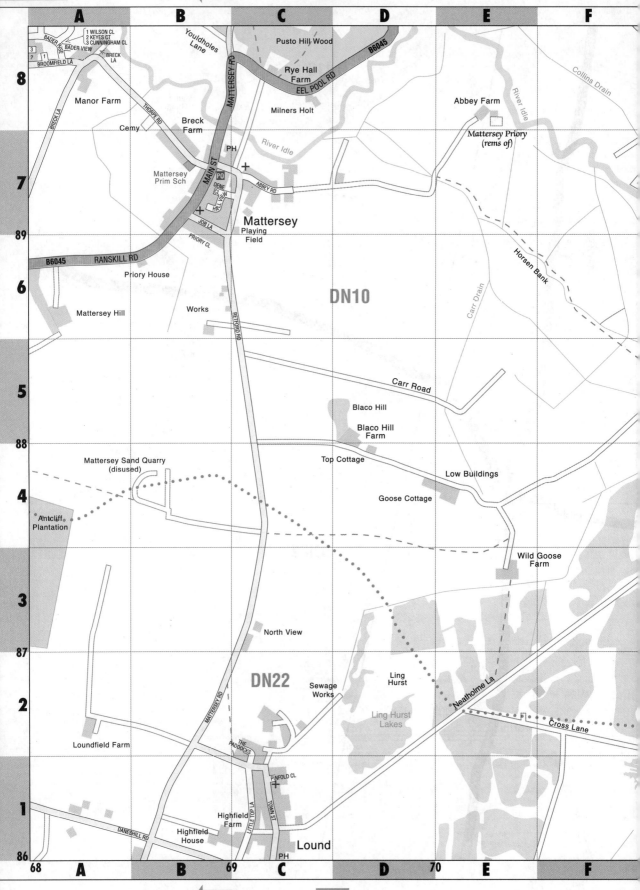

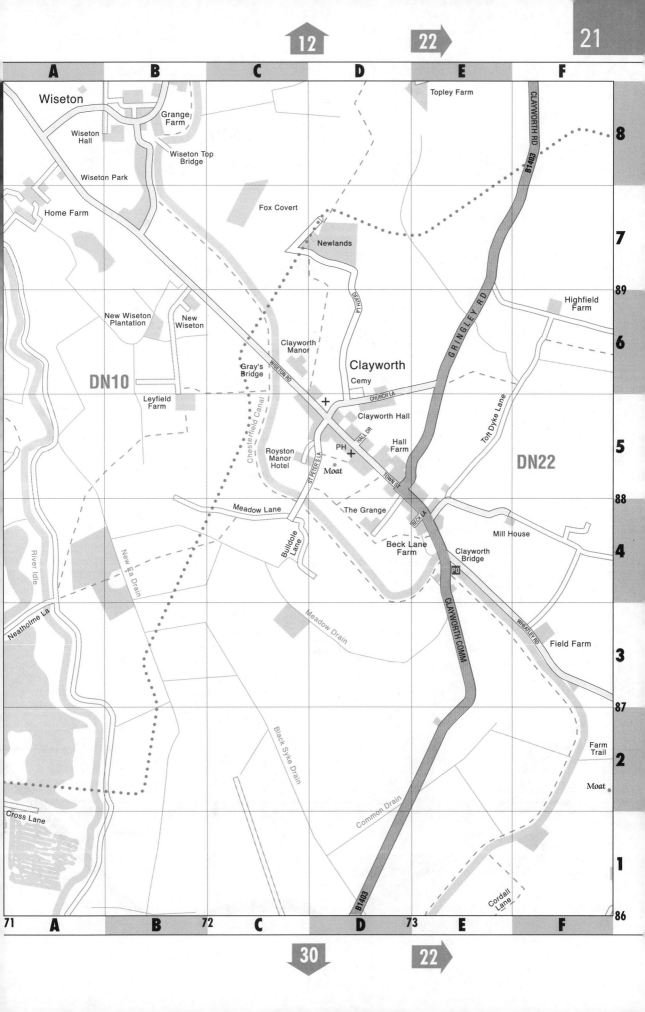

A B C D E F

8
7
89
6
5
88
4
3
87
2
1
86

Wiseton
Grange Farm
Wiseton Hall
Wiseton Top Bridge
Wiseton Park
Home Farm
Topley Farm
CLAYWORTH RD
B1403
Fox Covert
Newlands
DEATH LA
New Wiseton Plantation
New Wiseton
Clayworth Manor
Clayworth
Highfield Farm
GRINGLEY RD
DN10
Gray's Bridge
WISETON RD
Cemy
CHURCH LA
Tott Dyke Lane
Leyfield Farm
Chesterfield Canal
Clayworth Hall
HALL DR
Hall Farm
DN22
Royston Manor Hotel
ST PETER'S LA
PH
Moat
TOWN ST
BECK LA
Meadow Lane
The Grange
Mill House
River Idle
New Ea Drain
Buildole Lane
Beck Lane Farm
Clayworth Bridge
Neatholme La
Meadow Drain
CLAYWORTH COMM
PO
WHEATLEY RD
Field Farm
Black Syke Drain
Farm Trail
Moat
Common Drain
Cross Lane
Cordall Lane
B1403

A B C D E F

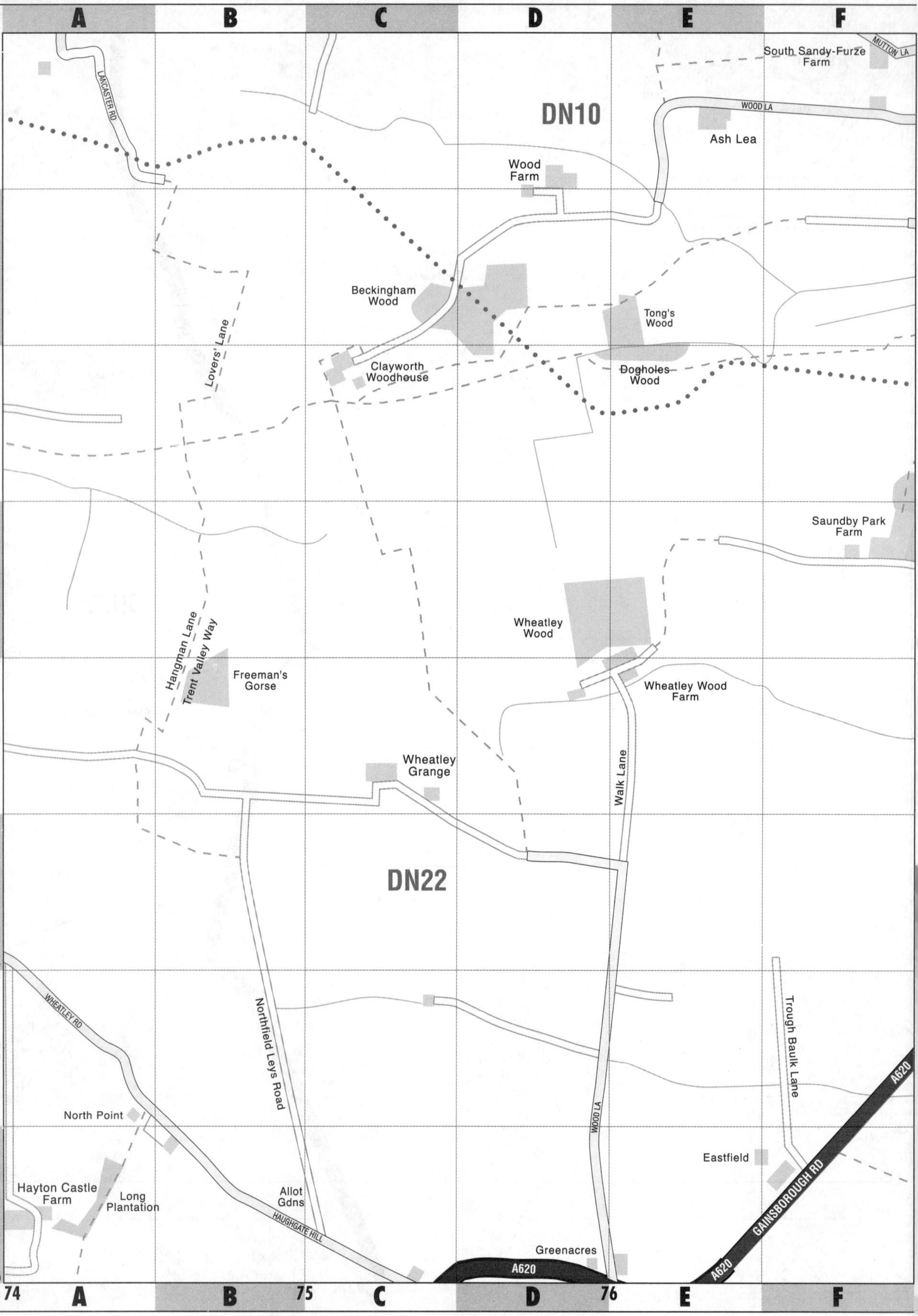

8

DN10

South Sandy-Furze Farm

MUTTON LA

WOOD LA

Ash Lea

Wood Farm

LANCASTER RD

7

Beckingham Wood

Tong's Wood

89

Lovers' Lane

Clayworth Woodhouse

Dogholes Wood

6

Saundby Park Farm

5

Wheatley Wood

88

Hangman Lane

Trent Valley Way

Freeman's Gorse

Wheatley Wood Farm

4

Wheatley Grange

Walk Lane

DN22

3

87

Wheatley Rd

Northfield Leys Road

Trough Baulk Lane

2

A620

North Point

Wood La

Eastfield

GAINSBOROUGH RD

1

Hayton Castle Farm

Long Plantation

Allot Gdns

HAUGHGATE HILL

Greenacres

A620

A620

86

74 A B 75 C D 76 E F

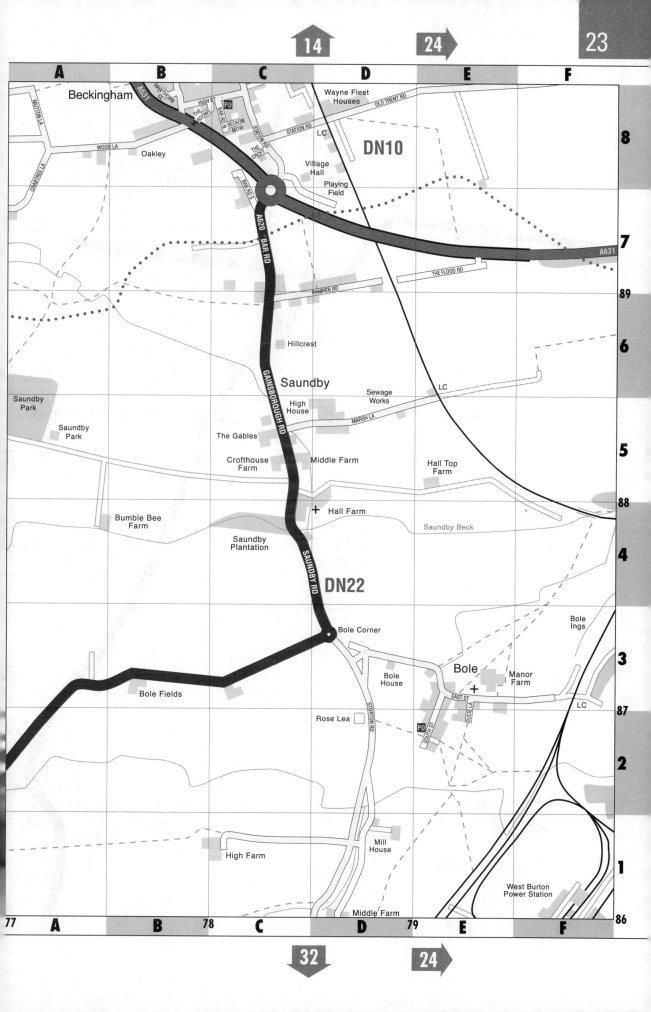

A B C D E F

Beckingham

Oakley

WOOD LA

MUTTON LA

CRABTREE LA

HAWTHORN CL

THE MEADOWS

HIGH ST

BAR RD N

PO

BECKON MDW

THE CROFT

STATION RD

STATION RD

Wayne Fleet Houses

OLD TRENT RD

LC

DN10

Village Hall

Playing Field

BAR RD S

A620 BAR RD

THE FLOOD RD

A631

RAMPER RD

Hillcrest

Saundby

GAINSBOROUGH RD

High House

Sewage Works

LC

MARSH LA

Saundby Park

Saundby Park

The Gables

Crofthouse Farm

Middle Farm

Hall Top Farm

Bumble Bee Farm

Hall Farm

Saundby Beck

Saundby Plantation

SAUNDBY RD

DN22

Bole Corner

Bole Ings

Bole Fields

Bole House

Bole

Manor Farm

STURTON RD

EAST ST

DUCIE LA

LC

Rose Lea

PO

SOUTH ST

High Farm

Mill House

West Burton Power Station

Middle Farm

8
7
89
6
5
88
4
3
87
2
1
86

77 A B 78 C D 79 E F 86

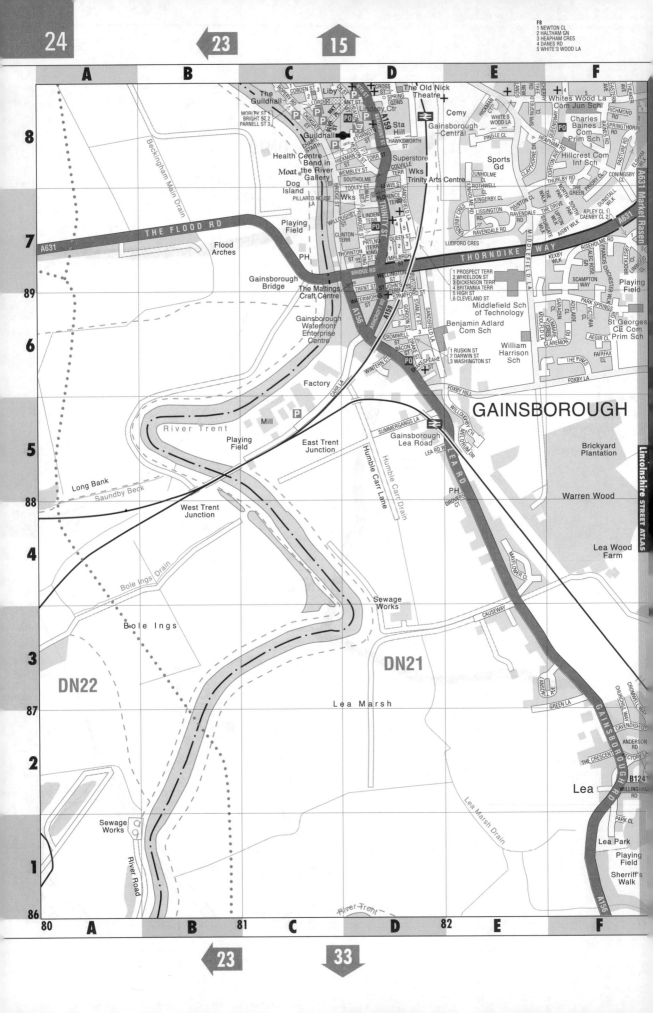

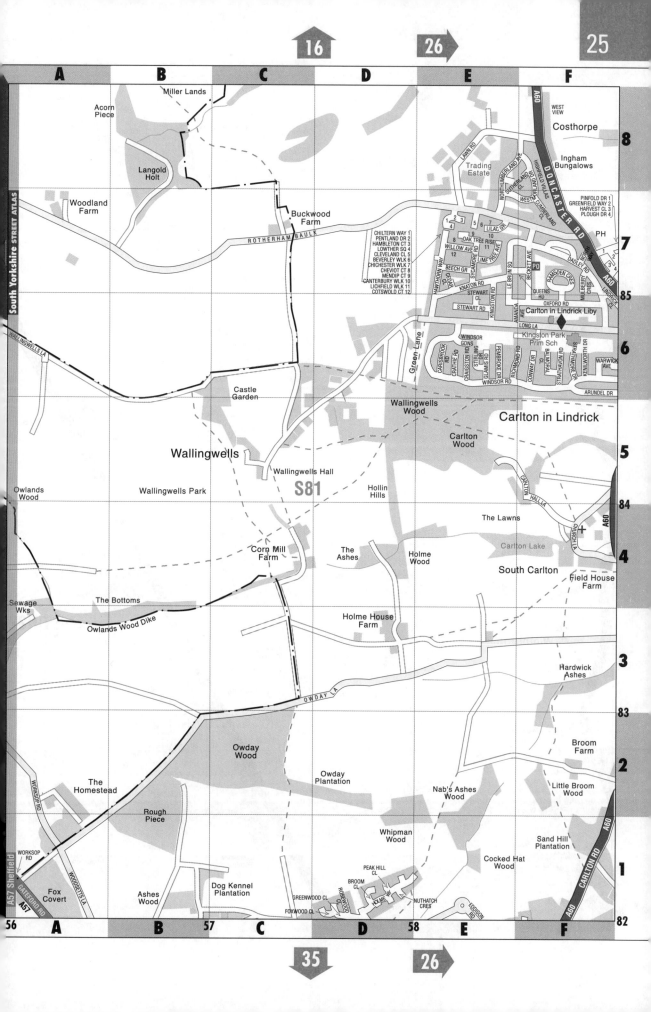

A | B | C | D | E | F

8 Costhorpe

WEST VIEW

Ingham Bungalows

PINFOLD DR 1
GREENFIELD WAY 2
HARVEST CL 3
PLOUGH DR 4

PH

7

Acorn Piece

Miller Lands

Woodland Farm

Langold Holt

Buckwood Farm

ROTHERHAM BAULK

LAWN RD

Trading Estate

NORTHUMBERLAND AVE
SUTHERLAND CL
WESTMORLAND
CUMBERLAND

DONCASTER RD

HIGHFIELD VILLAS

A60

DADLEY RD

CHILTERN WAY 1
PENTLAND DR 2
HAMBLETON CT 3
LOWTHER SQ 4
CLEVELAND CL 5
BEVERLEY WLK 6
CHICHESTER WLK 7
CHEVIOT CT 8
MENDIP CT 9
CANTERBURY WLK 10
LICHFIELD WLK 11
COTSWOLD CT 12

OAK TREE RISE
LILAC GR
WILLOW AVE
LIME TREE AVE

BEECH GR

HAWTHORN WAY

KNATON RD

SYCAMORE RD

LE BRUN RD

BECKETT AVE
RAMSDEN CRES

PO

QUEENS
RD

MILBERRY CRES

LINDRICK
CL

85

STEWART CL

STEWART RD

KINGSTON RD

AMANDA
AVE

OXFORD RD

Carlton in Lindrick Liby

Long La

6

Green Lane

WINDSOR GDNS

CARISBROOK RD

CRATHIE RD

CRAIGSTON RD

STIRLING DR

GLAMIS RD

PEMBROKE DR

RICHMOND RD

CONWAY DR

THORN HILL

STRATHAVON DR

STRATHORD RD

KENILWORTH DR

Kingston Park Prim Sch

WARWICK AVE

Castle Garden

WINDSOR RD

ARUNDEL DR

Wallingwells Wood

Carlton in Lindrick

5 Wallingwells

Wallingwells Hall

S81

Wallingwells Park

Carlton Wood

Carlton Wood

CARLTON HALL LA

CHURCH LA

84

Owlands Wood

Hollin Hills

The Lawns

A60

4

Corn Mill Farm

The Ashes

Holme Wood

Carlton Lake

South Carlton

Field House Farm

The Bottoms

Sewage Wks

Owlands Wood Dike

Holme House Farm

3 Hardwick Ashes

OWDAY LA

83

Broom Farm

2 The Homestead

Owday Wood

Owday Plantation

Nab's Ashes Wood

Little Broom Wood

WORKSOP RD

WOODSETTS LA

Rough Piece

Whipman Wood

Sand Hill Plantation

CARLTON RD

A60

1

A57 Sheffield

Worksop RD

GATEFORD RD

A57

Fox Covert

Ashes Wood

Dog Kennel Plantation

PEAK HILL CL

BROOM CL

ROSEWOOD

HOLME WY

GREENWOOD CL

FOXWOOD CL

NUTHATCH CRES

EDDISON RD

Cocked Hat Wood

82

56 | A | B | 57 | C | D | 58 | E | F

South Yorkshire STREET ATLAS

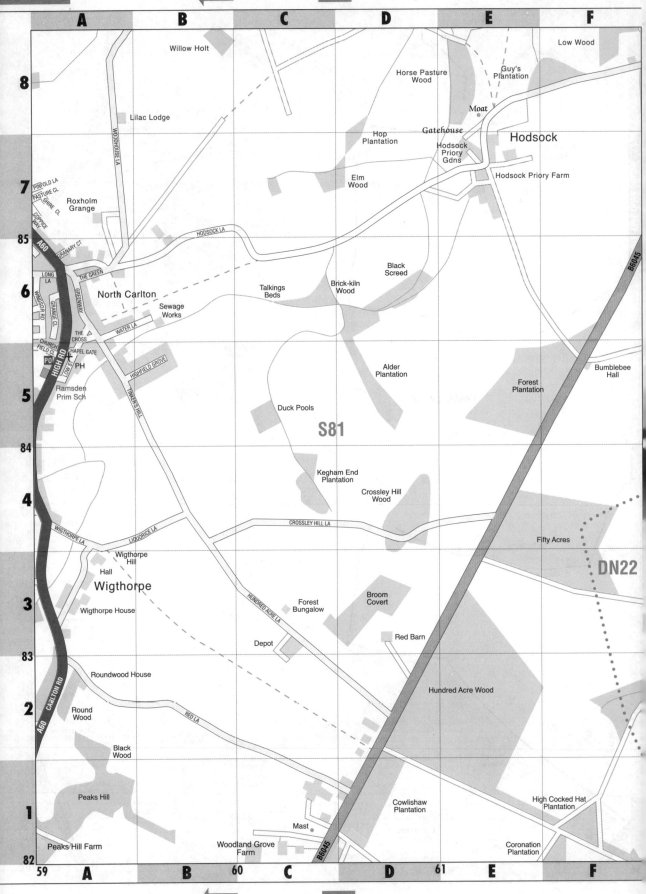

A B C D E F

8 7 85 6 5 84 4 83 2 1 82

Willow Holt

Horse Pasture Wood

Low Wood

Guy's Plantation

Lilac Lodge

WOODHOUSE LA

Hop Plantation

Gatehouse

Moat

Hodsock

Hodsock Priory Gdns

Hodsock Priory Farm

Elm Wood

Roxholm Grange

PINFOLD LA
PASTURE CL
SHIRE CL
COPPICE WAY

HODSOCK LA

GRANARY CT

A60

THE GREEN

LONG LA
WINDSOR RD
GRANGE CL
GREENWAY

North Carlton

WATER LA

Talkings Beds

Brick-kiln Wood

Black Screed

Sewage Works

B6045

THE CROSS

CHURCH FIELD CL
CHAPEL GATE

PO
HIGH RD
LOW ST
PH

HIGHFIELD GROVE

Alder Plantation

Forest Plantation

Bumblebee Hall

Ramsden Prim Sch

TINKER'S HILL

Duck Pools

S81

Kegham End Plantation

Crossley Hill Wood

Fifty Acres

DN22

WIGTHORPE LA

LIQUORICE LA

CROSSLEY HILL LA

Wigthorpe Hill

Hall

Wigthorpe

HUNDRED ACRE LA

Forest Bungalow

Broom Covert

Red Barn

Wigthorpe House

Depot

CARLTON RD

A60

Roundwood House

RED LA

Round Wood

Hundred Acre Wood

Black Wood

Peaks Hill

Cowlishaw Plantation

High Cocked Hat Plantation

Mast

Peaks Hill Farm

Woodland Grove Farm

B6045

Coronation Plantation

59 A B 60 C D 61 E F

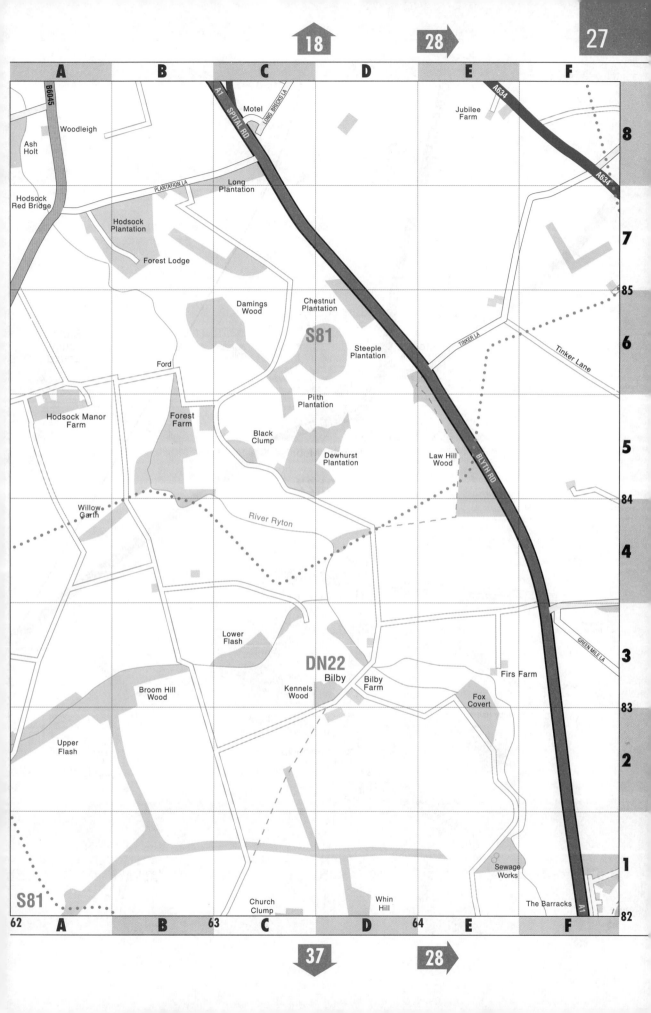

A B C D E F

8

7

85

6

5

84

4

3

83

2

1

82

S81

DN22

B6045

SPITAL RD

A1

LONG BRECKS LA

Motel

Woodleigh

Ash
Holt

Hodsock
Red Bridge

PLANTATION LA

Long
Plantation

Hodsock
Plantation

Forest Lodge

Damings
Wood

Chestnut
Plantation

S81

Steeple
Plantation

Ford

Pilth
Plantation

Hodsock Manor
Farm

Forest
Farm

Black
Clump

Dewhurst
Plantation

Law Hill
Wood

Willow
Garth

River Ryton

Lower
Flash

DN22
Bilby

Kennels
Wood

Bilby
Farm

Broom Hill
Wood

Fox
Covert

Firs Farm

Upper
Flash

Sewage
Works

Church
Clump

Whin
Hill

The Barracks

Jubilee
Farm

A634

A634

TINKER LA

Tinker Lane

BLYTH RD

GREEN MILE LA

A1

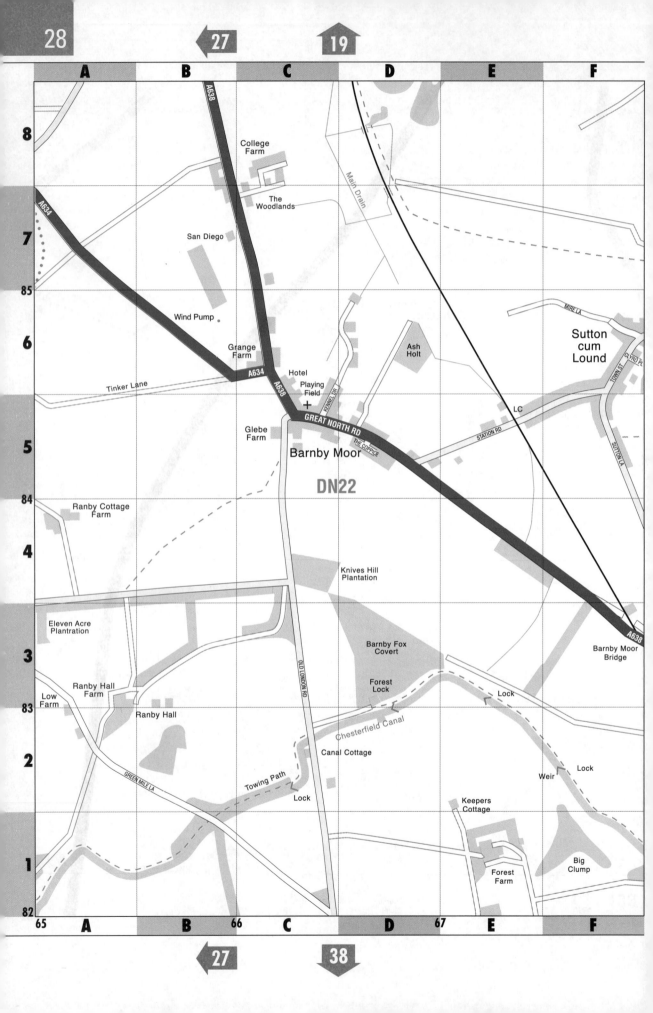

A   B   C   D   E   F

8

A638

College Farm

The Woodlands

Main Drain

San Diego

7

A634

85

Wind Pump

6

Grange Farm

Ash Holt

Sutton cum Lound

MIRE LA

TOWN ST

GLYPH PL

A634

Tinker Lane

A638

Hotel

Playing Field

KENNEL DR

Station Rd

LC

SUTTON LA

GREAT NORTH RD

5

Glebe Farm

Barnby Moor

THE COPPICE

DN22

84

Ranby Cottage Farm

4

Knives Hill Plantation

Eleven Acre Plantation

3

Barnby Fox Covert

Barnby Moor Bridge

A638

Ranby Hall Farm

Low Farm

83

Ranby Hall

Forest Lock

Lock

Chesterfield Canal

2

GREEN MILE LA

Canal Cottage

Towing Path

Lock

Weir

Lock

Keepers Cottage

OLD LONDON RD

1

Forest Farm

Big Clump

82

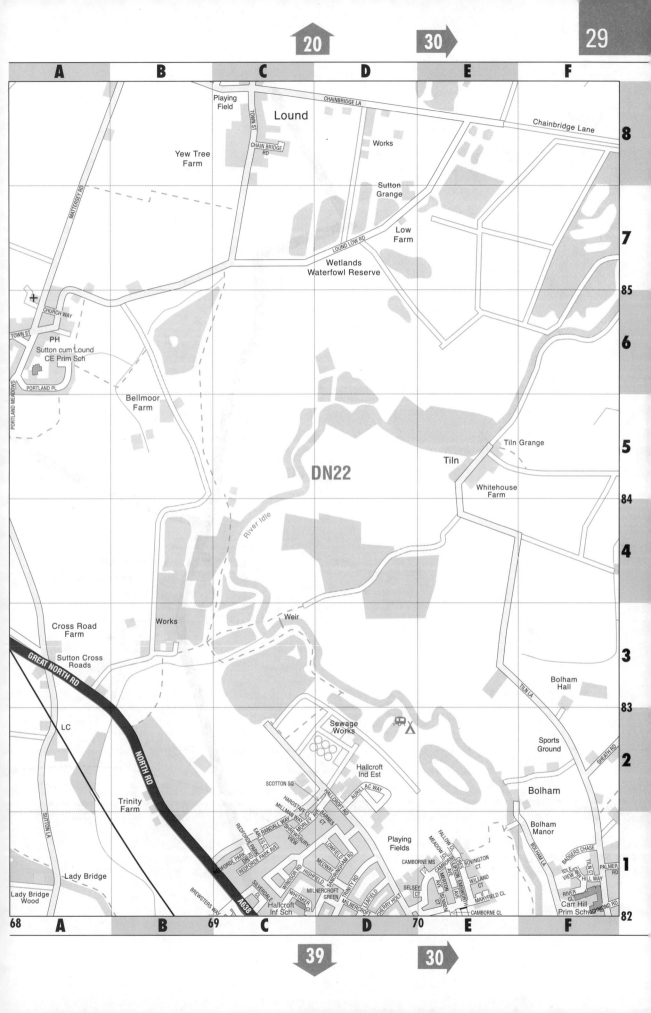

A | B | C | D | E | F

8

Chainbridge Nature Reserve

Chainbridge Lane

River Idle

Folly Dyke

7

B1403

Townend Bridge

BURNTLEYS RD

Cordall Lane

Hollinhill Lane

85

Bridge Farm

PH

Old Ea Drain

Scotter Lane

MAIN ST

Lovers' Walk

Goit Lane

6

Hanging side Lane

TOPYARD LA

Hayton

Tiln Holt

Meadow Lane

Sewage Works

CHURCH LA

VICARAGE DR

5

Guns Beck

Church Lane

Church Bridge

B1403

CLARBOROUGH HILL

A620

Hill Top Farm

84

DN22

4

SMEATH LA

PH

Sewage Works

BROAD GORES

GORES

BROAD

GILL GREEN WLK

PEAR TREE LA

PH

PO

MILLERS CT

HILLVIEW CRES

Clarborough

HOWBECK LA

SMEATH RD

Markfield Farm

ST JOHN'S DR

SOUTH VIEW DR

BROAD GORES

BIG LA

Clarborough Prim Sch

CHURCH LA

Works

3

Barcroft Lane

Church Farm

Bolham Farm

Bolham Cottage Farm

WHINLEYS RD

83

Chesterfield Canal

Clarborough Hall

2

BONEMILL LA

Bonemill Farm

Meadow Farm

The Baulk

Market Hill

Moorgate Farm

Longholme Farm

1

DURHAM GR

PALMER RD

CORNWALL RD

WINSTON GR

BIGSBY RD

THE DRIVE

PARK LA

RICHMOND RD

ELMWOOD CL

PARK LA

LONGHOLME RD

Whitsunday Pie Lock

Pinfolds Farm

Sewage Works

A620

Welham

A620

82

71 | A | B | 72 | C | WELHAM RD | D | 73 | E | F

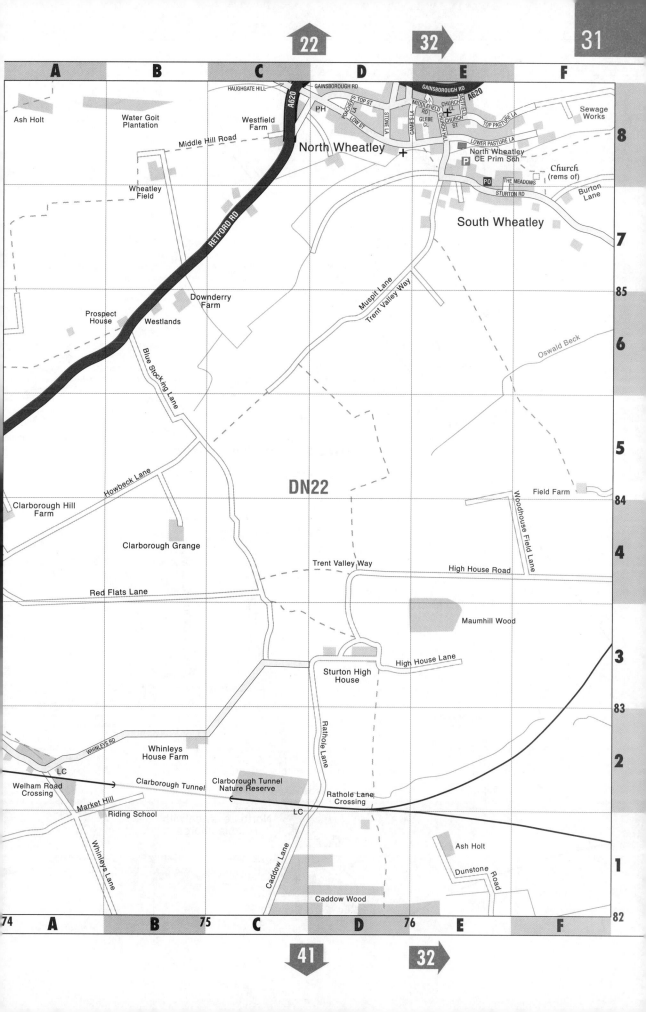

A B C D E F

Ash Holt

Water Goit Plantation

Westfield Farm

HAUGHGATE HILL

GAINSBOROUGH RD

A620

GAINSBOROUGH RD

A620

TOP ST

LOW ST

POUCHER'S LA

STONE LA

CAMB ST

MIDDLEFIELD RD

GLEBE CL

CHURCH CL

WESTFIELD

CHURCH HILL

CHURCH ST

TOP PASTURE LA

Sewage Works

PH

Middle Hill Road

North Wheatley

LOWER PASTURE LA

P

North Wheatley CE Prim Sch

PO

THE MEADOWS

STURTON RD

Church (rems of)

Burton Lane

Wheatley Field

South Wheatley

8

7

85

Downderry Farm

Muspit Lane

Trent Valley Way

Oswald Beck

Prospect House

Westlands

RETFORD RD

Blue Stocking Lane

6

5

Howbeck Lane

DN22

Field Farm

Woodhouse Field Lane

84

Clarborough Hill Farm

Clarborough Grange

4

Red Flats Lane

Trent Valley Way

High House Road

Maumhill Wood

3

High House Lane

Sturton High House

Rathole Lane

83

WHINLEYS RD

Whinleys House Farm

2

LC

Welham Road Crossing

Clarborough Tunnel

Clarborough Tunnel Nature Reserve

Rathole Lane Crossing

Market Hill

LC

Riding School

Whinleys Lane

Caddow Lane

Ash Holt

Dunstone Road

1

Caddow Wood

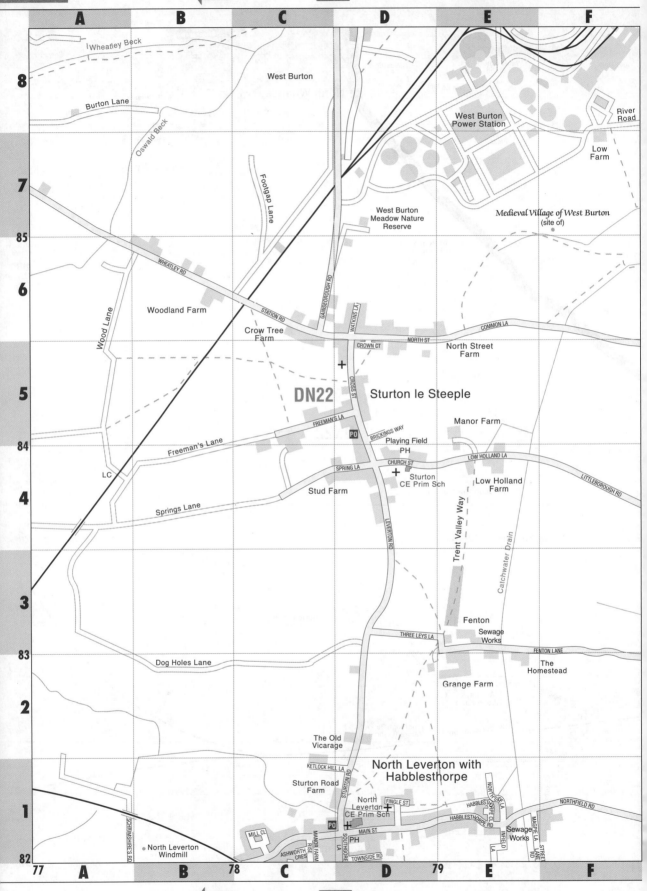

Wheatley Beck

West Burton

Burton Lane

Oswald Beck

West Burton
Power Station

River
Road

Low
Farm

Footgap Lane

West Burton
Meadow Nature
Reserve

Medieval Village of West Burton
(site of)

Wheatley Rd

Woodland Farm

Wood Lane

Station Rd

Gainsborough Rd

Crow Tree
Farm

Watkins La

North St

Common La

North Street
Farm

Crown Ct

DN22

Sturton le Steeple

Cross St

Manor Farm

Freeman's La

PO

Brickings Way

Playing Field

PH

Freeman's Lane

Spring La

Church St

Sturton
CE Prim Sch

Low Holland La

Low Holland
Farm

Littleborough Rd

LC

Stud Farm

Springs Lane

Leverton Rd

Trent Valley Way

Catchwater Drain

Fenton
Sewage
Works

Dog Holes Lane

Three Leys La

Fenton Lane

The
Homestead

Grange Farm

The Old
Vicarage

North Leverton with
Habblesthorpe

Ketlock Hill La

Sturton Rd

Fingle St

Habblesthorpe Cl

Northside La

Northfield Rd

Sturton Road
Farm

North
Leverton
CE Prim Sch

PO

Habblesthorpe Rd

Sewage
Works

Magpie La

Mill Cl

Manor Farm Rise

Southorpe La

Main St

PH

Infield La

Street
Lane Rd

North Leverton
Windmill

Scrimshire's Rd

Ashworth Cres

Townside Rd

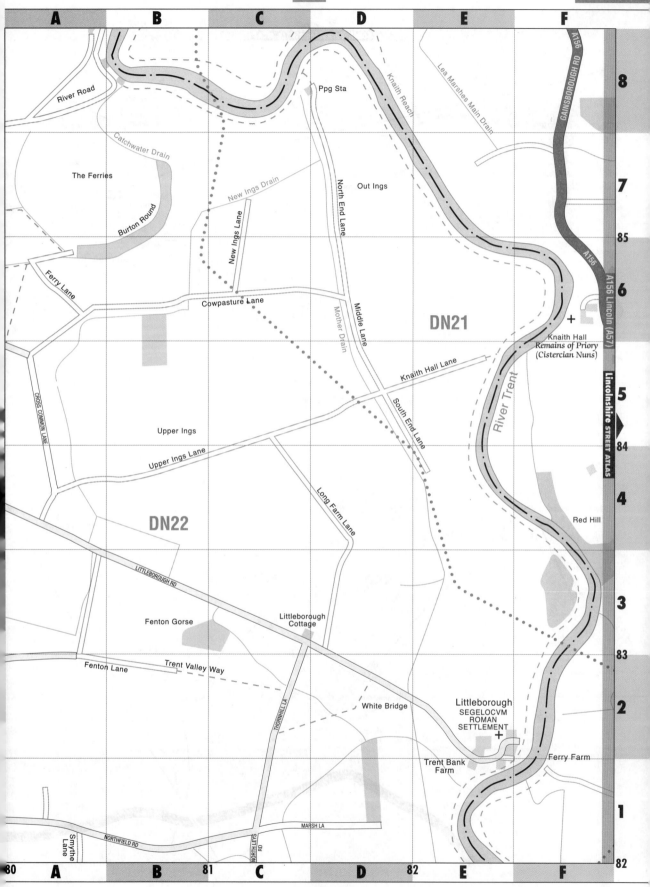

A B C D E F

River Road

Catchwater Drain

The Ferries

Burton Round

Ferry Lane

New Ings Drain

New Ings Lane

Cowpasture Lane

North End Lane

Out Ings

Ppg Sta

Knaith Reach

Lea Marshes Main Drain

GAINSBOROUGH RD

A156

A156

A156 Lincoln (A57)

DN21

Mother Drain

Middle Lane

Knaith Hall Lane

South End Lane

Upper Ings

Upper Ings Lane

DN22

Long Farm Lane

CROSS COMMON LANE

Knaith Hall
Remains of Priory
(Cistercian Nuns)

River Trent

Red Hill

Lincolnshire STREET ATLAS

LITTLEBOROUGH RD

Fenton Gorse

Littleborough
Cottage

Fenton Lane

Trent Valley Way

THORNHILL LA

White Bridge

Littleborough
SEGELOCVM
ROMAN
SETTLEMENT

Trent Bank
Farm

Ferry Farm

Smythe
Lane

NORTHFIELD RD

NORTH LEYS RD

MARSH LA

80 81 82

A B C D E F

8 85 7 6 5 84 4 3 83 2 1 82

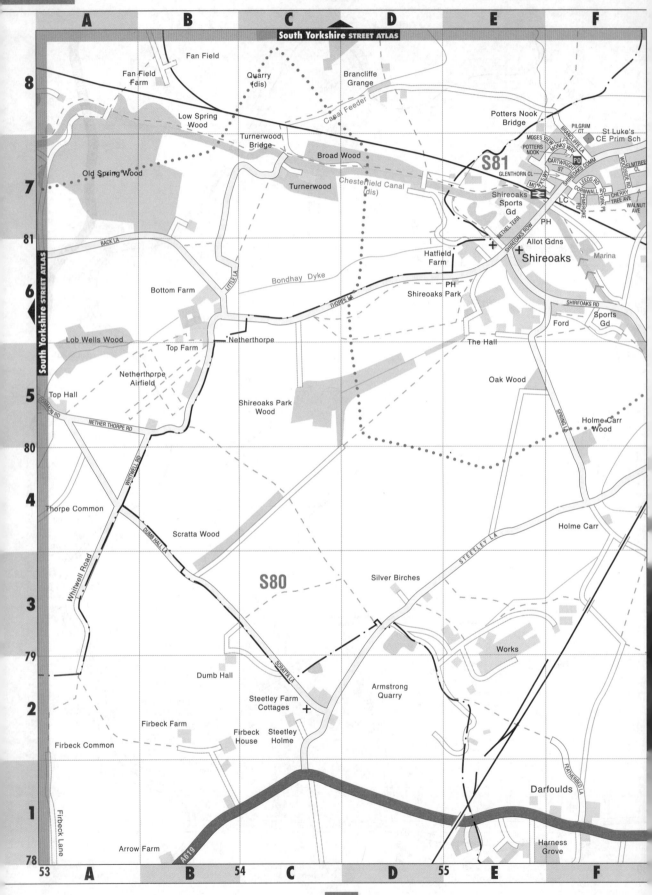

8

Fan Field

Fan Field Farm

Quarry (dis)

Brancliffe Grange

Canal Feeder

Low Spring Wood

Turnerwood Bridge

Broad Wood

Potters Nook Bridge

PILGRIM CT

St Luke's CE Prim Sch

MOSES VIEW

BRANCLIFFE LA

MONKS WAY

POTTERS NOOK

CARTWRIGHT ST

PO

ELMTREE CL

S81

GLENTHORN CL

MOSS WY

SHIREOAKS COMM

WOODSIDE RD

CORNWALL RD

LEEDS RD

YORK PL

CHERRY TREE AVE

WALNUT AVE

7

Old Spring Wood

Turnerwood

Chesterfield Canal (dis)

Shireoaks Sports Gd

LC

COPPERIDGE RD

PH

81

BACK LA

Bondhay Dyke

Hatfield Farm

BETHEL TERR

SHIREOAKS ROW

Allot Gdns

Marina

Shireoaks

6

LITTLE LA

Bottom Farm

THORPE LA

PH

Shireoaks Park

SHIRFOAKS RD

Ford

Sports Gd

Lob Wells Wood

Top Farm

Netherthorpe

The Hall

5

Netherthorpe Airfield

Shireoaks Park Wood

Oak Wood

SPRING LA

Holme Carr Wood

Top Hall

COMMON RD

NETHER THORPE RD

80

WHITWELL RD

4

Thorpe Common

DUMB HALL LA

Scratta Wood

STEETLEY LA

Holme Carr

Whitwell Road

S80

Silver Birches

3

Works

79

Dumb Hall

SCRATTA LA

Armstrong Quarry

2

Steetley Farm Cottages

Firbeck Farm

Firbeck House

Steetley Holme

FEATHERBED LA

Firbeck Common

Darfoulds

1

Firbeck Lane

Arrow Farm

A619

Harness Grove

78

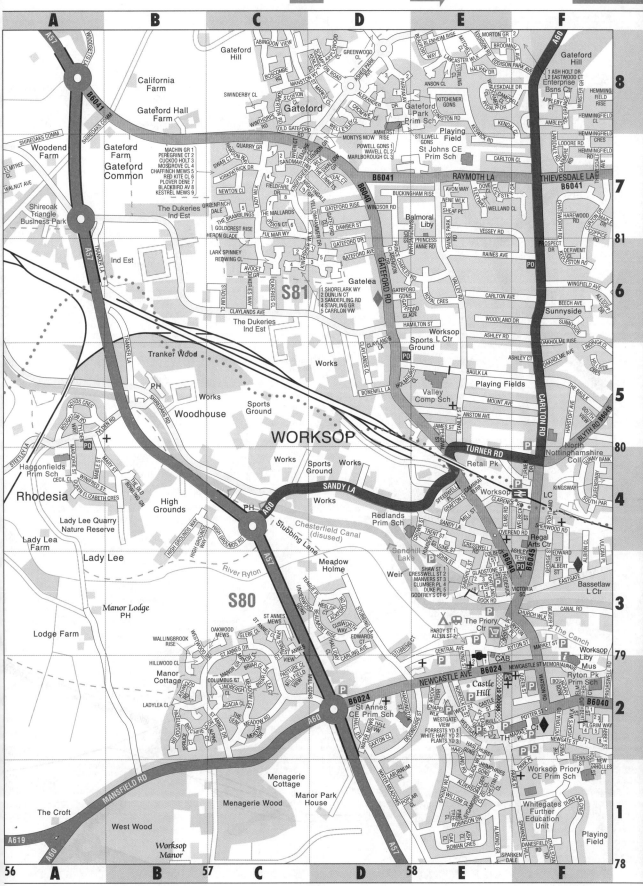

F2
1 LANGLEY ST
2 MELROSE WLK
3 LANERCOST MEWS
4 BUSHMEAD MEWS
5 NEWBURY MEWS
6 NOSTELL MEWS
7 EVESHAM MEWS
8 LAVENHAM MEWS

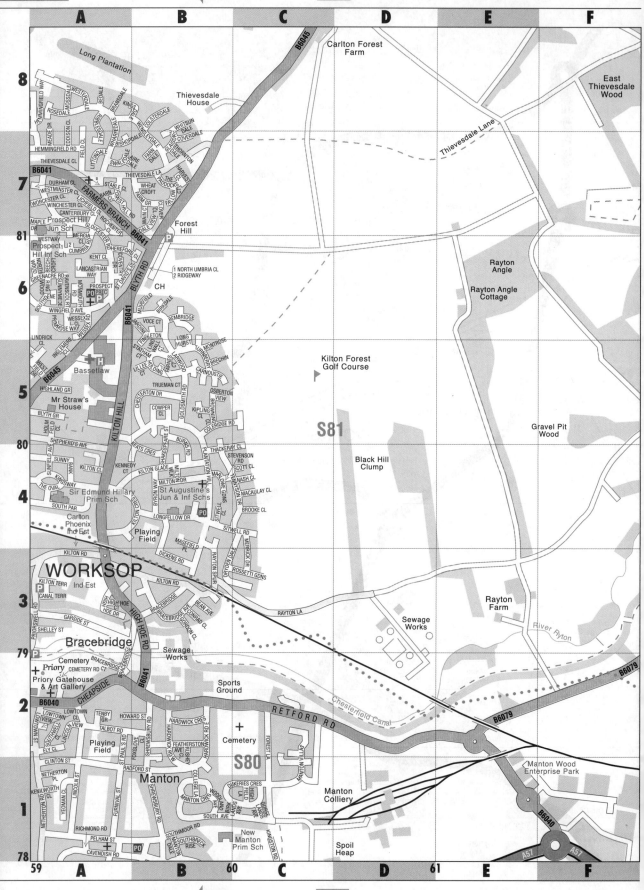

A B C D E F

8

Long Plantation

Carlton Forest Farm

East Thievesdale Wood

Thievesdale House

B6045

Thievesdale Lane

7

FARMERS BRANCH

B6041

B6041

The Paddocks

Forest Hill

Rayton Angle

81

Prospect Hill Jun Sch

Prospect Hill Inf Sch

BLYTH RD

Rayton Angle Cottage

1 NORTH UMBRIA CL
2 RIDGEWAY

CH

6

PO P REC

Kilton Forest Golf Course

KILTON HILL

Long Hurst

5

B6045

Bassetlaw H

Mr Straw's House

S81

Gravel Pit Wood

Black Hill Clump

80

Sir Edmund Hillary Prim Sch

St Augustine's Jun & Inf Schs

4

Carlton Phoenix Ind Est

Playing Field

WORKSOP

Ind Est

3

KILTON TERR

CANAL TERR

KILTON RD

HIGH HOE RD

RAYTON LA

Rayton Farm

Sewage Works

Rayton Farm

River Ryton

Bracebridge

79

Cemetery

Priory

Priory Gatehouse & Art Gallery

CHEAPSIDE

B6041

Sewage Works

Sports Ground

Chesterfield Canal

B6079

B6079

2

B6040

RETFORD RD

Playing Field

Cemetery

S80

Manton Villas

Manton Wood Enterprise Park

Manton

Manton Colliery

B6040

1

New Manton Prim Sch

Spoil Heap

A57

A57

78

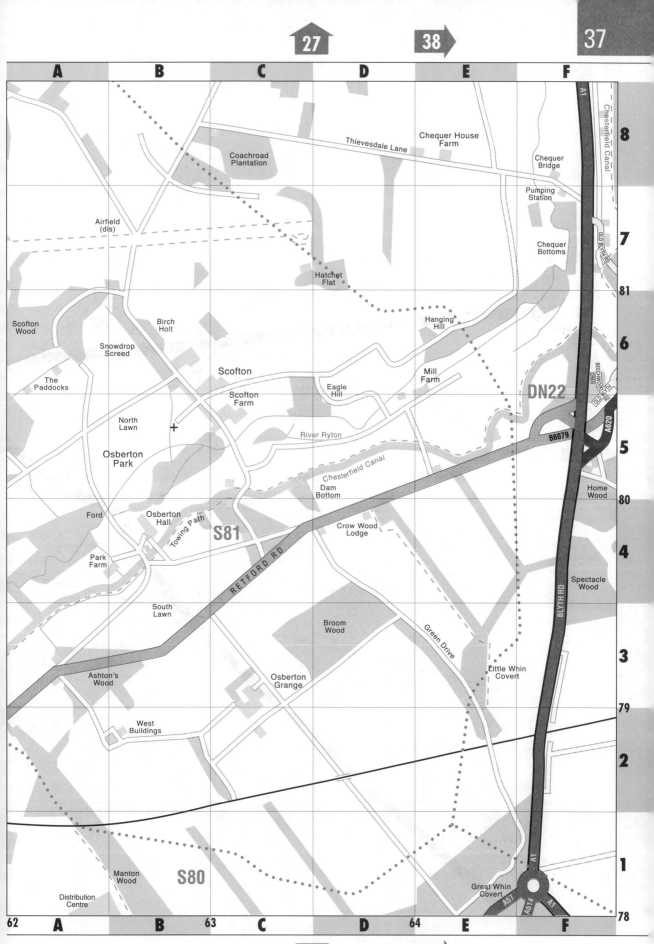

A B C D E F

8

Chequer House Farm

Thievesdale Lane

Coachroad Plantation

Chequer Bridge

7

Airfield (dis)

Pumping Station

Chequer Bottoms

81

Hatchet Flat

Hanging Hill

6

Scofton Wood

Birch Holt

Snowdrop Screed

Scofton

Mill Farm

DN22

The Paddocks

Scofton Farm

Eagle Hill

North Lawn

+

River Ryton

5

Osberton Park

B6079

A620

OLD BLYTH RD

BEECHWOOD CRES

OLD BLYTH RD

Chesterfield Canal

Dam Bottom

Home Wood

80

Ford

Osberton Hall

Towing Path

S81

Crow Wood Lodge

4

Park Farm

RETFORD RD

Spectacle Wood

BLYTH RD

South Lawn

Broom Wood

Green Drive

3

Ashton's Wood

Osberton Grange

Little Whin Covert

79

West Buildings

2

Manton Wood

S80

1

Great Whin Covert

A1

Distribution Centre

A57

A614

A1

78

62 A 63 B C 64 D E F

37
28

A   B   C   D   E   F

8

Green Mile Farm

GREEN MILE LA

7

OLD LONDON RD

Bowman Hill

Ranby CE Prim Sch

Ranby House Sch

Sewage Works

81

PH

H M Prison

New Plantation

6

OLD BLYTH RD

RETFORD RD

A620

Ranby

STRAIGHT MILE

PILGRIM CL

A620

BEECHWOOD DR

Walker's Wood

The Rectory

Beech Wood Farm

GREEN LA

Dunstons Clump

5

Chestnut Hill

DN22

Morton

B6420

Morton Hall Gardens

80

Kaye's Wood

Rushey Inn Wood

4

Morton Park

Forest Farm

LC

LC

Mansfield Road Crossing

OLD LONDON RD

3

Works

MANSFIELD RD

79

Little Morton Farm

2

Morton Hill Farm

1

78

B6420

65   A   B   66   C   D   67   E   F

37
49

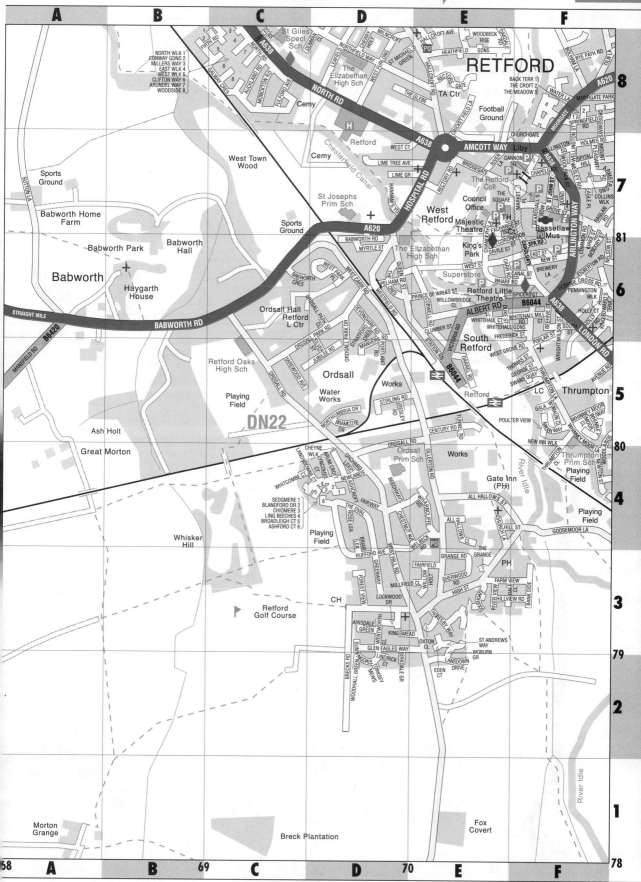

A   B   C   D   E   F

8
7
81
6
5
80
4
3
79
2
1

RETFORD

NORTH WLK 1
CONWAY GDNS 2
MILLERS WAY 3
EAST WLK 4
WEST WLK 5
CLIFTON WAY 6
ARUNDEL WAY 7
WOODSIDE 8

St Giles Specl Sch
The Elizabethan High Sch
TA Ctr
Retford
West Town Wood
Chesterfield Canal
Cemy
Cemy
WEST CT
LIME TREE AVE
LIME GR

BACK TERR 1
THE CROFT 2
THE MEADOW 3

Football Ground
Moorgate Park
CHURCHGATE
AMCOTT WAY
Liby
The Retford Coll
The Square
Council Office
Majestic Theatre
West Retford
King's Park
The Elizabethan High Sch
Bassetlaw Mus
Superstore
Retford Little Theatre
ALBERT RD
South Retford
B6044
Retford

Sports Ground
Babworth Home Farm
Babworth Park
Babworth Hall
Babworth
Haygarth House
St Josephs Prim Sch
Sports Ground
A620
BABWORTH RD
MYRTLE ST
BABWORTH RD
STRAIGHT MILE
B6420
MANSFIELD RD
Ordsall Hall Retford L Ctr
Retford Oaks High Sch
DN22
Ordsall
Playing Field
Water Works
Ash Holt
Great Morton
Works
STIRLING RD
BRAMCOTE DR
NORTHUMBRIA DR
CENTURY RD
TUNNEL RD

SEDGMERE 1
BLANDFORD DR 2
CHIOMERE 3
LING BEECHES 4
BROADLEIGH CT 5
ASHFORD CT 6

Ordsall RD
Ordsall Prim Sch
Works
Gate Inn (PH)
River Idle
Thrumpton Prim Sch
Playing Field
Thrumpton
LC
New Inn Wlk
POULTER VIEW
Playing Field

Whisker Hill
Playing Field
CH
Retford Golf Course
ALL HALLOWS ST
THE GRANGE
PH
GOOSEMOOR LA
Playing Field

Morton Grange
Breck Plantation
Fox Covert
River Idle

68   A   B   69   C   D   70   E   F   78

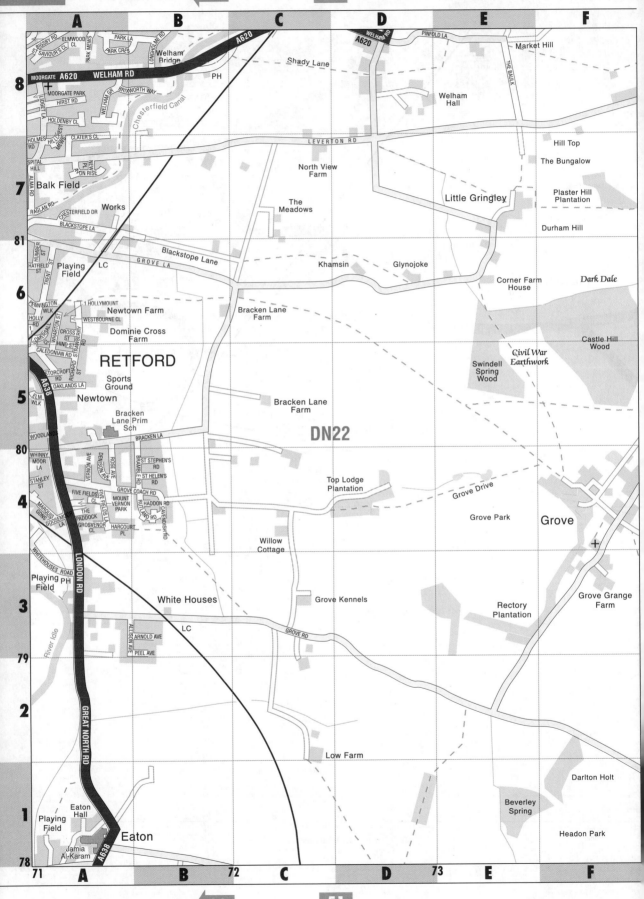

A   B   C   D   E   F

8

Moorgate A620 WELHAM RD

S BIGSBY RD
ELMWOOD CL
SAVIOUR'S CL
PARK MEWS
PARK LA
PARK CRES
LONGHOLME RD
Welham Bridge
PH
A620
Shady Lane
A620
PINFOLD LA
Market Hill
THE BAULK

LUDGATE
MELCHESTER
HIRST RD
Moorgate Park
BRIXWORTH WAY
WELHAM GR
Chesterfield Canal
Welham Hall

HOLDENBY CL
HOLMES RD
CLATER'S CL
NEW PL
NEWTON RISE
LEVERTON RD
Hill Top
The Bungalow

SPITAL HILL
ALMA RD
7 Balk Field
North View Farm
Little Gringley
Plaster Hill Plantation

RAGLAN RD
CHESTERFIELD DR
Works
The Meadows
Durham Hill

81
BLACKSTOPE LA
Blackstope Lane
Khamsin
Glynojoke

HUMBER ST
TRENT ST
HATFIELD ST
Playing Field
LC
GROVE LA
Corner Farm House
Dark Dale

6
PENNINGTON WLK
HOLLY RD
1 HOLLYMOUNT
Newtown Farm
WESTBOURNE CL
Bracken Lane Farm
Swindell Spring Wood
Civil War Earthwork
Castle Hill Wood

GOMERSALL
WHARTON ST
CROSS ST
HIND ST
STRAWBERRY
Dominie Cross Farm

CALEDONIAN RD
RICHARD ST
RETFORD

A638
STORCROFT RD
OAKLANDS LA
Sports Ground

5
ELM WLK
Newtown
Bracken Lane Farm
DN22

WOODLANDS
Bracken Lane Prim Sch
BRACKEN LA

80
WHINNY MOOR LA
VERNON AVE
DENISON AVE
ROSE AVE
BRAMBLE RD
ST STEPHEN'S RD
ST HELEN'S RD
Top Lodge Plantation

STANLEY ST
FIVE FIELDS CL
FIVE FIELDS LA
GROVE COACH RD
MOUNT VERNON PARK
RUTLAND RD
HADDON RD
CAVENDISH RD
Grove Drive

4
MARQUIS GDNS
GOOSEMOOR LA
THE PADDOCK
GROSVENOR CL
HARCOURT PL
Grove Park
Grove

WHITEHOUSES ROAD
Playing Field
PH
Willow Cottage
Rectory Plantation
Grove Grange Farm

3
LONDON RD
White Houses
LC
Grove Kennels
GROVE RD

ALLISON AVE
ARNOLD AVE
PEEL AVE

River Idle
79

GREAT NORTH RD

2
Low Farm
Darlton Holt

1
Playing Field
Eaton Hall
Beverley Spring
Headon Park

Jamia Al-Karam
A638
Eaton
78

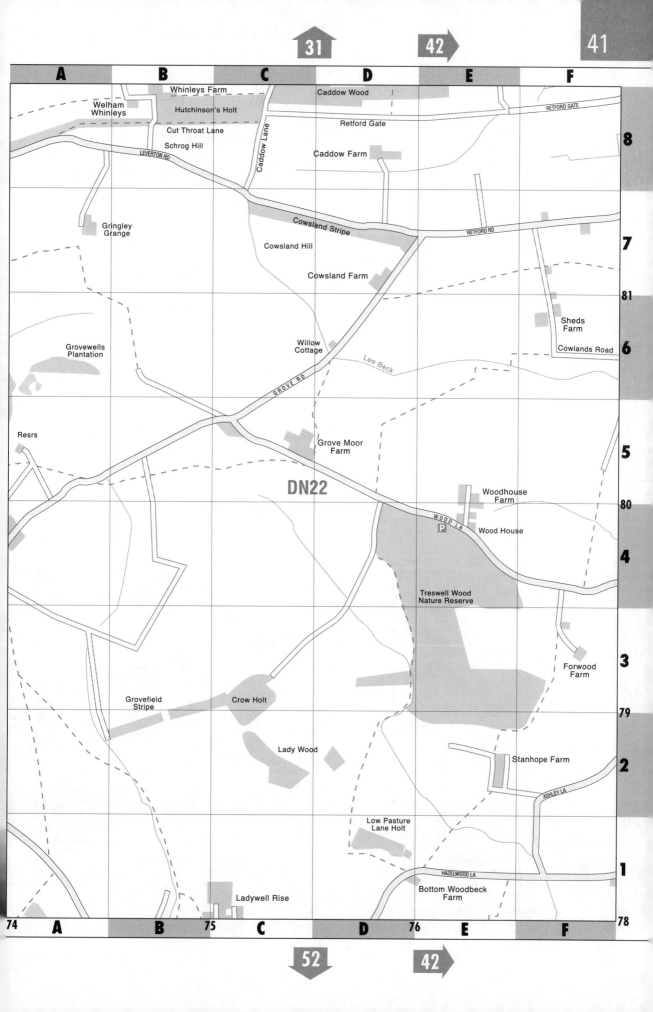

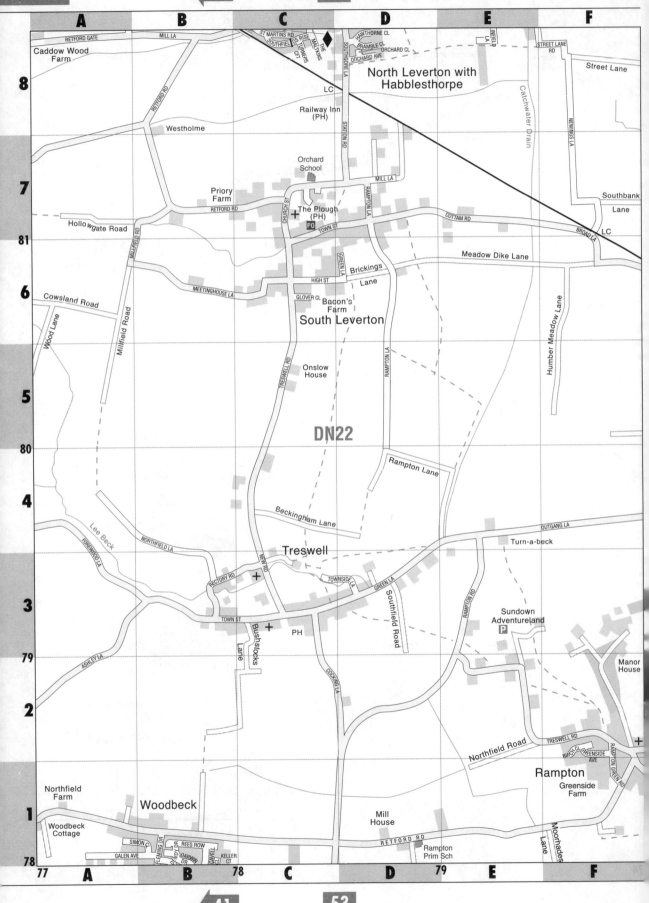

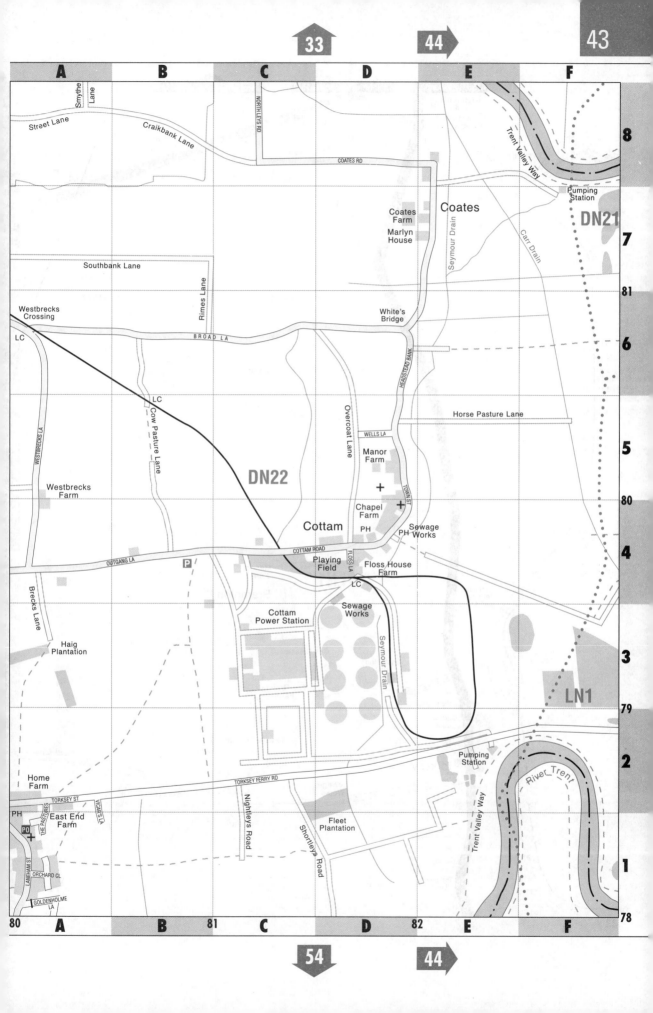

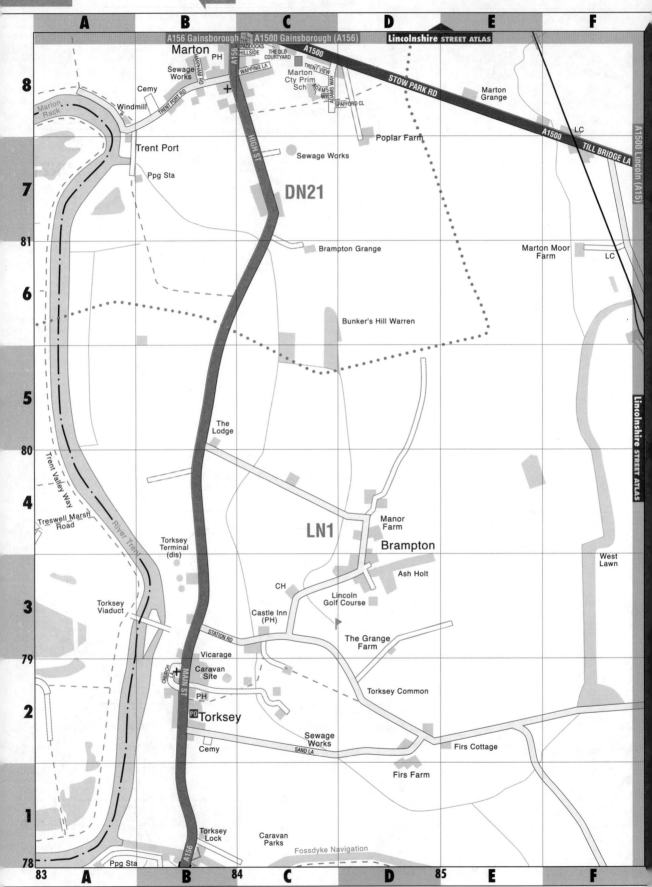

A   B   C   D   E   F

8

A156 Gainsborough   A1500 Gainsborough (A156)

Marton

THE PADDOCKS
HILLSIDE
THE OLD COURTYARD

PH

A156

WAPPING LA

A1500

STOW PARK RD

Marton Grange

Sewage Works

Cemy

Windmill

TRENT PORT RD

Marton Cty Prim Sch

TRENT VIEW
ADAMS WAY
ADAMS WY

SPAFFORD CL

A1500

LC

Marlon Rack

7

Trent Port

HIGH ST

Poplar Farm

TILL BRIDGE LA

A1500 Lincoln (A15)

Ppg Sta

Sewage Works

DN21

81

Brampton Grange

Marton Moor Farm

LC

6

Bunker's Hill Warren

Lincolnshire STREET ATLAS

5

The Lodge

80

Trent Valley Way

River Trent

Treswell Marsh Road

4

Torksey Terminal (dis)

Manor Farm

LN1

Brampton

West Lawn

Ash Holt

3

Torksey Viaduct

CH

Lincoln Golf Course

Castle Inn (PH)

STATION RD

The Grange Farm

79

Vicarage

CHURCH LA
MAIN ST

Caravan Site

Torksey Common

2

PH

PO Torksey

Cemy

Sewage Works

SAND LA

Firs Cottage

Firs Farm

1

Torksey Lock

A156

Caravan Parks

Fossdyke Navigation

78   Ppg Sta

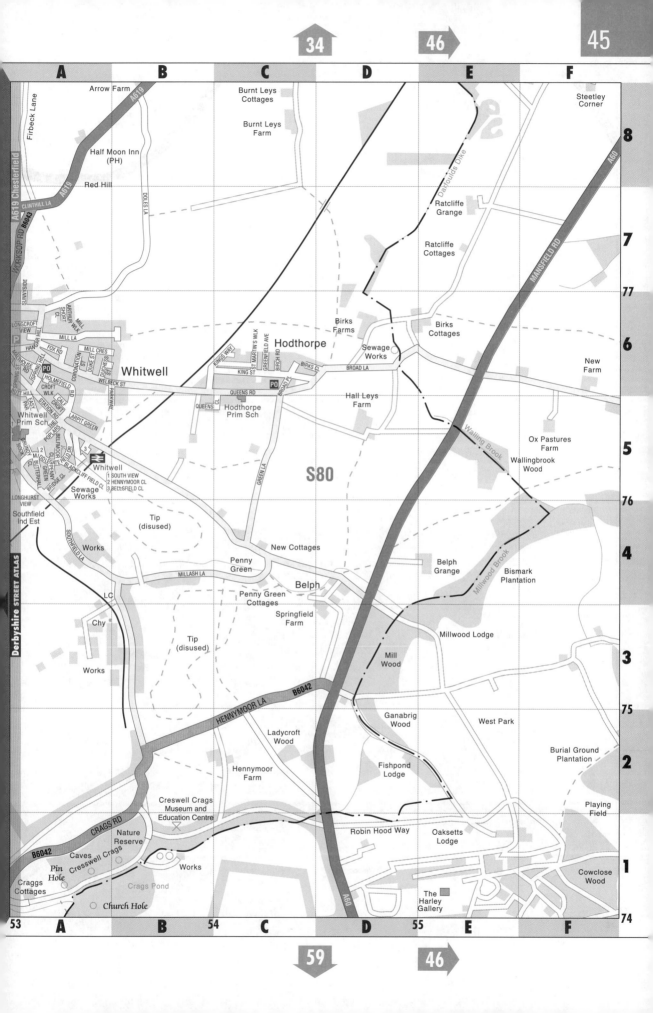

A **B** **C** **D** **E** **F**

Firbeck Lane

Arrow Farm

A619

Burnt Leys Cottages

Burnt Leys Farm

Steetley Corner

8

A619 Chesterfield

Half Moon Inn (PH)

Red Hill

CLINTHILL LA
B6043

DOLES LA

Darfoulds Dike

Ratcliffe Grange

MANSFIELD RD

A60

7

WORKSOP RD

Ratcliffe Cottages

77

SUNNYSIDE

LONGCROFT VIEW

MILL LA

ARTHUR WLK
SPINKHILL CL

MILL CRES

Whitwell

Hodthorpe

Birks Farms

Sewage Works

Birks Cottages

New Farm

6

MALTHOUSE RD
SPRING HILL RD
HANGAR HILL
FOX RD
MILL CL

CORONATION ST
DUKE ST
DUCHESS ST

P
PO

Whitwell Prim Sch.

HOLMEFIELD RD
CROFT WLK
STATION RD
CROFT

WELBECK ST
PARKWAY
LARPIT GREEN

KINGS WAY
ST MARTIN'S WLK
GREENFIELD AVE
BIRCH RD

KING ST

QUEENS RD
QUEENS CL

PO
BIRKS CL

BROAD LA
BROAD PL

Hall Leys Farm

Walling Brook

Ox Pastures Farm

Wallingbrook Wood

5

Whitwell Prim Sch

POPLARS
BELMOOR RD
BLACKCLIFF FIELD CL
BRIDGE CL
PENNY GREEN
BUTTERHALL
MIDDLEGATE

Hodthorpe Prim Sch

Whitwell
1 SOUTH VIEW
2 HENNYMOOR CL
3 BELLSFIELD CL

GREEN LA

S80

76

LONGHURST VIEW

Sewage Works

Southfield Ind Est

SOUTHFIELD LA

Works

Tip (disused)

New Cottages

Penny Green

MILLASH LA

Belph

Belph Grange

Millwood Brook

Bismark Plantation

4

LC

Chy

Works

Tip (disused)

Penny Green Cottages

Springfield Farm

Mill Wood

Millwood Lodge

3

B6042

HENNYMOOR LA

Ladycroft Wood

Ganabrig Wood

West Park

75

Hennymoor Farm

Fishpond Lodge

Burial Ground Plantation

2

Creswell Crags Museum and Education Centre

Playing Field

CRAGS RD

Nature Reserve

Robin Hood Way

Oaksetts Lodge

Cowclose Wood

1

B6042

Caves

Pin Hole

Cresswell Crags

Works

A60

The Harley Gallery

Craggs Cottages

Crags Pond

Church Hole

Derbyshire STREET ATLAS

A B C D E F

8

7

77

6

5

76

4

3

75

2

1

74

MANSFIELD RD
A60

Worksop Manor

Manor Park

A57

HARLEY CL
WATER MEADOWS
SOUTHERN WOOD
SPARKEN CL
SPARKEN DALE
DUNSTAN CRES
ATHELSTAN RD

Portland Sch

Hawk's Nest

Manor Croft

SPARKEN HILL
A57

Hawk's Nest Screed

Pudding Hill Wood

Rock Cottage

CASTLE FARM LA

Castle Farm

Oak Wood

Plain Piece

BROAD LA

Sloswicks Springs

South African Piece

S80

Manor Hills

Sloswicks Farm

Hill Wood

South Lodge

DRINKING PIT LA

Drinking Pit Lane

Robin Hood Way

Duchess' Plantation

Busaco

Wedding Drive

Robin Hood Way

Lord St Vincent Wood

White Deer Park

Porter Oaks

St Cuthbert's in the Woods

Lord Harley's Wood

Welbeck Woodhouse

White Stone Piece

Lady Harriet's Plantation

Lawn Wood

Valley Clump

Shrubbery Lake

Hagg Hill

Playing Field

Welbeck Park

Long Drive Wood

Long Valley

Welbeck Abbey

Wingfield Wood

8

7

77

6

S80

5

76

4

3

75

2

1

74

A57

Spoil Heap

Windmill Wood

Spoil Heap

Forest Farm Plantation North

Holy Family RC Prim Sch

Worksop Golf Course

OLD COACH RD

Forest Farm Plantation South

Manton Forest Farm

Cemy

Lowtown Plantation

Nature Reserve

Hannah Park Wood

WINDMILL LA

CH

Sparken Hill Farm

Worksop Coll

Kidney Clump

CH

Playing Fields

College Pines Golf Course

Clumber Road End Wood

Clumber Lane Farm

Forest Cottages Plantation

Clumber Park Country Park

Old Lings

Clumber Old Wood

Burnt Oak Plantation

Pheasant Wood

CLUMBER RD

Truman's Lodge

Cottage Plantation

Clumber Cottage

Robin Hood Way

Drinking Pit Lane

Robin Hood Way

Truman's Brake

Sod Banks

OLLERTON RD

Clumber Lane

Burnt Oak Wood

Forest Screed

Thrall Hill Plantation

Blackhill Clump

Lady Anne's Plantation

Sir James Saumarez Plantation

Woodcockhill Plantation

LIMETREE AVE

Whitwell Round

Haddon Pasture

Holywell Wood

Scotland Farm

New Road

Westfield Wood

Lord Howe's Plantation

Long Valley Screed

B6034

Long Valley Lodge

NETHERTON RD

B6034

SPARKEN HILL

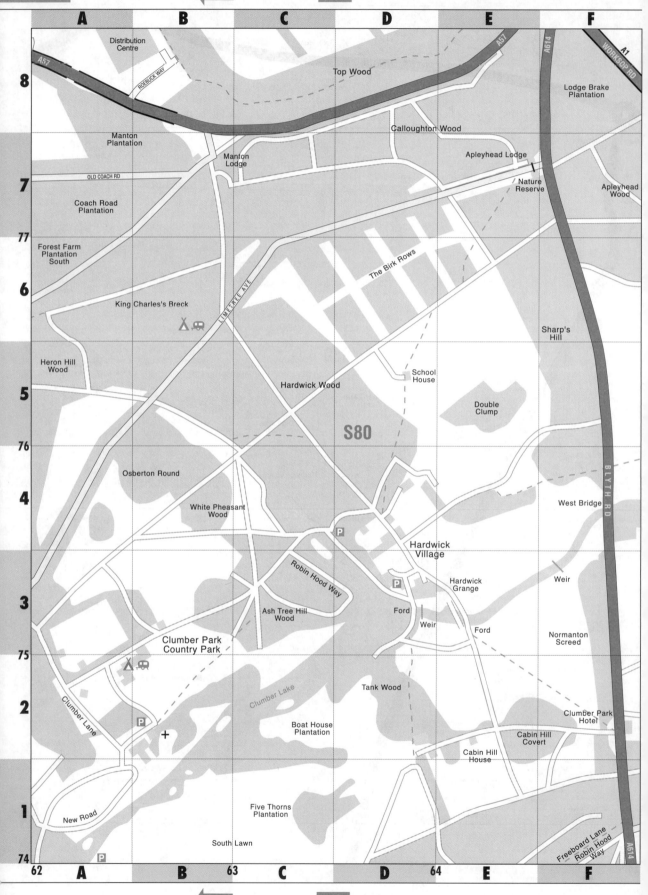

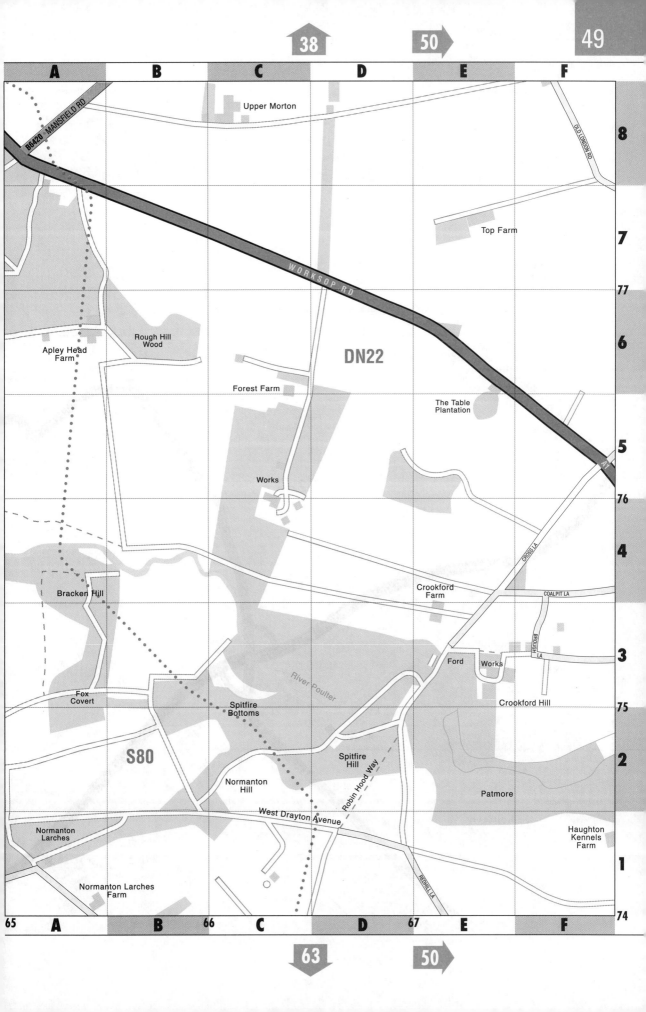

A B C D E F

B6420 MANSFIELD RD

OLD LONDON RD

Upper Morton

Top Farm

WORKSOP RD

DN22

Rough Hill Wood

Apley Head Farm

Forest Farm

The Table Plantation

A1

Works

CROSS LA

Crookford Farm

COALPIT LA

Bracken Hill

BROUGH LA

Ford

Works

Crookford Hill

River Poulter

Fox Covert

Spitfire Bottoms

S80

Spitfire Hill

Robin Hood Way

Normanton Hill

Patmore

West Drayton Avenue

Normanton Larches

Haughton Kennels Farm

REDHILL LA

Normanton Larches Farm

A B C D E F

8

7

77

6

Morton Grange

Eaton Breck
Farm

Clevelandhouse
Farm

Eaton
Bogs

Apple Pie
Plantation

OLD LONDON RD

BRICK YARD RD

River Idle

Gamston Covert

Jockey
House

Works

Playing
Field

MUTTONSHIRE HILL

B6387

JOCKEY LA

Saw Mill

Retford
(Gamston Airport)

OLLERTON RD

RECTORY LA

Gamston
CE
Prim Sch

5

A1

DN22

Church Farm

MANOR CL

76

Dover
Holt

Church LA

4

WORKSOP RD

COALPIT LA

HOLLY BUSH
CL

HIGH ST

Ind
Est

Bunker's Hill

Church Lane

SANDY LA

HEADLAND AVE

ELM
TREE
PL

YEW TREE RD

LIME TREE RD

BEECH
WALK

MAPLE DR

TWYFORD LA

PARK LA

DOVER BOTTOM

Pepperley
Hill

CEDAR TREE
RD

Elkesley
Prim Sch

Elkesley

TWYFORD LA

Twyford
Bridge

River Maun

LAWNWOOD
LA

LAWNWOOD AVE

Playing
Field

Battery Lane

River Poulter

3

Dobdykes
Lane

BROUGH LA

Park View
Farm

OLD LONDON RD

75

Sewage
Works

Elkesley Wood

Haughton
Park Farm

School
Farm

Little Birch
Holt

CHURCH LA

2

Broom Hill

Haughton Kennels
Farm

Beggar's Rest

West Drayton Avenue

River Meden

LAWSON CL

GRAVEL PIT LA

Robin Hood Way

Cocked Hat
Plantations

Great Birch
Holt

Fox
Covert
Lane

A1

1

B6387

Colliery

74

68 A B 69 C D 70 E F

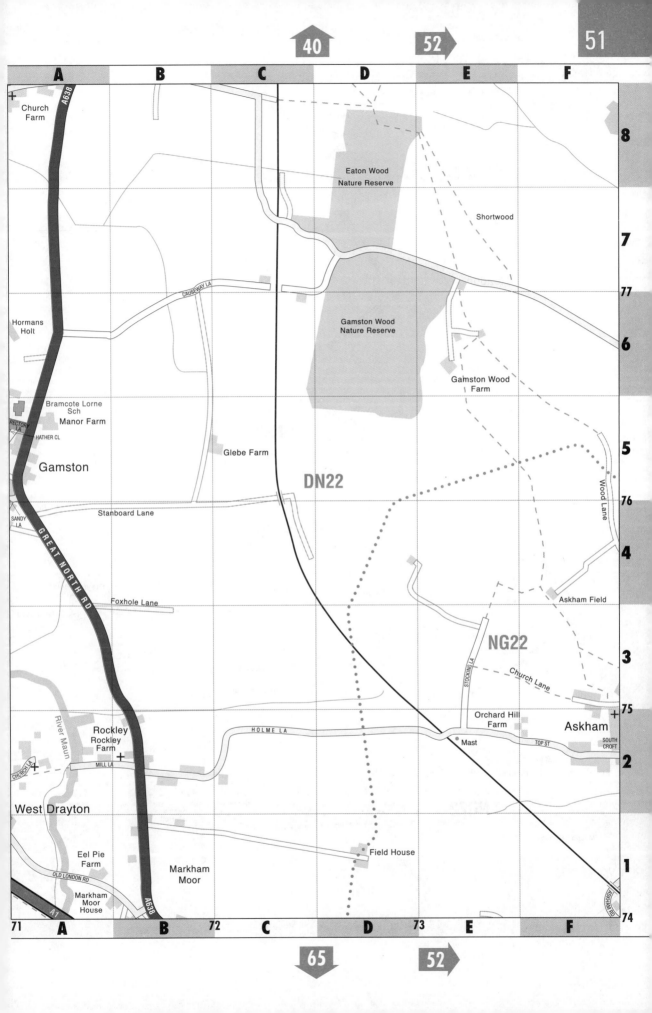

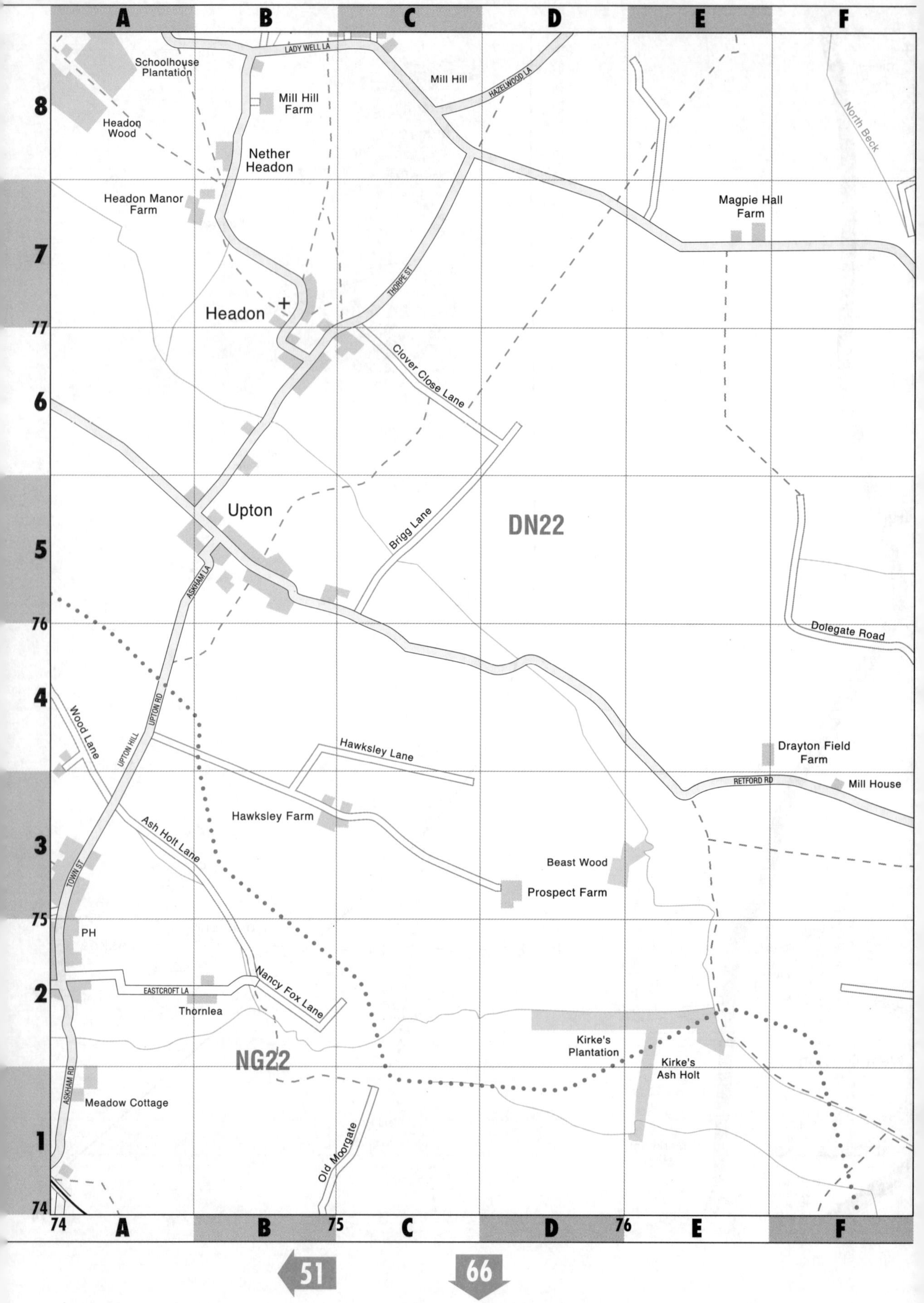

51
41

A B C D E F

8
7
77
6
5
76
4
3
75
2
1
74

LADY WELL LA
Schoolhouse Plantation
Mill Hill
Mill Hill Farm
Headon Wood
Nether Headon
HAZELWOOD LA
Headon Manor Farm
Magpie Hall Farm
North Beck
Headon +
THORPE ST
Clover Close Lane
Upton
Brigg Lane
DN22
ASKHAM LA
Dolegate Road
Wood Lane
UPTON RD
UPTON HILL
Hawksley Lane
Drayton Field Farm
RETFORD RD
Mill House
Ash Holt Lane
Hawksley Farm
Beast Wood
Prospect Farm
TOWN ST
PH
Nancy Fox Lane
EASTCROFT LA
Thornlea
NG22
Kirke's Plantation
Kirke's Ash Holt
ASKHAM RD
Meadow Cottage
Old Moorgate

74 A B 75 C D 76 E F

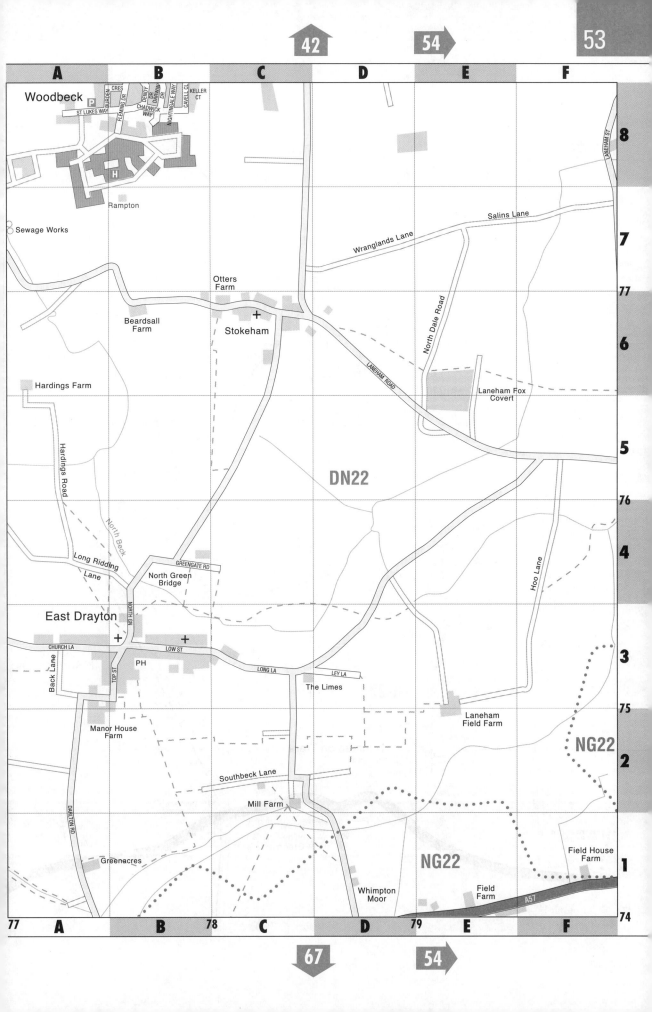

Woodbeck

A B C D E F

CRES
BURDEN
FLEMING DR
DENDY
DR DARWIN
NIGHTINGALE WAY
CAVELL CL
KELLER
CT
CHADWICK
WAY
St LUKES WAY

P

H

8

Rampton

Sewage Works

7

Salins Lane

Wranglands Lane

77

Otters
Farm

Beardsall
Farm

Stokeham

North Dale Road

Laneham Road

6

Hardings Farm

Laneham Fox
Covert

5

DN22

Hardings Road

North Beck

76

Long Ridding
Lane

GREENGATE RD

North Green
Bridge

Hoo Lane

4

East Drayton

NORTH GN

LOW ST

CHURCH LA

Back Lane

TOP ST

PH

LONG LA

LEY LA

The Limes

Laneham
Field Farm

3

75

Manor House
Farm

NG22

2

Southbeck Lane

Mill Farm

DARLTON RD

Greenacres

Whimpton
Moor

NG22

Field House
Farm

Field
Farm

A57

1

74

A B C D E F
77 78 79

A B C D E F

8

LANEHAM ST
GOLDENHOLME LA

Sewage Works

HELENSHIP LA

Broading Farm

Trentfield Farm

7

Maltkilns

Clayhough Lane

77

Rushmoor Farm

Manor House

DN22

RAMPTON RD

BROADINGS LA

Holly Folly Farm

6

MOOR LANE

Ferry Boat Inn (PH)

Laneham

Laughterton Marsh

River Trent

Church Laneham

Manor Farm

5

PH

MAIN ST

Sewage Works

LN1

Ring O'Bells

DUNHAM RD

76

Mill House

Trent Valley Way

MARSH LANE

4

Chequers Lane

Dunham Rack

3

NG22

Marsh Lane

75

Manor Farm

CHEQUERS LA

Dunham on Trent

2

White Swan (PH)

Hall

Playing Field

Bridge Inn (PH)

CARTWRIGHT CL

LANEHAM RD

UPPER ROW

Flears Farm

Dunham Bridge Toll

Green Lane

Dunham on Trent CE Prim Sch

TALL GABLES

Pumping Sta

PO

The Green

DUNHAM RD

1

LEACH CL

A57

A57

74

ROBERTS CL

80 A B 81 C D 82 E F

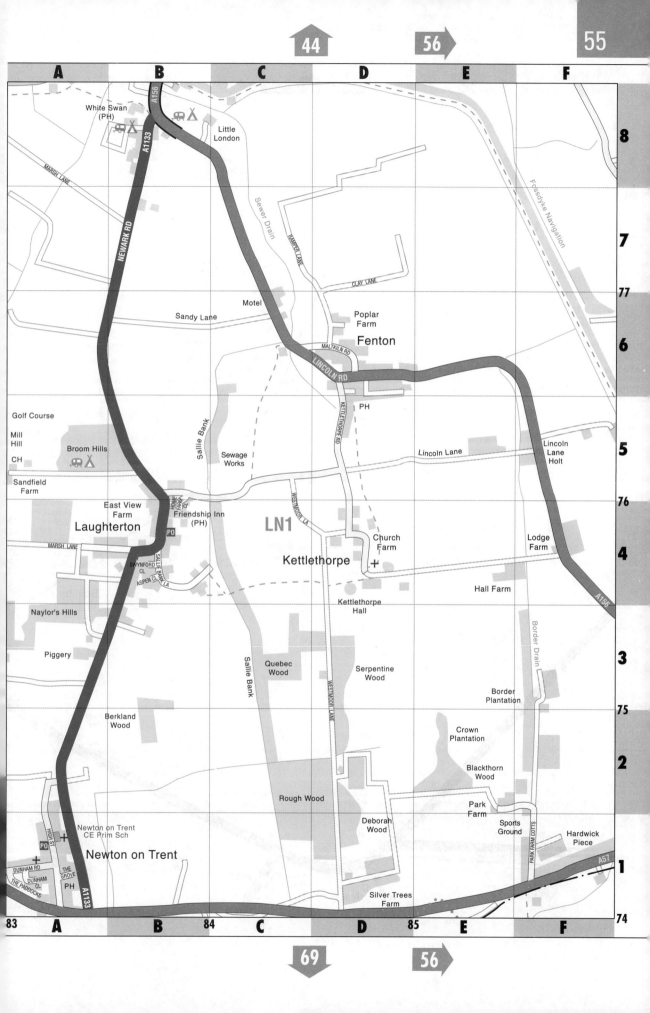

A
B
C
D
E
F

8
7
77
6
5
76
4
3
75
2
1
74

White Swan
(PH)

Little
London

MARSH LANE

NEWARK RD

A1133

A156

Sewer Drain

BAMPER LANE

CLAY LANE

Motel

Sandy Lane

MALTKILN RD

Poplar
Farm

Fenton

LINCOLN RD

PH

KETTLETHORPE RD

Golf Course

Mill
Hill

CH

Broom Hills

Sandfield
Farm

Sallie Bank

Sewage
Works

Lincoln Lane

Lincoln
Lane
Holt

East View
Farm

Laughterton

HOME FARM CL

Friendship Inn
(PH)

PO

LN1

WESTMOOR LA

Church
Farm

Kettlethorpe

Lodge
Farm

MARSH LANE

SWYNFORD CL

SALLIE BANK LA

ASPEN CL

Hall Farm

A156

Naylor's Hills

Kettlethorpe
Hall

Piggery

Border Drain

Sallie Bank

Quebec
Wood

WESTMOOR LANE

Serpentine
Wood

Border
Plantation

Berkland
Wood

Crown
Plantation

Blackthorn
Wood

Rough Wood

Deborah
Wood

Park
Farm

Sports
Ground

PARK FARM COTTS

Hardwick
Piece

HIGH ST

PO

Newton on Trent
CE Prim Sch

Newton on Trent

DUNHAM RD

DUNHAM CL

THE PADDOCKS

THE GROVE

PH

A1133

Silver Trees
Farm

A57

83
84
85
74

A
B
C
D
E
F

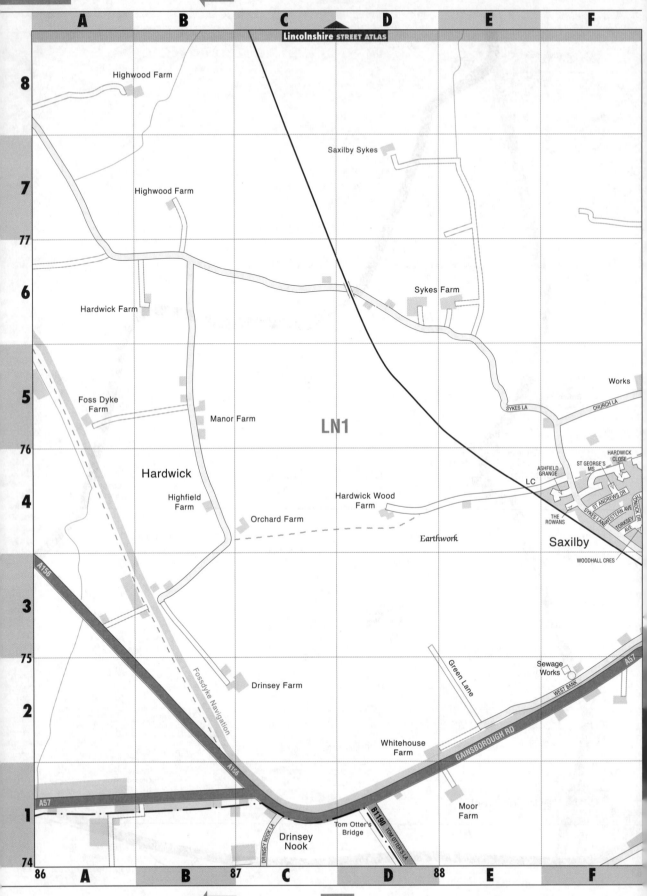

Highwood Farm

Saxilby Sykes

Highwood Farm

Sykes Farm

Hardwick Farm

Works

Foss Dyke Farm

SYKES LA

CHURCH LA

LN1

Manor Farm

HARDWICK CLOSE

ST GEORGE'S MS

ASHFIELD GRANGE

Hardwick

LC

ST ANDREWS DR

WESTERN AVE

CHUCK DR

Highfield Farm

Hardwick Wood Farm

SYKES LANE

TORKSEY AVE

THE ROWANS

Orchard Farm

Earthwork

Saxilby

WOODHALL CRES

A156

Green Lane

Sewage Works

A57

WEST BANK

Drinsey Farm

GAINSBOROUGH RD

Fossdyke Navigation

Whitehouse Farm

A156

A57

Moor Farm

B1190

DRINSEY NOOK LA

Drinsey Nook

Tom Otter's Bridge

TOM OTTER'S LA

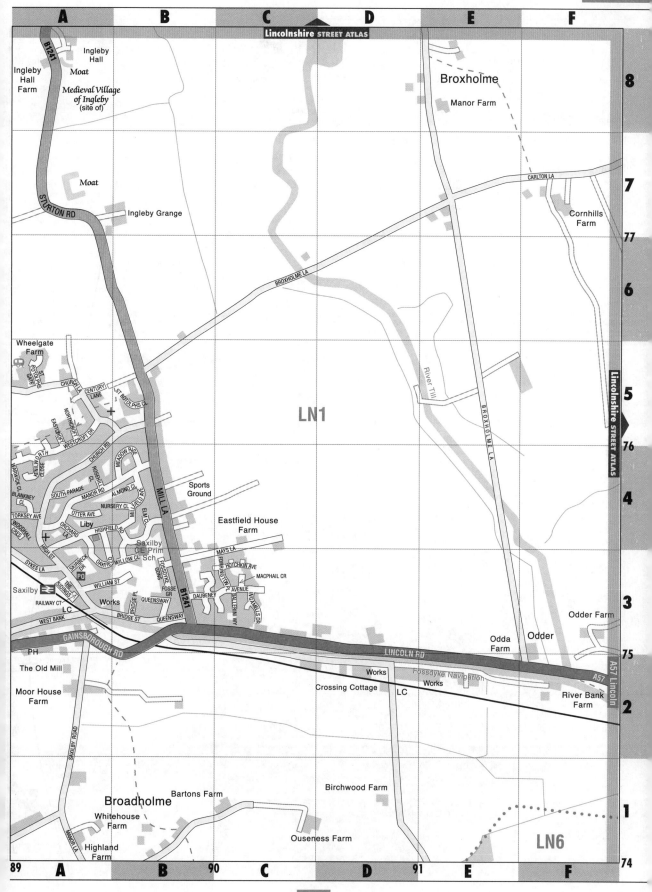

Lincolnshire STREET ATLAS

Broxholme

Ingleby Hall

Ingleby Hall Farm

Moat

Medieval Village of Ingleby (site of)

Manor Farm

Moat

CARLTON LA

STURTON RD

Ingleby Grange

Cornhills Farm

BROXHOLME LA

River Till

Wheelgate Farm

LN1

BROXHOLME LA

ST BOTOLPHS GATE

CHURCH LA

CENTURY LANE

ST BOTOLPHS CL

NORTHCROFT

WESTCROFT DR

EASTCROFT

CHURCH RD

MEADOW RIG

WESTFIELD AVE

MILL LA

Sports Ground

Eastfield House Farm

KENILWORTH CLOSE

ROSEHILL CL

SOUTH PARADE

MANOR RD

ALMOND CL

NURSERY CL

ELM CL

MAYS LA

WARWICK CL

BLANKNEY CL

OTTER AVE

MILL FIELD

HOTCHKIN AVE

TORKSEY AVE

Liby

HIGHFIELD

FORRINGTON PL

MACPHAIL CR

WOODHILL CRES

ORCHARD LA

HIGH ST

SKIRBECK DR

PO

OAKTREE

WILLOW CL

Saxilby CE Prim Sch

FOSSDYKE GDNS

DAUBENEY

AVENUE

INGOMELLS DR

BALLERINI WY

SYKES LA

THE SIDINGS

WILLIAM ST

FOSSE GR

Saxilby

RAILWAY CT

LC

Works

BRIDGE PL

QUEENSWAY

B1241

WEST BANK

BRIDGE ST

QUEENSWAY

Odder Farm

Odda Farm

Odder

GAINSBOROUGH RD

LINCOLN RD

A57 Lincoln

PH

The Old Mill

Works

Fossdyke Navigation

Works

River Bank Farm

Moor House Farm

Crossing Cottage

LC

SAXILBY ROAD

Broadholme

Bartons Farm

Birchwood Farm

Whitehouse Farm

MANOR LA

Highland Farm

Ouseness Farm

LN6

Lincolnshire STREET ATLAS

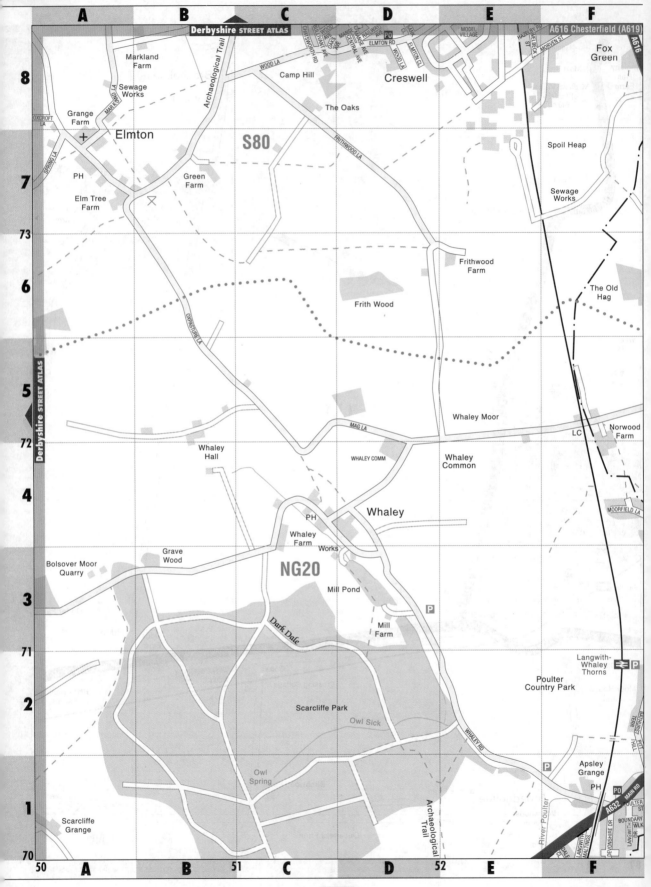

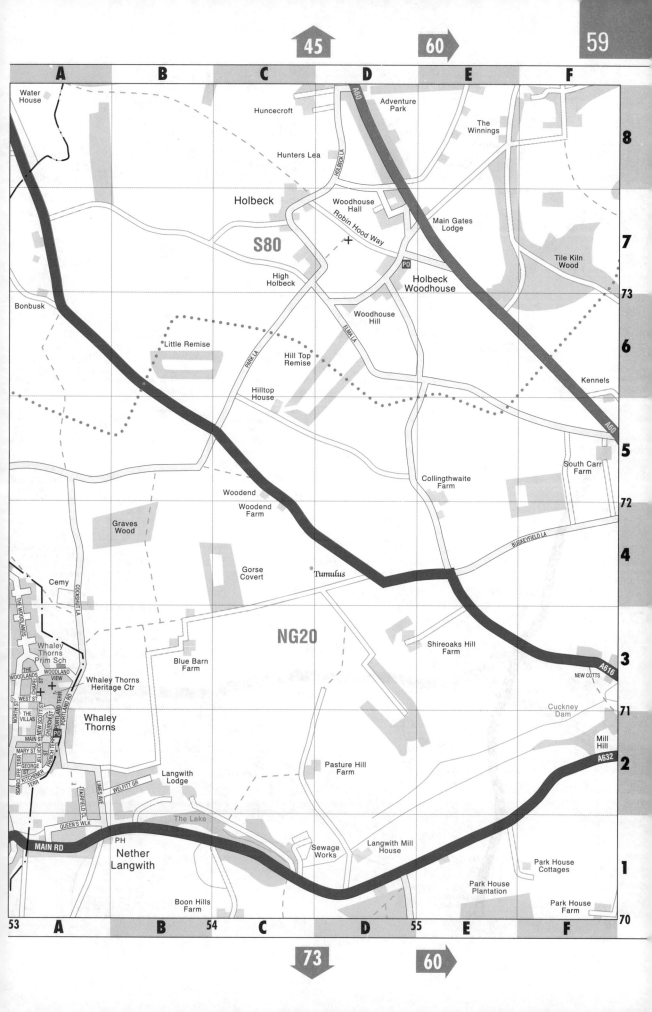

A B C D E F

8
7
73
6
5
72
4
3
71
2
1
70

Water House

Huncecroft

Adventure Park

The Winnings

Hunters Lea

Holbeck

Woodhouse Hall

Main Gates Lodge

HOLBECK LA

A60

Tile Kiln Wood

S80

Robin Hood Way

PO

Holbeck Woodhouse

High Holbeck

Bonbusk

Woodhouse Hill

Little Remise

Hill Top Remise

ELMA LA

PARK LA

Kennels

A60

Hilltop House

South Carr Farm

Woodend

Collingthwaite Farm

Woodend Farm

BUSKEYFIELD LA

Graves Wood

Gorse Covert

Tumulus

NG20

Shireoaks Hill Farm

A616

NEW COTTS

Cemy

Whaley Thorns Prim Sch

Blue Barn Farm

COOKSHUT LA

THE WOODLANDS

WOODLAND VIEW

CHAPEL ST

Whaley Thorns Heritage Ctr

Cuckney Dam

THE WOODLANDS

WEST ST

THE VILLAS

Whaley Thorns

PORTLAND TERR

PORTLAND RD

NEW SCOTT ST

CHURCH ST

Mill Hill

A632

NORTH ST

MAIN ST

MARY ST

JELLICOE TERR

PO

GEORGE ST

FRENCH TERR

SCARCLIFFE TERR

KITCHENER TERR

Langwith Lodge

Pasture Hill Farm

LIMES AVE

WELFITT GR

FAIRFIELD CL

QUEEN'S WLK

The Lake

Langwith Mill House

Park House Cottages

MAIN RD

PH

Nether Langwith

Sewage Works

Park House Plantation

Park House Farm

Boon Hills Farm

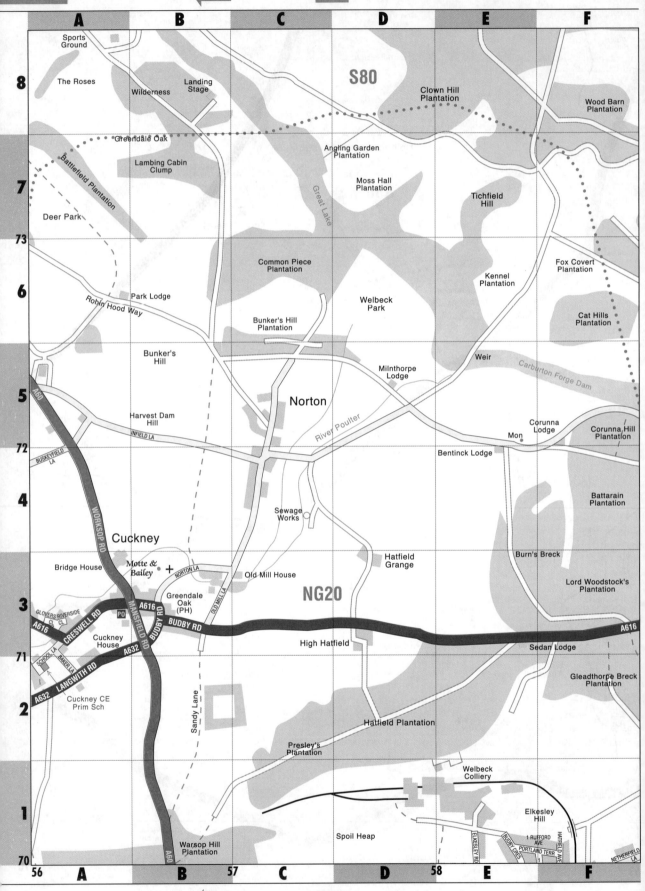

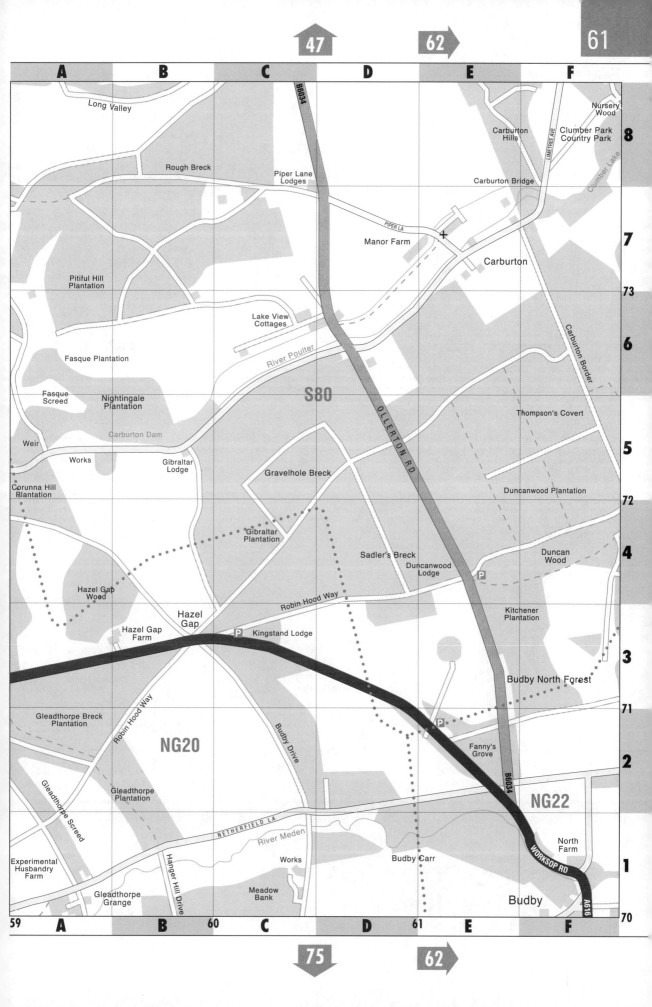

A B C D E F

8
7
73
6
5
72
4
3
71
2
1
70

Weir
Clumber Bridge
Thorney Hill
Claypit Wood
Little Oak Square
Clumber Park Country Park
Great Oak Square
Thoresby Border
Freeboard Lane
The Aviaries
Robin Hood Way
Blyth Corner
S80
Catwhins
Budby Corner Plantations
South Lodge
Carburton Corner
Morris Dancer's Plantation
Morris Dancer's Lodge
Day's Corner
Shepherd's Lodge
Piperwell Wood
Holders Grove
Charcoal Plantation
Osland Wood
Perlethorpe
Mary's Grove
River Meden
Weir
NG22
Thoresby Hall
Thoresby Home Farm
Thoresby Park
Thoresby Gallery (Pierrepont Art Gallery)
Weir
Perlethorpe Environment Education Centre
Cameleon Lodge
Weir
Weir
Spready Oaks
Deer Barn
Thoresby Lake
Pierrepoint Bridge
The Woodyard
Kingston Island
Nelson's Grove
Nelson's Lodge

BLYTH RD
A614

A B C D E F

8

7

73

Bothamsall

REDHILL LA

CHURCH LA

MAIN ST

MEDEN BANK

S80

Spittalmoor Forest Farm

MEADOW LA

River Meden

DN22

Ramillies Plantation

A614

Mill House Farm

6

B6387

Haughton

Conjure Alders

River Maun

Crow Park

5

72

Gosling Carr

Haughton Warren

Pickin's Bridge

Middle Ashes

Blackcliffe Hill Plantation

Robin Hood Way

4

Oakham Poultry Farms

Sports Ground

FOREST LA

Forest Lane

3

71

BLYTH RD

NG22

Anthony's Orchard

Whitewater

Whitemoor Farm

Robin Hood's Cave

Broom Covert

NEW HILL 1
KENNEDY RISE 2

1
2

RETFORD RD

2

Briers Lodge

MILL LA

Henrys Grove

Druids Cottage

WHITEWATER LA

Whitewater Bridge

New England

Walesby Forest

Breck Cottages

BRAKE RD

BRAKE RD

PH

1

The White Lodge

A614

B6387

70

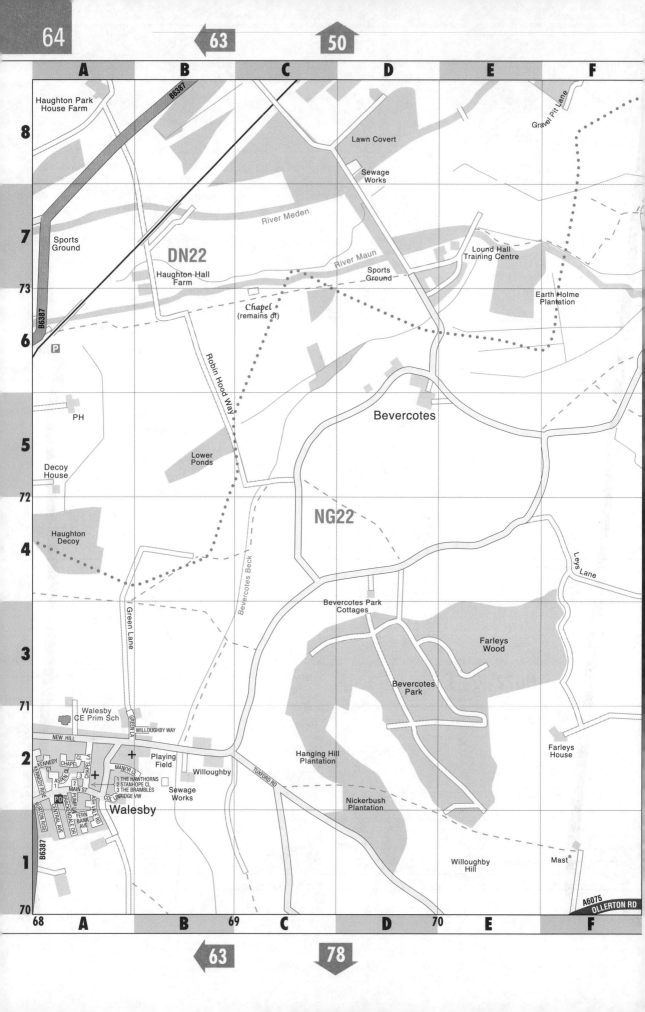

A   B   C   D   E   F

8

Haughton Park
House Farm

B6387

Lawn Covert

Gravel Pit Lane

Sewage
Works

7

Sports
Ground

B6387

DN22

River Meden

River Maun

Lound Hall
Training Centre

Sports
Ground

73

Haughton Hall
Farm

Chapel
(remains of)

Earth Holme
Plantation

6

B6387

P

Robin Hood Way

Bevercotes

PH

5

Decoy
House

Lower
Ponds

72

Haughton
Decoy

NG22

Bevercotes Beck

4

Leys Lane

Bevercotes Park
Cottages

Farleys
Wood

Green Lane

3

Bevercotes
Park

71

Walesby
CE Prim Sch

Green La

WILLOUGHBY WAY

Farleys
House

NEW HILL

2

KENNEDY CL
KENNEDY CT
CHAPEL LA
ASPEN
MAIN ST
ASH VALE RD

MANOR CL
1 THE HAWTHORNS
2 STANHOPE CL
3 THE BRAMBLES
COLINRIDGE VW

Playing
Field

Willoughby

TUXFORD RD

Hanging Hill
Plantation

Sewage
Works

BURTON RISE
PUMP LA
P O
CENTRAL AVE
BRACKENDALE DR
FERN BANK AVE

Walesby

Nickerbush
Plantation

1

B6387

Willoughby
Hill

Mast

A6075
OLLERTON RD

70

68   A   B   69   C   D   70   E   F

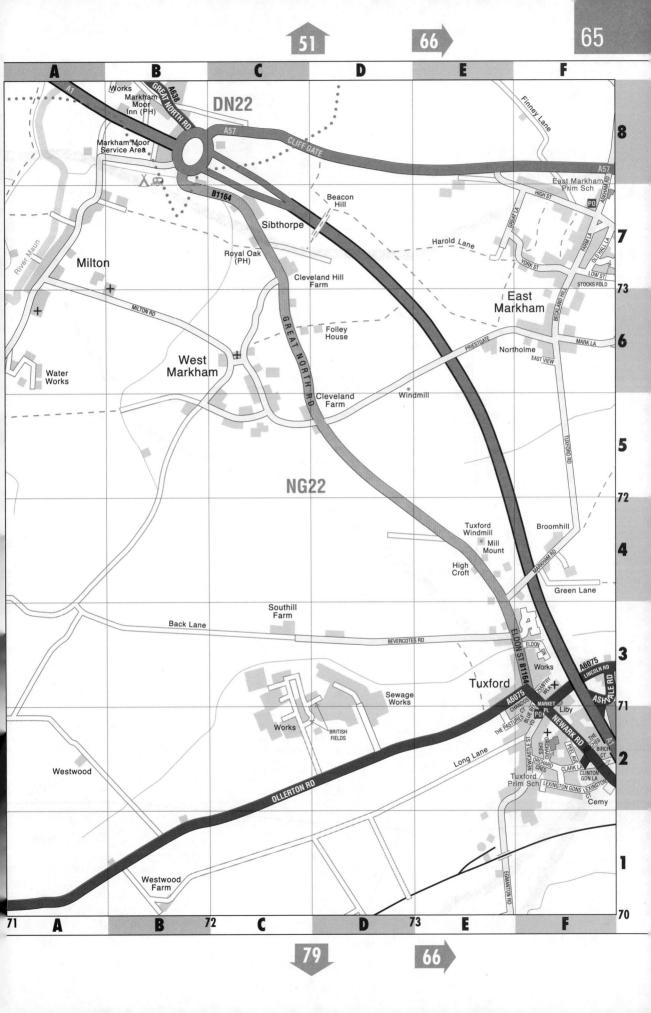

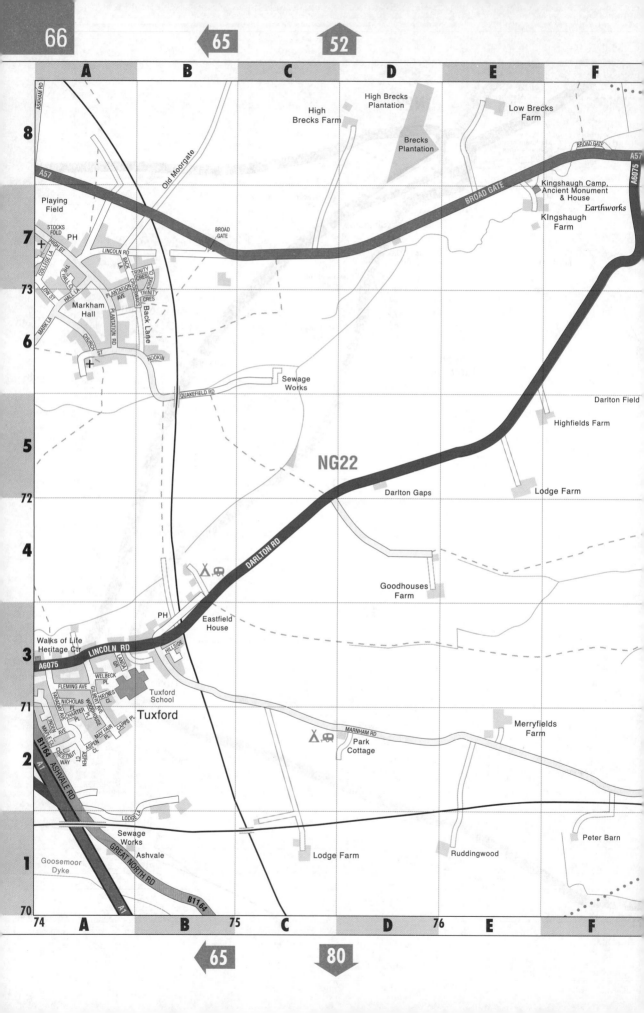

A   B   C   D   E   F

8

ASKHAM RD

High
Brecks Farm

High Brecks
Plantation

Brecks
Plantation

Low Brecks
Farm

BROAD GATE

A57

A6075

Old Moorgate

BROAD GATE

Kingshaugh Camp,
Ancient Monument
& House

Earthworks

Playing
Field

STOCKS
FOLD

PH

Kingshaugh
Farm

7

+   HIGH ST

LINCOLN RD

BROAD
GATE

HALL CT

COLLEGE LA

TRINITY CRES

TRINITY CRES

CROSSWAYS

BACK LA

73

LOW ST

MARK LA

PLANTATION AVE

TRINITY
CRES

Markham
Hall

PLANTATION RD

Back Lane

6   +   CHURCH ST

NOOKIN

QUAKEFIELD RD

Sewage
Works

Darlton Field

Highfields Farm

5

NG22

Darlton Gaps

Lodge Farm

72

DARLTON RD

4

⚐ ⛺

Goodhouses
Farm

PH

Eastfield
House

3   Walks of Life
Heritage Ctr

LINCOLN RD

HILLSIDE

A6075

LANDA
GR

WELBECK
PL

FLEMING AVE

GILBERT AVE

HAYNES
CL

WOODHOUSE
PL

Tuxford
School

71   NICHOLAS
PL

CHARTER
PL

CAPPS PL

Tuxford

MARNHAM RD

Merryfields
Farm

FARADAY AV

LINDEN
AVE

MAY FAIR
PL

ASPEN
CL

⚐ ⛺

Park
Cottage

2   A1

B1164

ASHVALE RD

MAPLE CL

CHESTNUT
WAY

ASPEN
CT

LODGE LA

Peter Barn

Sewage
Works

GREAT NORTH RD

Ashvale

Lodge Farm

Ruddingwood

1   Goosemoor
Dyke

A1

B1164

70

A B C D E F

8

Medieval Village
of Whimpton
(site of)

A57

BYRON CL
BROAD GATE

Darlton

Low Farm

Grange Farm

Farhill Farm   Farhill Lane

7

Grange Farm

73

Vicarage Farm

6

Fledborough Beck

Field Farm

America Farm

WOODCOATES RD

NG22

5

North Farm

Majors Farm

Top Farm

GREEN LA

72

Gibraltar

4

FAR RD

Wells
Farm

Woodcoates

Crabtree Lane

Station
Cottages

3

71

Babbington Springs
Farm

CRABTREE LA

2

NG23

POLLY TAYLOR'S RD

LC

Skegby

1

SKEGBY RD

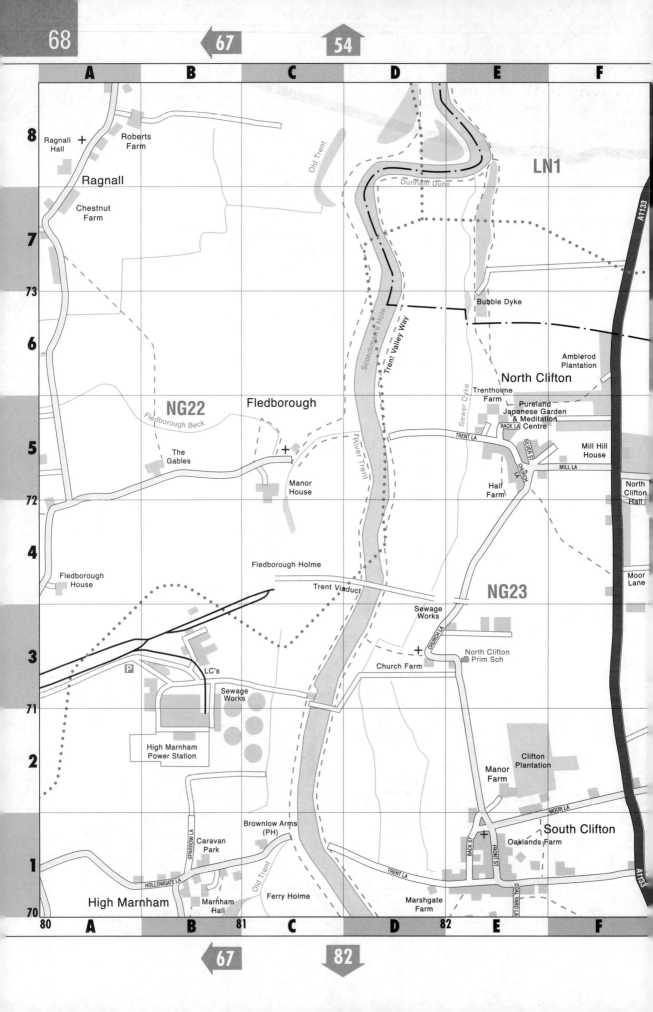

A   B   C   D   E   F

8

Ragnall Hall +

Roberts Farm

Ragnall

Chestnut Farm

Old Trent

LN1

Dunham Dubs

7

73

Bubble Dyke

6

Scotchman's Hole

Trent Valley Way

Amblerod Plantation

North Clifton

NG22

Fledborough

Fledborough Beck

Trentholme Farm

Sewer Dyke

Pureland Japanese Garden & Meditation Centre

BACK LA

5

The Gables

+

Manor House

River Trent

TRENT LA

SILVER ST

CHURCH LA

Mill Hill House

MILL LA

North Clifton Hall

72

Hall Farm

4

Fledborough House

Fledborough Holme

Trent Viaduct

NG23

Moor Lane

Sewage Works

3

P

LC's

Sewage Works

Church Farm

CHURCH LA

+

North Clifton Prim Sch

71

2

High Marnham Power Station

Manor Farm

Clifton Plantation

MOOR LA

South Clifton

Brownlow Arms (PH)

SPARROW LA

Caravan Park

BACK ST

FRONT ST

+

Oaklands Farm

COAL YARD LA

1

HOLLOWGATE LA

Old Trent

TRENT LA

A1133

70

High Marnham

Marnham Hall

Ferry Holme

Marshgate Farm

80   A   B   81   C   D   82   E   F

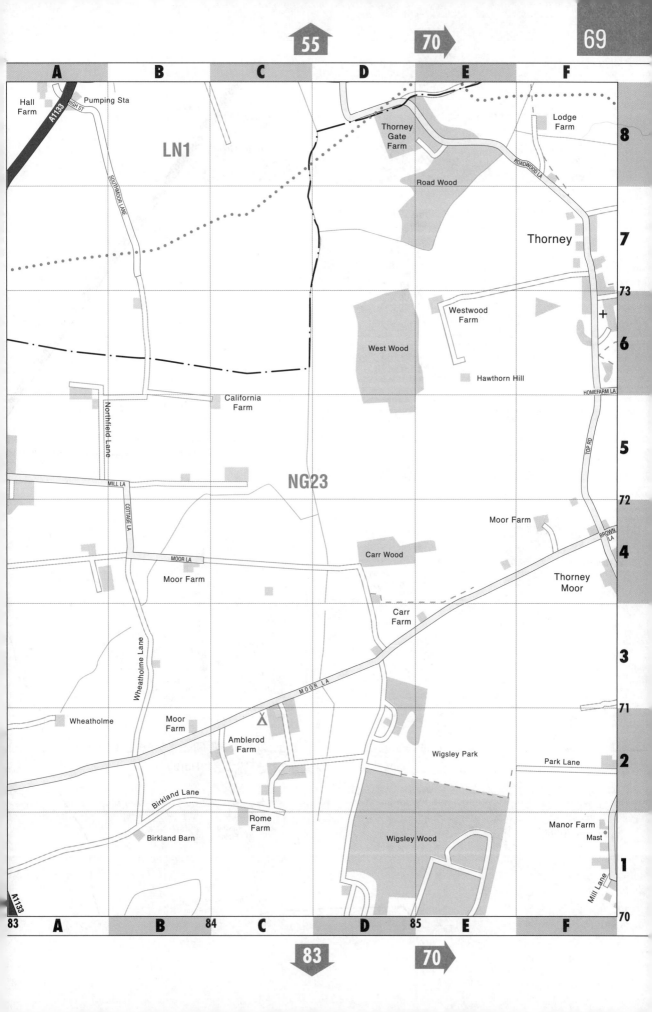

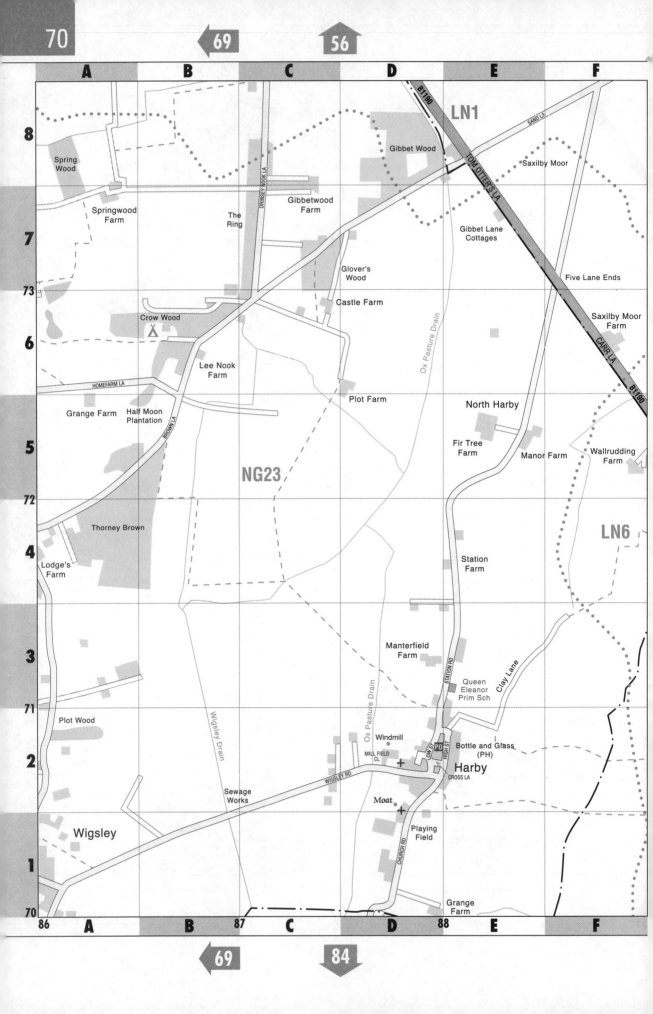

LN1

B1190

SAND LA

Spring Wood

Springwood Farm

The Ring

DRINSEY NOOK LA

Gibbetwood Farm

Gibbet Wood

Saxilby Moor

TOM OTTER'S LA

Gibbet Lane Cottages

Glover's Wood

Castle Farm

Ox Pasture Drain

Five Lane Ends

Crow Wood

Lee Nook Farm

Saxilby Moor Farm

CARR LA

B1190

HOMEFARM LA

Grange Farm

Half Moon Plantation

BROWN LA

Plot Farm

North Harby

Fir Tree Farm

Manor Farm

Wallrudding Farm

NG23

LN6

Thorney Brown

Station Farm

Lodge's Farm

Manterfield Farm

STATION RD

Queen Eleanor Prim Sch

Clay Lane

Plot Wood

Wigsley Drain

Windmill

LOW ST

HIGH ST

Bottle and Glass (PH)

MILL FIELD CL

PO

Harby

CROSS LA

Sewage Works

WIGSLEY RD

Moat

Ox Pasture Drain

Wigsley

CHURCH RD

Playing Field

Grange Farm

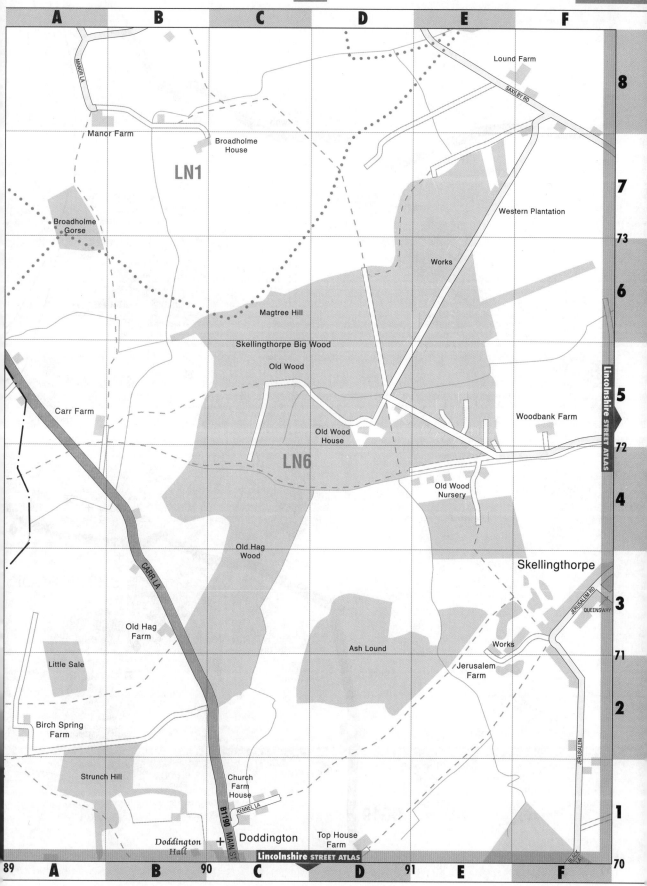

A B C D E F

8
7
73
6
5
72
4
3
71
2
1
70

MANOR LA

Manor Farm

Broadholme House

LN1

Broadholme Gorse

Lound Farm

SAXILBY RD

Western Plantation

Works

Magtree Hill

Skellingthorpe Big Wood

Old Wood

Carr Farm

Old Wood House

LN6

Woodbank Farm

Old Wood Nursery

Skellingthorpe

Lincolnshire STREET ATLAS

Old Hag Wood

CARR LA

Old Hag Farm

Ash Lound

Jerusalem Farm

Works

JERUSALEM RD

QUEENSWAY

Little Sale

Birch Spring Farm

JERUSALEM

Strunch Hill

Church Farm House

KENNEL LA

B1190 MAIN ST

Doddington Hall

Doddington

Top House Farm

BLACK LA

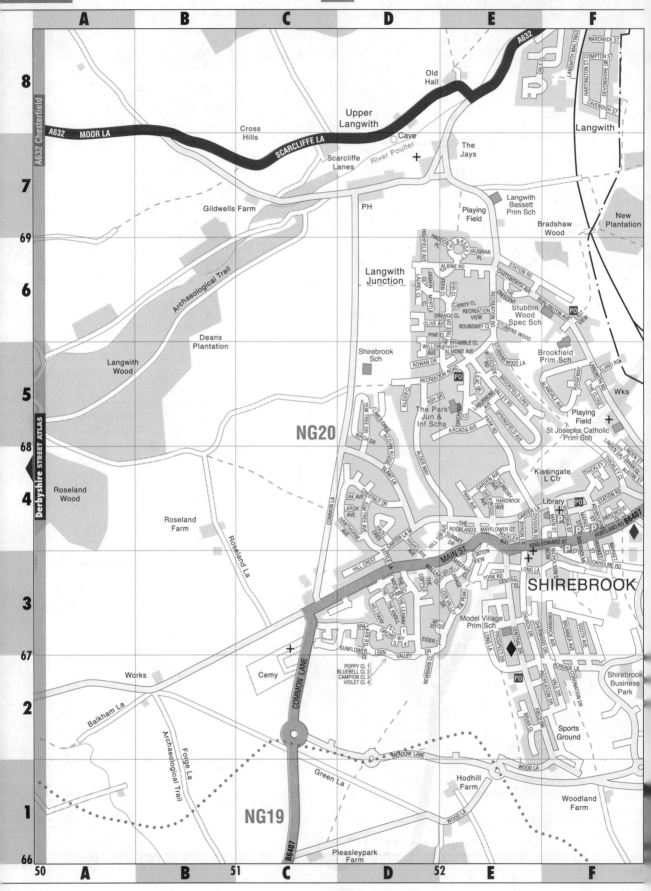

Derbyshire STREET ATLAS

A632 Chesterfield

A B C D E F

8

MOOR LA

Cross Hills

Upper Langwith

SCARCLIFFE LA

Old Hall

A632

Langwith Maltings

HARDWICK ST

COMPTON ST

DALE CL

HARTINGTON ST

DEVONSHIRE DR

CAVENDISH ST

Langwith

7

Gildwells Farm

Scarcliffe Lanes

River Poulter

Cave

PH

The Jays

Playing Field

Langwith Bassett Prim Sch

Bradshaw Wood

New Plantation

69

Archaeological Trail

Langwith Junction

HIGHFIELD AVE

HADDON PL

THE BASSET

VAUGHAN PL

ALBINE RD

STATION RD

CHATSWORTH AVE

THE CRESCENT

BURLINGTON AVE

STATION RD

PO

6

Deans Plantation

JASMIN CL

MYRTLE CL

FERN CL

ORANGE CL

OLIVE AVE

PINE CL

CHERRY CL

RECREATION VIEW

LAUREL CL

PEAR TREE DR

BRAMBLE CL

WILLOW AVE

ALMOND AVE

ROWAN DR

BOUNDARY CL

STUBBINS WOOD LA

Stubbin Wood Spec Sch

Stubbins Wood

WOODSIDE

Brookfield Prim Sch

LANGWITH RD

THE CLOSE

Wks

5

Langwith Wood

Shirebrook Sch

RECREATION ROAD

ASH GR

ALDER CL

PO

The Park Jun & Inf Schs

ORCHARD CL

LABURNUM CL

VALLEY RD

BROOKFIELD CRES

SPRINGFIELD AVE

ALDANDALE AVE

RIDGEWAY

Playing Field

St Josephs Catholic Prim Sch

LINDEN GR

BANK CL

LINDEN RD

68

Roseland Wood

YEW TREE DR

LIMES CRES

ACORN RIDGE

SLANT LA

BIRCH AVE

ARCADIA AVE

GARDEN AVE

PARK RD

Kissingate L Ctr

THICKLEY CL

AUSTIN ST

THICKLEY CT

STATION RD

4

Roseland Farm

Roseland La

COMMON LA

OAK AVE

LARCH AVE

ELM TREE AVE

HAZEL

CARTER LA W

HIGHCLIFFE

CHESTNUT DR

HAWTHORNE AVE

THE ROCKLANDS

MAYFLOWER CT

THORESBY AVE

SHERWOOD AVE

Hardwick

CARTER LA E

DIVISION ST

BYRON ST

MAIN ST

Library

PO

P P P

MARKET ST

ASHBOURNE RD

HEREWOOD

SOOKHOLME CL

Portland RD

B6407

3

Cemy

HILL CREST

LITTLE LA

CARTER LA

MALLARD CL

THE LEAWAY

NOOK LA

THE SPINNEY

THE KNOLL

HILLSWAY

ORCHID WY 3

BRA

LEEN CT

THE COPPICE

THE SUMMIT

THE PEAK

STATION VIEW

THE ROCKLEY

VICARAGE

WELFARE

King Edward St

NICHOLSON'S DR

CENTRAL AVE

Long La

SOOKHOLME RD

SHIREBROOK

GEORGIA ST

SWANWICK AVE

SHERWOOD DR

SOUTH AVE

Shirebrook Business Park

67

Works

COMMON LANE

SUNFLOWER CL

LEEN VALLEY

EIDER CL

POPPY CL 1

BLUEBELL CL 2

CAMPION CL 3

VIOLET CL 4

NEWBARN CL

Model Village Prim Sch

LONG LA

PROSPECT DR

CENTRAL DR

CHURCH DR

ACREAGE LA

CORONATION DR

VALE DR

BRIAR DR

FIELD DR

BRUNNER AVE

PO

2

Balkham La

Forge La

Archaeological Trail

Green La

MEADOW LANE

Hodhill Farm

WOOD LA

Sports Ground

1

NG19

B6407

Pleasleypark Farm

WOOD LA

Woodland Farm

66

50 A B 51 C D 52 E F

NG20

NG19

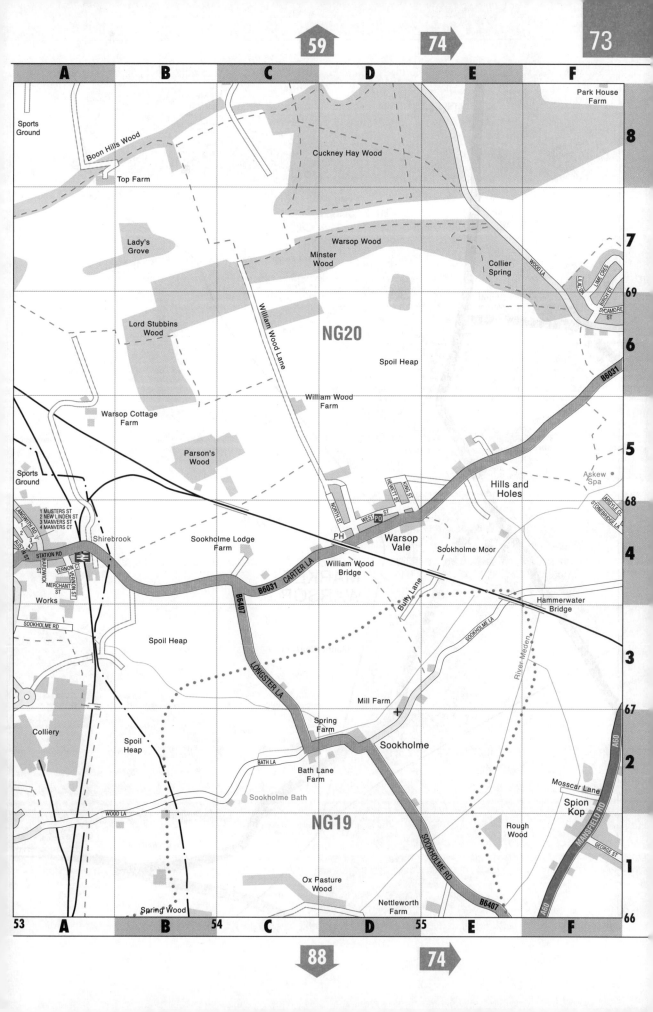

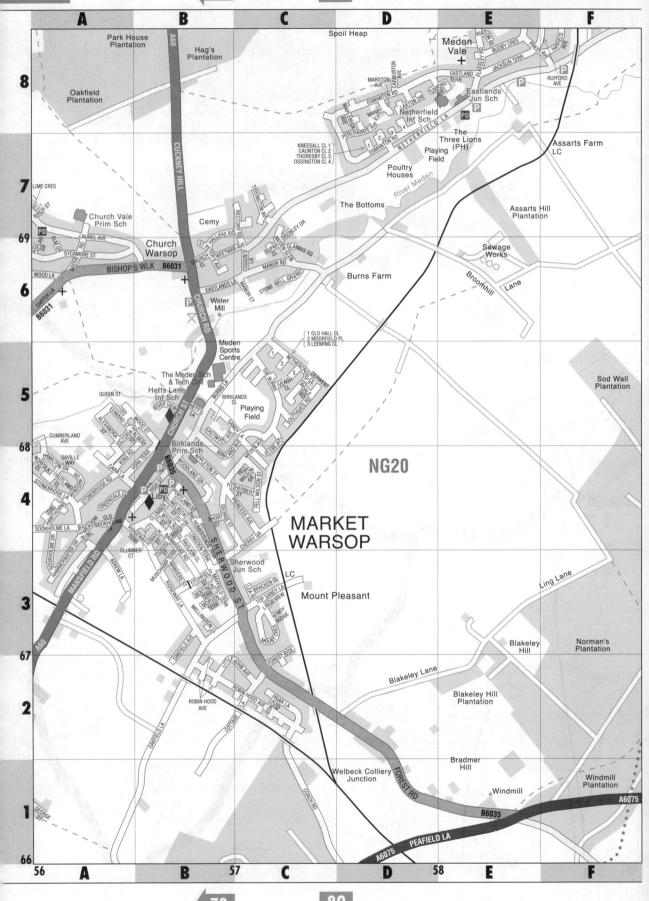

A   B   C   D   E   F

Park House Plantation
Hag's Plantation
A60 CUCKNEY HILL
Spoil Heap
Meden Vale
KIRTON CL
BUDBY CRES
ELKESLEY RD
PRIEST AVE
HATFIELD AVE
JACKSON TERR
EASTLAND TERR
RUFFORD AVE

8

Oakfield Plantation

MARSTON AVE
CARBURTON AVE
MAPLEBECK AVE
PERLTHORPE AVE
EGMANTON RD
MANBY CT
AXTON DR
TUXFORD AVE
Netherfield Inf Sch
Eastlands Jun Sch
NETHERFIELD LA
PO
Eastlands Jun Sch

KNEESALL CL 1
CAUNTON CL 2
THORESBY CL 3
OSSINGTON CL 4
7 6 5
4 3 2 1
EGMANTON RD

The Three Lions (PH)
Playing Field

Assarts Farm LC

7

LIME CRES
BIRCH ST
Church Vale Prim Sch
PO
POPLAR GR
ELM GR
LAUREL AVE
SYCAMORE ST
SPRUCE RD
Cemy
TISSINGTON AVE
RECTORY RD
ST PETER'S AVE
HALLIFAX AVE
WEETMAN AVE
CLIPARD GLEN
BROMLEY DR
GLANNIS SQ

Poultry Houses
River Meden
The Bottoms

Assarts Hill Plantation

69

Church Warsop

ST JOSEPH'S AVE
ST JUDOD
MANOR RD
MANOR CT
EASTLANDS LA
STONE MILL GRANGE

Sewage Works
○○○

WOOD LA
CARTER LA
B6031
BISHOP'S WLK
B6031
Water Mill
PO
CHURCH RD

Burns Farm
Broomhill
Lane

6

1 OLD HALL CL
2 MOORFIELD PL
3 LEEMING CL
NETHERCROSS CL
DERWENT
2 3 1

Sod Wall Plantation

Meden Sports Centre
The Meden Sch & Tech Coll
Hetts Lane Inf Sch
QUEEN ST
RIVER VIEW
HETTS LA
BURNS LA
BIRKLANDS CL
THE BURNS
IVEAGH
SOUTHGATE RD

5

CUMBERLAND AVE
HAMILTON DR
SAVILLE WAY
EDWARD ST
ALEXANDRA
ST ALBERT
VICTORIA ST
WOOD ST
KING RD
YORK TERR
CHURCH ST
HETTS LA
Birklands Prim Sch
EASTWOOD AVE
BIRKLAND AVE
SANDY LA
APPLETON ST
MEDEN AVE
Playing Field

NG20

68

NORFOLK CL
RUTLAND CL
THE WOODS
STONEBRIDGE LA
STONEBRIDGE RD
CARR LA
GREENDALE RD
B6035
HIGH ST
PO
P
Liby
WOODLAND GR
FITZHERBERT ST
FELL WILSON ST
WELSON ST

4

THE HAWTHORNS
SOOKHOLME LA
MEADOW DR
OLD SOOKHOLME LA
CLUMBER ST
PORTLAND ST
FENWICK
RIDGEWAY
STONE HOMESTEAD CL
WELTON ST
FAULION CL
LONGDEN TERR
GEORGE ST
SHORTER ST
PRINCESS AVE
CHERRY GR

MARKET WARSOP

MANSFIELD RD
A60
HAMMERWATER DR
SOOKHOLME LA
ASKEW LA
CLUMBER CT
VICKERS
MUSGRAVE TERR
MANVERS ST
RIDGEWAY LA
TITCHFIELD ST
BENTINCK TERR
MORVEN TERR
WELLINGTON CL
SHERWOOD ST
BRAMLEY CL
LINGS RD
Sherwood Jun Sch
LC
Mount Pleasant

3

A60
67
OAKFIELD AVE
LITTLE JOHN AVE
ROBIN HOOD AVE
ROBIN HOOD AVE
FRIAR LA
TOP SANDY LA
LINGS VIEW
WINDY RIDGE
MOUNT CRES
FOREST RISE

BLAKELEY Lane
FOREST RD
Blakeley Hill
Ling Lane
Norman's Plantation

2

ROBIN HOOD AVE
OAKFIELD LA
COTTAGE

Blakeley Hill Plantation

Welbeck Colliery Junction
COACH RD
Bradmer Hill
Windmill
Windmill Plantation

1

GEORGE ST
A6075
PEAFIELD LA
B6035
A6075
A6075

66

A   B   C   D   E   F

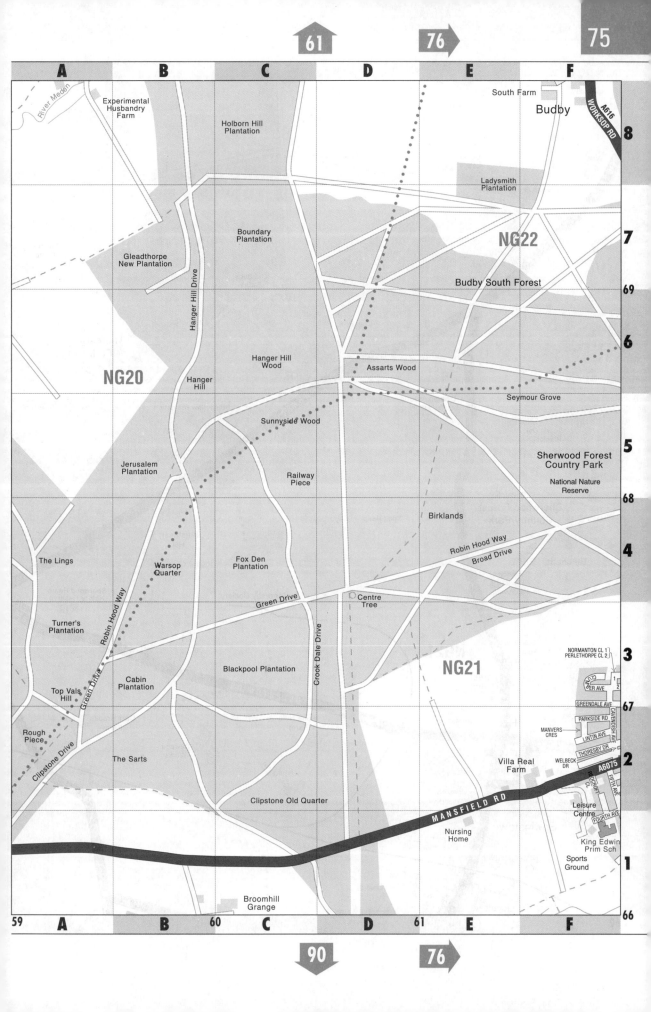

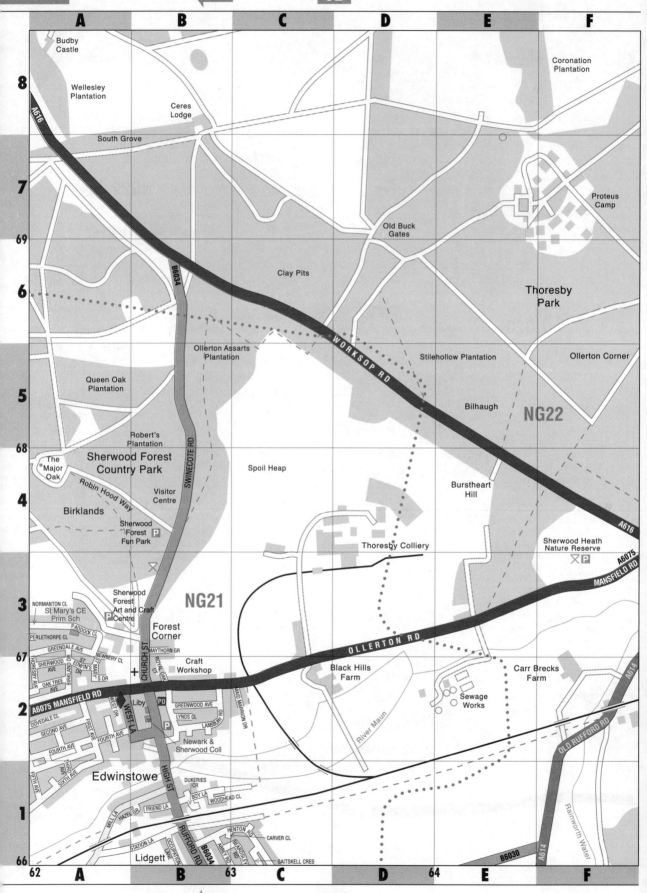

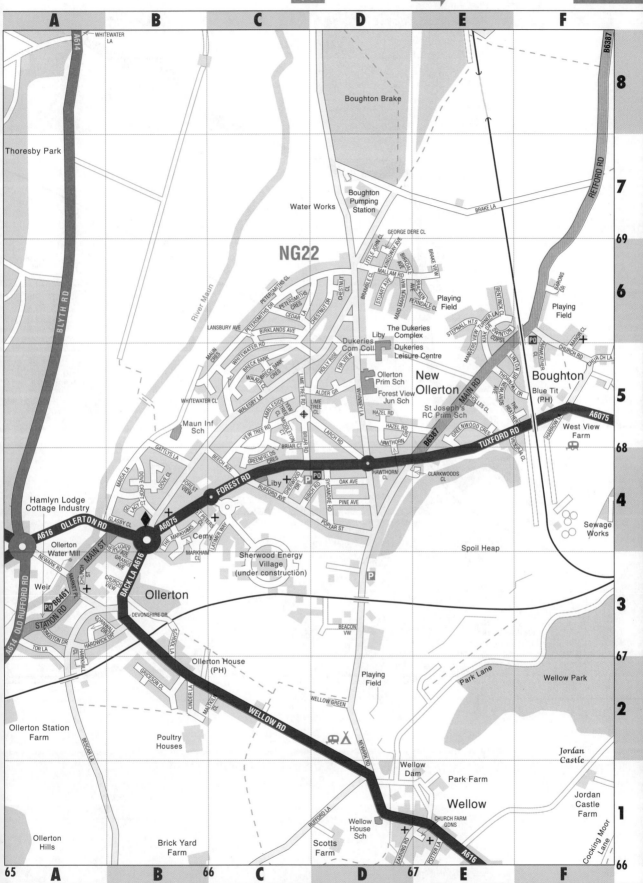

A B C D E F

8
7
69
6
5
68
4
3
67
2
1
66

WHITEWATER LA
A614

Thoresby Park

BLYTH RD

River Maun

NG22

Boughton Brake

Boughton Pumping Station

Water Works

BRAKE LA

RETFORD RD
B6387

GEORGE DERE CL

LITTLE JOHN CL
KINGSWAY CL
STUART AVE
MALLAM RD
MAID MARION WY
BRAKE VIEW
BIRCLE DALE
FERNDALE CL
BRACKEN AVE

Playing Field

BARONS DR

Playing Field

BENTINCK CL
STEPNALL H.T.S
MANNERS VIEW
SWANTON COPSE

CHURCH RD
PO
CHURCH LA
MANOR CL

Boughton

Blue Tit (PH)

West View Farm

A6075

SEWAGE Works

PETERSMITHS CL
PETERSMITHS DR
PETERSMITHS CRES
CEDAR LA
CHESTNUT DR
CHESTNUT CL
BRAMBLE CL

LANSBURY AVE
BIRKLANDS AVE

Liby
Dukeries Com Coll

The Dukeries Complex

Dukeries Leisure Centre

Ollerton Prim Sch

New Ollerton

St Joseph's RC Prim Sch

LINTON DR
THORN LA
NEVLANDS AVE
THE HEATHER
GREENWOOD CRES
HARROW RD
VICTORIA CL

MAIN CRES
WHITEWATER RD
BRECK BANK
BRECK BANK CRES
WALESBY LA
AMBLESIDE
NEW TREE VIEW
MIDDLE TON
HOLLY RISE
FIR VIEW
WHINNEY LA
HAZEL AVE
HAZEL CL
HAWTHORN
HAWTHORN CL

LIME TREE RD
LIME TREE CL
ALDER GR
LARCH RD

Forest View Jun Sch

MAIN RD
KIRK AVE
ICKLES CL

WHITEWATER CL

Maun Inf Sch

YEW TREE RD

BEECH AVE
GREENFIELDS CRES
BRIAR CT
SHERWOOD DR
RUFFORD AVE
BIRCH RD
SYCAMORE RD
OAK AVE
PINE AVE
POPLAR ST

GATTLY'S LA
DOVE CROFT
DOVE CL
FOREST VIEW
DE LACY CT
GLASBY CL
MAIDA LA
THE MARKHAMS
ST PETERS
LATIMER WAY
MARKHAM CL

FOREST RD

Liby
PO

B6387

CLARKWOODS CL

TUXFORD RD

Spoil Heap

Hamlyn Lodge Cottage Industry

OLLERTON RD
A616

Ollerton Water Mill

NEWARK RD
MAIN ST
MARKET PL
KINGHOLM
HEREFORD AVE
GRANGE AVE
CHURCH VIEW
BACK LA A616

A6075

Cemy

Sherwood Energy Village (under construction)

P

Weir

PO
B6461
STATION RD
KINGSTON DR
TOR LA
HAWKHILL CL
CORNWALL DR
HARDWICK DR

Ollerton

DEVONSHIRE DR

BEACON VW

BEACON VW

Ollerton House (PH)

Park Lane

Wellow Park

A614 OLD RUFFORD RD
BESSAR LA

SCHOOL LA
CINDER LA
GRICESON CL
MALTKILN CL

Playing Field

WELLOW GREEN

Jordan Castle

WELLOW RD

Poultry Houses

NEWARK RD

Wellow Dam

Park Farm

Jordan Castle Farm

Ollerton Station Farm

Wellow

Ollerton Hills

Brick Yard Farm

RUFFORD LA

Scotts Farm

Wellow House Sch

EAKRING RD
POTTER LA
CHURCH FARM GDNS
A616

Cocking Moor Lane

A B C D E F

A B C D E F

8

TUXFORD RD
A6075
OLLERTON RD

Collinridge Wood

Priors Park Farm

Manor Farm

7

Pasture Farm and Victorian Carriages

PH

Goosemoor Dyke

Hall Farm

69

RECTORY GDNS

SANDFIELD LA

KIRTON PARK

Kirton

Winson Hill

6

Doncaster Farm

CHARLOTTE CL

KIRTON CT

Manor Farm

CHURCH LA

MAIN ST

THE FURZE

PRIMROSE LA

Kirton Wood Nature Reserve

NG22

5

A6075

Boughton Ind Est

68

Cocking Hill Farm

Brick Works

Marl Pit

Norton Wood

TRENT RD

MEDEN RD

MAUN WAY

BROUGHTON CL

4

Sports Ground

Golden Hill

West Field

COCKING HILL

Birkhill Wood

3

Wellow Park

Mounds

Laxton Common

67

The Holocaust Centre

Westwood Farm

ACRE EDGE RD

Cocking Moor

2

Jordan Castle Farm

Cocking Moor La

Ompton Lodge

1

SHORTWOOD LA

66

68 A B 69 C D 70 E F

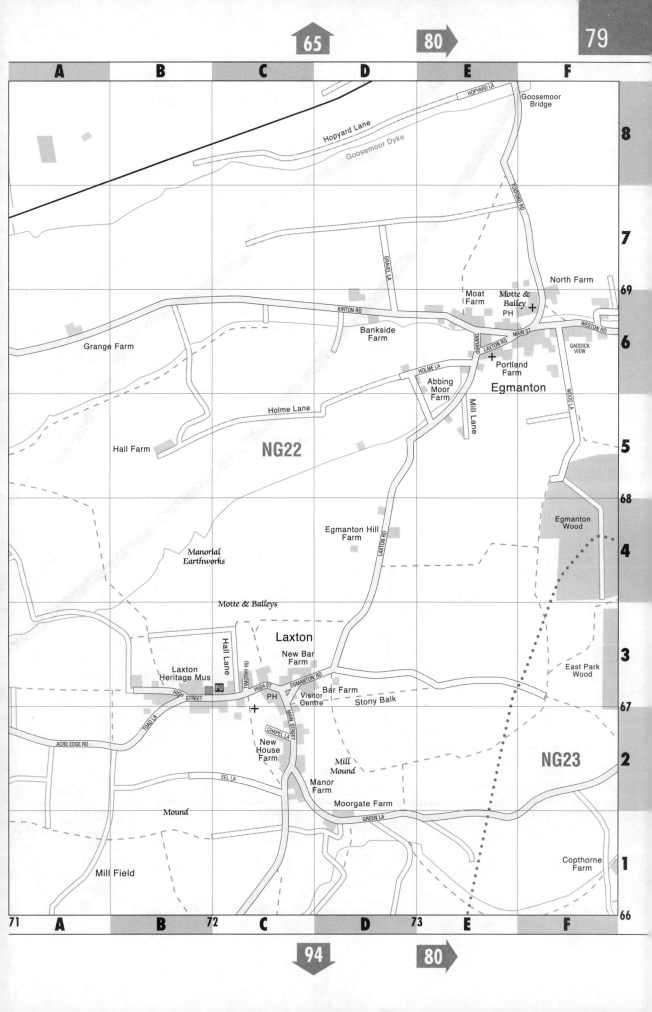

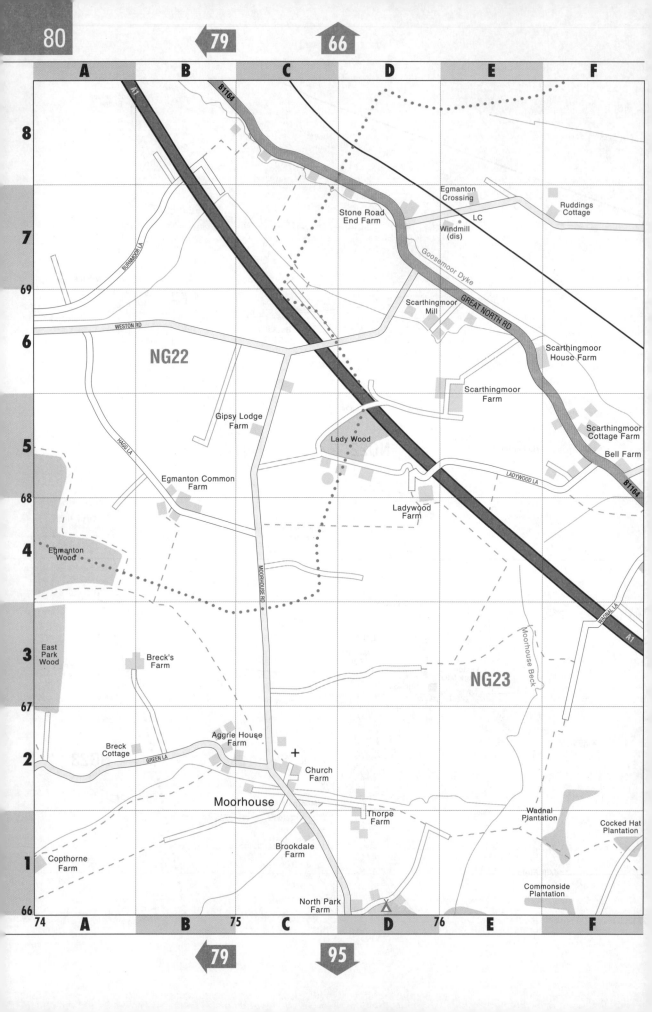

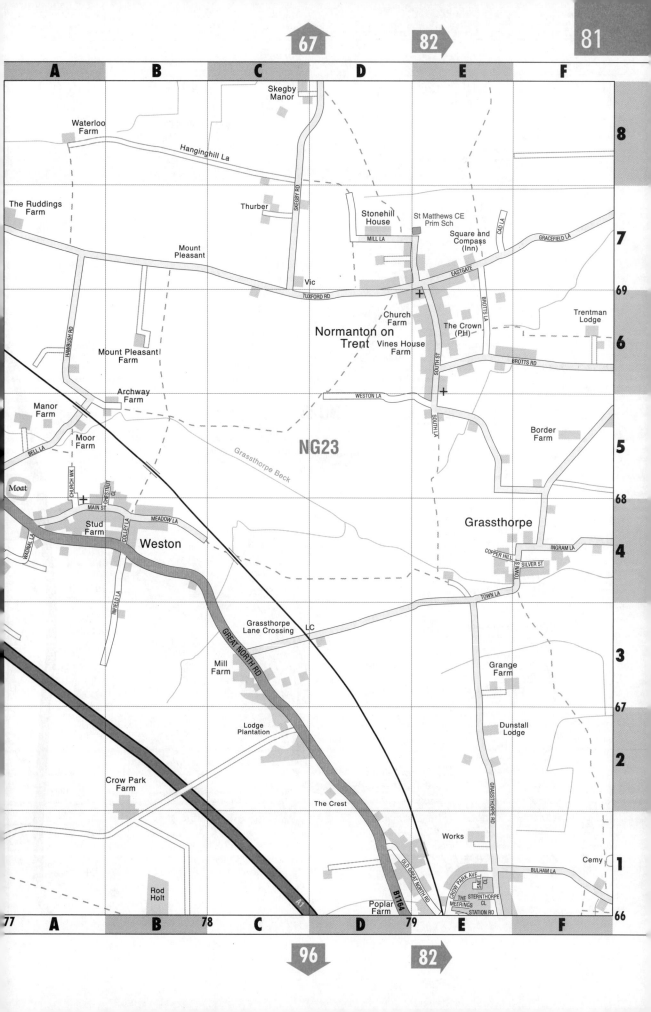

A   B   C   D   E   F

8

Waterloo Farm

Skegby Manor

Hanginghill La

The Ruddings Farm

Thurber

Stonehill House

St Matthews CE Prim Sch

Square and Compass (Inn)

CAD LA

GRACEFIELD LA

7

69

SKEGBY RD

Mount Pleasant

MILL LA

EASTGATE

Vic

TUXFORD RD

Church Farm

BROTTS LA

Trentman Lodge

Normanton on Trent

The Crown (P.H)

6

HAWBUSH RD

Mount Pleasant Farm

Vines House Farm

SOUTH ST

BROTTS RD

Archway Farm

WESTON LA

SOUTH LA

Manor Farm

Moor Farm

Border Farm

5

BELL LA

Grassthorpe Beck

NG23

68

Moat

CHURCH WK

CHESTNUT CL

MAIN ST

MEADOW LA

Stud Farm

COLLEY LA

Grassthorpe

Weston

INGRAM LA

4

WADNAL LA

COPPER HILL

TOWN S

SILVER ST

INFIELD LA

TOWN LA

Grassthorpe Lane Crossing

LC

GREAT NORTH RD

Mill Farm

Grange Farm

3

67

Lodge Plantation

Dunstall Lodge

GRASSTHORPE RD

2

Crow Park Farm

The Crest

Works

Cemy

1

OLD GREAT NORTH RD

BULHAM LA

Rod Holt

A1

B1164

Poplar Farm

CROW PARK AVE

SNELL CL

THE MEERINGS

STERNTHORPE CL

STATION RD

81
68

A B C D E F

8

Low Marnham

The Grange

Holme Farm

COAL YARD LA

Marshgate Farm

Clifton Hill

Old Trent

Marnham Holme

HOLME LA

Church Farm

Old Trent

7

69

Holly Farm

Marnham Meadow

6

BROTTS RD HOPYARD LA

River Trent

A1133

NG23

Girton Grange

HOLME LA

Marnham Road Farm

5

Normanton Holme

68

Grassthorpe Beck

Trent Valley Way

Green Lane

NEW LA

4

MEADOW LA

Highfield Farm

Holme Lane

Sand & Gravel Pit

Works

Boating Lake

3

Grassthorpe Holme

INGRAMS LA

Lower Girton Stakes

67

2

North Holme

Upper Girton Stakes

Oak Doors

TRENT LA

Weecar Home Farm

NEW LA

The Fleet

Girton

GAINSBOROUGH RD

Cemy

Smithy Marsh

WEST LA

HIGH ST

Baxter Bridge

1

CHURCH ST

PROCTERS DR

Baxter Bridge Farm

A1133

66

80 A B 81 C D 82 E F

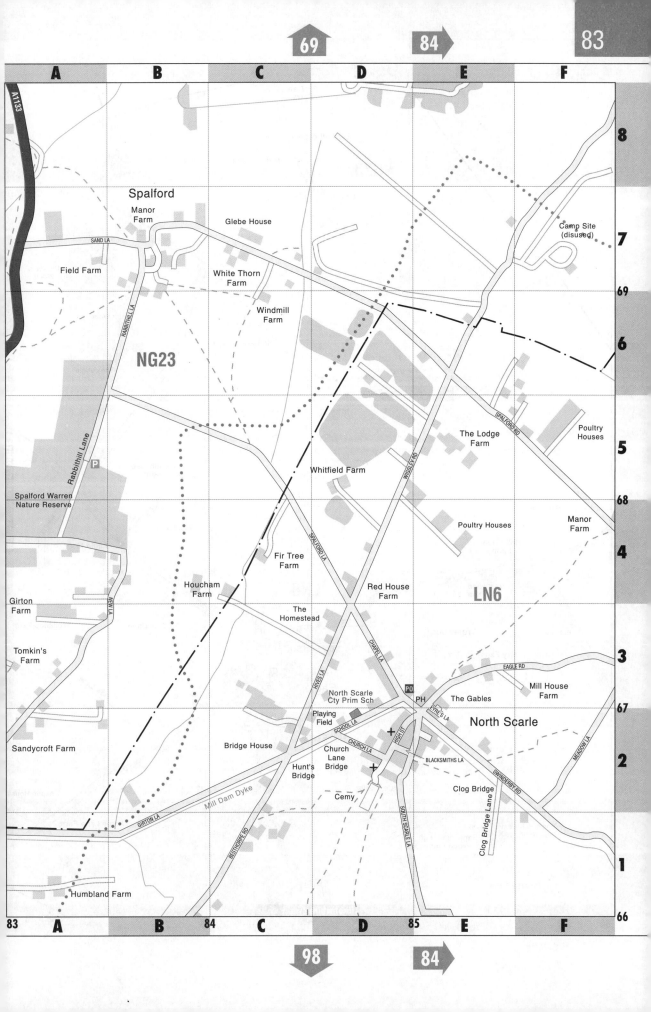

A B C D E F

8

7

69

6

5

68

4

3

67

2

1

66

86 A B 87 C D 88 E F

NG23

Swinethorpe

Fir Tree Farm

Middle Farm

Corner Farm

Fox Holt

Cock Pit

Crow Wood

Parson's Wood

Hurn Wood

Old Farm

The Jungle

Wigsley Drain

Large Farm

Woodhouse Farm

Lincolnshire STREET ATLAS

Plots Farm

Holly Tree Farm

Mill Farm

MILL LA

EAGLE MOOR

Eagle Moor

GREEN LA

SPALFORD RD

Enfield Farm

Westwood Farm

EAGLE RD

LN6

EAGLE RD

The Poplars

Westwood

SCARLE LA

HILLTOP CL

Fir Tree Farm

Wellands Farm

Cherry Farm

Eagle Cty Prim Sch

William & Henry Mews

PO

PH

FALCON CL

New Lane

MEADOW LA

Eagle

CHURCH LA

HIGH ST

MANOR CL

Playing Field

TANGLEWOOD

KESTREL RISE

Back Lane

Enfield Farm

THORPE LA

Slack's Hill

SWINDERBY RD

Aspen House

JOB'S LA

Eagle Hall High Wood

Eagle Hall High Wood Farm

Thorpe Lane Farm

BEEHIVE LA

Preston Farm

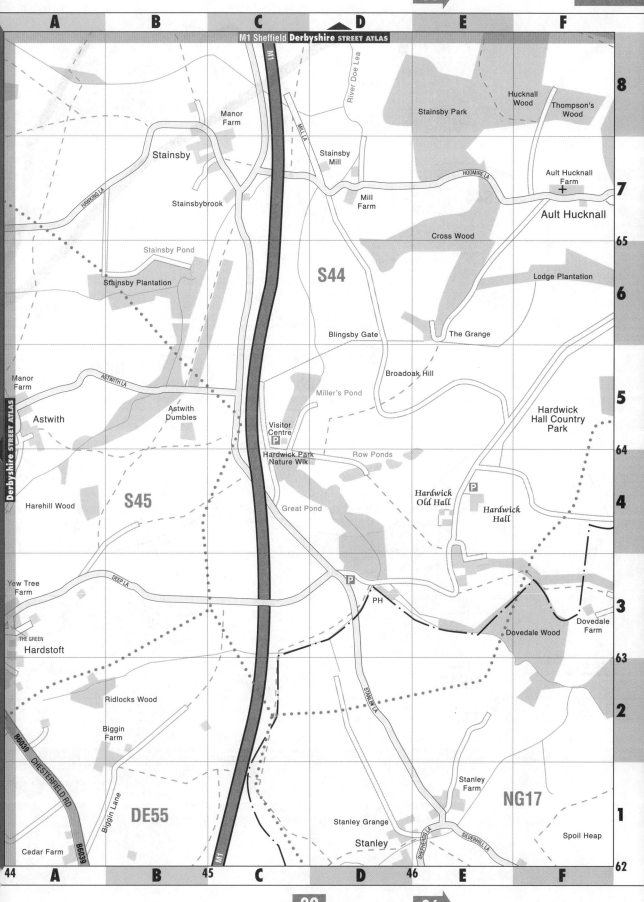

M1 Sheffield **Derbyshire** STREET ATLAS

A B C D E F

8
Hucknall Wood
Thompson's Wood
Stainsby Park
River Doe Lea
M1
MILL LA
Manor Farm
Stainsby
Stainsby Mill
HODMIRE LA
Ault Hucknall Farm
7
HAWKING LA
Stainsbybrook
Mill Farm
Ault Hucknall
65
Cross Wood
Stainsby Pond
S44
Lodge Plantation
6
Stainsby Plantation
The Grange
Blingsby Gate
Manor Farm
ASTWITH LA
Broadoak Hill
Hardwick Hall Country Park
5
Astwith Dumbles
Miller's Pond
Astwith
Visitor Centre
Row Ponds
64
Hardwick Park Nature Wlk
Harehill Wood
S45
Hardwick Old Hall
Hardwick Hall
4
Great Pond
Yew Tree Farm
DEEP LA
Dovedale Farm
3
PH
Dovedale Wood
THE GREEN
Hardstoft
63
Ridlocks Wood
STANLEY LA
2
Biggin Farm
B6039 CHESTERFIELD RD
Stanley Farm
NG17
Biggin Lane
DE55
Stanley Grange
1
Cedar Farm
B6039
Stanley
SHEPHERDS LA
SILVERHILL LA
Spoil Heap
62

44 A B 45 C D 46 E F

Derbyshire STREET ATLAS

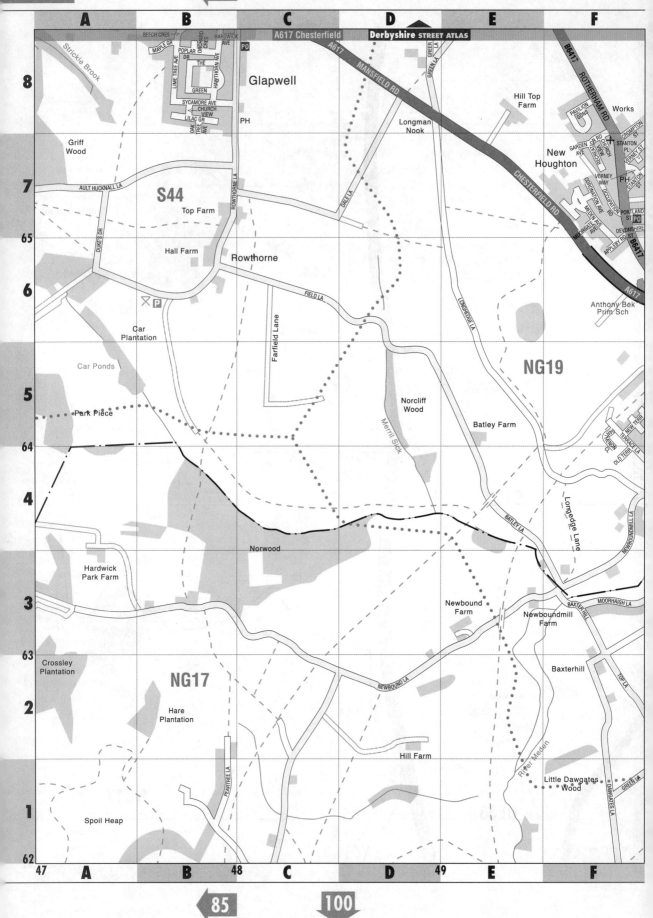

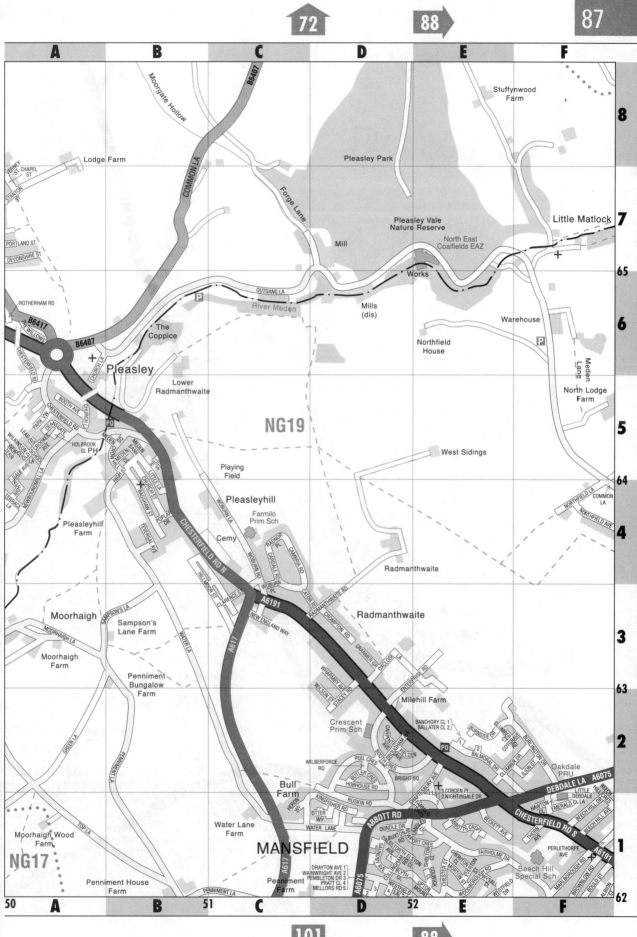

A   B   C   D   E   F

8

VERLEY ST
CHAPEL ST
STANTON ST

Moorgate Hollow

Lodge Farm

B6407

COMMON LA

Stuffynwood Farm

Pleasley Park

7

PORTLAND ST
DEVONSHIRE ST

Forge Lane

Pleasley Vale Nature Reserve

North East Coalfields EAZ

Little Matlock

ROTHERHAM RD

B6417
THE WILLOWS

Mill

Works

65

B6407

CHESTERFIELD RD

The Coppice

Outgang La

River Meden

Mills (dis)

Warehouse

6

Pleasley

Lower Radmanthwaite

Northfield House

Meden Lane

P

North Lodge Farm

BOOTH AVE
PARK VW
CHESTERFIELD RD
CHURCH LA
LEAS AVE
CROOKES AVE
WILKINSON AVE
BIRCHITT
LOW AVE
SALE AVE
TERRACE LA
NEWBOUNDARY LA

HOLBROOK CL PH
PO

MEDEN CRDY
MEDEN BANK
IRISH ST
LITTLE LA
CHURCH ST
BAGSHAW ST
POPLAR DR

NG19

West Sidings

5

64

Pleasleyhill Farm

Playing Field

Pleasleyhill

WOBURN LA

Farmilo Prim Sch

RAINOR PL
CARDALE RD
CAMBRIA RD

Radmanthwaite

NORTHFIELD
COMMON LA
NORTHFIELD AVE

4

Moorhaigh

MOORHAIGH LA

Sampson's Lane Farm

WATER LA

Cemy

CHESTERFIELD RD N
HILLMOOR ST
WOBURN RD
WOBURN PL
CLARENCE S

A6191

CATOR RD
RADMANTHWAITE RD
CROMPTON RD

Radmanthwaite

3

Moorhaigh Farm

Penniment Bungalow Farm

SAMPSON'S LA

A617

NEW ENGLAND WAY

CRANMER GR
OXCLOSE LA
ENTERPRISE RD

Milehill Farm

63

GREEN LA

PENNIMENT LA

WHARMBY AVE
WILSON AVE
STACEY RD

Crescent Prim Sch

BANCHORY CL 1
BALLATER CL 2

PO

CLUMBER
CRES
COTGRAVE RD
BURNSIDE DR
CLUMBER DR
ILION ST
BURLINGTON DR

Oakdale PRU

2

WILBERFORCE RD

PEEL CRES
BUTLER CRES
HOBHOUSE RD
BOOT CRES
BRIGHT SQ

CARPENTER AVE
TOM FIELDEN
BROMDALE
SHAFTESBURY AVE

BALMORAL DR

1 COBDEN PL
2 NIGHTINGALE DR

DEBDALE LA
A6075

LITTLE DEBDALE
EMERALD CL LA

Bull Farm

HEPON LA

KINGFISHER WY

RUSKIN RD

ABBOTT RD

OUNDLE DR
NEWPORT CRES

ABBOT'S CROFT

BECKETT AVE

FAIRHOLME DR

CHESTERFIELD RD S

HAWTON CL
THORN AVE

BEECH HILL DR CRES
BEECH HILL AVE

1

Moorhaigh Wood Farm

Water Lane Farm

OTTER WY

WATER LANE

BUXTON DR
CHESTORTH RD
EASTON RD

COLLINGHAM RD
BLYTH

SHAFFIELD
CANGLE RD

CHERITON
CHESTER ST
MORTON CL

WOODBOROUGH RD
WYSALL
EVERTON
WESTFIELD DR

Beech Hill Special Sch

PERLETHORPE AVE

MARLBOROUGH RD
BROWNLOW RD

A6191

NG17

MANSFIELD

A617

Penniment Farm

A6075

DRAYTON AVE 1
WAINWRIGHT AVE 2
PEMBLETON DR 3
PRATT CL 4
MELLORS RD 5

WESTFIELD LA

UPTON MOUNT

RONALD ST
ALBION ST

62

50   A   B   51   C   D   52   E   F

Penniment House Farm

PENNIMENT LA

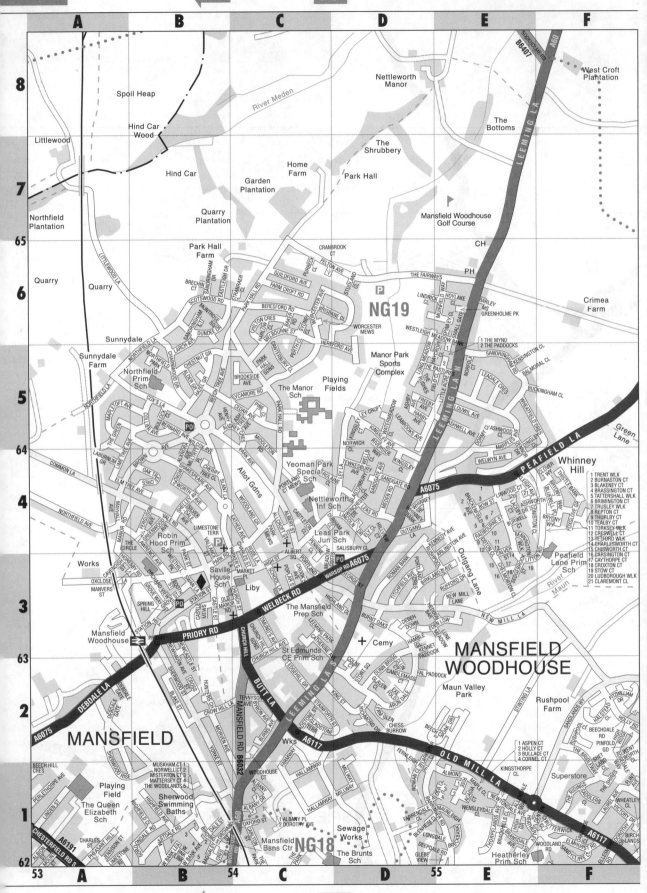

A B C D E F

8

7

65

6

5

64

4

63

3

2

1

62

53 54 55

A B C D E F

Littlewood

Spoil Heap

Hind Car Wood

Hind Car

Garden Plantation

Quarry Plantation

River Meden

Nettleworth Manor

The Shrubbery

Park Hall

Home Farm

The Bottoms

West Croft Plantation

LEEMING LA

B6407

A60

SOODHOLME RD

Mansfield Woodhouse Golf Course

CH

PH

Crimea Farm

Northfield Plantation

Quarry

Quarry

Sunnydale

Sunnydale Farm

Northfield Prim Sch

Park Hall Farm

CRANBROOK CT

FELTON AVE

GUILDFORD AVE

FARM CROFT RD

THE FAIRWAYS

NG19

LINDRICK WAY

HOYLAKE

BARLEY
MS
GREENHOLME PK

WESTLEIGH MEADOW

Manor Park Sports Complex

The Manor Sch

Playing Fields

Green Lane

Whinney Hill

PEAFIELD LA

Yeoman Park Special Sch

Nettleworth Inf Sch

Leas Park Jun Sch

A6075

Peafield Lane Prim Sch

River Maun

1 TRENT WLK
2 BURNASTON CT
3 BLAKENEY CT
4 BRASSINGTON CT
5 TATTERSHALL WLK
6 BRIMINGTON CT
7 TRUSLEY WLK
8 REPTON CT
9 THURLBY CT
10 TEALBY CT
11 TORKSEY WLK
12 CRESWELL CT
13 TETFORD WLK
14 CHARLESWORTH CT
15 CHISWORTH CT
16 CARSINGTON CT
17 CAYTHORPE CT
18 CROXTON CT
19 STOW CT
20 LUDBOROUGH WLK
21 CLAREMONT CL

Works

Robin Hood Prim Sch

Saville House Sch

Liby

WELBECK RD

The Mansfield Prep Sch

PO
WARSOP RD A6075

NEW MILL LA

Outgang Lane

NEW MILL LANE

MANSFIELD WOODHOUSE

Mansfield Woodhouse

PRIORY RD

St Edmunds CE Prim Sch

Cemy

Maun Valley Park

Rushpool Farm

DEBDALE LA

A6075

MANSFIELD

BUTT LA

LEEMING LA S

MANSFIELD RD B6032

A6117

OLD MILL LA

A6117

Superstore

BEECH HILL CRES

MUSKHAM CT 1
NORWELL CT 2
MISTERTON CT 3
MATTERSEY CT 4
THE WOODLANDS 5

Sherwood Swimming Baths

Playing Field

The Queen Elizabeth Sch

WOODHOUSE

HALLAM WAY

HALLAM WAY

MILLWAY

MILLWAY

Sewage Works

The Brunts Sch

Kingsthorpe CL

1 ASPEN CT
2 HOLLY CT
3 BULLACE CT
4 CORNEL CT

Heatherley Prim Sch

1 ALBANY PL
2 DOROTHY AVE

Mansfield Bsns Ctr

NG18

GLEBE VIEW

CHESTERFIELD RD S
A6191

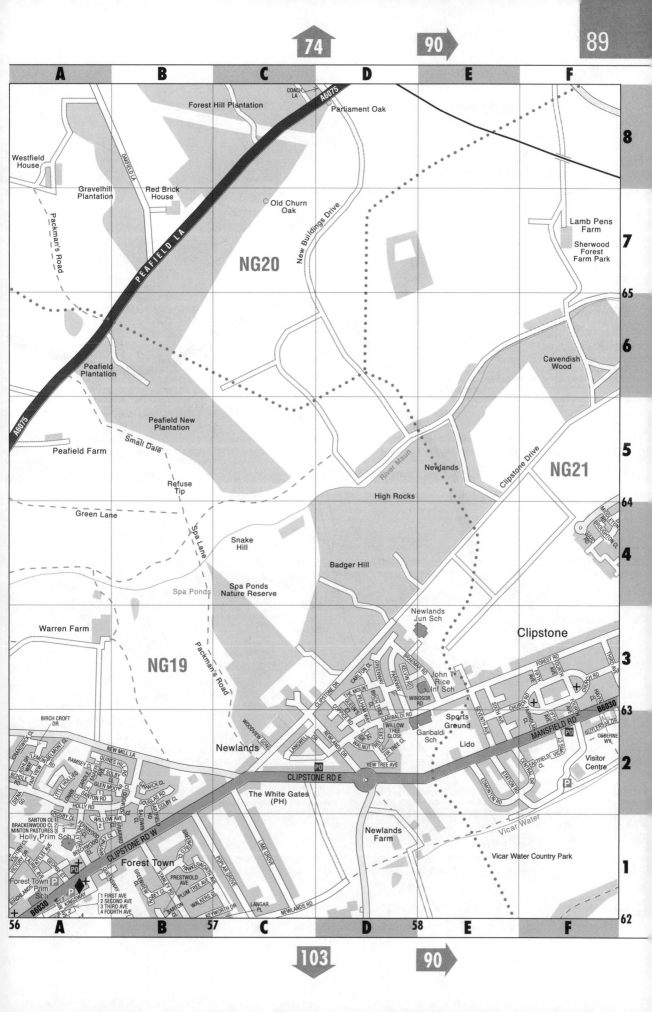

A B C D E F

8

7

65

6

5

64

4

3

63

2

1

62

COACH LA
A6075
Forest Hill Plantation
Parliament Oak

Westfield House

Gravelhill Plantation

Red Brick House

OAKFIELD LA

Old Churn Oak

New Buildings Drive

PEAFIELD LA

NG20

Lamb Pens Farm

Sherwood Forest Farm Park

Packman's Road

A6075

Peafield Plantation

Peafield New Plantation

Small Dale

Peafield Farm

Refuse Tip

Green Lane

Spa Lane

Snake Hill

Spa Ponds

Spa Ponds Nature Reserve

River Maun

Newlands

High Rocks

Badger Hill

Clipstone Drive

NG21

Cavendish Wood

MIDDLETON CL
BROUGHTON CL
WARD

Newlands Jun Sch

Clipstone

Warren Farm

NG19

Packman's Road

Newlands

BIRCH CROFT DR

WOODVIEW GDNS

LANGWELL DR

CLIPSTONE DR

CARLTON CL
GREENWAY
THE MOUNT
PELHAM WAY
BIRCH TREE CL
LEAS
COPPICE RD
CRES
PARKWAY
KELVIN RD
BRAEMAR RD

John T Rice Inf Sch

WINDSOR RD

GARIBALDI RD
WILLOW TREE CLOSE
FIR TREE CL

Garibaldi Sch

Sports Ground

Lido

FOREST RD
FIFTH AVE
FOURTH AVE
THIRD AVE
CHURCH RD
FIFTH AVE
FOURTH AVE

SEVENTH AVE
SIXTH AVE
CHURCH RD

MANSFIELD RD
B6030

PO

GUYLERS HILL DR
OSBERNE WY
EASTFIELD CL
VICK

Visitor Centre

P

NEW MILL LA
ORANGSWICK CL
BELMONT CL
RAMSEY CL
QUINES HILL RD
SULBY CL
GLEN MOOR
CL
AVE
FISH GH
FAIR VIEW
BCHILE
SIENA
RD
LOMM
LITTLE HOLLIES
HOLLYSIDE
SANTON RD
CARWICK CL
DARTLE
SNAEFEL
DOUGLAS RD
COLBY CL
DATFIELD
HOLLY RD
CROSBY CL
SANTON CL
BRACKENWOOD CL 2
MINTON PASTURES 3
FERNWOOD
WILLOW AVE
BEECHWOOD
BRIARWD
HOLLY CL
GREENWD
COTWD
CLIPSTONE RD W

Holly Prim Sch

Forest Town

VICTORY CL
BIRCHLANDS
VICTORIA
FAIRFIELD AVE
GEORGE ST
PO
QUEENSWAY
KINGSWAY

Forest Town Prim Sch

P

B6030

1 FIRST AVE
2 SECOND AVE
3 THIRD AVE
4 FOURTH AVE

GREENVIEW
STANLEY RD
GREY CL
HANKESWORTH DR
PRESTWOLD AVE
PLUM TREE AVE
BARTON
WALKERS CL
KEYWORTH DR
POPLAR GROVE
LANGAR PL

LIME GROVE

NEWLANDS RD

The White Gates (PH)

CLIPSTONE RD E
PO

YEW TREE AVE
WALNUT TREE CL

NEWLANDS DR

Newlands Farm

Vicar Water

Vicar Water Country Park

STATION RD
EDMONTON RD
CENTRAL DR

A   B   C   D   E   F

Broomhill Gorse

New Lodge Plantation

Robin Hood Way

8

Gorsethorpe

Forge Bridge

Clipstone Junction

Halfmoon Plantation

7

Lawn Hills

Eastfield Farm

Eastfield Cottage

River Maun

ARCHWAY RD

65

SQUIRES LA

PH

B6030

Cavendish Lodge

SQUIRES CROFT

King John's Palace (rems of)

6

Clipstone Dr

Old Clipstone

Forest Walks Cycle Route

Culloden Farm

Cavendish Wood

NG21

Culloden

Culloden Plantation

5

Intake Wood

MANSFIELD RD

Waterfield Farm

Lindleys Plantation

64

EMMERSON DRIVE

ROCKLEY CL

DOOSLEY WAY

BOUNDLEY WAY

Vicar Water

P ✕

4

Clipstone

WOODLAND CL

DAVIS CL

SHERWOOD PL

HIGHFIELD RD

HIGHFIELD DR

KING JOHN'S RD

GORSEWAY

PIKE RD

BAULKER LA

GREENDALE CRES

Cemy

Sherwood Pines Visitor Centre

Samuel Barlow Prim Sch

Library

THE CIRCLE

Go Ape!

Forestry Office

Sherwood Pines Forest Pk

3

CHURCH RD

FIRST AVE

NORTH CR

SECOND AVE

THE DRIVE

SOUTH CRES

Colliery

Forestry Holdings

63

THIRD AVE

B6030

Clipstone Forest

Vicar Pond

NG22

2

Spoil Heap

1

Sherwood Forest Golf Course

62

59   A   B 60 C   D 61 E   F

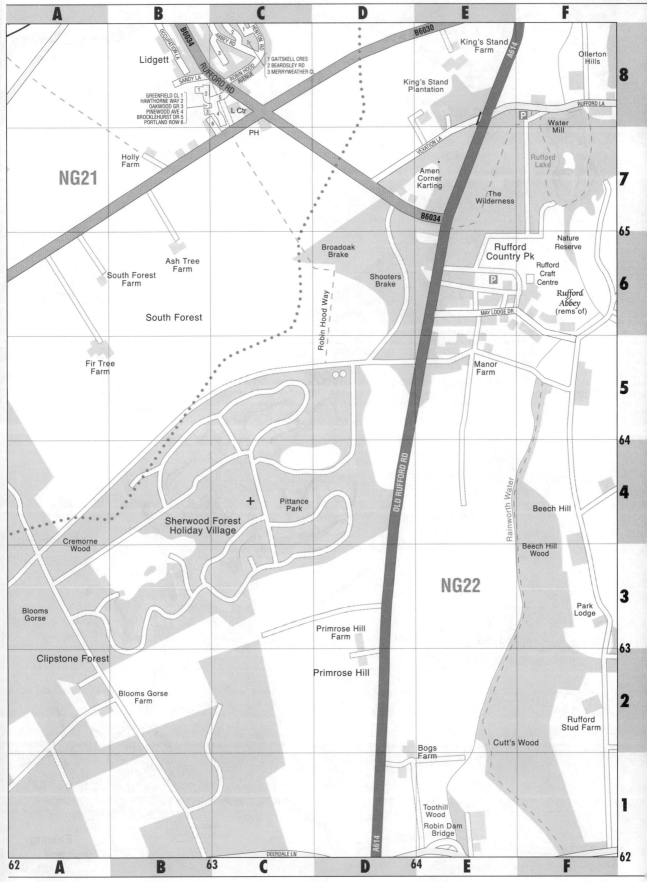

A B C D E F

8
7
65
6
5
64
4
3
63
2
1
62

B6030

King's Stand Farm

Ollerton Hills

A614

King's Stand Plantation

RUFFORD LA

Lidgett

OCCUPATION LA
B6034
ABBEY RD
HENTON RD
SANDY LA
RUFFORD RD
ROBIN HOOD AVENUE

1 GAITSKELL CRES
2 BEARDSLEY RD
3 MERRYWEATHER CL

GREENFIELD CL 1
HAWTHORNE WAY 2
OAKWOOD GR 3
PINEWOOD AVE 4
BROCKLEHURST DR 5
PORTLAND ROW 6

L Ctr

PH

VEXATION LA

Water Mill

Rufford Lake

NG21

Holly Farm

Amen Corner Karting

The Wilderness

Nature Reserve

Ash Tree Farm

Broadoak Brake

Rufford Country Pk

Rufford Craft Centre

Rufford Abbey (rems of)

South Forest Farm

Shooters Brake

B6034

P

P

South Forest

Robin Hood Way

MAY LODGE DR

Manor Farm

Fir Tree Farm

Rainworth Water

Beech Hill

Cremorne Wood

Pittance Park

Sherwood Forest Holiday Village

Beech Hill Wood

OLD RUFFORD RD

Blooms Gorse

NG22

Park Lodge

Clipstone Forest

Primrose Hill Farm

Blooms Gorse Farm

Primrose Hill

Rufford Stud Farm

Cutt's Wood

Bogs Farm

Toothill Wood

A614

Robin Dam Bridge

DEERDALE LN

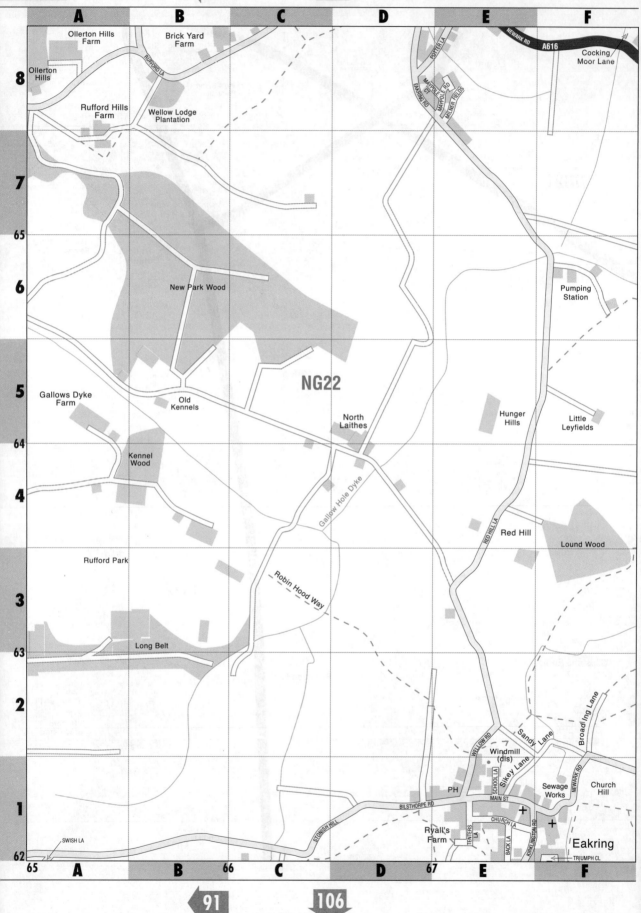

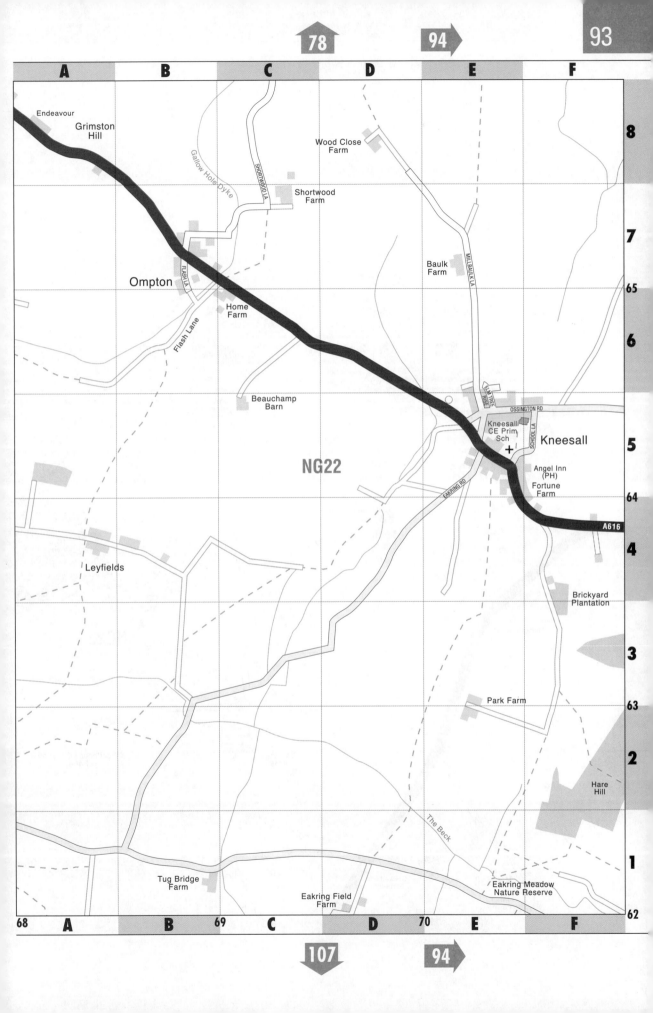

A B C D E F

8

7

65

6

Endeavour

Grimston
Hill

Gallow Hole Dyke

SHORTWOOD LA

Wood Close
Farm

Shortwood
Farm

MILBAULK LA

Baulk
Farm

Ompton

FLASH LA

Home
Farm

Flash Lane

Beauchamp
Barn

NG22

ELM TREE RISE

OSSINGTON RD

Kneesall
CE Prim
Sch

SCHOOL LA

Kneesall

5

Angel Inn
(PH)

Fortune
Farm

64

EAKRING RD

A616

4

Leyfields

Brickyard
Plantation

3

63

Park Farm

2

The Beck

Hare
Hill

1

Tug Bridge
Farm

Eakring Field
Farm

Eakring Meadow
Nature Reserve

62

68 A B 69 C D 70 E F

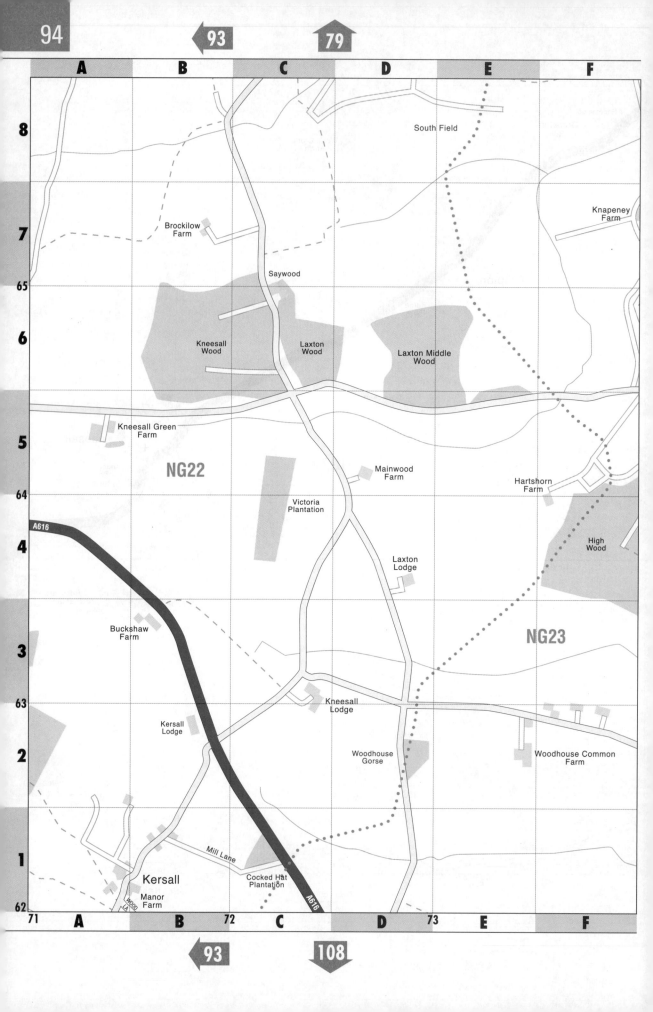

A B C D E F

8

South Field

Knapeney
Farm

7
Brockilow
Farm

65
Saywood

6
Kneesall
Wood

Laxton
Wood

Laxton Middle
Wood

5
Kneesall Green
Farm

NG22

Mainwood
Farm

Hartshorn
Farm

64
Victoria
Plantation

High
Wood

4
A616

Laxton
Lodge

3
Buckshaw
Farm

NG23

63
Kneesall
Lodge

Kersall
Lodge

2
Woodhouse
Gorse

Woodhouse Common
Farm

1
Mill Lane

Kersall

Cocked Hat
Plantation

A616

62
Manor
Farm

71 A B 72 C D 73 E F

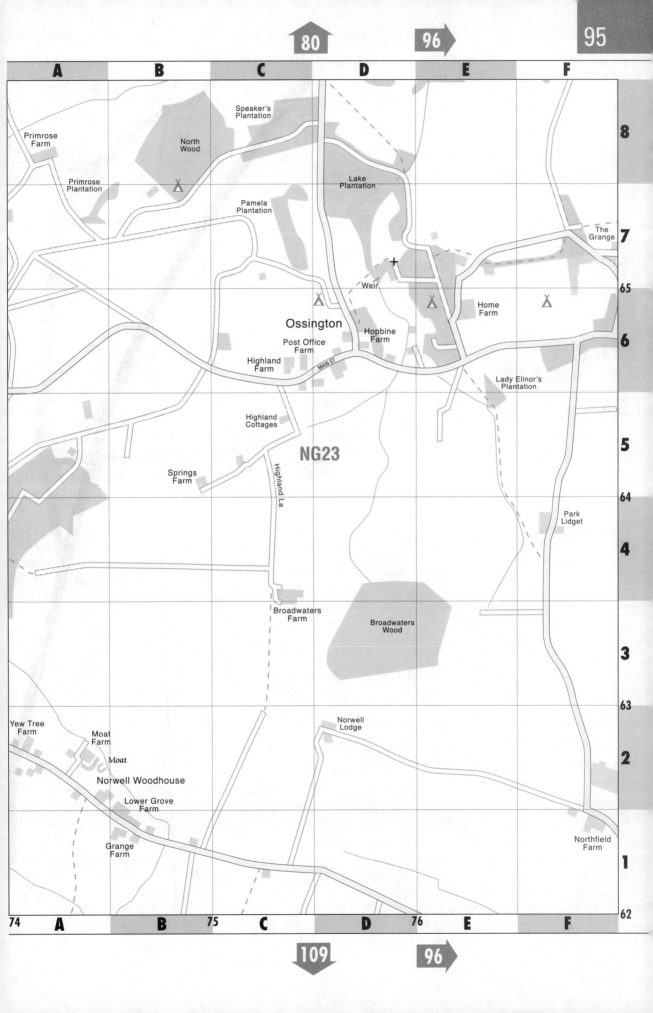

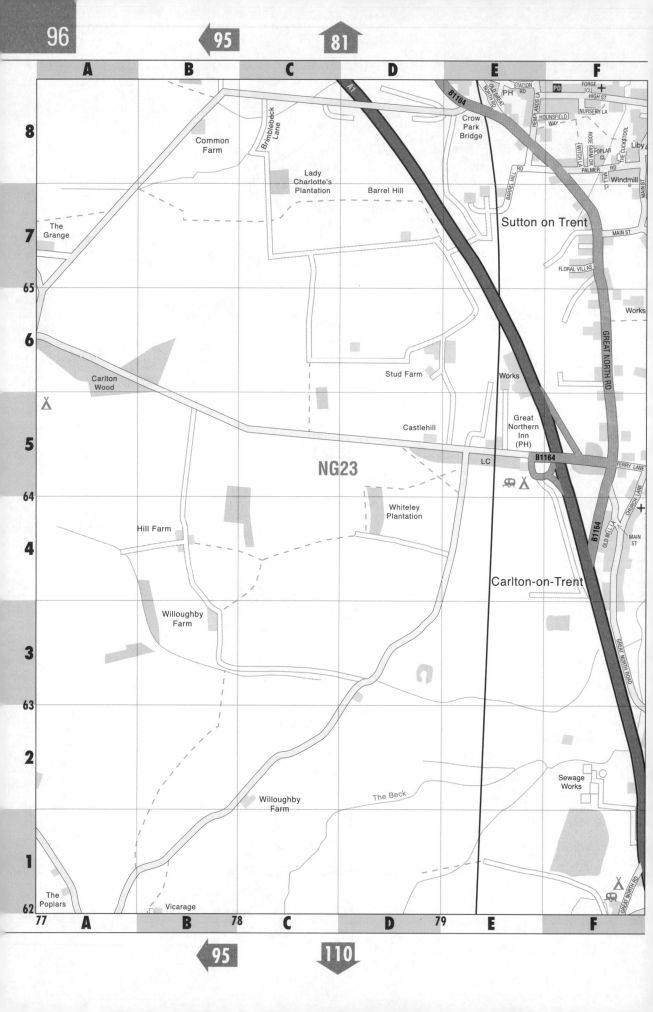

A B C D E F

8

The Grange
7

65

6
Carlton Wood

5

64

4

3

63

2

1

62

77 78 79

NG23

Common Farm

Brimbleback Lane

Lady Charlotte's Plantation

Barrel Hill

Crow Park Bridge

STATION RD
PH
OLD GREAT NORTH RD
HEMPLANDS LA
HOUNSFIELD WAY
PO
FORGE CL
HIGH ST
NURSERY LA
THE CUCKSTOOL
Liby

Sutton on Trent

BARREL HILL RD
ROSE FARM DR
POPLAR CL
TWITCH LA
PALMER RD
MILL CL
MAIN ST
Windmill

MAIN ST

FLORAL VILLAS

Works

GREAT NORTH RD

Stud Farm

Works

Castlehill

Great Northern Inn (PH)

LC

B1164

FERRY LANE

CHURCH LANE

OLD BELLA
B1164
MAIN ST

Whiteley Plantation

Hill Farm

Willoughby Farm

Carlton-on-Trent

Willoughby Farm

The Beck

Sewage Works

GREAT NORTH ROAD

The Poplars

Vicarage

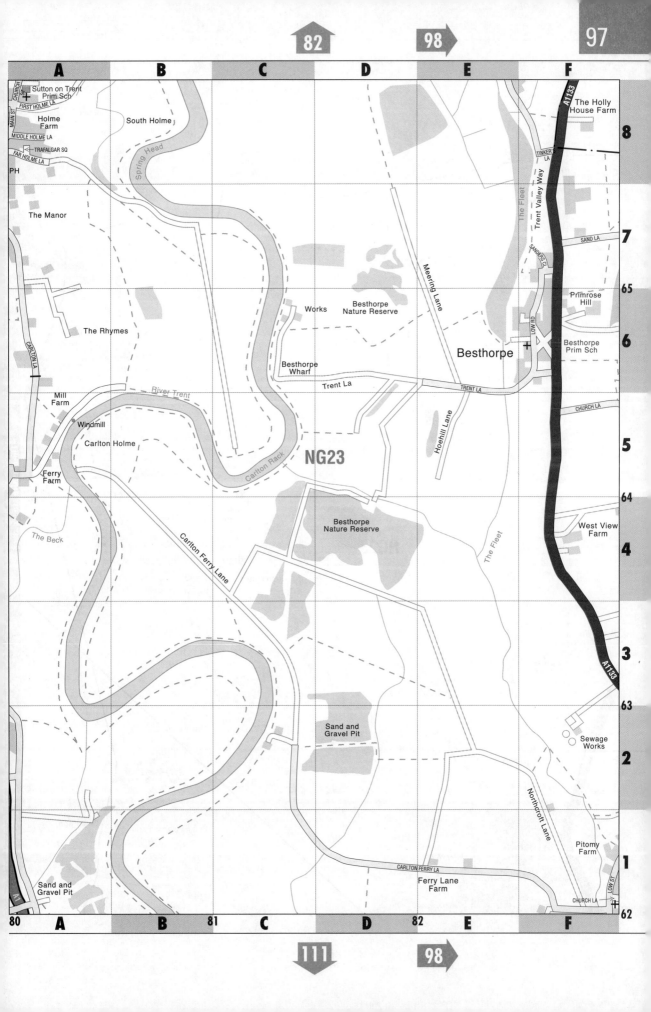

A B C D E F

8
7
65
6
5
64
4
3
63
2
1
62

The Holly House Farm

A1133

Trent Valley Way

TINKER'S LA

SAND LA

The Fleet

SANDERS CL

Primrose Hill

LOW RD

Besthorpe Prim Sch

Besthorpe

CHURCH LA

West View Farm

A1133

The Fleet

Northcroft Lane

Sewage Works

LOW ST

Pitomy Farm

CHURCH LA

Sutton on Trent Prim Sch

CHURCH

MAIN ST

FIRST HOLME LA

Holme Farm

South Holme

MIDDLE HOLME LA

TRAFALGAR SQ

FAR HOLME LA

PH

The Manor

Spring Head

CARLTON LA

The Rhymes

Works

Besthorpe Nature Reserve

Meering Lane

Besthorpe Wharf

Trent La

TRENT LA

Hoehill Lane

River Trent

Mill Farm

Windmill

Carlton Holme

Carlton Rack

NG23

Ferry Farm

The Beck

Carlton Ferry Lane

Besthorpe Nature Reserve

Sand and Gravel Pit

Sand and Gravel Pit

A1

CARLTON FERRY LA

Ferry Lane Farm

A B C D E F

8

7

65

6

5

64

4

3

63

2

1

62

Field Farm

BESTHORPE RD

FOLLY LA

Holme Farm

The Firs

SAND LA

Grange Farm

Windmill

Mill Farm

MOOR LA

Holly House Farm

Lodge Farm

CHURCH LA

South Scarle

Cemy

NG23

Amos Farm

Hill Farm

Trent Valley Way

SOUTH SCARLE RD

Ox Pasture Plantation

Collingham

Cross (rems of)

BESTHORPE RD

A1133

HIGH ST

RUE DE L'YONNE

SHAFTESBURY WAY

BROOKLANDS CL

LOW RD

QUEEN ST

VICARAGE CL

CHURCH LA

WOODHILL RD

DENBIGH CL

BROWN CT

CURTIS CL

MEERING CL

MANOR RD

DENBIGH CT

PINFOLD

THE ROOKERY

HEMPLANDS

THE LAWNS

BULLER CL

FOSTER RD

BARNFIELD RD

MOOR RD

CROSS LA

MONKWOOD CL

CAWTHORNE CL

BLACKBURN CL

PETERBOROUGH RD

POCKLINGTON RD

FISHER RD

LN6

SOUTH SCARLE LA

Grange Farm

Clay Farm

NORTH SCARLE RD

MOOR LA

Eagle Hall Wood

Long Plantation

LOW WOOD LA

SWINDERBY RD

Willow Farm

PO

Church Farm

AMOS LA

PLOT LA

Plots Farm

Bolting Holme Farm

SWINDERBY RD

COLLINGHAM RD

Dale Farm

BULPIT LA

Lincolnshire STREET ATLAS

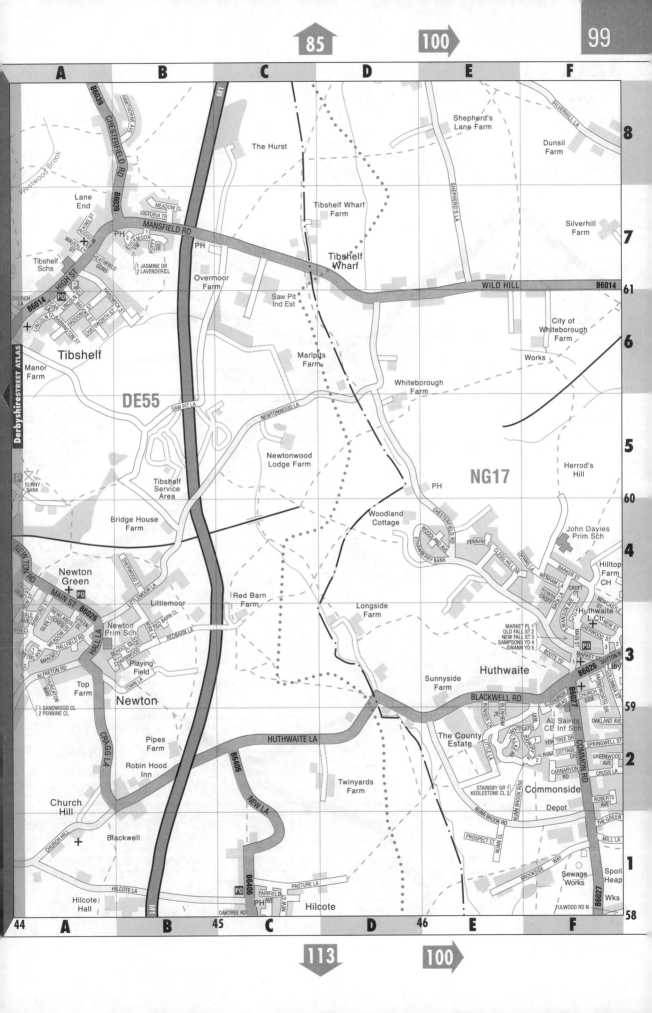

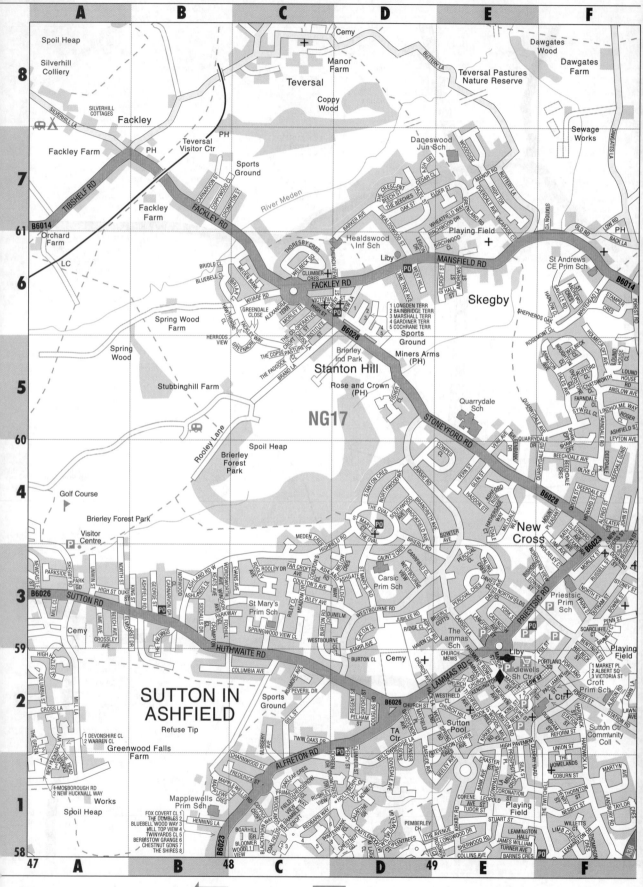

A   B   C   D   E   F

8

Spoil Heap

Silverhill Colliery

SILVERHILL COTTAGES

SILVERHILL LA

Fackley

Fackley Farm

Teversal

Manor Farm

Coppy Wood

Cemy

Dawgates Wood

Dawgates Farm

Teversal Pastures Nature Reserve

DAWGATES LA

Sewage Works

7

Fackley Farm

PH

Teversal Visitor Ctr

PH

Sports Ground

River Meden

CARNARVON ST

COPPYWOOD CL

CROMPTON ST

FACKLEY RD

Daneswood Jun Sch

WOODSIDE

Playing Field

St Andrews CE Prim Sch

OLD RD

LOW RD

PH

BACK LA

B6014

61

TIBSHELF RD

B6014

Orchard Farm

LC

MEDEN BANK

WIJARF RD

BRIDLE CL

BLUEBELL CL

BRIAR CL

HAWTHORNE

FACKLEY WAY

GREENDALE CLOSE

GREENMOOR

HERRODS VIEW

THORESBY CRES

WELBECK ST

CLUMBER CRES

ALEXANDRA TERR

MORLEY ST

VICTORIA'S

HIGH ST

CHURCH VIEW

FACKLEY RD

THE CO-OPERATIVE

CROFT

INSTITUTE

THE COPSE

THE PADDOCK

PASTURE

BRAND LA

B6028

Healdswood Inf Sch

Liby

PO

WEST HILL

LIME TREE AVE

MANSFIELD RD

GILCROFT

ELDER ST

HALL ST

ST ANDREWS

THE CRESCENT

BEECH ST

THE BEECHES

OAK ST

CEDAR CL

HAZEL CL

BIRCHWOOD DR

BIRCHWOOD CL

LEGION RD

OVERDALE AVE

VICARAGE CL

HIGH TOR

MANOR RD

BUTTERY LA

STATION YD

Skegby

St Andrews

SHEPHERDS OAK

ANDREWS RD

WHITEFORD RD

HAW OW

SAVILE RD

STAMPER CRES

FOREST RD

6

Spring Wood Farm

Spring Wood

Stubbinghill Farm

1 LONGDEN TERR
2 BAINBRIDGE TERR
3 MARSHALL TERR
4 GARDINER TERR
5 COCHRANE TERR

Sports Ground

Brierley Ind Park

Stanton Hill

Rose and Crown (PH)

Miners Arms (PH)

FISHER ST

Quarrydale Sch

STONEYFORD RD

COWPES CL

ROSEMOINT CL

ABINGTON AVE

WELBECK AVE

RUFFORD AVE

CHATSWORTH

OVERSTONE CL

DALES AVE

LOUND HOUSE RD

ANSLOW AVE

FARNDALE

SYWELL CL

ASHFIELD ST

LINDHOLME WAY

ROGER CL

LEYTON AVE

QUARRYDALE AVE

SHAW CL

DEEPDALE

OLIVE CT

BEECHDALE AVE

BEECHDALE CRES

TEECHDALE GDNS

DEEPDALE ST

5

Rooley Lane

Brierley Forest Park

Spoil Heap

NG17

STANTON CRES

NORTHWOOD AVE

SOUTHWOOD AVE

BRANDRETH AVE

BROOKFIELD AVE

BRIERLY RD

CARSIC RD

FERN ST

GLEN ST

HADDON ST

ASHFORD RISE

HATHERSAGE

WILLOW CL

MILL DALE

VERE AVE

EMBANK DR

QUARRYDALE AVE

MOUNT PLEASANT

New Cross

60

Golf Course

Brierley Forest Park

Visitor Centre

MEDEN CRES

HIGHFIELD RD

ROOLEY AVE

THE OVAL

St Mary's

PO

THE OVAL

SOWTER AVE

CAUNT'S AVE

CARNELL CL

WESTBOURNE AVE

PERCIVAL CRES

PALING ST

DAVIES ST

BISHOP ST

NORTHERN DR

CAVENDISH ST

WOLSELEY ST

MORLEY ST

RUSSELL ST

NORTH ST

DOWNING ST

STONEY ST

BOWNE ST

SLATER ST

B6028

B6023

4

PARKSIDE

SKEGBY RD

PARK GD

UNWIN ST

NORTH ST

HIGH ST

DUKE ST

GEORGE ST

CARNARVON GR

ASHLAND RD W

NORWOOD CL

WORDSWORTH AVE

KEATS AVE

WINDSOR AVE

ASHLAND RD

SIDDALLS DR

CRAMPTON

PARKWAY

FOXHILL

RILEY AVE

COULTON'S AVE

BURTON RD

DUNELM DR

ASHGATE RD

St Mary's Rd

MDWS CRES

FAR CROFT AVE

Carsic Prim Sch

JUBILEE RD

RIDGE CL

BRIERLY COTTS

ASHLEY RD

CARSIC LA

YORK ST

THE LAMMAS SCH

CHURCH MEWS

FRIAR'S ROW

MARION AVE

Priestsic Prim Sch

PENN ST

SCARCLIFFE CT

WELBECK ST

Playing Field

1 MARKET PL
2 ALBERT SQ
3 VICTORIA ST

Croft Prim Sch

3

B6026

SUTTON RD

Cemy

LIME AVE

BEECH AVE

CROSSLEY AVE

ELMARST DR

THE FAIRINGS

ASHFIELD RD

HUTHWAITE RD

COLUMBIA AVE

EVANS AVE

MEADOW DR

SPRINGWOOD VIEW CL

CATON CL

STARR AVE

WESTBOURNE RD

BURTON CL

Cemy

CHURCH AVE

CHURCH ST

LAMMAS RD

Idlewells Sh Ctr

Liby

LOW ST

PORTLAND SQ

PORTLAND ST

OUTRAM ST

FOREST ST

L Ctr

STATION RD

HARDWICK LA

LAWN CL

STATION ST

59

High La

COLUMBIA CT

CROSS LA

MILL LA

ASHLANDS

THE HEADS

THE GREEN

SUTTON IN ASHFIELD

Refuse Tip

Sports Ground

COLUMBIA AVE

PEVERIL DR

GILL ST

NURSERY AVE

ASHMORE AVE

PELHAM

TWIN OAKS DR

DOUGLAS ST

REGENT ST

CROSS ST

CHURCH ST

B6026

TA Ctr

Sutton Pool

WESTFIELD LA

KING ST

MAFIELD

NEW ST

KINGSLEY CL

CHURCH HILL

LUTHER

KINGSWAY

KIRKBY RD

HIGH PAVEMENT

DEVONSHIRE SQ

PARLIAMENT ST

PROSPECT ST

REFORM ST

QUARRY YARD

THE HOMELANDS

COBURN ST

UNION ST

Sutton Ctr Community Coll

MARTYN ST

LANSBURY RD

TAYLOR CRES

2

1 DEVONSHIRE CL
2 WARREN CL

Greenwood Falls Farm

1-MOSBOROUGH RD
2 NEW HUCKNALL WAY

Works

Spoil Heap

CHARNWOOD ST

FREDERICK ST

MAPPLEWELLS CRES

HENNING LA

ALFRETON RD

PRIMROSE CT

OAKLEAF CRES

BRAMBLE CROFT

HEDGEROW

RUSHLEY VIEW

MOLLYBERRY

PERCY ST

GREEN LA

LICKING LA

DOVEDALE AVE

WILLOWBRIDGE LA

COPPICE RD

GARSIDE ST

BEELEY AVE

STEVENSON PL

LEOPOLD ST

CORONATION ST

CORENE AVE

STUART ST

TUDOR ST

Playing Field

LEAMINGTON HALL

NESBITT ST

WILLETTS ST

LIM B CRES

THE THICKINGS

LEAMINGTON DR

1

MAPPLEWELLS PRIM SCH

FOX COVERT CL 1
THE DUMBLES 2
BLUEBELL WOOD WAY 3
MILL TOP VIEW 4
TWINYARDS CL 5
BERGISTOW GRANGE 6
CHESTNUT GDNS 7
THE SHIRES 8

HENNING LA

BOARHILL GR

BLOOMER WOOD VIEW

COAL PIT LA

WINTERBECK

CASTLEWOOD GR

GREENTREES

Pemberley Ch

LONGWOOD DR

SHERWOOD RD

COLLINS AVE

JAMES WILLIAM TURNER AVE

BARNES CRES

LEAMINGTON CRES

58

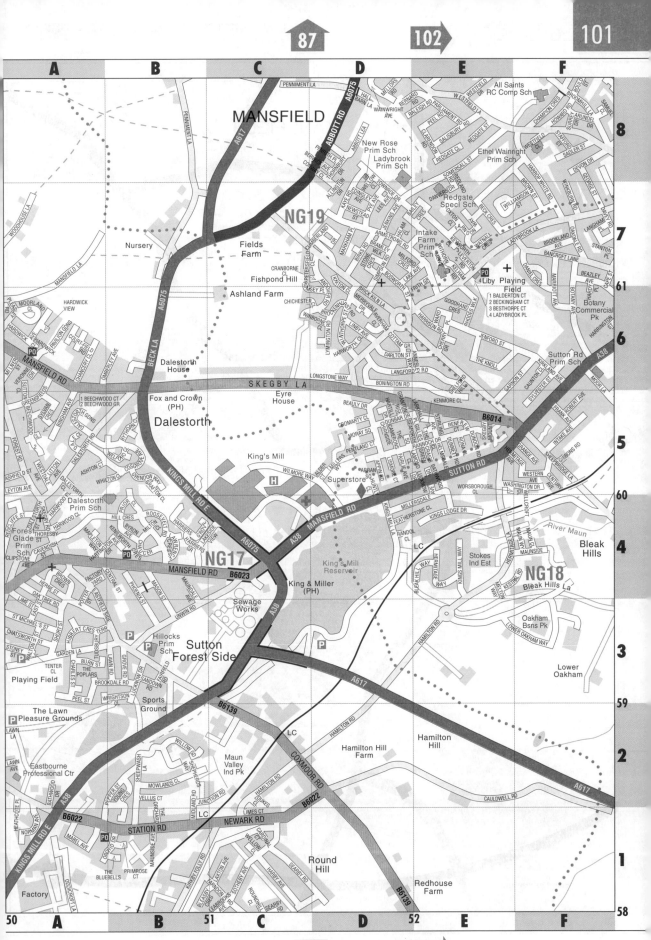

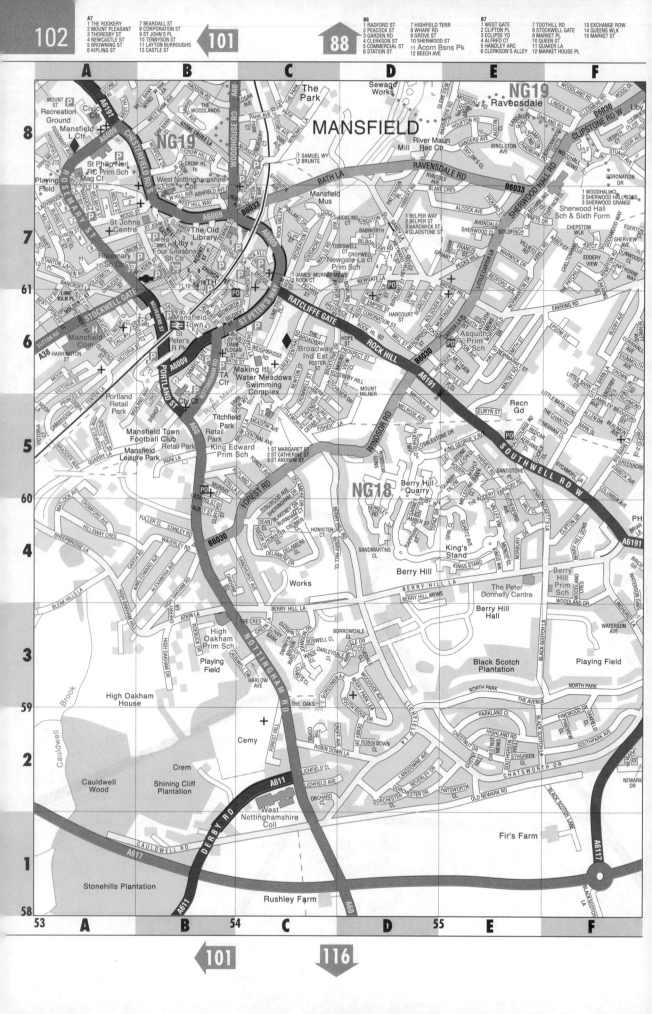

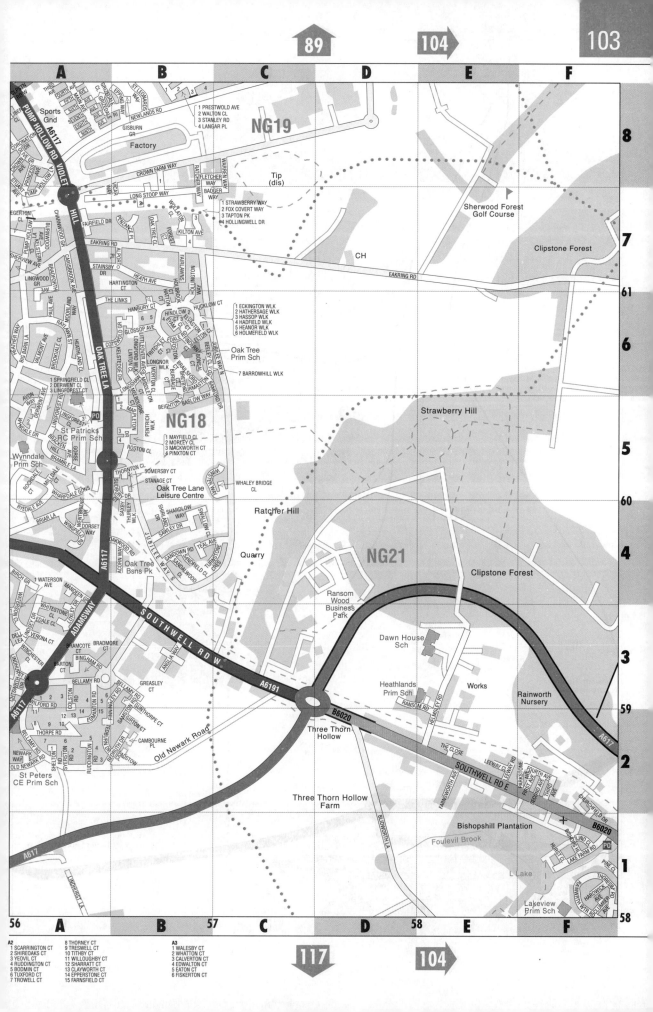

A2
1 SCARRINGTON CT
2 SHIREOAKS CT
3 YEOVIL CT
4 RUDDINGTON CT
5 BODMIN CT
6 TUXFORD CT
7 TROWELL CT

8 THORNEY CT
9 TRESWELL CT
10 TITHBY CT
11 WILLOUGHBY CT
12 SHARRATT CT
13 CLAYWORTH CT
14 EPPERSTONE CT
15 FARNSFIELD CT

A3
1 WALESBY CT
2 WHATTON CT
3 CALVERTON CT
4 EDWALTON CT
5 EATON CT
6 FISKERTON CT

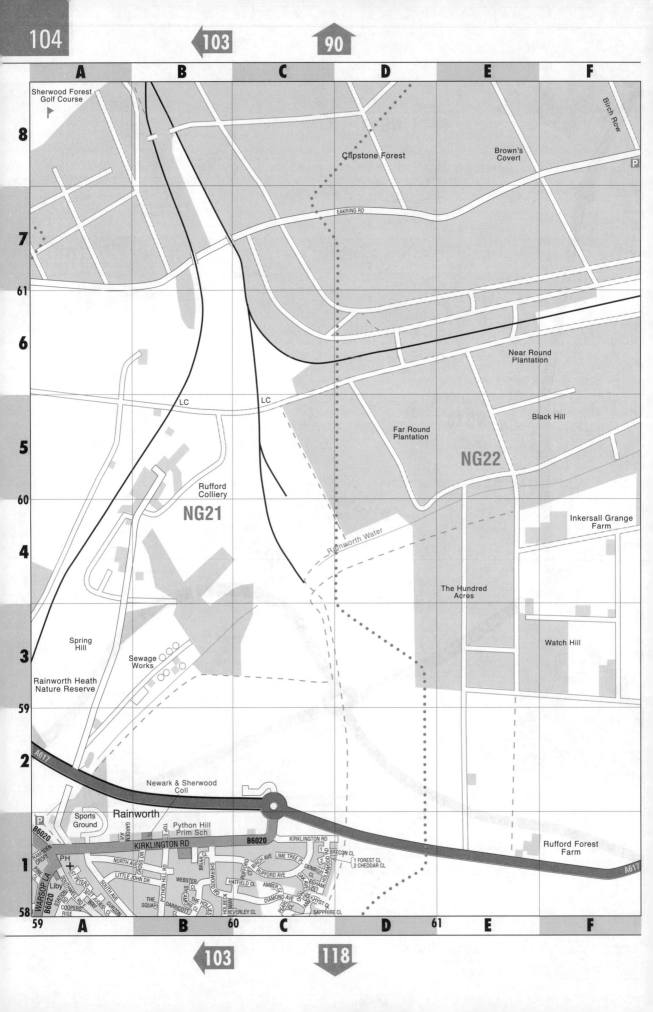

A   B   C   D   E   F

Sherwood Forest
Golf Course

8

Clipstone Forest

Brown's
Covert

Birch Row

P

EAKRING RD

7

61

6

Near Round
Plantation

LC

LC

Far Round
Plantation

Black Hill

5

NG22

60

Rufford
Colliery

NG21

Inkersall Grange
Farm

Rainworth Water

4

The Hundred
Acres

Watch Hill

Spring
Hill

3

Sewage
Works

Rainworth Heath
Nature Reserve

59

2

A617

Newark & Sherwood
Coll

Rufford Forest
Farm

P

Sports
Ground

Rainworth

Python Hill
Prim Sch

KIRKLINGTON RD

B6020

KIRKLINGTON RD

B6020

1 FOREST CL
2 CHEDDAR CL

A617

1

B6020

RAMSDEN CROFT

WARSOP LA

B6020

PH

Liby

SOUTHWELL RD E

STATION RD

ST PETERS ST

SOUTH AVE

NORTH AVE

CROSS DR

CURZON

JUBS

LITTLE JOHN DR

TOP ST

PYTHON HILL RD

SHERWOOD RD

WEBSTER

BRIAR

SYCAMORE CL

THE HOLLIES

DARRICOTT

HATFIELD CL

RUFFORD AVE

BIRCH AVE

LIME TREE P

DENBIGH CT

BRECON CL

AMBER

EGHAM

OAK AVE

PERO

AMETHYST CL

BEVERLEY CL

DIAMOND AVE

SAPPHIRE CL

THE SQUARE

COOPERS RISE

PINE AVE

GARDEN AVE

58

59   A   B   60   C   D   61   E   F

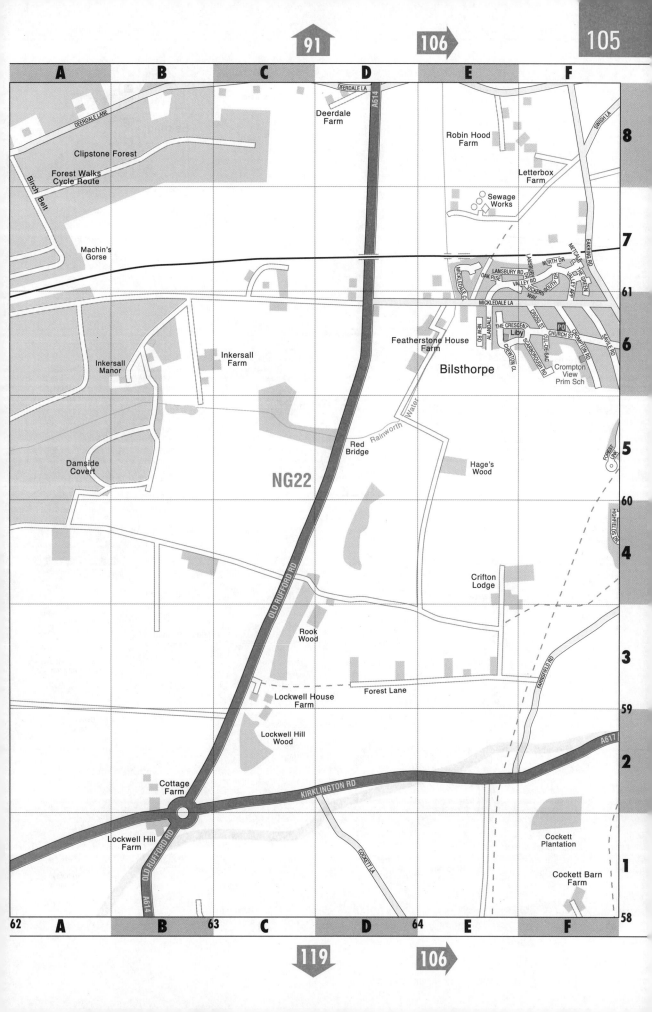

A　B　C　D　E　F

8

7

61

6

5

60

4

3

59

2

1

58

DEERDALE LA

Deerdale Farm

DEERDALE LANE

Clipstone Forest

Forest Walks Cycle Route

Birch Belt

Machin's Gorse

Inkersall Manor

Inkersall Farm

Damside Covert

NG22

A614

Robin Hood Farm

Letterbox Farm

SWISH LA

Sewage Works

METCALF CT

EAKRING RD

THE GREEN

LANSBURY DR

NORTH DR

VALLEY RD

VICKERS SOUTH

VALLEY APP

OAK RISE

MICKLEDALE CL

MICKLEDALE LA

DOT WAY

NEW RD

ALANDALE

THE CRESCENT

CHENTON CL

SCARBOROUGH RD

CROSS ST

CHURCH ST

CUL-DE-SAC

CROMPTON RD

SAVILE RD

Liby

PO

Crompton View Prim Sch

Featherstone House Farm

Bilsthorpe

Water

Rainworth

Red Bridge

Hage's Wood

FOREST LINK

HIGHFIELDS DR

Crifton Lodge

OLD RUFFORD RD

Rook Wood

Forest Lane

FARNSFIELD RD

Lockwell House Farm

Lockwell Hill Wood

A617

A614

Cottage Farm

KIRKLINGTON RD

COCKETT LA

Lockwell Hill Farm

Cockett Plantation

Cockett Barn Farm

62　A　B　63　C　D　64　E　F

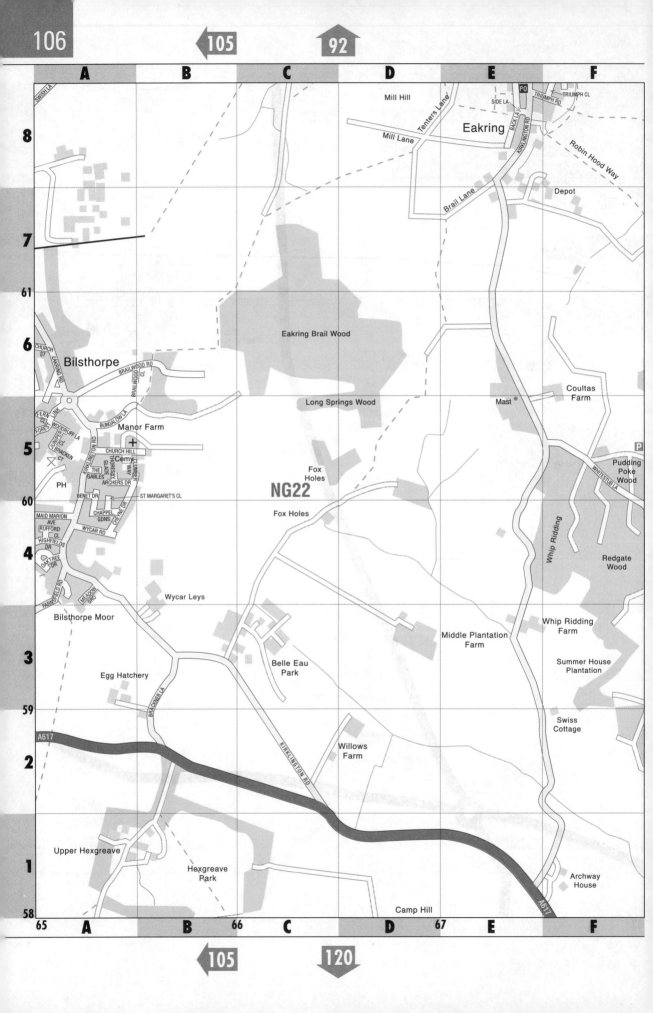

105
92

A B C D E F

8

Mill Hill

Tenters Lane

SIDE LA

PO

TRIUMPH CL

TRIUMPH RD

Eakring

Mill Lane

BACK LA

KIRKLINGTON RD

Robin Hood Way

Brail Lane

Depot

7

61

6

Eakring Brail Wood

CHURCH ST

EAKRING RD

Bilsthorpe

BRAILWOOD RD

BRAILWOOD CL

Long Springs Wood

Mast

Coultas Farm

FERN LINK

WOODRUFF LA

FOREST CT

JUNIPER CT

BUNGALOW LA

Manor Farm

KIRKLINGTON RD

CHURCH HILL

THORESBY GLADE

CLUMBER WAY

BRACKEN CT

Cemy

THE GABLES

ARCHERS DR

NG22

Fox Holes

Mast

P

WHITESTUB LA

Pudding Poke Wood

5

PH

BENET DR

CHEINE DR

ST MARGARET'S CL

60

MAID MARION AVE

RUFFORD CL

HIGHFIELDS DR

CHAPPEL GDNS

Fox Holes

Whip Ridding

Redgate Wood

4

OAK TREE DR

FARNSFIELD RD

INEADON GRO

WYCAR RD

Wycar Leys

Whip Ridding Farm

Summer House Plantation

Bilsthorpe Moor

Wycar Leys

Middle Plantation Farm

3

Egg Hatchery

BRACKNER LA

Belle Eau Park

59

A617

Swiss Cottage

KIRKLINGTON RD

Willows Farm

2

Upper Hexgreave

1

Hexgreave Park

Archway House

A617

58

Camp Hill

105
120

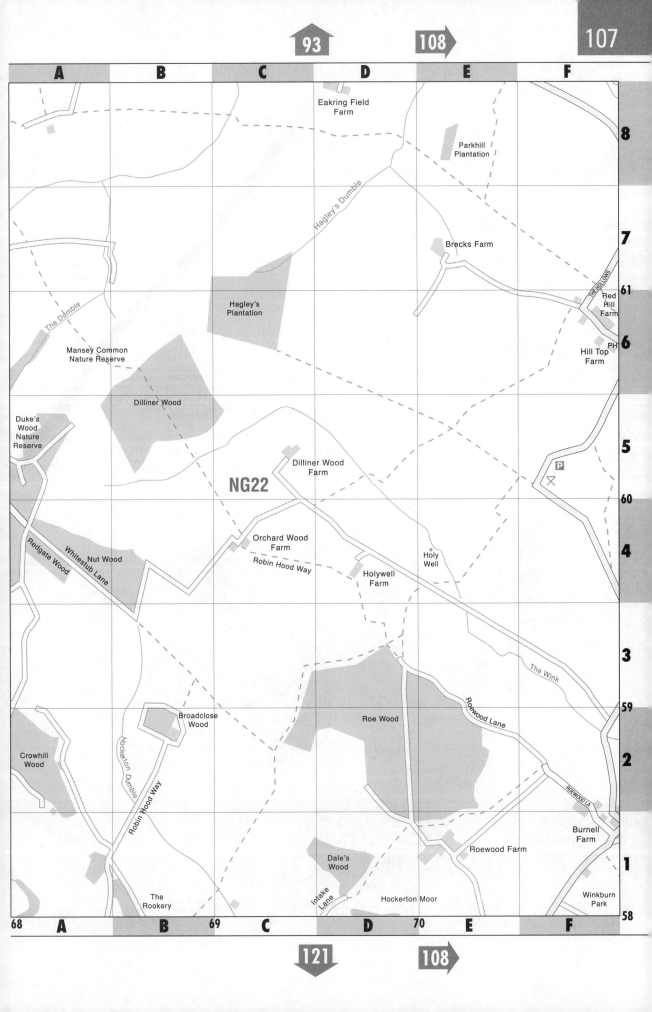

A B C D E F

8 7 61 6 5 60 4 3 59 2 1 58

Eakring Field Farm

Parkhill Plantation

Hagley's Dumble

Brecks Farm

The Hollows

Red Hill Farm

PH

Hill Top Farm

The Dumble

Hagley's Plantation

Mansey Common Nature Reserve

Dilliner Wood

Duke's Wood Nature Reserve

Dilliner Wood Farm

NG22

P

Orchard Wood Farm

Robin Hood Way

Nut Wood

Redgate Wood

Whitestub Lane

Holywell Farm

Holy Well

The Wink

Roewood Lane

Broadclose Wood

Hockerton Dumble

Robin Hood Way

Roe Wood

Crowhill Wood

ROEWOOD LA

Dale's Wood

Roewood Farm

Burnell Farm

The Rookery

Intake Lane

Hockerton Moor

Winkburn Park

68 69 70 58

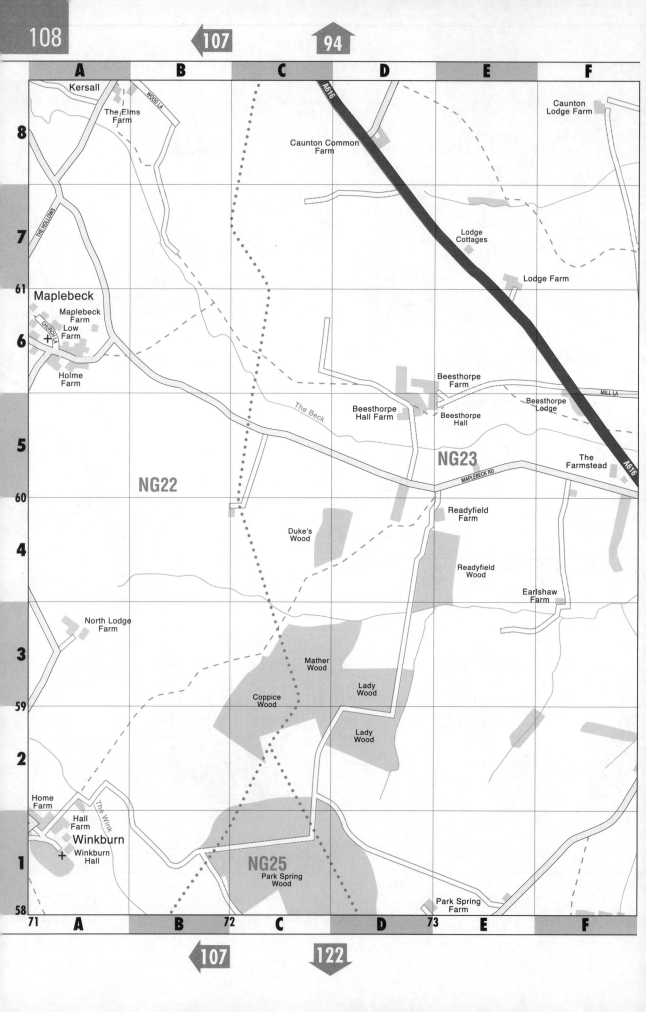

107

94

A   B   C   D   E   F

Kersall

The Elms
Farm

WOOD LA

Caunton
Lodge Farm

8

Caunton Common
Farm

A616

THE HOLLOWS

7

Lodge
Cottages

Lodge Farm

61

Maplebeck

Maplebeck
Farm
Low
Farm

CHURCH LA

6

Holme
Farm

Beesthorpe
Farm

Beesthorpe
Lodge

MILL LA

The Beck

Beesthorpe
Hall Farm

Beesthorpe
Hall

NG23

NG22

The
Farmstead

5

MAPLEBECK RD

A616

60

Readyfield
Farm

Duke's
Wood

4

Readyfield
Wood

Earlshaw
Farm

North Lodge
Farm

3

Mather
Wood

Lady
Wood

Coppice
Wood

59

Lady
Wood

2

Home
Farm

THE WINK

Hall
Farm

Winkburn

NG25

Winkburn
Hall

1

Park Spring
Wood

Park Spring
Farm

58

71   A   B   72   C   D 73 E   F

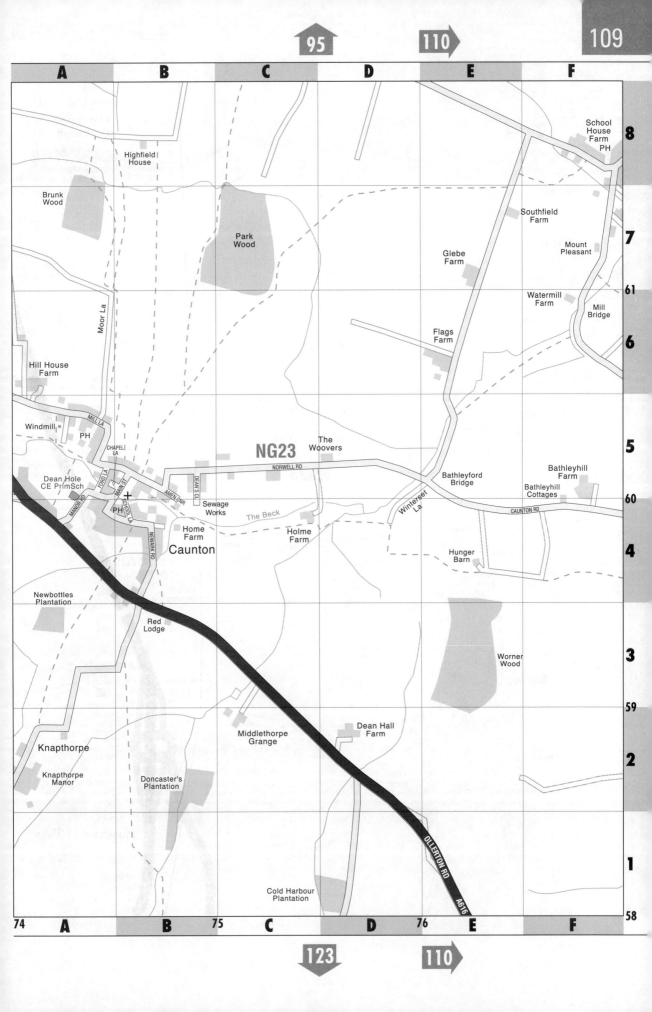

A   B   C   D   E   F

8
Model Farm
WILLOUGHBY CT
PO
Church Farm
Norwell CE Prim Sch
SCHOOL LA
OLD HALL LA
FAIR VALE
Beck Bridge
New Farm
NORWELL LA
LC
Milestone Farm
Laurels Farm
Cromwell
MAIN ST
Cromwell House Farm
Vina Cooke Museum of Dolls & Bygone Childhood
CHURCH LA

Norwell
The Beck

7

61

6
Fox Covert

GREAT NORTH RD
A1

5
Foxholes Farm
NG23
Lodge Farm

60
Sunnybrook Farm
CAUNTON RD
Mousehole Corner

4
Fallows End
Manor Farm
VICARAGE LA
Bracken Farm
LC
Norwell Crossing
EDGE CL
DICKENSON WAY
MANOR HO DR

3
Cogley Lane
Bathley
MAIN ST
CHAPEL LA
THE PARK
THE GRANGE
CHAPEL LA
PO
Northroad Farm
GREAT NORTH RD
WILLOW DR
WALTON'S LA
Trent Farm

59
PH
MUSKHAM LA
GREEN LA
Cordon Lodge
BATHLEY LA
Lord Nelson (PH)
Playing Field
TRENT CL
MACKLEYS LA
River Trent

2
The Cottage
Mill House
LC
NELSON LA
MAIN ST
FERRY LA
PH
Muskham Prim Sch
EASTFIELD
ST WILFREDS CL
PEETS DR

Oak Farm
LC
Downside Cottage
The Old Hall
MARSH LA

Hopyard Lane
BATHLEY LA
Moorhouse Lane
Moor House
GREAT NORTH RD
North Muskham
MEADOW CL

1
Mill Lane
Mill House
PH
MILL LA
CRAB LA

58
B6325
A1
CHURCH LA

77   A   B   78   C   D   79   E   F

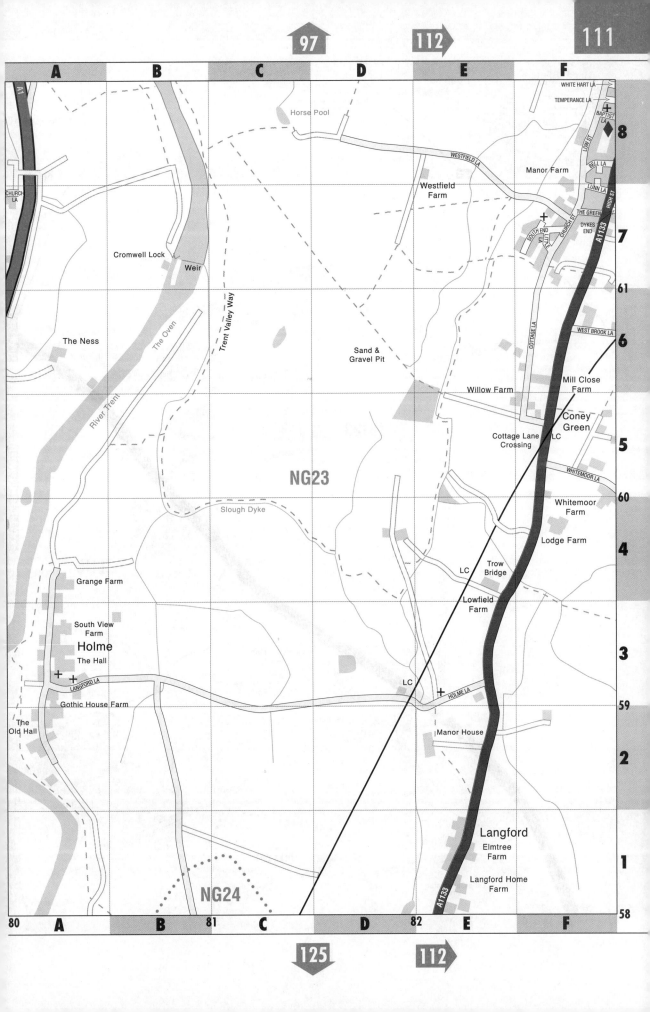

A1

A B C D E F

WHITE HART LA

TEMPERANCE LA

BAPTIST
LA

8

Horse Pool

WESTFIELD LA

Manor Farm

LOW ST

BELL LA

HIGH ST

Westfield
Farm

LUNN LA

CHURCH
LA

THE GREEN

CHURCH ST

DYKES
END

A1133

7

SOUTH END

LITTLE
HILL

61

Cromwell Lock

COTTAGE LA

WEST BROOK LA

Weir

6

The Ness

The Oven

Trent Valley Way

Sand &
Gravel Pit

Mill Close
Farm

Coney
Green

River Trent

Willow Farm

LC

Cottage Lane
Crossing

NG23

Whitemoor
Farm

WHITEMOOR LA

5

60

Slough Dyke

Lodge Farm

4

LC

Trow
Bridge

Grange Farm

LC

Lowfield
Farm

South View
Farm

Holme

The Hall

LANGFORD LA

LC

HOLME LA

3

59

Gothic House Farm

Manor House

The
Old Hall

2

NG24

Langford

A1133

Elmtree
Farm

1

Langford Home
Farm

58

80 A B 81 C D 82 E F

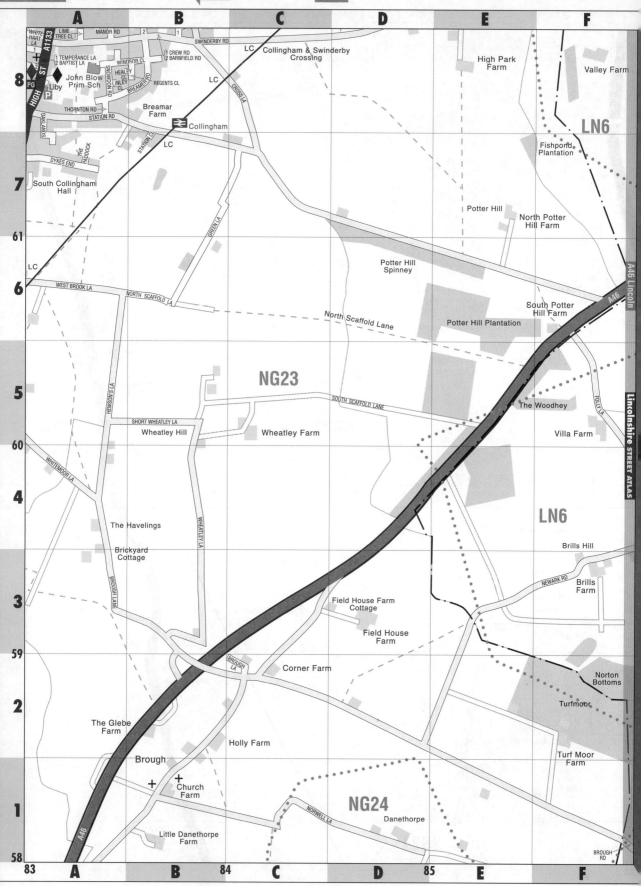

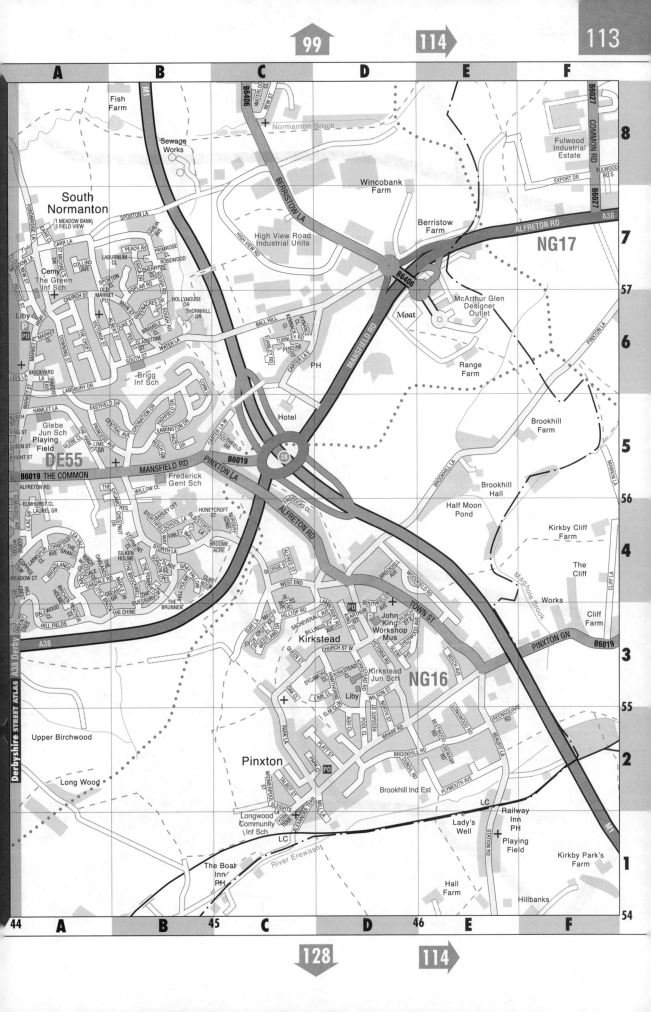

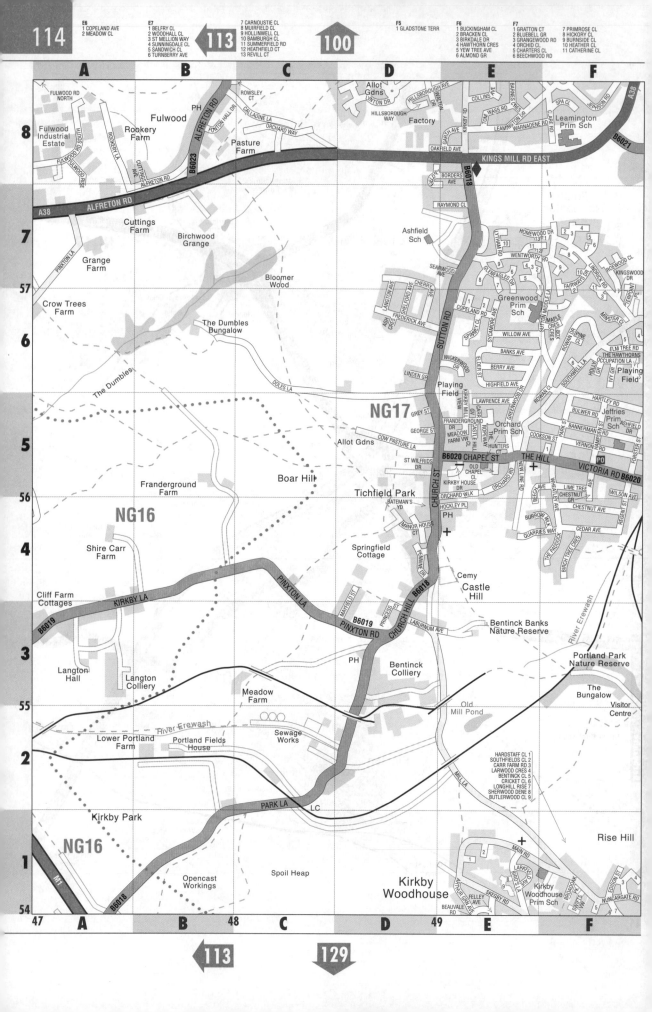

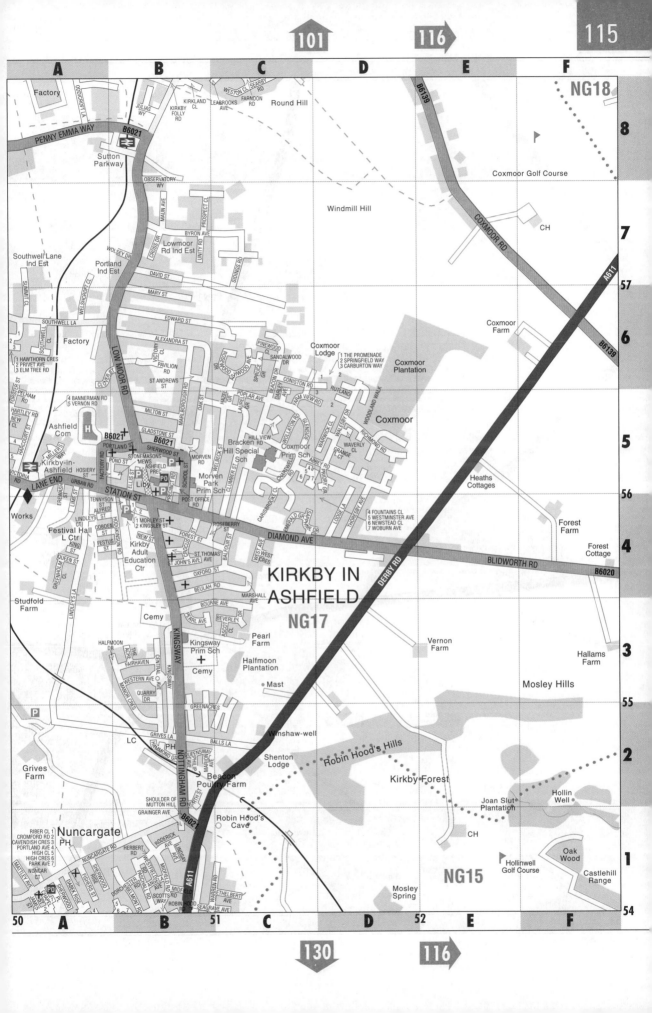

NG18

A B C D E F

8

Factory

Kirkland CL WESTON CL SEARBY
LEABROOKS FARNDON Round Hill
JULIAS AVE RD
WY KIRKBY
FOLLY
RD

PENNY EMMA WAY B6021

Sutton
Parkway

OBSERVATORY
WY

Windmill Hill

Coxmoor Golf Course

7

CH

Southwell Lane
Ind Est

WOLSEY DR

Lowmoor
Rd Ind Est

MAUN AVE
CROSS ST
BYRON AVE
UNITY RD
SIDINGS RD

57

Portland
Ind Est

DAVID ST

MARY ST

Coxmoor
Farm

6

SUMMIT CL
SOUTHWELL LA

Factory

EDWARD ST

ALEXANDRA ST

PINEWOOD
CL

Coxmoor
Lodge

1 THE PROMENADE
2 SPRINGFIELD WAY
3 CARBURTON WAY

1 HAWTHORN CRES
2 PRIVET AVE
3 ELM TREE RD

VICTORY
CL

PAVILION
RD

ST ANDREWS
RD

SANDALWOOD
DR

Coxmoor
Plantation

A611

B6139

FORSTER
RD

PELHAM
RD

HARTLEY RD
NEW
CL

LOW MOOR RD

CLOVER ST

4 BANNERMAN RD
5 VERNON RD

MILTON ST

MARLBOROUGH RD
OAK ST
HAZEL GR
LAUREL GR
SPRUCE GR

POPLAR AVE

CONISTON RD

RUTLAND

Coxmoor

5

HARCOURT ST

Ashfield
Com

H

B6021

GLADSTONE ST

SHERWOOD ST

PORTLAND RD
POND ST
FACTORY RD
STONEMASONS
MEWS
ELLIS ST

P

MORVEN ST
WELBECK RD
CLUMBER ST

HILL VIEW
RD

Bracken
Hill Special
Sch

Coxmoor
Prim Sch

WARWICK CL
WOLSEY DR

WAVERLY
GRANGE
CL CT

RICHMOND RD

WOODLAND WALK

Heaths
Cottages

56

MILLERS
WAY

Kirkby-in-
Ashfield

VICTORIA
RD

HOSIERY
ST

P
P
PO
P
P

ASHFIELD
PREC

CARISBROOKE CL

Morven
Park Prim Sch

POST OFFICE
RD

CARIUS CL
EMERALD GR
PRIORY GR
ABBEY RD

4 FOUNTAINS CL
5 WESTMINSTER AVE
6 NEWSTEAD CL
7 WOBURN AVE

Forest
Farm

Forest
Cottage

4

Works

LANE END

EREWASH ST
LIME ST

URBAN RD

TENNYSON
ST
ALFRED
ST

LINDLEYS ST

STATION ST

1 MORLEY ST
2 KINGSLEY ST

NEW ST

ROSEBERRY
AVE

BALFOUR ST

DIAMOND AVE

WEST AVE
WEST
CRES

LODGE LA

THORESBY AVE

DERBY RD

BLIDWORTH RD

B6020

Festival Hall
L Ctr

GREENHOLM
CL
QUEEN ST
KING
ST

COBDEN ST
FESTUM
ST

Kirkby
Adult
Education
Ctr

CROCUS ST
ST JOHN'S AVE
ST THOMAS
AVE

FOREST ST

OXFORD ST

BEULAH RD

MARSHALL
AVE

KIRKBY IN
ASHFIELD
NG17

Vernon
Farm

Hallams
Farm

3

Studfold
Farm

LINDLEY'S LA

Cemy

BOURNE AVE

PEARL AVE
ASCOT CL

BEVERLEY
DR

Pearl
Farm

Mosley Hills

Halfmoon
Plantation

55

Kingsway
Prim Sch

Cemy

Mast

KINGSWAY

HALFMOON
DR
THE
ACRE
FAIRHAVEN

CENTRAL O AVE

WESTERN AVE

MANOR CRES

QUARRY
DR

GREENACRES

Winshaw-well

Robin Hood's Hills

Kirkby Forest

2

Grives
Farm

P

LC

GRIVES LA

BALLS LA

NOTTINGHAM RD

HAMMOND GR
QUEENSWAY

PHILLIP
ST
MARION
ST

PH

Shenton
Lodge

Joan Slut
Plantation

Hollin
Well

SHOULDER OF
MUTTON HILL

GRAINGER AVE

B6021

Beacon
Poultry Farm

Robin Hood's
Cave

CH

Hollinwell
Golf Course

Oak
Wood

Castlehill
Range

1

RIBER CL 1
CROMFORD RD 2
CAVENDISH CRES 3
PORTLAND AVE 4
HIGH CL 5
HIGH CRES 6
PARK AVE 7
NUNCAR
ST

Nuncargate
PH

MATTLEY AVE

JAMES ST
PO
SHERWOOD
DEREK RISE

NUNCARGATE RD

SHERWOOD
WESTFIELD
FISHERS ST

RODERICK
AVE
HERBERT
RD

LINDSEY
AVE

DORCHESTER RD
BELMONT RD
ANGELL
PASCAL RD

A611

WARBETH RD
ETHELBERT AVE
SCOTTS WAY
ROBIN HOOD
MIDFIELD RD
SEAGRAVE AVE

Mosley
Spring

NG15

54

115
102

A   B   C   D   E   F

8

Stonehills Farm

A611

DERBY RD

Forest Stone

BLACK SCOTCH LA

Works

7

A611

Two Oaks Farm

NOTTINGHAM RD

A60

THE SPINNEY

MAPLE DR

PINES WY

OAK VIEW RISE

POPLARS WY

LIME TREE DR

Harlow Wood

NG18

Thieves' Wood

CHESTNUT CL

57

Greenwood Craft Centre

Forest Walks

6

B6139

Fountaindale Specl Sch

P

Portland Coll

COXMOOR RD

Robin Hood Way

NG21

Sheppard's Stone

Woodlands Farm

5

Nomanshill Wood

56

P

Little Nomanshill Wood

Forest Walks

RICKET LA

Holly Lodge

4

NG17

P

B6139

Campfield Farm

LITTLE RICKET LA

MANSFIELD RD

PH

The Larch Farm

Twin Hill

B6020

BLIDWORTH RD

KIRKBY RD

BEECH AVE

3

B6020

MAIN RD

WOODSIDE RD 1
HASLEMERE GDNS 2

ROSEDALE LA

BYRON CRES

SUMMERCOURT DR

WESTBROOK

HIGHLEYS DR

FAIRFIELD DR

FAIRFIELD COPSE CL

Haggnook Wood

NOTTINGHAM RD

LINWOOD CRES

CAMBOURNE GDNS

DOVER BECK CL

SWINTON DR

55

Gosford Plantation

NG15

Gunthorpe Hagg Wood

2

SHEPWALK

CHURCH DR

PILGRIM CL

THE HOLLIES

MILTON CR

Liby

MILTON DR

PO

P

Knightcross Dale

Monksbarn Farm

1

Reedwater

Newstead Park

Swinecotte Dale

Pilgrim Oak

Hotel

MANSFIELD RD

LONGDALE LA

VERNON CRES

VERNON AVE

Knightcross

Lady Wildman's Wood

A60

MISTERTON CRES

REGINA CRES

54

Castle Wood

Upper Lake

53   A   B   54   C   D   55   E   F

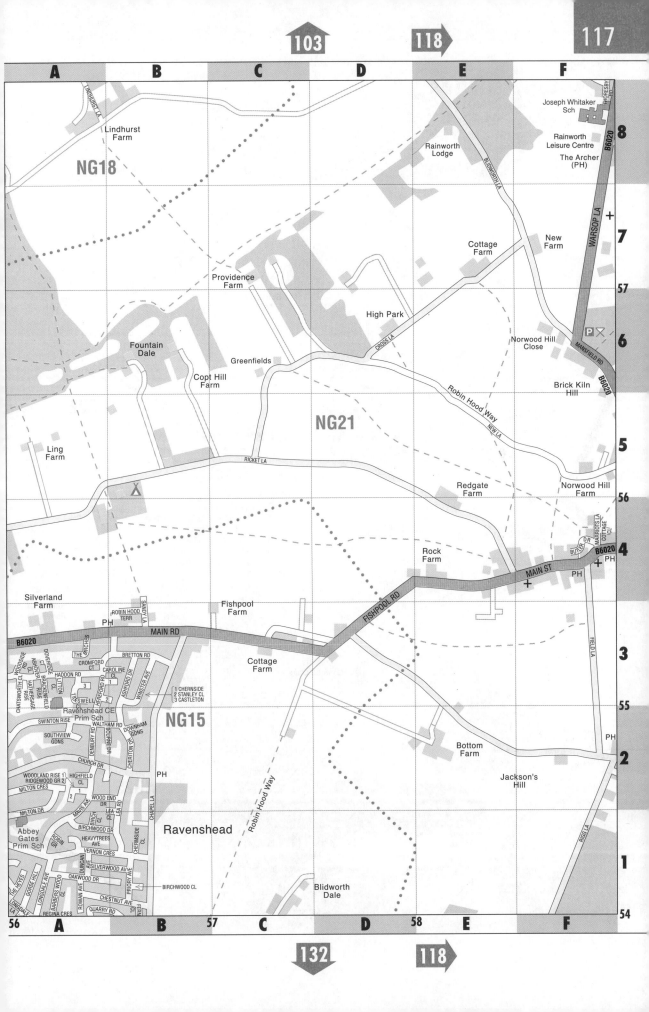

A   B   C   D   E   F

8
7
57
6
5
56
4
3
55
2
1
54

NG18

Lindhurst
Farm

LINDHURST LA

Joseph Whitaker
Sch

THORESBY RD

Rainworth
Lodge

Rainworth
Leisure Centre

The Archer
(PH)

BLIDWORTH LA

WARSOP LA

B6020

New
Farm

Cottage
Farm

Providence
Farm

High Park

Norwood Hill
Close

P

Mansfield Rd

B6020

CROSS LA

NG21

Fountain
Dale

Greenfields

Copt Hill
Farm

Robin Hood Way

NEW LA

Brick Kiln
Hill

Ling
Farm

RICKET LA

Redgate
Farm

Norwood Hill
Farm

56

MARRIOTS LA

COTTAGE
CL

BUTLER DR

B6020

PH

Rock
Farm

Main St

PH

+

FIELD LA

PH

Silverland
Farm

Robin Hood
Terr

SANDY LA

PH

Fishpool
Farm

FISHPOOL RD

B6020

MAIN RD

THE ARCHES

Cottage
Farm

DOVERIDGE CL

WOODROSE CL

ASHOVER RD

HATHERSAGE RISE

BRACKENFIELD

CHATSWORTH CL

CROMFORD CT

HADDON RD

LITTON CL

TISSWELL CL

HEREFORD RD

BRETTON RD

CAROLINE

ASHFORD DR

RISE

WINSTER AVE

1 CHERNSIDE
2 STANLEY CL
3 CASTLETON

Ravenshead CE
Prim Sch

SWINTON RISE

SOUTHVIEW
GDNS

DEHBURY RD

BOURNE DR

WALTHAM RD

CHERITON DR

DOWNHAM
GDNS

NG15

CHURCH DR

PH

Bottom
Farm

WOODLAND RISE 1
RIDGEWOOD GR 2
HIGHFIELD CL

MILTON CRES

WOOD END
DR

CHAPEL LA

Jackson's
Hill

MILTON DR

MAVIS AVE

BIRCH CL

LEA RD

BIRCHWOOD DR

Robin Hood Way

Abbey
Gates
Prim Sch

ROBIN
GR

HEAVYTREES
AVE

VERNON CRES

CHERNSIDE
CL

Ravenshead

RIGG LA

THE HEXES

GORSE HILL

BARBERS WOOD

LONGDALE AVE

LONGDALE LA

DUNCAN

SILVERWOOD AVE

OAKWOOD DR

PRIORY AVE

Blidworth
Dale

REGINA CRES

ROWAN AVE

CHESTNUT AVE

QUARRY RD

BIRCHWOOD CL

56   A   B   57   C   D   58   E   F   54

A B C D E F

8
7
57
6
57
5
56
4
3
55
2
1
54

59 60 61

Blidworth

NG21
NG22
NG25

Little Allamoor Farm
Allamoor Farm
Boundary Farm
Lurcher Farm
Forest Farm
Baulker Farm
Far Baulker Farm
Sewage Works
Jolly Friar (PH)
Robin Hood Way
Mansfield Rd
Baulker La
Forest Wlks
Haywood Oaks
Blidworth Bottoms
Gorse Covert
Syke Breck Farm
Long Wood
Beck Lane
Robin Hood Way
Old Rufford Rd
A614

Newark & Sherwood Coll
Blidworth Ind Pk
Robert Jones Jun Sch
Robert Jones Inf Sch

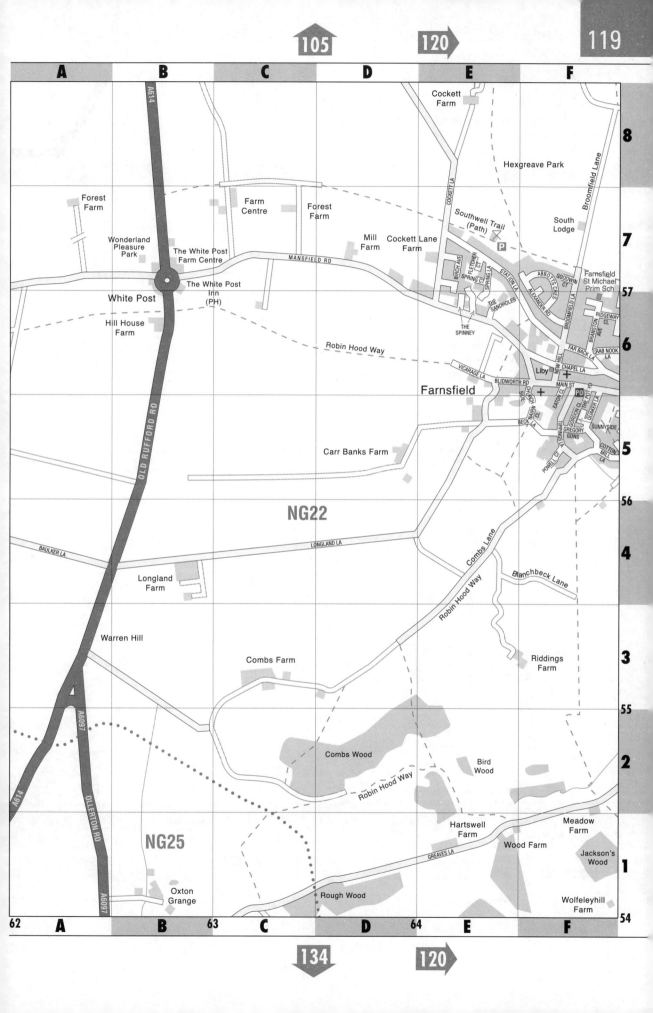

A B C D E F

8

Lower Hexgreave
Farm

Hexgreave
Park

A617 KIRKLINGTON RD

Home
Farm

NEWARK RD

Kirklington

Park
Plantation

Kirklington
Prim Sch

Mill Farm

SCHOOL

SOUTHWELL RD

THE GREEN

7

Moor Farm

River Greet

Robin Hood Way

57

RIDGEWAY CL
D'AYNCOURT WLK

MEADOW CL

LONG MEADOW

Osmanthorpe
Manor

6

THE RIDGEWAY
WOODLAND CL
GREENVALE

MILLDALE RD

GREENWOOD CL

WOODSIDE

NETHER CT

BRICKYARD LA

Pumping
Station

Southwell Trail

Spring's
Farm

Osmanthorpe
Nature Reserve

Collyeat
House

Farnsfield

1 CRAB NOOK LANE
2 CHAPEL LA
3 MAIN ST

Cotton Mill Dyke

Edingley Beck

STATION RD

P

NG22

5

PARK DRIVE

IRVING CL

CARDING CL

COTTON MILL LA

SOUTHWELL RD

Sewage
Works

Edingley
Mill

Valley
Farm
PH

Moat

STATION RD

Harlow
Fields

56

MANSFIELD RD

BELFIELDS VW

MAIN ST

4

Cotton Mill
Farm

ALLESFORD LA

Manor House
Farm

Edingley

EDINGLEY HILL

HOLME LA

Diamond
Cottage
Farm

GREAVES LA

LITTLE LA

Halam
Mill

3

New Manor
Farm

GREAVES LA

Woodendale

Grange
Farm

Littledale

Old
Hall
Farm

55

New Hall
Farm

ST HELEN'S LA

PH

2

CARVER'S HOLLOW

Little Turn Croft
Farm

NEWHALL LA

Robin Hood Way

Halam Beck

Halam CE
Prim Sch

SCHOOL LA

PH

BACK LA

HALAM HILL

GRAY LA

Middlebeck
Farm

Halam

ST MICHAEL'S CL

CHURCH LA

1

Wolveleyhill La

Turncroft
Farm

Brockley
Farm

Machin's
Farm

Manor
Farm

RADLEY RD

Halam House
Farm

Cutlersforth

54

65 A 66 B C 67 D E F

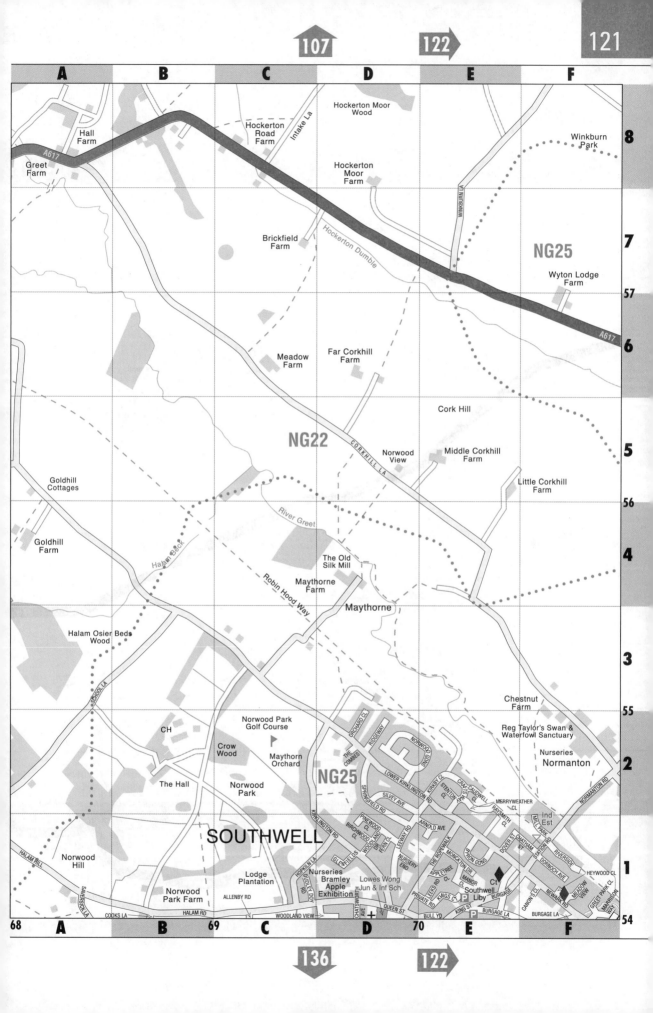

107
122
136
122

A B C D E F

Hall Farm

Greet Farm

A617

Hockerton Moor Wood

Hockerton Road Farm

Intake La

Hockerton Moor Farm

Winkburn Park

8

Winkburn La

NG25

7

Brickfield Farm

Hockerton Dumble

Wyton Lodge Farm

57

A617

6

Meadow Farm

Far Corkhill Farm

Cork Hill

NG22

CORKHILL LA

Norwood View

Middle Corkhill Farm

Little Corkhill Farm

5

56

Goldhill Cottages

River Greet

Halam Beck

4

The Old Silk Mill

Maythorne Farm

Maythorne

Goldhill Farm

Robin Hood Way

Halam Osier Beds Wood

SCHOOL LA

3

Chestnut Farm

55

CH

Norwood Park Golf Course

Reg Taylor's Swan & Waterfowl Sanctuary

Crow Wood

Maythorn Orchard

NG25

Nurseries Normanton

2

NORMANTON RD

The Hall

Norwood Park

SOUTHWELL

ORCHARD CL

RIDGEWAY

THE COMBES

NORWOOD GDNS

LOWER KIRKLINGTON RD

KIRBY CL

STENTOR CL

CRAG ST

CAUDWELL CL

RAYSMITH

MERRYWEATHER CL

Ind Est

MILL PARK RD

SPRINGFIELD RD

SILVEY AVE

BIRCHWOOD CL

PINEWOOD CL

WOODLAND

LEEWAY RD

CHATHAM

DOVER ST

STATION RD

RIVERSIDE

1

Norwood Hill

SAVERSICK LA

HALAM HILL

Norwood Park Farm

Lodge Plantation

ALLENBY RD

KIRKLINGTON RD

HOPKILN LA

DUDLEY DOY

GLENFIELDS

Nurseries Bramley Apple Exhibition

Lowes Wong Jun & Inf Sch

NURSERY END

THE ROPEWALK

MONCKTON DR

BYRON GDNS

APPLETREE

MANOR CL

Southwell Liby

CHATSWORTH AVE

Queen St

BULL YD

LEEKS RD

KNGS CL

PRIVATE RD

KING ST

BURGAGE LA

CANON CL

NEWARK RD

MORRISON

MEADOW VIEW

GREET PARK CL

HEYWOOD CL

54

68 A B 69 C D 70 E F 54

A B C D E F

8
7
57
6
5
56
4
3
55
2
1
54

NG22

Winkburn Park

Park Spring Wood

Newlands Farm

Newfields Farm

Park Leys

Sunnybank Farm

A617

THE PADDOCKS

HOCKERTON HTS

CAUNTON RD

Hockerton

PH

Woodside Farm

Hockerton Grange

Manor Farm

NG25

Hockerton Dumble

Cheverals

Cheveral Wood

The Wink

WHEATGRASS HILL

Gorse Hill

NG23

Upton Lodge

Lodge Farm

Spring Wood Farm

A617

NG22

Hockerwood

Hopyard Farm

Car Dyke

The Mill

HOCKERTON RD

The Hall

NORMANTON RD

GALLEY HILL RD

Upton Field

HOCKERWOOD LA

Upton Road

Hockerwood Farm

Cliffe Farm

British Horological Institute

Time Mus

Upton Hall

Upton

The Close

PH

CHURCH LA

CHURCH WLK

The Workhouse

Greet Bridge

Caudwell House

UPTON RD

Hopyard Farm House

A612

MAIN RD

MILL LA

A612

Cross Keys (PH)

Trent Valley Way

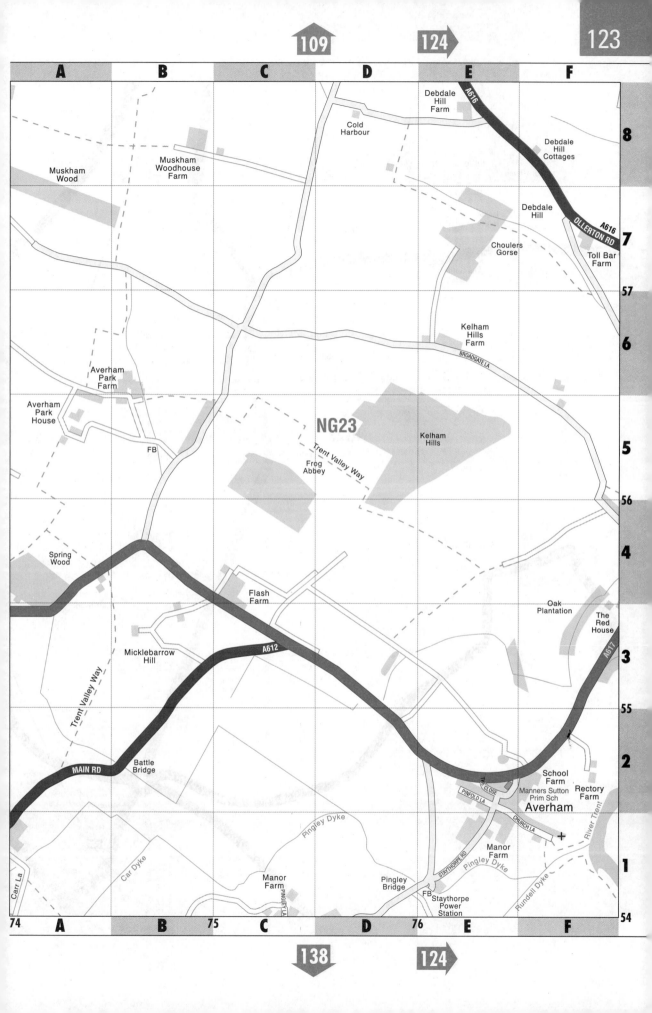

109

124

A **B** **C** **D** **E** **F**

8

Debdale
Hill
Farm

Cold
Harbour

Debdale
Hill
Cottages

A616

7

Debdale
Hill

OLLERTON RD

A616

Toll Bar
Farm

Choulers
Gorse

57

Muskham
Wood

Muskham
Woodhouse
Farm

6

Kelham
Hills
Farm

BROADGATE LA

Averham
Park
Farm

NG23

Kelham
Hills

5

Averham
Park
House

FB

Frog
Abbey

Trent Valley Way

56

4

Spring
Wood

Oak
Plantation

The
Red
House

Flash
Farm

Mickelbarrow
Hill

A612

A617

3

Trent Valley Way

55

MAIN RD

Battle
Bridge

2

School
Farm

PINFOLD LA

THE CLOSE

Manners Sutton
Prim Sch

Rectory
Farm

Averham

River Trent

Pingley Dyke

CHURCH LA

1

Car Dyke

PINGLEY LA

Manor
Farm

STAYTHORPE RD

Pingley
Bridge

Pingley Dyke

Rundell Dyke

Carr La

FB

Manor
Farm

Staythorpe
Power
Station

54

74 **A** **B** 75 **C** **D** 76 **E** **F**

138

124

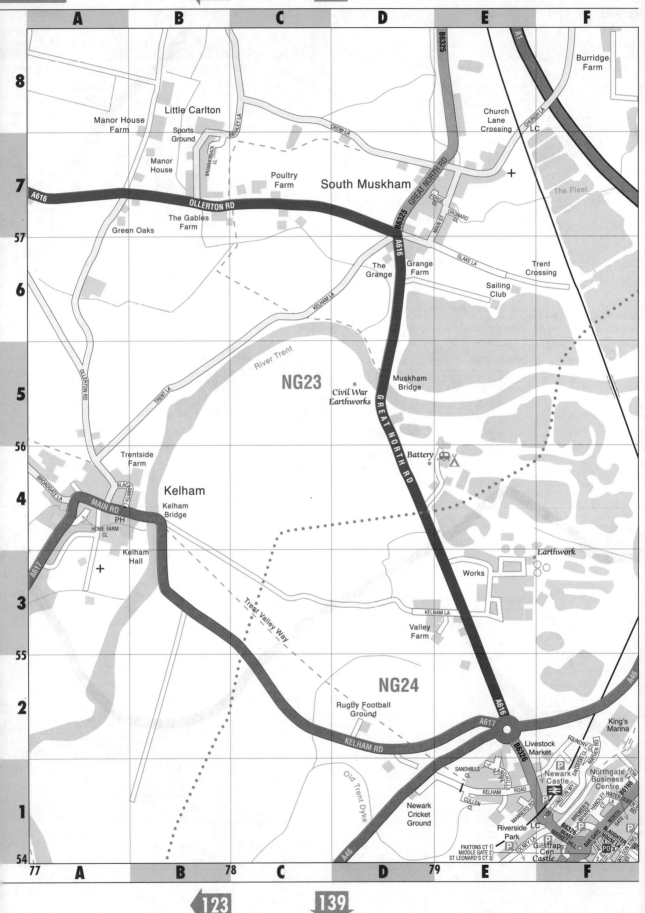

A   B   C   D   E   F

8

7

57

6

5

56

4

3

55

2

1

54

Manor House Farm

Little Carlton

Sports Ground

Manor House

BRAMMERSACK CL

BATHLEY LA

CROW LA

South Muskham

Church Lane Crossing

CHURCH LA

LC

Burridge Farm

Poultry Farm

A616 OLLERTON RD

B6325

GREAT NORTH RD

B6325

The Fleet

Green Oaks

The Gables Farm

The Grange

A616

FORGE CL

MAIN ST

ORCHARD CL

SLAKE LA

Grange Farm

Sailing Club

Trent Crossing

KELHAM LA

River Trent

NG23

Civil War Earthworks

Muskham Bridge

GREAT NORTH RD

Battery

TRENT LA

OLLERTON RD

Trentside Farm

BROADGATE LA

BLACKSMITH LA

Kelham

Kelham Bridge

MAIN RD

PH

HOME FARM CL

Kelham Hall

A617

Earthwork

Works

Trent Valley Way

KELHAM LA

Valley Farm

NG24

Rugby Football Ground

A616

Kelham Rd

Old Trent Dyke

KELHAM RD

A617

Livestock Market

B6326

SANDHILLS CL

SANDHILLS

KELHAM ROAD

CULLEN CL

MANERS RD

King's Marina

FOUNDRY CL

MATHER RD

SINCER'S CL

Newark Castle

P

Northgate Business Centre

B6166

Newark Cricket Ground

Newark Castle

LC

BREWER'S WHARF

HANDLEY WATER

P

CROSSING ONLY W?

P

B6326

BEAST MARKET HILL

BAR GATE

Riverside Park

P

Gilstrap Cen

Castle

TOLNEY LA

PAXTONS CT 1
MIDDLE GATE 2
ST LEONARD'S CT 3

NORTH GATE

ST AUGHTER HOUSE LA

WILSON

KINGS

A46

A617

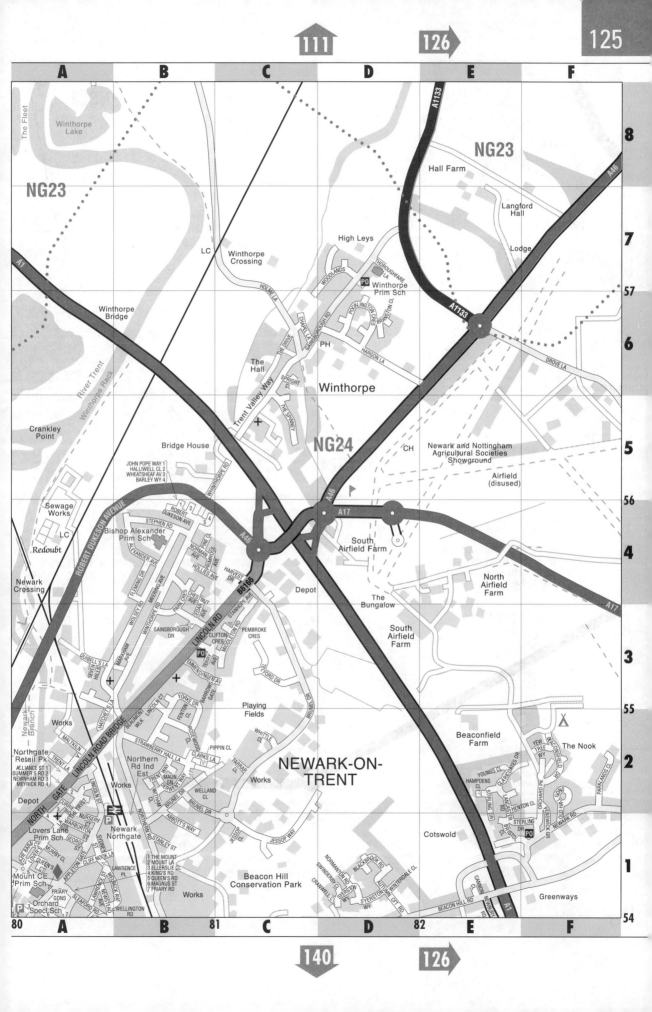

A B C D E F

8

NG23

NG23

Thorpe Field Farm

Danethorpe Hill

DANETHORPE LA

7

High Wood

Danethorpe Hill Farm

Little Danethorpe Farm

LN6

57

6

Lingspot Farm

Langford Moor Farm

Langford Moor

Stapleford Wood

NG24

CODDINGTON LA

5

Newark Air Museum

56

HIGHFIELD DR

4

Northlea

DROVE LA

Drove Cottage Farm

The Bungalow

A17

STAPLEFORD LA

3

Moor Brats

The Cottage

Moor Plantation

55

Flawford Farm

2

THE GREEN

MORGANS CL

THORPE CL

ROSS CL

PARKES CL

Sports Ground

Coddington Moor

The Tinderbox

Hall Farm

Coddington

SLEAFORD RD

A17

NEWARK RD

VALLEY VIEW

CHAPEL LA

MAIN ST

PH

BROWNLOW'S HILL

Manor Farm

Kelwick Wood

1

BALDERTON LA

Coddington CE Prim Sch

P

Newark Golf Course

LONG LA

Vale Farm

CH

54

83 A B 84 C D 85 E F

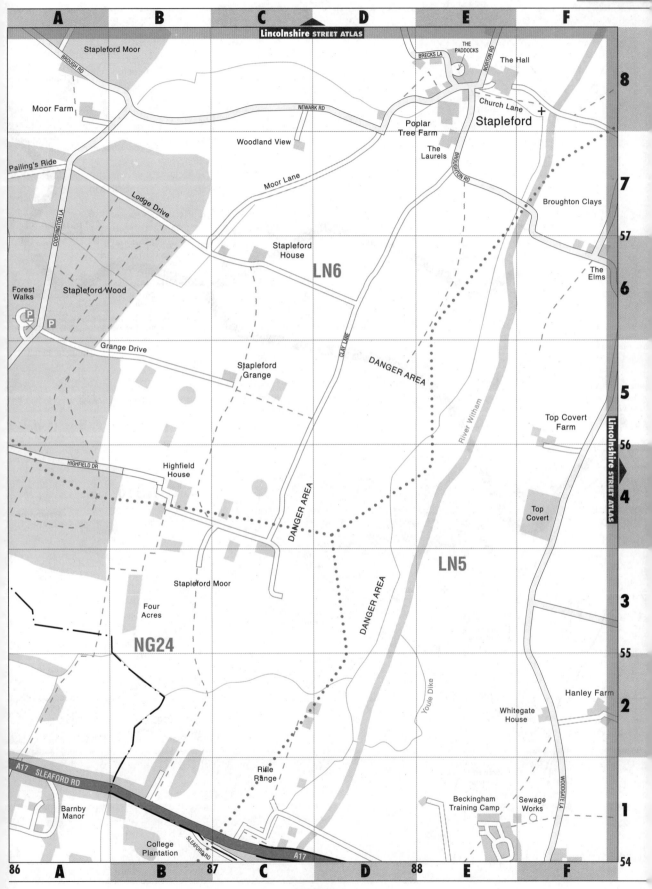

A B C D E F

8 7 57 6 5 56 4 3 55 2 1 54

Stapleford Moor

BROUGH RD

Moor Farm

Pailing's Ride

CODDINGTON LA

Lodge Drive

Woodland View

NEWARK RD

Moor Lane

THE PADDOCKS

BRECKS LA

The Hall

NORTON RD

Church Lane

Stapleford

Poplar
Tree Farm

The Laurels

BROUGHTON RD

Broughton Clays

Stapleford
House

LN6

The Elms

Forest
Walks

P

P

Stapleford Wood

Grange Drive

CLAY LANE

DANGER AREA

River Witham

Top Covert
Farm

Stapleford
Grange

HIGHFIELD DR

Highfield
House

DANGER AREA

Top
Covert

Stapleford Moor

DANGER AREA

LN5

Four
Acres

NG24

Youle Dike

Hanley Farm

Whitegate
House

WOODGATE LA

A17 SLEAFORD RD

Barnby
Manor

Rifle
Range

College
Plantation

SLEAFORD RD

A17

Beckingham
Training Camp

Sewage
Works

142

86 A B 87 C D 88 E F

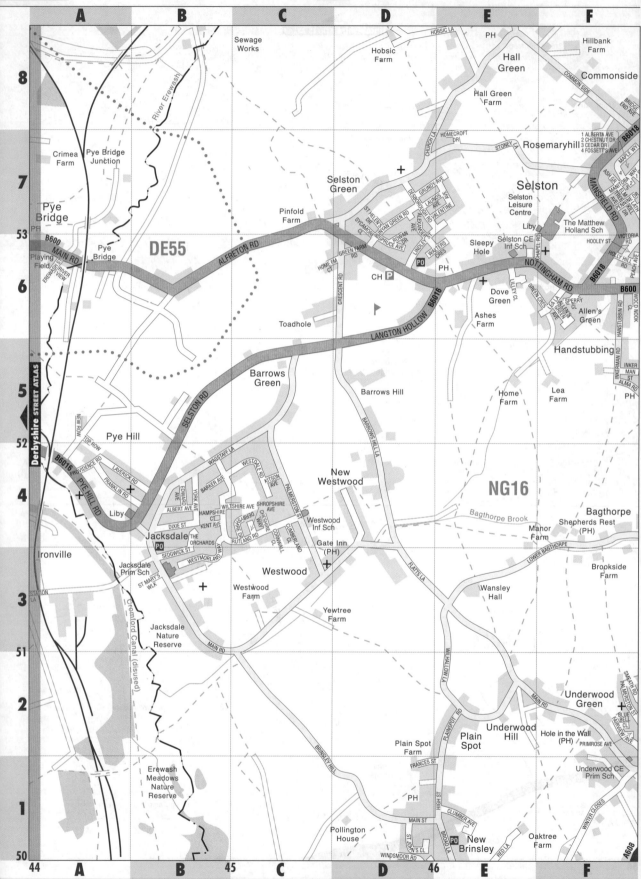

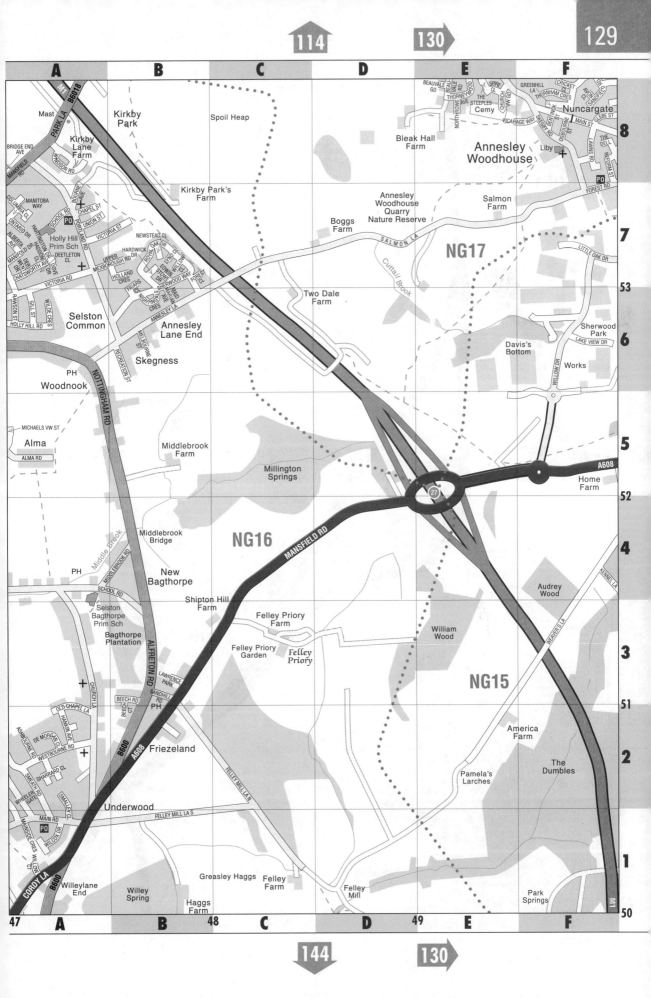

A B C D E F

M1 B6018

Mast

Kirkby Park

Spoil Heap

BEAUVALE GD
THE STEEPLES
Cemy

GREENHILL
CL
CRICKET
CL
Nuncargate

Bridge End Ave

Kirkby Lane Farm

PARK LA

WINDSOR RD

Bleak Hall Farm

Annesley Woodhouse

Liby

PO

8

MANSFIELD RD

COLUMBIA CT

MANITOBA WAY

Chapel St

SCHOOL RD

BOURNE AVE

PO

PORTLAND ST

UNION ST

VICTORIA ST

NEWSTEAD CL

Kirkby Park's Farm

Annesley Woodhouse Quarry Nature Reserve

Boggs Farm

SALMON LA

NG17

LITTLE OAK DR

7

ONTARIO DR

ALBERTA AVE

MANSFIELD RD

DERBY AVE

DOVE

CHATSWORTH AVE

Holly Hill Prim Sch

DEETLETON CL

HARDWICK DR

UPPER MEXBOROUGH RD

ROYAL OAK DR

FORD

LOWER MAID

FRIARS

HOLLAND CRES

SHERWOOD WAY

NIGHTINGALE

FOREST CL

Cuttail Brook

53

VICTORIA RD

RAWSON ST

GILL ST

WILDE CRES

HOLLY HILL RD

Selston Common

MELBOURNE ST

ANNESLEY LA

Annesley Lane End

Two Dale Farm

Sherwood Park

LAKE VIEW DR

6

RECREATION ST

Skegness

Davis's Bottom

WILLOW DR

Works

PH

Woodnook

5

NOTTINGHAM RD

MICHAELS VW ST

Alma

ALMA RD

Middlebrook Farm

Millington Springs

27

A608

Home Farm

52

Middle Brook

Middlebrook Bridge

NG16

MANSFIELD RD

KENNEL LA

4

PH

MIDDLEBROOK RD

New Bagthorpe

Audrey Wood

SCHOOL RD

Selston Bagthorpe Prim Sch

Shipton Hill Farm

Felley Priory Farm

William Wood

WEAVERS LA

3

Bagthorpe Plantation

ALFRETON RD

LAWRENCE PARK

SANDHILL RD

Felley Priory Garden

Felley Priory

NG15

51

CHURCH LA

OLD CHAPEL LA

BEECH RD

BEECH CT

PH

America Farm

2

DE MORGAN CL

HANKIN AVE

B600

A608

Friezeland

FELLEY MILL LA N

Pamela's Larches

The Dumbles

ASHBOURNE RD

WESTBOURNE RD

SHARRARD CL

WHEELER RD

SMALLEY CL

MAIN RD

PO

WILCOX DR

Underwood

FELLEY MILL LA S

1

SWEATH RD

MAINSIDE CRES

WILLOW CT

CORDY LA

B600

Willeylane End

Willey Spring

Haggs Farm

Greasley Haggs

Felley Farm

Felley Mill

Park Springs

M1

50

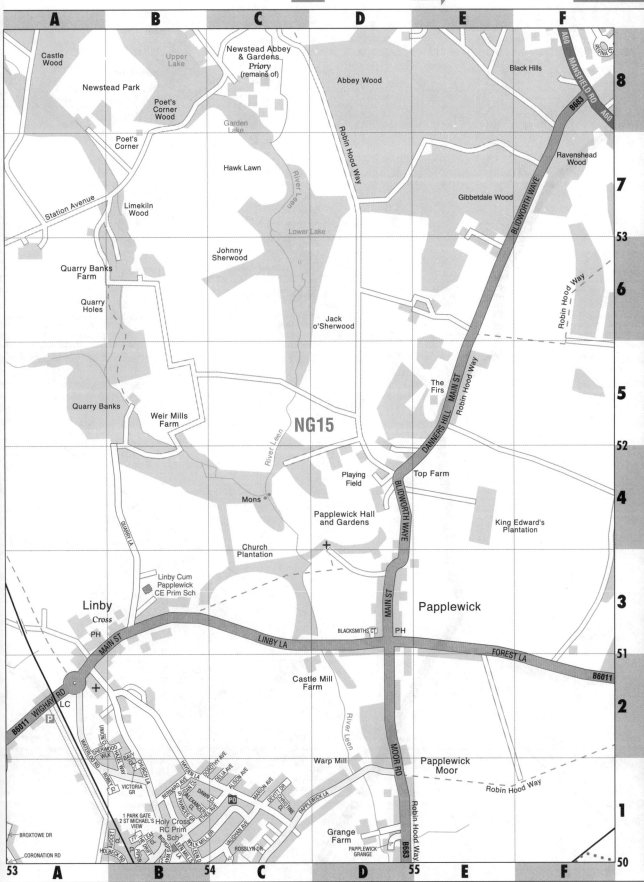

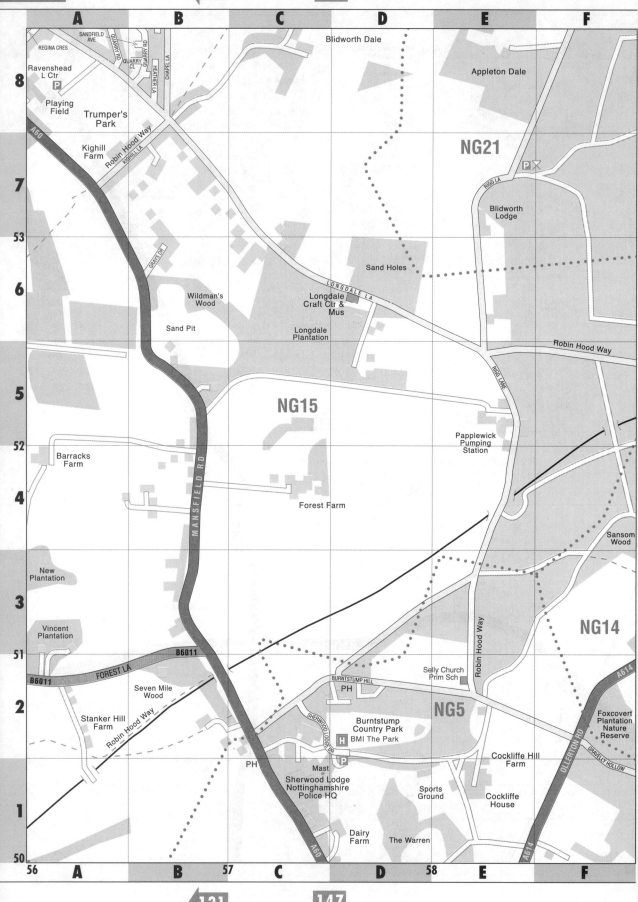

A   B   C   D   E   F

SANDFIELD AVE
REGINA CRES
QUARRY RD
QUARRY CL
HEATHER LA
CHAPEL LA

Ravenshead L Ctr

8

Playing Field

Trumper's Park

Kighill Farm

Robin Hood Way

KIGHILL LA

7

Blidworth Dale

Appleton Dale

NG21

RIGG LA

Blidworth Lodge

GRAYS DR

53

Wildman's Wood

LONGDALE LA

Sand Holes

Longdale Craft Ctr & Mus

6

Sand Pit

Longdale Plantation

Robin Hood Way

NG15

5

RIGG LANE

Papplewick Pumping Station

Barracks Farm

MANSFIELD RD

52

Forest Farm

4

New Plantation

Sansom Wood

Vincent Plantation

NG14

51

B6011

Robin Hood Way

FOREST LA

B6011

Seven Mile Wood

Selly Church Prim Sch

A614

Stanker Hill Farm

BURNTSTUMP HILL

PH

OLLERTON RD

Robin Hood Way

2

NG5

Foxcovert Plantation Nature Reserve

Burntstump Country Park

BMI The Park

H

SHERWOOD LODGE DR

Cockliffe Hill Farm

PH

Mast

P

GRAVELLY HOLLOW

Sherwood Lodge Nottinghamshire Police HQ

Sports Ground

Cockliffe House

1

Dairy Farm

The Warren

A614

A60

50

56   A   57   B   C   58   D   E   F

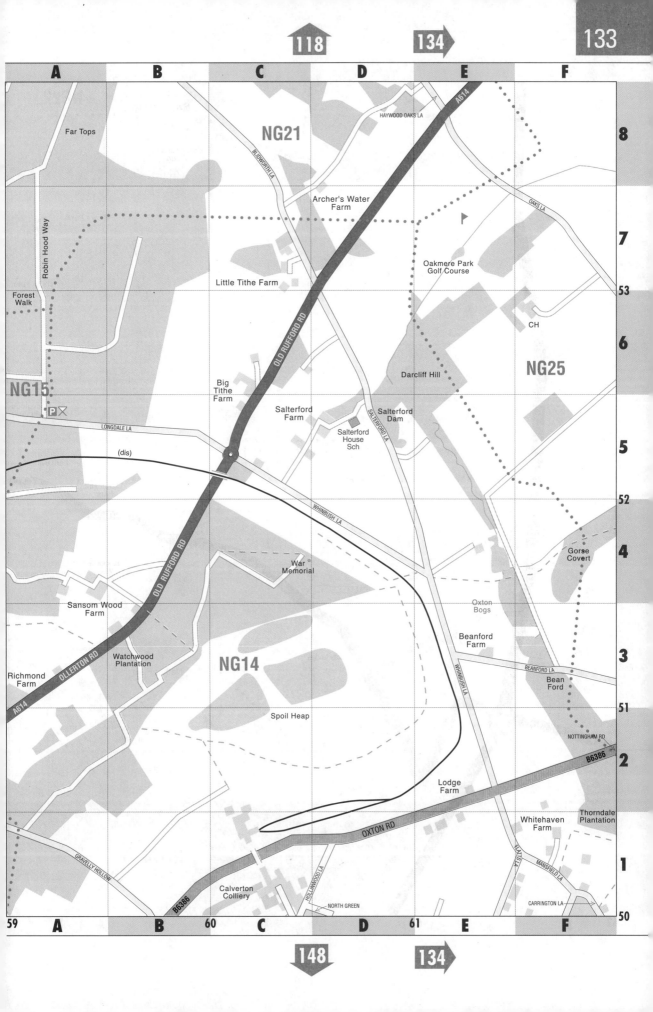

NG22

A B C D E F

8

Margaret's Spring

Robin Hood Way

Loath Hill

Horsepasture
Wood

Robin Hood
Hill

7

Moorfields
Farm

Fallows Farm

Far
Leys
Holt

OLLERTON RD

A6097

GREAVES LA

53

Dairy Farm

OAKS LA

OXTON BY-PASS

6

Godson
Plantation

Oxton Dumble

Cockglode
Plantation

HONEYKNAB LA

NG25

Far Leys

5

FOREST RD

WINDMILL HILL

Windmill
Hill

B6386

52

Oxton Hill
Farm

OXTON HILL

Deer
Leap

Birkhouse
Wood

Hatfield Lane

CHAPEL LA

SOUTHWELL RD

P

4

THE ORCHARDS

Oxton

PO

BLIND LA

MANOR CL

+

ELMCROFT

MAIN ST

NEW RD

SANDY LA

Holly Lodge

Rossellewood
Farm

3

BEANFORD LA

PH

WATER LA

Nether Field

51

Park Farm

B6386

NOTTINGHAM RD

SOUTHWELL RD

2

Thorndale
Plantation

NG14

Mill Farm

EPPERSTONE RD

1

Dover Beck

Epperstone Park

A6097

50

62 A B 63 C D 64 E F

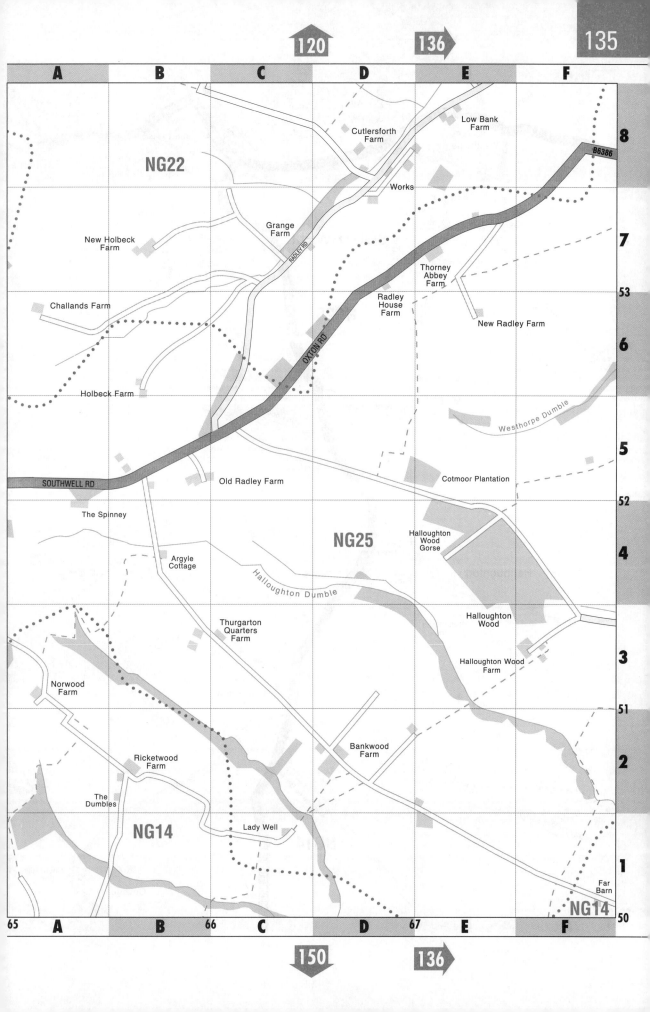

A B C D E F

8

NG22

Cutlersforth
Farm

Low Bank
Farm

Works

B6386

New Holbeck
Farm

Grange
Farm

7

RADLEY RD

Thorney
Abbey
Farm

53

Challands Farm

Radley
House
Farm

New Radley Farm

6

OXTON RD

Holbeck Farm

Westhorpe Dumble

5

SOUTHWELL RD

Old Radley Farm

Cotmoor Plantation

52

The Spinney

NG25

Halloughton
Wood
Gorse

4

Argyle
Cottage

Halloughton Dumble

Thurgarton
Quarters
Farm

Halloughton
Wood

Halloughton Wood
Farm

3

Norwood
Farm

51

Ricketwood
Farm

Bankwood
Farm

2

The
Dumbles

NG14

Lady Well

1

Far
Barn

NG14

50

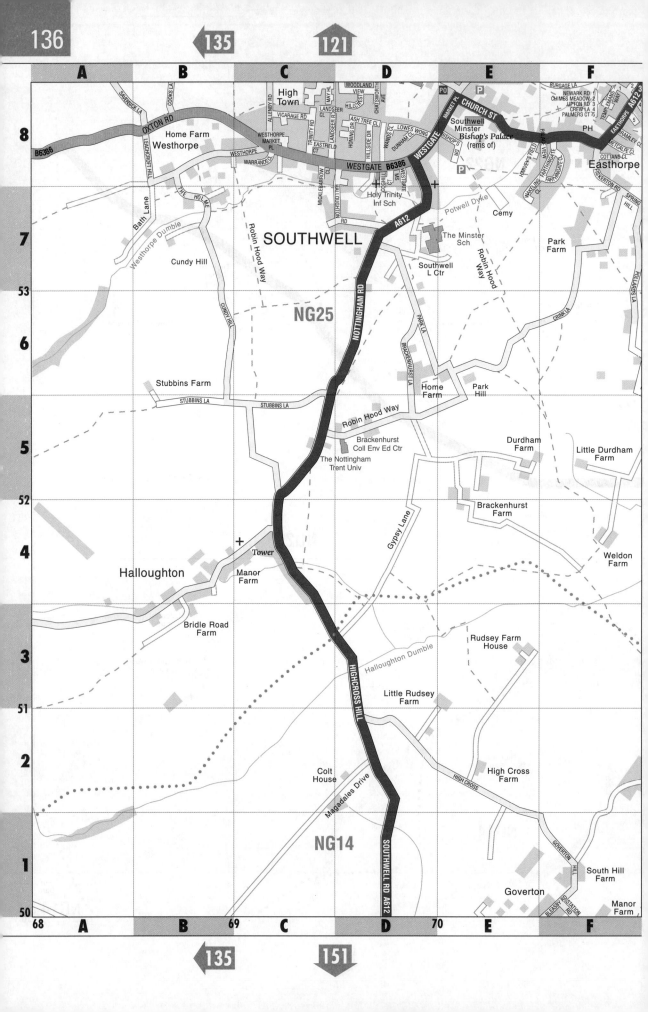

A B C D E F

8

SALTERSICK LA
COOKS LA
OXTON RD
B6386
Home Farm
Westhorpe
High Town
WOODLAND VIEW
ALLENBY RD
VICARAGE RD
MAY H
LANDSEER
CHATSWORTH AVE
HILLCRS
ASH TREE CL
HONING DR
LANDSEER RD
TRINITY RD
EASTFIELD CT
WANDS CL
DUNHAM CL
LOWES WONG
HILLSIDE DR
WESTGATE
MICKLEBARROW
HALLOUGHTON RD
MS
WESTGATE
BISHOP'S RD
MARKET PL
CHURCH ST
Southwell Minster
Bishop's Palace (rems of)
PO
P
BURGAGE LA
NEWARK RD
CHIMES MEADOW 2
UPTON RD 3
CREW LA 4
PALMERS CT 5
TEMPLE LANS
A612
WAY 1
EASTHORPE
BRAMLEY CL
PH
METCALFE CL
COTTANS DR
Easthorpe
PALME VIEW
HARVEY'S FIELD
FARTHINGATE CL
FARTHINGATE
MARLING CL
WESTHORPE MARKET PL
WESTHORPE
WARRANDS CL
WESTGATE
B6386
Holy Trinity Inf Sch
Cemy
FISKERTON RD
SPRING HILL

7

Bath Lane
THE HOLME
Westhorpe Dumble
Westhorpe Dumble
Cundy Hill
Robin Hood Way
SOUTHWELL
A612
Potwell Dyke
The Minster Sch
Southwell L Ctr
Robin Hood Way
Park Farm
POLLARDS LA

53

NG25

6

CUNDY HILL
NOTTINGHAM RD
PARK LA
BRACKENHURST LA
CRINKLA

Stubbins Farm
STUBBINS LA
STUBBINS LA
Home Farm
Park Hill

5

Brackenhurst Coll Env Ed Ctr
The Nottingham Trent Univ
Robin Hood Way
Durdham Farm
Little Durdham Farm

52

Brackenhurst Farm

4

Tower
Halloughton
Manor Farm
GYPSY LANE
Weldon Farm

Bridle Road Farm

3

HIGHCROSS HILL
Halloughton Dumble
Rudsey Farm House

51

Little Rudsey Farm

2

Colt House
MAGDALES DRIVE
HIGH CROSS
High Cross Farm

1

NG14
SOUTHWELL RD A612
GOVERTON HILL
BLEASBY RD
Goverton
South Hill Farm
Manor Farm

50

68 A B 69 C D 70 E F

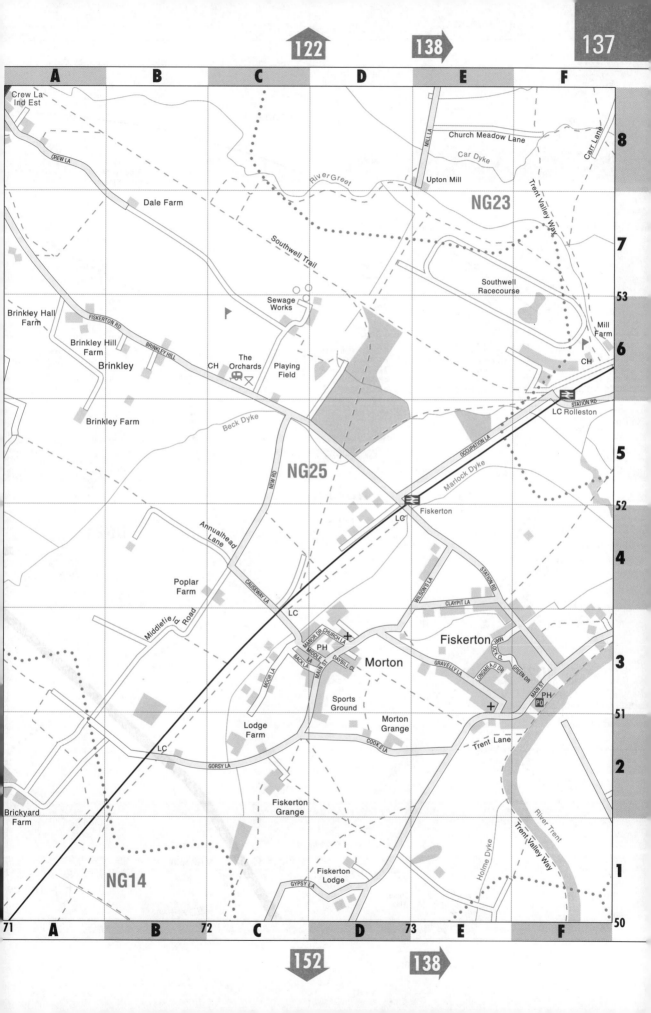

Crew La
Ind Est

CREW LA

Dale Farm

Southwell Trail

River Greet

MILL LA

Church Meadow Lane

Car Dyke

Upton Mill

NG23

Trent Valley Way

8

7

53

Brinkley Hall
Farm

FISKERTON RD

Brinkley Hill
Farm

BRINKLEY HILL

Brinkley

CH

The
Orchards

Sewage
Works

Playing
Field

Southwell
Racecourse

Mill
Farm

CH

6

Brinkley Farm

Beck Dyke

NEW RD

NG25

LC Rolleston

STATION RD

5

Occupation La

Marlock Dyke

Annualhead
Lane

CAUSEWAY LA

LC

Fiskerton

52

Poplar
Farm

Middlefield Road

LC

WILSON'S LA

STATION RD

CLAYPIT LA

Fiskerton

4

MANOR DR CHURCH LA

PH

MOOR LA

BACK LA

MIDDLE

MAIN ST

DAYBILL CL

Morton

Sports
Ground

GRAVELLY LA

LOCK CL

LONGMEAD DR

GREEN DR

MAIN ST

PH
PO

3

Lodge
Farm

Morton
Grange

51

LC

GORSY LA

COOK'S LA

Trent Lane

2

Brickyard
Farm

Fiskerton
Grange

Holme Dyke

River Trent

Trent Valley Way

NG14

GYPSY LA

Fiskerton
Lodge

1

50

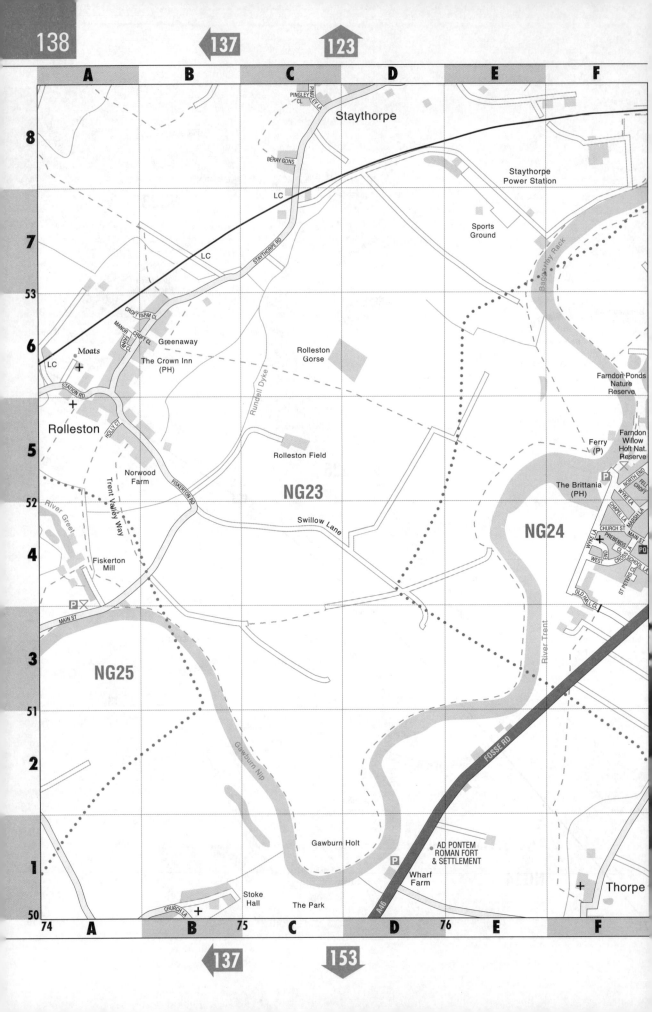

Staythorpe

PINGLEY CL
PINGLEY LA

BERAY GDNS

LC

Staythorpe
Power Station

Sports
Ground

Bargarsley Rack

STAYTHORPE RD

LC

CROFT FARM CL

Moats

Greenaway

CROFT FARM CL

MANOR FARM CL

The Crown Inn
(PH)

Rolleston
Gorse

Farndon Ponds
Nature
Reserve

LC

STATION RD

Rolleston

HOLLY CT

Rundell Dyke

Rolleston Field

Ferry
(P)

Farndon
Willow
Holt Nat.
Reserve

The Brittania
(PH)

Norwood
Farm

FISKERTON RD

Trent Valley Way

River Greet

NG23

Swillow Lane

NORTH END

FELL CROFT

WYKE LA

CHAPEL LA

CHURCH ST

MAIN ST

PREBENDS CL

WYKE LA

CROSS LA

ST PETER'S CL

SCHOOL LA

WEST END

NG24

Fiskerton
Mill

River Trent

OLD HALL CL

MAIN ST

NG25

Gawburn Nip

FOSSE RD

River Trent

Gawburn Holt

AD PONTEM
ROMAN FORT
& SETTLEMENT

Wharf
Farm

A46

CHURCH LA

Stoke
Hall

The Park

Thorpe

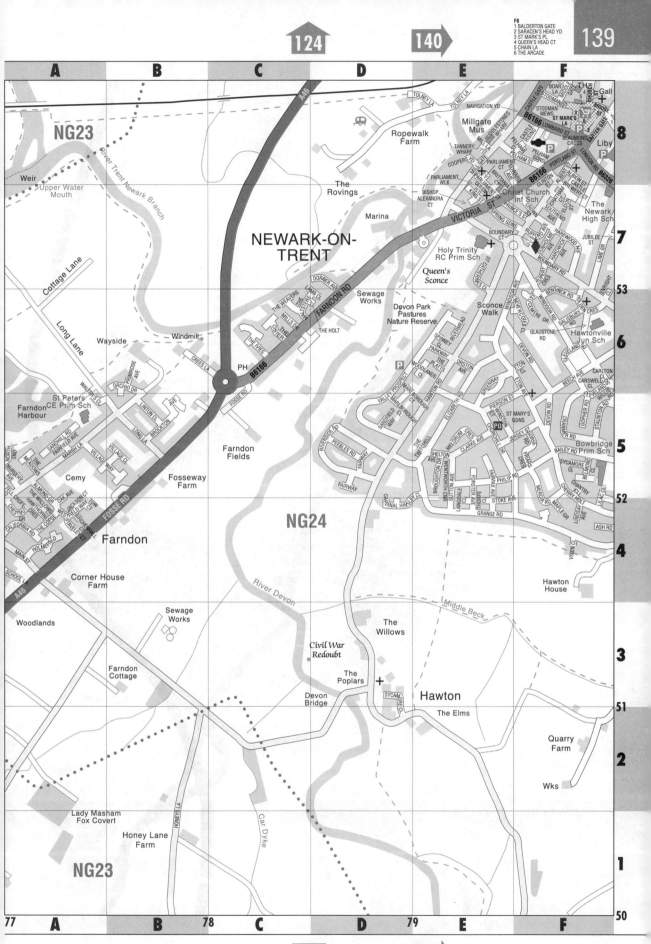

139

F8
1 BALDERTON GATE
2 SARACEN'S HEAD YD
3 ST MARK'S PL
4 QUEEN'S HEAD CT
5 CHAIN LA
6 THE ARCADE

124 ◀   140 ▶

NG23

NEWARK-ON-TRENT

NG24

NG23

Weir

Upper Water Mouth

Cottage Lane

Long Lane

Wayside

Windmill

River Trent Newark Branch

The Rovings

Ropewalk Farm

Millgate Mus

Marina

Sewage Works

Queen's Sconce

Holy Trinity RC Prim Sch

Christ Church Inf Sch

The Newark High Sch

Sconce Walk

Hawtonville Jun Sch

Bowbridge Prim Sch

St Mary's GDNS

Devon Park Pastures Nature Reserve

Farndon Fields

St Peters CE Prim Sch

Farndon Harbour

Cemy

Fosseway Farm

Farndon

Corner House Farm

Woodlands

Sewage Works

Farndon Cottage

River Devon

Civil War Redoubt

Devon Bridge

The Poplars

The Willows

Middle Beck

Hawton

The Elms

Hawton House

Quarry Farm

Wks

Lady Masham Fox Covert

Honey Lane Farm

Car Dyke

FARNDON RD

FOSSE RD

B6166

A46

VICTORIA ST

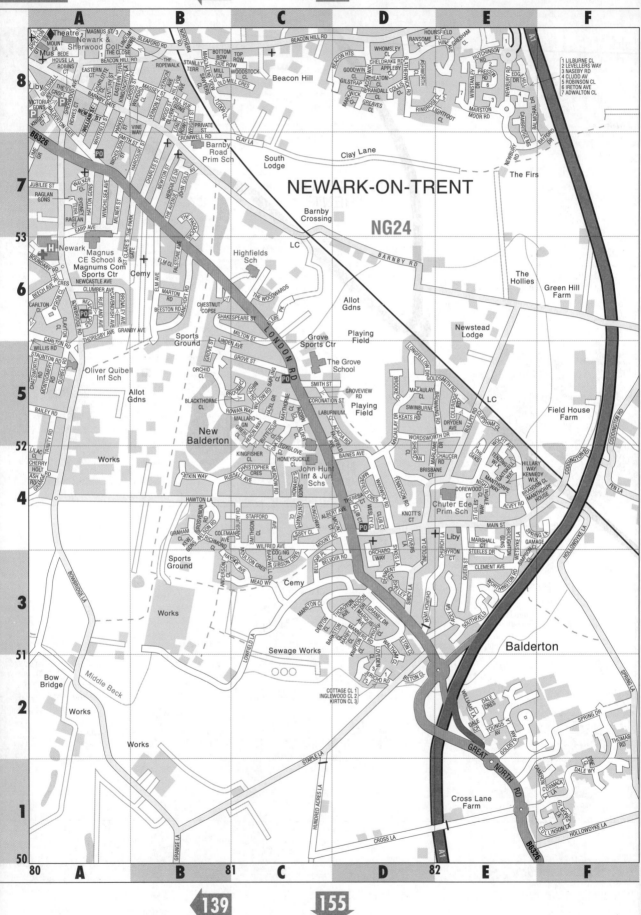

NEWARK-ON-TRENT

NG24

Beacon Hill

Clay Lane

South Lodge

The Firs

Barnby Crossing

LC

The Hollies

Green Hill Farm

Highfields Sch

Barnby Rd

Allot Gdns

Newstead Lodge

Grove Sports Ctr

Playing Field

The Grove School

LC

Field House Farm

Newark Magnus CE School & Magnums Com Sports Ctr

Cemy

Sports Ground

Oliver Quibell Inf Sch

Allot Gdns

New Balderton

Playing Field

Sports Ground

Works

Works

John Hunt Inf & Jun Schs

Chuter Ede Prim Sch

Liby

COTTAGE CL 1
INGLEWOOD CL 2
KIRTON CL 3

Works

Cemy

Sewage Works

Balderton

Bow Bridge

Middle Beck

Works

Works

Cross Lane Farm

GREAT NORTH RD

1 LILBURNE CL
2 LEVELLERS WAY
3 NASEBY RD
4 CLUDD AV
5 ROBINSON CL
6 IRETON AVE
7 ADWALTON CL

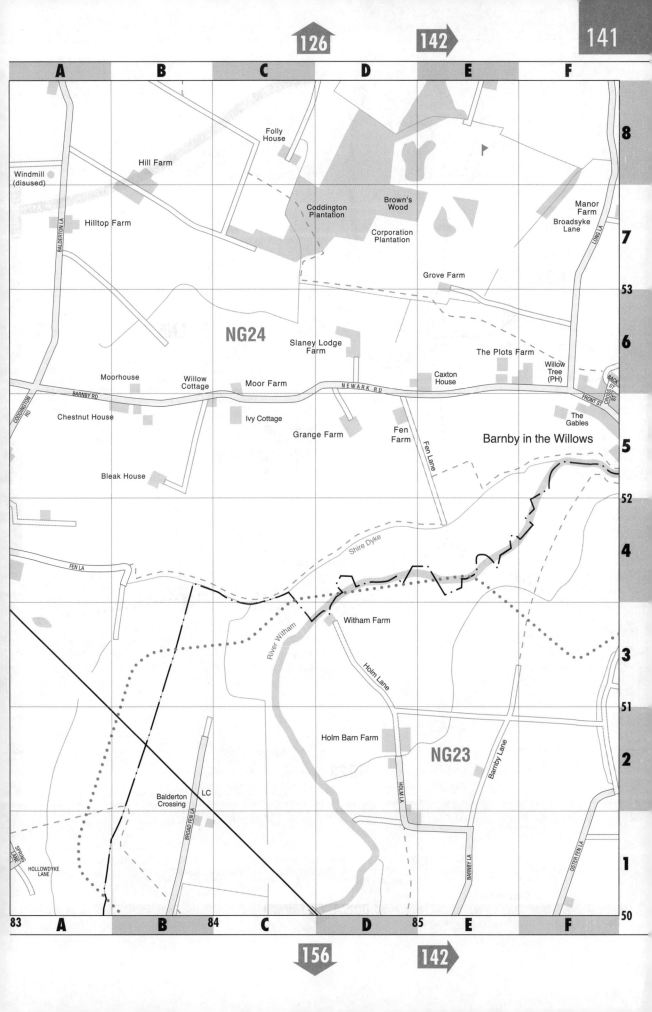

A   B   C   D   E   F

8

Folly
House

Windmill
(disused)

Hill Farm

7

Hilltop Farm

Coddington
Plantation

Brown's
Wood

Manor
Farm

Broadsyke
Lane

Corporation
Plantation

53

Grove Farm

NG24

6

Slaney Lodge
Farm

The Plots Farm

Willow
Tree
(PH)

BALDERTON LA

CODDINGTON RD

BARNBY RD

Moorhouse

Willow
Cottage

Moor Farm

NEWARK RD

Caxton
House

FRONT ST

BACK ST

CROSS ST

LONG LA

5

Chestnut House

Ivy Cottage

Grange Farm

Fen
Farm

The
Gables

Barnby in the Willows

Bleak House

FEN LANE

52

Shire Dyke

4

FEN LA

River Witham

Witham Farm

3

Holm Lane

51

Holm Barn Farm

NG23

2

HOLM LA

BARNBY LA

BARNBY Lane

OSTER FEN LA

BROAD FEN LA

Balderton
Crossing

LC

SPRING
LANE

HOLLOWDYKE
LANE

1

50

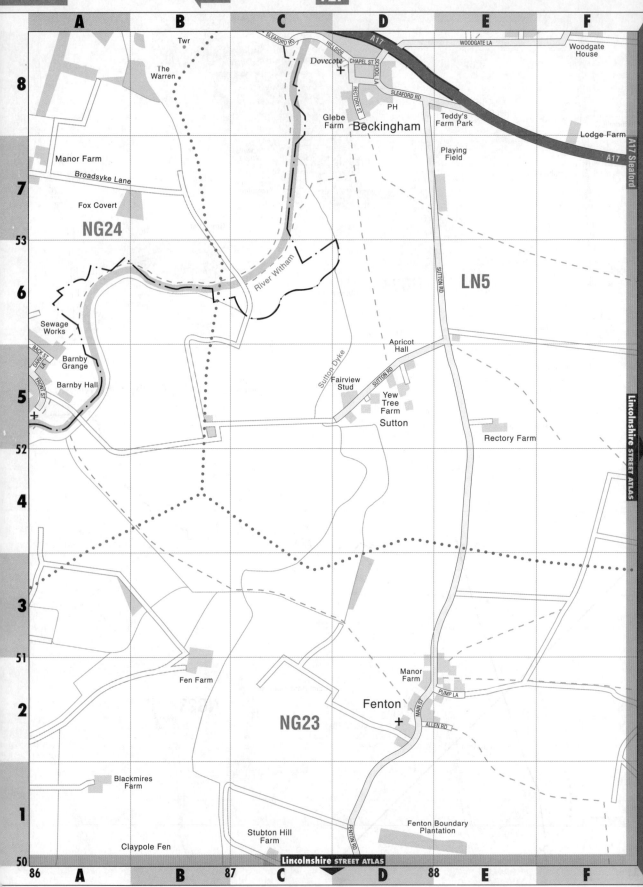

A B C D E F

8

7

53

6

52

5

4

51

3

2

1

50

86 A 87 B C 87 D 88 E F

Twr
The Warren

Manor Farm
Broadsyke Lane

Fox Covert

NG24

Sewage Works

BACK ST
DARK LA
FRONT ST

Barnby Grange

Barnby Hall

River Witham

SLEAFORD RD
HILLSIDE
A17
WOODGATE LA
Woodgate House

Dovecote
CHAPEL ST
SCHOOL LA

Glebe Farm

RECTORY ST

Beckingham

PH
SLEAFORD RD

Teddy's Farm Park

Playing Field

Lodge Farm

A17 Sleaford

LN5

SUTTON RD

Apricot Hall

Sutton Dyke

Fairview Stud

SUTTON RD

Yew Tree Farm

Sutton

Rectory Farm

Fen Farm

Manor Farm

PUMP LA

Fenton

MAIN ST

ALLEN RD

NG23

Blackmires Farm

Stubton Hill Farm

Claypole Fen

FENTON RD

Fenton Boundary Plantation

Lincolnshire STREET ATLAS

Lincolnshire STREET ATLAS

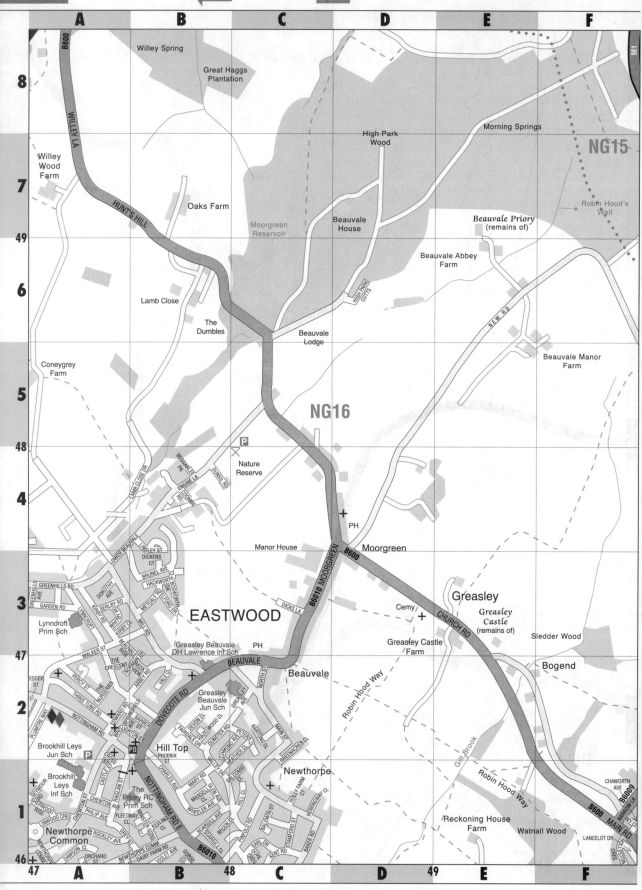

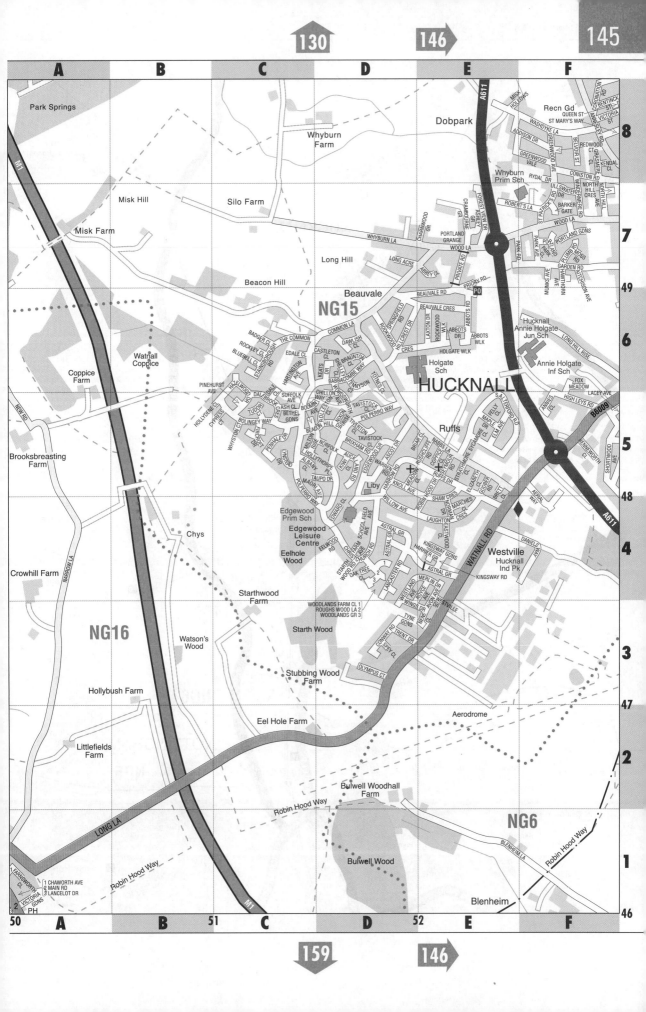

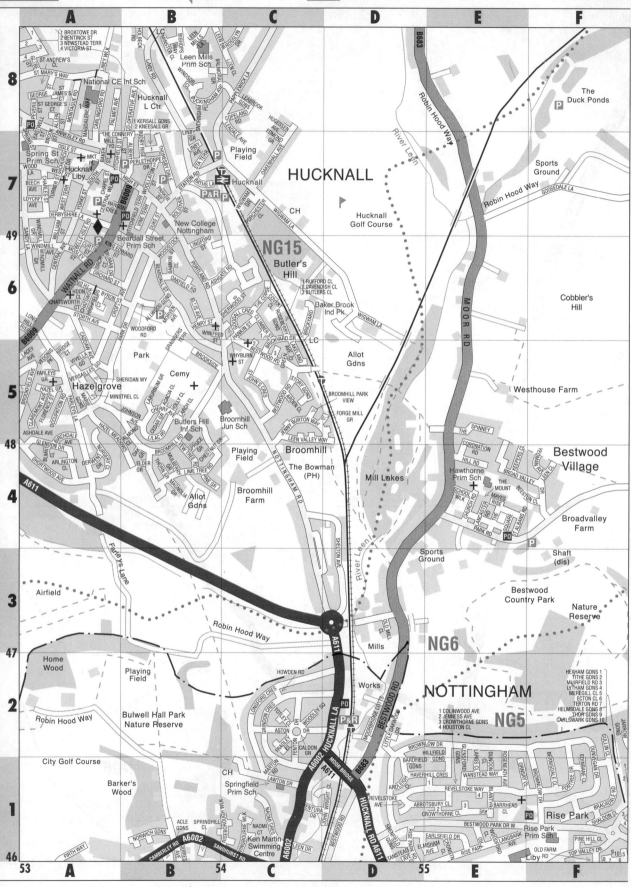

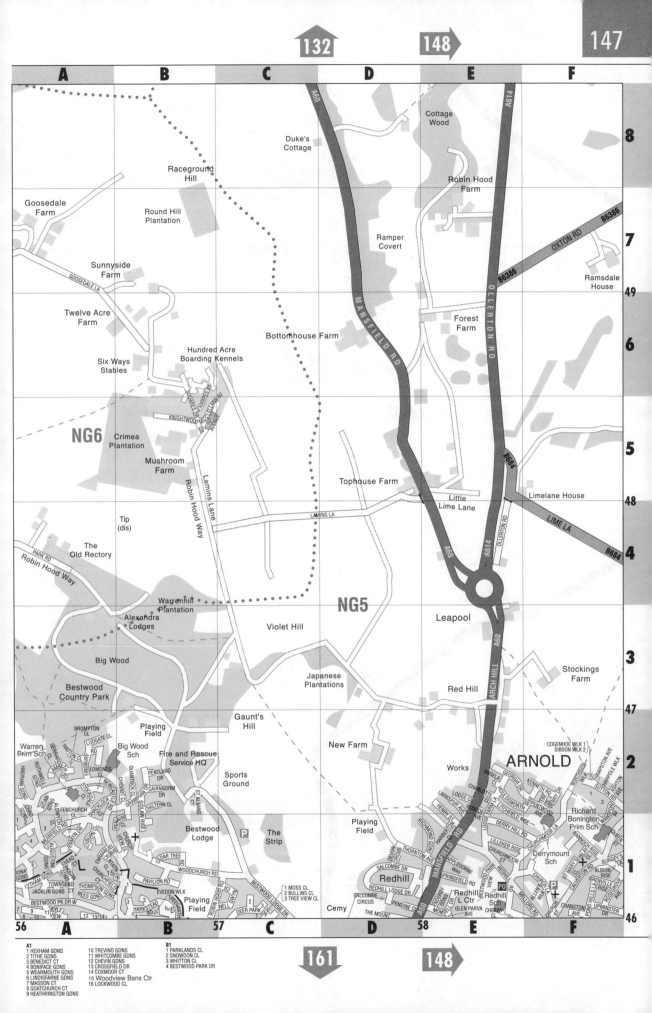

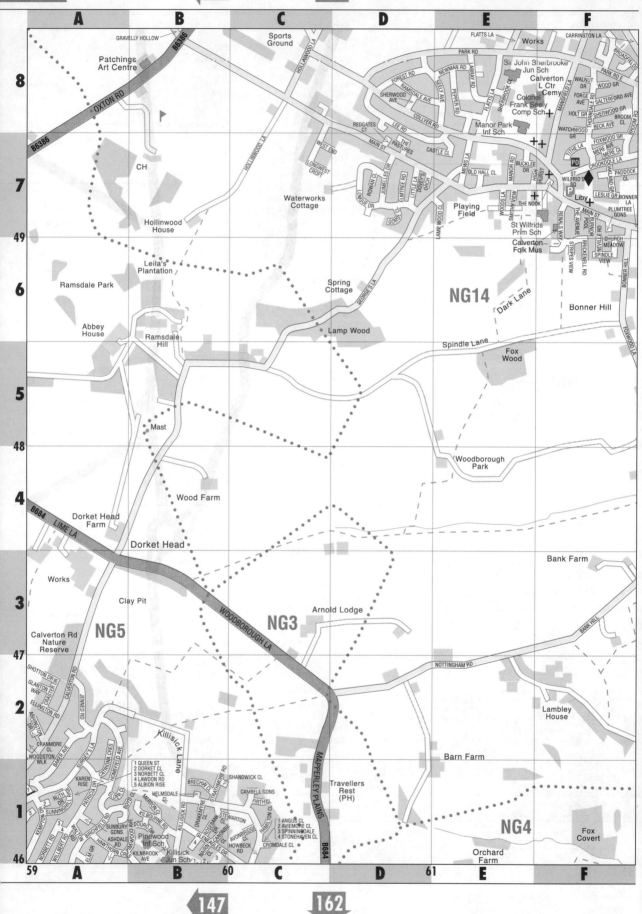

147

133

A   B   C   D   E   F

8

7

49

6

5

48

4

3

47

2

1

46

59   A   B   60   C   D   61   E   F

147

162

Gravelly Hollow
B6386
Sports Ground
HOLLINWOOD LA
FLATTS LA
Works
CARRINGTON LA
Patchings Art Centre
BROADFELLS
Sir John Sherbrooke Jun Sch
PARK RD
FOREST RD
NEWMAN RD
ARRAY RD
Calverton L Ctr
Calverton Cemy
WALNUT DR
WOOD GR
PARK RD E
OXTON RD
SHERWOOD AVE
RAMSDALE AVE
SEELY AVE
PEPPER RD
FLATTS LA
MANSFIELD LA
FORGE AVE
SALTERFORD AVE
Colonel Frank Seely Comp Sch
HOLT GR
SHERWOOD GR
BECK AVE
BROOM GR
B6386
REDGATES CT
LEE RD
COLLYER RD
Manor Park Inf Sch
WATCHWOOD GR
FOXWOOD GR
CH
WEST END
LONGWEST CROFT
MAIN ST
THE PASTURES
CASTLE CL
MEWS LA
OLD HALL CL
MANOR RD
BUCKLEE DR
HIGH HURST
TITHE LA
MERE AVE
MERE CL
MERE GR
PO
CROOKDOLE LA
OAKLAND LA
PADDOCK CL
HOLLINWOOD LA
ROWAN CL
JUMELLES DR
ELMTREE RD
LITTLE LA
DOVEYS ORCH
WOODS LA
SMITHY VIEW
THE NOOK
ST WILFRID'S SQ
Liby
LESLIE GR
BONNER LA
PLUMTREE GDNS
Hollinwood House
LONGUE DR
GORSE CL
Playing Field
St Wilfrids Prim Sch
RENALS WAY
MAIN RD
THE AVENUE
BONNER HILL
Leila's Plantation
ELMTREE RD
Calverton Folk Mus
STRIPES VIEW
BRICKENELL RD
CHURCH MEADOW
SPINDLE VIEW
Ramsdale Park
Spring Cottage
GEORGE'S LA
NG14
Dark Lane
Bonner Hill
Abbey House
Ramsdale Hill
Lamp Wood
Spindle Lane
Fox Wood
FOXWOOD LA
Waterworks Cottage
LAMP WOOD CL
Mast
Woodborough Park
Wood Farm
Dorket Head Farm
B684
LIME LA
Dorket Head
Bank Farm
Works
Clay Pit
WOODBOROUGH LA
NG3
Arnold Lodge
BANK HILL
Calverton Rd Nature Reserve
NG5
Nottingham Rd
SHOTTON DR
GLANTON WAY
ELLINGTON RD
CALVERTON RD
JENNED RD
Lambley House
ASHINGTON DR
CRANMORE CL
WOODSTON WLK
SURGEY'S LA
BAKER AVE
Killisick Lane
MAPPERLEY PLAINS
Barn Farm
KAREN RISE
RUTH DR
PATRICIA DR
CATFROOM CRES
HOMEFIELD AVE
ROSEMARY CRES
BRECHIN CL
SHANDWICK CL
STRATHMORE RD
CAMBELL GDNS
HAMILTON CL
FIRTH CL
Travellers Rest (PH)
NG4
Fox Covert
KEMPTON RD
SUNNINGHILL DR
WALTON DR
ELM AVE
WILLBERT RD
BIRCHFIELD RD
ASHDALE RD
SUNBURY GDNS
HAWTHORN CRES
KILBROOK RD
DOURO DR
MERTON CL
DRAKEMYRE CL
GLENEAGLES DR
WARWICK CL
AVONBRIDGE CL
HOWBECK RD
CROMDALE CL
Orchard Farm
B684

1 QUEEN ST
2 DORKET CL
3 NORBETT CL
4 LAWDON RD
5 ALBION RISE

1 ANGUS CL
2 AVIEMORE CL
3 SPINNINGDALE
4 STONEHAVEN CL

Pinewood Inf Sch
Killisick Jun Sch

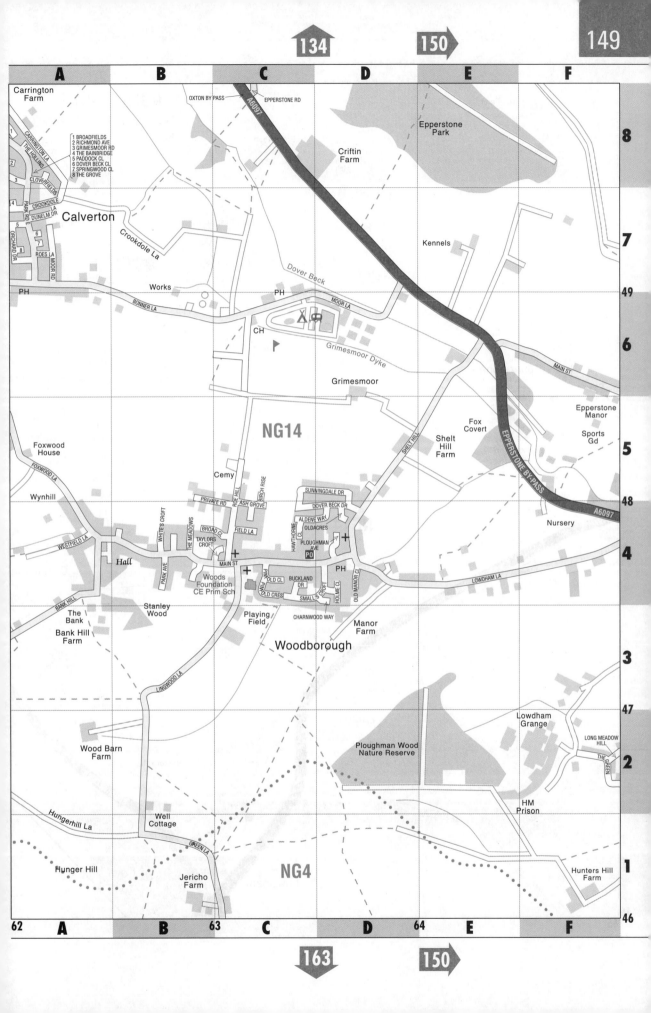

A   B   C   D   E   F

8
7
49
6
5
48
4
3
47
2
1
46

Carrington Farm

1 BROADFIELDS
2 RICHMOND AVE
3 GRIMESMOOR RD
4 THE BAINBRIDGE
5 PADDOCK CL
6 DOVER BECK CL
7 SPRINGWOOD CL
8 THE GROVE

CARRINGTON LA
THE HOLLINS
CLOVERFIELDS
CROOKDOLE LA
DUNELM DR
PARK RD
ROES LA
MOOR RD
ORCHARD DR

Calverton

Crookdole La

Works

PH

BONNER LA

OXTON BY PASS
EPPERSTONE RD
A6097

Dover Beck

PH

CH

MOOR LA

Grimesmoor Dyke

Grimesmoor

Criftin Farm

Epperstone Park

Kennels

Epperstone Manor

Sports Gd

Main St

NG14

Foxwood House

Wynhill

FOXWOOD LA

WESTFIELD LA

Hall

BANK HILL

The Bank

Bank Hill Farm

Stanley Wood

Cemy

PRIVATE RD
ROE HILL
ASH GROVE
BIRCH RISE

WHITE'S CROFT
THE MEADOWS
BROAD CL
TAYLORS CROFT
FIELD LA
MAIN ST
PARK AVE

Woods Foundation CE Prim Sch

PINFOLD CL
PINFOLD CRES
OLD CL
SMALL'S CROFT
BUCKLAND DR
HOLME CL

Playing Field

CHARNWOOD WAY

SUNNINGDALE DR
DOVER BECK DR
ALDENE WAY
OLDACRES
HAWTHORNE CL
PLOUGHMAN AVE
PO

PH

OLD MANOR CL

Shelt Hill Farm

SHELT HILL

Fox Covert

EPPERSTONE BI-PASS

A6097

Nursery

LOWDHAM LA

Woodborough

Manor Farm

LINGWOOD LA

Wood Barn Farm

Hungerhill La

Well Cottage

GREEN LA

Hunger Hill

Jericho Farm

NG4

Ploughman Wood Nature Reserve

Lowdham Grange

LONG MEADOW HILL

THE GREEN

HM Prison

Hunters Hill Farm

A B C D E F

NG25

Hill Farm

Thurgarton Beck

Brockwood Farm

Starling Hall

Foxhole Wood

8

Cottage Farm

Thistly Coppice

Green Acres

7

Souther Wood

Southerwood Barn

49

Eastwood Farm

Hagg Farm

Hagg Lane

Chapel La

NEEPS CROFT

Order Beck

6

Hagg Cottage

CHURCH LA

Bentley Wood

Epperstone

PH

PO

MAIN ST

HAGG'S LA

PARR LA

BLAND LA

DOVE LA

Dovecote

Netherfield Farm

5

Order Beck

LOWDHAM RD

Playing Field

Netherfield Farm House

48

Wash Bridge

NG14

Leland's Dumble

A6097

LOWDHAM LA

4

Nursery

EPPERSTONE BY-PASS

OLD EPPERSTONE RD

Car Holt Farm

Gonalston

GONALSTON LA

Dover Beck

Lowdham Mill

Carr Beck Barn

Eliment Hill Farm

Nurseries

3

The Hermitage

Cliff Mill

A612

Vicarage

The Hut

47

Cliff Mill Farm

Cemy

EPPERSTONE RD

Grove Farm

Lowdham CE Prim Sch

The Old Hall

THE LEYS

MOUNT PLEASANT

NURSURY GDNS

Barker Hill

Long Meadow Hill

CHURCH LA

Liby

RISE HILL

ST FRANCIS CL

BARKER HILL

Norrisdene

2

HILL SYKE

ROCKLEYS VIEW

Motte

ST MARY'S CL

THE PRIORS

SOUTHWELL RD

Blackthorne Dr

STONEY BANK

TON LA

PLOUGH LA

MANOR HOUSE CL

PH

PO

CRANLEIGH DR

1 Nottingham Rd
2 Victoria Ave
3 Worcester Cl

Cocker Beck

LAMBLEY RD

PH

RED LA

MAIN ST

MAGNA CL

WILLOW HOLT

A612

1

BROOKSIDE

THE CORNER

MORLEY'S CL

PH

OLD TANNERY DRIVE

LIME TREE GDNS

LAMBOURNE CRES

PH

Lowdham

A6097

ST MERIVALE CL

NEWTON CL

BLENHEIM AVE

STATION RD

BECKSIDE RD

RUSSEY CL

CAYTHORPE RD

46

65 66 67

A B C D E F

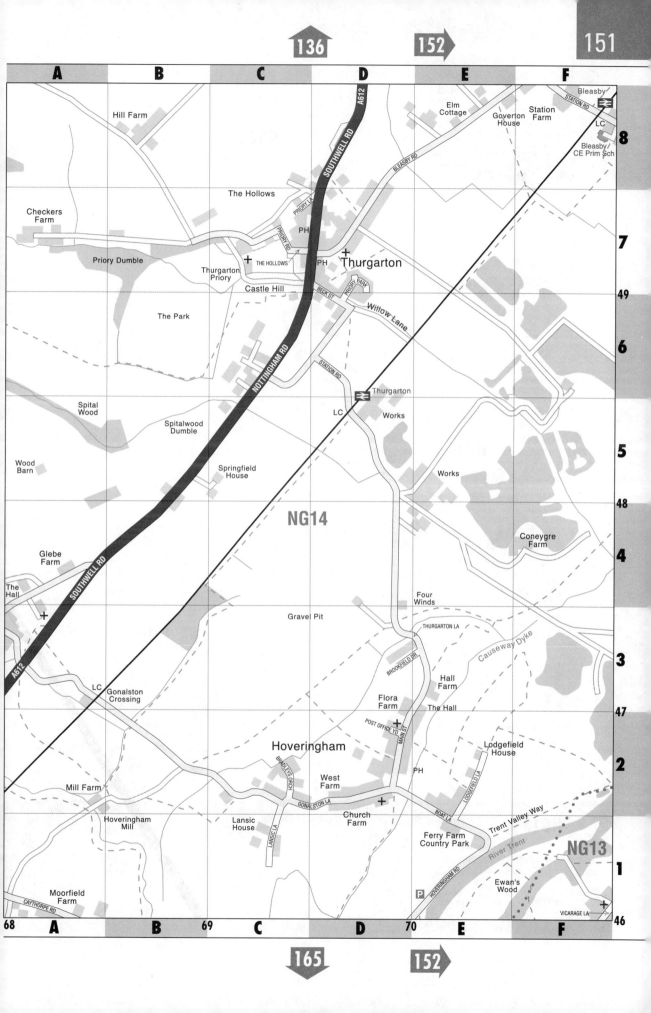

← 151
137

A **B** **C** **D** **E** **F**

8

MANOR CL
SHALE LA
OAK TREE
STATION RD
ELMORE'S ROW
ORCHARD CL
PO
SYCAMORE LA
BORROW BREAD LA

North Farm

Wadham Cottage

NG25

New Lock House

Ladies Piece

Bleasby

PH

GIPSY LA

Vicarage

MAIN ST

The Hall

Holme Dyke

Weir

Hazelford Lock

7

The Nabbs

Weir

BOAT LA

Hazelford Ferry

49

Gibsmere

Hazelford Ferry Hotel

Longhedge Lane

Trent Lane

6

Primrose Plantation

Glebe Farm

Trent Valley Way

River Trent

Flintham Wood

NG14

5

48

Syerston Airfield

4

NG23

3

47

Coneygre Wood

College Wood

2

Ann's Wood

Trent Hills

Trent Hills Farm

CONEYGREY SPINNEY

INHOLMS GDNS
INHOLMS RD

SLACK'S LA

NG13

Charles's Wood

Shipman's Wood

The Park

1

Flintham Hall

Cemy

Thornton's Wood

VICARAGE LA
BRIDGFORD RD

Kneeton

A46

46

71 **A** **B** **72** **C** **D** **73** **E** **F**

← 151
166

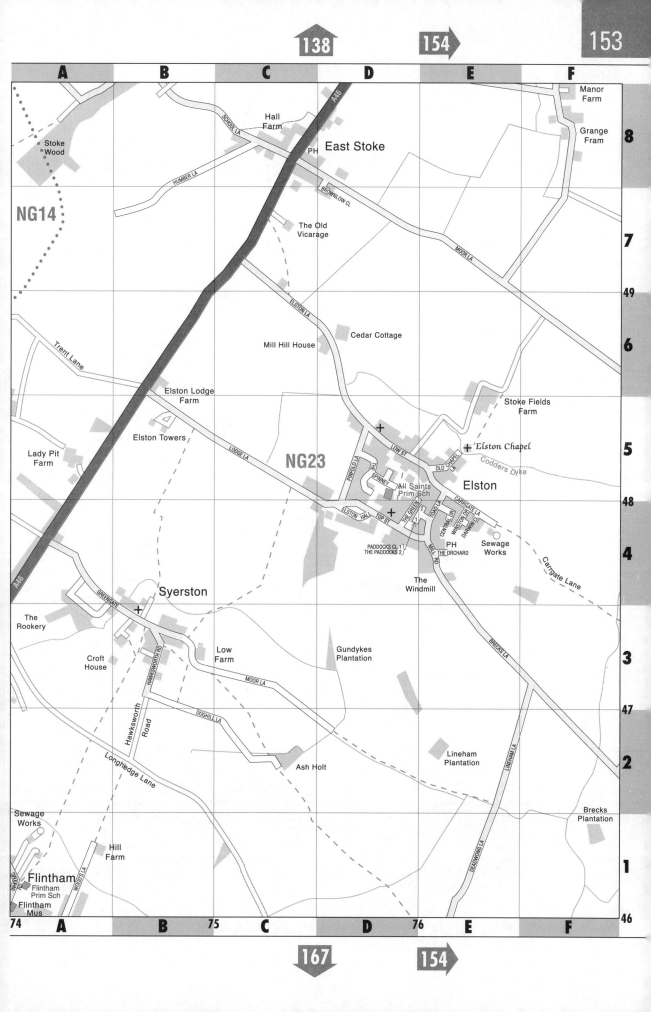

A   B   C   D   E   F

8

NG14

7

49

6

5

48

4

3

47

2

1

46

A   B   C   D   E   F

74   75   76

Stoke Wood

SCHOOL LA

Hall Farm

A46

East Stoke

PH

HUMBER LA

BROWNLOW CL

The Old Vicarage

MOOR LA

ELSTON LA

Trent Lane

Cedar Cottage

Mill Hill House

Elston Lodge Farm

Stoke Fields Farm

Elston Towers

LODGE LA

NG23

Elston Chapel

Codders Dyke

Lady Pit Farm

Low St

Old Chapel La

Elston

PINFOLD LA

SPINNEY

All Saints Prim Sch

Carrgate La

Carrgate Lane

A46

ELSTON HALL

TOP ST

THE GREEN

TOAD LA

CENTRAL DR

WINSTOW DR

DARWIN CL

Sewage Works

PADDOCKS CL

THE PADDOCKS 2

PH

THE ORCHARD

GREENGATE

Syerston

MILL RD

The Windmill

The Rookery

Croft House

HAWKSWORTH RD

Low Farm

Gundykes Plantation

BRECKS LA

Hawksworth Road

MOOR LA

DOGHILL LA

Ash Holt

Lineham Plantation

LINEHAM LA

DEADWONG LA

Brecks Plantation

Longhedge Lane

Sewage Works

WOODS LA

Hill Farm

Flintham

Flintham Prim Sch

Flintham Mus

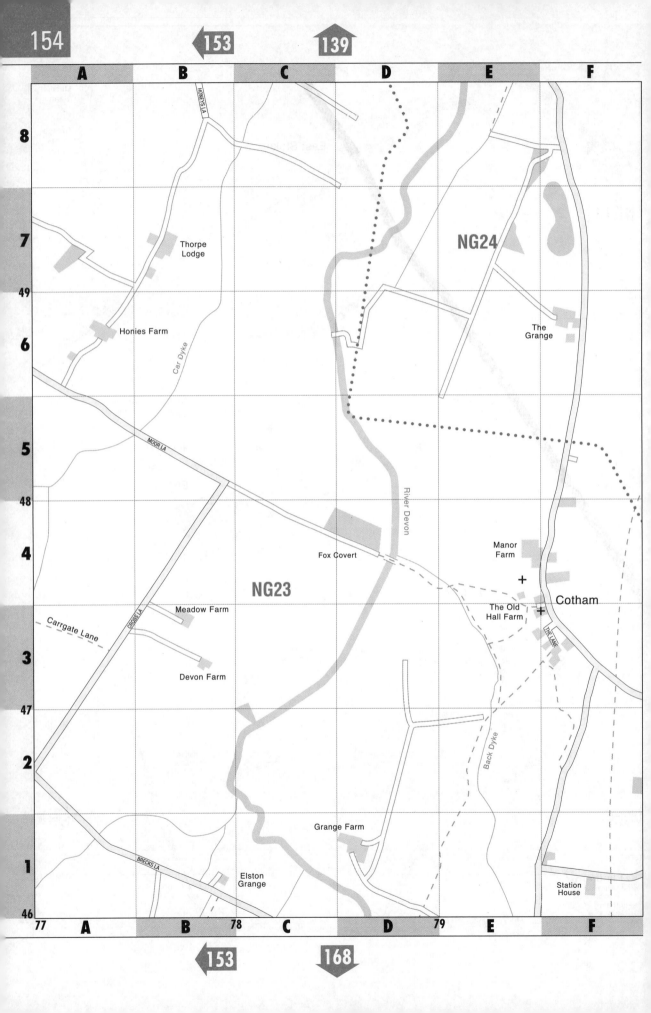

A   B   C   D   E   F

8

7

Thorpe
Lodge

49

Honies Farm

Car Dyke

6

NG24

The
Grange

5

MOOR LA

River Devon

48

NG23

Fox Covert

Manor
Farm

4

Carrgate Lane

CROSS LA

Meadow Farm

The Old
Hall Farm

Cotham

THE LANE

3

Devon Farm

47

2

Back Dyke

Grange Farm

1

BRECKS LA

Elston
Grange

Station
House

46

77   A   B   78   C   D   79   E   F

HONIES LA

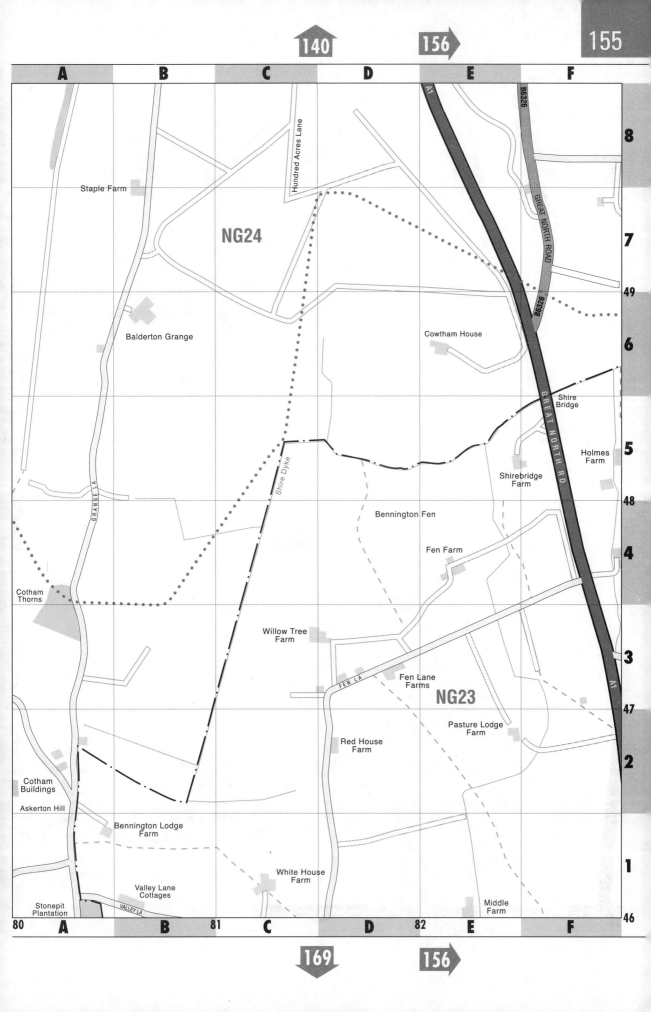

140
156

A B C D E F

8
7
49
6
5
48
4
3
47
2
1
46

NG24

Staple Farm

Hundred Acres Lane

Balderton Grange

GRANGE LA

Shire Dyke

Cotham Thorns

Cotham Buildings

Askerton Hill

Bennington Lodge Farm

Valley Lane Cottages

Stonepit Plantation

VALLEY LA

Willow Tree Farm

Red House Farm

White House Farm

FEN LA

Fen Lane Farms

NG23

Bennington Fen

Fen Farm

Shirebridge Farm

Cowtham House

Shire Bridge

GREAT NORTH ROAD

GREAT NORTH RD

B6326

A1

Holmes Farm

Pasture Lodge Farm

Middle Farm

80 81 82

169
156

A   B   C   D   E   F

NG24

8

Balderfields

Sewage Works

Balderfield

Cross Lane

7

BROAD FEN LA

SHIRE LA

Well Fen Lane

Liberty Gates Crossing

LC

Claypole

Brunts Farm

Piggery

Witham View

WELL FEN LA

CHAPEL LA

ALLEN CL

SWALLOW DR

SCOTT CL

REVIL CL

SCHOOL LA

SCHOOL LA

Playing Field

Claypole CE (Cont) Prim Sch

LC

OSTER FEN LA

BARNBY LA

49

GRETTON CL

CHURCH MD

Claypole Bridge

MAIN ST

BACK LA

TOWN ST

DODDINGTON LA

MOORE CL

PH

RECTORY LA

COULBY CL

REDTHORN WAY

TINSLEY CL

LC

STUBTON RD

LC

6

Hough Lane

Mill Road

DODDINGTON LA

5

Sandhills

48

Mill Farm

Weir

River Witham

NG23

4

Holmes Lane

3

The Willows

Doddington Bridge

Coach Road

47

DODDINGTON LA

Long Lane

2

A1

GREAT NORTH RD

A1

Bridge Farm

Syke Lane

Manor Farm

MANOR HOUSE LA

CLAYPOLE LA

VALE VW

MAIN ST

GREEN LA

Red House Farm

HOUGHAM RD

CLENSEY LA

The Wheatsheaf (PH)

Dry Doddington

Hill Farm

1

46

A   B   C   D   E   F

8

NG16

Marlpool Inf Sch

ILKESTON RD   A6007 Ripley (A610)

A6007 HARDY BARN

DE75

HASSOCK LA N

The Shipley Boat (PH)

Canal (disused)

Factory

Braemar Ave

Main St

Newmanleys Rd S

Hufton's Coppice

Hufton's Dr

Algrave Hall Farm

Purdy House Farm

7

Poplars Farm

45

The Coppice Inn

THE FIELD

Shipley

Michael House - Rudolf Steiner Sch

SCHOOL WOODS CL

PIT LA

HASSOCK LA S

Cotmanhay Wood

Erewash Canal

6

Shipley Lake

The American Adventure Theme Park

Chapel Hill Farm

Cotmanhay Wood

Hartington Pl 1
Millersdale Ave 2
Birchover Pl 3
Castleton Ave 4
Devonshire Cl 5

THE COPPICE

Beauvale Dr

Ashford

Dovedale Circ

Skevington's La

Canon Cl

5

Playing Field

Cotmanhay Inf & Jun Sch

Hopewell Wk

44

Shipley Country Park

Chapel Hill Farm

Shipley Wood

WOODSIDE CRES

LANGLEY AVE

CAPRICE AVE

CHURCH DR

PEACOCK

ROSSENDALE

CHURCH ST

Cotmanhay

Mount Pleasant

Richmond Ave

Bennerley Fields Sch

Bridge St

Stratford St

Bennerley Sch

4

Lodge Farm

Ilkeston Com
H

VICARAGE AVE

Milton Ave

Milton

Bennerley Ave

Vernon St

Shipley Common

SHIPLEY COMMON LA

ELVERDON DR

WYNDALE DR

AUDLEY CL

NESTEAD RD N

COTTAGE DR

Primrose

Archer St

Portland St

Raleigh St

Jervis Ct

Mountbatten

3

Head House Farm

HARLECH CL

WARWICK DR

ATHERTON RD

FARRIERS CROFT

CHAMPION AVE

HOUGHTON

FOXTON CL

BARCLAY CL

MONKTON CL

MOUTH

MILLBANK

SKIPTON CL

SEPTON

NEWSTEAD RD S

High Holborn

HADDON CL

THORPE ST

DUKE ST

OCHBROOK CT

MUSKHAM AV

RISLEY CT

43

Mapperley Brook

The Brook

CHERITON DR

EMSWORTH CL

WHITEHEAD CL

SUMMERFIELDS WAY

BROUGHTON CL

HADDON

Granby Jun Sch

Charlotte St

Charlotte Inf Sch

EYRE'S GDNS

REDLAND

2

West Hallam

DE7

REVILL CL

WOOLISCROFT WAY

WATSHUCKERBY CL

TURNBERRY CL

BARLING DR

HORSECROFT

WESTFIELD DR

HOLME

HAYS CL

MASON RD

Sports Ground

ILKESTON

Allotment Gardens

Mast

Works

SPRING GARDEN TERR

BARKER GATE

ABBEY

A6096

Ind Est

LOWER BLOOMSGROVE

RUTLAND ST

1

West Hallam

PH

Manners Ind Est

BIRKDALE CL

FALCON CT

MANNERS AVE

EREWASH

ELIZABETH CT

HARCOURT

Orchard Bsns Pk

Victoria Pk L Ctr

B6007

PELHAM

MANNERS RD

CHALONS WAY

P

PO

P

ALBION ST

A6007

CHAPEL ST

A609

HIGH LA CENTRAL   HIGH LA E

KNIVETON LA

Victoria Ct

DRUMMOND RD

B6007

A6007 Ilkeston

42

44   A   B   45   C   46   D   E   F   42

Derbyshire STREET ATLAS

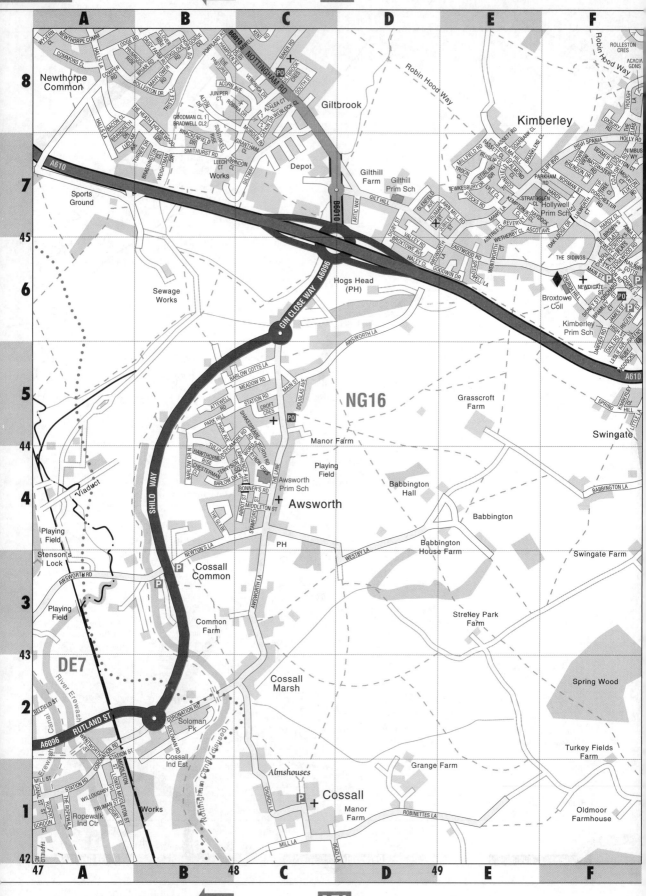

A   B   C   D   E   F

8   Newthorpe Common   Giltbrook   Robin Hood Way   Kimberley

Wyvern Cl   Newthorpe Comm
Commons Cl   Halls La
   Lodge Rd
   Daisy Farm St   Portland Rd   Baker Rd   Kent Av
   Primrose Rise   Thorne Gro   NOTTINGHAM RD   B6010
   Briar Rd   Foxglove Gro   Hampden St
   Mayflower Rd   Clover Rise   Veronica Dr
   Rolleston Dr   Acorn Av   Azalea Ct   Rolleston Cres
   Comper   Bacon Cl   Juniper Ct   Acacia Gdns
   Brandreth Dr   Alton Ct   Robina Dr   Robin Hood Way   Oxbury Rd
   The Heath   Holmefield Dr   Southwell Rise   Morden Cl   Rolleston Cres
   Goodman Cl 1   Grantham Cl   Nimbus Wy
   Bradwell Cl2   Brackenfield Rise   Holly La
   Smithurst Rd   Leech Ct
   Swindon Cl
   Brassington Cl   Weightman Dr   Gilt Way   Depot
7   Sports Ground   A610   Works   Giltway   B6010   Artic Way   Gilt Hill   Gilthill Farm   Gilthill Prim Sch

45   Sewage Works   GIN CLOSE WAY   A6096   Hogs Head (PH)   Broxtowe Coll   Kimberley Prim Sch

6

5   Barlow Cotts La   Meadow Rd   Main St   Douglas Av   NG16   Grasscroft Farm   Swingate
   Attewell Rd   Station Rd   Croft Cres   PO
   Park Hill   Shakespeare Rd   Manor Farm   Spring Hill Cl

44   Barlow Dr N   Hawthorne Rise   Tulip Av   Sycamore Rd   The Lane   Playing Field   Babbington Hall   Babbington La
   Chesterman Cl   Tennyson Av   Lawrence Av   Smithy Rd   Awsworth Prim Sch
4   The Glebe   Barlow Dr S   Bonner's Rd   Abbot Cl   Stamford St   Middleton St   Awsworth   Babbington   Swingate Farm
   Newton's La   Babbington House Farm
   Westry La

3   Playing Field   Answorth Rd   P   Cossall Common   P   Awsworth La   PH   Stanley Park Farm
   Stenson's Lock

   Common Farm

43   DE7   River Erewash   Spring Wood
   Canal

2   Belfield St   Rutland St   A6096   Wentworth Rd   Coronation Rd   Soloman Pk   Cossall Marsh   Grange Farm   Turkey Fields Farm
   Station St   Soloman Rd
   Cossall Ind Est

1   Mill St   The Ropewalk   Station Rd   Willoughby St   Lower Middleton St   Truman St   Digby St   Works   Almshouses   Church La   P   Cossall   Manor Farm   Robinettes La   Oldmoor Farmhouse
   Rupert St   Gordon St   Coronation Rd   Middleton St
   Gairfield Cl   Ropewalk Ind Ctr   Mill La   Road La

42

47   A   48   B   C   D   49   E   F

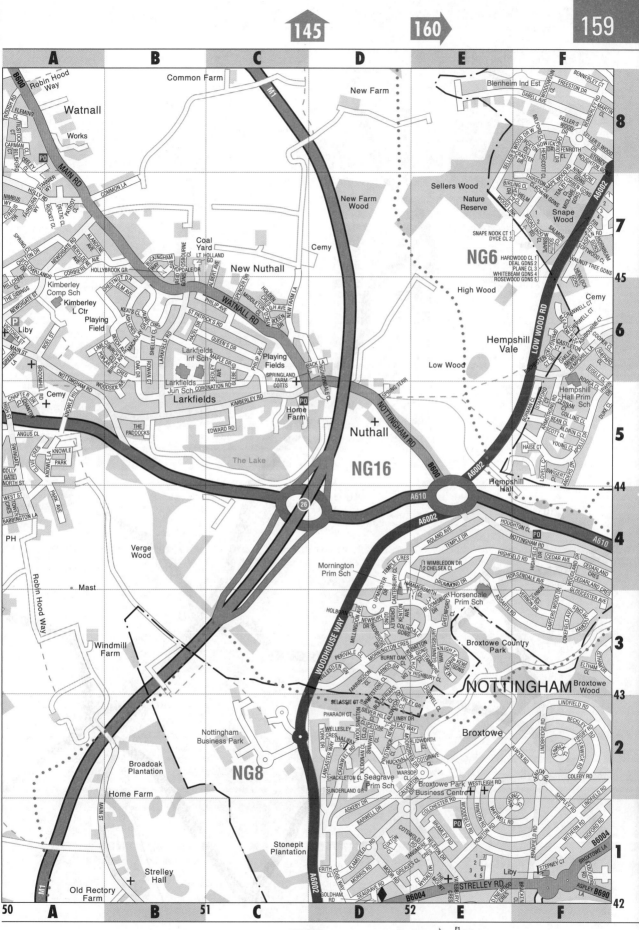

E1
1 ROSEMARY CL
2 LAVENDER CL
3 MAGNOLIA CL
4 HONEYSUCKLE CL
5 JASMINE CL
6 BRIDGE GREEN WALK
7 LILAC CL

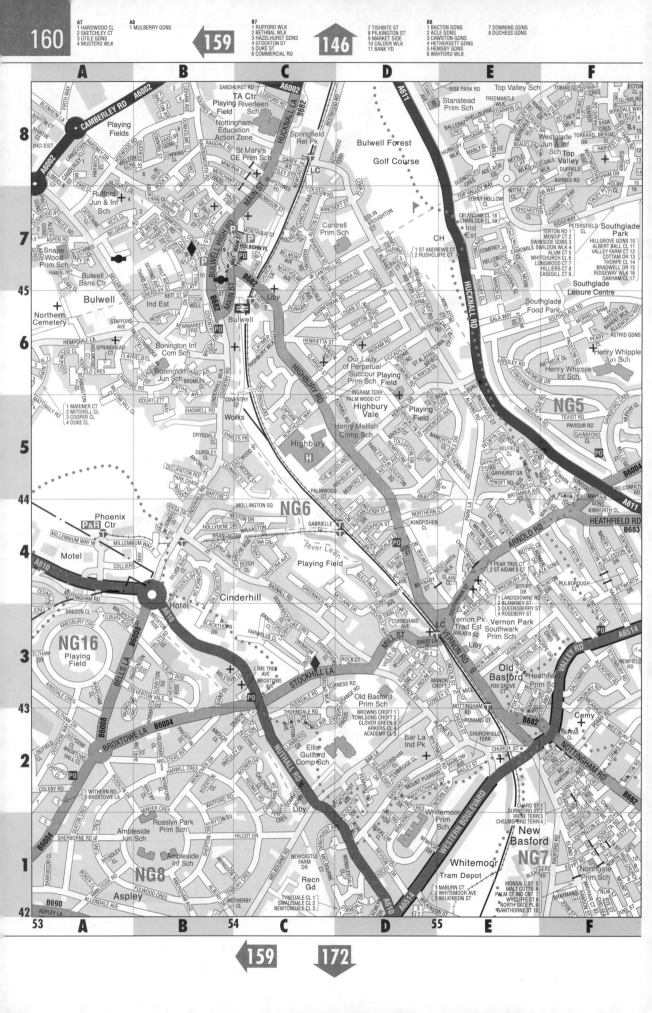

	A7				A8			7 DOLPHIN CT	14 HILLGROVE GDNS			C8	7 FALCONERS WLK	
	1 HENDRE GDNS	7 MADRYN WLK		1 RICKLOW CT			8 ELDER GDNS	15 WINSCALE GDNS		B8	1 CARNFORTH CT		D8	
	2 TUDWAL WLK	8 TOWYN CT		2 YATES GDNS			9 BIRKDALE WAY	16 VALLEY FARM CT		1 SHORESWOOD CL	2 CALDERHALL WLK		1 HEDDINGTON GDNS	
	3 GWNDY GDNS	9 EDERN GDNS		3 SWEENEY CT			10 CASPER CT	17 RIDGEWAY WLK		2 REEDHAM WLK	3 CAPENWRAY GDNS		2 SLOWTHORNE GDNS	
	4 PENLLECH WLK	10 DARON GDNS		4 HUGGET GDNS			11 PADGHAM CT	18 THORPE CL		3 GOATHLAND CL	4 CATLOW WLK		3 KNOWLES WLK	
	5 CADLAN CT	11 MONROE WLK		5 NICKLAUS CT			12 WEETMAN GDNS	B7		4 STAMFORD CT	5 CODRINGTON GDNS			
	6 COLMON WLK	12 WALGRAVE WLK		6 ANDERSON CT			13 HENNING GDNS	1 CALDBECK WLK		C7	6 STINSFORD CL			
										1 MAYTHORNE WLK				

 147   **162**   **161**

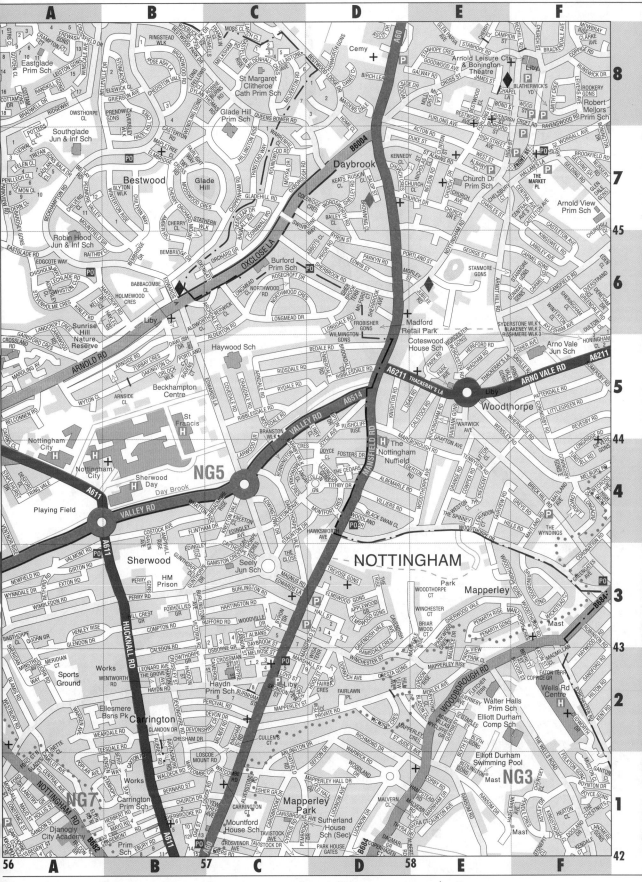

56   A   **57**   B   C   D   **58**   E   F   **42**

A1		B1			C2		C3		D2	
1 ALTHEA CT		1 ASH VILLAS	10 WESLEY GRN		1 BUTTERMERE CT		1 HARDWICK RD		1 TRELAWN CL	
2 POYSER CL		2 LOSCOE GDNS	11 HAMILTON GDNS		2 WOODVILLE RD		2 OSBORNE RD			
3 ST AUGUSTINES CL		3 ELTON RD	12 WESLEY ST		3 DRAYTON ST		3 DRAYBROOK AVE		D3	
4 SHAFTESBURY ST		4 ERSKIN RD	13 SELKIRK WAY		4 BROXTOWE ST		4 KANSINGTON CT		1 THE FIRS	
5 HEDLEY VILLAS		5 RAMSEY CT	14 JENNER ST		5 DERWENT TERR		5 NEWSTEAD ST		2 BULLER TERR	
6 FALCON ST		6 MAY CT	15 NEW ST		6 VICTOR TERR		6 NEWSTEAD ST		3 HOOLEY PL	
7 MEYNELL GR		7 FERN AVE			7 ORMONDE TERR		7 WINCHESTER TERR		4 CRAMWORTH DR	
		8 WESTMORELAND CT			8 PENNHOME AVE				5 SHERWOOD AVE	
		9 CAITHNESS CT			9 BANBURY MT					

 173   **162**

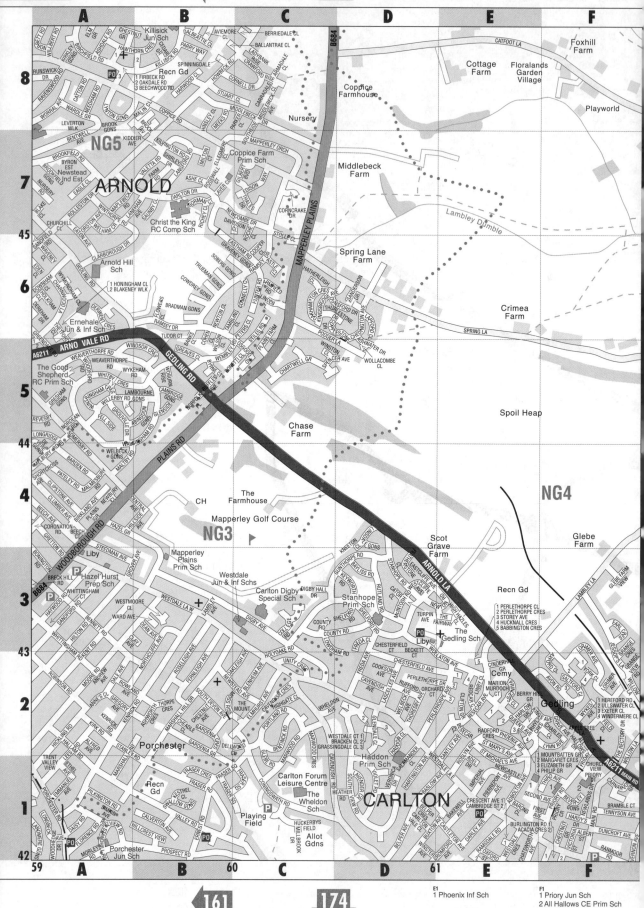

E1
1 Phoenix Inf Sch

F1
1 Priory Jun Sch
2 All Hallows CE Prim Sch

A B C D E F

NG14

8

Bateman House

Harlow Wood Farm

Nursery

Cocker Beck

THE DUMBLES

GREEN LA

CATFOOT LA

Lambley

PARK LA

Works

ORCHARD RISE

CHURCH ST

STEELES WAY

COCKER BECK

Broughton Park

7

Lambley Prim Sch

CHAPEL LA

TRINITY CRES

WILLOW CRES

Cemy

Cornwall's Hill

Stockhill Farm

Bulcote Wood

PH

MILL LA

MAIN ST

ROSS LA

GRANGE CL

45

FLAMSTEAD AVE

Lambley Dumble

NEGUS CT

CROMWELL CRES

Bulcote Lodge Farm

6

SPRING LA

Wicketwood Hill

Stockhill Farm

LAMBLEY BRIDLE RD

LAMBLEY LA

Lodge Farm

The Mount

5

Wood Farm

NG4

BLACKACRE GREENACRE

HILCREST GDNS

FOXHILL RD

CORSEY CL

OLIVE GR

ORCHARD CL

LANGHAM

CARNARVON

HILLSIDE DR

GLEN RD

PADLEYS LA

WILLOW PONDS

BIRCHWOOD CL

LAMBLEY LA

BRIDLE RD

COVERT CL

ROSE COTTS

GROVE CL

MAYFIELD AVE

A612

44

Crock Dumble

BROOKLYN AVE

Burton Joyce Prim Sch

WOODSIDE

WHEATSHEAF

PO

Liby

Gedling Wood

Barron's Plantation

NG14

Burton Joyce

MAIN ST

LENDRUM CT

CHURCH RD

CHESTNUT

WINIFRED

4

VICARAGE DR

PARK AV

ST HELEN'S CRES

Glebe Farm

CRAGMOOR RD

CROW PARK DR

ASH CL

MARIS DR

ST HELEN'S GR

STATION RD

LC

3

Gedling Wood

GLEBE DR

BULCOTE DR

FRENCHMAN GDNS

MASSEY CL

MILL FIELD CL

Burton Joyce

P

NG12

Gedling Wood Farm

WOODSIDE RD

New Plantation

NOTTINGHAM RD

Sports Ground

43

White Gates

Gedling House

River Trent

2

GRANGE VIEW

OAK TREE

ALMOND WLK

JAYNE CL

ADCOCK DR

ACORN DR

MAPLE DR

THE CL

TAMARBIX

BLACKTHORN

WHITWORTH DR

Willow Farm Prim Sch

Gedling House Woods Nature Reserve

STOKE LA

YEW TREE LA

MAPLE CL

WILLOW LA

WATERHOUSE LA

1

WILLOW CRES

WATERHOUSE LA

PO

MAIN RD

THE ORCHARD

CONISBROUGH AVE

BURTON RD

LINDEN GR

P

Carlton le Willows Comp Sch

HENDERSONS

BEAUMARIS DR

Sewage Works

Ferry Boat Inn (PH)

P

Trent Valley Way

VERNON AVE

STATION AVE

CORONATION WLK

SHEARING HILL

A6211

BRAEMAR DR

CAISTBROOKE

RAGLAN DR

THE CHESTNUTS

HARRINGTON CL

FLORENCE RD

STOKE LA

STOKE FERRY LA

A612

42

◄ 163
150 ▲

A B C D E F

8

LAMBLEY RD

Lowdham Lodge

SKITHORNE RISE

A612

Brakes Farm

VICTORIA AVE
THE ORCHARDS
LONG MOOR AVE
STATION RD
GUNTHORPE RD

PH

Lowdham

LC

PAVILION CT
CAYTHORPE RD

Playing Field

Marlock Bridge

COTTAGE PASTURE LA

LC

Marlock House Farm

7

Sibthorpe House

Beecroft Farm

NOTTINGHAM RD

LOWDHAM RD

Holly Farm

45

Hill Farm

Grange Farm

Parklands

6

Bulcote

OLD MAIN RD
REDMAN'S DR

The Manor House

NG14

THE AVENUE

The Cedars

Cocker Beck

Bulcote Hill Plantation

Old Main Rd

SHELFORD RD
PORTLAND AVE
THE RIDINGS
SHELLEBURY AVE
THE SPINNEY
THE LEES

Bulcote Crossing

LC

Bulcote Farm

FEARON CL

MAIN ST

HOBSON'S CL
THE PADDOCK

5

MAIN ST

Gunthorpe

FARNSFIELD AVE
CHESTERFIELD AVE
GORDON RD
WELLINGTON RD

CHURCH RD

Works

44

A612
CARNARVON DR
CRIFTIN RD

LC

Trent Lane

BYE PASS RD A6097

4

TRENT GDNS

TRENT LA

Trent La

Burton Meadows

River Trent

Shelford Manor

Long Plantation

3

The Holmes

43

NG12

The Hams

MANOR LA

2

Moor Close Plantation

PH

Trent Valley Way

WATER LA

NG13

1

NG14

STOKE FERRY LA

The Dam

Earthwork

CHURCH ST
BURTON CL
MAIN LA
MILLERS CL
JULIAN LA
WATERFURROWS LA

Shelford

Waterfurrows Plantations

PINFOLD LA

Bosworth Farm

42

65 A B 66 C D 67 E F

◄ 163
176 ▲

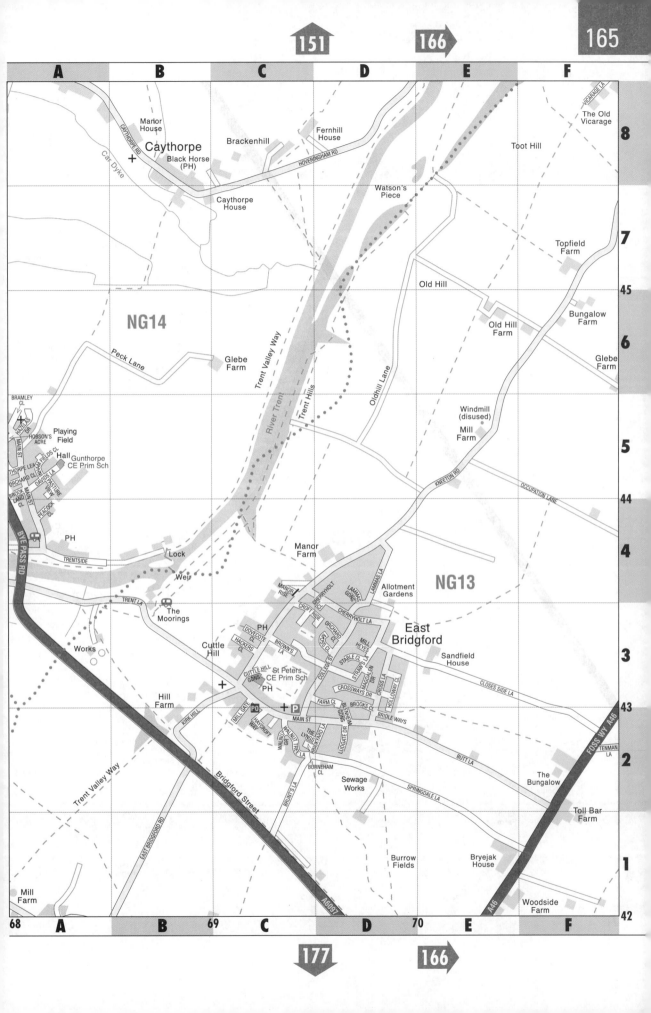

A   B   C   D   E   F

8

Manor House
Caythorpe   Brackenhill   Fernhill House
Car Dyke   Black Horse (PH)   HOVERINGHAM RD
Caythorpe House   Watson's Piece   Toot Hill   The Old Vicarage

7
Topfield Farm
Old Hill
45
NG14   Bungalow Farm
6
Peck Lane   Glebe Farm   Old Hill Farm   Glebe Farm

Oldhill Lane
Windmill (disused)
Mill Farm
5
BRAMLEY CL
Playing Field
HOBSON'S ACRE
Hall   Gunthorpe CE Prim Sch   KNEETON RD   OCCUPATION LANE
44
Trent Valley Way   River Trent   Trent Hills

4
PH   Manor Farm   LAMMAS LA   NG13
TRENTSIDE   Lock   Allotment Gardens
Weir   MANOR RISE   CHERRYHOLT
The Moorings   CROFT RISE   LAMMAS GDNS
TRENT LA   ORCHARD CL   CHERRYHOLT LA
Works   PH   East Bridgford
Cuttle Hill   DOVECOTE CL   BROWN'S LA   MILL HEYES
HACKERS CL   COLLEGE ST   ORCHARD CL   Sandfield House   3
CUTTLE HILL GDNS   St Peters CE Prim Sch   STABLE CL   MAGDALEN DR   CLOSES SIDE LA
Hill Farm   PH   STRAWS LA   CROSS LA   HOLLOWAY CL
KIRK HILL   MILL GATE   PO   FARM CL   BROOKS CL   43
BYE PASS RD   HAYCROFT WAY   P   BRIDLE WAYS
Trent Valley Way   WALNUT TREE LA   THE LYNGS   LUDGATE DR   BLENHEIM GDNS   BUTT LA   2
Bridgford Street   BORNEHAM CL   BRICKYARD LA   The Bungalow   TENMAN LA
BRUNT'S LA   Sewage Works   SPRINGDALE LA   Toll Bar Farm
EAST BRIDGFORD RD   A6097   Burrow Fields   Bryejak House   1
Mill Farm   A46   FOSS WY A46   Woodside Farm   42

68   A   B   69   C   D   70   E   F

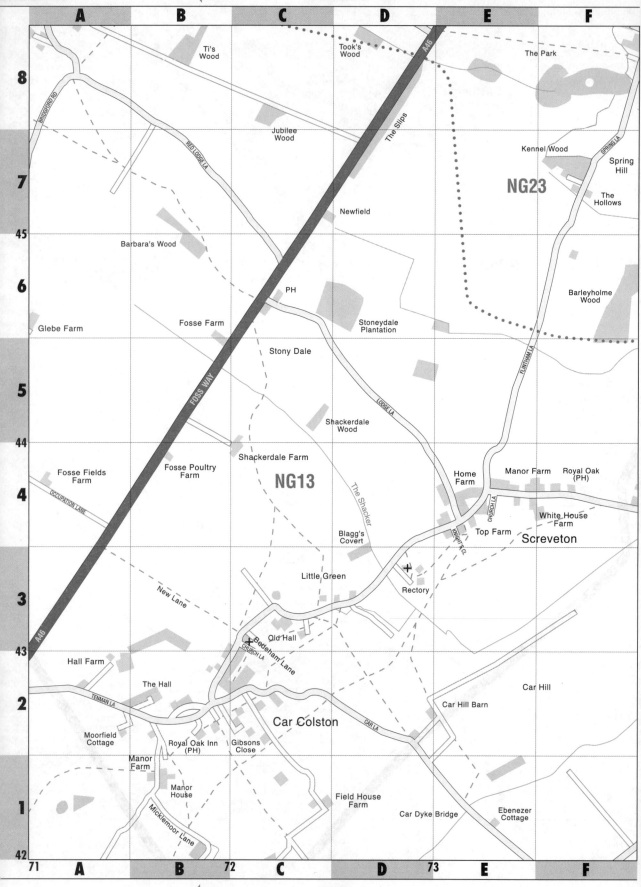

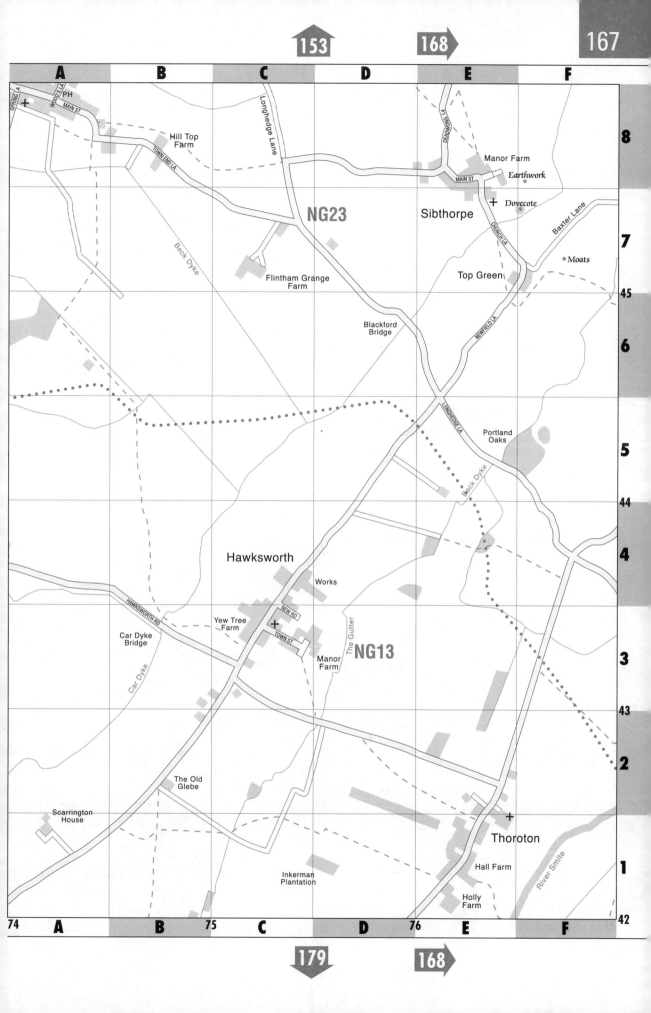

153
168

A B C D E F

8
7
45
6
5
44
4
3
43
2
42

SPRING LA
WOOD'S LA
PH
MAIN ST
Hill Top
Farm
TOWN END LA
Longhedge Lane
NG23
Beck Dyke
Flintham Grange
Farm
Blackford
Bridge
DEADWONG LA
Manor Farm
Earthwork
MAIN ST
Sibthorpe
CHURCH LA
Dovecote
Baxter Lane
Moats
Top Green
NEWFIELD LA
LONGHEDGE LA
Portland
Oaks
Back Dyke
Hawksworth
Works
The Gutter
NG13
HAWKSWORTH RD
Yew Tree
Farm
Car Dyke
Bridge
Car Dyke
NEW RD
TOWN ST
Manor
Farm
The Old
Glebe
Scarrington
House
Inkerman
Plantation
Thoroton
Hall Farm
River Smite
Holly
Farm

74 A B 75 C D 76 E F 42

179
168

A B C D E F

8

7

45

6

5

44

4

3

43

2

1

42

77 78 79

Firs Farm

Wensor Bridge

Booth's Farm

Fox Covert

Limekiln Covert

Staunton Grange

Back Dyke

NG23

Shelton

Shelton House Farm

Hall Farm

The Hall

ST ANN'S WAY

PO

Manor Farm

Little Orchard

Fishpond Plantation

River Smite

Fourteen Acre Covert

Staunton Works

Top Farm

Fairfields

Brickyard Plantation

River Devon

Works

Greenacres

Shelton Lodge Farm

NG13

Lane Side

Flawborough

LONGHEDGE LA

Oscar Bridge

Flawborough Hall

Manor Farm

Manor Farm

Stonehouse Farm

Sunnymede

MILL LA

Chestnut Farm

Grange Farm

Alverton

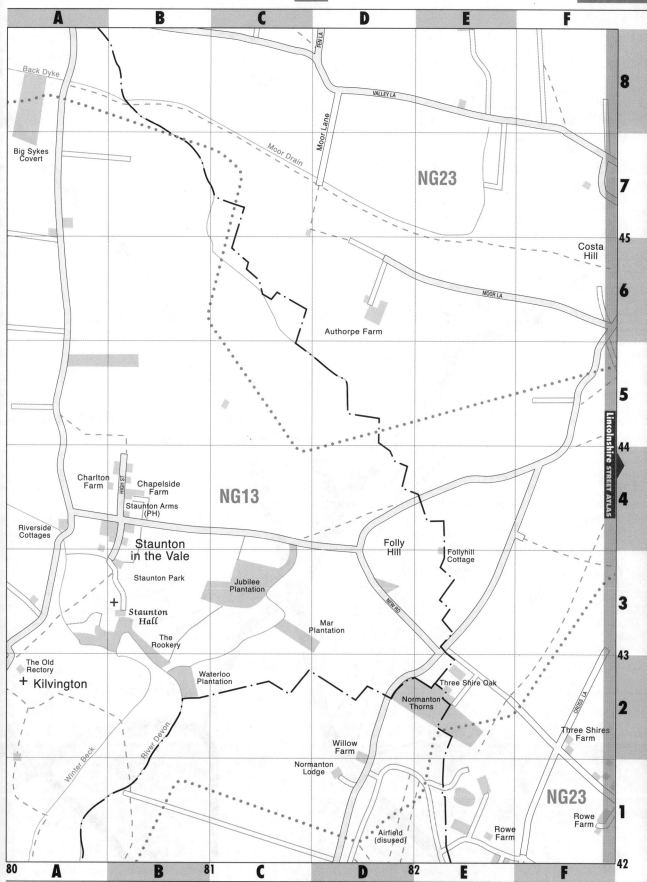

A B C D E F

8

7

45

6

5

44

4

43

3

2

1

42

Back Dyke

Big Sykes
Covert

NG23

Costa
Hill

Moor Lane

FEN LA

VALLEY LA

Moor Drain

MOOR LA

Authorpe Farm

Charlton
Farm

HIGH ST

Chapelside
Farm

Staunton Arms
(PH)

NG13

Folly
Hill

Follyhill
Cottage

Riverside
Cottages

Staunton
in the Vale

Staunton Park

Jubilee
Plantation

Mar
Plantation

NEW RD

Staunton
Hall

The Rookery

The Old
Rectory

Waterloo
Plantation

Three Shire Oak

Normanton
Thorns

CROSS LA

Three Shires
Farm

Kilvington

River Devon

Winter Beck

Willow
Farm

Normanton
Lodge

Airfield
(disused)

Rowe
Farm

NG23

Rowe
Farm

80 A B 81 C D 82 E F

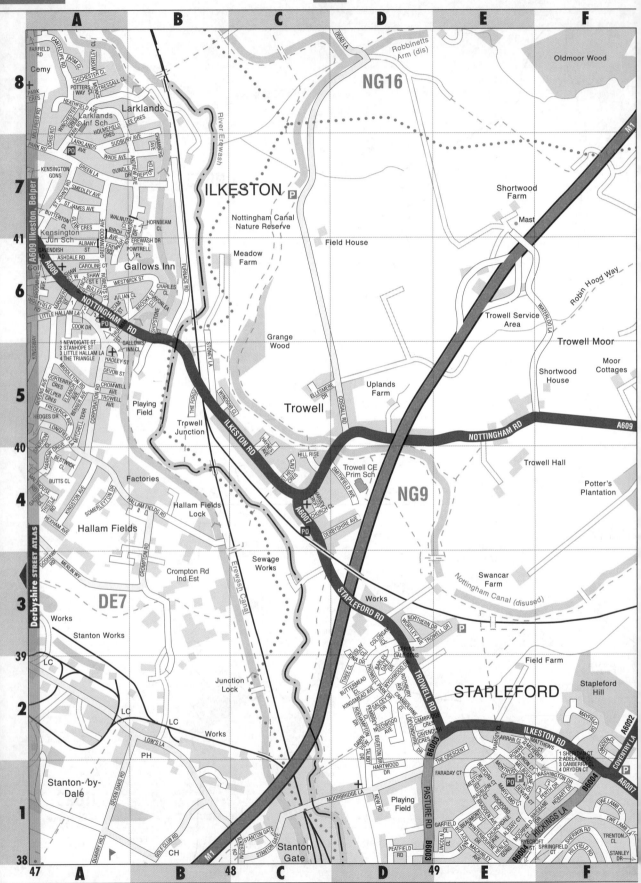

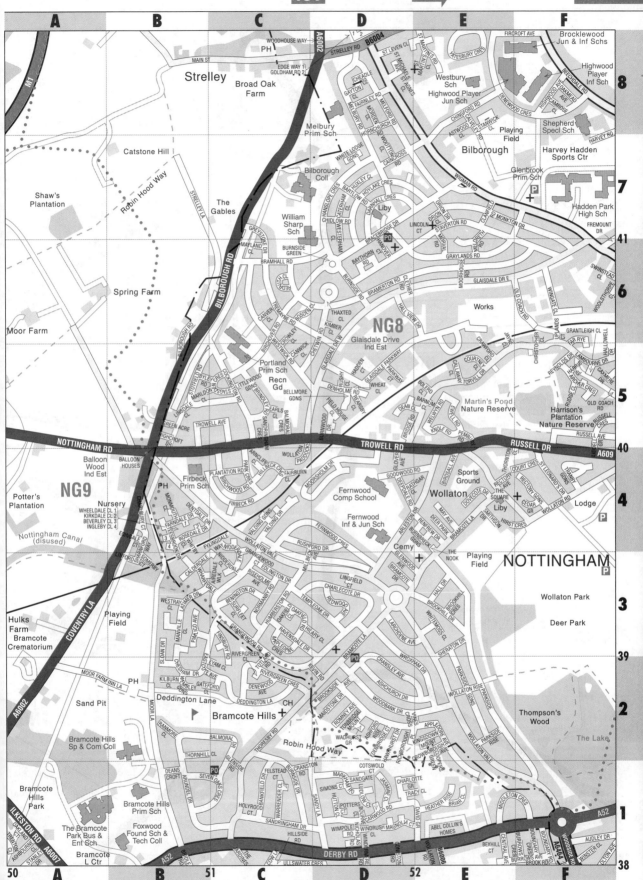

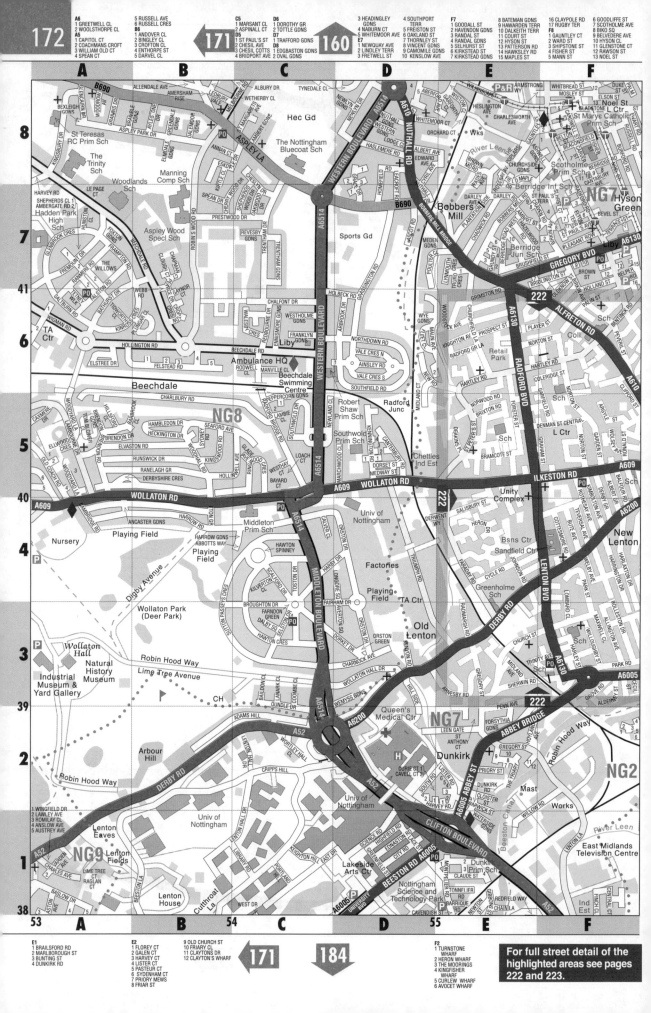

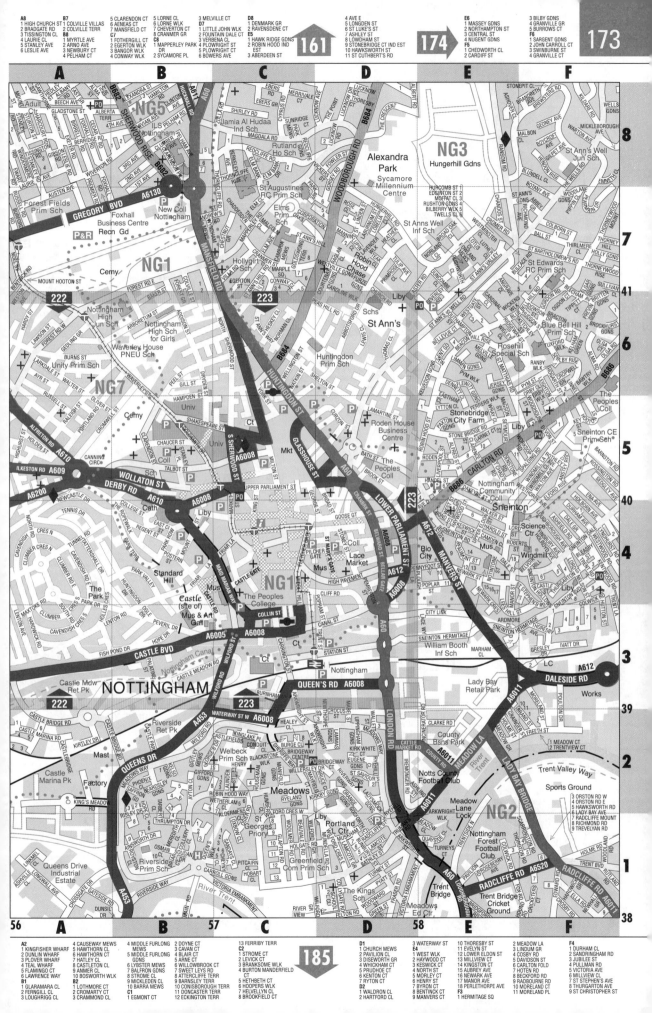

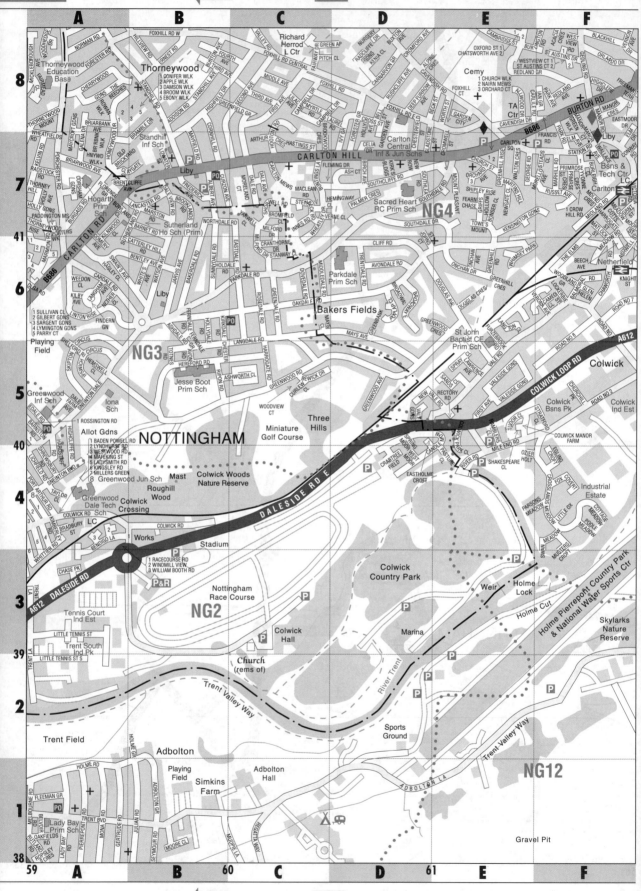

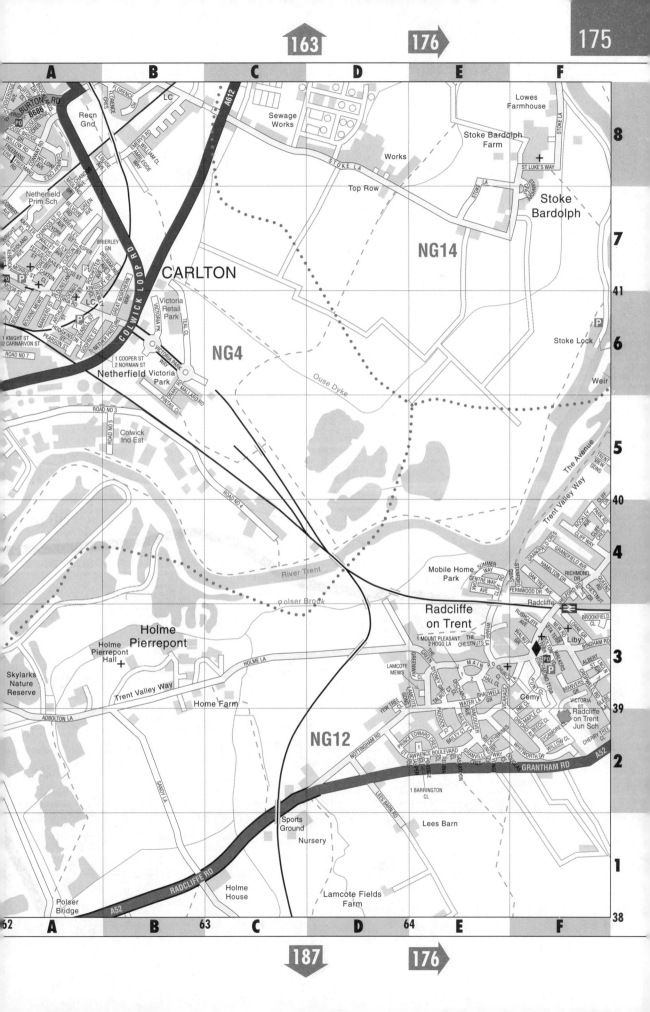

175
164

A **B** **C** **D** **E** **F**

NG13

NG14

Trent Valley Way

Field Lane

Bosworth Farm

Ashdown

MAIN RD

SHELFORD HILL

Newton Airfield

No Joke Plantation

Malkin Hill

River Trent

Lawson's Barn Farm

Shelford Lodge Farm

The Cliffs

Weir

Jubilee Plantation

OATFIELD LA

RIDGE LA

VALLEY RD

SHELFORD RD

Shelford Road Farm

TRENT VIEW GDNS

CLIFF DR

HOPEWELL CL

Spellow Hill

NG12

NG13

PARK RD

WESTCLIFFE AVE

BECK RD

CLUMBER DR

CHATSWORTH AVE

BUTLER

NEUST EAD AVE

WAKEFIELD AVE

PENRITH AVE

THORESBY CL

Spellow Farm

HADDON WAY

A52

Hill Farm

BIRKIN AVE

MALKIN AVE

CRAIG MORAY

QUEEN'S RD

DOWSON CL

HUDSON SOUTH

FENIMORE CT

Brickyard Plantation

CARNABY CL

PIMLICO CL

HENSON CL

GRANTHAM RD

NEWTON AVE 1

SHELFORD CL 2

NURSERY CL

PO

NURSERY CL

WOODSIDE RD

THOMAS AVE

NORTHFIELD AVE

RTON CL

MO

MORTON GDNS

SAXONDALE DR

GROSVENOR CL

KING

BRAXTON

NTPL

THE CRESCENT SINGD

BINGHAM RD

CARTER AVE

BRICKYARD LA

WOODSIDE AVE

DORMY CL

HAREB

CL

MEADOW END

Parr's Barn Farm

BERKELEY CR

WESTMINSTER DR

BUCKINGHAM

REGENT GDNS

GOLF RD

HAREWOOD

JOHNS RD

BLAKENEY RD

WOODLAND

OXERT CRES

MAYFAIR

SHAFTESBURY AVE

Cropwell Lings

GLEBE LA

CROPWELL GDNS

EASTWOOD RD

HILLSIDE RD

Radcliffe on Trent Inf Sch

Harlequin

HAMMERSMITH CL

QUEEN MARY'S CL

SERPENTINE CL

Upper Saxondale or St James's Pk

HENSON LA

Saxton's Lings

A52

Dayncourt Sch

Dewberry Hill

CH

DEWBERRY LA

High Thorpe

CROPWELL RD

The Fields

Hall Farm

Radcliffe Barn Farm

A46

A **B** **C** **D** **E** **F**
175
188

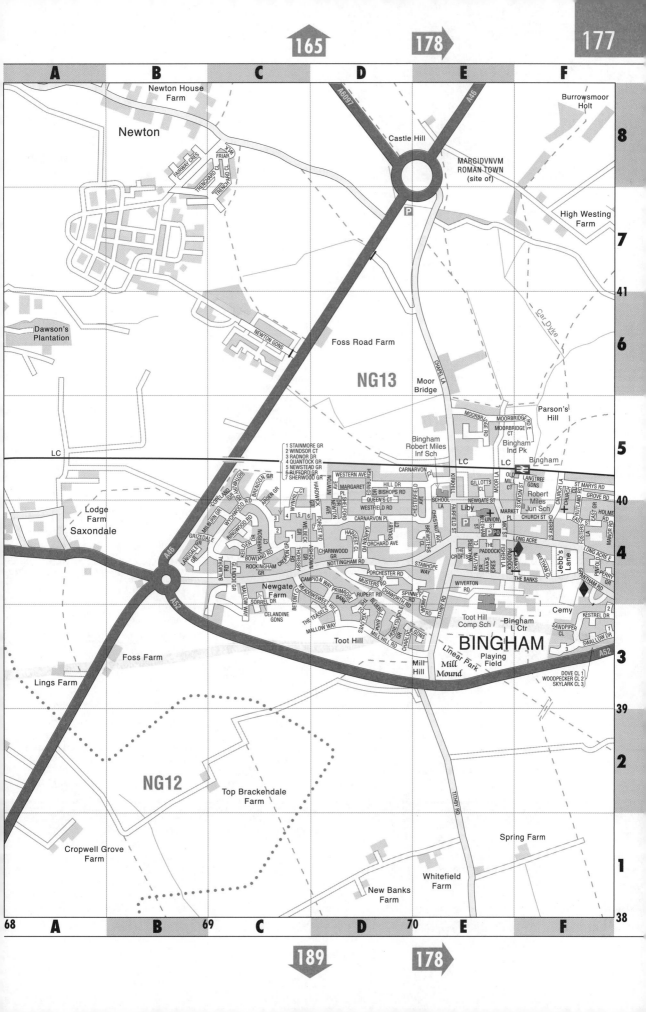

A B C D E F

8

Thoroughfare Holt

Longmoor La

Hall

The Old Vicarage

HAWKSWORTH RD

Scarrington

7

Bottom Plantation

Manor Farm

MAIN ST
THE SAUCERS

MILL LA

41

6

Holme Farm

NEW LA

5

LC

Sewage Works

MOOR LA

NG13

Archbishop Cranmer CE Prim Sch

ABBEY LA

WALNUT CL

GROVE RD
ST MARYS RD
BUTT RD
HOLME RD
CROW CT

PRIORS CL

BROWNES RD

VICTORIA CL

CARR RD

DOUGLAS RD

ABBEY RD

COGLEY LA

Abbey Farm

FIELDS DR

ABBEY CL
THE CAPES

40

4

NURSERY LA

BANES RD

Carnarvon Prim Sch

LC

Aslockton Hall

BEVERLEYS AVE

GREEN WLK
SMITE CL

COTTAGE AVE

LONG ACRE E
DARK LA
RAYMOND DR
ASH CL
CEDAR

ROWAN CL

LARCH CL
MAPLE CL

ASPEN CL

JUNIPER CL

POPLAR CL

OAK AVE

HOLLY CL

WILLOW RD

BEECH AVE

HAZEL CL

BLACKTHORN CL

DERRY LA

Nursery

Brocker Farm

HM Young Offender Institution

Sewage Works

3 ELM AV
GRANTHAM RD

Nursery

BELVOIR

CROMWELL RD

CRANMER AVE

SWALLOW DR
NIGHTINGALE WY

A52

GRANTHAM RD

A52

1 AVOCET CL
2 MALLARD CL
3 SYCAMORE CL
4 GOLDCREST CL

Aslockton Grange

39

2

GRANBY LA

River Smite

CONERY LA

Thorough Bridge

Starnhill Farm

Starnhill Plantation

1

Vicars Croft

38

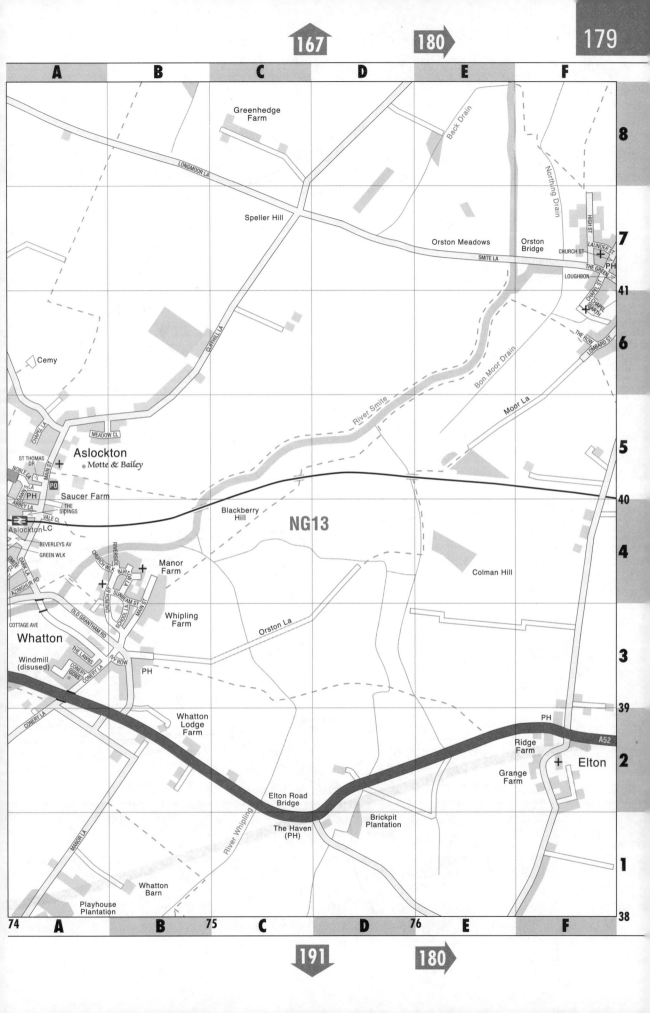

A B C D E F

8
7
41
6
5
40
4
3
39
2
1
38

Greenhedge Farm

Back Drain

Northing Drain

LONGMOOR LA

Speller Hill

Orston Meadows

Orston Bridge

SMITE LA

HIGH ST

LAUNDER ST

CHURCH ST

PH

THE GREEN

LOUGHBON

CHAPEL ST

CHAPEL GARTH

THE ROW

LOMBARD ST

CLIFF HILL LA

Cemy

CHAPEL LA

MEADOW CL

Aslockton

• Motte & Bailey

St THOMAS DR

MAIN ST

NOBLE LA

LINDY'S LA

PO

PH

Saucer Farm

ABBEY LA

THE SIDINGS

VALE CL

Aslockton LC

Blackberry Hill

NG13

Bon Moor Drain

Moor La

River Smite

BEVERLEYS AV

GREEN WLK

RIVERSIDE

CHURCH WLK

BURTON LA

Manor Farm

Colman Hill

SMITE CL

DAIRY LA

AZINGHUR RD

FORTH'D

SCHOOL LA

SUNBEAM ST

MAIN ST

Whipling Farm

Orston La

COTTAGE AVE

Whatton

OLD GRANTHAM RD

IVY ROW

Windmill (disused)

THE LAWNS

CONERY GDNS

CONERY LA

PH

Whatton Lodge Farm

PH

A52

Ridge Farm

Elton

Grange Farm

CONERY LA

Elton Road Bridge

River Whipling

The Haven (PH)

Brickpit Plantation

MANOR LA

Whatton Barn

Playhouse Plantation

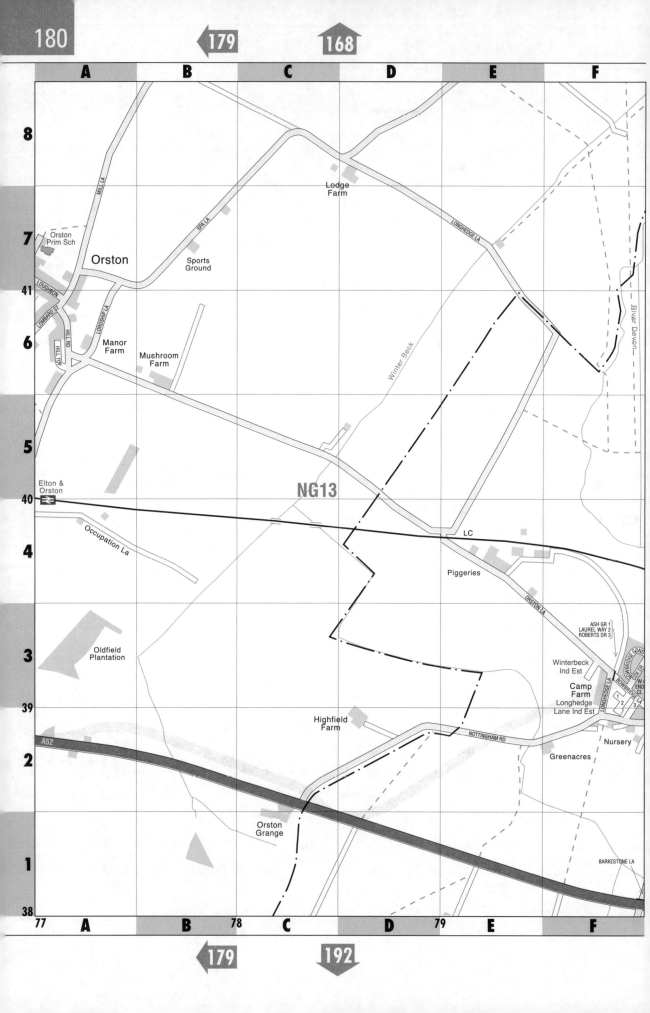

179
168

A B C D E F

8

Lodge
Farm

LONGHEDGE LA

River Devon

7
Orston
Prim Sch

Orston

SPA LA

Sports
Ground

41

LOUGHBON

LOMBARD ST

HILL RD

LORDSHIP LA

6
HILL TOR

Manor
Farm

Mushroom
Farm

Winter Beck

5

NG13

Elton &
Orston

40

LC

Occupation La

4

Piggeries

ORSTON LA

ASH GR 1
LAUREL WAY 2
ROBERTS DR 3

3
Oldfield
Plantation

Winterbeck
Ind Est

Camp
Farm
Longhedge
Lane Ind Est

LONGHEDGE LA

BOWBRIDGE GDNS

39

Highfield
Farm

NOTTINGHAM RD

Nursery

2
A52

Greenacres

Orston
Grange

1

BARKESTONE LA

38

77 A B 78 C D 79 E F

A B C D E F

8
7
41
6
5
40
4
3
39
2
1
38

NG23

NG13

Lincolnshire STREET ATLAS

River Devon

Piggery

Airfield
(disused)

Ease
Drain

Normanton
Hall

Normanton
House

Peacock
Farm

Little Covert
Farm

Normanton

Elm Farm

Home Farm

Sewage
Works

Beacon Hill

Rectory
Farm

The
Nook
COX RD

Beckingthorpe

Works

LC

LC

Bottesford

Bottesford

WIMBISHTHORPE

Ford

Liby

PH

1 WEST END CL
2 NOTTINGHAM RD
3 BOWBRIDGE LA

WALNUT
RD

SILVERWOOD RD

The Elms

Manor
Farm

Easthorpe

South
View

River Devon

Belvoir
High Sch

Castleview
Farm

Winterbeck
Bridge

Corner
Farm

Hospital
Farm

Muston

A52

A52

A52 Grantham

CASTLE VIEW RD

MUSTON LA

EASTHORPE LA

GRANTHAM RD

RUTLAND LA

EASTHORPE RD

MANOR RD

GREEN LA

CASTLE VIEW RD

VAUGHAN AVE

FLEMING AVE

OLD STATION YD

STATION RD

CHURCH ST

MARKET ST

QUEEN ST

ALBERT ST

HIGH ST

CHAPEL ST

NORMANTON LA

BEACON VIEW

STROUD CT

SPIRE VIEW

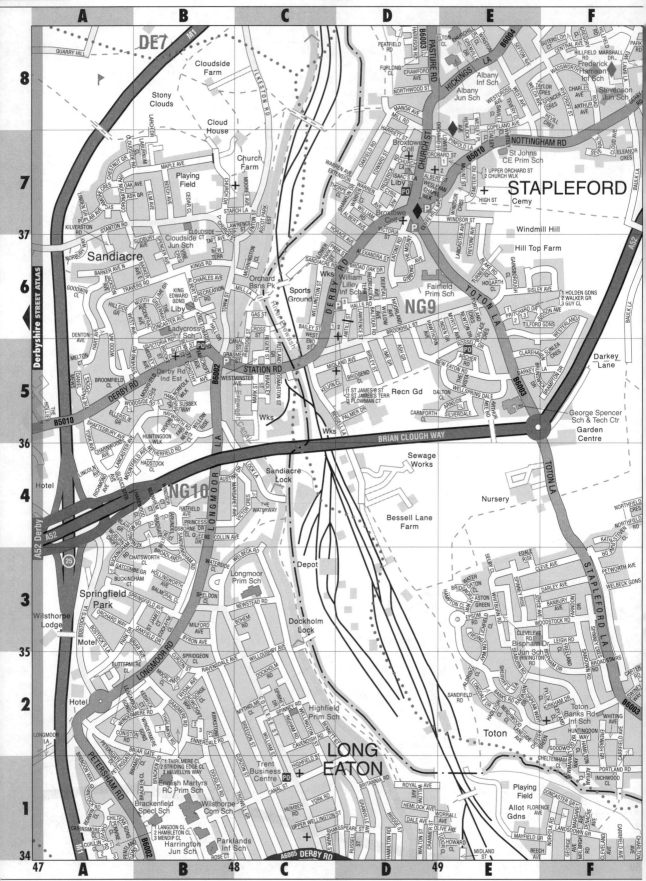

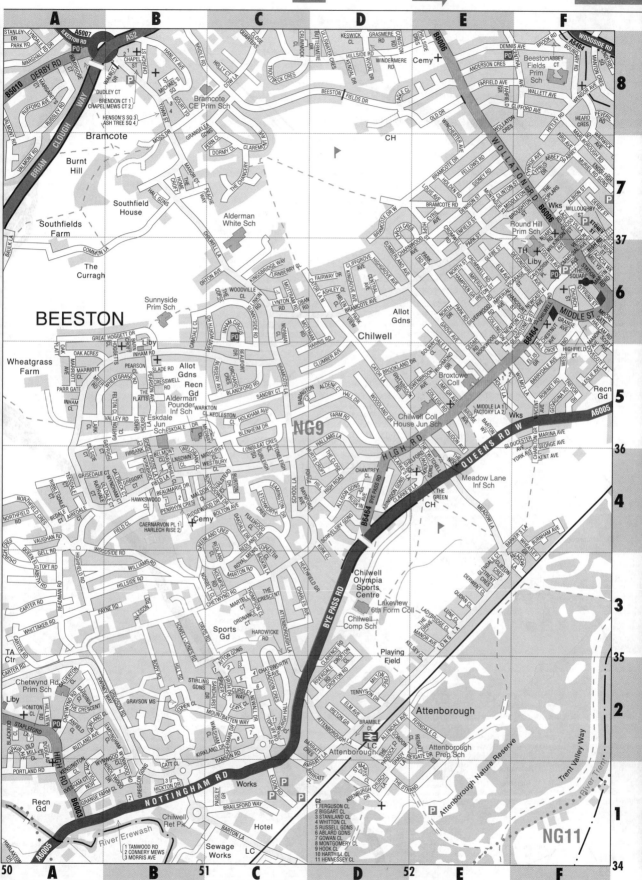

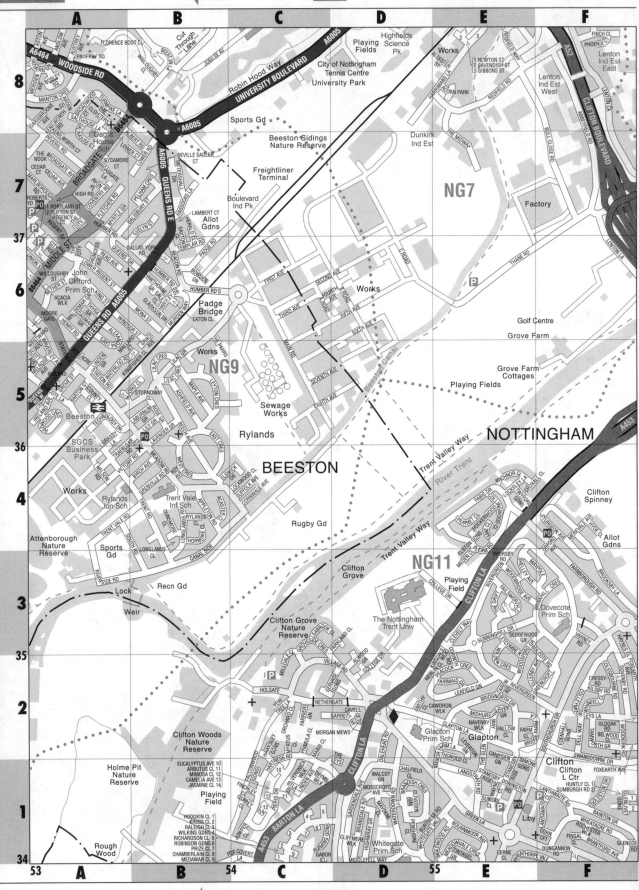

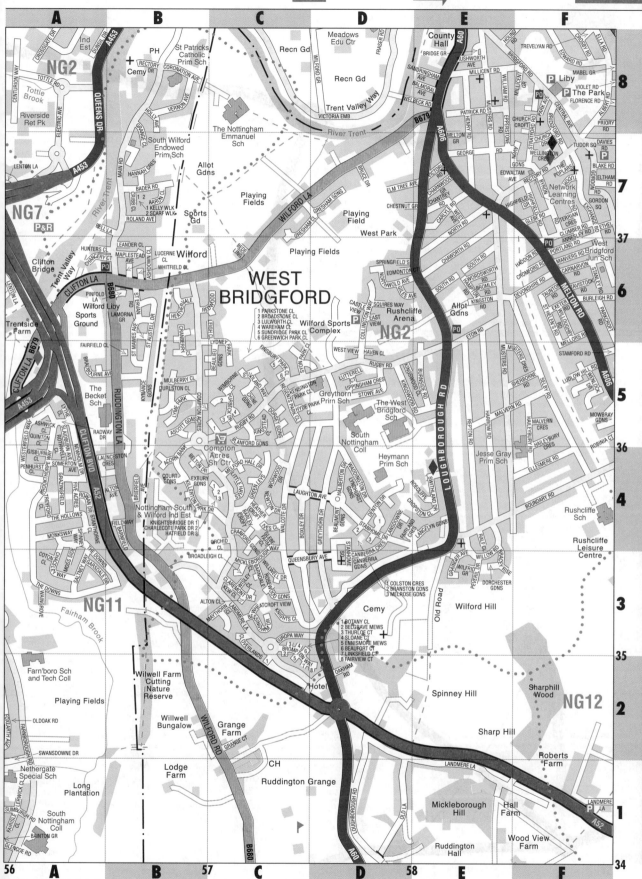

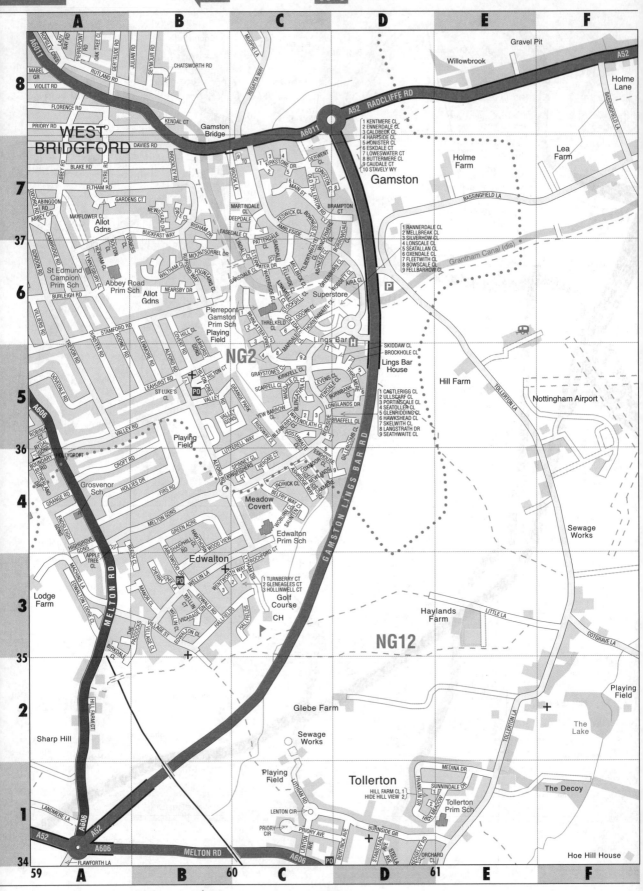

A B C D E F

RADCLIFFE RD A52

NATHANS LA

Bassingfield

Polser Brook

Shepherd's (PH)

Sewage Works

Thornton's Holt Farm

North Farm

Nursery

Cotgrave Place

CH

Thurlbeck Dyke

Grantham Canal (dis)

Cotgrave Bridge

P

NG12

Peashill Farm

Windmill Hill

Sewage Works

MILL
MAIN RD
BLACKSMITH LA
MORKINSHIRE LA

CHICHESTER DR
MORKINSHIRE CRES

THE PARK
PINFOLD CL
THE OLD PARK

Cotgrave CE Prim Sch

VINE FARM CL
EAST ACRES
HOLLYGATE LA
COLSTON GATE

CHURCH LA
Miller Hives Cl
THE CROSS
PH
PO
WALNUT GR
BINGHAM RD
LAWRENCE CL
SCOTLAND BANK
CANDLEBY CT
Liby
THE PRECINCT
AVONDALE

RECTORY RD
WOODGATE LA
BAKER'S HOLLOW
WOODGATE CL
HALES CL
Cemy
PLUMTREE RD
SCRIMSHIRE LA
CHERRY OR
THURMAN DR
RISEGATE
RISEGATE GDNS
GOOSE GATE
FOREST CL
CANDLEBY LA

Cotgrave Manvers Jun Sch
Cotgrave Int Sch
Highfield Prim Sch

LAMPLANDS
GREENFIELDS DR
Ash Lea Special Sch

PLUMTREE RD

Cotgrave

WHITE FURROWS
FERN LEA AVE
HAWTHORN AVE
WOODLAND CL
SPINNEY CL
ASH LEA CL
FLAGHOLME
CARTBRIDGE
RING LEAS

MARIN
MANNS LEYS
TOFT CL
CORN
DALESIDE
HIGH HILL
SANDSIDE
MANORWOOD RD
OWTHORPE RD
RUNCIE CL

MILLERS BRIDGE 1
INGLEBY CL 2
BONNY MEAD
THE DIAL
WESTWAY
THE WARREN
GRIPPS COMM

COTGRAVE LA

COTGRAVE RD

Tollerton Wood

GILLOTT LA
CHURCH GATE

Clipston

Manor Farm

Blackberry Farm
Wolds La

Mill Lane

Brickyard Plantation

WOLDS CL
SAXON WAY
KINGSTON DR
WARWICK GDNS
Scotton's Hill

Hoehill Farm

187
176

A   B   C   D   E   F

8

Cropwell
Court

Barn Farm
Court

The Grove

Stragglethorpe

7

The Limes

Barnsfield
Farm

37

Cotgrave
Country Park

Brown's
Cottages

6

Foss
Bridge

Berry
Hill

Sports
Gd

Hollygate
Farm

Hoe
Hill

5

HOLLYGATE LA

Mann's
Bridge

NG12

36

Hollygate
Bridge

4

Hollygate
Ind Park

NOTTINGHAM RD

Works

Cropwell
Bridge

COLSTON GATE

Playing
Field

RIVERMEAD
HAZELWOOD
GLENBROOK
TROUTBECK
DEANSCOURT

3

Gypsum
Quarry

AVONDALE
LINGFORD
SPRING MEADOW
THORNTONS
GRASSMERE
WILLOWDENE
PIT DALE
CROSSHILL

Hazeldean
Cottage

Foss
House

35

Cotgrave
Leisure
Centre

WOODVIEW
CHENNEL NOOK
RITCHIE
LITTLE MEADOW

2

Smith's
Round
Hill

Cotgrave
Gorse

Long
Plantation

Wolds
Farm

Groundwells
Farm

Wks

WHITELANDS
BRAMBLEWAY
CLOVERDALE
RING LEAS
PRIORIDGE
BURYHILL
FLAXENDALE

Limekiln Inn
(PH)

THIRLBECK
WEST FURLONG
HUCKNALL WAY
SAXON WAY
EASTWOLD
MARLWOOD
BRIAR GV
FOSSE WALK

Cropwell
Wolds

COLSTON RD

SWAB'S LA

1

EDGINGTON CL
EAST
MOOR

Stone Pit
Plantation

Limekiln
Farm

34

OWTHORPE RD

A46

The Old
Farm House

65   A   B   66   C   D   67   E   F

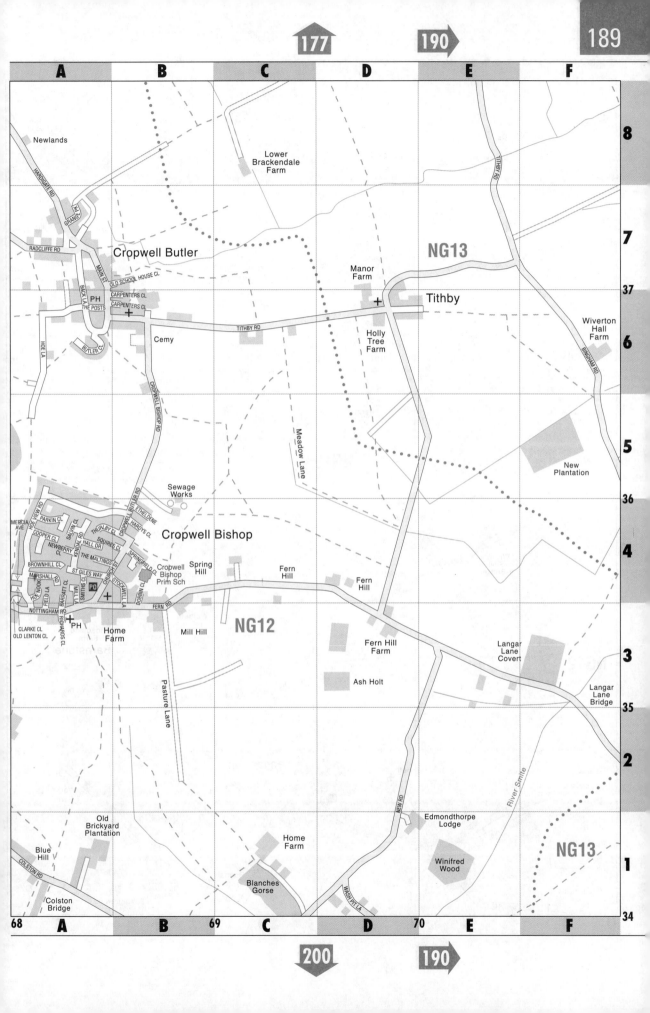

A   B   C   D   E   F

8

Newlands

Lower
Brackendale
Farm

7

HARDIGATE RD

GRANGE

RADCLIFFE RD

Cropwell Butler

NG13

MAIN ST

BACK LA

OLD SCHOOL HOUSE CL

Manor
Farm

Tithby

37

PH
THE POSTS

CARPENTERS CL
CARPENTERS CL

HOE LA

BUTLER CL

Cemy

TITHBY RD

Holly
Tree
Farm

Wiverton
Hall
Farm

6

TITHBY RD

BINGHAM RD

CROPWELL BISHOP RD

Meadow Lane

New
Plantation

5

Sewage
Works

36

MERCIA AVE
HOE VIEW RD
PARKIN CL

CROPWELL BUTLER RD
ETHELDENE
HARDYS CL

Cropwell Bishop

COOPER CL
THURLBY CL
SQUIRES CL
KENDAL RD
HALL DR
SAVIN CL

NEWBERRY CL
THE MALTINGS
SPRINGFIELD CL

Spring
Hill

Fern
Hill

Fern
Hill

4

BROWNHILL CL
MARSHALL RD
ST GILES WAY

Cropwell
Bishop
Prim Sch

DOBBIN LA
CHURCH ST
STOCKWELL LA

FERN RD

FERN RD

Langar
Lane
Covert

HCK
NOOK LA
FIELD LA
BARRATT CL
MILL LA
RICHARDS CL

PO

NG12

Fern Hill
Farm

3

CLARKE CL
OLD LENTON CL

NOTTINGHAM RD
PH

Home
Farm

Mill Hill

Ash Holt

Langar
Lane
Bridge

35

Pasture Lane

River Smite

2

NEW RD

WASH PIT LA

Old
Brickyard
Plantation

Home
Farm

Edmondthorpe
Lodge

NG13

1

Blue
Hill

Winifred
Wood

COLSTON RD

Colston
Bridge

Blanches
Gorse

34

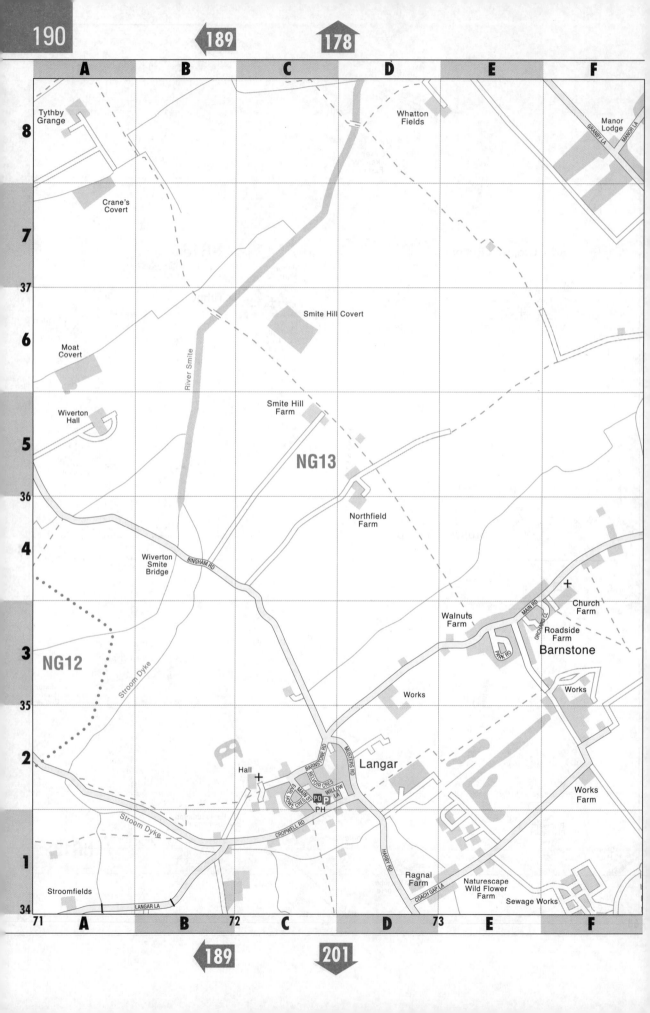

A   B   C   D   E   F

8

Tythby
Grange

Crane's
Covert

Whatton
Fields

Manor
Lodge

GRANBY LA

MANOR LA

7

37

Smite Hill Covert

6

Moat
Covert

River Smite

Wiverton
Hall

Smite Hill
Farm

NG13

5

36

Northfield
Farm

4

Wiverton
Smite
Bridge

BINGHAM RD

Walnuts
Farm

MAIN RD

ORCHARD CT

Church
Farm

Roadside
Farm

PARK RD

Barnstone

3

NG12

Stroom Dyke

35

Works

Works

2

Hall

BARNSTONE RD

MUSTERS RD

Langar

BELVOIR CRES

WILLOW LA

MAIN ST

EAST HOME CRES

PO

P

PH

Works
Farm

Stroom Dyke

CROPWELL RD

HARBY RD

Ragnal
Farm

COACH GAP LA

Naturescape
Wild Flower
Farm

Sewage Works

1

34

Stroomfields

LANGAR LA

71   A   B   72   C   D   73   E   F

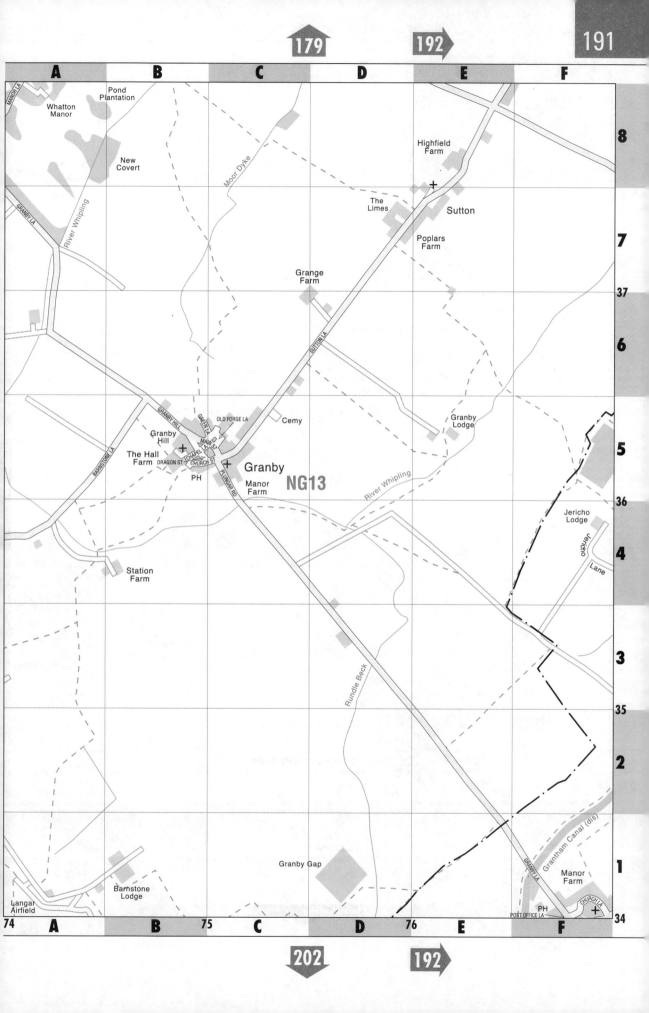

A B C D E F

8

Whatton Manor

Pond Plantation

Highfield Farm

New Covert

Sutton

The Limes

7

River Whipling

Moor Dyke

GRANBY LA

Poplars Farm

37

Grange Farm

SUTTON LA

6

BARNSTONE LA

GRANBY HILL

OLD FORGE LA

Cemy

Granby Lodge

5

Granby Hill

GREEN LA

The Hall Farm

DRAGON ST

CHAPEL LA

MAIN ST

CHURCH ST

PH

Granby

NG13

River Whipling

Manor Farm

PLUNGAR RD

36

Jericho Lodge

4

Station Farm

Jericho Lane

Rundle Beck

3

35

2

Granby Gap

1

Langar Airfield

Barnstone Lodge

Grantham Canal (dis)

Manor Farm

GRANBY LA

CHURCH LA

PH

POST OFFICE LA

34

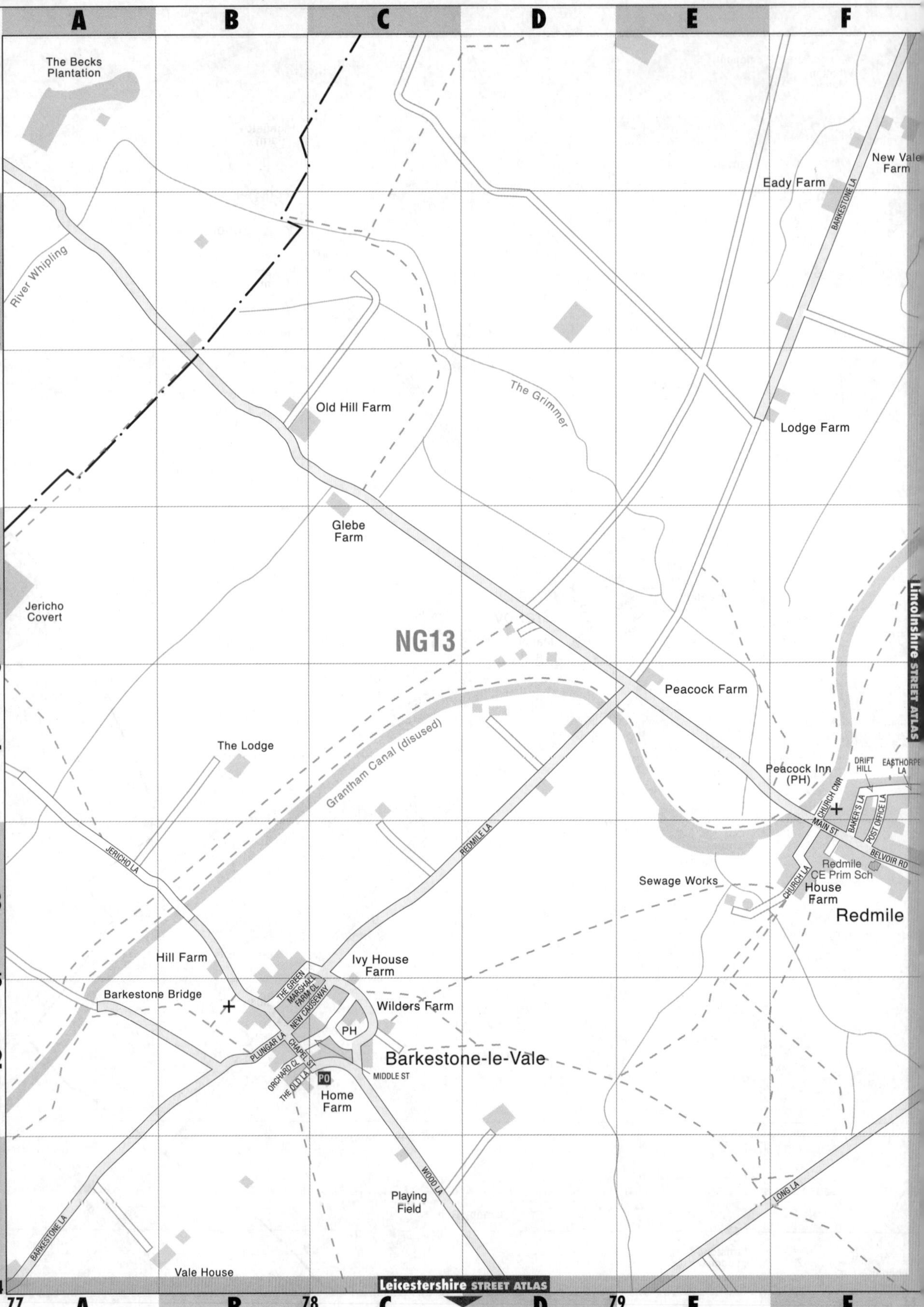

The Becks Plantation
River Whipling
Old Hill Farm
The Grimmer
Eady Farm
New Vale Farm
BARKESTONE LA
Lodge Farm
Glebe Farm
Jericho Covert
NG13
Peacock Farm
Lincolnshire STREET ATLAS
The Lodge
Grantham Canal (disused)
Peacock Inn (PH)
DRIFT HILL
EASTHORPE LA
CHURCH CNR
BAKER'S LA
POST OFFICE LA
MAIN ST
BELVOIR RD
JERICHO LA
REDMILE LA
Redmile CE Prim Sch
Sewage Works
CHURCH LA
House Farm
Redmile
Hill Farm
Ivy House Farm
THE GREEN
MARSHALL FARM CL
NEW CAUSEWAY
Barkestone Bridge
Wilders Farm
PH
PLUNGAR LA
CHAPEL ST
Barkestone-le-Vale
ORCHARD CL
THE OLD LA
PO
MIDDLE ST
Home Farm
WOOD LA
Playing Field
LONG LA
BARKESTONE LA
Vale House
Leicestershire STREET ATLAS
A
B
C
D
E
F
8
7
37
6
5
36
4
3
35
2
1
34
77
78
79

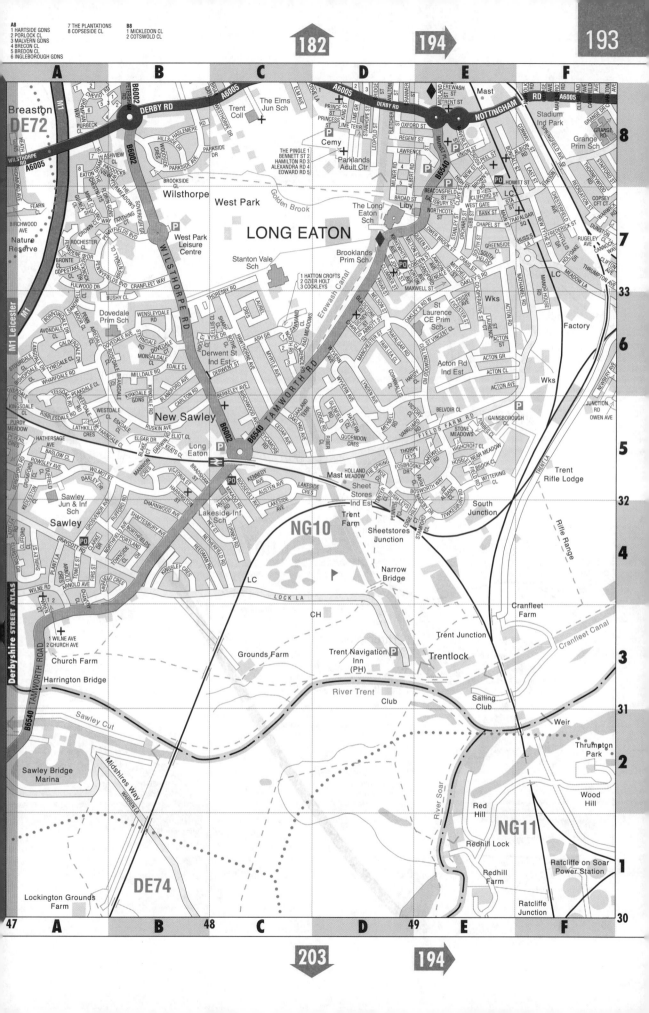

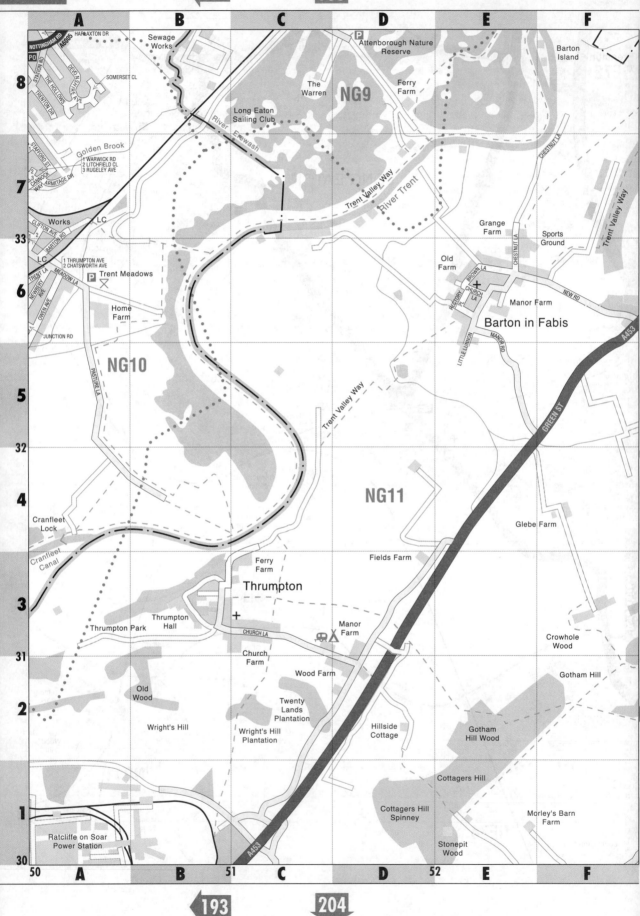

A   B   C   D   E   F

8

NOTTINGHAM RD   A6005   HARLAXTON DR
Sewage Works
Barton Island

STATION RD   PO
DEVON ST
THE HOLLINS
SOMERSET CL
TRENTON DR

The Warren   NG9   Ferry Farm

Long Eaton Sailing Club

River Erewash

7

Golden Brook
1 WARWICK RD
2 LITCHFIELD CL
3 RUGELEY AVE

STAFFORD ST
CANNOCK WAY   ARMITAGE DR

Trent Valley Way   River Trent

Grange Farm

Sports Ground

CHESTNUT LA

Trent Valley Way

33

Works   LC

CLIFTON AVE
BARTON RD

LC

1 THRUMPTON AVE
2 CHATSWORTH AVE

P   Trent Meadows

Old Farm

CHURCH LA
BROWN LA
CHESTNUT LA
NEW RD

6

TRENT LA
MEADOW LA
NEWBERY AVE
OWEN AVE

Home Farm

Manor Farm

RECTORY PL

Barton in Fabis

A453

JUNCTION RD

NG10

LITTLE LUNNON   MANOR RD

5

PASTURE LA

Trent Valley Way

GREEN ST

32

NG11

Glebe Farm

4

Cranfleet Lock

Fields Farm

Crowhole Wood

3

Cranfleet Canal

Ferry Farm

Thrumpton

Gotham Hill

Thrumpton Hall
Manor Farm

31

Thrumpton Park

Church Farm

CHURCH LA

Wood Farm

Gotham Hill

2

Old Wood

Twenty Lands Plantation

Hillside Cottage

Gotham Hill Wood

Wright's Hill

Wright's Hill Plantation

Cottagers Hill

Morley's Barn Farm

1

Ratcliffe on Soar Power Station

A453

Cottagers Hill Spinney

Stonepit Wood

30

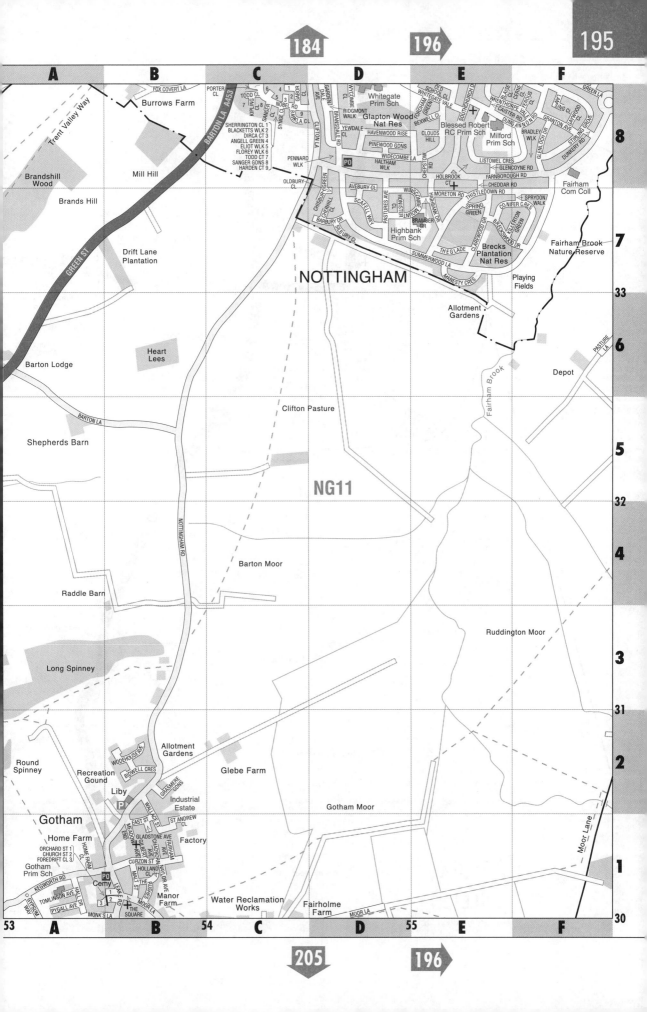

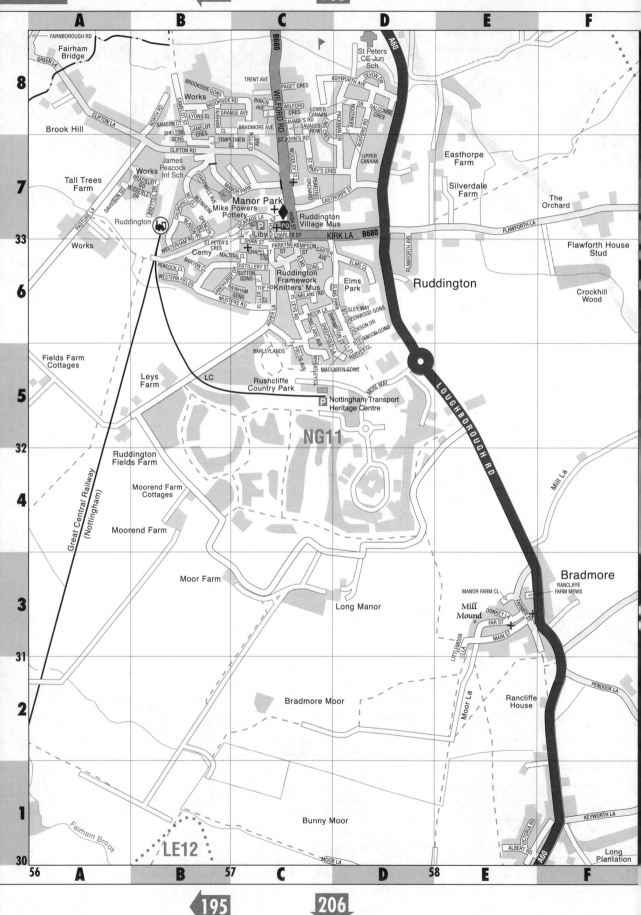

A B C D E F

8

FARNBOROUGH RD

Fairham
Bridge

GREEN LA

Brook Hill

CLIFTON LA

BROOKSIDE GDNS

Works

TRENT AVE

PAGET CRES

St Peters
CE Jun
Sch

ASHWORTH AVE

DEVON DR

NORTH RD

CAMELOT DR

BROOKSIDE RD

BIRKIN
AVE

WILFORD
CRES

LOWER
CANAAN

SALCOMBE
CRES

Easthorpe
Farm

7

Tall Trees
Farm

PASTURE LA

DAVIDSON LOW
WIBBERLEY DR
BRADBURY
RD

Works

Ruddington

SAMSON CT ST
SHELTON
GDNS
LYONS CL

GRANGE AVE

FAIRHAM

CLIFTON RD

CAMELOT
CRES

BRADMORE AVE

TEMPLEMEN
CL

CLIFTON
AVE

ST JOHN'S RD

SAVAGE'S RD
SAVAGES
ROW

WOODLEY ST

WILFORD RD

PICKMAN
DR

RUFFORD RD
ABINGDON
DR
LING CT

ST MARY'S CRES

UPPER
CANAAN

PEARTREE
ORCHARD

Silverdale
Farm

The
Orchard

FLAWFORTH LA

James
Peacock
Inf Sch

CHARTWELL AVE

MANOR PARK

Mike Powers
Pottery

Manor Park

BLENHEIM
BLADON DR
HO CL
CHURCHILL DR
SPENCER DR
STREETSIDE

VICARAGE LA

HIGH ST

Ruddington
Village Mus

EASTHORPE ST

FLAWFORTH AVE

Flawforth House
Stud

33

Works

WESTERHAM RD PL

ST PETER'S
CRES

SHAW ST

CHAPEL ST

Liby

CHARLES ST
PARKYNS
ST

KEMPSON
ST

CARTER
AVE

KIRK LA

B680

Ruddington

6

WESTERN FIELDS

PEACOCK CL

BARTON CL

Cemy

MALTING CL

DISTILLERY ST
SUTTON
GDNS
SANDHURST
RAINHAM
GDNS

TOP RD
FULLER
CL

ASHER LA

Ruddington
Framework
Knitters' Mus

MUSTERS RD

ELMS
GDNS

MOOR LA

DUNBLANE RD

WESLEY WAY
GREENWOOD GDNS
DICKSON DR

ELMS CL

ELMS PARK

Elms
Park

STEVENSON GDNS

Crockhill
Wood

Fields Farm
Cottages

Leys
Farm

LC

BARLEYLANDS

FIELDS AVE

LEYS RD

SHRIMPTON CT
SHEPPTON CL
ISLLANS AVE

HARVEY CL

MACLAREN GDNS

WHENTLEY CL

MERE WAY

LOUGHBOROUGH RD

5

Rushcliffe
Country Park

Nottingham Transport
Heritage Centre

32

Great Central Railway
(Nottingham)

Ruddington
Fields Farm

NG11

Mill La

4

Moorend Farm
Cottages

Moorend Farm

3

Moor Farm

Long Manor

Mill
Mound

MANOR FARM CL

DONKEY LA

FAR ST

FARMERS ST

Bradmore

RANCLIFFE
FARM MEWS

31

MAIN ST

LITTLEMOOR LA

Rancliffe
House

PENDOCK LA

2

Bradmore Moor

MOOR LA

A60

1

Fairham Brook

LE12

Bunny Moor

KEYWORTH LA

30

VICTORIA RD

ALBERT RD

A60

Long
Plantation

56 A B 57 C D 58 E F

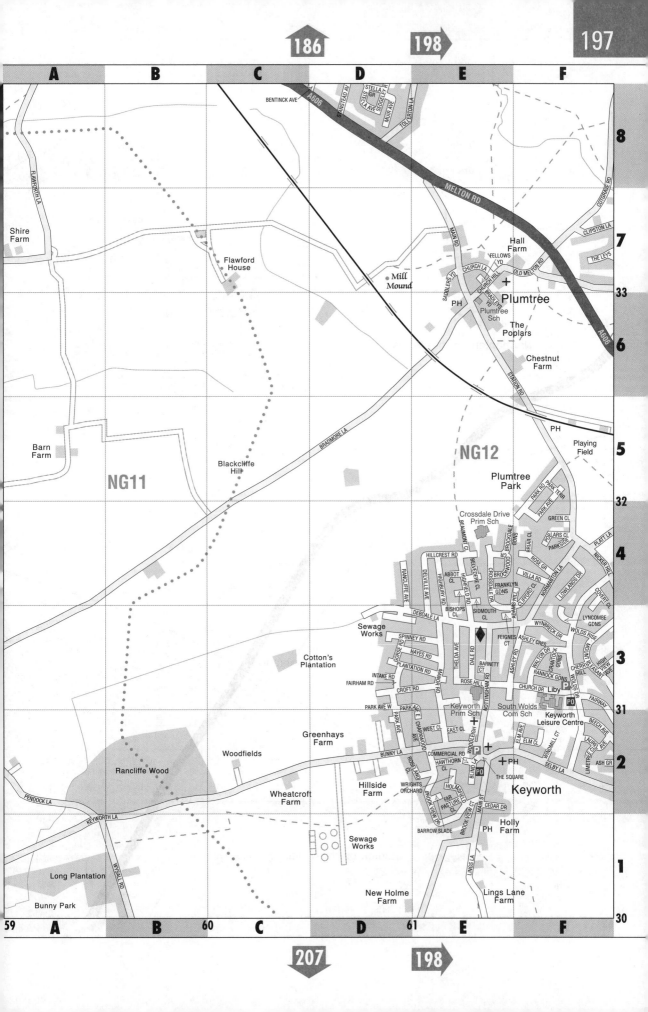

A B C D E F

8

7

33

6

5

32

4

3

31

2

1

30

BENTINCK AVE

A606

STELLA
GR
STANSTEAD AV
STELLA
AVE
SEDGELEY
MUIR AVE
TOLLERTON LA

MELTON RD

A606

Shire
Farm

FLAWFORTH LA

Flawford
House

Mill
Mound

MAIN RD
CHURCH LA
SADDLER'S YD
FELLOWS
YD
CHURCH HILL
BRADLEY'S
YD
OLD MELTON RD

CLIPSTON LA

THE LEYS

Hall
Farm

Plumtree
Sch

PH

Plumtree

The
Poplars

STATION RD

Chestnut
Farm

PH

Playing
Field

Barn
Farm

NG11

Blackcliffe
Hill

BRADMORE LA

NG12

Plumtree
Park

PARK RD
PARK TERR
PARK AVE
GREEN CL

Crossdale Drive
Prim Sch

BROOKDALE
GDNS
BRIAR CL
POSLARS CL
PARKSIDE
PLATT LA

HILLCREST RD

RANCLIFFE AVE
DELVILLE AVE
HIGHBURY RD
BELVEDERE CL
HIGHFIELD RD
ABBOT
CL
BISHOPS
CL
DEBDALE LA
CROSSDALE DR
BROS
WOOD
ROSE GR
VILLA RD
FRANKLYN
GDNS
CLIFFORD CL
ADAMS HILL
SIDMOUTH
CL
NORMANTON LA
LOWLANDS DR
NICKER HILL
COVERT CL
LYNCOMBE
GDNS
WOLDS RISE

Sewage
Works

SPINNEY RD
GORSE RD
HAYES RD
PLANTATION RD
INTAKE RD
THE LDA AVE
MANOR RD
DALE RD
BARNETT
CT
FEIGNES
CT
ASHLEY CRES
WYNBRECK DR
ASHLEY RD
VALTON DR
RANNOCK GDNS
CRANTOCK
GDNS
CHERRY
HILL
PLEASANT
AVE
HIGH
VIEW

Cotton's
Plantation

FAIRHAM RD
CROFT RD
NOTTINGHAM RD
ROSE HILL
CHURCH DR
Liby
PO
FAIRWAY

PARK AVE W
PARK AVE
PARK AVE E
CHADWOOD
AVE
WEST CL
EAST CL
Keyworth
Prim Sch
South Wolds
Com Sch
Keyworth
Leisure Centre
BEECH AVE
WINDMILL CT
LAUREL AVE
ASH GR
LIMETREE CRE
SELBY LA

Greenhays
Farm

Woodfields

BUNNY LA

ROSE LANE
HAWTHORN
CL
COMMERCIAL RD
BLIND LA
WOODLEIGH
ELM RD
ELM CL
PH
THE SQUARE

PO

Rancliffe Wood

Wheatcroft
Farm

Hillside
Farm

WRIGHTS
ORCHARD
HOLMEFIELD
FAR
PASTURE
CL
BROOK LANE
BROOK VIEW CT
MAIN ST
CEDAR DR
PH
Holly
Farm

Keyworth

PENDOCK LA

KEYWORTH LA

WYSALL RD

Sewage
Works

BARROW SLADE

LINGS LA

Long Plantation

Bunny Park

New Holme
Farm

Lings Lane
Farm

A B C D E F

8

←COTGRAVE RD

CHURCH GATE

Glebe Farm

Mill Lane

Hoe Hill

Smallthorne Plantation

7

THE LEYS

Cotgrave Forest

Grange Plantation

Blackberry Hill

Wolds La

33

THE LEYS

Avenue Farm

Wolds Farm

6

BACK LA

Normanton-on-the-Wolds

PH

A606

Plumtree Wolds

5

Playing Field

PLATT LA

Wolds Farm

NG12

LAMING GAP LA

32

Clipston Wolds

4

Normanton Wolds

British Geological Survey

MELTON RD

MOUNT PLEASANT

Hill Farm

3

HIGH VIEW AVE

NICKER HILL

MEADOW DR

THE RIDINGS

MOUNT PLS

PHEASANT

LABURNUM AVE

LARCH WAY

31

MOUNT PLEASANT

FAIRWAY

ROMAN DR

MAPLE CL

ALDER WY

LILAC CL

BEECH AVE

WILLOW BROOK

Bank Farm

2

ASH GROVE

BEECH AVE

SELBY LA

GOLF COURSE RD

STANTON LA

CH

Willow Brook Prim Sch

Laurel Farm

BROWNS LA

Stanton Tunnel

1

Manor Farm

Business Park

Stanton-on-the-Wolds

Nursery

Black Plantation

The Pastures

THURLBY LA

A606

30

62 A B 63 C D 64 E F

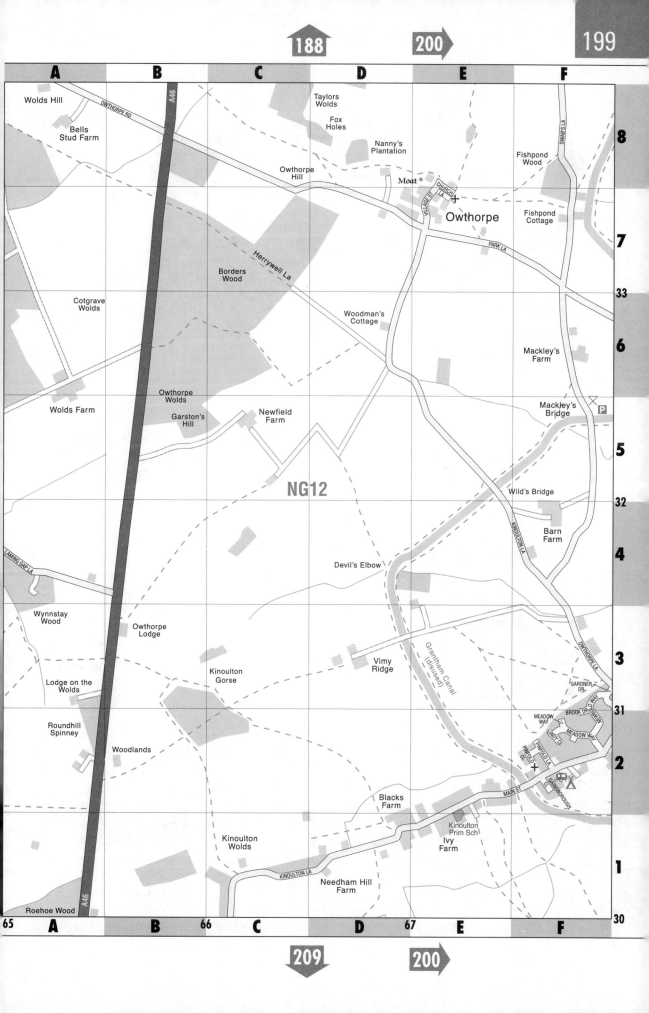

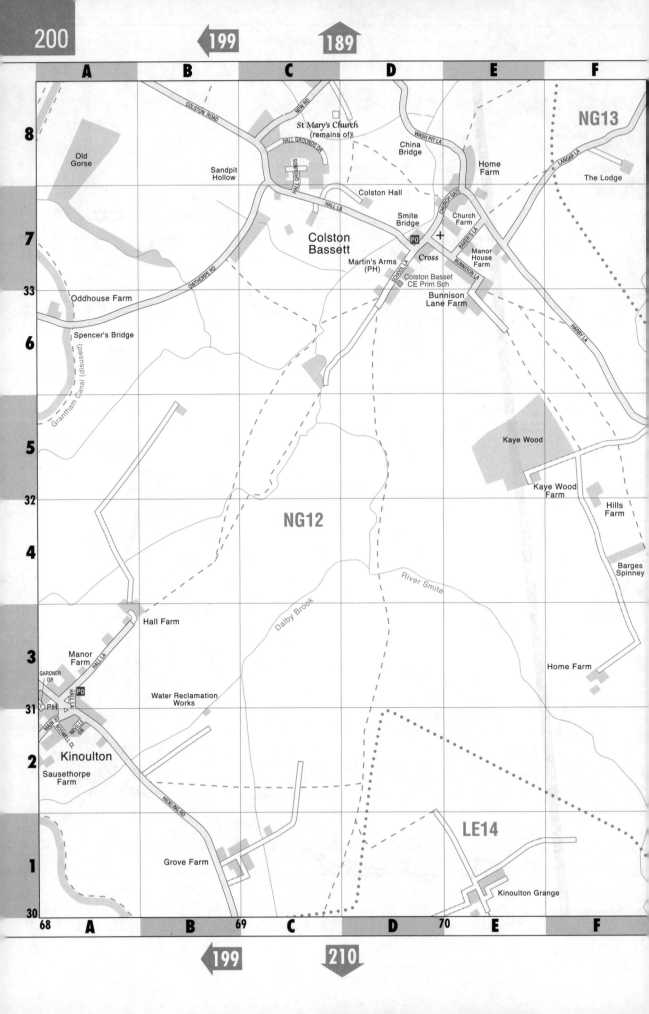

A B C D E F

NG13

8

Old
Gorse

COLSTON ROAD

NEW RD

St Mary's Church
(remains of)

WASH PIT LA

China
Bridge

Home
Farm

LANGAR LA

The Lodge

Sandpit
Hollow

HALL GROUNDS DR

Colston Hall

HALL GROUNDS

7

Colston
Bassett

HALL LA

Smite
Bridge

PO

CHURCH GATE

Church
Farm

Church
Farm

BAKER'S LA

Cross

Manor
House
Farm

OWTHORPE RD

Martin's Arms
(PH)

SCHOOL LA

Colston Basset
CE Prim Sch

BUNNISON LA

33

Oddhouse Farm

Bunnison
Lane Farm

6

Spencer's Bridge

HARBY LA

Grantham Canal (disused)

Kaye Wood

5

Kaye Wood
Farm

Hills
Farm

32

NG12

4

River Smite

Barges
Spinney

Dalby Brook

Hall Farm

3

Manor
Farm

HALL LA

Home Farm

GARDNER
DR

PO

Water Reclamation
Works

31

PH

HALL LA

MAIN ST

BISWELL CL

NEVILLE DR

2

Kinoulton

Sausethorpe
Farm

HICKLING RD

LE14

1

Grove Farm

Kinoulton Grange

30

68 A 69 B C 70 D E F

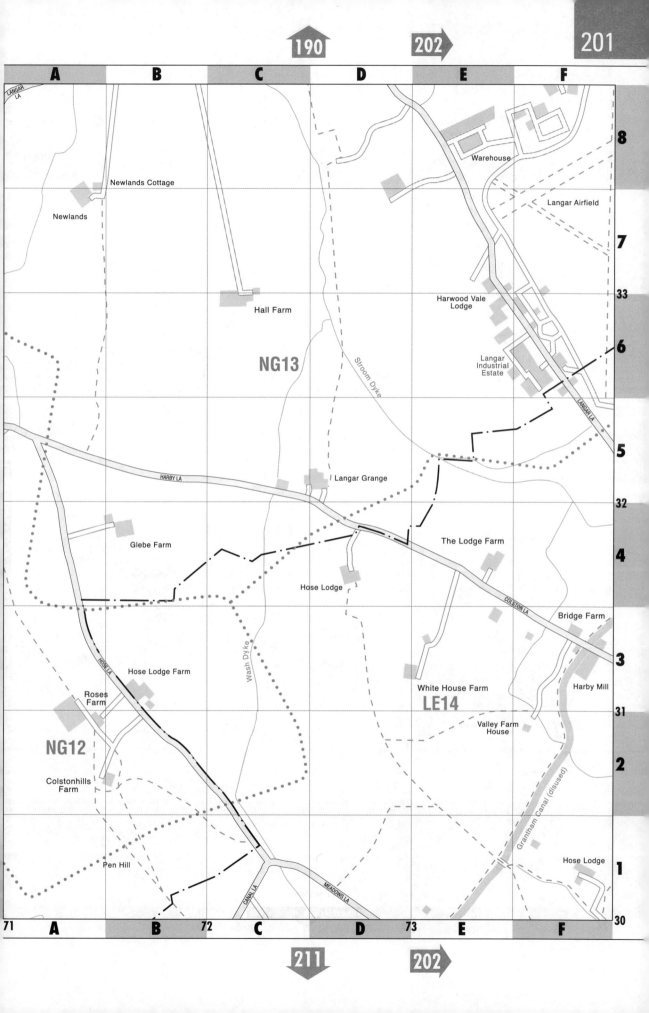

A B C D E F

8

7

33

6

5

32

4

3

31

2

1

30

Langar La

Newlands Cottage

Newlands

Hall Farm

NG13

Stroom Dyke

Warehouse

Langar Airfield

Harwood Vale Lodge

Langar Industrial Estate

Langar La

Harby La

Langar Grange

Glebe Farm

The Lodge Farm

Hose Lodge

Colston La

Bridge Farm

Wash Dyke

Hose La

Hose Lodge Farm

White House Farm

LE14

Harby Mill

Roses Farm

Valley Farm House

NG12

Colstonhills Farm

Grantham Canal (disused)

Hose Lodge

Pen Hill

Canal La

Meadows La

A   B   C   D   E   F

8

NG13

Anchor
Inn
(PH)
Home
Farm

Plungar

7

Small Farm
Ctr

Lodge
Farm

33

Woodland Farm

6

HARBY LA

Stathern Lodge

Stathern
Bridge

P

Rundle Beck

5

White House

32

LE14

Glebe Farm

Grantham Canal (disused)

Lodge
Farm

4

Washdyke
Farm

PENN LA

Langar Bridge

Canal
Farm

Kimberley
Farm

Stathern

3

Harby
CE Prim
Sch

P

BOYER'S ORCHARD

PINFOLD PL

STATHERN RD

HARBY LA

CITY RD

PO

GAS WALK

PINFOLD

SWALLOWS DR

COLSTON LA

NETHER ST

SCHOOL LA

WATSON'S LA

BURTON CL

BURDEN LA

WALNUT PADDOCK

TINKMAN'S LA

PH

31

White Hart
Inn
(PH)

MAIN ST

STATHERN LA

THE RED
CAUSEWAY

GREEN LA

2

Sewage
Works

Harby

1

HOSE LA

WALTHAM LA

Lodge Farm

Pasture Lane

Willow Farm

30

Leicestershire STREET ATLAS

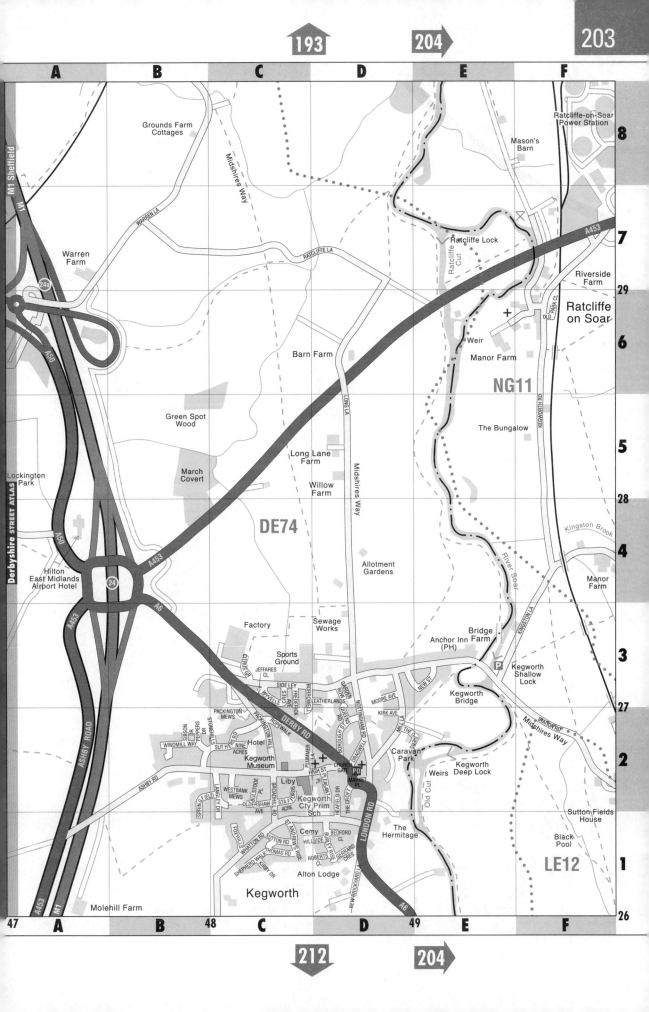

A B C D E F

Ratcliffe-on-Soar
Power Station

A453

Fox Covert

8

Winking Hill
Farm

Winking Hill

Stonepit
Farm

KEGWORTH RD

Woodlands

A453

Gotham
Wood

Hillside
Farm

WOOD LA

7

Kingston
Spinney

The Odells

Cuckoo Bush
Farm

29

Hillside

6

Moor
Wood

New
Kingston

NG11

Kingston
Works

Kingston
Spinney

W. LEAKE LA

Crownend Wood

Whitehills
Farm

WOSSOCK LANE

5

The Cottage

Lodge

Kingston
Park

Kingston Fields
Farm

KINGSTON CT

28

Kingston
Hall

Lumbry
Wood

Lodge

Church
Farm

KEGWORTH RD

4

THE GREEN

LONG
ROW

The Pool

WOSSOCK LA

Kingston
on Soar

3

Station
Plantation

Woodside

STATION RD

Scotland
Farm

27

DE74

Scotland
Wood

DARK LA

Cattle
Breeding
Centre

LE12

Moulter Hill

2

STATION RD

Playing
Field

MELTON LA

Kingston Brook

Midshires Way

VILLAGE FARM CL

MAIN ST

COLLEGE RD

PITHOUSE LA

Moat

1

Sewage
Works

Froghole
Farm

Domleo's
Spinney

PH

BRICKYARD LA

26

LANDCROFT LA

TROWELL LA

Univ of Nottingham
Sutton Bonington
Campus

50 A 51 B C 52 D E F

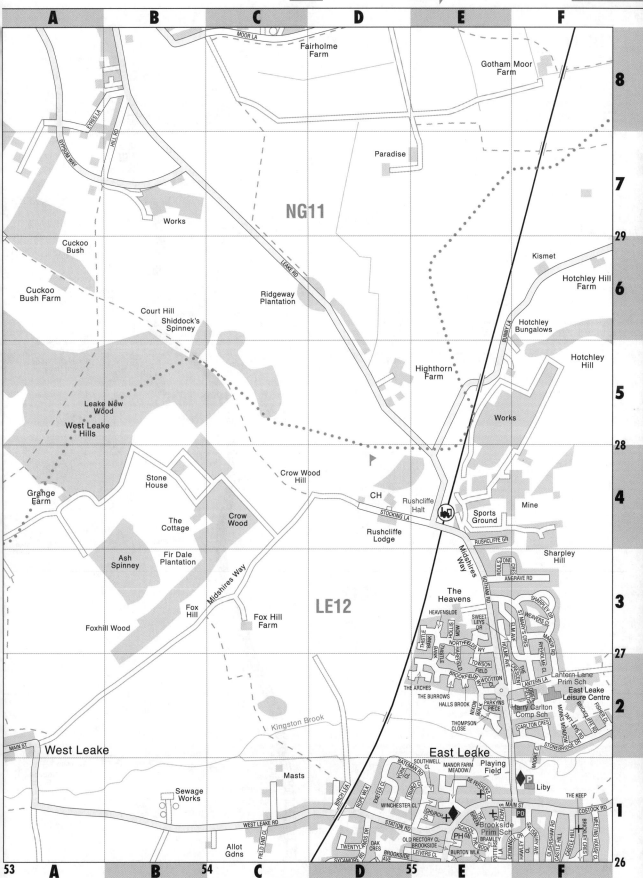

A B C D E F

NG11

8

Bunny Moor

The Walled Garden

Bunny CE Prim Sch

MOOR LA

Moor End Farm

MOOR VIEW

Bunny Park

Moor View

Grange Farm

CHURCH ST

MAIN ST

A60

LOUGHBOROUGH RD

Bunny Hall

PH

THOMAS PARKYN CL

PO

Bunny

Football Ground

7

Fairham Brook

NG11

Welldale Farm

BUNNY LA

GOTHAM LA

Midshires Way

Silver Seal Mine

29

Works

Woodside Farm

6

Hotchley Hill

Rough Hill

Works

Water House

New Wood

Chestnut Farm

Midshires Way

Bunny Old Wood Nature Reserve

5

Bunny Hill

BUNNY HILL

ASH LA

28

ASH LA

Hill Top Farm

Midshires Way

4

White Gates

Intake Wood

Highfields

3

LE12

Taft Leys

Grange Farm

Lantern Lane

27

The Cottage

Costock Hill

Field Farm

2

Stonebridge Dr

Sheep Plank Lane

Brook Furlong Farm

NOTTINGHAM RD

Fulwell Farm

Cemy

WYSALL RD

Westview

MANOR CL

CHURCH LA

CHAPEL

A60

OLD MAIN RD

Hotel

Nouvelle Farm

1

COSTOCK RD

LEAKE RD

MAIN ST

THE SQUARE

Glebe Farm

GABLES FARM DR

MILLER'S LA

LOUGHBOROUGH RD

The Elms Farm

BARS HILL

Costock CE Prim Sch

Costock

26

56 A B 57 C D 58 E F

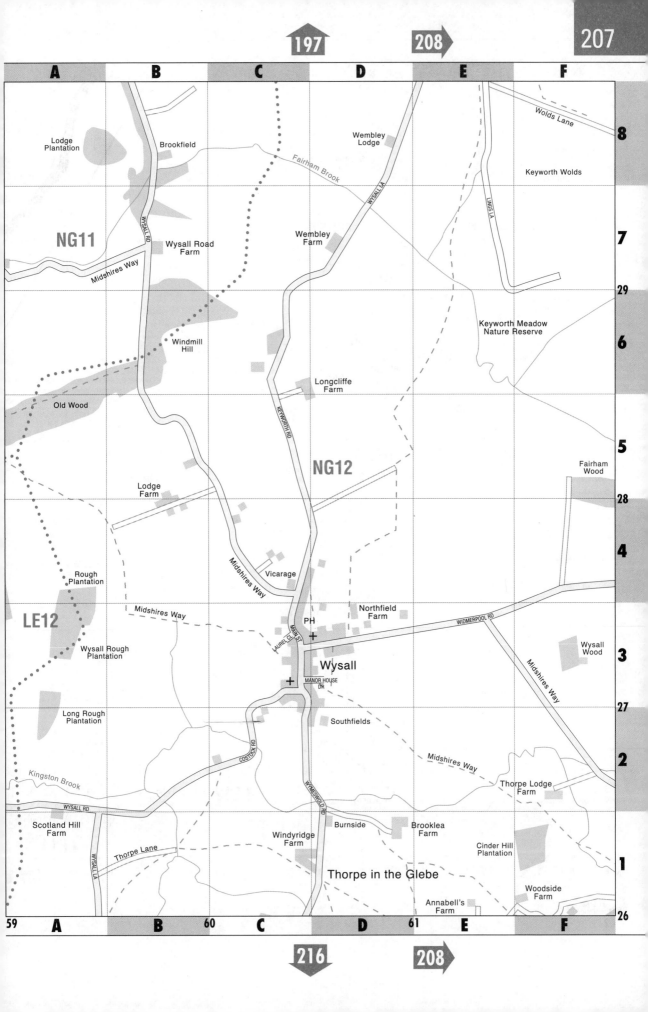

A B C D E F

8

Wolds Lane

Lodge
Plantation

Brookfield

Wembley
Lodge

Keyworth Wolds

Fairham Brook

NG11

7

WYSALL RD

Wysall Road
Farm

WYSALL LA

Wembley
Farm

LINGS LA

29

Midshires Way

Windmill
Hill

6

Keyworth Meadow
Nature Reserve

Old Wood

Longcliffe
Farm

KEYWORTH RD

5

Fairham
Wood

NG12

Lodge
Farm

28

Midshires Way

4

Rough
Plantation

Vicarage

Northfield
Farm

LE12

Midshires Way

PH

Wysall Rough
Plantation

MAIN ST

LAUREL CL

WIDMERPOOL RD

Wysall
Wood

Midshires Way

3

Wysall

Long Rough
Plantation

MANOR HOUSE
DR

27

Southfields

COSTOCK RD

Midshires Way

2

Kingston Brook

Thorpe Lodge
Farm

WYSALL RD

WYMESWOLD RD

Scotland Hill
Farm

Burnside

Brooklea
Farm

Cinder Hill
Plantation

WYSALL LA

Thorpe Lane

Windyridge
Farm

1

Woodside
Farm

Thorpe in the Glebe

Annabell's
Farm

26

A B C D E F

8

Wolds Lane

Keyworth Wolds

Stanton Lodge
Farm

THURLBY LA

A606

MELTON RD

Roehoe
Lodge

The
Borders

A606

7

Wolds Farm

Roehoe Brook

Hill Farm

Schooner
Inn
(PH)

29

North Lodge
Farm

NG12

Queensgate
Wood

STATION RD

6

The
Stonepits

Crow Hill

Widmerpool
Hall

5

Morris's
Plantation

Park
Farm

OLD HALL DR

KEYWORTH RD

The Grange

Flint
Hill

Manor
Farm

CHURCH LA

BROOKLANDS

28

Widmerpool

Fairham Brook

Fields Farm

PEN LA

4

Sports
Ground

WYSALL RD

WIDMERPOOL RD

Green Hill

Greenhill
Plantation

South
Lodge

3

Magpie
Plantation

WILLOUGHBY RD

27

Manor Farm

LE12

Willoughby
Lodge

2

Willoughby
Lodge

Lodge
Farm

LE14

1

Homeward

Midshires Way

The Grey
House

Kingston Brook

MELLA

Fosse
Lodge

26

Thorpe
Plantation

62 A 63 B C 64 D E F

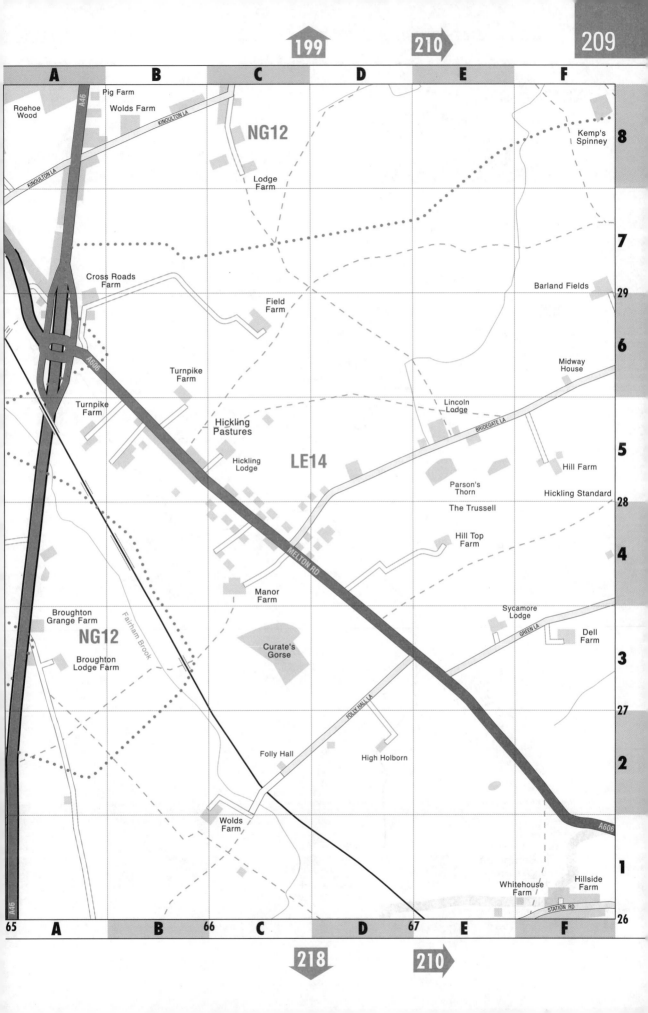

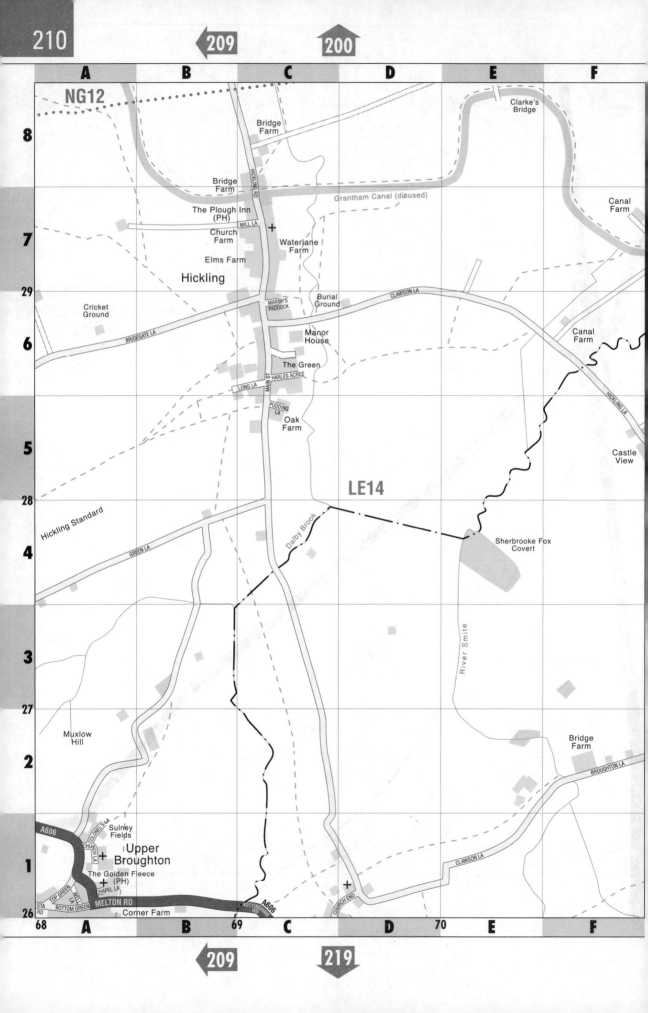

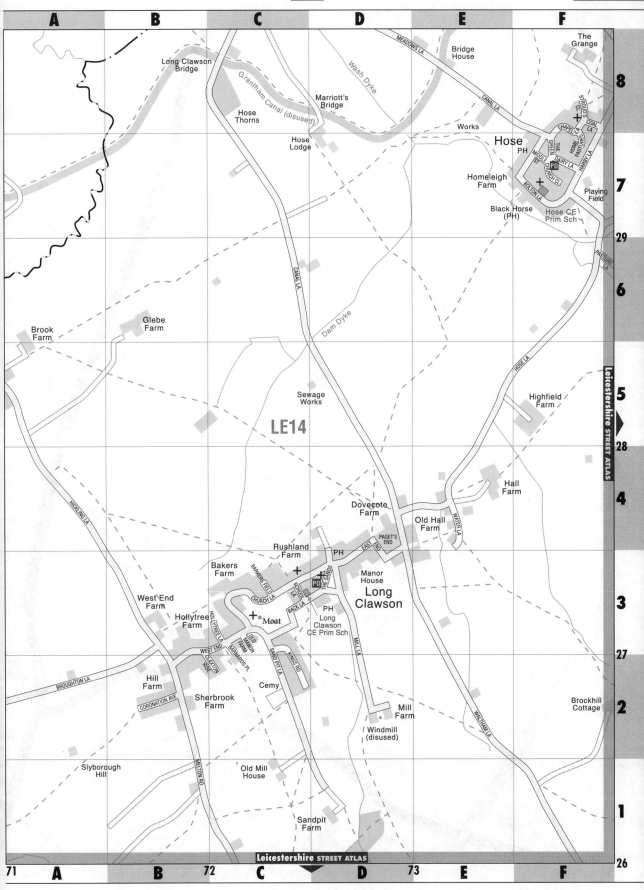

The Grange

8

Long Clawson
Bridge

Grantham Canal (disused)

Marriott's
Bridge

Wash Dyke

MEADOWS LA

Bridge
House

CANAL LA

Hose
Thorns

Hose
Lodge

Works

Hose

Homeleigh
Farm

Black Horse
(PH)

Hose CE
Prim Sch

Playing
Field

7

29

6

Brook
Farm

Glebe
Farm

Dam Dyke

CANAL LA

Sewage
Works

HOSE LA

Highfield
Farm

5

28

LE14

HICKLING LA

Hall
Farm

4

Dovecote
Farm

Old Hall
Farm

WATER LA

Rushland
Farm

PH

EAST END

PAGET'S
END

Manor
House

Bakers
Farm

West End
Farm

Hollytree
Farm

Moat

Long
Clawson

Long
Clawson
CE Prim Sch

MILL LA

3

27

BROUGHTON LA

Hill
Farm

Cemy

Sherbrook
Farm

Mill
Farm

WALTHAM LA

Brockhill
Cottage

2

Windmill
(disused)

Slyborough
Hill

MELTON RD

Old Mill
House

Sandpit
Farm

1

26

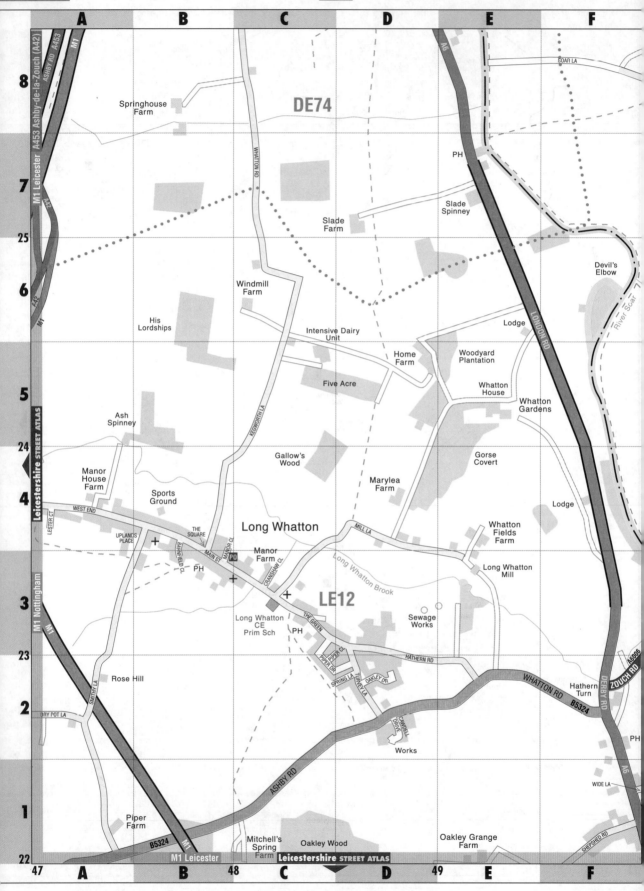

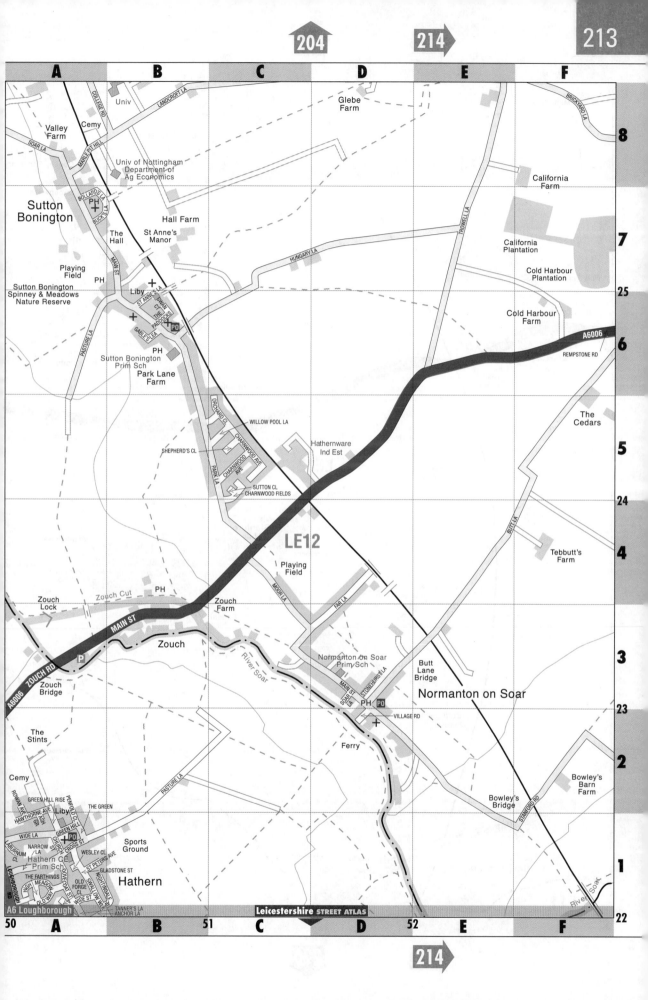

A B C D E F

8

Glebe
Farm

BRICKYARD LA

College Rd

Univ

Landcroft La

Valley
Farm

Cemy

California
Farm

Soar La

Maple Pit Hill

Univ of Nottingham
Department of
Ag Economics

7

Sutton
Bonington

Hall Farm

St Anne's
Manor

The Hall

California
Plantation

Hungary La

Trowell La

Cold Harbour
Plantation

25

Playing
Field

PH

Buck's La

Main St

Liby

St Anne's La

Swan La

Sutton Bonington
Spinney & Meadows
Nature Reserve

The Paddocks

PO

Cold Harbour
Farm

6

Pasture La

PH

Gable La

Flea La

Sutton Bonington
Prim Sch

A6006

Rempstone Rd

Park Lane
Farm

The
Cedars

5

Orchard Cl

Willow Pool La

Hathernware
Ind Est

Charnwood Ave

Shepherd's Cl

Park La

Charnwood Ave

Sutton Cl
Charnwood Fields

24

LE12

Butt La

Tebbutt's
Farm

4

Playing
Field

Moor La

Zouch Cut

PH

Far La

Zouch
Lock

Zouch Farm

MAIN ST

3

Zouch

Normanton on Soar
Prim Sch

Butt
Lane
Bridge

A6006 ZOUCH RD

River Soar

Main St

Stonehurst La

P

Zouch
Bridge

Normanton on Soar

PH PO

23

The
Stints

Village Rd

Cemy

Ferry

2

Rowan Ave

Green Hill Rise

Penfold Cl

Pasture La

Bowley's
Barn
Farm

Hawthorne Ave

Liby

The Green

Green Hill

Stanford Rd

Bowley's
Bridge

Wide La

PO

Narrow
La

Cross St

Church St

Sports
Ground

Wesley Cl

Laburnum
Cl

Hathern CE
Prim Sch

St Peters Ave

Gladstone St

1

The Farthings

High St

Dovecote St

Shallow La

Nightingale

Old
Forge
Cl

Loughborough Rd

Old Way

Meadow

Hathern

Tanner's La

Anchor La

A6 Loughborough

Leicestershire STREET ATLAS

22

50 A B 51 C 52 D E F

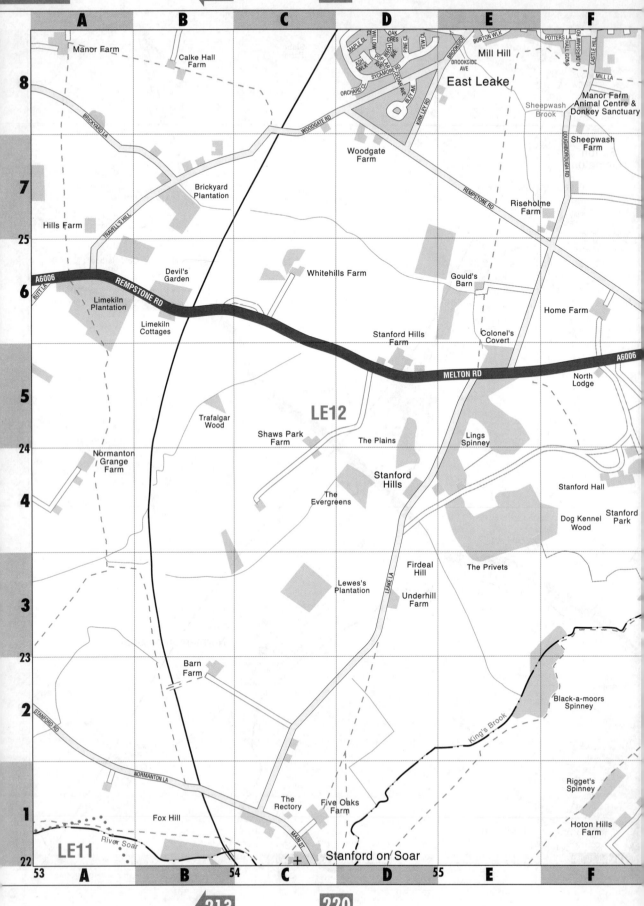

A B C D E F

8

7

25

6

5

24

4

3

23

2

1

22

53   A   B   54   C   55   D   E   F

Manor Farm

Calke Hall Farm

BRICKYARD LA

Woodgate RD

MAPLE CL
ASH WLK
ORCHARD CL
SYCAMORE RD
POP LAR AVE
BIRCH AVE
PINE CL
CEDAR AVE
OAK CRES
YEW CL
MO TT IMA
BROOKSIDE
BROOKSIDE AVE
BURTON WLK
POTTERS LA
THILL GDNS
OLDERSHAW RD
CASTLE HILL
MILL LA

Mill Hill

East Leake

Woodgate Farm

Manor Farm Animal Centre & Donkey Sanctuary

Sheepwash Brook

Sheepwash Farm

LOUGHBOROUGH RD

Brickyard Plantation

REMPSTONE RD

Riseholme Farm

Hills Farm

TRAFELL'S HILL

BUTT LA

A6006

REMPSTONE RD

Devil's Garden

Whitehills Farm

Gould's Barn

Home Farm

Limekiln Plantation

Limekiln Cottages

Stanford Hills Farm

Colonel's Covert

MELTON RD

A6006

North Lodge

LE12

Trafalgar Wood

Shaws Park Farm

The Plains

Lings Spinney

Normanton Grange Farm

The Evergreens

Stanford Hills

Stanford Hall

Dog Kennel Wood

Stanford Park

Lewes's Plantation

LEAKE LA

Firdeal Hill

The Privets

Underhill Farm

Barn Farm

Black-a-moors Spinney

King's Brook

STANFORD RD

NORMANTON LA

The Rectory

Five Oaks Farm

Rigget's Spinney

Fox Hill

MAIN ST

Hoton Hills Farm

LE11

River Soar

Stanford on Soar

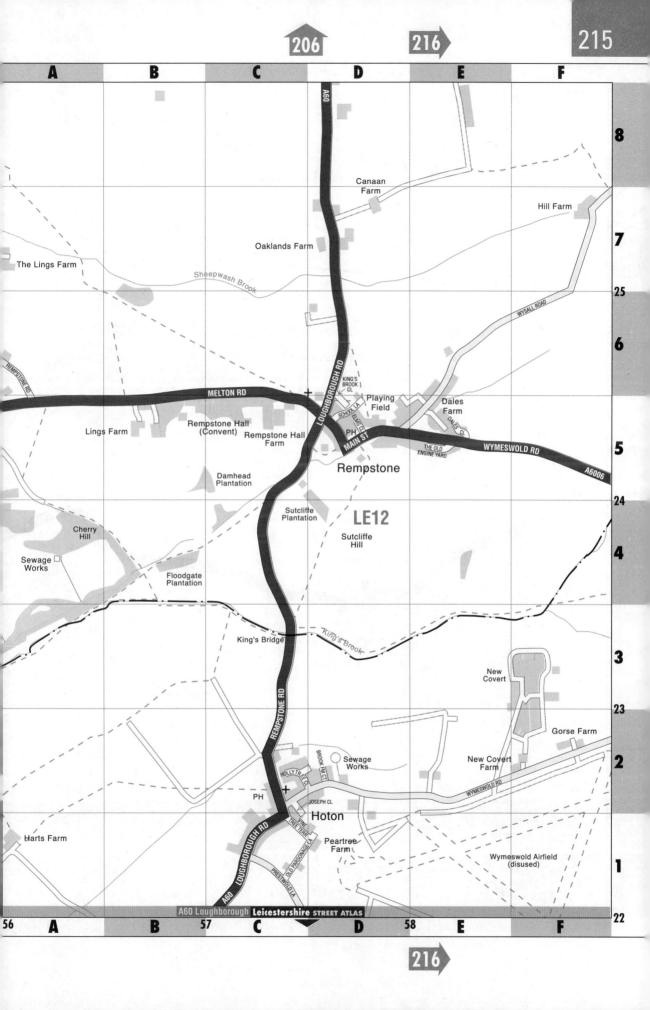

A   B   C   D   E   F

8

7

25

6

A60

Canaan Farm

Hill Farm

Oaklands Farm

The Lings Farm

Sheepwash Brook

WYSALL ROAD

LOUGHBOROUGH RD

KING'S BROOK CL

Playing Field

Dales Farm

MELTON RD

SCHOOL LA

ELMS CL

DALES CL

Lings Farm

Rempstone Hall (Convent)

Rempstone Hall Farm

PH

MAIN ST

WYMESWOLD RD

A6006

THE OLD ENGINE YARD

Rempstone

5

Damhead Plantation

Sutcliffe Plantation

LE12

24

Cherry Hill

Sutcliffe Hill

4

Sewage Works

Floodgate Plantation

REMPSTONE RD

King's Bridge

King's Brook

New Covert

3

23

Gorse Farm

New Covert Farm

Sewage Works

WYMESWOLD RD

2

BROOK FM CT

HOLLY TR

BEECH

PH

JOSEPH CL

Hoton

Harts Farm

LOUGHBOROUGH RD

PRESTWOLD LA

OLD PARSONAGE LA

TREE TERR

Peartree Farm

Wymeswold Airfield (disused)

1

A60

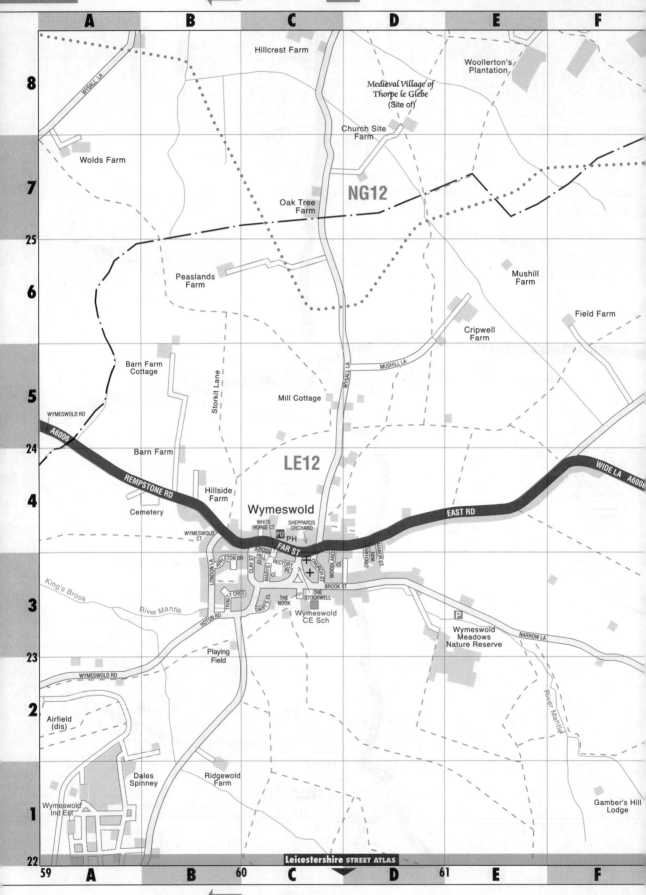

8

7

25

6

5

24

4

3

23

2

1

22

Hillcrest Farm

Woollerton's
Plantation

Medieval Village of
Thorpe le Glebe
(Site of)

Church Site
Farm

NG12

WYSALL LA

Wolds Farm

Oak Tree
Farm

Peaslands
Farm

Mushill
Farm

Field Farm

Barn Farm
Cottage

Storkit Lane

Mill Cottage

WYSALL LA

MUSHILL LA

Cripwell
Farm

WYMESWOLD RD

A6006

Barn Farm

LE12

WIDE LA A600

REMPSTONE RD

Hillside
Farm

Wymeswold

EAST RD

Cemetery

WHITE
HORSE CT

SHEPPARDS
ORCHARD

PO

FAR ST

PH

MANOR CT

ORCHARD WAY

WYMESWOLD
CT

APPLETON DR

LONDON LA

CROSS
HILL

CLAY ST

MARY'S CL

RECTORY
PL

CHURCH ST

WOODLANDS
CL

King's Brook

River Mantle

HOTON RD

TRINITY CRES

SWAN'S CL

THE
NOOK

THE
STOCKWELL

BROOK ST

Wymeswold
CE Sch

P

Wymeswold
Meadows
Nature Reserve

NARROW LA

River Mantle

Playing
Field

WYMESWOLD RD

Airfield
(dis)

Dales
Spinney

Ridgewold
Farm

Gamber's Hill
Lodge

Wymeswold
Ind Est

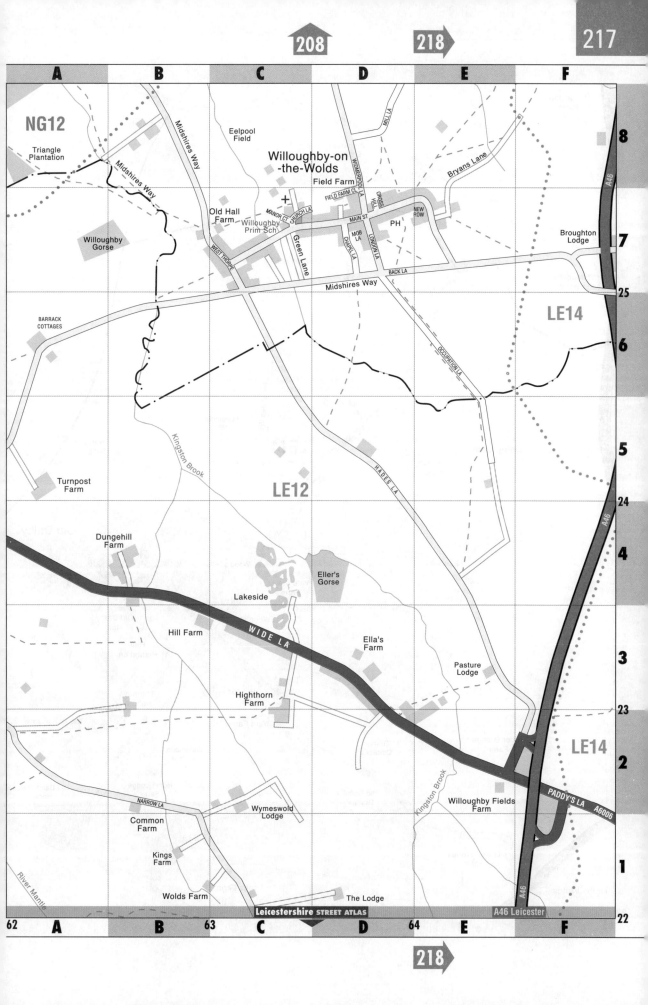

A   B   C   D   E   F

NG12

Triangle
Plantation

Midshires Way

Midshires Way

Eelpool
Field

Willoughby-on
-the-Wolds

Field Farm

Old Hall
Farm

WEST THORPE

Willoughby
Prim Sch

MANOR CT

CHURCH LA

Green Lane

Field Farm Cl

MAIN ST

CHAPEL LA

MOB LA

LONDON LA

WIDMERPOOL LA

MILL LA

CROSS HILL

NEW ROW

Bryans Lane

PH

Broughton
Lodge

Willoughby
Gorse

BACK LA

Midshires Way

LE14

25

BARRACK
COTTAGES

OCCUPATION LA

6

Kingston Brook

Turnpost
Farm

LE12

HADES LA

5

24

Dungehill
Farm

4

Eller's
Gorse

Lakeside

Hill Farm

WIDE LA

Ella's
Farm

Pasture
Lodge

A46

3

Highthorn
Farm

23

LE14

2

NARROW LA

Wymeswold
Lodge

Kingston Brook

Willoughby Fields
Farm

PADDY'S LA

A6006

Common
Farm

Kings
Farm

River Mantle

Wolds Farm

The Lodge

A46

A46 Leicester

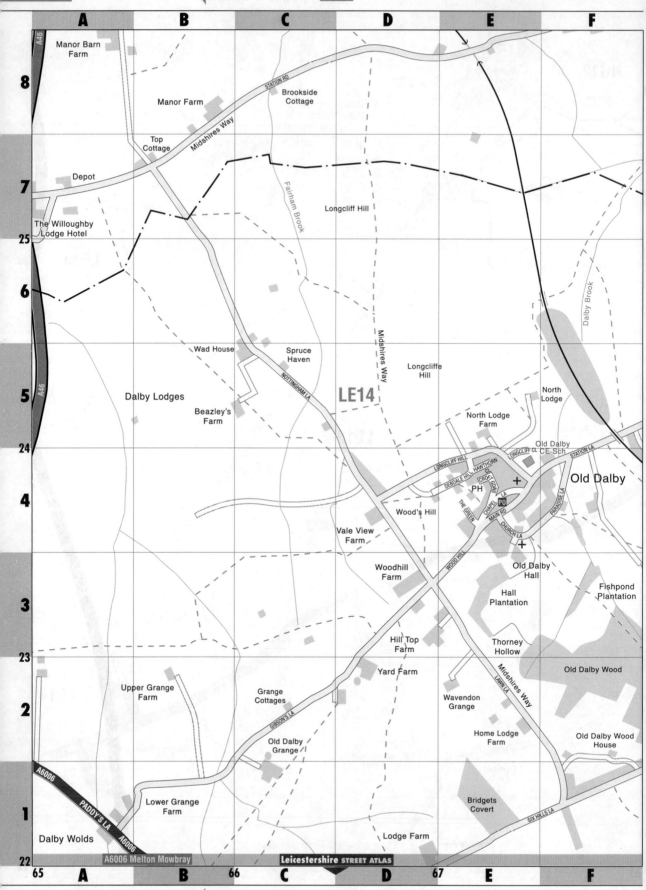

A   B   C   D   E   F

Manor Barn Farm

8

Manor Farm

Brookside Cottage

STATION RD

Midshires Way

Top Cottage

Depot

7

The Willoughby Lodge Hotel

Fairham Brook

Longcliff Hill

25

A46

6

Wad House

Spruce Haven

NOTTINGHAM LA

Midshires Way

Dalby Lodges

Beazley's Farm

LE14

Longcliffe Hill

North Lodge

North Lodge Farm

5

A46

Old Dalby CE Sch

STATION LA

24

Longcliff Hill

DEBDALE HILL

HAWTHORN CL

CROS GDNS

LONGCLIFF CL

Old Dalby

4

Wood's Hill

THE GREEN

PH

CHAPEL LA

MAIN RD

PO

CHURCH LA

PARADISE LA

Vale View Farm

Woodhill Farm

WOOD HILL

Old Dalby Hall

Hall Plantation

Fishpond Plantation

3

Thorney Hollow

Old Dalby Wood

23

Hill Top Farm

Upper Grange Farm

Grange Cottages

Yard Farm

Wavendon Grange

LAWN LA

Midshires Way

2

GIBSON'S LA

Old Dalby Grange

Home Lodge Farm

Old Dalby Wood House

A6006

PADDY'S LA

A6006

Lower Grange Farm

Bridgets Covert

1

SIX HILLS LA

Dalby Wolds

Lodge Farm

22

65 A   B 66 C   D 67 E   F

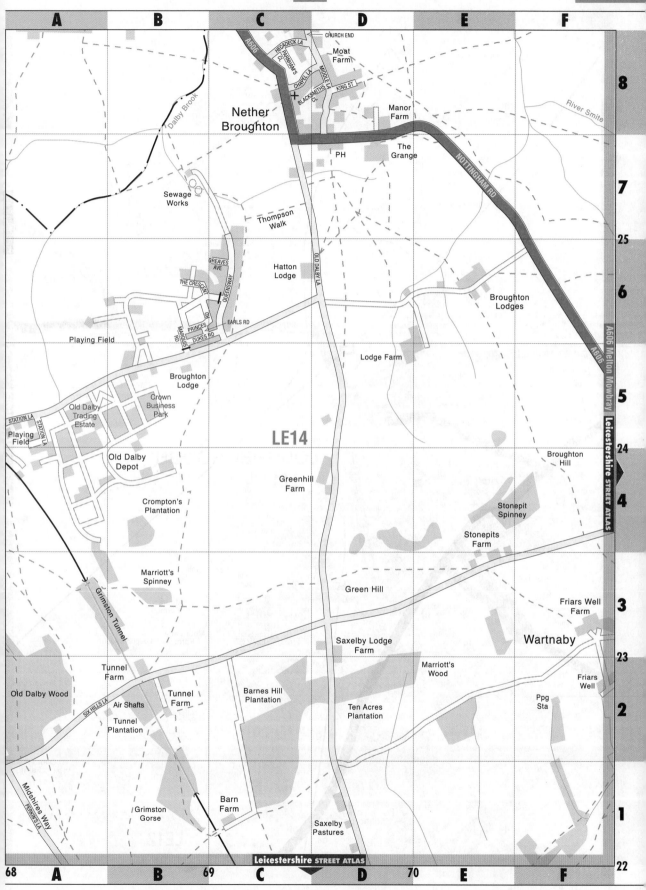

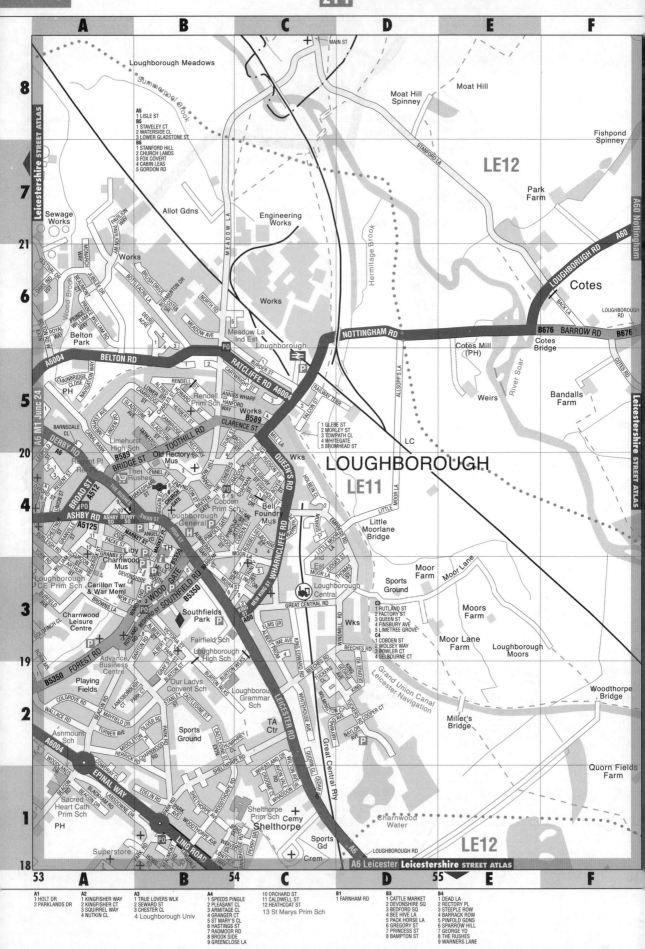

A5
1 LISLE ST
B5
1 STAVELEY CT
2 WATERSIDE CL
3 LOWER GLADSTONE ST
B6
1 STANFORD HILL
2 CHURCH LANDS
3 FOX COVERT
4 CABIN LEAS
5 GORDON RD

LE12

Moat Hill
Spinney

Moat Hill

Fishpond
Spinney

Park
Farm

Loughborough Meadows

Sewage
Works

Allot Gdns

Engineering
Works

Cotes

Belton
Park

Works

Works

NOTTINGHAM RD

BARROW RD

Cotes Mill
(PH)

Cotes
Bridge

BELTON RD

Meadow La
Ind Est

Loughborough

Weirs

Bandalls
Farm

RATCLIFFE RD A6004

B589

TOOTHILL RD

CLARENCE ST

Works

1 GLEBE ST
2 MORLEY ST
3 TOWPATH CL
4 WHITEGATE
5 BROMHEAD ST

LC

LOUGHBOROUGH

LE11

Limehurst
High Sch

Old Rectory
Mus

The
Rushes

Wks

Little
Moorlane
Bridge

Moor
Farm

BROAD ST

ASHBY RD

A5125

Cobden
Prim Sch

Bell
Foundry
Mus

Loughborough
General

Sports
Ground

Moors
Farm

Liby

Charnwood
Mus

WOOD GATE

SOUTHFIELD RD

B5350

Loughborough
Central

C3
1 RUTLAND ST
2 FACTORY ST
3 QUEEN ST
4 FINSBURY AVE
5 LIMETREE GROVE
C4
1 COBDEN ST
2 WOLSEY WAY
3 BOWLER CT
4 SELBOURNE CT

Moor Lane
Farm

Loughborough
Moors

Charnwood
Leisure
Centre

Southfields
Park

GREAT CENTRAL RD

Wks

Charnwood
CE Prim Sch

Fairfield Sch

BEECHES RD

Grand Union Canal
Leicester Navigation

Woodthorpe
Bridge

FOREST RD

Advance
Business
Centre

Loughborough
High Sch

Our Ladys
Convent Sch

Loughborough
Grammar
Sch

B5350

Playing
Fields

LEICESTER RD

Miller's
Bridge

Ashmount
Sch

A6004

Sports
Ground

TA
Ctr

Quorn Fields
Farm

EPINAL WAY

Sacred
Heart Cath
Prim Sch

LING ROAD

Shelthorpe
Prim Sch

Shelthorpe

Cemy

Charnwood
Water

LE12

Superstore

Sports
Gd

Crem

A6 Leicester Leicestershire STREET ATLAS

A1
1 HOLT DR
2 PARKLANDS DR

A2
1 KINGFISHER WAY
2 KINGFISHER CT
3 SQUIRREL WAY
4 NUTKIN CL

A3
1 TRUE LOVERS WLK
2 SEWARD ST
3 CHESTER CL
4 Loughborough Univ

A4
1 SPEEDS PINGLE
2 PLEASANT CL
3 ARMITAGE CL
4 GRANGER CT
5 ST MARY'S CL
6 HASTINGS ST
7 RADMOOR RD
8 BROOK SIDE
9 GREENCLOSE LA

10 ORCHARD ST
11 CALDWELL ST
12 HEATHCOAT ST
13 St Marys Prim Sch

B1
1 FARNHAM RD

B3
1 CATTLE MARKET
2 DEVONSHIRE SQ
3 BEDFORD SQ
4 BEE HIVE LA
5 PACK HORSE LA
6 GREGORY ST
7 PRINCESS ST
8 BAMPTON ST

B4
1 DEAD LA
2 RECTORY PL
3 STEEPLE ROW
4 BARRACK ROW
5 PINFOLD GDNS
6 SPARROW HILL
7 GEORGE YD
8 THE RUSHES
9 WARNERS LANE

Nottingham approaches

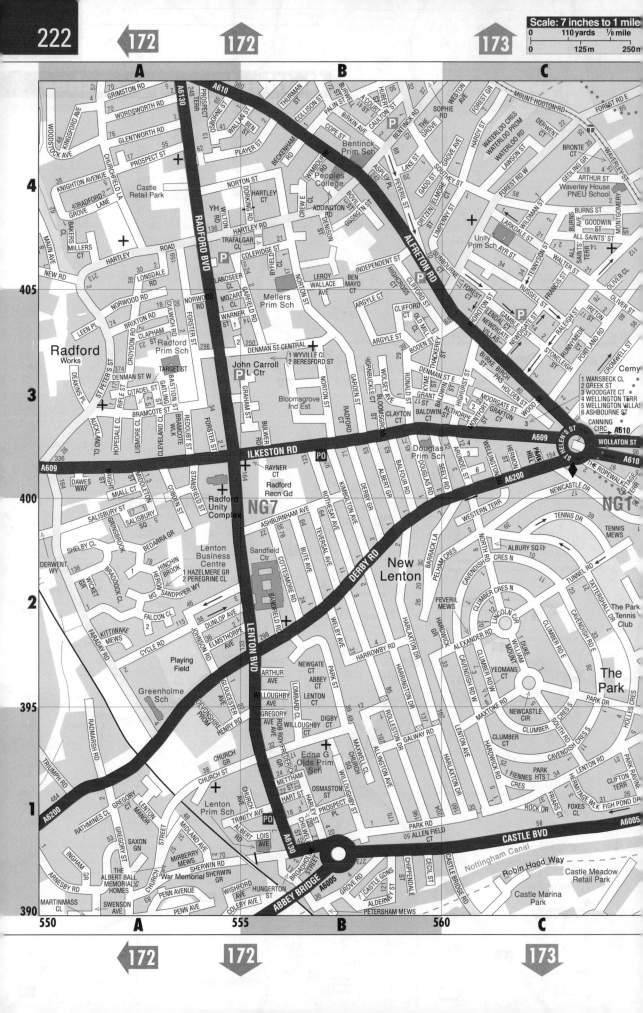

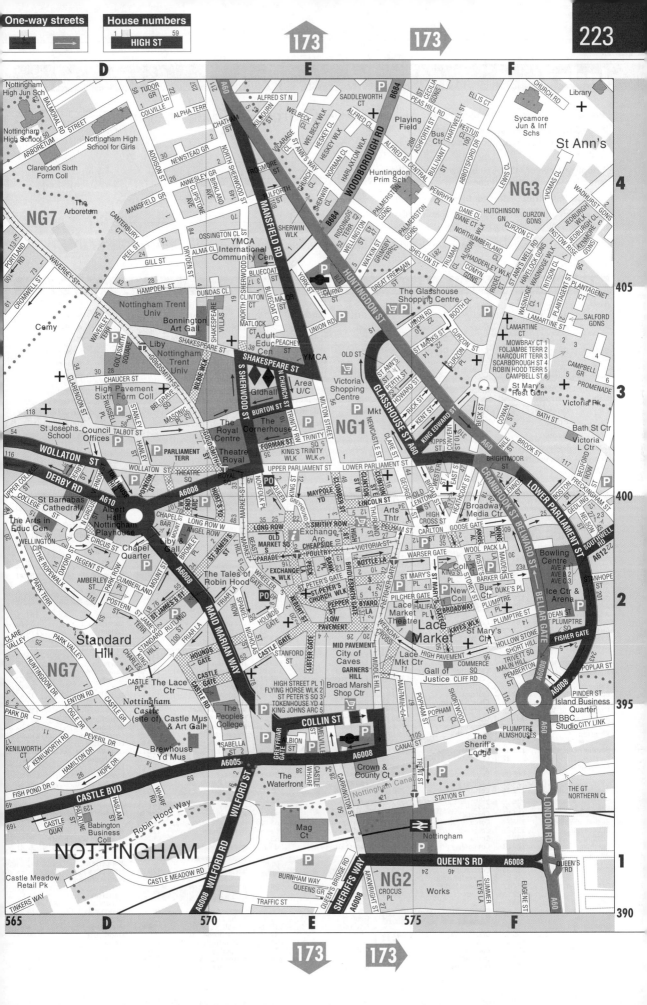

Index

Place name May be abbreviated on the map

Location number Present when a number indicates the place's position in a crowded area of mapping

Locality, town or village Shown when more than one place has the same name

Postcode district District for the indexed place

Page and grid square Page number and grid reference for the standard mapping

Church Rd 6 Beckenham BR2..........**53** C6

Public and commercial buildings are highlighted in **magenta**   **Places of interest** are highlighted in **blue** with a star★

Abbreviations used in the index

Acad	**Academy**	Comm	**Common**	Gd	**Ground**	L	**Leisure**	Prom	**Promenade**
App	**Approach**	Cott	**Cottage**	Gdn	**Garden**	La	**Lane**	Rd	**Road**
Arc	**Arcade**	Cres	**Crescent**	Gn	**Green**	Liby	**Library**	Recn	**Recreation**
Ave	**Avenue**	Cswy	**Causeway**	Gr	**Grove**	Mdw	**Meadow**	Ret	**Retail**
Bglw	**Bungalow**	Ct	**Court**	H	**Hall**	Meml	**Memorial**	Sh	**Shopping**
Bldg	**Building**	Ctr	**Centre**	Ho	**House**	Mkt	**Market**	Sq	**Square**
Bsns, Bus	**Business**	Ctry	**Country**	Hospl	**Hospital**	Mus	**Museum**	St	**Street**
Bvd	**Boulevard**	Cty	**County**	HQ	**Headquarters**	Orch	**Orchard**	Sta	**Station**
Cath	**Cathedral**	Dr	**Drive**	Hts	**Heights**	Pal	**Palace**	Terr	**Terrace**
Cir	**Circus**	Dro	**Drove**	Ind	**Industrial**	Par	**Parade**	TH	**Town Hall**
Cl	**Close**	Ed	**Education**	Inst	**Institute**	Pas	**Passage**	Univ	**University**
Cnr	**Corner**	Emb	**Embankment**	Int	**International**	Pk	**Park**	Wk, Wlk	**Walk**
Coll	**College**	Est	**Estate**	Intc	**Interchange**	Pl	**Place**	Wr	**Water**
Com	**Community**	Ex	**Exhibition**	Junc	**Junction**	Prec	**Precinct**	Yd	**Yard**

Index of localities, towns and villages

A

Adbolton	174	B2
Aldercar	143	A4
Annesley	130	C8
Annesley Woodhouse	129	E8
Arnold	162	A7
Askham	51	F2
Aslockton	179	A5
Astwith	85	A5
Attenborough	183	E2
Ault Hucknall	85	F7
Austerfield	3	C2
Averham	123	F2
Awsworth	158	C4

B

Babworth	39	A6
Bakers Fields	174	C6
Balderton	140	E3
Barkestone-le-Vale	192	C2
Barnby in the Willows	141	F5
Barnby Moor	28	C5
Barnstone	190	F3
Barton in Fabis	194	E6
Bathley	110	A3
Bawtry	10	B7
Beckingham		
Lincs	142	D8
Notts	14	B1
Beechdale	172	B6
Beeston	183	A6
Besthorpe	97	E6
Bestwood	161	B7
Bestwood Village	146	F4
Bilborough	171	E7
Bilsthorpe	105	E6
Bingham	177	E3
Bircotes	9	D4
Bleasby	152	B8
Blidworth	118	B4
Blyth	18	A3
Bobbers Mill	172	E7
Bole	23	E3
Bothamsall	63	E7
Bottesford	181	C3
Boughton	77	F5
Bracebridge	36	A3
Bradmore	196	F3
Bramcote	183	A4
Bramcote Hills	171	C2
Breaston	193	A8
Brinsley	143	E7

Broadholme	57	B1
Brough	112	B1
Broxholme	57	E8
Budby	75	F8
Bulcote	164	A6
Bulwell	160	A6
Bunny	206	E7
Burton Joyce	163	E4

C

Calverton	149	A7
Car Colston	166	C2
Carlton	162	D1
Carlton in Lindrick	25	F5
Carlton-on-Trent	96	E4
Carr Hill	11	A4
Carrington	161	B2
Caunton	109	B4
Caythorpe	165	B4
Chilwell	183	D6
Church Warsop	74	A7
Cinderhill	160	B4
Clarborough	30	E4
Claypole	156	D7
Clayworth	21	D6
Clifton	184	F1
Clipston	187	C1
Clipstone	89	F3
Coates	43	E7
Coddington	126	A2
Collingham	98	A2
Colston Bassett	200	C7
Colwick	174	F5
Cossall	158	C1
Costock	206	C1
Cotes	220	F6
Cotgrave	187	E2
Cotham	154	F4
Cotmanhay	157	E4
Cottam	43	D4
Creswell	58	D8
Cromwell	110	E7
Cropwell Bishop	189	A6
Cropwell Butler	189	B7
Cuckney	60	A4

D

Dalesworth	101	B5
Darlton	67	B7
Daybrook	161	D7
Doddington	71	C1
Drakeholes	11	F1

Dry Doddington	156	E1
Dunham on Trent	54	C2
Dunkirk	172	E2

E

Eagle	84	C3
Eakring	92	F1
East Bridgford	165	D3
East Drayton	53	A3
East Leake	205	E2
East Markham	65	F7
East Stockwith	7	E1
East Stoke	153	D8
Eastwood	143	E3
Eaton	40	A1
Edingley	120	C4
Edwalton	186	B3
Edwinstowe	76	A1
Egmanton	79	E6
Elkesley	50	B3
Elmton	58	A7
Elston	153	E5
Epperstone	150	A6
Everton	11	C3

F

Farndon	139	B4
Farnsfield	119	E6
Fenton		
Balderton	142	D2
Saxilby	55	D6
Firbeck	16	A6
Fiskerton	137	E3
Flawborough	168	C2
Fledborough	68	C5
Flintham	153	A1
Forest Town	89	B1

G

Gainsborough	24	E5
Gamston		
Retford	51	A5
West Bridgford	186	D7
Gedling	162	F2
Giltbrook	158	C8
Girton	82	E1
Glapwell	86	C8
Gotham	195	A1
Granby	191	C5
Grassthorpe	81	E4

Greasley	144	E3
Gringley on the Hill	12	E1
Grove	40	F4
Gunthorpe	164	F5

H

Halam	120	E1
Halloughton	136	B4
Harby		
Leics	202	B2
Notts	70	E2
Hardstoft	85	A3
Harwell	11	A4
Harworth	8	F5
Hathern	213	B1
Haughton	63	F6
Hawksworth	167	C4
Hawton	139	E3
Hayton	30	D6
Headon	52	B7
Heanor	143	B2
Hempshill Vale	159	E6
Hickling	210	B7
High Marnham	68	B1
Hilcote	99	C1
Hockerton	122	B6
Hodsock	26	E7
Hodthorpe	45	C6
Holbeck	59	C7
Holme	111	A3
Holme Pierrepont	175	B3
Hose	211	F7
Hoton	215	D1
Hoveringham	151	D2
Hucknall	145	E6
Huthwaite	99	E3
Hyson Green	172	F7

I

Ilkeston	170	B7

K

Kegworth	203	C1
Kelham	124	B4
Kersall	94	B1
Kettlethorpe	55	C4
Keyworth	197	F2
Kimberley	158	E8
Kingston on Soar	204	A4
Kinoulton	200	A2

Kirkby in Ashfield	115	C4
Kirkby Woodhouse	114	D1
Kirklington	120	E8
Kirkstead	113	D3
Kirton	78	C6
Kneesall	93	F5
Kneeton	152	A1

L

Lambley	163	C8
Laneham	54	B6
Langar	190	D2
Langford	111	E1
Langley Mill	143	B3
Langold	16	E4
Langwith	72	F8
Laughterton	55	A4
Laxton	79	C3
Lea	24	F2
Letwell	16	A3
Lidgett	91	B8
Linby	131	A3
Little Carlton	124	B8
Ilkeston	157	D2
Long Clawson	211	D3
Long Eaton	193	C7
Long Whatton	212	C4
Loughborough	220	C4
Lound	29	C8
Lowdham	150	D1
Low Marnham	82	A8
Ironville	128	A3

M

Mansfield	102	C8
Mansfield Woodhouse	88	C4
Manton	36	B1
Maplebeck	108	A6
Mapperley	161	E4
Mapperley Park	161	E3
Market Warsop	74	C4
Marton	44	B8
Mattersey	20	C7
Meadows	173	C2
Meden Vale	74	E8
Misson	4	B2
Misterton	6	F1
Moorhouse	80	C2
Morton		
Lincs	15	C4
Notts	137	D3
Muston	181	F1

N

Nether Broughton......219 C8
Netherfield...........175 B6
Nether Langwith.......59 B1
Newark-on-Trent......140 C7
New Balderton........140 B5
New Cross...........100 E4
New Houghton.........86 F7
Newington...........10 E8
New Lenton..........172 F4
New Ollerton.........77 E5
Newstead...........130 E5
Newton.............99 B3
Newton on Trent......55 A1
Normanton on Soar....213 E3
Normanton-on-the-
  Wolds.............198 A6
Normanton on Trent....81 D6
North Clifton.........68 E6
North Leverton with
  Habblesthorpe......42 D8
North Muskham.......110 E1
North Scarle.........83 E2
North Wheatley.......31 D8
Norwell............110 A7
Nottingham..........173 B3
Nuncargate..........115 A1
Nuthall............159 D5

O

Old Clipstone........90 C6
Oldcotes............17 A6
Old Dalby..........218 F4
Old Lenton..........172 D3
Ollerton............77 B3
Ompton.............93 B7
Orston............180 A7
Ossington...........95 D6

Owthorpe...........199 E7
Oxton.............134 C4

P

Papplewick.........131 D3
Perlethorpe.........62 F3
Pinxton...........113 C2
Pleasley............87 B6
Pleasleyhill.........87 B4
Plumtree..........197 E6
Plungar..........202 F8
Porchester........162 B2
Pye Bridge.........128 A7

R

Radcliffe on Trent....175 E3
Radford...........222 A3
Radmanthwaite.......87 D3
Ragnall............68 A8
Rainworth..........104 A1
Rampton...........42 F1
Ranby.............38 A6
Ranskill...........19 B4
Ratcliffe on Soar....203 F6
Ravenshead........117 B1
Redmile...........192 F3
Rempstone........215 D5
Retford...........39 E8
Rhodesia..........35 A4
Rockley...........51 A2
Rolleston.........138 A5
Ruddington........196 D6

S

St Ann's..........173 D6
Sandiacre.........182 A6

Saundby...........23 C6
Sawley...........193 A4
Saxilby...........56 F4
Saxondale.........177 A4
Scarrington.......178 F8
Screveton.........166 E4
Scrooby..........10 A2
Selston..........128 E7
Shelford.........164 C1
Shelton..........168 C6
Sherwood.........161 B3
Shipley..........157 B6
Shirebrook........72 F3
Shireoaks.........34 E6
Sibthorpe........167 E7
Skegby..........100 E6
Skellingthorpe.....71 F3
Sneinton.........173 E4
South Clifton......68 E1
South Leverton.....42 C6
South Muskham....124 D7
South Normanton...113 A7
South Scarle......98 C5
Southwell.........121 C1
South Wheatley....31 E7
Spalford..........83 B7
Stainsby.........85 B7
Stanford on Soar....214 D1
Stanley..........85 D1
Stanton-by-Dale....170 A1
Stanton Hill.......100 C5
Stanton-on-the-Wolds.198 C1
Stapleford
  Lincs...........127 E8
  Notts..........182 E7
Stathern.........202 F3
Staunton in the Vale.169 B4
Staythorpe........138 D8
Stoke Bardolph....175 F7
Strelley.........171 B8
Sturton le Steeple...32 D5
Styrrup..........8 D1

Sutton Bonington....213 A7
Sutton cum Lound...28 F6
Sutton Forest Side...101 B3
Sutton in Ashfield...100 B2
Sutton on Trent.....96 E7
Syerston.........153 B4

T

Teversal..........100 C8
The Park.........173 A4
Thorney..........69 F7
Thorneywood......174 B8
Thoroton.........167 E2
Thorpe..........138 F1
Thorpe Salvin......34 A6
Thrumpton........194 C3
Thurgarton.......151 D7
Tibshelf.........99 A6
Tickhill...........8 B8
Tithby..........189 E6
Tollerton.........186 D1
Torksey..........44 B2
Torworth.........19 B2
Toton...........182 E2
Treswell.........42 C3
Trowell..........170 C5
Tuxford..........66 B2

U

Upper Broughton...210 B2
Upper Langwith....72 D8
Upton...........122 F1

W

Walesby..........64 A1
Walkeringham......13 F5

Walkerith.........14 D7
Wallingwells.......25 C5
Warsop Vale.......73 D4
Watnall..........159 A8
Wellow..........77 E1
West Bridgford....186 A7
West Drayton......51 A2
West Hallam.......157 A1
West Leake.......205 A1
West Markham.....65 B6
Weston..........81 B4
West Stockwith.....7 D2
Westwood........128 C3
Whaley..........58 D4
Whaley Thorns.....59 A2
Whatton.........179 A3
Whitwell.........45 B6
Widmerpool......208 B5
Wilford..........185 B6
Willoughby-on-the-
  Wolds.........217 D8
Winkburn........108 A1
Winthorpe.......125 D6
Wollaton........171 E4
Woodbeck........53 A8
Woodborough.....149 C3
Woodthorpe......161 E5
Worksop.........35 C5
Wymeswold.......216 C4
Wysall..........207 D3

Z

Zouch...........213 B3

Index of streets, hospitals, industrial estates, railway stations, schools, shopping centres, universities and places of interest

1st Ave NG7.........173 B8
2nd Ave NG7........173 B8
3rd Ave NG7........173 B8
4th Ave NG7........173 B8

A

Aaron Cl NG11.......185 B7
Abba Cl NG16.......158 F7
Abbey Bridge NG7....172 E2
Abbey Cir NG2......186 A7
Abbey Cl
  Aslockton NG13....178 F5
  Hucknall NG15.....145 E7
Abbey Ct
  Beeston NG9......183 F8
  Mansfield NG18....102 F7
  Nottingham NG7...222 B2
Abbeydale Dr NG18..102 D3
Abbey Dr NG9......183 F7
Abbeyfield Rd NG7...184 F8
Abbey Gates Prim Sch
  NG15............117 A1
Abbey Gr NG3.......173 F7
Abbey La NG13......178 F5
Abbey Rd
  Beeston NG9......183 F7
  Bingham NG13.....178 A4
  Blidworth NG21....118 B5
  Eastwood NG16....144 B2
  Kirkby in A NG17...115 D5
  Mansfield NG18....102 F7
  Mattersey DN10....20 C7
  Newstead NG15....130 E6
  West Bridgford NG2..186 A7
Abbey Road Prim Sch
  NG2.............186 A6
Abbey St
  Ilkeston DE7......157 F2
  Nottingham NG7...172 E2
  Worksop S80......35 F2
Abbot Cl NG12......197 E4
Abbotsbury Cl NG5...146 E1
Abbots Cl NG5......161 D6
Abbots Dr NG15.....145 E6
Abbotsford Dr NG3...223 E4
Abbotsford Mews DE7.157 D3
Abbotsford Rd NG15..145 E6
Abbot St NG16......158 C4
Abbots Wlk NG15....145 E6
Abbott Lea NG19....101 D8
Abbotts Cres NG22...119 F6
Abbotts Croft NG19..87 E1
Abbott St NG10.....193 D6
Abbotts Way NG8....172 C4
Abbott's Way NG24...125 B1
Abel Collin's Homes
  NG8............171 E1
Abercarn Cl NG6....160 B7
Aberconway St NG21..118 A5
Aberdeen St 3 NG3..173 E5
Aberford Ave NG8...172 D8
Abingdon Dr NG11...196 D8
Abingdon Gdns
  Arnold NG5.......162 B5
  Beeston NG9......183 D4

Abingdon Rd NG2....186 A7
Abingdon Sq NG8....160 B1
Abingdon View S81...35 C8
Abington Ave NG17..100 F5
Ablard Gdns 6 NG9..183 C2
Acacia Ave
  Annesley Woodhouse
    NG17..........130 A8
  Gainsborough DN21.15 D1
Acacia Cl
  Hucknall NG15.....146 B5
  Worksop S80......35 C2
Acacia Cres NG4....162 F1
Acacia Ct NG19.....88 C1
Acacia Gdns NG16...158 F8
Acacia Wlk NG9.....183 F6
Academy Cl NG6....160 D2
Acaster Cl NG9.....184 B4
Acer Cl NG16.......113 C3
Ackford Dr S80.....35 D3
Acland St DN21.....15 C1
Acle Gdns NG6......146 B1
Acorn Ave NG16....158 B8
Acorn Bank NG2....185 B4
Acorn Bsns Pk 11 NG18.102 B6
Acorn Cl NG24......140 C5
Acorn Dr NG4......163 A2
Acorn Pk NG7......184 E8
Acorn Ridge NG20...72 D5
Acorn Way NG18....103 B4
Acourt St NG7......222 B4
Acreage La NG20....72 F2
Acre The NG17......115 B3
Acton Ave
  Long Eaton NG10..193 E6
  Nottingham NG6...160 D4
Acton Cl NG10......193 E6
Acton Gr NG10......193 E6
Acton Rd
  Arnold NG5.......161 E7
  Long Eaton NG10..193 E6
Acton Rd Ind Est NG10.193 E6
Acton St NG10......193 E6
Adams Ct DE7......157 E3
Adams Hill
  Keyworth NG12....197 F3
  Nottingham NG7...172 C2
Adam St DE7.......170 A6
Adamsway NG18....103 A3
Adams Way DN21....44 C8
Adbolton Ave NG4...162 E1
Adbolton Gr NG12...174 B1
Adbolton La NG12...174 D1
Adderley Cl NG5....161 A6
Addington Ct NG12..176 A2
Addington Rd NG7...222 B4
Addison Dr NG15....145 F8
Addison Rd NG4....174 B8
Addison St
  Nottingham NG1...223 D4
  Tibshelf DE55.....99 A7
Addison Villas NG16..143 E1
Adelaide Cl
  Gainsborough DN21.24 F6
  Stapleford NG9....170 F1
Adelaide Gr NG5....160 E8

Adel Dr NG4........162 E1
Adenburgh Dr NG9...183 D1
Adrian Cl NG9......182 F1
Adrians Cl NG18....102 E5
Advance Bsns Ctr LE12.220 A2
Adwalton Cl 7 NG24.140 E8
Aegir Cl DN21......24 F6
Aeneas Ct 6 NG5....173 B8
Aerial Way NG15....145 F5
Agnes Villas NG3....161 E2
Aidan Gdns NG5.....147 A2
Ainsdale Cres NG8...160 A3
Ainsdale Gn DN22...39 D3
Ainsley Rd NG8.....172 D6
Ainsworth Dr NG2...173 B1
Aintree Cl NG16.....158 E7
Aira Cl NG2........186 D6
Aisby Wlk DN21.....24 F7
Aitchison Ave NG15..145 F7
Alandale NG22......105 E6
Alandale Ave NG20..72 F5
Alandene Ave NG16..159 A7
Albany Cl
  Arnold NG5.......161 E7
  Hucknall NG15.....145 C5
  Mansfield Woodhouse NG19.88 C1
Albany Ct NG9......170 E1
Albany Dr NG19.....88 C1
Albany Inf Sch NG9..182 E8
Albany Jun Sch NG9..182 E8
Albany Pl NG19.....88 C1
Albany Rd NG7......173 A8
Albany St
  Gainsborough DN21..15 C2
  Ilkeston DE7......170 A6
Albemarle Rd NG5...161 D4
Alberta Ave NG16...129 A7
Alberta Terr NG7....173 A8
Albert Ave
  Balderton NG24....140 C4
  Carlton NG4......174 B7
  Nottingham NG8...172 D8
  Nuthall NG16.....159 C6
  Stapleford NG9....182 D7
  Westwood NG16....128 B4
Albert Ball Cl NG5...160 F8
Albert Dr NG7......222 B3
Albert Hall NG1.....223 D2
Albert Pl LE11......220 B3
Albert Prom LE11...220 C3
Albert Rd
  Beeston NG9......184 B7
  Bunny NG11.......196 E1
  Long Eaton NG10..193 D8
  Nottingham, Alexander Park
    NG3...........173 D8
  Nottingham NG7...222 A1
  Retford DN22......39 E6
  Sandiacre NG9.....182 B6
  West Bridgford NG2.185 F8
Albert Sq NG17.....100 E2
Albert St
  Bottesford NG13...181 A3

Albert St continued
  Carlton NG4......162 F1
  Eastwood NG16....143 F3
  Hucknall NG15.....146 B7
  Loughborough LE11.220 B3
  Mansfield NG18....102 B6
  Mansfield Woodhouse NG19.88 C4
  Market Warsop NG20.74 A5
  Newark-on-T NG24..139 F8
  Nottingham NG1...223 E2
  Radcliffe on T NG12.175 E3
  South Normanton DE55.113 B6
  Stanton Hill NG17..100 C6
  Stapleford NG9....182 D7
  Worksop S80......35 F3
Albine Rd NG20.....72 E6
Albion Cl S80.......35 F3
Albion Rd
  Long Eaton NG10..193 F8
  Sutton in A NG17..100 F2
Albion Rise NG5.....147 F1
Albion St
  Beeston NG9......183 F7
  Ilkeston DE7......157 F1
  Mansfield NG19....87 F1
  Newark-on-T NG24..139 F8
  Nottingham NG1...223 E1
Albion Terr DN10....7 B1
Albury Cl NG8......160 B1
Albury Dr NG8......160 B1
Albury Sq NG7......222 C2
Alcester St NG7.....184 E8
Alcock Ave NG18....102 E7
Aldene Ct NG9......183 D5
Aldene Way NG14...149 C4
Aldercar Com Lang Coll
  NG16............143 A4
Aldercar Flash Nature
  Reserve NG16.....143 B6
Aldercar Inf Sch NG16.143 A4
Aldercar La NG16....143 A6
Alder Cl
  Mansfield NG19....88 D1
  New Balderton NG24.140 C4
  Shirebrook NG20...72 D5
  Worksop S80......35 E1
Alder Ct NG19......101 D5
Alder Gdns NG6.....160 A7
Alder Gr
  Mansfield Woodhouse
    NG19..........88 B5
  New Ollerton NG22.77 D5
Alderman Pounder Inf Sch
  NG9............183 B5
Alderman White Sch
  NG9............183 C7
Aldermens Cl NG2...173 C2
Alderney St NG7....222 B1
Alderson Cl DN11...8 B8
Alderson Dr DN11...8 B8
Alderson Rd S80....35 E1
Alders The 5 DN21..15 F1
Alderton Rd NG5....161 C6
Alder Way
  Keyworth NG12....198 A2
  Shirebrook NG20...72 D4
  Sutton in A NG17..100 D3
Aldgate Cl NG6.....160 A8
Aldred's La DE75...143 B2

Aldridge Cl NG9.....182 E2
Aldrin Cl NG6.......159 F5
Aldworth Cl NG5....161 C6
Aldwych Cl
  Nottingham NG5...147 A1
  Nuthall NG16.....159 D2
Alec Rose Gr DN21..24 F2
Alexander Ave
  Newark-on-T NG24.125 B4
  Selston NG16......128 D7
Alexander Cl NG15..131 B1
Alexander Rd
  Farnsfield NG22...119 F6
  Nottingham NG7...222 C2
Alexander St NG16..143 F2
Alexander Terr NG16.113 C1
Alexandra Ave
  Mansfield NG18....102 B4
  Mansfield Woodhouse NG19.88 B5
  Sutton in A NG17..100 F4
Alexandra Cres NG9.184 A6
Alexandra Rd
  Bircotes DN11.....9 B4
  Long Eaton NG10..193 D8
Alexandra St
  Kirkby in A NG17...115 B6
  Market Warsop NG20.74 A5
  Nottingham NG5...173 B8
  Stapleford NG9....182 D6
Alexandra Terr NG17.100 C6
Alford Cl NG9......184 B5
Alford Rd NG2......186 B5
Alfred Ave NG3.....162 A2
Alfred Cl NG3......223 E4
Alfred Ct 4 NG18...102 B7
Alfred St Central NG3.223 E4
Alfred St N NG3....223 E4
Alfred St S NG3.....173 E5
Alfred St
  Gainsborough DN21.15 C1
  Kirkby in A NG17...115 A4
  Loughborough LE11.220 B3
  Pinxton NG16......113 C4
  Sutton in A NG17..100 F4
Alfreton Rd
  Huthwaite NG17....113 F7
  Newton DE55......99 A3
  Nottingham NG7...222 B4
  Pinxton NG16......113 C4
  Selston, Selston Green DE55,
    NG16..........128 C6
  Selston, Underwood NG16 129 B3
  South Normanton DE55..113 A5
  Sutton in A NG17..100 C1
Alison Ave NG15....131 C1
Alison Wlk NG3.....223 F4
Allcroft St NG19....88 C4
Allenby Rd NG25....136 C8
Allen Cl NG23......156 D7
Allendale Ave
  Beeston NG9......183 D2
  Nottingham NG8...160 A1
Allendale Rd NG21..118 B8
Allendale Way NG19.88 E1
Allen Dr NG18......102 F5

Allen Field Ct NG7 . . . . 222 B1
Allen Rd NG23 . . . . 142 D2
Allen's Gn Ave NG16. . . . . . 128 F6
Allen St
  Hucknall NG15. . . . . 146 A8
  Worksop S80 . . . . 35 E3
Allen's Wlk NG5. . . . . 147 F1
Allesford La NG22. . . . . . . 120 B4
All Hallows CE Prim Sch **2**
  NG4. . . . . 162 F1
All Hallows Cl DN22 . . . . . . 39 E4
All Hallows Dr NG4. . . . . . . 162 F2
All Hallows St DN22 . . . . . . 39 E4
Alliance St NG12 . . . . 125 A2
Allington Ave NG7 . . . . 222 B1
Allington Dr NG19 . . . . 101 D7
Allison Ave DN22 . . . . 40 B3
Allison Gdns NG9 . . . . 183 D4
All Saints CE Inf Sch
  NG17. . . . . 99 F2
All Saints Prim Sch
  NG23. . . . . 153 D5
All Saints RC Comp Sch
  NG19. . . . . 101 F8
All Saints' St NG7 . . . . 222 C4
All Saints' Terr NG7 . . . . . . 222 C4
Allsopp Dr S81. . . . . 35 F6
Allsopp's La LE11 . . . . 220 D5
Allwood Dr NG4 . . . . 174 E8
Allwood Gdns NG15 . . . . . 146 B6
Alma Cl
  Carlton NG4. . . . . 163 A2
  Nottingham NG1 . . . . 223 E4
Alma Hill NG16 . . . . 158 E7
Alma Rd
  Nottingham NG3 . . . . 173 F6
  Retford DN22. . . . . 40 A7
  Selston NG16. . . . . 129 A5
Alma St NG7. . . . . 173 A8
Almond Ave NG20. . . . . . . 72 E5
Almond Cl
  Hucknall NG15. . . . . 146 B5
  Kimberley NG16. . . . . 158 E7
  Saxilby LN1 . . . . 57 B4
Almond Gr
  Farndon NG24 . . . . 139 A5
  6 Kirkby in A NG17 . . . . 114 F6
  Worksop S80 . . . . 35 E1
Almond Rise NG19 . . . . . . 88 E1
Almond Wlk NG4 . . . . 163 A2
Alnwick Cl NG6 . . . . 160 D6
Alpha Terr NG1 . . . . 223 E4
Alpine Cres NG4 . . . . 174 D8
Alpine Ct S80 . . . . 35 C2
Alpine St NG6 . . . . 160 E2
Alport Pl NG18. . . . . 103 B7
Althea Ct **1** NG7. . . . . 161 A1
Althorpe St NG7 . . . . 222 C4
Alton Ave NG11 . . . . 185 B4
Alton Cl NG11. . . . . 185 C3
Alton Dr NG16 . . . . 158 B8
Alum Ct NG5. . . . . 160 F8
Alvenor St NG7 . . . . 157 F1
Alverstone Rd NG3. . . . . . 161 C1
Alvey Rd NG24 . . . . 140 E4
Alwood Gr NG11 . . . . 184 D2
Alwyn Rd NG8 . . . . 159 F2
Amanda Ave S81. . . . . 25 E6
Amanda Rd DN11 . . . . 8 F4
Amber Cl NG21 . . . . 104 C1
Amber Dr NG16 . . . . 143 B2
Ambergate Rd NG8 . . . . . . 172 A7
Amber Hill NG5 . . . . 161 B7
Amberley St NG1 . . . . 223 D2
Amber St NG18 . . . . 102 C5
Ambleside
  New Ollerton NG22. . . . . . 77 C5
  West Bridgford NG2 . . . . . 186 C7
Ambleside Dr NG16 . . . . . 143 D3
Ambleside Grange S81. . . . 35 F8
Ambleside Inf Sch NG8. . . 160 B1
Ambleside Jun Sch NG8 160 A1
Ambleside Rd NG8 . . . . . . 160 A1
Ambleside Way NG18 . . . 175 B8
Amcott Ave DN10 . . . . 14 A8
Amcott Way DN22. . . . . . . 39 E7
Amen Cnr NG23. . . . . 109 B5
Amen Cnr Karting NG22 . . 91 E7
American Adventure Theme
  Pk The DE75 . . . . 157 B5
Amersham Rise NG8 . . . . . 160 B1
Amesbury Circ NG8 . . . . . 160 A3
Amethyst Cl NG21 . . . . . . 104 C1
Amhurst Rise S81. . . . . . . 35 D8
Amos La NG23 . . . . 98 D4
Ampthill Rise NG5 . . . . . . 161 B4
Anastasia Cl DN21 . . . . . . 15 C3
Ancaster Gdns NG8 . . . . . 172 A4
Anchor Cl NG8. . . . . 160 B2
Anchor Rd NG16 . . . . 143 D2
Anders Dr NG6. . . . . 159 F5
Anderson Cl NG24 . . . . . . 140 B3
Anderson Cres NG9 . . . . . 183 E8
Anderson Ct **6** NG5. . . . . . 161 A8
Anderson Rd DN21. . . . . . 24 F2
Andover Cl **1** NG8. . . . . . 172 B6
Andover Rd
  Mansfield NG19 . . . . 101 D7
  Nottingham NG5 . . . . 160 E5
Andrew Ave
  Ilkeston DE7 . . . . 170 B7
  Nottingham NG3 . . . . 162 A2
Andrew Dr NG21 . . . . 118 A4
Andrews Dr NG16. . . . . . . 143 A3
Anfield Cl NG9. . . . . 183 A2

Anford Cl NG6 . . . . 160 B5
Angela Ave NG17. . . . . . . 115 B1
Angela Cl NG5 . . . . 147 E2
Angel Alley NG1 . . . . 223 F2
Angell Gn NG11. . . . . 195 C8
Angel Row NG1. . . . . 223 E2
Angel Row Gall NG1. . . . 223 D2
Angel Yd LE11 . . . . 220 B4
Anglia Way NG18 . . . . 103 B3
Angrave Cl NG3 . . . . 173 E7
Angus Cl
  Arnold NG5 . . . . 148 B1
  Kimberley NG16. . . . . 159 A5
Anmer Cl **9** NG2. . . . . . . 173 B1
Annan Ct NG8 . . . . 172 B8
Anne's Cl NG3 . . . . 162 A2
Annesley Cutting NG15. . 130 C7
Annesley Gr NG1 . . . . 223 D4
Annesley La NG16. . . . . . . 129 B6
Annesley Prim Sch NG17 130 B8
Annesley Rd
  Hucknall NG15. . . . . 145 F8
  West Bridgford NG2 . . . . . 185 F7
Annesley Way NG19 . . . . 101 D6
Annesley Woodhouse Quarry
  Nature Reserve NG17 . . 129 D7
Annie Holgate Inf Sch
  NG15. . . . . 145 F6
Annies Cl NG15 . . . . 145 F5
Annies Wharf LE11. . . . . 220 B5
Anslow Ave
  Beeston NG9 . . . . 184 A8
  Sutton in A NG17. . . . . . . 100 F5
Anson Wlk DE7 . . . . 157 F3
Anstee Rd NG10 . . . . 193 C4
Anstey Rise NG3 . . . . 173 F5
Anston Ave S81. . . . . 35 E5
Anthony Bek Prim Sch
  NG19. . . . . 86 F6
Antill St NG9 . . . . 182 D6
Apley Cl DN21 . . . . 24 F7
Apollo Dr NG6 . . . . 159 F5
Appin Rd NG19 . . . . 101 D5
Appleby Cl NG24 . . . . 140 D8
Appleby Ct S81 . . . . 35 F8
Appleby Rd NG19 . . . . 86 F6
Appledore Ave NG8 . . . . . 171 E2
Appledorne Way NG5 . . . 147 E1
Appleton Dr LE12 . . . . 216 B3
Appleton Gate NG24 . . . . 125 A1
Appleton Rd
  Beeston NG9 . . . . 184 B4
  Blidworth NG21. . . . . 118 B5
Appleton St NG20 . . . . 74 B4
Appletree Cl NG25 . . . . . . 121 E1
Apple Tree Cl NG12 . . . . . 186 A4
Apple Tree La NG4. . . . . . 162 F2
Apple Wlk NG4 . . . . 174 A8
Applewood Cl S81 . . . . 35 D8
Applewood Gr NG5 . . . . . 161 D3
Arboretum St NG1 . . . . . . 223 D4
Arbrook Dr NG8 . . . . 172 D6
Arbutus Cl NG11 . . . . 184 C1
Arcade The NG24 . . . . 139 F8
Arcadia Ave NG20 . . . . . . 72 E5
Archbishop Cranmer CE Prim
  Sch NG13 . . . . 178 F5
Archdale Rd NG5 . . . . 161 C6
Archer Cres NG8. . . . . 171 F5
Archer Rd NG9. . . . . 182 E5
Archers Dr NG22. . . . . . . 106 A5
Archer St DE7 . . . . 157 E3
Arches The LE12 . . . . 205 E2
Arch Hill NG5. . . . . 147 E3
Archway Rd NG21. . . . . . . 90 D7
A Rd NG9. . . . . 184 C6
Arden Cl
  Beeston NG9 . . . . 184 A8
  Hucknall NG15. . . . . 146 C5
Arden Gr NG13. . . . . 177 C5
Ardleigh Cl NG5 . . . . 146 D1
Ardmore Cl NG3 . . . . 173 F3
Ardsley Cl DE75. . . . . 143 A2
Argosy Cl DN10 . . . . 9 F8
Argyle Cl NG20 . . . . 73 F4
Argyle Ct NG7 . . . . 222 B3
Argyle St
  Langley Mill NG16 . . . . . . 143 C4
  Mansfield NG18 . . . . 102 E6
  Nottingham NG7 . . . . 222 B3
Ariel Cl NG6 . . . . 160 F5
Arkers Cl NG6 . . . . 160 D3
Arklow Cl NG8. . . . . 160 B2
Arkwright St
  Gainsborough DN21 . . . . . 15 C1
  Nottingham NG2 . . . . 173 C3
Arkwright Wlk NG2 . . . . . 173 C2
Arleston Dr NG8 . . . . 171 D4
Arlington Ave NG19 . . . . . 88 E4
Arlington Cl NG15. . . . . . . 146 A4
Arlington Dr NG3 . . . . 161 C2
Arlington Way DN22 . . . . . 39 F7
Armadale Cl NG5 . . . . 162 C8
Armfield Rd NG5 . . . . 162 C6
Armitage Cl **3** LE11. . . . . 220 A4
Armitage Dr NG10 . . . . . . 194 A7
Armstrong Rd
  Mansfield NG19. . . . . 101 D7
  Nottingham NG6 . . . . 159 F5
  Retford DN22. . . . . 39 F7
Arncliff Cl NG8 . . . . 171 C4
Arndale Rd NG5 . . . . 161 C5
Arne Ct **5** NG2 . . . . 173 C1
Arnesby Rd NG7 . . . . 222 A1
Arno Ave **2** NG7. . . . . . . 173 B8
Arnold Ave
  Long Eaton NG10. . . . . . . 193 A4
  Retford DN22. . . . . 40 B3

Arnold Ave continued
  Southwell NG25. . . . . . . 121 E1
Arnold Cres NG10. . . . . . . 193 A4
Arnold Hill Sch NG5. . . . . 162 A6
Arnold La NG3 . . . . 162 D4
Arnold L Ctr NG5. . . . . . . 161 E8
Arnold Rd NG5. . . . . 161 A5
Arnold View Prim Sch
  NG5. . . . . 161 F7
Arnos Gr NG8. . . . . 159 D3
Arnot Hill Rd NG5. . . . . . . 161 E6
Arno Vale Gdns NG5 . . . . 161 E5
Arno Vale Jun Sch NG5. . 161 F5
Arno Vale Rd NG5. . . . . . . 161 F5
Arnside NG9. . . . . 182 E5
Arnside Cl NG5 . . . . 161 B5
Arnside Rd NG5. . . . . 161 B5
Arran Cl NG9 . . . . 170 A2
Arran Sq NG19 . . . . 101 D5
Arthur Ave
  Nottingham NG7 . . . . 222 B2
  Stapleford NG9 . . . . 182 F8
Arthur Cres NG4 . . . . 174 C7
Arthur Gn Ave NG17. . . . . 114 E1
Arthur Mee Rd NG9 . . . . . 182 E5
Arthur Rd DN21. . . . . 15 D2
Arthur Short Cl S80 . . . . . 45 A6
Arthur St
  Carlton NG4. . . . . 175 A6
  Mansfield NG18 . . . . 102 C6
  Nottingham NG7 . . . . 222 C4
  Pinxton NG16. . . . . 113 D3
Artic Way NG16 . . . . 158 D7
Arum Croft DN22 . . . . 39 D4
Arun Dale NG19 . . . . 88 D2
Arundel Ct
  Gainsborough DN21 . . . . . 15 C3
  Sandiacre NG10. . . . . . . 182 B4
Arundel Dr
  Beeston NG9 . . . . 171 B1
  Carlton in L S81. . . . . 25 F6
  Mansfield NG19 . . . . 101 A4
  Ranskill DN22 . . . . 19 B5
Arundel St NG7 . . . . 222 C3
Arundel Way DN22 . . . . . . 39 C8
Arundel Wlk DN11 . . . . 9 A5
Ascot Ave NG16 . . . . 158 E7
Ascot Cl NG17 . . . . 115 C3
Ascot Dr
  Arnold NG5 . . . . 161 D8
  Hucknall NG15. . . . . 145 D5
Ascot Pk Est NG10 . . . . . 182 B4
Ascot Rd NG8. . . . . 172 D7
Ascott Gdns NG2. . . . . . . 185 A5
Ashbourne Cl NG9 . . . . . . 171 A1
Ashbourne Ct NG6 . . . . . . 159 F6
Ashbourne Rd NG16. . . . . 129 A2
Ashbourne St
  Nottingham NG7 . . . . 222 C3
  Shirebrook NG20. . . . . . . 72 F4
Ashburnham Ave NG7. . . . 222 B2
Ashby Ave NG19 . . . . 88 D5
Ashby Rd
  Kegworth DE74 . . . . 203 A2
  Kegworth DE74. . . . . 203 B2
  Long Whatton LE12 . . . . . 212 C1
  Loughborough LE11 . . . . . 220 A4
Ashby Sq LE11 . . . . 220 A4
Ashchurch Dr NG8 . . . . . . 171 D2
Ash Cl
  Bingham NG13. . . . . 178 A4
  Burton Joyce NG14 . . . . . 163 E4
  Hucknall NG15. . . . . 145 C5
  Pinxton NG16. . . . . 113 D2
  Worksop S80 . . . . 35 E1
Ash Cres
  Kirkby in A NG17 . . . . 114 D6
  Nuthall NG16 . . . . 159 B6
Ashcroft DN22 . . . . 39 D4
Ashcroft Rd DN21 . . . . 24 D6
Ash Ct NG4 . . . . 174 D7
Ashdale Ave NG15 . . . . . . 146 A5
Ashdale Rd
  Arnold NG5 . . . . 162 A8
  Ilkeston DE7 . . . . 170 A6
  Nottingham NG3 . . . . 174 B6
Ashdown Cl NG11 . . . . . . 185 B6
Ashdown Gr NG13. . . . . . . 177 D4
Ashdown Way DN10. . . . . . 6 A2
Ashe Cl NG5 . . . . 162 B7
Asher La NG11 . . . . 196 C6
Ashes Pk Ave S81. . . . . . . 35 D8
Ashfield Ave
  Beeston NG9 . . . . 184 B5
  Mansfield NG18 . . . . 102 B7
Ashfield Com Hospl
  NG17. . . . . 115 A5
Ashfield Dr NG17 . . . . 114 F5
Ashfield Grange LN1. . . . . 56 F4
Ashfield Prec NG17. . . . . . 115 B5
Ashfield Rd
  Huthwaite NG17. . . . . . . 100 B3
  Nottingham NG2 . . . . 173 F4
Ashfield Sch NG17. . . . . . 114 D7
Ashford Ct DN22 . . . . 39 C6
Ashford Dr NG15. . . . . 117 B3
Ashford Pl DE7 . . . . 157 E5
Ashford Rise
  Nottingham NG8 . . . . 171 B6
  Sutton in A NG17. . . . . . . 100 E4
Ashforth Ave DE75 . . . . . 143 A1
Ashforth St NG3. . . . . 223 F4
Ashgate NG17. . . . . 100 D3
Ashgate Rd NG15 . . . . . . 146 B5
Ash Gr
  Brinsley NG16 . . . . 143 D8

Ash Gr continued
  Gainsborough DN21 . . . . . 15 D2
  Hathern LE12. . . . . 213 A1
  Keyworth NG12 . . . . 198 A2
  Long Eaton NG10. . . . . . . 193 C6
  Sandiacre NG10. . . . . . . 182 A7
  Selston NG16. . . . . 128 C8
  Shirebrook NG20. . . . . . . 72 D5
  Stapleford NG9. . . . . 182 D5
  Sutton in A NG17. . . . . . . 100 D7
  Woodborough NG14 . . . . 149 D4
Ash Holt Dr S81. . . . . 35 F8
Ashington Dr NG5. . . . . . . 148 A2
Ash La LE12 . . . . 206 C4
Ashland Rd NG17 . . . . . . 100 C3
Ashland Rd W NG17. . . . . 100 B3
Ashlands Cl NG17 . . . . . . 100 B3
Ashlea DN10 . . . . 6 E1
Ash Lea Cl NG12 . . . . 187 F2
Ash Lea Specl Sch NG12 187 F2
Ashleigh Way NG19 . . . . . 89 A2
Ashley Cl NG9 . . . . 183 D6
Ashley Cres NG12 . . . . . . 197 F3
Ashley Ct S81. . . . . 35 F5
Ashley Gr NG15 . . . . 145 E2
Ashley La DN22 . . . . 41 F2
Ashley Rd
  Keyworth NG12 . . . . 197 E3
  Worksop S81 . . . . 35 E6
Ashley St **7** NG3. . . . . . . 173 E5
Ashley Terr S80. . . . . 35 F3
Ashling St NG2 . . . . 173 D2
Ashmore Ave NG17. . . . . . 100 C2
Ash Mount Rd NG16. . . . . 143 B3
Ashmount Sch LE11 . . . . 220 A1
Ashness Cl NG2. . . . . 186 C6
Ashover Cl
  Nottingham NG3 . . . . 173 E8
  Ravenshead NG15 . . . . . . 117 B3
Ash Rd NG24. . . . . 139 F4
Ashridge Way NG2. . . . . . 186 C4
Ash St DE7 . . . . 157 E4
Ashton Ave NG5 . . . . 147 F2
Ashton Ct NG17 . . . . 101 A5
Ash Tree Ave
  Bawtry DN10 . . . . 9 F7
  Mansfield Woodhouse NG19 88 C5
Ash Tree Cl NG25 . . . . . . 136 D8
Ash Tree Sq NG9. . . . . . . 183 B8
Ashvale Rd NG22. . . . . . . 66 A2
Ash Vale Rd NG22. . . . . . . 64 A2
Ashview Cl NG10. . . . . . . 193 A8
Ash Villas **1** NG7 . . . . . . 161 B1
Ashville Cl NG2 . . . . 173 A1
Ashwater Dr NG3 . . . . 162 D5
Ashwell Ave NG19. . . . . . . 88 E5
Ashwell Gdns NG7 . . . . . . 172 E8
Ashwell St NG4 . . . . 174 F6
Ashwick Cl NG11. . . . . . . 185 A5
Ash Wlk LE12 . . . . 214 D8
Ashwood Ave NG17 . . . . . 115 C6
Ashwood Cl NG19. . . . . . . 88 E5
Ashwood Rd S80. . . . . 35 B2
Ashworth Ave NG11 . . . . . 196 C8
Ashworth Bsns Ctr NG1 . 223 F4
Ashworth Cl
  Newark-on-T NG24 . . . . . 140 D8
  Nottingham NG3 . . . . 174 C5
Ashworth Cres
  North Leverton w H DN22.. 32 C1
  Nottingham NG3 . . . . 162 B2
Ashworth Dr NG19 . . . . . . 88 E4
Askeby Dr NG8 . . . . 159 D1
Askew La NG20 . . . . 74 A3
Askham La DN22 . . . . 52 B5
Askham Rd NG22. . . . . . . 51 F1
Aslockton Dr NG8. . . . . . . 160 D2
Aslockton Sta NG13 . . . . 179 A4
Aspen Cl
  Bingham NG13. . . . . 178 A4
  Laughterton LN1 . . . . 55 B4
  Tuxford NG22. . . . . 66 A2
Aspen Ct
  Gainsborough DN21 . . . . . 15 F2
  Mansfield NG19. . . . . 88 E1
  Tuxford NG22. . . . . 66 A2
Aspen Rd NG6 . . . . 159 F7
Asper St NG4 . . . . 175 A7
Aspinall Ct **2** NG8 . . . . . 172 C5
Aspley La NG8 . . . . 172 C8
Aspley Pk Dr NG8 . . . . . . 172 B8
Aspley Pl NG7 . . . . 222 B4
Aspley Rd NG17. . . . . 100 D3
Asquith Mews NG18 . . . . 102 E6
Asquith Prim Sch NG18 . 102 E6
Asquith St
  Gainsborough DN21 . . . . . 15 B2
  Mansfield NG18. . . . . 102 E6
Assarts Rd NG16 . . . . 159 E3
Astcote Cl DE75. . . . . 143 A1
Aster Rd NG3 . . . . 173 E7
Astle Ct NG5. . . . . 162 C6
Astley Cl NG17. . . . . 130 A8
Astley Dr NG3 . . . . 161 F1
Aston Ave NG9. . . . . 172 A1
Aston Ct DE7 . . . . 157 F1
Aston Dr NG6. . . . . 146 C2
Aston Gn NG9 . . . . 182 E3
Astral Gr NG15. . . . . 145 E4
Astrid Gdns NG5 . . . . 160 F6
Astwith La S44, S45. . . . . 85 B5
Astwood Cl NG8 . . . . 171 E8
Athelstan Rd S80 . . . . 35 F1
Atherfield Gdns NG16 . . . 143 F3
Atherton Rd DE7. . . . . . . 157 C3

Atherton Rise NG8 . . . . . 160 B3
Athorpe Gr NG6. . . . . 160 E3
Atkin La NG18 . . . . 102 B3
Attenborough La NG9. . . 183 C3
Attenborough Nature
  Reserve NG9 . . . . 183 E1
Attenborough Prep Sch
  NG9. . . . . 183 E1
Attenborough Sta NG9. . 183 D2
Attercliffe Terr **8** NG2 . . 173 C1
Attewell Rd NG16 . . . . . . 158 B5
Attlee Ave NG19 . . . . 89 A1
Aubrey Ave **15** NG2. . . . . 173 E4
Aubrey Rd NG5 . . . . 161 B2
Auckland Cl NG7. . . . . . . 222 A3
Auckland Rd
  Hucknall NG15. . . . . 145 D5
  Retford DN22. . . . . 39 C8
Audley Cl DE7 . . . . 157 D3
Audley Dr NG9. . . . . 171 F1
Audon Ave NG9. . . . . 183 E5
Audrey Cres NG19 . . . . . . 88 C5
Augustine Gdns NG5. . . . 147 A1
Ault Hucknall La S44. . . . . 86 A7
Aumberry Gap LE11. . . . . 220 B4
Aurillac Way DN22 . . . . . . 29 D2
Austen Ave
  Long Eaton NG10. . . . . . . 193 C5
  Nottingham NG7 . . . . 173 A4
Austin Cl NG18. . . . . 102 E8
Austins Dr NG10 . . . . 182 B4
Austin St
  Nottingham NG6 . . . . 160 C7
  Shirebrook NG20. . . . . . . 73 A4
Austrey Ave NG9. . . . . . . 184 A8
Autumn Cft Rd NG24 . . . 125 D1
Avalon Cl NG6 . . . . 160 E6
Ave A NG1. . . . . 223 F2
Ave B NG1. . . . . 223 F2
Avebury Cl NG11. . . . . . . 195 D8
Ave C NG1. . . . . 223 F2
Ave D NG1. . . . . 173 E4
Ave E **4** NG1. . . . . 173 E5
Avenue Cl NG5. . . . . 160 F8
Avenue Rd DN22 . . . . 39 F5
Avenue The
  Calverton NG14 . . . . 148 F7
  Gainsborough DN21 . . . . . 15 E2
  Gunthorpe NG14 . . . . . . 164 F6
  Mansfield NG18. . . . . 102 E3
  Newark-on-T NG24 . . . . . 140 B7
  Sutton in A NG17. . . . . . . 100 E1
Averham Cl NG19 . . . . . . 101 D6
Averton Sq NG8. . . . . 172 D3
Aviemore Cl NG5 . . . . 162 B8
Avocet Cl
  Bingham NG13. . . . . 178 A3
  Hucknall NG15. . . . . 131 B1
Avocet Gr S81 . . . . 35 C6
Avocet Wharf **6** NG7 . . . 172 F2
Avon Ave NG15 . . . . 145 E4
Avonbridge Cl NG5. . . . . . 148 C1
Avon Cl NG17 . . . . 129 F8
Avondale
  Cotgrave NG12 . . . . 188 A3
  Mansfield NG18. . . . . 102 E7
Avondale Cl NG10. . . . . . . 193 A6
Avondale Rd NG4 . . . . . . 174 D6
Avon Gdns NG2 . . . . 185 F7
Avonlea Cl DE7 . . . . 170 B6
Avon Pl NG9 . . . . 184 A7
Avon Rd
  Carlton NG4. . . . . 162 F2
  Nottingham NG3 . . . . 174 B5
Avon Rise DN22 . . . . 40 A7
Avon Vale Rd LE11 . . . . . 220 C1
Avon Way
  Mansfield NG18. . . . . 103 A3
  Worksop S81 . . . . 35 E7
Awsworth La NG16 . . . . . 158 C6
Awsworth Prim Sch
  NG16. . . . . 158 C4
Awsworth Rd DE7. . . . . . . 157 F2
Axford Cl NG4 . . . . 162 F2
Aylesham Ave NG5. . . . . . 161 F6
Aylestone Dr NG8 . . . . . . 172 B8
Ayr St NG7 . . . . 222 C4
Ayscough Ave NG16. . . . . 159 C6
Ayton Cl NG2 . . . . 173 B2
Ayton Gdns NG9 . . . . 183 C2
Azalea Ct NG16 . . . . 158 C8
Azimghur Rd NG13. . . . . . 179 A4

B

Babbacombe Cl NG5 . . . . 161 B6
Babbacombe Way NG15 . 145 D6
Babbington Cres NG4 . . . 162 E2
Babbington La NG16 . . . . 158 F4
Babbington St DE55. . . . . 99 A6
Babington Ct NG9. . . . . . . 183 C5
Babington Cres DN22 . . . . 39 C6
Babworth Ct NG18 . . . . . 102 D7
Babworth Rd DN22. . . . . . 39 B6
Back La
  Claypole NG23 . . . . 156 D6
  Cotes LE12. . . . . 220 F6
  Cropwell Butler NG12 . . . 189 A6
  Eakring NG22. . . . . 106 E8
  East Markham NG22 . . . . 66 A7
  Halam NG22 . . . . 120 F2
  Huthwaite NG17. . . . . 99 F3
  Ilkeston DE7. . . . . 157 E2
  Keyworth NG12. . . . . 198 A6
  Long Clawson LE14 . . . . . 211 C3
  Misson DN10. . . . . 4 B2
  Morton NG25. . . . . 137 C3

Back La *continued*
North Clifton NG23 . . . . 68 E5
Nuthall NG16 . . . . 159 D6
Ollerton NG22 . . . . 77 B3
Ranskill DN22 . . . . 19 A4
Sutton in A NG17 . . . . 100 F6
Thorpe Salvin S80 . . . . 34 A6
Willoughby-on-t-W LE12 . . 217 D7
Back St
Barnby in t W NG24 . . . . 142 A5
East Stockwith DN21 . . . . 7 D1
South Clifton NG23 . . . . 68 E1
Back Terr DN22 . . . . 39 F8
Bacon Cl NG16 . . . . 158 A8
Bacon St DN21 . . . . 24 D6
Bacton Ave NG6 . . . . 160 B8
Bacton Gdns [1] NG6 . . . . 160 B8
Baden Powell Rd NG2 . . 174 A4
Bader NG11 . . . . 185 B7
Bader Rise DN10 . . . . 20 A8
Bader View DN10 . . . . 20 A8
Badger Cl NG15 . . . . 145 C6
Badgers Chase DN22 . . . . 29 F1
Badger Way NG19 . . . . 103 B7
Baggaley Cres NG19 . . . . 88 B1
Bagnall Ave NG5 . . . . 161 C7
Bagnall Rd NG6 . . . . 160 C4
Bagshaw St NG19 . . . . 87 B4
Bagthorpe Cl NG5 . . . . 161 A3
Baildon Cl NG8 . . . . 172 C3
Bailey Brook Cres NG16 . 143 A4
Bailey Brook Dr NG16 . . 143 A3
Bailey Brook Wlk NG16 . . 143 A3
Bailey Cl NG5 . . . . 161 D7
Bailey Cres NG19 . . . . 101 E7
Bailey Ct NG12 . . . . 175 E2
Bailey Gr Rd NG16 . . . . 143 D2
Bailey La NG12 . . . . 175 E2
Bailey Rd NG24 . . . . 139 F5
Bailey St
Carlton NG4 . . . . 175 A7
Nottingham NG6 . . . . 160 E2
Stapleford NG9 . . . . 182 C6
Bainbridge Rd
Loughborough LE11 . . . . 220 C1
Market Warsop NG20 . . . . 74 B4
Bainbridge Terr NG17 . . 100 D6
Bainbridge The NG14 . . . 149 A7
Baines Ave NG24 . . . . 140 D4
Baines Rd DN21 . . . . 24 F8
Bainton Gr NG7 . . . . 184 F1
Baker Ave NG5 . . . . 148 A2
Baker Brook Ind Pk
NG15 . . . . 146 C6
Bakerdale Rd NG3 . . . . 174 B6
Baker La NG20 . . . . 60 A2
Baker Rd
Eastwood NG16 . . . . 144 C1
Mansfield Woodhouse NG19 88 C6
Bakers Cl NG7 . . . . 222 A4
Baker's Hollow NG12 . . . . 187 E3
Baker's La
Colston Bassett NG12 . . . . 200 E7
Redmile NG13 . . . . 192 F3
Baker St
Hucknall NG15 . . . . 146 A7
[13] Ilkeston DE7 . . . . 157 F1
Nottingham NG1 . . . . 173 B7
Bakewell Ave NG4 . . . . 162 E1
Bakewell Cl NG24 . . . . 140 C4
Bakewell Dr NG5 . . . . 160 E7
Bakewell Rd NG10 . . . . 193 E5
Bala Dr NG5 . . . . 161 A7
Balderton Ct NG19 . . . . 101 E7
Balderton Gate NG24 . . . . 140 A8
Balderton La NG24 . . . . 141 A7
Baldwin Cl NG19 . . . . 89 B2
Baldwin Ct NG7 . . . . 222 B3
Baldwin St
Eastwood NG16 . . . . 144 C1
Nottingham NG7 . . . . 222 C3
Balfour Rd
Nottingham NG7 . . . . 222 B3
Stapleford NG9 . . . . 182 D6
Balfour St
Gainsborough DN21 . . . . 15 C1
Kirkby in A NG17 . . . . 115 C4
Balfron Gdns [7] NG2 . . . . 173 B2
Ballantrae Cl NG5 . . . . 162 B8
Ballater Cl NG19 . . . . 87 E2
Ballerat Cres NG5 . . . . 160 E8
Ballerini Way LN1 . . . . 57 C3
Ball Hill DE55 . . . . 113 C6
Balloon Houses NG9 . . . . 171 B4
Balloon Wood Ind Est
NG8 . . . . 171 A4
Balls La NG17 . . . . 115 C2
Ball St NG3 . . . . 173 F7
Balmoral Ave NG2 . . . . 185 E8
Balmoral Cl
Carlton in L S81 . . . . 25 F6
Mansfield Woodhouse NG19 88 E5
Sandiacre NG10 . . . . 182 B3
Balmoral Cres NG8 . . . . 171 C5
Balmoral Ct DN11 . . . . 9 B5
Balmoral Dr
Beeston NG9 . . . . 171 C2
Mansfield NG19 . . . . 87 E2
Newark-on-T NG24 . . . . 140 E8
Balmoral Gr NG15 . . . . 146 B8
Balmoral Rd
Bingham NG13 . . . . 177 C4
Carlton NG4 . . . . 174 F6
Nottingham NG1 . . . . 223 D4
Bamburgh Cl [10] NG17 . . . 114 E7
Bamford Dr NG18 . . . . 103 B6
Bamford St DE55 . . . . 99 A3
Bamkin Cl NG15 . . . . 146 B6
Bampton St [8] LE11 . . . . 220 B3
Banbury Ave NG9 . . . . 182 F3
Banbury Mount [9] NG5 . . 161 C2
Banchory Cl NG19 . . . . 87 E2
Bancroft La NG18 . . . . 101 F7
Bancroft Rd NG24 . . . . 140 B6
Bancroft St NG6 . . . . 160 C7
Banes Rd NG13 . . . . 178 B4
Bangor Wlk [3] NG3 . . . . 173 C7
Bank Ave NG17 . . . . 100 E1
Bank Cl
Creswell S80 . . . . 58 D8
Shirebrook NG20 . . . . 72 F4
Bank End Rd DN10 . . . . 1 C4
Bankfield Dr NG9 . . . . 171 C1
Bank Hill NG14 . . . . 149 A4
Bank Pl NG1 . . . . 223 E2
Banks Ave NG17 . . . . 114 E6
Banks Cl NG5 . . . . 162 B6
Banks Cres NG13 . . . . 177 E4
Bank Side DN22 . . . . 39 F3
Banks Paddock NG13 . . . 177 F4
Banks Rd NG9 . . . . 182 E2
Bank St
Langley Mill NG16 . . . . 143 C3
Long Eaton NG10 . . . . 193 E7
Banks The NG13 . . . . 177 F4
Bankwood Cl NG8 . . . . 160 A1
Bank Yd [11] NG6 . . . . 160 B7
Bannerman Rd
Kirkby in A NG17 . . . . 114 F5
Nottingham NG6 . . . . 160 C6
Baptist La NG23 . . . . 111 F8
Barbara Sq NG15 . . . . 130 F1
Barber Cl DE7 . . . . 157 F3
Barber St NG16 . . . . 144 B2
Barbers Wood Cl NG15 . . 117 A1
Barbrook Cl NG8 . . . . 172 A5
Barbury Dr NG11 . . . . 195 D7
Barclay Ct DE7 . . . . 157 C3
Barden Rd NG3 . . . . 162 A4
Bardfield Gdns NG5 . . . . 146 D1
Bardney Dr NG6 . . . . 160 A8
Bardsey Gdns NG5 . . . . 161 A7
Barent Cl NG5 . . . . 160 F6
Barent Wlk NG5 . . . . 160 F6
Bar Gate NG24 . . . . 124 F1
Barker Ave
Sutton in A NG17 . . . . 100 D7
Westwood NG16 . . . . 128 B4
Barker Ave E NG10 . . . . 182 A6
Barker Ave N NG10 . . . . 182 A6
Barker Gate
Hucknall NG15 . . . . 145 F7
Ilkeston DE7 . . . . 157 F2
Nottingham NG1 . . . . 223 F2
Barker Hades Rd S81 . . . . 16 B3
Barker Hill NG14 . . . . 150 E2
Barkers Field LE14 . . . . 211 C3
Barker's La NG9 . . . . 183 E4
Barker St NG17 . . . . 99 F4
Barkestone La
Barkestone-le-V NG13 . . . . 192 A1
Bottesford NG13 . . . . 181 A1
Barkla Cl NG11 . . . . 195 C8
Barkston Cl NG24 . . . . 140 D3
Bar La NG6 . . . . 160 D2
Bar La Ind Pk NG6 . . . . 160 D2
Barley Croft
South Normanton DE55 . . . . 113 B4
West Bridgford NG2 . . . . 185 C4
Barley Dale Dr NG9 . . . . 170 D2
Barleylands NG11 . . . . 196 C6
Barley Ms NG19 . . . . 88 E6
Barley Wy [4] NG24 . . . . 125 B4
Barling Dr DE7 . . . . 157 C2
Barlock Rd NG6 . . . . 160 E4
Barlow Cotts La NG16 . . . 158 B5
Barlow Dr N NG16 . . . . 158 B4
Barlow Dr S NG16 . . . . 158 B4
Barnards Pl LE14 . . . . 211 C3
Barnby Gate NG24 . . . . 140 A8
Barnby La NG23 . . . . 156 E8
Barnby Rd NG24 . . . . 140 D6
Barnby Road Prim Sch
NG24 . . . . 140 B7
Barnby Wlk NG5 . . . . 161 C4
Barn Cl
Cotgrave NG12 . . . . 187 E2
Mansfield NG18 . . . . 102 F5
Worksop S81 . . . . 36 A7
Barn Croft NG9 . . . . 183 B5
Barndale Cl NG2 . . . . 185 C3
Barnes Cres NG17 . . . . 114 E8
Barnes Ct DN22 . . . . 29 D2
Barnes Rd NG5 . . . . 160 E8
Barnet Rd NG3 . . . . 174 B7
Barnett Ct NG12 . . . . 197 E3
Barnfield NG11 . . . . 185 B4
Barnfield Cl LE12 . . . . 212 B4
Barnfield Rd NG23 . . . . 98 B1
Barnsdale Cl LE11 . . . . 220 A5
Barnsley Terr [9] NG2 . . . 173 C1
Barnstone La NG13 . . . . 191 A5
Barnstone Rd NG13 . . . . 190 C2
Barnston Rd NG2 . . . . 174 A5
Barnum Cl NG8 . . . . 171 E5
Barons Cl NG4 . . . . 162 E1
Barons Dr NG22 . . . . 77 F6
Barrack Cotts LE12 . . . . 217 A6
Barrack La NG7 . . . . 222 B2
Barrack Row [4] LE11 . . . . 220 B4
Barra Mews [10] NG2 . . . . 173 B2
Barratt Cl
Beeston NG9 . . . . 183 D1
Cropwell Bishop NG12 . . . . 189 A4
Barratt Cres NG9 . . . . 183 D2
Barratt La NG9 . . . . 183 D1
Bar Rd DN10 . . . . 23 C7
Bar Rd N DN10 . . . . 23 C8
Bar Rd S DN10 . . . . 23 C8
Barrel Hill Rd NG23 . . . . 96 E7
Barrhead Cl NG5 . . . . 146 E1
Barringer Rd NG19 . . . . 88 D1
Barrington Cl NG12 . . . . 175 E2
Barrique Rd NG7 . . . . 172 E1
Barrowhill Wlk NG18 . . . 103 B6
Barrow Rd LE12 . . . . 220 F6
Barrows Gate NG24 . . . . 125 B3
Barrows Hill La NG16 . . . 128 D5
Barrow Slade NG12 . . . . 197 E2
Barrow St LE11 . . . . 220 B3
Barrydale Ave NG9 . . . . 183 F5
Barry St NG6 . . . . 160 B7
Bars Hill LE12 . . . . 206 C1
Bartlow Rd NG8 . . . . 171 D7
Barton Cl
Mansfield Woodhouse
NG19 . . . . 89 B1
Ruddington NG11 . . . . 196 B6
Barton La
Barton in F NG11 . . . . 195 A5
Beeston NG9 . . . . 183 C1
Nottingham NG11 . . . . 184 C1
Barton Rd NG10 . . . . 194 A6
Bartons Cl NG16 . . . . 144 C2
Barton St NG9 . . . . 184 A5
Barton Wy NG9 . . . . 183 E5
Barwell Dr NG8 . . . . 159 D1
Basa Cres NG5 . . . . 160 F8
Basford Rd NG6 . . . . 160 D2
Baskin La NG9 . . . . 183 C3
Baslow Ave NG4 . . . . 162 D1
Baslow Cl NG10 . . . . 193 A5
Baslow Dr NG9 . . . . 172 A1
Baslow Way NG18 . . . . 103 B5
Bassetlaw District General
Hospl S81 . . . . 36 A5
Bassetlaw L Ctr S80 . . . . 35 F3
Bassetlaw Mus DN22 . . . . 39 F7
Bassett Cl NG16 . . . . 158 E7
Bassett Rd NG16 . . . . 158 E7
Bassett The NG20 . . . . 72 E6
Bassingfield La NG12 . . . . 186 F8
Bastion St NG7 . . . . 222 A3
Bateman Gdns [8] NG7 . . . 172 F7
Bateman Rd LE12 . . . . 205 E1
Bateman's Yd NG17 . . . . 114 D4
Bath La
Mansfield NG18 . . . . 102 C8
Market Warsop NG19 . . . . 73 C2
Bathley La
Little Carlton NG23 . . . . 124 C7
South Muskham NG23 . . . . 110 B1
Bathley St NG2 . . . . 173 D1
Baths La NG15 . . . . 146 B7
Bath St
Ilkeston DE7 . . . . 157 E1
Mansfield NG18 . . . . 102 B6
Nottingham NG1 . . . . 223 F3
Sutton in A NG17 . . . . 100 F4
Bath Street Ctr NG1 . . . . 225 F5
Bathurst Dr NG8 . . . . 172 A6
Bathurst Terr NG20 . . . . 58 F2
Bathwood Dr
Mansfield NG17, NG18 . . . 101 E5
Sutton in A NG17, NG18 . . 101 A2
Batley La NG19 . . . . 86 E4
Baulker La
Blidworth NG21 . . . . 118 E4
Clipstone NG21 . . . . 90 B4
Farnsfield NG22 . . . . 119 A4
Baulk La
Beeston NG9 . . . . 183 A6
Harworth DN11 . . . . 8 F5
Torworth DN22 . . . . 19 A2
Worksop S81 . . . . 35 E5
Baulk The
Clarborough DN22 . . . . 40 E8
Worksop S81 . . . . 35 F5
Baum's La NG18 . . . . 102 C5
Bawtry Cl DN11 . . . . 8 F4
Bawtry Rd
Bawtry DN10 . . . . 10 C8
Bircotes DN10 . . . . 9 C1
Blyth S81 . . . . 18 A6
Everton DN10 . . . . 11 A3
Harworth DN11 . . . . 9 A5
Misson DN10 . . . . 4 A3
Tickhill DN11 . . . . 8 E7
Bawtry Wlk NG3 . . . . 173 F6
Baxter Hill NG19 . . . . 86 F3
Baxter St LE11 . . . . 220 B4
Bayard Ct NG8 . . . . 172 C5
Bayard St DN21 . . . . 15 C1
Bayford Dr NG24 . . . . 140 F7
Bayliss Rd NG4 . . . . 162 D3
Bayswater Rd NG16 . . . . 158 F7
Baythorn Rd NG8 . . . . 171 D6
Beacon Dr
Kirkby in A NG17 . . . . 115 C6
Loughborough LE11 . . . . 220 A1
Beacon Hill Conservation
Park NG24 . . . . 125 C1
Beacon Hill Dr NG15 . . . . 145 D5
Beacon Hill Rd
Gringley on t H DN10 . . . . 13 A2
Newark-on-T NG24 . . . . 140 C8
Beacon Hill Rise NG3 . . . . 173 E6
Beacon Hts NG24 . . . . 140 D8
Beacon Rd
Beeston NG9 . . . . 184 B6
Loughborough LE11 . . . . 220 A2
Beaconsfield Dr NG24 . . . 125 F2
Beaconsfield St
Long Eaton NG10 . . . . 193 E7
Beaconsfield St *continued*
Nottingham NG7 . . . . 172 F8
Beacon View NG13 . . . . 181 B3
Beacon Vw NG22 . . . . 77 D3
Beacon Way NG24 . . . . 140 D8
Bean Ave S80 . . . . 36 B3
Bean Cl NG6 . . . . 159 F5
Beanford La
Calverton NG14 . . . . 133 F3
Oxton NG25 . . . . 134 A3
Beardall St
Hucknall NG15 . . . . 146 B6
[7] Mansfield NG18 . . . . 102 A7
Beardall Street Prim Sch
NG15 . . . . 146 B6
Beardsall's Row DN22 . . . . 39 F7
Beardsley Gdns NG2 . . . . 173 B2
Beardsley Rd NG21 . . . . 76 C1
Beardsmore Gr NG15 . . . . 130 F1
Beast Mkt Hill
Newark-on-T NG24 . . . . 124 F1
Nottingham NG1 . . . . 223 E2
Beatty Wlk DE7 . . . . 157 F3
Beauclerk Dr NG5 . . . . 160 E8
Beaufit La NG16 . . . . 113 E2
Beaufort Ct NG11 . . . . 185 C3
Beaufort Dr NG9 . . . . 183 C5
Beaufort Gdns DN10 . . . . 9 F7
Beaufort St DN21 . . . . 15 C3
Beaufort Way S81 . . . . 35 E8
Beaulieu Gdns NG2 . . . . 185 C5
Beauly Dr NG19 . . . . 101 D5
Beaumaris Dr
Beeston NG9 . . . . 183 B4
Carlton NG4 . . . . 163 B1
Beaumond Cross NG24 . . 139 F8
Beaumont Ave NG18 . . . . 102 F5
Beaumont Cl
Keyworth NG12 . . . . 197 E4
Stapleford NG9 . . . . 170 E1
Beaumont Ct LE11 . . . . 220 A6
Beaumont Gdns NG2 . . . . 185 D4
Beaumont Rd LE11 . . . . 220 B1
Beaumont Rise S80 . . . . 35 D3
Beaumont St
Gainsborough DN21 . . . . 24 D8
Nottingham NG2 . . . . 173 E4
Beaumont Wlk NG24 . . . . 125 B2
Beauvale NG16 . . . . 144 C2
Beauvale Cres NG15 . . . . 145 E6
Beauvale Dr DE7 . . . . 157 E5
Beauvale Rd
Annesley Woodhouse
NG17 . . . . 129 E8
Hucknall NG15 . . . . 145 E6
Nottingham NG2 . . . . 173 C1
Beauvale Rise NG16 . . . . 144 A3
Beaver Pl S80 . . . . 35 F3
Beazley Ave NG18 . . . . 101 F7
Beck Ave NG14 . . . . 148 F8
Beck Cres
Blidworth NG21 . . . . 118 A4
Mansfield NG19 . . . . 101 E7
Beckenham Rd NG7 . . . . 222 B4
Becket Sch The NG11 . . . 185 A5
Beckett Ave
Carlton in L S81 . . . . 25 F7
Gainsborough DN21 . . . . 15 E2
Mansfield NG19 . . . . 87 E1
Beckett Ct NG4 . . . . 162 D3
Beckford Rd [8] NG2 . . . . 173 F3
Beckhampton Ctr NG5 . . 161 B5
Beckhampton Rd NG5 . . 161 A7
Beckingham Ct NG19 . . . . 101 E7
Beckingham Prim Sch
DN10 . . . . 14 B1
Beckingham Rd DN10 . . . . 14 A4
Beckingthorpe Dr NG13 . 181 B3
Beck La
Blidworth NG21 . . . . 118 A4
Clayworth DN22 . . . . 21 E4
Farnsfield NG22 . . . . 119 F5
Sutton in A NG17, NG19 . . 101 B6
Beckland Hill NG22 . . . . 65 F6
Beckley Rd NG8 . . . . 159 F2
Beckon Mdw DN10 . . . . 23 C8
Beckside
Lowdham NG14 . . . . 150 E1
West Bridgford NG2 . . . . 186 C5
Beck St
Carlton NG4 . . . . 174 E8
Nottingham NG1 . . . . 223 F3
Thurgarton NG14 . . . . 151 D7
Bedale S81 . . . . 36 A8
Bedale Ct NG9 . . . . 183 A4
Bedale Rd NG5 . . . . 161 D5
Bedarra Gr NG7 . . . . 222 A2
Bede House La NG24 . . . . 140 A8
Bede Ling NG2 . . . . 185 C6
Bedford Ave NG18 . . . . 102 E7
Bedford Cl DE74 . . . . 203 D1
Bedford Ct
Bawtry DN10 . . . . 9 F7
Stapleford NG9 . . . . 170 E1
Bedford Gr NG6 . . . . 160 D5
Bedford Row NG1 . . . . 223 F3
Bedford Sq [3] LE11 . . . . 220 B3
Bedford St LE11 . . . . 220 B3
Bedlington Gdns NG3 . . . 161 E1
Beecham Ave NG3 . . . . 173 F7
Beech Ave
Beeston NG9 . . . . 184 B5
Bingham NG13 . . . . 178 A4
Carlton NG4 . . . . 174 F6
East Leake LE12 . . . . 214 D8
Gainsborough DN21 . . . . 15 D2
Hucknall NG15 . . . . 146 A7
Huthwaite NG17 . . . . 100 A3
Beech Ave *continued*
Keyworth NG12 . . . . 198 A2
Kirkby in A NG17 . . . . 114 F5
Long Eaton NG10 . . . . 182 F1
[12] Mansfield NG18 . . . . 102 B6
New Ollerton NG22 . . . . 77 C4
Nottingham, Hyson Green
NG7 . . . . 173 A8
Nottingham, Mapperley
NG3 . . . . 162 A4
Nuthall NG16 . . . . 159 B6
Pinxton NG16 . . . . 113 E3
Ravenshead NG15 . . . . 116 F3
Sandiacre NG10 . . . . 182 B7
Tickhill DN11 . . . . 8 B7
Worksop S81 . . . . 35 F6
Beech Cl
Gringley on t H DN10 . . . . 12 F2
Nottingham NG6 . . . . 160 C4
Radcliffe on T NG12 . . . . 175 F2
West Bridgford NG12 . . . . 186 A4
Beech Cres
Glapwell S44 . . . . 86 B8
Mansfield Woodhouse
NG19 . . . . 88 D2
Beechcroft S81 . . . . 36 A6
Beech Ct
Nottingham NG3 . . . . 162 A4
Selston NG16 . . . . 129 B3
Beechdale Ave NG17 . . . . 100 F4
Beechdale Cres NG17 . . . 100 F4
Beechdale Rd
Mansfield Woodhouse
NG19 . . . . 89 A2
Nottingham NG8 . . . . 172 B7
Beechdale Swimming Ctr
NG8 . . . . 172 C6
Beecher La DN10 . . . . 14 B1
Beeches Rd LE11 . . . . 220 C2
Beeches The
Carlton NG3 . . . . 174 A8
Sutton in A NG17 . . . . 100 D7
Tuxford NG22 . . . . 65 F2
Beech Gr
Blidworth NG21 . . . . 118 C5
Carlton in L S81 . . . . 25 E7
South Normanton DE55 . . . . 113 B5
Beech Hill Ave NG19 . . . . 87 F1
Beech Hill Cres NG19 . . . . 87 F1
Beech Hill Dr NG19 . . . . 87 F1
Beech Hill Specl Sch
NG19 . . . . 87 F1
Beech Rd
Harworth DN11 . . . . 9 A5
Selston NG16 . . . . 129 B3
Beech St NG17 . . . . 100 D7
Beech Tree Ave NG19 . . . . 88 B5
Beechways DN22 . . . . 39 D4
Beech Wlk DN22 . . . . 50 B4
Beechwood Cl
Mansfield Woodhouse
NG19 . . . . 89 A1
Sutton in A NG17 . . . . 101 A5
Beechwood Cres DN22 . . . 37 F6
Beechwood Ct NG17 . . . . 101 A5
Beechwood Dr DN22 . . . . 38 D6
Beechwood Gr NG17 . . . . 101 A5
Beechwood Rd
Arnold NG5 . . . . 162 A8
[6] Kirkby in A NG17 . . . . 114 F7
Beehive La LN6 . . . . 84 F1
Bee Hive La [4] LE11 . . . . 220 B3
Beehive St DN22 . . . . 39 F6
Beeley Ave NG17 . . . . 100 E1
Beeley Cl NG18 . . . . 103 B6
Beeston Cl NG6 . . . . 146 F4
Beeston Ct NG6 . . . . 160 D6
Beeston Fields Dr NG9 . . 183 D8
Beeston Fields Prim Sch
NG9 . . . . 183 F8
Beeston La NG9 . . . . 184 B8
Beeston Rd
Newark-on-T NG24 . . . . 140 B5
Nottingham NG7 . . . . 172 D1
Beeston Sidings Nature
Reserve NG11 . . . . 184 C7
Beeston Sta NG9 . . . . 184 A5
Beethan Cl NG13 . . . . 177 F4
Beggarlee Pk NG16 . . . . 144 B4
Behay Gdns NG23 . . . . 138 C8
Beighton Ct NG18 . . . . 103 B5
Beighton St NG17 . . . . 100 F3
Belconnen Rd NG5 . . . . 161 A5
Belfields Yd NG22 . . . . 120 C4
Belfmoor Cl S80 . . . . 45 A5
Belford Cl NG6 . . . . 159 F8
Belfry Cl [1] NG17 . . . . 114 E7
Belfry Way NG2 . . . . 186 C4
Belgrave Ct DN10 . . . . 9 F7
Belgrave Mews NG11 . . . . 185 C3
Belgrave Rd NG6 . . . . 160 A7
Belgrave Sq NG1 . . . . 223 D3
Bella Cl NG16 . . . . 143 B4
Bellamy Rd NG18 . . . . 103 A2
Bellar Gate NG1 . . . . 223 F2
Belle-Isle Rd NG15 . . . . 146 A7
Belleville Dr NG5 . . . . 161 B8
Bellevue Ct NG3 . . . . 173 E6
Belle Vue La NG21 . . . . 118 A6
Bell Foundry Mus LE11 . . 220 C4
Bell La
Collingham NG23 . . . . 111 F8
Nottingham NG11 . . . . 185 A7
Weston NG23 . . . . 81 A5
Bellmore Gdns NG8 . . . . 171 D5

Bellsfield Cl S80 . . . . 45 A5
Bells La NG8 . . . . 160 A3
Bell St NG4 . . . . 174 D8
Belmond Cl NG24 . . . . 139 F5
Belmont Ave NG6 . . . . 160 C7
Belmont Cl
 Beeston NG9 . . . . 183 B4
 Hucknall NG15 . . . . 146 A4
 Mansfield Woodhouse NG19 89 A2
Belmont Rd NG17 . . . . 115 B1
Belper Ave NG4 . . . . 162 D1
Belper Cres NG4 . . . . 162 D1
Belper Rd NG7 . . . . 172 F7
Belper St NG18 . . . . 102 D7
Belper Way NG18 . . . . 102 D7
Belsay Rd NG5 . . . . 161 A7
Belsford Ct NG16 . . . . 159 A8
Belton Cl NG10 . . . . 182 B4
Belton Dr NG2 . . . . 185 B4
Belton Rd LE11 . . . . 220 A5
Belton Rd W Extension
 LE11 . . . . 220 A6
Belton St NG7 . . . . 172 F8
Belt Rd The DN21 . . . . 15 E3
Belvedere Ave **9** NG7. . 172 F8
Belvedere St NG18 . . . . . . 102 B6
Belvoir Ave NG13 . . . . 181 A1
Belvoir Cl
 Aslockton NG13 . . . . 178 E3
 Long Eaton NG10 . . . . . . 193 E5
Belvoir Cres
 Langar NG13 . . . . 190 C2
 Newark-on-T NG24 . . . . . 140 A6
Belvoir High Sch NG13 . . . 181 A1
Belvoir Hill NG2 . . . . 173 F4
Belvoir Pl NG24 . . . . 140 D4
Belvoir Rd
 Balderton NG24 . . . . 140 D3
 Bottesford NG13 . . . . 181 A2
 Carlton NG4 . . . . 175 A4
 Redmile NG13 . . . . 192 F3
 West Bridgford NG2 . . . . 174 A1
Belvoir St
 Hucknall NG15 . . . . 145 F8
 Nottingham NG3 . . . . 161 F2
Belvoir Terr DN21 . . . . 15 B4
Belward St NG1 . . . . 223 F2
Belwood Cl NG7 . . . . 184 F2
Bembridge S81 . . . . 36 B6
Bembridge Ct NG9 . . . . 183 A8
Bembridge Dr NG5 . . . . 161 B6
Bendigo La NG2 . . . . 174 A4
Benedict Ct **3** NG5 . . . . 147 A1
Benet Dr NG22 . . . . 106 A5
Benington Dr NG8 . . . . 171 C3
Benjamin Adlard Com Sch
 DN21 . . . . 24 E6
Ben Mayo Ct NG7 . . . . 222 B4
Benner Ave DE7 . . . . 170 A5
Bennerley Ave DE7 . . . . . . 157 F4
Bennerley Ct NG6 . . . . 159 F8
Bennerley Rd NG6 . . . . 159 F8
Bennett Ave NG18 . . . . 102 F6
Bennett Rd NG3 . . . . 162 A3
Bennett St
 Long Eaton NG10 . . . . . . 182 C2
 Nottingham NG3 . . . . 161 F2
 Sandiacre NG10 . . . . 182 B5
Benneworth Cl NG15 . . . . . 145 F5
Bennington Wlk NG19 . . . . . 88 E4
Ben St NG7 . . . . 222 B4
Bentick St NG18 . . . . 102 D7
Bentinck Ave NG12 . . . . . . 186 D1
Bentinck Banks Nature
 Reserve NG17 . . . . 114 E3
Bentinck Cl
 Annesley Woodhouse
  NG17. . . . . 114 F1
 Boughton NG22 . . . . 77 E6
Bentinck Ct **8** NG4 . . . 173 E4
Bentinck Prim Sch NG7 . 222 B4
Bentinck Rd
 Carlton NG4 . . . . 162 C2
 Newark-on-T NG24 . . . . . 139 F6
 Nottingham NG7 . . . . 222 B4
Bentinck St
 Annesley Woodhouse
  NG17. . . . . 129 F8
 Hucknall NG15 . . . . 145 F8
 Sutton in A NG17 . . . . . . 100 F3
Bentinck Terr NG20 . . . . 74 B3
Bentley Ave NG3 . . . . 174 B6
Bentwell Ave NG5 . . . . 162 A7
Beresford Dr DE7 . . . . 157 E5
Beresford Rd
 Long Eaton NG10 . . . . . . 193 A5
 Mansfield Woodhouse NG19 88 C6
Beresford St
 Mansfield NG18 . . . . 102 D6
 Nottingham NG7 . . . . 222 A3
Berkeley Ave
 Long Eaton NG10 . . . . . . 193 C6
 Nottingham NG3 . . . . 173 C8
Berkeley Cres NG12 . . . . . 176 D3
Berkeley Rd NG18 . . . . 102 C5
Bernard Ave
 Hucknall NG15 . . . . 131 B1
 Mansfield Woodhouse NG19 88 B5
Bernard Rd NG19 . . . . 101 E8
Bernard St NG5 . . . . 161 B1
Bernisdale Cl NG5 . . . . 146 F1
Berridge Adult Ctr The
 NG7. . . . . 173 A8
Berridge Inf Sch NG7 . . . 172 E7
Berridge Jun Sch NG7 . . . 172 E7

Berridge Rd NG7 . . . . 173 A8
Berridge Rd W NG7 . . . . . 172 E7
Berriedale Cl NG5 . . . . 162 C8
Berristow Grange NG17 . 100 D1
Berristow La DE55 . . . . 113 C7
Berry Ave NG17 . . . . 114 E6
Berry Hill Cl NG18 . . . . 102 C4
Berry Hill Gdns NG18 . . . . 102 F4
Berry Hill Gr NG4 . . . . 162 E2
Berry Hill La NG18 . . . . 102 D4
Berry Hill Mews NG18 . . . 102 D4
Berry Hill Prim Sch
 NG18. . . . . 102 F4
Berry Hill Rd NG18 . . . . . . 102 C4
Berry Pk Lea NG18 . . . . . . 102 D3
Berwick Ave NG19 . . . . 101 D8
Berwick Cl NG5 . . . . 161 C6
Berwin Cl NG10 . . . . 182 A1
Beryldene Ave NG16 . . . . . 159 A7
Bescar La NG22 . . . . 77 A2
Bescoby St DN22 . . . . 39 F6
Besecar Ave NG4 . . . . 162 E2
Besecar Cl NG4 . . . . 162 E2
Bessell La NG9 . . . . 182 D5
Bessingham Dr NG11 . . . . 185 C3
Besthorpe Nature Reserve
 (North) NG23 . . . . 97 D6
Besthorpe Nature Reserve
 (South) NG23 . . . . 97 D4
Besthorpe Prim Sch NG23 97 F6
Besthorpe Rd
 Collingham NG23 . . . . . . 98 A2
 North Scarle LN6 . . . . 83 C1
Bestwick Ave DE75 . . . . . . 143 B1
Bestwick Cl DE7 . . . . 170 A4
Bestwood Ave NG5 . . . . . . 161 E8
Bestwood Cl NG5 . . . . 161 E8
Bestwood Ctry Pk NG6 . . 146 F3
Bestwood Lodge Dr NG5 161 D8
Bestwood Park Drive 4
 NG5 . . . . 147 B1
Bestwood Pk Dr NG5 . . . . 161 B8
Bestwood Pk Dr W NG5 . 146 E1
Bestwood Pk View NG5 . 147 E1
Bestwood Rd
 Hucknall NG15 . . . . 146 C5
 Nottingham NG6 . . . . 146 D2
 Pinxton NG16 . . . . 113 C2
Bestwood Terr NG6 . . . . . . 160 C8
Bethel Gdns NG15 . . . . 145 C5
Bethel Terr S80 . . . . 34 E7
Bethnal Wlk **2** NG6 . . . 160 B7
Betony Cl NG13 . . . . 177 C4
Betula Cl NG11 . . . . 184 C1
Beulah Rd NG17 . . . . 115 B4
Bevan Cl NG21 . . . . 118 B8
Bevel St NG7 . . . . 172 F7
Bevercotes Cl NG24 . . . . . 139 F6
Bevercotes Rd NG22 . . . . . 65 D3
Beverley Cl
 Nottingham NG8 . . . . 171 B4
 Rainworth NG21 . . . . 104 B1
Beverley Dr
 Kimberley NG16 . . . . 158 E7
 Kirkby in A NG17 . . . . . . 115 C3
 Mansfield NG18 . . . . 102 D2
Beverley Gdns NG4 . . . . . 162 F1
Beverley Rd DN11 . . . . 9 A4
Beverleys Ave NG13 . . . . . 178 F4
Beverley Sq NG3 . . . . 173 E2
Beverley Wlk S81 . . . . 25 E7
Bewcastle Rd NG5 . . . . . . 147 A2
Bewick Dr NG3 . . . . 174 C5
Bexhill Ct NG8 . . . . 171 E1
Bexwell Cl NG11 . . . . 195 E8
Biant Cl NG8 . . . . 160 B3
Bidford Rd NG8 . . . . 159 F1
Bidwell Cres NG11 . . . . . . 195 B2
Big Barn La NG18 . . . . 102 F5
Biggart Cl **2** NG9 . . . . 183 C2
Biggin St LE11 . . . . 220 B4
Big La DN22 . . . . 30 D3
Bigsby Rd DN22 . . . . 30 A1
Big Wood Sch NG5 . . . . . . 147 B2
Biko Sq **8** NG7 . . . . 172 F8
Bilberry Wlk NG3 . . . . 173 E7
Bilbie Wlk NG1 . . . . 223 D3
Bilby Gdns **3** NG3 . . . . 173 F5
Billesdon Dr NG5 . . . . 160 F4
Billingsley Ave NG16 . . . . 113 D3
Bilsthorpe Rd NG22 . . . . . . 92 D1
Bilton Cl NG24 . . . . 140 D2
Binbrook Ct DN10 . . . . 9 F6
Bingham Ave NG17 . . . . . . 101 A5
Bingham Ind Pk NG13 . . . 177 E5
Bingham L Ctr NG13 . . . . 177 F3
Bingham Rd
 Cotgrave NG12 . . . . 187 F3
 Langar NG13 . . . . 190 B4
 Mansfield NG18 . . . . 103 A3
 Nottingham NG5 . . . . 161 C2
 Radcliffe on T NG12 . . . . 176 A3
Bingham Robert Miles Inf
 Sch NG13 . . . . 177 E5
Bingham Sta NG13 . . . . . . 177 F5
Bingley Cl **2** NG8 . . . . . 172 B6
BioCity NG8 . . . . 173 E4
Birch Ave
 Beeston NG9 . . . . 184 B4
 Carlton NG4 . . . . 174 D7
 Farnsfield NG22 . . . . 119 E7
 Ilkeston DE7 . . . . 170 A7
 Nuthall NG16 . . . . 159 B6
 Rainworth NG21 . . . . 104 C1

Birch Cl
 Nuthall NG16 . . . . 159 B6
 Rampton DN22 . . . . 42 F2
 Ravenshead NG15 . . . . . 117 A1
Birch Croft Dr NG19 . . . . . . 89 A2
Birch Ct NG22 . . . . 65 F2
Birchdale Ave NG15 . . . . . 146 A5
Birchenhall Ct NG24 . . . . . 139 A4
Birchen Holme DE55 . . . . 113 A4
Birches The NG15 . . . . 117 A3
Birchfield Dr S80 . . . . 35 B2
Birchfield Rd NG5 . . . . 148 A1
Birch Gr
 Gainsborough DN21 . . . . 15 D2
 Mansfield NG18 . . . . 103 A4
 Shirebrook NG20 . . . . 72 D5
Birchlands NG19 . . . . 88 F1
Birch Lea
 Arnold NG5 . . . . 161 D8
 East Leake LE12 . . . . . . 205 D1
Birchover Pl DE7 . . . . 157 E5
Birchover Rd NG8 . . . . 171 C6
Birch Pas NG7 . . . . 222 C3
Birch Rd
 Hodthorpe S80 . . . . 45 C6
 New Balderton NG24 . . . 140 C5
 New Ollerton NG22 . . . . 77 D4
Birch Rise NG14 . . . . 149 C5
Birch St NG20 . . . . 73 F6
Birch Tree Cl NG19 . . . . 89 D3
Birch Tree Cres NG17 . . . . 114 F4
Birchwood Ave
 Breaston NG10 . . . . 193 A7
 Long Eaton NG10 . . . . . . 193 C5
Birchwood Cl
 Ravenshead NG15 . . . . . 117 B1
 South Normanton DE55 . 113 A4
 Southwell NG25 . . . . 121 D1
 Sutton in A NG17 . . . . . . 100 E6
Birchwood Dr
 Ravenshead NG15 . . . . . 117 A1
 Sutton in A NG17 . . . . . . 100 D7
Birchwood Rd NG8 . . . . . . 171 C4
Birchwood View DN21 . . . . 15 F1
Bircotes & Harworth Com
 Sch DN11 . . . . 9 C5
Bircotes L Ctr DN11 . . . . . . 9 C4
Bird Cl NG18 . . . . 102 C3
Birding St NG19 . . . . 88 B1
Birdsall Ave NG8 . . . . 171 E4
Bird's La NG17 . . . . 114 E1
Birkdale Cl
 Ilkeston DE7 . . . . 157 D1
 West Bridgford NG12 . . . 186 A3
Birkdale Dr **3** NG17 . . . 114 F6
Birkdale Gr DN22 . . . . 39 D2
Birkdale Way
 Nottingham NG5 . . . . 160 F8
 9 Nottingham NG5 . . 161 A8
Birkin Ave
 Beeston NG9 . . . . 183 A2
 Nottingham NG7 . . . . 172 F7
 Radcliffe on T NG12 . . . . 176 A4
 Ruddington NG11 . . . . . . 196 C8
Birkland Ave
 Mansfield Woodhouse
  NG19. . . . . 88 D3
 Market Warsop NG20 . . . . 74 B4
 Nottingham, Mapperley
  NG3. . . . . 162 A4
 Nottingham, St Ann's NG1. 223 E4
Birkland Dr NG21 . . . . 76 A2
Birklands Ave
 New Ollerton NG22 . . . . 77 C6
 Worksop S80 . . . . 36 C1
Birklands Cl NG20 . . . . 74 B5
Birklands Prim Sch NG20. 74 B5
Birkland St NG18 . . . . 102 D7
Birks Cl S80 . . . . 45 C6
Birks Rd NG19 . . . . 101 D7
Birley St NG9 . . . . 182 D5
Birling Cl NG6 . . . . 159 F7
Birrell Rd NG7 . . . . 173 A8
Birrel St DN21 . . . . 15 B2
Bisham Dr NG2 . . . . 186 A7
Bishop Alexander Prim Sch
 NG24. . . . . 125 A4
Bishop Alexandra Ct
 NG24 . . . . 139 E7
Bishopdale S81 . . . . 36 A7
Bishopdale Cl NG10 . . . . . 193 A6
Bishopdale Dr NG16 . . . . . 159 B7
Bishopfield La DN22 . . . . . 19 A5
Bishops Cl NG12 . . . . 197 E4
Bishop's Dr NG25 . . . . 136 E8
Bishops Hill NG21 . . . . 103 F1
Bishops Rd NG13 . . . . 177 D5
Bishop St
 Eastwood NG16 . . . . 143 F4
 Loughborough LE11 . . . . 220 C4
 Mansfield NG18 . . . . 102 B5
 Sutton in A NG17 . . . . . . 100 E3
Bishops Way NG15 . . . . . . 146 B8
Bishop's Wlk NG20 . . . . . . 74 A4
Bispham Dr NG9 . . . . 182 F2
Bispham Dr Jun Sch
 NG9. . . . . 182 E3
Blackacre NG14 . . . . 163 E5
Blackbird Av **8** S81. . . . 35 C7
Blackbrook Rd NG24 . . . . 125 D1
Blackburn Cl NG23 . . . . . . 98 B1
Blackburn Pl DE7 . . . . 157 E3
Blackcliff Field Cl S80 . . . . 45 A5
Blacketts Wlk NG11 . . . . . 195 C8
Blackfriars Cl NG8 . . . . . . 159 D3

Blackham Rd LE11 . . . . . . 220 A1
Blackhill Dr NG4 . . . . 174 F8
Black La LN6 . . . . 71 F1
Blackrod Cl NG9 . . . . 183 A2
Black Scotch La
 Mansfield NG18 . . . . 102 E3
 Ravenshead NG18 . . . . . 116 F8
Blacksmith Ct NG12 . . . . . 187 E4
Blacksmith La
 Kelham NG23 . . . . 124 A4
 Torworth DN22 . . . . 19 B2
Blacksmiths Cl LE14 . . . . . 219 D8
Blacksmiths Ct NG15 . . . . 131 D3
Blacksmiths La LN6 . . . . . . 83 D2
Blackstone Wlk NG2 . . . . . 173 C2
Blackstope La DN22 . . . . . . 40 A7
Black Swan Cl NG5 . . . . . . 161 D4
Blackthorn Cl
 Bingham NG13 . . . . 178 B4
 Carlton NG4 . . . . 163 A2
 1 Gainsborough DN21. 15 F1
Blackthorn Dr NG6 . . . . . . 160 B3
Blackthorne Cl NG24 . . . . 140 B5
Blackthorne Dr NG14 . . . . 150 D2
Blackthorn Way NG100 . . . 100 C1
Blackwell Rd NG17 . . . . . . 99 E3
Bladon Cl NG3 . . . . 161 E2
Bladon Rd NG11 . . . . 196 B7
Blair Ct **4** NG2 . . . . 173 C1
Blair Gr NG10 . . . . 182 A4
Blaise Cl NG11 . . . . 195 E8
Blake Rd
 Stapleford NG9 . . . . 182 E6
 West Bridgford NG2 . . . . 186 A7
Blake St
 Ilkeston DE7 . . . . 157 F1
 Mansfield Woodhouse NG19 88 B2
Blandford Ave NG10 . . . . . 193 B5
Blandford Dr DN22 . . . . . . 39 D4
Blandford Gdns NG2 . . . . . 185 C5
Blandford Rd NG9 . . . . 183 C5
Bland La NG14 . . . . 150 A5
Blankney Cl LN1 . . . . 57 A4
Blankney St NG5 . . . . 160 E4
Blantyre Ave NG5 . . . . 146 E1
Blatherwick Rd NG24 . . . . 140 D8
Blatherwick's Yd NG5 . . . . 161 F8
Bleaberry Cl NG2 . . . . 186 C5
Bleachers Yd NG7 . . . . 160 F1
Bleak Hill Way NG18 . . . . 101 E4
Bleasby CE Prim Sch
 NG14. . . . . 151 F8
Bleasby Cres NG17 . . . . . 101 B1
Bleasby Rd NG14 . . . . 151 D8
Bleasby St NG2 . . . . 173 F4
Bleasby Sta NG14 . . . . . . 151 F8
Bleasdale Cl NG4 . . . . 163 A2
Blencathra Cl NG2 . . . . . . 186 C5
Blenheim Ave
 Lowdham NG14 . . . . 150 E1
 Nottingham NG3 . . . . 162 C2
Blenheim Cl
 Mansfield NG19 . . . . 88 D1
 Ruddington NG11 . . . . . . 196 B7
Blenheim Dr NG9 . . . . 183 C5
Blenheim Gdns NG15 . . . . 165 D2
Blenheim Ind Est NG6 . . . 159 F8
Blenheim La NG6,NG15 . . 145 E1
Blenheim Pl NG17 . . . . 99 E3
Blenheim Rise
 Bawtry DN10 . . . . 9 F6
 Worksop S81 . . . . 35 E8
Blenheim St NG10 . . . . . . 182 B5
Blessed Robert RC Prim Sch
 NG11. . . . . 195 E8
Bley Ave LE12 . . . . 214 D8
Blidworth Cl NG8 . . . . 159 E2
Blidworth Ind Pk NG21 . . 118 B6
Blidworth La
 Blidworth NG21 . . . . 133 C8
 Mansfield NG21 . . . . 103 D1
 Rainworth NG21 . . . . 117 E8
Blidworth Rd
 Farnsfield NG22 . . . . 119 E6
 Kirkby in A NG15 . . . . . . 115 D8
Blidworth Waye NG15 . . . 131 F7
Blind La
 Keyworth NG12 . . . . 197 E2
 Oxton NG25 . . . . 134 C4
Bloomgrove Rd DE7 . . . . . 157 F2
Bloomsbury Dr NG16 . . . . 159 E3
Bloomsgrove Ind Est
 NG7. . . . . 222 B3
Bloomsgrove St NG7 . . . . 222 B3
Bluebell Bank NG13 . . . . 177 D3
Bluebell Cl
 Hucknall NG15 . . . . 145 C6
 Selston NG16 . . . . 128 F2
 Shirebrook NG20 . . . . 72 D3
 Stanton Hill NG17 . . . . . 100 B6
Bluebell Gr **2** NG17 . . . 114 F7
Blue Bell Hill Prim Sch
 NG3. . . . . 173 F6
Blue Bell Hill Rd NG3 . . . 173 E6
Bluebell Pl NG19 . . . . 88 F4
Bluebells The NG17 . . . . . 101 B1
Bluebell Wood Way
 NG17. . . . . 100 C1
Blue Bell Yd NG22 . . . . 65 F3
Bluecoat Cl NG1 . . . . 223 E3
Bluecoat St NG1 . . . . 223 E4

Blundell Cl NG3 . . . . 173 F8
Blyth Cl NG19 . . . . 87 D1
Blyth Gdns NG3 . . . . 161 E2
Blyth Gr S81 . . . . 36 A5
Blyth Rd
 Blyth, Bilby S81, DN22. . . 27 E5
 Blyth, Nornay S81 . . . . . . 18 A7
 Elkesley S80 . . . . 48 F4
 Harworth DN11 . . . . 8 F3
 New Ollerton NG22 . . . . . 77 A6
 Oldcotes S81 . . . . 16 F6
 Ranskill DN22 . . . . 19 A4
 Walesby NG22 . . . . 63 A3
 Worksop, Kilton S81 . . . . 36 B6
Blyth St NG3 . . . . 161 E2
Blyton Wlk NG5 . . . . 161 B7
BMI The Park Hospl
 NG5. . . . . 132 D2
Boar La NG24 . . . . 139 F8
Boat La
 Aldercar NG16 . . . . 143 A7
 Bleasby NG14 . . . . 152 C7
 Hoveringham NG14 . . . . 151 E2
Boatmans Cl DE7 . . . . 157 F2
Bobbers Mill Bridge
 NG7. . . . . 172 D7
Bobbers Mill Rd NG7 . . . . 172 E7
Boden Dr NG16 . . . . 159 C6
Boden St NG7 . . . . 222 B3
Bodmin Ave NG15 . . . . . . 145 C5
Bodmin Ct **5** NG18 . . . . 103 A2
Bodmin Dr NG8 . . . . 160 C2
Body Rd NG9 . . . . 183 B2
Bohem Rd NG10 . . . . 182 C3
Bold Cl NG6 . . . . 160 B8
Bolero Cl NG8 . . . . 171 E5
Bolham La DN22 . . . . 29 F1
Bolingey Way NG15 . . . . . 145 C5
Bollard's La LE12 . . . . 213 A7
Bolsover St
 Hucknall NG15 . . . . 146 B7
 Mansfield NG18 . . . . 102 D6
Bolton Ave NG9 . . . . 183 C4
Bolton Cl NG2 . . . . 186 A7
Bolton La NG14 . . . . 211 F7
Bolton Terr NG12 . . . . 175 F3
Bond Cl LE11 . . . . 220 C1
Bond St
 Arnold NG5 . . . . 161 E8
 Nottingham NG2 . . . . 173 E4
Bonemill La
 Clarborough DN22 . . . . . . 30 D2
 Worksop S81 . . . . 35 D5
Bonetti Cl NG5 . . . . 162 C5
Boniface Gdns **4** NG5. . 147 A1
Bonington Art Gall NG1 . 223 D3
Bonington Dr NG5 . . . . . . 161 F7
Bonington Inf Com Sch
 NG6. . . . . 160 B6
Bonington Jun Sch NG6. 160 B6
Bonington Rd
 Mansfield NG19 . . . . 101 E6
 Nottingham NG3 . . . . 162 A3
Bonington Theatre NG5. 161 E8
Bonner Hill NG14 . . . . 148 F6
Bonner La NG14 . . . . 149 B6
Bonner's Rd NG16 . . . . . . 158 C4
Bonnington Cl NG6 . . . . . . 160 A6
Bonnington Cres NG5 . . . 161 C4
Bonny Mead NG12 . . . . . . 187 E2
Bonsal Ct NG18 . . . . 103 B6
Bonsall St NG10 . . . . 193 E8
Bonser Cl NG4 . . . . 174 E7
Bonser Cres NG17 . . . . 99 E2
Bonser Gdns NG17 . . . . . 100 D2
Booth Ave NG19 . . . . 87 A5
Booth Cl NG3 . . . . 223 F3
Booth Cres NG19 . . . . 87 D2
Booth St NG19 . . . . 88 B3
Boots Yd NG17 . . . . 99 F3
Borders Ave NG17 . . . . . . 114 E8
Borlace Cres NG9 . . . . 182 E6
Borman Cl NG6 . . . . 159 F5
Borough St DE74 . . . . 203 D2
Borrow Bread La NG14 . . 152 B2
Borrowdale Cl NG2 . . . . . . 186 D6
Borrowdale Dr NG10 . . . . . 193 A6
Borrowell DE74 . . . . 203 C3
Boscombe Rd S81 . . . . 35 C8
Boscowan Ct DE7 . . . . 157 F4
Bosden Cl NG8 . . . . 171 C6
Bosley Sq NG9 . . . . 184 A8
Bostock's La NG10 . . . . . . 182 A3
Boston St NG1 . . . . 223 F3
Boswell Cl
 Kinoulton NG12 . . . . 200 A2
 Mansfield NG18 . . . . 102 C3
Bosworth Dr NG16 . . . . . . 144 B3
Bosworth St NG19 . . . . . . 101 D7
Bosworth Way NG10 . . . . 193 E5
Bosworth Wlk **10** NG2 . 173 B1
Botany Ave
 Mansfield NG18 . . . . 101 F6
 Nottingham NG3 . . . . 173 F7
Botany Cl NG11 . . . . 185 C2
Botany Dr DE7 . . . . 157 F5
Bothe Cl NG10 . . . . 193 C6
Bottesford Sta NG13 . . . . 181 C3
Bottleacre La LE11 . . . . . . 220 B6
Bottle La NG1 . . . . 223 E2
Bottom Gn LE14 . . . . 210 A1
Bottom Row NG24 . . . . . . 140 B8
Boughton Cl NG17 . . . . . . 100 F5
Boughton Ind Est NG22 . 78 B5
Boughton Ppg Sta NG22. 77 D2
Boughton Rd S80 . . . . 35 A5
Bould St NG19 . . . . 87 F1

Boulevard Ind Pk NG7 184 C7
Boundary Cl NG20 72 E6
Boundary Cres
Beeston NG9 171 F1
Blidworth NG21 118 B5
Boundary Ct NG24 139 F7
Boundary La NG16 143 C3
Boundary Rd
Beeston NG9 183 F8
Newark-on-T NG24 139 F7
West Bridgford NG2 185 F4
Boundary Row S80 35 F2
Boundary Wlk NG20 58 F1
Bourne Ave
Kirkby in A NG17 115 B3
Selston NG16 129 A7
Bourne Cl NG9 171 D1
Bourne Dr NG15 117 A2
Bourne Mews NG4 175 A6
Bourne St NG4 175 A6
Bournmoor Ave NG7 184 E1
Bovill St NG7 222 B4
Bovington Ct DN22 29 E1
Bowbridge Gdns NG13 181 A3
Bowbridge La
Bottesford NG13 180 F3
New Balderton NG24 140 A3
Bowbridge Prim Sch NG24 139 F5
Bowbridge Rd NG24 140 A6
Bowden Dr NG9 184 B6
Bowers Ave 6 NG3 173 D7
Bowes Well Rd DE7 157 E2
Bowland Cl NG3 174 A7
Bowland Rd NG13 177 C4
Bowler Ct 3 LE11 220 C4
Bowling Gn Rd DN21 15 B1
Bowling St NG18 102 D6
Bowlwell Ave NG5 160 F8
Bowness Ave NG6 160 C2
Bowness Cl NG2 186 C7
Bowne St NG17 100 F3
Bowscale Cl NG2 186 C5
Bow St NG19 88 E4
Box Cres NG17 114 F6
Boxley Dr NG2 185 C4
Boyce Gdns NG3 161 F1
Boycroft Ave NG3 173 F8
Boyd Cl NG5 148 A1
Boyer's Orch LE14 202 B3
Boyer St LE11 220 C4
Boy La NG21 76 B1
Boynton Dr NG3 161 F1
Bracadale Rd NG5 146 F1
Bracebridge S80 36 B3
Bracebridge Ave S80 36 B3
Bracebridge Ct S80 36 A2
Bracebridge Dr NG8 171 D7
Bracey Rise NG2 185 E3
Bracken Ave NG22 77 E6
Bracken Cl
Carlton NG4 162 D2
Gainsborough DN21 15 B3
2 Kirkby in A NG17 114 F6
Long Eaton NG10 182 B1
Market Warsop NG20 74 C3
Nottingham NG8 159 F1
Bracken Ct
Bilsthorpe NG22 106 A5
Harworth DN11 8 E4
Brackendale Ave NG5 161 F8
Brackendale Dr NG22 64 A2
Brackenfield Ave NG19 88 E4
Brackenfield Dr NG16 158 B7
Brackenfield Rise NG15 117 A3
Brackenfield Specl Sch NG10 182 B1
Bracken Hill NG18 103 A5
Bracken Hill La
Austerfield DN10 3 F7
Misson DN10 4 A5
Bracken Hill Specl Sch NG17 115 C5
Brackenhurst Coll Env Ed Ctr NG25 136 D5
Brackenhurst La NG25 136 D6
Bracken La DN22 40 B5
Bracken Lane Prim Sch DN22 40 A5
Bracken Rd
Long Eaton NG10 182 B1
Shirebrook NG20 72 D3
Bracken Way DN11 8 E4
Brackenwood Cl NG19 89 A1
Brackhills Cl NG19 88 E1
Bracknell Cres NG8 160 D1
Brackner La NG22 106 B3
Bracton Dr NG3 173 F6
Bradbourne Ave NG11 185 A5
Bradbury Gd NG11 196 B7
Bradbury St NG2 174 A4
Bradden Ave NG9 170 E1
Bradder Way NG18 102 A5
Braddock Cl NG7 222 A2
Bradfield Rd NG8 159 F1
Bradforth Ave NG18 103 A7
Bradgate Cl NG10 182 B4
Bradgate Rd 2 NG7 173 A8
Bradleys Orch NG14 151 C2
Bradley St NG10 182 C5
Bradman Gdns NG5 162 B6
Bradmore Ave NG11 196 C8
Bradmore Ct NG18 103 A3
Bradmore La NG12 197 D5
Bradmore Rise NG5 161 C4
Bradshaw St NG10 193 B5
Bradwell Cl NG16 158 C8
Bradwell Dr NG5 161 A8
Braefell Cl NG2 186 D5
Braemar Ave NG16 143 F1
Braemar Dr NG4 163 B1
Braemar Rd
Clipstone NG19 89 E3
Nottingham NG6 160 C7
Brailsford Ct NG18 103 B6
Brailsford Rd 1 NG7 172 E1
Brailsford Way NG9 183 C1
Brailwood Cl NG22 106 A6
Brailwood Rd NG22 106 A6
Brake La NG22 77 E7
Brake Rd NG22 63 D1
Brake View NG22 77 E6
Bramber Gr NG11 195 E7
Bramble Cl
Beeston NG9 183 D2
Long Eaton NG10 182 B1
New Ollerton NG22 77 D6
North Leverton with Habblesthorpe DN22 42 D8
Nottingham NG6 160 D3
Shirebrook NG20 72 E6
South Normanton DE55 113 B6
Bramble Croft NG17 100 C1
Bramble Ct NG4 162 F1
Bramble Dr NG3 174 B8
Bramble Gdns NG8 172 A8
Bramble La NG18 103 A5
Bramble Rd DN22 40 B4
Brambles The NG22 64 A2
Brambleway NG12 188 A2
Bramble Way DN11 8 E4
Brambling Cl NG18 102 E7
Bramblings The S81 35 C7
Bramcote Ave NG9 183 D6
Bramcote CE Prim Sch NG9 183 B8
Bramcote Ct NG18 103 A3
Bramcote Dr
Beeston NG9 183 E7
Nottingham NG8 171 D3
Retford DN22 39 D5
Bramcote Dr W NG9 183 D7
Bramcote Hills Prim Sch NG9 171 B1
Bramcote Hills Sp & Com Coll NG9 171 B2
Bramcote La
Beeston NG9 183 C5
Nottingham NG8 171 D3
Bramcote L Ctr NG9 171 A1
Bramcote Lorne Sch DN22 51 A5
Bramcote Park Bus & Ent Sch The NG9 171 A1
Bramcote Rd NG9 183 E7
Bramcote St NG7 222 A3
Bramcote Wlk NG7 222 A3
Bramerton Rd NG8 171 D6
Bramhall Rd NG8 171 C6
Bramley Apple Ex NG25 121 D1
Bramley Cl
East Leake LE12 205 E1
Gunthorpe NG14 165 A5
Southwell NG25 136 F8
Bramley Ct
Gainsborough DN21 15 E1
Kimberley NG16 158 F6
Sutton in A NG17 100 F3
Bramley Rd NG8 159 E1
Bramley Wlk NG19 101 D7
Brammersack Cl NG23 124 B7
Brampton Ave DE75 143 A2
Brampton Ct NG2 186 C7
Brampton Dr NG9 182 F5
Brancaster Cl NG6 160 B4
Brancliffe La S81 34 F7
Brandish Cres NG11 184 D1
Brand La NG17 100 C5
Brandon Cl NG24 140 E4
Brandreth Ave
Nottingham NG3 173 F8
Sutton in A NG17 100 D4
Brandreth Dr NG16 158 A8
Brand St NG2 173 F2
Branklene Cl NG16 158 E7
Branksome Wlk 3 NG2 173 C2
Bransdale S81 36 A8
Bransdale Ave NG19 88 E1
Bransdale Cl NG10 193 B6
Bransdale Rd NG11 184 D1
Branston Ave NG22 119 F6
Branston Cl NG24 125 D6
Branston Gdns NG2 185 D4
Branston Wlk NG5 161 C4
Brantford Ave NG7 184 F1
Brantingham Gdns DN10 3 A1
Brassington Cl NG16 158 B7
Brassington Ct NG19 88 E4
Braunton Cl NG15 145 D6
Brayton Cres NG6 160 D5
B Rd NG9 184 D6
Breach Rd DE75 157 A8
Breadsall Ct DE7 157 F3
Breamer Rd NG23 112 B8
Brechin S81 36 B5
Brechin Cl NG5 148 B1
Brechin Ct NG19 88 B6
Breckbank NG19 88 E1
Breck Bank NG22 77 C5
Breck Bank Cres NG22 77 C5
Breck Hill Rd NG3 161 F4
Breck La DN10 20 A8
Brecknock Dr NG10 193 A7
Brecks La
Elston NG23 154 B1
Stapleford LN6 127 E8
Brecks Plantation Nature Reserve NG11 195 D8
Brecks Rd DN22 39 D3
Breckswood Dr NG11 195 E7
Brecon Cl
4 Long Eaton NG10 193 A8
Nottingham NG8 160 A3
Rainworth NG21 104 C1
Bredon Cl 5 NG10 193 A8
Breedon St NG10 182 C2
Brendon Ct NG9 183 B8
Brendon Dr
Kimberley NG16 158 F7
Nottingham NG8 172 A5
Brendon Gdns NG8 172 A5
Brendon Gr NG13 177 C5
Brendon Rd NG8 172 A5
Brendon Way NG10 182 A1
Brentcliffe Ave NG3 174 A7
Brentnall Cl NG10 193 B7
Bretby Ct NG18 103 B6
Brett Cl NG15 145 E5
Bretton Rd NG15 117 B3
Brettsil Dr NG11 196 B7
Brewer's Wharf NG24 124 F1
Brewery La
Everton DN10 11 C3
Retford DN22 39 F6
Brewery St NG16 158 F6
Brewhouse Yd Mus-The Mus of Nottingham Life NG7 223 D1
Brewsters Cl NG13 177 E4
Brewsters Rd NG3 173 F8
Brewsters Way DN22 29 C1
Brewsters Wlk DN10 10 A8
Brian Clough Way NG9 182 D5
Briar Ave NG10 182 B3
Briarbank Ave NG3 174 A8
Briarbank Wlk NG3 174 A7
Briar Cl
Beeston NG9 171 E1
Hucknall NG15 145 E5
Keyworth NG12 197 F4
Rainworth NG21 104 B1
Stanton Hill NG17 100 C6
Worksop S80 35 C2
Briar Ct
Harworth DN11 8 E4
New Ollerton NG22 77 C5
Nottingham NG2 173 B1
Briar Gate
Cotgrave NG12 188 A2
Long Eaton NG10 182 B2
Briar Gn DN11 8 E4
Briar La NG18 103 A4
Briar Lea
Retford DN22 39 D4
Worksop S80 35 C2
Briar Rd
Eastwood NG16 158 B8
New Ollerton NG22 77 C5
Briars The DN10 4 B3
Briarwood Ave NG3 174 A7
Briarwood Cl NG19 89 B1
Briarwood Ct NG3 161 E3
Briber Hill S81 18 A1
Briber Rd S81 18 A2
Brickcliffe Rd LE12 205 F2
Brickenell Rd NG14 148 F6
Brickenhole La DN10 13 F5
Brickings Way DN22 32 D5
Brick Kiln La NG18 101 D7
Brickley Cres LE12 205 F1
Brickyard NG15 146 C6
Brickyard Dr NG15 146 C5
Brickyard La
East Bridgford NG13 165 C2
East Leake LE12 214 A8
Farnsfield NG22 120 B6
Misson DN10 4 D4
Radcliffe on T NG12 176 B3
South Normanton DE55 113 A6
Sutton Bonington LE12 213 F8
Walkeringham DN10 13 C6
Brick Yd Rd DN22 50 C6
Bride Church La DN11 8 A7
Bridegate La LE14 209 E5
Bridge Ave NG9 183 E5
Bridge Cl S80 45 A5
Bridge Ct NG15 146 A5
Bridge End Ave NG16 128 F8
Bridge Farm La NG7 184 E2
Bridgegate DN22 39 E7
Bridge Gn Wlk 6 NG8 159 E1
Bridge Gr NG2 185 E8
Bridgend Cl NG9 182 D5
Bridge Pl
Saxilby LN1 57 B3
Worksop S80 35 E3
Bridge Rd
Gainsborough DN21 24 D7
Nottingham NG8 171 D5
Bridge St
Gainsborough DN21 24 C7
Ilkeston DE7 157 F4
Langley Mill NG16 143 C3
Long Eaton NG10 182 D1
Loughborough LE11 220 A4
Mansfield NG18 102 C7
Newark-on-T NG24 139 F8
Sandiacre NG10 182 B6
Saxilby LN1 57 B3
Worksop S80 35 E2
Bridgeway Ct NG2 173 D2
Bridgeway Ctr NG2 173 C2
Bridgford Rd
Kneeton NG13 166 A8
Bridgford Rd *continued*
West Bridgford NG2 185 F8
Bridgford St NG18 102 F5
Bridgnorth Dr NG7 184 E2
Bridgnorth Way NG9 182 E3
Bridle Cl NG17 100 B6
Bridle Rd
Beeston NG9 183 B8
Burton Joyce NG14 163 E5
Bridlesmith Gate NG1 223 E2
Bridle Ways NG13 165 D2
Bridleway The NG19 88 F1
Bridlington St NG7 172 F7
Bridport Ave 4 NG8 172 D5
Brielen Rd NG12 176 A3
Brierfield Ave NG11 185 B4
Brierley Forest Pk NG17 100 A2
Brierley Gn NG4 175 A7
Brierly Cotts NG17 100 E3
Brierly Rd NG17 100 D4
Brigg Inf Sch DE55 113 B6
Brightmoor St NG1 223 F3
Bright Sq NG19 87 D2
Bright St
Gainsborough DN21 24 C8
Ilkeston DE7 157 E3
Nottingham NG7 222 A3
South Normanton DE55 113 A5
Brimington Ct NG19 88 E4
Brindley Rd NG8 171 C5
Brinkhill Cres NG11 184 F3
Brinkley Hill NG25 137 B6
Brinsley Cl NG8 160 A1
Brinsley Hill NG16 128 C2
Brinsley Prim Sch NG16 143 E8
Brisbane Cl NG19 88 C6
Brisbane Ct NG24 140 D4
Brisbane Dr
Nottingham NG5 160 E8
Stapleford NG9 170 E1
Bristol Cl NG24 125 E1
Bristol Rd DE7 157 E1
Britannia Ave NG6 160 E5
Britannia Rd NG10 182 D1
Britannia Terr DN21 24 D7
British Fields NG22 65 D3
British Horological Inst NG23 122 E2
Brittania Ct NG24 139 E8
Britten Gdns NG3 173 F6
Brixham Rd NG15 145 D5
Brixton Rd NG7 222 A3
Brixworth Way DN22 40 B8
Broad Cl NG14 149 C4
Broad Eadow Rd NG6 159 F7
Broad Fen La NG23 156 B8
Broadfields NG14 148 F8
Broadgate NG9 184 A7
Broad Gate NG22 66 E7
Broadgate Ave NG9 184 A7
Broadgate La
Beeston NG9 184 A7
Kelham NG23 123 E6
Broad Gores DN22 30 D3
Broadhill Rd DE74 203 C2
Broadholme St NG7 222 B1
Broadhurst Ave NG6 160 D2
Broadings La DN22 54 A6
Broad La
Brinsley NG16 143 E8
Hodthorpe S80 45 D6
South Leverton DN22 43 B6
Broadlands
Sandiacre NG10 182 B3
South Normanton DE55 113 A4
Broadleigh Cl NG11 185 C3
Broadleigh Ct DN22 39 D4
Broad Marsh Sh Ctr NG1 223 E2
Broadmead NG14 163 F5
Broad Meer NG12 187 E3
Broad Oak Cl NG3 173 E7
Broad Oak Dr
Brinsley NG16 143 E8
Stapleford NG9 182 D6
Broadoak Pk NG17 114 F1
Broad Pl S80 45 C6
Broad St
Long Eaton NG10 193 D7
Loughborough LE11 220 A4
Nottingham NG1 223 F3
Broadstairs Rd NG9 182 F2
Broadstone Cl NG2 185 C5
Broad Valley Dr NG6 146 E4
Broadway
Carlton NG3 174 D6
Ilkeston DE7 157 E3
Nottingham NG1 223 F2
Broadway E NG4 174 D6
Broadway Ind Est NG18 102 C6
Broadway Media Ctr NG1 223 F2
Broadway The NG18 102 C6
Broad Wlk NG6 160 C3
Broadwood Ct NG9 184 A8
Broadwood Rd NG5 161 B8
Brockdale Gdns NG12 197 E4
Brockenhurst Rd NG19 101 D6
Brockhall Rise DE75 143 A1
Brockhole Cl NG2 186 D5
Brockhurst Gdns NG3 173 F6
Brocklehurst Dr NG21 91 C8
Brocklesby Cl DN21 24 F7
Brocklewood Inf Sch NG8 171 F8
Brocklewood Jun Sch NG8 171 F8
Brockley Rd NG2 186 B7
Brockton Ave NG24 139 B5
Brockwell The DE55 113 B4
Brockwood Cres NG12 197 E4
Bromfield Cl NG3 174 C7
Bromhead St LE11 220 C5
Bromley Ave NG24 140 A6
Bromley Cl NG6 160 B6
Bromley Pl NG1 223 D2
Bromley Rd NG2 185 E6
Brompton Cl NG5 147 A2
Brompton Way NG11 185 C3
Bronte Cl NG10 193 A7
Bronte Ct NG7 222 C4
Brook Ave NG5 162 B8
Brook Cl
Eastwood NG16 144 B1
Long Eaton NG10 193 E5
Nottingham NG6 160 B6
Brook Cotts DE7 157 F3
Brook Ct NG16 143 B2
Brookdale Ct NG5 161 D5
Brookdale Rd NG17 101 B3
Brook Dr NG12 199 F2
Brooke Cl
Balderton NG24 140 D5
Worksop S81 36 C4
Brooke St
Ilkeston DE7 170 B6
Sandiacre NG10 182 B5
Brookfield Ave
Hucknall NG15 146 A5
Sutton in A NG17 100 D4
Brookfield Cl NG12 175 F3
Brookfield Cres NG20 72 E5
Brookfield Ct 8 NG2 173 C2
Brookfield Dr NG14 151 D3
Brookfield Gdns NG5 162 A7
Brookfield Rd NG5 162 A7
Brookfields Way LE12 205 E2
Brookfield Way DE75 143 B1
Brook Gdns NG5 162 A8
Brookhill Ave NG16 113 D4
Brookhill Cres NG8 171 E3
Brookhill Dr NG8 171 E3
Brookhill Ind Est NG16 113 D2
Brookhill La NG16 113 E5
Brookhill Leys Inf Sch NG16 144 A1
Brookhill Leys Jun Sch NG16 144 A2
Brookhill Leys Rd NG16 143 E1
Brookhill Rd NG16 113 D2
Brookhill St NG9 182 D6
Brook La NG2 186 C7
Brookland Ave NG18 101 F7
Brookland Cl NG14 165 A5
Brookland Dr NG9 183 D5
Brooklands NG12 208 C4
Brooklands Cl NG23 98 A1
Brooklands Cres NG4 163 A1
Brooklands Dr NG4 163 A1
Brooklands Prim Sch NG10 193 D7
Brooklands Rd NG3 174 B7
Brooklyn Ave NG14 163 E5
Brooklyn Cl NG6 160 D5
Brooklyn Rd NG6 160 D5
Brook Rd NG9 183 F8
Brooksby La NG11 184 F3
Brooks Cl NG13 165 D3
Brookside
East Leake LE12 214 E8
Eastwood NG16 143 F4
Hucknall NG15 146 B5
Lowdham NG14 150 D1
Brook Side 8 LE11 220 A4
Brookside Ave
East Leake LE12 205 D1
Mansfield Woodhouse NG19 88 C5
Nottingham NG8 171 D2
Brookside Cl NG10 193 B8
Brookside Gdns NG11 196 B8
Brookside Rd NG11 196 B8
Brookside Way NG17 99 F1
Brookside Wlk DN11 9 B4
Brook St
Hucknall NG15 146 A7
Nottingham NG1 223 F3
Sutton in A NG17 100 E2
Tibshelf DE55 99 A6
Wymeswold LE12 216 C3
Brook Terr S80 35 E1
Brookthorpe Way NG11 185 A4
Brookvale Cl NG18 103 A6
Brook Vale Rd NG16 143 C2
Brook View Ct NG12 197 E1
Brook View Dr NG12 197 E2
Brookwood Cres NG4 174 C7
Broom Cl
Calverton NG14 148 F8
Carlton in L S81 25 D1
Tickhill DN11 8 B7
Broome Acre DE55 113 C4
Broome Cl NG24 140 B5
Broomfield Cl NG10 182 A5
Broomfield La
Farnsfield NG22 119 F6
Mattersey DN10 19 E7
Broomhill Ave
Ilkeston DE7 170 A6
Worksop S81 35 F8
Broomhill Jun Sch NG15 146 B5
Broomhill La NG19 101 F8
Broomhill Pk View NG15 146 C5
Broomhill Rd
Hucknall NG15 146 B4

Broomhill Rd *continued*
Kimberley NG16 159 A6
Nottingham NG6 160 D6
Broom Rd NG14 148 F8
Broomston La DN9 2 E2
Broom Wlk NG4 174 B8
Brora Rd NG6 160 D7
Brotts La NG23 81 F6
Brotts Rd NG23 81 F6
Brougham Ave NG19 87 D2
Brough La
Brough NG23 112 B3
Brough NG23 112 C2
Elkesley DN22 50 B3
Brough Rd LN6 127 A8
Broughton Cl
Clipstone NG21 89 F4
Ilkeston DE7 157 D2
Broughton Dr
Newark-on-T NG24 139 E5
Nottingham NG8 172 C3
Broughton Gdns NG24 140 E4
Broughton La LE14 211 A2
Broughton Rd LN6 127 E7
Broughton St NG9 183 F7
Broughton Way NG22 78 A4
Brown Ave NG19 88 B4
Brown Cres NG17 101 A4
Brownes Rd NG13 178 A5
Brownhill Cl NG12 189 A4
Browning Cl
Arnold NG5 161 D7
Worksop S81 36 B5
Browning Rd NG24 140 E5
Browning St 5 NG18 102 A7
Brown La
Barton in F NG11 194 E6
Thorney NG23 70 B5
Brownlow Cl NG23 153 D7
Brownlow Dr NG5 146 F1
Brownlow Rd NG19 87 F1
Brownlow's Hill NG24 126 A1
Brown Md Rd NG8 172 E8
Browns Croft NG6 160 D3
Brown's Flats NG16 158 F7
Browns La
Loughborough LE11 220 A3
Stanton-on-t-W NG12 198 D2
Brown's La NG13 165 C3
Brown's Rd NG10 193 E8
Brown St
Mansfield NG19 101 F7
Nottingham NG7 172 F7
Broxholme La LN1 57 C6
Broxton Rise NG8 160 B3
Broxtowe Ave
Kimberley NG16 158 D6
Nottingham NG8 160 C2
Broxtowe Coll
Beeston & Stapleford NG9 183 E5
Kimberley NG16 158 F6
Stapleford NG9 182 D7
Broxtowe Ctry Pk NG8 159 E3
Broxtowe Dr
Hucknall NG15 131 A1
Mansfield NG18 102 C6
Broxtowe Hall Cl NG8 160 A2
Broxtowe La NG8 160 A2
Broxtowe Pk Bsns Ctr NG8 159 E2
Broxtowe St 4 NG5 161 C2
Bruce Cl NG2 173 D2
Bruce Dr NG2 185 D7
Brunel Ave NG16 144 B3
Brunel Cl DN11 8 F2
Brunel Dr NG24 125 C2
Brunel Gate DN11 8 F2
Brunnen The DE55 113 B4
Brunner Ave NG20 72 F3
Brunswick Dr NG9 182 E5
Brunts NG18 102 C8
Brunt's La NG13 165 C2
Brunts Sch The NG18 88 D1
Brunts St NG18 102 C6
Brush Dr LE11 220 B6
Brushfield St NG7 172 E7
Brussels Terr 1 DE7 157 E1
Brusty Pl NG14 163 E5
Bryans Cl La DN10 3 F3
Brynsmoor Rd NG16 143 E7
Bryony Way NG19 88 F4
Buckfast Way NG2 186 B7
Buckingham Ave NG15 146 B8
Buckingham Cl
1 Kirkby in A NG17 114 F6
Mansfield Woodhouse NG19 88 E5
Buckingham Ct NG10 182 A3
Buckingham Dr NG12 176 E3
Buckingham Rd
Arnold NG5 161 E5
Sandiacre NG10 182 A3
Buckingham Rise S81 35 E7
Buckingham Way NG16 159 B7
Buckland Dr NG14 149 C4
Bucklee Dr NG14 148 E8
Bucklow Cl NG8 160 D1
Buck's La LE12 213 A7
Budby Ave NG18 102 F6
Budby Cres NG20 74 E8
Budby Rd NG20 60 B3
Budby Rise NG15 146 B7
Bulcote Dr NG14 163 D3
Bulcote Rd NG11 184 E3
Bulgrave Mews NG2 185 C3
Bulham La NG23 81 F1
Bullace Ct NG19 88 E1
Bullace Rd NG3 173 E7
Bull Cl Rd NG7 184 F7
Buller Cl NG23 98 B1
Buller St DE7 170 A6
Buller Terr 2 NG5 161 D3
Bullfinch Rd NG6 160 D4
Bullins Cl NG5 147 C1
Bullivant Ave S80 58 C8
Bullivant St NG3 223 F4
Bullock Cl NG19 88 B5
Bullpit Rd NG24 140 E5
Bull Yd
Southwell NG25 121 E1
Worksop S80 35 E2
Bulpit La LN6 98 F5
Bulstode Pl DE74 203 C2
Bulwell Bsns Ctr NG6 160 A7
Bulwell Hall Pk Nature Reserve NG6 146 B2
Bulwell High Rd NG6 160 B7
Bulwell La NG6 160 D4
Bulwell Sta NG6 160 C6
Bulwer Rd
Kirkby in A NG17 114 F5
Nottingham NG7 222 B3
Bunbury St NG2 173 D1
Bungalow La NG22 106 A5
Bunnison La NG12 200 E7
Bunny CE Prim Sch NG11 206 E8
Bunny Hill LE12, NG11 206 D5
Bunny La
East Leake NG11 205 E6
Keyworth NG12 197 D2
Bunny Wood Nature Reserve NG11 206 F5
Buntings La NG4 174 C7
Bunting St 3 NG7 172 E1
Bunyan Gn Rd NG16 128 D7
Burbage Ct NG18 103 B6
Burden Cres DN22 53 B8
Burden La
Harby LE14 202 B3
Shelford NG12 164 C1
Burder St LE11 220 C5
Burfield Ave LE11 220 A3
Burford Prim Sch NG5 161 C6
Burford Rd NG7 172 F8
Burford St NG5 161 E8
Burgage NG25 121 E1
Burgage La NG25 121 E1
Burgass Rd NG3 174 A7
Burge Cl NG2 173 C2
Burgh Hall Cl NG9 183 C2
Burhill NG12 188 A2
Burke St NG7 222 C3
Burleigh Cl NG4 174 F7
Burleigh Rd
Loughborough LE11 220 A4
West Bridgford NG2 186 A6
Burleigh Sq NG9 183 C4
Burleigh St 1 DE7 157 F1
Burley Rise DE74 203 D1
Burlington Ave
Nottingham NG5 161 B3
Shirebrook NG20 72 F6
Burlington Dr NG19 87 F2
Burlington Rd
Carlton NG4 174 F8
Nottingham NG5 161 C3
Burma Rd NG21 118 A6
Burmaston Rd NG18 103 B6
Burnaby St NG6 160 D4
Burnaston Ct NG19 88 E4
Burnbank Cl NG2 186 D5
Burnbreck Gdns NG8 171 E4
Burndale Wlk NG5 160 E8
Burneham Cl NG13 165 C2
Burnham Ave NG9 183 F4
Burnham Ct NG18 102 C4
Burnham St NG5 161 C2
Burnham Way NG2 223 E1
Burnham Wy NG1 173 C3
Burnmoor La NG22 80 A7
Burnor Pool NG14 148 F7
Burns Ave
Mansfield Woodhouse NG19 88 C2
Nottingham NG7 222 C4
Burnside Cl 9 NG17 114 F7
Burnside Dr
Beeston NG9 171 C1
Mansfield NG19 87 E2
Burnside Gn NG8 171 D6
Burnside Gr NG12 186 D1
Burnside Rd
Nottingham NG8 171 D6
West Bridgford NG2 185 E5
Burns La NG20 74 B5
Burns Rd S81 36 B4
Burns St
Gainsborough DN21 15 B2
Mansfield NG18 102 A7
Nottingham NG7 222 C4
Burn St NG17 101 A3
Burns The NG20 74 C5
Burntleys Rd DN22 30 D7
Burnt Oak Cl NG16 159 D3
Burnt Oaks Cl NG19 88 D3
Burntstump Ctry Pk NG5 132 D1
Burntstump Hill NG5 132 D2
Burnwood Ave NG18 103 A7
Burnwood Dr NG8 171 D5
Burr La 12 DE7 157 F1
Burrows Ave NG9 171 F1
Burrows Cres NG9 171 F1
Burrows Ct NG3 173 F5
Burrows The LE12 205 E2
Burrow Wlk NG17 114 E4
Burtness Rd NG7 184 D1
Burton Ave NG4 174 A7
Burton Cl
Carlton NG4 175 A8
Harby LE14 202 A3
Burton Dr NG9 183 C4
Burton Joyce Prim Sch NG14 163 F4
Burton Joyce Sta NG14 163 E3
Burton La NG13 179 B4
Burton Manderfield Ct 4 NG2 173 C2
Burton Rd
Carlton NG4 175 A8
Sutton in A NG17 100 C3
Burton Rise
Annesley NG17 130 A8
Walesby NG22 64 A1
Burton St
Gainsborough DN21 24 D7
Loughborough LE11 220 B2
Nottingham NG1 223 E3
Burton Wlk LE12 214 E8
Burton Wlks LE11 220 B2
Burwell Ct NG19 88 E4
Burwell St NG7 222 B4
Bush Cl NG5 160 F8
Bushmead Mews 4 S80 35 F2
Bushy Cl NG10 193 A6
Buskeyfield La NG20 59 F4
Bute Ave NG7 222 B2
Butler Ave NG12 176 A4
Butler Cl NG12 189 A6
Butler Cres NG19 87 D2
Butler Dr NG21 117 F4
Butlers Cl NG15 146 C5
Butlers Hill Inf Sch NG15 146 B5
Butlerwood Cl 9 NG17 114 E1
Butten Mdw DN10 3 C2
Buttercup Cl NG24 140 C5
Butterhall Cl S80 45 A5
Buttermarket Sh Ctr NG24 139 F8
Buttermead Cl NG9 170 D2
Buttermere Cl
Long Eaton NG10 182 A2
West Bridgford NG2 186 D7
Buttermere Ct 1 NG5 161 C2
Buttermere Dr NG9 183 D8
Butterton Cl DE7 170 A7
Butterwick Cl NG19 88 F1
Buttery La NG17 100 E7
Butt Hill S80 45 A6
Butt La
East Bridgford NG13 165 E2
Mansfield Woodhouse NG19 88 C2
Normanton on S LE12 213 E4
Butt Rd NG13 178 A4
Butts Cl DE7 170 A4
Butt St NG10 182 B5
Buxton Ave NG4 162 D1
Buxton Ct DE7 157 D1
Buxton Rd NG19 87 D1
Byard La NG1 223 E2
Bycroft Rd DN21 15 C4
Bye Pass Rd
Beeston NG9 183 D3
Gunthorpe NG14 164 F5
Bye Path Rd DN22 39 F8
Byfield Cl NG7 222 B4
Byford Cl NG3 161 E2
Byley Rd NG8 171 B5
Byrne Ct NG5 162 B5
Byron Ave
Kirkby in A NG17 115 B7
Long Eaton NG10 182 B3
Mansfield Woodhouse NG19 88 C2
Sutton in A NG17 101 B4
Byron Cl
Darlton NG22 67 A8
Newark-on-T NG24 140 A6
Byron Cres
Awsworth NG16 158 C4
Ravenshead NG15 116 E3
Byron Ct
Balderton NG24 140 E3
7 Nottingham NG2 173 E4
Stapleford NG9 170 E2
Byron Est NG5 162 A7
Byron Gdns NG25 121 E1
Byron Gr NG5 161 C3
Byron Rd
Annesley NG15 130 C8
West Bridgford NG2 185 F7
Byron St
Arnold NG5 161 D6
Blidworth NG21 118 B5
Hucknall NG15 146 A6
Ilkeston DE7 157 F1
Mansfield NG18 102 A7
Newstead NG15 130 D6
Shirebrook NG20 72 E4
Byron Way S81 36 B4
Bythorn Cl NG17 101 B5

C

Cabin Leas 4 LE11 220 B5
Caddaw Ave NG15 146 A5
Cad La NG23 81 E7
Cadlan Cl NG5 161 A7
Cadlan Ct 5 NG5 161 A7
Caenby Cl DN21 24 F7
Caernarvon Pl NG9 183 B4
Caincross Rd NG8 171 D7
Cairngorm Dr NG5 147 B2
Cairns Cl NG5 161 A5
Cairnsmore Cl NG10 182 A1
Cairns St NG1 223 E3
Cairo St NG7 160 F1
Caister Rd NG11 195 E8
Caithness Ct 9 NG5 161 B1
Calcroft Cl NG8 160 C2
Caldbeck Cl NG2 186 C7
Caldbeck Ct NG9 183 B4
Caldbeck Wlk 1 NG5 161 B7
Calderdale NG8 171 B3
Calderdale Dr NG10 193 A6
Calderhall Gdns 2 NG5 161 C8
Calder Wlk 10 NG6 160 B7
Caldon Gn NG6 146 C2
Caldwell St 11 LE11 220 A4
Caledonian Rd DN22 40 A5
Caledon Rd NG5 161 B3
Calf Croft S80 45 A5
California Rd NG24 139 A4
Calke Ave NG17 99 E2
Calladine Cl NG17 100 D1
Calladine Gr NG17 100 D1
Calladine La NG17 114 C8
Callaway Cl NG8 171 E5
Calstock Rd NG5 161 E5
Calveley Rd NG8 171 E8
Calver Cl NG8 172 C4
Calver St NG19 88 E4
Calvert Cl NG16 143 B3
Calverton Ave NG4 162 B1
Calverton Cl NG9 183 A2
Calverton Ct 3 NG18 103 A3
Calverton Dr NG8 159 D2
Calverton Folk Mus NG14 148 E7
Calverton Forum L Ctr NG4 162 C1
Calverton Rd
Arnold NG5 148 A2
Blidworth NG21 118 A2
Calverton Road Nature Reserve NG5 148 A3
Cambell Gdns NG5 148 C1
Camberley Ct NG6 160 A8
Camberley Rd NG6 160 A8
Camborne Cl DN22 29 E1
Camborne Cres DN22 29 E1
Camborne Dr NG8 160 C2
Camborne Ms DN22 29 E1
Cambourne Gdns NG15 116 F2
Cambourne Pl NG18 103 B2
Cambrai Terr S80 35 E4
Cambria Mews NG3 173 C7
Cambria Rd NG19 87 C4
Cambridge Cl NG21 118 B8
Cambridge Cres NG9 170 D2
Cambridge Gdns NG5 162 B5
Cambridge Ms NG24 140 E8
Cambridge Rd
Harworth DN11 8 F4
Nottingham NG8 172 A4
Rainworth NG21 118 A8
West Bridgford NG2 186 A6
Cambridge St
Carlton NG4 174 E8
Loughborough LE11 220 B5
Mansfield NG18 102 A5
Camb's La DN22 31 D8
Camdale Cl NG9 183 B6
Camden Cl NG2 173 E4
Camelia Ave NG11 184 C1
Camelot Ave NG5 161 A1
Camelot Cres NG11 196 B8
Camelot St NG11 196 B8
Cameo Cl NG4 174 F6
Cameron La NG24 140 E1
Cameron St NG5 161 C2
Camerons The NG19 101 D5
Camomile Cl NG5 160 E7
Camomile Gdns 9 NG7 172 E7
Campbell Cl S81 35 F8
Campbell Dr NG4 174 C8
Campbell Gr NG3 223 F3
Campbell St
Gainsborough DN21 15 B1
Langley Mill NG16 143 C4
Nottingham NG3 223 F3
Campden Gn NG7 184 E2
Campion Cl NG20 72 D3
Campion St NG5 161 E8
Campion Way NG13 177 D4
Camrose Cl NG8 171 F8
Canal La
Harby NG13 202 D5
Hose LE14 211 C6
West Stockwith DN10 7 D2
Canal Rd S80 35 F3
Canal Side NG9 184 B3
Canal St
Ilkeston DE7 158 A1
Long Eaton NG10 182 C1
Nottingham NG1 223 E1
Retford DN22 39 F6
Sandiacre NG10 182 C5
Canal Terr S80 36 A3
Canberra Cl NG9 170 F1
Canberra Cres NG2 185 D3
Canberra Gdns NG2 185 D3
Candleby Cl NG12 187 F3
Candleby Ct NG12 187 F3
Candleby La NG12 187 F3
Candlemass Ct NG19 88 D2
Candle Mdw NG2 174 D5
Canning Circ NG7 222 C3
Cannock Way NG10 194 A7
Cannon Cl NG24 125 E1
Cannon Sq DN22 39 F8
Cannon St NG5 161 C3
Canonbie Cl NG5 148 B1
Canon Cl DE7 157 F5
Canon's Cl NG25 121 F1
Cantabury Ave NG7 172 F8
Cantelupe Rd DE7 170 A8
Canterbury Cl
Mansfield Woodhouse NG19 88 C5
Nuthall NG16 159 D3
Worksop S81 36 A7
Canterbury Ct NG1 223 D4
Canterbury Rd NG8 172 D5
Canterbury Wlk S81 25 E7
Cantley Ave NG4 162 E2
Cantrell Prim Sch NG6 160 C7
Cantrell Rd NG6 160 C7
Canver Cl NG8 171 C6
Canwick Cl NG8 171 C5
Capenwray Gdns 3 NG5 161 C8
Cape St NG18 101 F7
Capes The NG13 178 F4
Capitol Ct 1 NG8 172 A5
Caporn Cl NG6 160 C5
Capps Pl NG22 66 A2
Capt Ball Meml Homes NG7 222 A1
Carburton Ave NG20 74 D8
Carburton Border S80 61 F6
Carburton Way NG17 115 D6
Cardale Rd
Nottingham NG3 174 A6
Radmanthwaite NG19 87 C4
Cardiff St 2 NG3 173 F5
Cardinal Cl NG3 173 E6
Cardinal Hinsley Cl NG24 139 D4
Carding Cl NG22 120 A5
Cardington Cl NG5 146 E1
Cardle Cl NG19 89 A2
Cardwell St NG7 172 F8
Carew Rd NG7 184 E2
Carey Rd NG6 160 C8
Carisbrook Ave NG18 103 A7
Carisbrooke Ave
Beeston NG9 184 A8
Carlton NG4 163 B1
Nottingham NG3 161 C1
Carisbrooke Cl NG17 115 C5
Carisbrooke Dr NG3 161 C1
Car La NG13 166 D2
Carlile Rd NG4 174 E8
Carling Ave S80 35 D3
Carlingford Rd NG15 146 A8
Carlin St NG6 160 B7
Carlisle Ave NG6 160 C7
Carlisle St DN21 15 D1
Carlswark Gdns NG5 146 F1
Carlton Ave S81 35 E6
Carlton Bsns & Tech Ctr NG4 174 F7
Carlton Central Inf & Jun Schs NG4 174 D8
Carlton Central Jun Sch NG4 174 D8
Carlton Cl
Clipstone NG19 89 D3
Heanor DE75 143 A3
Newark-on-T NG24 139 F6
Worksop S81 35 E7
Carlton Cres LE12 205 F2
Carlton Digby Specl Sch NG3 162 C3
Carlton Dr DN10 9 F6
Carlton Ferry La NG23 97 D1
Carlton Fold 6 NG2 173 F3
Carlton Forum L Ctr NG4 162 C1
Carlton Hall La S81 25 F5
Carlton Hill NG4 174 C7
Carlton La
Broxholme LN1 57 F7
Sutton on T NG23 97 A6
Carlton le Willows Comp Sch NG4 163 A1
Carlton Mews NG4 174 C7
Carlton Phoenix Ind Est S80 36 A4
Carlton Rd
Long Eaton NG10 193 B5
Newark-on-T NG24 140 A5
Nottingham NG3 173 E5
Worksop S80, S81 35 F5
Carlton Sq NG4 174 E7
Carlton St
Mansfield Woodhouse NG19 88 C1
Nottingham NG1 223 F2
Carlton Sta NG4 174 F7
Carlton Vale Cl NG4 162 D1
Carlyle Rd NG2 185 E7
Carman Cl NG16 159 A8
Carmel Gdns NG5 161 F6
Carnaby Cl NG12 176 E3
Carnarvon Cl NG13 177 E5
Carnarvon Dr NG14 164 A5
Carnarvon Gr
Carlton, Gedling NG4 162 F1
Carlton, Thorneywood NG4 174 D8
Sutton in A NG17 100 B3
Carnarvon Pl NG13 177 D4
Carnarvon Prim Sch NG13 178 B4

Carnarvon Rd
Huthwaite NG17 . . . 99 F2
West Bridgford NG2 . . . 185 F6
Carnarvon St
Carlton NG4 . . . 175 A6
Teversal NG17 . . . 100 B7
Carnforth Cl NG9 . . . 182 D5
Carnforth Ct 1 NG5 . . . 161 C8
Carnoustie S81 . . . 36 B5
Carnoustie Cl 7 NG17 . . 114 E7
Carnwood Rd NG5 . . . 161 A5
Carolgate DN22 . . . 39 F6
Caroline Cl NG15 . . . 117 B3
Caroline Ct DE7 . . . 170 A6
Caroline Wlk NG3 . . . 173 D6
Carpenter Ave NG19 . . . 87 D2
Carpenters Cl NG12 . . . 189 B6
Carradale Cl NG5 . . . 162 C8
Carr Cl DE55 . . . 113 A7
Carr Farm Rd NG17 . . . 114 F1
Carrfield Ave NG10 . . . 182 F1
Carrfield Cl NG17 . . . 100 D3
Carrgate La NG23 . . . 153 E5
Carr Gr NG17 . . . 114 E5
Carr Hill Prim Sch DN22 . . 29 F1
Carr Hill Way DN22 . . . 29 F1
Carrington Ct NG5 . . . 161 C1
Carrington La NG14 . . . 149 A8
Carrington Prim Sch NG5 . . . 161 B1
Carrington St NG1 . . . 223 E1
Carr La
Blyton DN21 . . . 15 C8
Doddington LN6 . . . 71 B3
East Stockwith DN21 . . . 7 E1
Gainsborough DN21 . . . 24 C6
Market Warsop NG20 . . . 74 A4
Misterton DN10 . . . 6 E2
South Normanton DE55 . . . 113 A7
Carrlon Vw 5 S81 . . . 35 D6
Carroll Gdns NG2 . . . 173 C1
Carr Rd
Bingham NG13 . . . 178 B5
Gringley on t H DN10 . . . 12 C6
Retford DN22 . . . 39 E6
Carr View DN10 . . . 11 C3
Carsic La NG17 . . . 100 E3
Carsic Prim Sch NG17 . . . 100 D3
Carsic Rd NG17 . . . 100 D4
Carsington Ct NG19 . . . 88 E3
Carson Rd DN21 . . . 15 C2
Carswell Cl NG24 . . . 139 F6
Cartbridge NG12 . . . 187 F2
Carter Ave
Radcliffe on T NG12 . . . 176 B3
Ruddington NG11 . . . 196 C6
Carter Gate NG24 . . . 139 F8
Carter La
Mansfield NG18 . . . 102 E6
Shirebrook NG20 . . . 72 E4
Warsop Vale NG19 . . . 73 C4
Carter La E DE55 . . . 113 C6
Carter La W
Shirebrook NG20 . . . 72 D4
South Normanton DE55 . . . 113 C5
Carter Rd NG9 . . . 183 A3
Carters Wood Dr NG16 . . 159 F3
Cartwright Cl NG22 . . . 54 A2
Cartwright St
Loughborough LE11 . . . 220 C5
Shireoaks S81 . . . 34 F7
Carver Cl NG21 . . . 76 B1
Carver's Hollow NG22 . . 120 A2
Carver St NG7 . . . 172 F8
Carwood Rd NG9 . . . 171 D1
Caskgate St DN21 . . . 24 C8
Casper Ct 10 NG5 . . . 161 A8
Castellan Rise NG5 . . . 161 C8
Casterton Rd NG5 . . . 161 B7
Castle Brewery Ct NG24 . 139 F7
Castlebridge NG2 . . . 173 A2
Castle Bridge Rd NG2 . . 173 A2
Castle Bvd NG7 . . . 222 C1
Castle Cl
Bottesford NG13 . . . 181 D2
Calverton NG14 . . . 148 E7
Castledine St Extension LE11 . . . 220 B2
Castledine St LE11 . . . 220 B2
Castle Farm La S80 . . . 46 D7
Castlefields NG2 . . . 173 C2
Castle Gate
Newark-on-T NG24 . . . 139 F8
Nottingham NG1 . . . 223 E2
Tickhill DN11 . . . 8 A7
Castle Gdns NG7 . . . 222 B1
Castle Gr NG7 . . . 223 D1
Castle Hill LE12 . . . 205 F1
Castle Hill Cl NG17 . . . 114 E5
Castle Marina Pk NG2 . . 173 A2
Castle Marina Rd NG2 . . 173 A2
Castle Mdw Rd NG2 . . . 223 D1
Castle Mdw Ret Pk NG7 . 222 C1
Castle Mews NG19 . . . 88 B3
Castle Mus & Art Gall NG7 . . . 223 D1
Castle Pk NG2 . . . 173 B2
Castle Pl NG1 . . . 223 D2
Castle Quay NG7 . . . 223 D1
Castle Rd NG1 . . . 223 D2
Castlerigg Cl NG2 . . . 186 C5
Castle Rising NG24 . . . 139 F8
Castle St
Eastwood NG16 . . . 144 A1
12 Mansfield NG18 . . . 102 A7
Mansfield Woodhouse NG19 88 B3
Nottingham NG2 . . . 173 F4
Worksop S80 . . . 35 E2
Castleton Ave
Arnold NG5 . . . 161 F6
Carlton NG4 . . . 162 E1
Ilkeston DE7 . . . 157 E5
Castleton Cl
Hucknall NG15 . . . 145 D6
Mansfield Woodhouse NG19 88 C4
8 Nottingham NG2 . . . 173 B1
Ravenshead NG15 . . . 117 A3
Castleton Ct NG6 . . . 159 F6
Castle View
Aldercar NG16 . . . 143 A4
West Bridgford NG2 . . . 185 D6
Castle View Rd NG13 . . . 181 C1
Caterham Cl NG8 . . . 171 D7
Catfoot La NG4 . . . 162 E8
Catherine Ave NG19 . . . 88 C3
Catherine Cl
11 Kirkby in A NG17 . . . 114 F7
Nottingham NG6 . . . 160 A7
Catkin Dr NG16 . . . 158 C8
Catkin Way NG24 . . . 140 B4
Catlow Wlk 4 NG5 . . . 161 C8
Caton Cl NG17 . . . 100 D3
Cator Cl NG4 . . . 162 D3
Cator La NG9 . . . 183 D5
Cator La N NG9 . . . 183 D6
Cator Rd NG19 . . . 87 C3
Catriona Cres NG5 . . . 148 A1
Catt Cl NG9 . . . 183 B1
Catterley Hill Rd NG3 . . 174 B6
Cattle Mkt 1 LE11 . . . 220 B3
Cattle Mkt Rd NG2 . . . 173 D2
Cattle Rd DN10 . . . 6 C1
Catton Rd NG5 . . . 162 A8
Caudale Ct NG2 . . . 186 C7
Caudwell Cl NG25 . . . 121 E2
Caudwell Dr NG18 . . . 102 C3
Cauldwell Rd NG17 . . . 101 E2
Caulton St NG7 . . . 222 B4
Caunton Ave NG3 . . . 161 E1
Caunton Cl
Mansfield NG18 . . . 101 F6
Meden Vale NG20 . . . 74 D7
Caunton Rd
Bathley NG23 . . . 109 E4
Hockerton NG25 . . . 122 B6
Caunt's Cres NG17 . . . 100 D3
Causeway DN21 . . . 24 E3
Causeway La
Gamston DN22 . . . 51 B7
Morton NG25 . . . 137 C4
Causeway Mews 4 NG2 . 173 B1
Cavan Ct 3 NG2 . . . 173 C1
Cavell Cl
Nottingham NG11 . . . 184 D2
Woodbeck DN22 . . . 53 B8
Cavell Ct NG7 . . . 172 D2
Cavendish Ave
Carlton NG4 . . . 162 D2
Edwinstowe NG21 . . . 75 F2
Newark-on-T NG24 . . . 140 A6
Nottingham NG5 . . . 161 D3
Sutton in A NG17 . . . 100 E3
Cavendish Cl
Bawtry DN10 . . . 9 F6
Hucknall NG15 . . . 146 C5
Cavendish Cres
Annesley Woodhouse NG17 . . . 130 A8
Carlton NG4 . . . 162 C2
Stapleford NG9 . . . 170 D2
Cavendish Cres N NG7 . . 222 C2
Cavendish Cres S NG7 . . 222 C1
Cavendish Dr
Carlton NG4 . . . 174 E8
Lea DN21 . . . 24 F2
Cavendish Pl NG9 . . . 183 F6
Cavendish Rd
Carlton NG4 . . . 162 C1
Ilkeston DE7 . . . 170 A6
Long Eaton NG10 . . . 182 C2
Retford DN22 . . . 40 B4
Worksop S80 . . . 47 A8
Cavendish Rd E NG7 . . . 222 C2
Cavendish Rd W NG7 . . . 222 C2
Cavendish St
Arnold NG5 . . . 161 E8
Langwith NG20 . . . 72 F8
Mansfield NG18 . . . 102 C5
Mansfield Woodhouse NG19 88 A3
Nottingham NG7 . . . 184 E8
Sutton in A NG17 . . . 101 A4
Cavendish Vale NG5 . . . 161 D3
Cave's La DN10 . . . 13 D6
Cawdell Dr LE12 . . . 212 D2
Cawdron Wlk NG7 . . . 184 E2
Cawston Gdns 3 NG6 . . . 160 B8
Cawthorne Cl NG23 . . . 98 B1
Cawthorne Way NG18 . . . 102 F7
Caxmere Dr NG8 . . . 171 F5
Caxton Cl NG4 . . . 175 A7
Caxton Rd NG5 . . . 161 B1
Caythorpe Cres NG5 . . . 161 C3
Caythorpe Ct NG19 . . . 88 E3
Caythorpe Rd NG14 . . . 150 F1
Caythorpe Rise NG5 . . . 161 C3
Cecil Cl S80 . . . 35 A4
Cecil St
Gainsborough DN21 . . . 15 C1
Nottingham NG7 . . . 222 B1
Cedar Ave
Beeston NG9 . . . 184 A7
East Leake LE12 . . . 214 D8
Kirkby in A NG17 . . . 114 F4
Long Eaton NG10 . . . 193 C5
Mansfield Woodhouse NG19 88 C5
Newark-on-T NG24 . . . 125 B3
Cedar Ave *continued*
Nuthall NG16 . . . 159 F4
Cedar Cl
Carlton in L S81 . . . 25 E7
Gainsborough DN21 . . . 15 B3
Sandiacre NG10 . . . 182 B7
Sutton in A NG17 . . . 100 D7
Cedar Ct NG9 . . . 184 A7
Cedar Dr
Keyworth NG12 . . . 197 E2
Selston NG16 . . . 128 F7
Cedar Gr
Arnold NG5 . . . 162 B8
Hucknall NG15 . . . 146 B5
Nottingham NG8 . . . 171 F4
South Normanton DE55 . . . 113 B4
Cedar La NG22 . . . 77 C6
Cedarland Cres NG16 . . . 159 F4
Cedar Rd
Beeston NG9 . . . 183 E5
Loughborough LE11 . . . 220 C1
Nottingham NG7 . . . 173 A8
Cedar St NG18 . . . 102 C5
Cedars The NG5 . . . 161 D4
Cedar Tree Rd
Elkesley DN22 . . . 50 A3
Nottingham NG5 . . . 147 B1
Celandine Cl NG5 . . . 160 E7
Celandine Gdns NG13 . . . 177 C4
Celia Dr NG4 . . . 174 D7
Cemetery Rd
Stapleford NG9 . . . 182 E7
Worksop S80 . . . 36 A2
Centenary Cl NG24 . . . 140 C4
Central Ave
Arnold NG5 . . . 161 F7
Beeston, Chilwell NG9 . . . 183 D6
Beeston NG9 . . . 183 F8
Blidworth NG21 . . . 118 B5
Creswell S80 . . . 58 D8
Hucknall NG15 . . . 146 A6
Kirkby in A NG17 . . . 115 B3
Mansfield NG18 . . . 102 C5
Nottingham, Mapperley NG3 . . . 162 A4
Nottingham, New Basford NG7, NG5 . . . 161 A1
Sandiacre NG10 . . . 182 B6
South Normanton DE55 . . . 113 B5
Stapleford NG9 . . . 182 F8
Walesby NG22 . . . 64 A1
West Bridgford NG2 . . . 185 F8
Worksop S80 . . . 35 E3
Central Ave S NG5 . . . 161 F7
Central Cl NG20 . . . 72 E3
Central Ct NG7 . . . 172 F1
Central Dr
Bawtry DN10 . . . 10 A8
Clipstone NG21 . . . 89 F2
Elston NG23 . . . 153 E4
Shirebrook NG20 . . . 72 E3
Central St
3 Nottingham NG3 . . . 173 E6
Sutton in A NG17 . . . 101 B4
Central Wlk NG15 . . . 146 A7
Centre Way NG12 . . . 175 E4
Centurion Way NG11 . . . 185 A8
Century Ave NG18 . . . 101 F5
Century La LN1 . . . 57 A5
Century Rd DN22 . . . 39 E5
Century St NG24 . . . 140 A8
Cernan Ct NG6 . . . 159 F5
Cerne Cl NG7 . . . 184 E1
Chaceley Way NG11 . . . 185 A3
Chadborn Ave NG11 . . . 195 B1
Chadburn Rd NG18 . . . 102 E8
Chaddesden The NG3 . . . 173 C7
Chad Gdns NG5 . . . 147 A2
Chadwick Rd NG7 . . . 172 E7
Chadwick Way DN22 . . . 53 B8
Chaffinch Cl NG18 . . . 102 F7
Chaffinch Mews S81 . . . 35 C7
Chainbridge Cl LE11 . . . 220 A5
Chainbridge La DN22 . . . 29 D8
Chainbridge Nature Reserve DN22 . . . 30 A8
Chain Bridge Rd DN22 . . . 29 C8
Chain La
5 Newark-on-T NG24 . . . 139 F8
Nottingham NG7 . . . 172 E1
Chalfield Cl NG11 . . . 184 D1
Chalfont Dr NG8 . . . 172 C6
Chalons Cl DE7 . . . 157 F1
Chamberlain Cl NG11 . . . 184 C1
Chambers Ave DE7 . . . 170 B7
Champion Ave DE7 . . . 157 C3
Champion Cres NG19 . . . 101 F8
Chancery Cl NG17 . . . 101 A6
Chancery Ct NG11 . . . 185 A6
Chancery La DN22 . . . 39 E6
Chancery The NG9 . . . 183 C7
Chandos Ave NG4 . . . 175 A8
Chandos Ct NG22 . . . 65 F3
Chandos St
Carlton NG4 . . . 175 A7
Nottingham NG3 . . . 173 E7
Chantrey Cl NG9 . . . 183 D4
Chantrey Rd NG2 . . . 185 E7
Chantry Cl
Kimberley NG16 . . . 159 A5
Long Eaton NG10 . . . 193 A4
Newark-on-T NG24 . . . 139 F5
Chantry The NG18 . . . 102 F5
Chantry Wlk NG22 . . . 65 F3
Chapel Bar NG1 . . . 223 D2
Chapel Baulk DN9 . . . 2 B1
Chapel Cl
Misterton DN10 . . . 6 F2
Chapel Cl *continued*
Walesby NG22 . . . 64 A2
Chapel Ct DE7 . . . 157 F4
Chapel Garth NG13 . . . 179 F6
Chapelgate DN22 . . . 39 F7
Chapel Gate S81 . . . 26 A5
Chapel La
Arnold NG5 . . . 161 E8
Aslockton NG13 . . . 179 A5
Bathley NG23 . . . 110 B3
Bingham NG13 . . . 177 E6
Caunton NG23 . . . 109 A5
Claypole NG23 . . . 156 D7
Coddington NG24 . . . 126 B1
Costock LE12 . . . 206 C1
Cotgrave NG12 . . . 187 F3
Epperstone NG14 . . . 150 A6
Everton DN10 . . . 11 C3
Farndon NG24 . . . 138 F4
Farnsfield NG22 . . . 119 F5
Granby NG13 . . . 191 B5
Hose LE14 . . . 211 F8
Lambley NG4 . . . 163 B7
Laxton NG22 . . . 79 C2
Misterton DN10 . . . 6 F2
Morton DN21 . . . 15 B4
Nether Broughton LE14 . . . 219 C8
North Scarle LN6 . . . 83 D3
Old Dalby LE14 . . . 218 E4
Oxton NG25 . . . 134 C4
Ravenshead NG15 . . . 117 B2
Scrooby DN10 . . . 10 A2
Upper Broughton LE14 . . . 210 A1
Walesby NG22 . . . 64 A2
Willoughby-on-t-W LE12 . . 217 D7
Winthorpe NG24 . . . 125 C6
Chapel Mews Ct NG9 . . . 183 B8
Chapel Pl NG16 . . . 158 F6
Chapel Quarter Bsns Development NG1 . . . 223 D2
Chapel Rd NG16 . . . 128 E6
Chapel St
Annesley Woodhouse NG17 . . . 115 A1
Barkestone-le-V NG13 . . . 192 B2
Beckingham LN5 . . . 142 D8
Beeston NG9 . . . 183 B8
Bottesford NG13 . . . 181 A3
Eastwood NG16 . . . 143 F1
Heanor DE75 . . . 157 A8
Hucknall NG15 . . . 146 A7
8 Ilkeston DE7 . . . 157 F1
Kimberley NG16 . . . 158 F6
Kirkby in A NG17 . . . 114 E5
Long Eaton NG10 . . . 193 E7
New Houghton NG19 . . . 87 A7
Orston NG13 . . . 179 F7
Ruddington NG11 . . . 196 C6
Selston NG16 . . . 129 A7
Whaley Thorns NG20 . . . 59 A3
Chapel Staith DN21 . . . 24 C8
Chapel Wlk S80 . . . 35 E2
Chapman Ct NG8 . . . 172 B7
Chapman St LE11 . . . 220 C4
Chappel Gdns NG22 . . . 106 A4
Chapter Dr NG16 . . . 159 A5
Chard St NG7 . . . 160 F2
Charlbury Ct NG9 . . . 171 B4
Charlbury Rd NG8 . . . 172 B5
Charlecote Dr NG8 . . . 171 D3
Charlecote Pk Dr NG2 . . . 185 C4
Charles Ave
Beeston, Chilwell NG9 . . . 183 C3
Beeston NG9 . . . 172 A1
Eastwood NG16 . . . 144 B1
Sandiacre NG10 . . . 182 B6
Stapleford NG9 . . . 182 F8
Charles Baines Com Prim Sch DN21 . . . 24 F8
Charles Cl
Carlton NG4 . . . 162 F2
Ilkeston DE7 . . . 170 B6
Charles Pk NG6 . . . 160 B5
Charles St
Arnold NG5 . . . 161 E7
Gainsborough DN21 . . . 15 D1
Hucknall NG15 . . . 146 A7
Long Eaton NG10 . . . 193 D6
Loughborough LE11 . . . 220 B5
Mansfield NG19 . . . 88 A1
Mansfield Woodhouse NG19 88 C3
Newark-on-T NG24 . . . 140 B7
Ruddington NG11 . . . 196 C7
Sutton in A NG17 . . . 101 A3
Charlesworth Ave NG7 . . 172 E8
Charlesworth Ct NG19 . . . 88 E3
Charlock Cl NG5 . . . 160 E7
Charlock Gdns NG13 . . . 177 D3
Charlotte Cl
Arnold NG5 . . . 147 E2
Kirton NG22 . . . 78 B6
Newark-on-T NG24 . . . 140 A8
Charlotte Gr NG9 . . . 171 D1
Charlton Ave NG10 . . . 182 F1
Charlton Gr NG9 . . . 183 F5
Charlton Rd S81 . . . 26 A2
Charnock Ave NG8 . . . 172 D3
Charnwood Ave
Beeston NG9 . . . 183 E6
Keyworth NG12 . . . 197 E2
Long Eaton NG10 . . . 193 B4
Sandiacre NG10 . . . 182 A4
Sutton Bonington LE12 . . . 213 C5
Charnwood Cres DE55 . . . 99 B3
Charnwood Fields LE12 . 213 C5
Charnwood Gr
Bingham NG13 . . . 177 D4
Hucknall NG15 . . . 145 E7
Charnwood Gr *continued*
Mansfield NG18 . . . 103 A7
Mansfield Woodhouse NG19 88 B5
West Bridgford NG2 . . . 185 E7
Charnwood La NG5 . . . 162 A6
Charnwood L Ctr LE11 . . 220 A3
Charnwood Mus LE11 . . . 220 A3
Charnwood Rd LE11 . . . 220 B2
Charnwood St NG17 . . . 100 C1
Charnwood Way NG14 . . . 149 D4
Charter Pl NG22 . . . 66 A2
Charters Cl 5 NG17 . . . 114 F7
Chartwell Ave NG11 . . . 196 B7
Chartwell Gr NG3 . . . 162 C5
Chartwell Rd NG17 . . . 115 C5
Chase Pk NG2 . . . 174 A3
Chatham Ct NG24 . . . 139 F7
Chatham St
Nottingham NG1 . . . 223 E4
Southwell NG25 . . . 121 F1
Chatsworth Ave
Beeston NG9 . . . 183 C2
Carlton NG4 . . . 162 E1
Long Eaton NG10 . . . 194 A6
Nottingham NG7 . . . 160 F2
Radcliffe on T NG12 . . . 176 A4
Selston NG16 . . . 129 A7
Shirebrook NG20 . . . 72 E6
Southwell NG25 . . . 121 D1
Chatsworth Cl
Mansfield NG18 . . . 102 E2
Ravenshead NG15 . . . 117 A3
Sandiacre NG10 . . . 182 B4
Sutton in A NG17 . . . 100 F5
Chatsworth Ct
Harworth DN11 . . . 9 B5
Hucknall NG15 . . . 146 A6
Chatsworth Dr
Hucknall NG15 . . . 146 A6
Mansfield NG18 . . . 102 E2
Chatsworth Rd
Creswell S80 . . . 58 C8
Newark-on-T NG24 . . . 140 A5
West Bridgford NG2 . . . 186 B8
Worksop S81 . . . 35 F7
Chatsworth St
Sutton in A NG17 . . . 101 A3
Tibshelf DE55 . . . 99 A6
Chaucer Cres NG17 . . . 101 B4
Chaucer Rd NG24 . . . 140 E4
Chaucer St
Ilkeston DE7 . . . 157 F1
Mansfield NG18 . . . 102 A7
Nottingham NG1 . . . 223 D3
Chaworth Ave NG16 . . . 145 A1
Chaworth Rd
Bingham NG13 . . . 177 D4
Carlton NG4 . . . 174 F6
West Bridgford NG2 . . . 185 E6
Chaworth St NG21 . . . 118 B5
Cheadle Cl
Nottingham, Bilborough NG8 . . . 171 D8
Nottingham, Portchester NG3 . . . 162 B2
Cheapside
Nottingham NG1 . . . 223 E2
Worksop S80 . . . 36 A2
Cheddar Cl NG21 . . . 104 C1
Cheddar Rd NG11 . . . 195 E8
Chedington Ave NG3 . . . 162 D6
Chediston Vale NG5 . . . 161 B8
Chedworth Cl 1 NG3 . . . 173 F5
Chelmorton Cl NG19 . . . 88 E3
Chelmsford Rd NG7 . . . 160 F2
Chelmsford Terr NG7 . . . 160 F2
Chelsea Cl NG16 . . . 159 E3
Chelsea St NG7 . . . 160 F1
Cheltenham Cl NG9 . . . 182 F1
Cheltenham Ct NG18 . . . 102 F7
Cheltenham St NG6 . . . 160 E4
Chennel Nook NG12 . . . 188 A2
Chepstow Rd NG11 . . . 195 E8
Chepstow Wlk NG18 . . . 102 F7
Chequers La NG22 . . . 54 B2
Cherhill Cl NG11 . . . 195 D7
Cheriton Cl NG19 . . . 87 E1
Cheriton Dr
Ravenshead NG15 . . . 117 B2
Shipley DE7 . . . 157 C3
Chermside Cl NG15 . . . 117 B1
Chernside NG15 . . . 117 A3
Cherry Ave
Hucknall NG15 . . . 146 B5
Kirkby in A NG17 . . . 114 D7
Cherry Cl
Arnold NG5 . . . 161 E8
Nottingham NG5 . . . 161 B7
Shirebrook NG20 . . . 72 E6
South Normanton DE55 . . . 113 B7
Cherry Gr
Mansfield NG18 . . . 101 E6
Market Warsop NG20 . . . 74 C4
Cherry Hill NG12 . . . 197 F3
Cherry Holt
Newark-on-T NG24 . . . 139 F5
Retford DN22 . . . 29 D1
Cherryholt Cl NG13 . . . 165 D4
Cherryholt La NG13 . . . 165 D3
Cherry La NG18 . . . 102 B3
Cherry Orch NG12 . . . 187 E3
Cherry Orch Mount NG5 . 161 B7
Cherry St NG13 . . . 177 F4
Cherry Tree Ave S81 . . . 34 F7

Cherry Tree Cl
Brinsley NG16 . . . . 143 E8
Mansfield Woodhouse NG16 . . . 88 B4
Radcliffe on T NG12 . . . . 175 F2
Cherry Tree La NG12 . . . . . . 186 B3
Cherry Tree Rd DN21 . . . . . . 15 E1
Cherry Tree Wlk DN22 . . . . . 19 C5
Cherry Wood Dr NG8 . . . . . 172 B7
Cherrywood Gdns NG3 . . . . 174 A8
Chertsey Cl NG3 . . . . 161 F1
Cherwell Ct NG6 . . . . 159 F6
Chesham Dr
Beeston NG9 . . . . 171 B2
Nottingham NG5 . . . . 161 B1
Cheshire Way NG16 . . . . . . 128 C4
Chesil Ave 2 NG8 . . . . 172 D5
Chesil Cotts 3 NG8 . . . . . . 172 D5
Cheslyn Dr NG8 . . . . 172 C8
Chesnut Cl NG23 . . . . 81 A4
Chesnut Gdn NG17 . . . . 100 D1
Chess Burrow NG19 . . . . 88 D2
Chester Cl 3 LE11 . . . . 220 A3
Chesterfield Ave
Bingham NG13 . . . . 177 E5
Carlton NG4 . . . . 162 D4
Long Eaton NG10 . . . . 193 F7
Chesterfield Ct NG4 . . . . . . 162 D3
Chesterfield Dr
Burton Joyce NG14 . . . . 164 A5
Retford DN22 . . . . 40 A7
Chesterfield Rd
Hardstoft DE55 . . . . 85 A1
Huthwaite NG17 . . . . 99 E4
New Houghton NG19 . . . . . . 86 E7
Pleasley NG19 . . . . 87 A5
Chesterfield Rd N NG19 . . 87 C4
Chesterfield Rd S NG18 . 102 B8
Chesterfield St NG4 . . . . . 174 D7
Chester Gn NG2 . . . . 182 E2
Chesterman Cl NG16 . . . . . 158 B4
Chester Rd NG3 . . . . 174 B5
Chester St NG19 . . . . 87 E1
Chesterton Dr S81 . . . . 36 B5
Chestnut Ave
Beeston NG9 . . . . 183 F6
Bingham NG13 . . . . 177 E4
Gainsborough DN21 . . . . 15 D2
Kirkby in A NG17 . . . . 114 F4
Newark-on-T NG24 . . . . 125 B4
Nottingham NG3 . . . . 162 B2
Ravenshead NG15 . . . . 117 B1
Retford DN22 . . . . 39 D4
Chestnut Cl
Bottesford NG13 . . . . 181 C3
New Ollerton NG22 . . . . 77 D6
Ravenshead NG18 . . . . 116 E7
Worksop S80 . . . . 35 E1
Chestnut Copse NG24 . . . 140 B6
Chestnut Dr
Bawtry DN10 . . . . 9 F7
Mansfield NG18 . . . . 102 E2
New Ollerton NG22 . . . . 77 D6
Nuthall NG16 . . . . 159 B6
Selston NG16 . . . . 128 F7
Shirebrook NG20 . . . . 72 D4
South Normanton DE55 . . . . 113 B4
Chestnut Gdns NG17 . . . . 100 D1
Chestnut Gr
Arnold NG5 . . . . 162 A8
Burton Joyce NG14 . . . . 163 F4
Carlton NG4 . . . . 162 F1
Farndon NG24 . . . . 139 A4
Hucknall NG15 . . . . 146 B4
Kirkby in A NG17 . . . . 114 F5
Mansfield Woodhouse NG19 . . 88 B5
Nottingham NG3 . . . . 173 C7
Radcliffe on T NG12 . . . . . . 175 F4
Sandiacre NG10 . . . . 182 A7
West Bridgford NG2 . . . . . . 185 D7
Chestnut Hill NG18 . . . . . 102 E2
Chestnut La NG11 . . . . 194 E6
Chestnut Mews NG18 . . . 102 E2
Chestnut Rd
Langley Mill NG16 . . . . 143 A3
Langold S81 . . . . 16 F4
Chestnut St LE11 . . . . 220 A4
Chestnuts The
Carlton NG4 . . . . 163 B1
Long Eaton NG10 . . . . 193 A8
Nottingham NG3 . . . . 161 F1
Radcliffe on T NG12 . . . . . . 175 E3
Chestnut Way NG22 . . . . . . 66 A2
Chettles Ind Est NG8 . . . . 172 D5
Chetwin Rd NG8 . . . . 171 D5
Chetwynd Rd
Beeston, Chilwell NG9 . . . . 183 C3
Beeston, Toton NG9 . . . . . . 183 A2
Chetwynd Road Prim Sch
NG9 . . . . 183 A2
Cheverton Ct 7 NG3 . . . . 173 C7
Chevin Gdns 12 NG5 . . . . 147 A1
Cheviot Cl NG5 . . . . 147 B2
Cheviot Ct S81 . . . . 25 E7
Cheviot Dr NG6 . . . . 159 F8
Cheviot Rd NG10 . . . . 182 A1
Chewton Ave NG16 . . . . . . 144 A1
Chewton Cl NG22 . . . . 105 E6
Chewton St NG16 . . . . 144 A1
Cheyne Dr NG22 . . . . 106 A4
Cheyne Wlk
Bawtry DN10 . . . . 9 F7
Retford DN22 . . . . 39 D4
Cheyny Cl NG2 . . . . 173 C1
Chichester Cl
Ilkeston DE7 . . . . 170 A8

Chichester Cl continued
Mansfield NG19 . . . . 101 D6
Nottingham NG5 . . . . 160 E7
Chichester Dr NG12 . . . . . 187 E4
Chichester Wlk S81 . . . . . . 25 E7
Chidlow Rd NG8 . . . . 171 D7
Chigwell Cl NG8 . . . . 159 E3
Chillon Way NG15 . . . . . . 145 D6
Chiltern Cl NG5 . . . . 147 B2
Chiltern Gdns NG10 . . . . . 182 A1
Chiltern Way
Carlton in L S81 . . . . 25 E7
Nottingham NG5 . . . . 161 B7
Chilton Cres NG19 . . . . 88 C6
Chilton Dr NG16 . . . . 159 A7
Chilvers Cl NG5 . . . . 161 A7
Chilwell Coll House Jun Sch
NG9 . . . . 183 D5
Chilwell Comp Sch NG9 183 D3
Chilwell Ct NG6 . . . . 160 D7
Chilwell La NG9 . . . . 183 C6
Chilwell Olympia NG9 . . . 183 D3
Chilwell Rd NG9 . . . . 183 F6
Chilwell Ret Pk NG9 . . . . 183 A2
Chilwell St NG7 . . . . 222 B1
Chimes Mdw NG25 . . . . . . 136 F8
Chine Gdns NG2 . . . . 185 C5
Chine The DE55 . . . . 113 B3
Chingford Rd NG8 . . . . 171 E8
Chiomere DN22 . . . . 39 D4
Chippendale St NG7 . . . . 222 B1
Chippenham Rd NG5 . . . . 161 C7
Chirnside NG19 . . . . 101 D5
Chisbury Gn NG11 . . . . . . 195 D7
Chisholm Way NG5 . . . . . . 161 A6
Chisworth Ct NG19 . . . . 88 E3
Christ Church Inf Sch
NG24 . . . . 139 E7
Christchurch Rd NG15 . . 145 D4
Christina Ave NG6 . . . . . . 160 C4
Christina Cres NG6 . . . . . . 160 C4
Christine Cl NG15 . . . . 131 C1
Christopher Cl NG8 . . . . . 171 F6
Christopher Cres NG24 . . 140 C4
Christ the King RC Comp Sch
NG5 . . . . 162 B7
Chrysalis Way NG16 . . . . . 143 C3
Church Ave
Arnold NG5 . . . . 161 E7
Long Eaton NG10 . . . . 193 A4
Nottingham NG7 . . . . 222 B1
Sutton in A NG17 . . . . 100 D2
Church Cl
Arnold NG5 . . . . 161 E7
Bingham NG13 . . . . 177 F5
Church Warsop NG20 . . . . . 74 B6
East Leake LE12 . . . . 205 E1
Hose LE14 . . . . 211 F7
North Wheatley DN22 . . . . . 31 E8
Nottingham NG3 . . . . 223 E4
Radcliffe on T NG12 . . . . . . 175 E3
Trowell NG9 . . . . 170 C4
Church Cnr NG13 . . . . 192 F4
Church Cres
Arnold NG5 . . . . 161 D7
Beeston NG9 . . . . 183 A3
Church Croft NG2 . . . . 185 F8
Churchdale Ave NG9 . . . . 170 E1
Church Dr
Arnold NG5 . . . . 161 E7
Hucknall NG15 . . . . 146 A7
Ilkeston DE7 . . . . 157 D4
Keyworth NG12 . . . . 197 F3
Misterton DN10 . . . . 6 E2
Nottingham NG5 . . . . 161 B1
Ravenshead NG15 . . . . 117 A2
Sandiacre NG10 . . . . 182 B7
Shirebrook NG20 . . . . 72 E3
West Bridgford NG2 . . . . . . 185 F7
Church Dr E NG5 . . . . 161 E7
Church Drive Prim Sch
NG5 . . . . 161 E7
Church End LE14 . . . . 210 C1
Church Farm Gdns NG22 77 E1
Church Field Cl S81 . . . . . . 26 A5
Churchfield Ct NG5 . . . . . 147 A1
Churchfield Dr NG21 . . . . 103 F2
Churchfield La NG7 . . . . . 222 A4
Churchfield Terr NG7 . . . . 160 C7
Churchgate DN22 . . . . 39 F7
Church Gate
Colston Bassett NG12 . . . . 200 E7
Cotgrave NG12 . . . . 198 C8
Kegworth DE74 . . . . 203 D2
Loughborough LE11 . . . . . . 220 A4
Loughborough LE11 . . . . . . 220 B4
Church Gr NG7 . . . . 222 A1
Church Hill
Bilsthorpe NG22 . . . . 106 A5
Keyworth NG12 . . . . 197 E3
Kimberley NG16 . . . . 158 F6
Kirkby in A NG17 . . . . 114 D3
Mansfield Woodhouse NG19 88 C3
Newton DE55 . . . . 99 A1
North Wheatley DN22 . . . . . 31 E8
Sutton in A NG17 . . . . 100 E2
Church Hill Ave NG19 . . . . 88 C3
Church Hill Gdns NG19 . . 88 C3
Churchill Cl NG5 . . . . 161 F6
Churchill Dr
Newark-on-T NG24 . . . . 139 E5
Ruddington NG11 . . . . 196 B7
Stapleford NG9 . . . . 182 E8
Churchill Pk NG4 . . . . 174 C3
Churchill Way DN21 . . . . . 24 F3
Church La
Arnold NG5 . . . . 147 F1
Averham NG23 . . . . 123 F1

Church La continued
Balderton NG24 . . . . 140 E4
Barton in F NG11 . . . . 194 E6
Beeston NG9 . . . . 183 D1
Besthorpe NG23 . . . . 98 B5
Bingham NG13 . . . . 177 F5
Bothamsall DN22 . . . . 63 F7
Bottesford NG13 . . . . 181 B3
Boughton NG22 . . . . 77 F5
Brinsley NG16 . . . . 143 E7
Car Colston NG13 . . . . 166 C3
Carlton in L S81 . . . . 25 F4
Carlton-on-Trent NG23 . . . . 96 F4
Clarborough DN22 . . . . 30 E3
Clayworth DN22 . . . . 21 D5
Collingham NG23 . . . . 98 A1
Cossall NG16 . . . . 158 C1
Costock LE12 . . . . 206 C1
Cotgrave NG12 . . . . 187 E3
Cromwell NG23 . . . . 110 F7
Eagle LN6 . . . . 84 D3
Eakring NG22 . . . . 92 E1
East Drayton DN22 . . . . 53 A3
East Stoke NG23 . . . . 138 B1
Epperstone NG14 . . . . 150 A6
Gamston DN22 . . . . 50 F4
Halam NG22 . . . . 120 F1
Harworth DN11 . . . . 8 E4
Hayton DN22 . . . . 30 C5
Hucknall NG15 . . . . 131 B1
Letwell S81 . . . . 16 A2
Long Clawson LE14 . . . . 211 C3
Lowdham NG14 . . . . 150 C2
Mansfield NG18 . . . . 102 C6
Maplebeck NG22 . . . . 108 A6
Misterton DN10 . . . . 6 E2
Morton NG25 . . . . 137 D3
North Clifton NG23 . . . . 68 D3
North Scarle LN6 . . . . 83 D2
Nottingham NG6 . . . . 160 C7
Old Dalby LE14 . . . . 218 E4
Owthorpe NG12 . . . . 199 E8
Pleasley NG19 . . . . 87 A6
Plumtree NG12 . . . . 197 E7
Plungar NG13 . . . . 191 F1
Redmile NG13 . . . . 192 F3
Retford DN22 . . . . 39 E4
Saxilby LN1 . . . . 56 F5
Screveton NG13 . . . . 166 E4
Scrooby DN10 . . . . 10 A2
Selston, Selston Green
NG16 . . . . 128 D7
Selston, Underwood NG16 129 A3
Sibthorpe NG23 . . . . 167 E2
South Muskham NG23 . . . . . 124 E7
Stapleford NG9 . . . . 182 D7
Sutton in A NG17 . . . . 100 E2
Thrumpton NG11 . . . . 194 C3
Tibshelf DE55 . . . . 99 A6
Tickhill DN11 . . . . 8 A7
Torksey LN1 . . . . 44 B2
Upper Broughton LE14 . . . . 210 A1
Upton NG23 . . . . 122 F1
West Drayton DN22 . . . . 50 F2
Widmerpool NG12 . . . . 208 C5
Willoughby-on-t-W LE12 . . 217 C7
Church Lands 2 LE11 . . . 220 B6
Church Mdw
Calverton NG14 . . . . 148 F7
Claypole NG23 . . . . 156 C6
Church Mead NG17 . . . . . . 99 F3
Church Mews
1 Nottingham NG2 . . . . . . 173 D1
Sutton in A NG17 . . . . 100 E2
Churchmoor Ct NG5 . . . . . 147 A1
Churchmoor La NG5 . . . . . 147 F1
Church Rd
Bestwood Village NG6 . . . . . 146 E4
Bircotes DN11 . . . . 9 C4
Burton Joyce NG14 . . . . 163 F4
Church Warsop NG20 . . . . . 74 B6
Clipstone NG21 . . . . 89 F3
Greasley NG16 . . . . 144 E3
Harby NG23 . . . . 70 D1
Nottingham NG3 . . . . 223 F4
Saxilby LN1 . . . . 57 A4
Church St E NG16 . . . . 113 D4
Church St W NG16 . . . . 113 D4
Church Side
Farnsfield NG22 . . . . 119 F6
Huthwaite NG17 . . . . 99 F3
Mansfield NG18 . . . . 102 C6
Churchside Gdns NG7 . . . 172 E8
Church Sq NG7 . . . . 222 B1
Church St
Arnold NG5 . . . . 161 F8
Bawtry DN10 . . . . 10 A6
Beckingham DN10 . . . . 14 B1
Beeston, Bramcote NG9 . . . 183 B8
Beeston NG9 . . . . 183 F6
Bilsthorpe NG22 . . . . 105 F6
Bingham NG13 . . . . 177 F4
Bottesford NG13 . . . . 181 B2
Bunny NG11 . . . . 206 E8
Carlton NG4 . . . . 174 E7
Collingham NG23 . . . . 111 F7
Cropwell Bishop NG12 . . . . 189 A4
East Markham NG22 . . . . . . 66 A6
Eastwood NG16 . . . . 143 F2
Edwinstowe NG21 . . . . 76 B2
Everton DN10 . . . . 11 C3
Farndon NG24 . . . . 138 F4
Gainsborough DN21 . . . . . . 15 C1
Gotham NG11 . . . . 195 B1
Granby NG13 . . . . 191 B5
Hathern LE12 . . . . 213 A1
Ilkeston DE7 . . . . 157 E4
Kirkby in A NG17 . . . . 114 D4

Church St continued
Lambley NG4 . . . . 163 C7
Langold S81 . . . . 16 E2
Mansfield NG18 . . . . 102 B7
Mansfield Woodhouse NG19 88 C3
Market Warsop NG20 . . . . . 74 B5
Misterton DN10 . . . . 6 E2
Newark-on-T NG24 . . . . 139 F8
North Wheatley DN22 . . . . . 31 E8
Nottingham NG7 . . . . 222 A1
Nottingham, Old Basford
NG6 . . . . 160 E2
Ollerton NG22 . . . . 77 A3
Orston NG13 . . . . 179 F7
Pleasleyhill NG19 . . . . 87 B4
Ruddington NG11 . . . . 196 C7
Sandiacre NG10 . . . . 182 B7
Shelford NG12 . . . . 164 C1
South Leverton DN22 . . . . . 42 C7
South Normanton DE55 . . . 113 A6
Southwell NG25 . . . . 136 E8
Stapleford NG9 . . . . 182 D7
Sturton le S DN22 . . . . 32 D4
Sutton in A NG17 . . . . 100 E2
Sutton on T NG23 . . . . 97 A8
Whaley Thorns NG20 . . . . . . 59 A2
Whatton NG13 . . . . 179 A3
Wymeswold LE12 . . . . 216 C3
Church Vale Prim Sch
NG20 . . . . 74 A7
Church View
Balderton NG24 . . . . 140 D3
Beckingham DN10 . . . . 14 B1
Bottesford NG13 . . . . 181 A3
Carlton NG4 . . . . 162 F1
Glapwell S44 . . . . 86 B8
New Houghton NG19 . . . . . 86 F7
Ollerton NG22 . . . . 77 B3
Scrooby DN10 . . . . 10 A2
Stanton Hill NG17 . . . . 100 D6
Church View Cl NG5 . . . . . 147 B1
Church Vw Gd NG17 . . . . 129 E8
Church Way DN22 . . . . 29 A6
Church Wlk
Bawtry DN10 . . . . 10 A7
Brinsley NG16 . . . . 143 E7
Carlton NG4 . . . . 174 E7
Eastwood NG16 . . . . 143 F2
Harworth DN11 . . . . 8 E4
Stapleford NG9 . . . . 182 E7
Upton NG23 . . . . 122 F1
Weston NG23 . . . . 81 A5
Whatton NG13 . . . . 179 B4
Worksop S80 . . . . 35 F3
Churnet Cl NG11 . . . . 184 E4
Chuter Ede Prim Sch
NG24 . . . . 140 E4
Cinderhill Gr NG4 . . . . 162 E2
Cinderhill Rd NG6 . . . . 160 B5
Cinderhill Wlk NG6 . . . . . 160 B5
Cinder La NG22 . . . . 77 B2
Circle The NG19 . . . . 88 B4
Cirrus Dr NG16 . . . . 159 A7
Citadel St NG7 . . . . 222 A3
Citrus Gr DE74 . . . . 203 C3
**City Gd (Nottingham Forest
FC) The** NG2 . . . . 173 E1
City Link NG1, NG2 . . . . . . 173 F3
City of Caves NG1 . . . . . . 223 E2
**City of Nottingham Tennis
Ctr** NG7 . . . . 184 C8
City Rd
Beeston NG9 . . . . 184 A6
Nottingham NG7 . . . . 172 D1
Stathern LE14 . . . . 202 F3
City The NG9 . . . . 184 A6
Clandon Dr NG5 . . . . 161 B2
Clanfield Rd NG8 . . . . 171 E7
Clapham St NG7 . . . . 222 A3
Clapton La NG7 . . . . 184 E2
Clara Mount Rd DE75 . . . 143 A1
Clarborough Dr NG5 . . . . 162 A6
Clarborough Hill DN22 . . 30 E4
Clarborough Prim Sch
DN22 . . . . 30 E3
**Clarborough Tunnel Nature
Reserve** DN22 . . . . 31 C2
Clare Cl NG6 . . . . 160 E4
Clarehaven NG9 . . . . 182 E5
Clare Hill NG21 . . . . 118 A4
Claremont Ave
Beeston NG9 . . . . 183 C7
Hucknall NG15 . . . . 146 A5
Claremont Dr NG11 . . . . . 185 C3
Claremont Prim Sch
NG5 . . . . 161 B1
Claremont Rd
Gainsborough DN21 . . . . . . 24 F6
Nottingham NG5 . . . . 161 B1
Claremount Cl NG19 . . . . . 88 E3
Clarence Rd
Beeston NG9 . . . . 183 D3
Long Eaton NG10 . . . . 193 C6
Worksop S80 . . . . 35 E4
Clarence St
Loughborough LE11 . . . . . . 220 C5
Mansfield NG18 . . . . 102 A6
Nottingham NG3 . . . . 173 E5
Pleasleyhill NG19 . . . . 87 C3
Clarendon Ct 5 NG5 . . . . 173 B8
Clarendon Dr S81 . . . . 35 D6
Clarendon Pk NG5 . . . . . . 173 B8
Clarendon Rd NG19 . . . . . 101 E8
Clarendon Sixth Form Coll
NG1 . . . . 223 D4

Clare Valley NG7 . . . . 223 D2
Clarewood Gr NG11 . . . . . 195 E7
Clarges St NG6 . . . . 160 C6
Claricoates Dr NG24 . . . . 125 E2
Clarke Ave
Arnold NG5 . . . . 161 F8
Newark-on-T NG24 . . . . 139 E5
Clarke Cl NG12 . . . . 189 A4
Clarke Dr NG10 . . . . 193 A4
Clarke Rd NG2 . . . . 173 E2
Clarke's La NG9 . . . . 183 D4
Clark La NG22 . . . . 65 F2
Clarks La NG24 . . . . 125 B2
Clarkson Dr NG9 . . . . 184 B6
Clarkwoods Cl NG22 . . . . . 77 E4
Clater's Cl DN22 . . . . 40 A8
Claude St NG7 . . . . 172 E1
Clawson La
Hickling LE14 . . . . 210 D6
Nether Broughton LE14 . . . 210 E1
Claxton Rise LE14 . . . . . . 211 C2
Clay Ave NG3 . . . . 162 A3
Claye St NG10 . . . . 193 E7
Clayfield Cl NG6 . . . . 160 A6
Claygate NG3 . . . . 174 A7
Clay La
Fenton LN1 . . . . 55 D7
Newark-on-T NG24 . . . . 140 C7
Claylands Ave S81 . . . . 35 C5
Claylands Cl S81 . . . . 35 D5
Claylands La S81 . . . . 35 D6
Claypit La NG25 . . . . 137 E3
Claypole CE (Cont) Prim Sch
NG23 . . . . 156 E2
Claypole La NG23 . . . . 156 E2
Claypole Rd 16 NG7 . . . . 172 F7
Clay St LE12 . . . . 216 C3
Claythorne Dr DN21 . . . . . 24 E8
Clayton Cl NG24 . . . . 140 A6
Clayton Ct NG7 . . . . 222 B3
Claytons Dr 11 NG7 . . . . 172 E2
Clayton's Wharf 12 NG7 . 172 E2
Clayworth Comm DN22 . . 21 E3
Clayworth Ct 13 NG18 . . 103 A2
Clayworth Rd DN10 . . . . . 12 F1
Clegg Hill Dr NG17 . . . . . . 99 E4
Clement Ave NG24 . . . . . . 140 E3
Clensey La NG23 . . . . 156 F2
Clerkson's Alley 6 NG18 102 B7
Clerkson St 4 NG18 . . . . 102 B6
Clether Rd NG8 . . . . 171 D6
Cleve Ave NG9 . . . . 182 E3
Cleveland Ave NG10 . . . . 182 F1
Cleveland Cl
Carlton in L S81 . . . . 25 E7
Nottingham NG7 . . . . 222 A3
Cleveland Sq NG20 . . . . . 139 F6
Cleveland St DN21 . . . . 24 D7
Cleveleys Rd NG9 . . . . 182 E3
Clevely Way NG11 . . . . 184 E3
Cliff Bvd NG16 . . . . 158 F7
Cliff Cres NG12 . . . . 175 F4
Cliff Dr NG12 . . . . 176 A5
Cliffe Hill Ave NG9 . . . . . . 182 D7
Cliff Gate NG22 . . . . 65 C8
Cliffgrove Ave NG9 . . . . . . 183 D6
Clifthill La NG13 . . . . 179 C6
Cliff La NG13 . . . . 113 F4
Cliffmere Wlk NG11 . . . . . 184 D1
Cliff Nook DE55 . . . . 113 B4
Cliff Nook La NG24 . . . . . . 125 A1
Clifford Ave NG9 . . . . 183 F8
Clifford Cl
Keyworth NG12 . . . . 197 F4
Long Eaton NG10 . . . . 193 A4
Clifford Ct NG7 . . . . 222 B3
Clifford St
Long Eaton NG10 . . . . 193 E7
Mansfield NG18 . . . . 102 B4
Nottingham NG7 . . . . 222 B3
Cliff Rd
Carlton NG4 . . . . 174 D6
Nottingham NG1 . . . . 223 F2
Radcliffe on T NG12 . . . . . . 175 E4
Cliff St NG18 . . . . 102 C7
Cliff The NG6 . . . . 160 B4
Cliff Way NG12 . . . . 175 F4
Clifton Ave
Long Eaton NG10 . . . . 194 A7
Ruddington NG11 . . . . 196 C7
Clifton Bvd NG7 . . . . 184 F8
Clifton Cres
Beeston NG9 . . . . 183 E3
Newark-on-T NG24 . . . . 125 B3
Clifton Gr
Carlton NG4 . . . . 162 E2
Mansfield NG18 . . . . 102 F4
Clifton Grove Nature Reserve
NG11 . . . . 184 C3
Clifton La
Nottingham NG11 . . . . 184 D1
Ruddington NG11 . . . . 196 A8
Clifton L Ctr NG11 . . . . . . 184 F1
Clifton Pl 2 NG18 . . . . . . 102 B7
Clifton Rd NG11 . . . . 196 B7
Clifton St NG9 . . . . 184 A6
Clifton Terr NG7 . . . . 222 C1
Clifton Way DN22 . . . . 39 C8
**Clifton Woods Nature
Reserve** NG11 . . . . 184 C3
Clinthill La S80 . . . . 45 A7
Clinton Ave
Brinsley NG16 . . . . 143 D6
Nottingham NG5 . . . . 173 B8
Clinton Ct NG1 . . . . 223 E3
Clinton Gdn La NG22 . . . . 65 F2
Clinton St E NG1 . . . . 223 E3
Clinton St W NG1 . . . . 223 E3

Clinton St
Arnold NG5 . . . . 161 E7
Beeston NG9 . . . . 183 E7
Newark-on-T NG24 . . . . . 139 F8
Worksop S80 . . . . 36 A1
Clinton Terr DN21 . . . . . 24 D7
Clipsham Cl NG24. . . . . . 140 E5
Clipstone Ave
Mansfield NG18. . . . . 102 C8
Nottingham, Mapperley
NG3. . . . . 162 A4
Nottingham NG1 . . . . . . 223 D4
Sutton in A NG17 . . . . . . 101 A4
Clipstone Cl NG8. . . . . . . 159 D2
Clipstone Dr NG19 . . . . . . 89 D3
Clipstone Rd E NG19 . . . . . 89 C2
Clipstone Rd W NG19 . . . . 89 B1
Clipston La NG12 . . . . . 197 F7
Clive Cres NG16 . . . . . . 159 A5
Cliveden Gn NG11 . . . . . 184 D1
Cloister St NG7 . . . . 172 E2
Cloisters The NG9 . . . . . 184 A8
Close Quarters NG9 . . . 183 C8
Closes Side La NG13 . . . 165 E3
Close The
Averham NG23. . . . . 123 E2
Beeston NG9 . . . . 183 D4
Mansfield NG21. . . . . 103 F2
Newark-on-T NG24 . . . . . 140 A8
Nottingham NG5 . . . . . . 161 C3
Shirebrook NG20. . . . . 72 F5
Upton NG23. . . . . 122 F1
Cloud Ave NG9 . . . . 182 F7
Clouds Hill NG11 . . . . . . 195 E8
Cloudside Ct NG10 . . . . 182 C7
Cloudside Jun Sch NG10 182 B6
Cloudside Rd NG10 . . . . 182 A7
Clough Ct NG8. . . . . 172 B7
Clover Cl S81 . . . . 36 B7
Cloverdale NG12 . . . . . . 188 A2
Cloverfields NG14. . . . . 149 A8
Clover Gn NG6. . . . . 160 D3
Cloverlands NG11 . . . . . 185 C3
Cloverlands Dr NG16 . . . 159 A7
Clover Rise NG16 . . . . . 158 B8
Clover St NG17 . . . . 115 A6
Clover Way NG19 . . . . . . 88 F4
Club Ct NG24 . . . . 140 D4
Cludd Ave NG24 . . . . . . 140 E8
Clumber Ave
Beeston NG9 . . . . 183 D5
Brinsley NG16 . . . . 128 E1
Carlton NG4. . . . . 175 A4
Edwinstowe NG21 . . . . . . 75 F3
Mansfield NG21. . . . . 103 F1
Newark-on-T NG24 . . . . . 140 A6
Nottingham, Hyson Green
NG5. . . . . 173 B8
Nottingham, Mapperley
NG3. . . . . 162 A4
Clumber Cres NG17. . . . 100 C6
Clumber Cres N NG7 . . . 222 C2
Clumber Cres S NG7 . . . 222 C1
Clumber Ct
Ilkeston DE7 . . . . 157 F5
Mansfield NG19. . . . . 87 E2
Market Warsop NG20 . . . . 74 B4
Nottingham NG7 . . . . . . 222 C1
Clumber Dr
Mansfield NG19. . . . . 87 E2
Radcliffe on T NG12. . . . . 176 A4
Clumber Pk Ctry Pk S80. . 48 B3
Clumber Pl S80. . . . . 35 E3
Clumber Rd
West Bridgford NG2 . . . . 185 F7
Worksop S80 . . . . 47 B5
Clumber Rd E NG7 . . . . 222 C2
Clumber Rd W NG7 . . . . 222 C2
Clumber St
Hucknall NG15. . . . . 146 C6
Kirkby in A NG17 . . . . . . 115 C5
Long Eaton NG10 . . . . . . 193 D7
Mansfield NG18. . . . . 102 B7
Market Warsop NG20 . . . . 74 B4
Nottingham NG1 . . . . . . 223 E3
Retford DN22. . . . . 39 E6
Sutton in A NG17 . . . . . . 100 D2
Clumber Way NG22 . . . . 106 A5
Clun Ct NG19 . . . . 88 D2
Clyro Pl DN22 . . . . 28 F6
Coach Dr NG16 . . . . 143 F4
Coach Gap La NG13 . . . . 190 D1
Coachmans Croft 2
NG8 . . . . 172 A5
Coach Rd NG16 . . . . 74 C1
Coalfields Cl NG17 . . . . 100 C1
Coal La LE14 . . . . 211 F8
Coalpit La DN22. . . . . 49 F4
Coal Yd La NG23 . . . . 82 E8
Coates Ave NG15. . . . . . 130 F1
Coatsby Rd NG16 . . . . . 158 F7
Coates Rd DN22 . . . . 43 D8
Cobblestone Dr NG18 . . 102 D5
Cobden Pl NG16 . . . . 87 E2
Cobden Prim Sch LE11 . 220 B4
Cobden St
Gainsborough DN21 . . . . . 24 C8
Kirkby in A NG17 . . . . . . 115 A4
Long Eaton NG10 . . . . . . 193 E7
1 Loughborough LE11 . . 220 C4
Nottingham NG7 . . . . . . 222 A3
Coburn St NG17. . . . . . . 100 F1
Cobwell Rd DN22 . . . . . . 39 E6
Cochrane Terr NG17. . . . 100 D6
Cockayne Cl NG10 . . . . . 182 B3
Cocker Beck NG4 . . . . . . 163 C7
Cockerhouse Rd NG16 . . 143 E4
Cockett La NG22 . . . . . . 119 E7

Cockhill Cl DN10 . . . . 10 A6
Cock Hill La DN10 . . . . . . 10 A6
Cocking Hill NG22 . . . . . 78 C4
Cocking La DN22 . . . . 42 C2
Cockington Rd NG8 . . . . 171 C5
Cockle Cl NG18 . . . . 102 E5
Cockleys NG10 . . . . 193 C6
Cockshut La NG20 . . . . . . 59 A4
Coddington CE Prim Sch
NG24. . . . . 126 A1
Coddington La LN6 . . . . 127 A6
Coddington Rd NG24 . . . 140 F5
Codrington Gdns 5
NG5 . . . . 161 C8
Cogenhoe Wlk NG5 . . . . 147 F2
Coggin's La NG20 . . . . . . 74 C6
Coghill Ct NG25 . . . . . . 136 D8
Coging Cl NG24. . . . . . . 140 C3
Cogley La NG13 . . . . 178 A4
Cohen Cl
Arnold NG5 . . . . 162 B6
Beeston NG9 . . . . 183 B2
Cokefield Ave NG16 . . . . 159 F3
Colbeck St S80 . . . . 35 E3
Colborn St NG3 . . . . 173 F7
Colby Cl NG19 . . . . 89 B2
Coleby Ave NG7. . . . . . . 222 A1
Coleby Rd NG8 . . . . 159 F2
Coledale NG2. . . . . 186 C6
Coleman Ave NG24. . . . . 140 B4
Coleridge Cres NG5 . . . . 161 D7
Coleridge Rd
Balderton NG24. . . . . 140 E5
Worksop S81. . . . . 36 B5
Coleridge St NG7 . . . . . . 222 B4
Colesbourne Rd NG7. . . . 184 F2
Colgrove Rd LE11 . . . . . . 220 A2
Colin Broughton Ct NG6 160 D7
Colindale NG16. . . . . . . 159 E3
Colinwood Ave NG5. . . . 146 E1
College Dr
Nottingham NG11 . . . . . . 184 D2
Nottingham NG11 . . . . . . 184 E3
College La
East Markham NG22 . . . . . 66 A7
Worksop S80. . . . . 36 B1
College Rd
Beeston NG9 . . . . 183 E5
Carlton NG3. . . . . 162 A4
Sutton Bonington LE12 . . 204 A1
College St
East Bridgford NG13 . . . . 165 D3
Long Eaton NG10 . . . . . . 182 C2
Nottingham NG1 . . . . . . 223 D2
Colley La NG23 . . . . 81 B4
Colleymoor Leys La NG7 184 F2
Collier Ave NG19. . . . . . . 88 B5
Colliers Way NG6 . . . . . . 160 A4
Colliers Wy NG12 . . . . . . 188 A5
Colliery Cl NG2 . . . . 173 B1
Colliery Rd DN11. . . . . 9 A3
Collin Ave NG10 . . . . 182 B4
Collingham Rd
Collingham LN6 . . . . 98 F1
Mansfield NG19. . . . . 87 D1
Collingham Sta NG23 . . 112 B8
Collin Gn NG5 . . . . 161 D4
Collington St NG9. . . . . . 183 F6
Collington Way NG2 . . . . 185 D6
Collingwood Cl NG11. . . . 184 E4
Collingwood Rd NG10 . . 193 E6
Collinridge View NG22 . . . 64 A2
Collins Ave
South Normanton DE55 . . 113 A7
Sutton in A NG17 . . . . . . 114 E7
Collins Cl NG6 . . . . 159 F5
Collinson La NG24 . . . . . 140 F1
Collin St
Beeston NG9 . . . . 183 F6
Nottingham NG1 . . . . . . 223 E1
Collins Wlk DN22 . . . . 39 F7
Collis Cl NG24 . . . . 140 E8
Collison St NG7 . . . . 222 B4
Collyer Rd NG14 . . . . . . 148 D8
Colly Gate NG16 . . . . . . 159 A5
Collygate Rd NG2 . . . . . 173 D1
Colmon Cl NG5 . . . . 161 A7
Colmon Wlk 6 NG5. . . . 161 A7
Colne Ct NG19 . . . . 88 D2
**Colonel Frank Seely Comp
Sch** NG14 . . . . 148 E8
Colonel's La LE14 . . . . . . 210 A1
Colonsay Ct NG9 . . . . . . 170 D3
Colsterdale S81. . . . . 36 B8
Colston Basset CE Prim Sch
NG12. . . . . 200 B8
Colston Cres NG2 . . . . . . 185 D4
Colston Gate NG12. . . . . 188 A3
Colston La LE14. . . . . . . 201 E4
Colston Rd
Colston Bassett NG12 . . . 200 B8
Cropwell Bishop NG12. . . 189 A1
Mansfield NG18. . . . . 103 A3
Nottingham NG6 . . . . . . 160 C7
Colton St DN10 . . . . 6 E2
Columbia Ave
Mansfield NG18. . . . . 102 F5
Sutton in A NG17. . . . . . . 100 C2
Columbia Cl NG16 . . . . . 129 A7
Columbia St NG17 . . . . . 100 A2
Columbus St S80 . . . . . . 35 C2
Colville St NG1 . . . . 173 B7
Colville Terr
Gainsborough DN21 . . . . . 24 D8
2 Nottingham NG1 . . . . . 173 B7
Colville Villas 1 NG1 . . 173 B7
Colwick Bsns Pk NG4 . . . 174 F5
Colwick Cl NG19 . . . . 87 E1

Colwick Ctry Pk NG2 . . . 174 D3
Colwick Hall NG2 . . . . . . 174 C3
Colwick Ind Est NG4 . . . 174 F5
Colwick Loop Rd NG4 . . . 175 B6
Colwick Manor Farm
NG4. . . . . 174 A5
Colwick Pk Cl NG4 . . . . . 174 E5
Colwick Rd
Nottingham NG2 . . . . 174 B4
West Bridgford NG2 . . . . 173 E1
**Colwick Woods Nature
Reserve** NG2 . . . . 174 B4
Combes The NG25 . . . . . 121 D2
Comery Ave NG3. . . . . . . 174 A6
Comfrey Cl NG5 . . . . 160 E7
Commerce Sq NG1. . . . . 223 F2
Commercial Ave NG9 . . . 183 F6
Commercial Gate NG18 . 102 B6
Commercial Rd
Keyworth NG12. . . . . 197 E2
6 Nottingham NG6. . . . . 160 B7
Commercial St 5 NG18 . 102 B6
Commodore Gdns NG8. . 160 C2
Common La
Beeston NG9 . . . . 183 A6
Blyth S81 . . . . 18 B4
Hucknall NG15. . . . . 145 E7
Mansfield Woodhouse NG19 88 A4
Ranskill DN22. . . . . 19 C4
Shirebrook NG20. . . . . 72 C2
Sturton le S DN22 . . . . . . 32 E6
Watnall NG16 . . . . 159 B7
Common Rd
Huthwaite NG17 . . . . 99 F2
Retford DN22. . . . . 39 F7
Thorpe Salvin S80 . . . . . . 34 A5
Commons Cl NG16 . . . . . 158 A8
Common Side NG16 . . . . 128 F8
Common The
Hucknall NG15. . . . . 145 C6
South Normanton DE55 . . 113 B6
Compton Acres NG2 . . . 185 B5
Compton Acres Sh Ctr
NG2. . . . . 185 C5
Compton Rd NG5 . . . . . . 161 B3
Compton St NG20 . . . . . . 72 F8
Comyn Gdns NG3 . . . . . 223 F4
Conduit Cl NG2 . . . . 173 C2
Conery Gdns NG13 . . . . . 179 A3
Conery La NG13. . . . . . . 178 F2
Coneygrey Spinney
NG23. . . . . 152 E2
Conifer Cres NG11 . . . . . 195 E7
Conifer Wlk NG3 . . . . . . 174 A8
Coningsby Cl DN21. . . . . . 24 F8
Coningsby Gdns E NG5. . 161 F4
Coningsby Rd NG5 . . . . . 161 F5
Coningswath Rd NG4. . . . 162 C1
Conisborough Terr 10
NG2. . . . . 173 C1
Conisbrough Ave NG4. . . 163 B1
Coniston Ave NG6. . . . . . 160 C2
Coniston Cl
Mansfield Woodhouse NG19 . . . . 88 E4
West Bridgford NG2 . . . . 186 C7
Coniston Rd
Beeston NG9 . . . . 183 D8
Hucknall NG15. . . . . 145 F8
Kirkby in A NG17 . . . . . . 115 C6
Long Eaton NG10 . . . . . . 182 A2
Worksop S81. . . . . 35 E8
Connaught Rd DN21. . . . . 15 D2
Connelly Cl NG5 . . . . 162 C6
Connery Mews NG9 . . . . 183 B1
Connery The NG15 . . . . . 146 A7
Conrad Cl S80 . . . . 36 B3
Constance St NG7. . . . . . 161 A1
Convent St NG1. . . . . . . 223 F3
Conway Ave NG4. . . . . . . 175 A7
Conway Cl
Mansfield NG19. . . . . 101 D8
Nottingham NG3 . . . . . . 173 C7
Conway Cres NG4 . . . . . . 175 A8
Conway Dr S81 . . . . 25 E8
Conway Gdns
Arnold NG5 . . . . 161 F6
Retford DN22. . . . . 39 B8
Conway Rd
Carlton NG4. . . . . 175 A8
Hucknall NG15. . . . . 145 D3
Conway St NG10 . . . . . . 193 F8
Conway Wlk 4 NG3. . . . . 173 C7
Cook Dr DE7. . . . . 170 A6
Cooks La
Fiskerton NG25 . . . . 137 D2
Southwell NG25. . . . . 136 B8
Cookson Ave NG4. . . . . . 162 D2
Cookson St NG17 . . . . . . 114 E5
Coombe Cl NG8. . . . . . . 172 C3
Coombe Rd NG16 . . . . . . 144 B8
Co-Operative Ave NG15 . 146 B8
Co-Operative St
Long Eaton NG10 . . . . . . 193 E6
Stanton Hill NG17 . . . . . . 100 C6
Cooper Cl
Arnold NG5 . . . . 162 C6
Cropwell Bishop NG12. . . 189 A4
Nottingham NG6 . . . . . . 159 F6
Cooper Ct LE11 . . . . 220 D2
Coopers Gn NG8 . . . . . . 171 C2
Coopers Rise NG21. . . . . 104 A1
Cooper St NG4. . . . . 175 A6
Coopers Yd NG24 . . . . . . 139 E8
Copeland Ave
1 Kirkby in A NG17 . . . . 114 E6
Stapleford NG9 . . . . 182 E8

Copeland Gr NG13 . . . . . 177 C5
Copeland Rd
Hucknall NG15. . . . . 146 C8
Kirkby in A NG17 . . . . . . 114 E6
Copenhagen Ct NG3 . . . . 161 D1
Cope St NG7. . . . . 222 B4
Copestake Cl NG10 . . . . 193 A7
Copper Hill NG23 . . . . . . 81 E4
Coppice Ave DE7 . . . . . . 157 D5
Coppice Cl NG15. . . . . . . 145 E5
Coppice Croft NG17 . . . . 100 C1
Coppice Dr NG16 . . . . . . 143 D3
Coppice Form Prim Sch
NG5. . . . . 162 B7
Coppice Gr NG3 . . . . 161 E1
Coppice Rd
Arnold NG5 . . . . 162 B8
Clipstone NG19 . . . . 89 D3
Worksop S81. . . . . 35 F7
Coppice The
Barnby Moor DN22 . . . . . . 28 D5
Shirebrook NG20. . . . . 72 D3
Coppice View DE55 . . . . 113 A4
Copplestone Dr NG3 . . . . 162 C6
Coppywood Cl NG17 . . . . 100 B7
Copse Cl
Burton Joyce NG14 . . . . . 163 F5
Ravenshead NG15 . . . . . . 116 C3
Copseside Cl 8 NG10 . . 193 A8
Copse The
Beeston NG9 . . . . 183 C6
Farndon NG24 . . . . 139 A4
Hucknall NG15. . . . . 146 A4
Ilkeston DE7 . . . . 157 D5
Mansfield NG18. . . . . 102 C6
Stanton Hill NG17 . . . . . . 100 C5
Copsewood DE55 . . . . . . 113 A4
Corben Gdns NG6 . . . . . 159 F7
Corbiere Ave NG16. . . . . 159 A7
Corby Rd NG3 . . . . 161 E1
Cordy La NG16 . . . . 143 F8
Corene Ave NG17 . . . . . . 100 E1
Coriander Dr NG6. . . . . . 160 D3
Corinth Rd NG7 . . . . 184 E2
Corkhill La NG22. . . . . . . 121 D5
Cormack La NG24 . . . . . . 140 F1
Corn Cft NG11 . . . . 184 F1
Corn Cl
Cotgrave NG12 . . . . 187 E2
South Normanton DE55 . . 113 A4
Corncrake Ave NG6. . . . . 160 D3
Corncrake Dr NG5 . . . . . . 162 C7
Cornell Dr NG5 . . . . 162 C8
Corner The NG14 . . . . . . 150 D1
Cornfield Ave DE55 . . . . 113 A4
Cornfield Rd NG16 . . . . . 158 E7
Cornhill Rd NG4 . . . . 174 B7
Cornley Rd DN10 . . . . 6 C3
Cornwall Ave
Beeston NG9 . . . . 184 C4
Mansfield NG18. . . . . 102 F6
Cornwall Cl NG16 . . . . . . 128 C4
Cornwall Dr NG22. . . . . . . 77 A3
Cornwallis Cl NG10 . . . . 193 D6
Cornwall Rd
Arnold NG5 . . . . 161 C7
Retford DN22. . . . . 30 A1
Shireoaks S81 . . . . 34 F7
Coronation Ave
Long Clawson LE14 . . . . . 211 B2
Misson DN10. . . . . 4 B3
New Houghton NG19. . . . . 86 F7
Nottingham NG11 . . . . . . 185 B8
Sandiacre NG10. . . . . 182 A7
Coronation Dr
Mansfield NG19. . . . . 103 A8
Shirebrook NG20. . . . . 72 F2
South Normanton DE55. . . 113 B6
Coronation Rd
Arnold NG5 . . . . 161 F3
Awsworth DE7. . . . . 158 A1
Bestwood Village NG6. . . 146 A4
Cossall NG16. . . . . 158 B2
Hucknall NG15. . . . . 145 F8
Nuthall NG16. . . . . 159 C5
Coronation St
Mansfield NG18. . . . . 102 D6
New Balderton NG24. . . . . 140 C5
Retford DN22. . . . . 39 E6
Sutton in A NG17. . . . . . . 100 E1
Whitwell S80 . . . . 45 A6
Coronation Wlk NG4 . . . . 163 A1
Corporation Oaks
NG3 . . . . 173 C7
Corporation Rd DE7. . . . . 170 A5
Corporation St 8
NG18 . . . . 102 A7
Corringham Rd DN21. . . . 15 F1
Corsham Gdns NG3 . . . . 174 A7
Cosby Rd 4 NG2. . . . . . . 173 F3
Cosgrove Ave NG17 . . . . 101 B5
Cossall Ind Est NG16. . . . 158 B2
Cossall Rd NG9 . . . . 170 D5
Costhorpe Ind Est S81. . . 16 E1
Costhorpe Villas S81. . . . 16 E1
Costock Ave NG5 . . . . . . 161 B4
Costock Rd
East Leake LE12 . . . . 206 A1
Wysall NG12. . . . . 207 C2
Cotes Dr LE12 . . . . 220 B6
Cotes Rd LE12 . . . . 220 F5
Coteswood House Sch
NG5. . . . . 161 E5
Cotgrave Ave NG4 . . . . . 162 F2
Cotgrave CE Prim Sch
NG12. . . . . 187 E3
Cotgrave Cl NG8 . . . . . . 159 E2

Cotgrave Ctry Pk NG12 . 188 A6
Cotgrave Inf Sch NG12 . . 187 F3
Cotgrave La NG12 . . . . . . 187 A2
Cotgrave L Ctr NG12 . . . 188 A3
Cotgrave Manvers Jun Sch
NG12. . . . . 187 F3
Cotgrave Rd
Cotgrave NG12 . . . . 187 A1
Mansfield NG19. . . . . 87 F2
Cotmanhay Rd DE7 . . . . 157 E3
Coton Cl
Mansfield Woodhouse NG19. . . . . 88 E4
Nottingham NG11 . . . . . . 185 A3
Cotswold Cl 2 NG10 . . . 193 B8
Cotswold Ct
Beeston NG9 . . . . 171 C1
Carlton in L S81. . . . . 25 E7
Cotswold Gr NG18 . . . . . 103 B6
Cotswold Rd NG8 . . . . . . 159 E1
Cottage Ave NG13. . . . . . 178 F4
Cottage Cl
Balderton NG24. . . . . 140 D2
Blidworth NG21 . . . . 117 F4
Ilkeston DE7 . . . . 157 D3
Cottage La
Collingham NG23 . . . . . . 111 F6
Market Warsop NG20 . . . . 74 C2
North Clifton NG23 . . . . . . 69 B4
Cottage Mdw NG4 . . . . . 174 F4
Cottage Pasture La
NG14. . . . . 164 E7
Cottage Terr NG1 . . . . . . 222 C3
Cottam Dr NG5 . . . . 161 A8
Cottam Gdns NG5. . . . . . 161 A8
Cottam Gr NG19 . . . . . . 101 D6
Cottam Rd
Cottam DN22. . . . . 43 C4
South Leverton DN22 . . . . 42 E7
Cottans Cl NG25 . . . . . . 136 F8
Cottesmore Rd NG7. . . . . 222 B2
Cotton Mill La NG22. . . . 120 A5
Coulby Cl NG23 . . . . 156 E6
Coulton's Ave NG17 . . . . 100 C3
Coulton's Cl NG17 . . . . . 100 C3
County Bsns Pk NG2 . . . 173 E2
County Cl NG9 . . . . 184 A5
County Rd
Carlton NG4. . . . . 162 C3
Nottingham NG2 . . . . . . 173 E2
Coupland Cl 6 DN21. . . . 15 F1
Court Cres NG8 . . . . 171 F4
Courtenay Gdns NG3 . . . 173 D7
Court-Field Rd NG17 . . . 101 A6
Court Gdns NG11 . . . . . . 185 B4
Courtney Cl NG8 . . . . 171 E5
Court St 11 NG7 . . . . 172 F7
Court Yd NG9 . . . . 183 B8
Covedale Rd NG5 . . . . . . 161 C5
Covent Gdns NG12 . . . . . 176 E3
Coventry Ct NG6 . . . . . . 160 C5
Coventry Dr S81 . . . . 36 A6
Coventry La NG9 . . . . . . 171 A3
Coventry Rd
Beeston NG9 . . . . 184 A7
Nottingham NG6 . . . . . . 160 B6
Cove Rd DN9 . . . . 2 E6
Coverdale S81. . . . . 36 B7
Covert Cl
Burton Joyce NG14 . . . . . 163 E5
Hucknall NG15. . . . . 146 C6
Keyworth NG12 . . . . 197 F4
Covert Rd NG2. . . . . 186 B6
Cowan St NG1. . . . . 223 F3
Cowdray Cl LE11. . . . . . . 220 A1
Cowdrey Gdns NG5 . . . . 162 B6
Cow La
Beeston NG9 . . . . 183 C8
Newark-on-T NG24 . . . . . 124 F1
Cowlairs NG5. . . . . 160 E7
Cowley St NG6. . . . . 160 D3
Cowpasture La NG17 . . . 100 E1
Cow Pasture La NG17 . . . 114 D5
Cowper Cl S81. . . . . 36 B5
Cowper Rd
Arnold NG5 . . . . 161 E4
Eastwood NG16 . . . . 158 A4
Cowpes Cl NG17 . . . . . . 100 E4
Cox Dr NG13. . . . . 180 F3
Coxmoor Cl NG2 . . . . . . 186 C4
Coxmoor Ct 14 NG5 . . . . 147 A1
Coxmoor Prim Sch
NG17. . . . . 115 C5
Coxmoor Rd NG17, NG15. 115 E2
Cox's Hill DN21 . . . . 15 D1
Cox's La NG19 . . . . 88 B3
Crab La NG23 . . . . 110 F1
Crab Nook La NG22 . . . . 119 F6
Crabtree Field NG2 . . . . . 174 D4
Crabtree La
Beckingham DN10. . . . . . . 23 A8
High Marnham NG23. . . . . 67 D2
Crabtree Rd NG6. . . . . . . 160 A6
Craddock St LE11. . . . . . 220 B4
Crafts Way NG25. . . . . . . 121 E1
Cragdale Rd NG5 . . . . . . 161 C5
Cragg La DE55 . . . . 99 A2
Cragmoor Rd NG14 . . . . 163 E3
Crags Rd S80 . . . . 45 A4
Craig Moray NG12 . . . . . 176 A4
Craigs Gn NG19 . . . . 101 E5
Craig St NG10 . . . . 193 E7
Craigston Rd S81 . . . . . . 25 E6
Crammond Cl 3 NG2 . . . 173 B2

Crampton Cl NG17 . . . . .100 B3
Crampton Ct NG5 . . . . . . .161 A8
Crampton Rd NG18 . . . . . .102 E8
Cramworth Dr **4** NG5. . .161 D3
Cranberry Cl NG2 . . . . . . .185 B5
Cranborne Cl NG19 . . . . . .101 D7
Cranbourne Cl NG9 . . . . . .170 D2
Cranbourne Gr NG15 . . . . .145 E7
Cranbrook St NG1 . . . . . . .223 F3
Cranfleet Way NG10. . . . . .193 B7
Cranford Gdns NG2 . . . . . .185 C4
Cranleigh Dr NG14 . . . . . .150 D1
Cranmer Ave NG13 . . . . . .178 E3
Cranmer Gr
  8 Nottingham NG3. . . . . .173 C7
  Radmanthwaite NG19 . . . . .87 D3
Cranmer Rd NG24 . . . . . . .139 F5
Cranmer St
  Ilkeston DE7 . . . . .157 F1
  Long Eaton NG10. . . . . . .182 D1
  Nottingham NG3 . . . . .173 C7
Cranmore Cl NG5 . . . . . . .148 A2
Cranshaw Cl LE12 . . . . . . .212 C3
Cransley Ave NG8 . . . . . . .171 D2
Cranston Ave NG5 . . . . . . .147 F1
Cranston Rd NG9 . . . . . . .171 C1
Cranswick Cl NG19 . . . . . . .89 A2
Cranthorne Dr NG3 . . . . . .174 C6
Crantock Gdns NG12 . . . . .197 F3
Cranwell Cl NG24 . . . . . . .125 D1
Cranwell St NG1 . . . . .223 D1
Cranwell Rd NG8 . . . . . . .159 D2
Craster Dr
  Arnold NG5 . . . . .148 A2
  Nottingham NG6 . . . . .159 F8
Craster St NG17 . . . . .100 E1
Crathie Rd S81 . . . . .25 E6
Craven Rd NG7 . . . . .172 E7
Crawford Ave NG9 . . . . . . .182 D8
Crawford Cl NG8 . . . . . . .171 E5
Crawford Rise NG5. . . . . . .162 C8
C Rd NG9 . . . . .184 D6
Crees La NG24 . . . . .139 B6
Crescent Ave NG4 . . . . . . .162 C6
Crescent Prim Sch NG19 . .87 D2
Crescent Rd NG16 . . . . . . .128 C6
Crescent The
  Arnold NG5 . . . . .161 E4
  Beckingham DN10 . . . . . . .14 B1
  Beeston, Chilwell NG9 . . . .183 C3
  Beeston, Toton NG9. . . . . .183 A2
  Bilsthorpe NG22 . . . . .105 E6
  Bircotes DN11 . . . . .9 C4
  Blidworth NG21. . . . . .118 B5
  East Leake LE12 . . . . .205 F2
  Eastwood NG16. . . . . .144 A2
  Lea DN21. . . . . .24 F2
  Mansfield NG18. . . . . .102 C3
  Newark-on-T NG24 . . . . . .140 A6
  Nottingham NG3 . . . . .173 D8
  Old Dalby LE14 . . . . .219 B6
  Radcliffe on T NG12. . . . . .176 A3
  Retford DN22. . . . . .39 D6
  Shirebrook NG20 . . . . .72 E6
  Stapleford NG9 . . . . .170 E2
  Sutton in A NG17 . . . . . . .100 D7
Cresswell Rd
  Beeston NG9 . . . . .183 B5
  Worksop S80 . . . . .35 E4
Cresswell St S80. . . . . .35 E3
Cressy Rd NG7 . . . . .184 F2
Cresta Gdns NG3 . . . . . . .161 D2
Creswell Crags Mus & Ed Ctr
  S80 . . . . .45 B1
Creswell Ct NG19 . . . . .88 E4
Creswell Rd NG20. . . . . . . .60 A3
Crewe Cl
  Blidworth NG21. . . . . .118 A6
  Nottingham NG7 . . . . .222 B4
Crewe Rd DN11 . . . . .9 B4
Crew La NG25 . . . . .137 A8
Crew La Ind Est NG25 . . . .137 A8
Crew Rd NG23 . . . . .98 B1
Cribb Cl NG11 . . . . .185 B7
Crich View
  Newton DE55. . . . . .99 A4
  Nottingham NG5 . . . . .161 C2
Cricket Cl NG17 . . . . .129 F8
Cricketers Ct NG2. . . . . . .173 F1
Cricket Field La DN22 . . . . .39 E8
Criftin Rd NG14 . . . . .164 A4
Crink La NG25 . . . . .136 F6
Cripps Hill NG7 . . . . .172 C2
Critchley St DE7 . . . . .157 F1
Critch's Flats NG16. . . . . .158 F6
Crocus St
  Kirkby in A NG17 . . . . . . .115 B4
  Nottingham NG2 . . . . .173 D2
Croft Ave
  Hucknall NG15 . . . . .146 A6
  Mansfield NG18. . . . . .102 C2
Croft Cl
  Pinxton NG16. . . . . .113 C3
  Rolleston NG23 . . . . .138 A6
Croft Cres NG16 . . . . .158 C5
Croft Ct NG17. . . . . .99 F4
Croft Dr DN11 . . . . .8 A8
Croft Farm Cl
  Everton DN10 . . . . .11 C3
  Rolleston NG23 . . . . .138 B6
Croft Gdns LE14 . . . . .218 E4
Crofton Cl
  Beeston NG9 . . . . .183 D3
  3 Nottingham NG8. . . . .172 B6

Crofton Rd NG9 . . . . .183 D2
Croft Prim Sch NG17 . . . . .100 F2
Croft Rd
  Arnold NG5 . . . . .161 F8
  Finningley DN10 . . . . .1 A1
  Keyworth NG12 . . . . .197 D3
  West Bridgford NG12 . . . . .186 A4
Croft Rise NG13. . . . . .165 C3
Crofts The NG13 . . . . .177 E4
Croft The
  Bockingham DN10 . . . . . . .23 C8
  Kegworth DE74 . . . . .203 D2
  Newark-on-T NG24 . . . . . .140 A8
  Retford DN22. . . . . .39 F8
  South Normanton DE55. . . .113 A6
  Stanton Hill NG17 . . . . . . .100 C5
Croft Way DN10 . . . . .11 C3
Croft Wlk S80 . . . . .45 A6
Cromarty Cl NG19. . . . . . .101 D5
Cromarty Ct **2** NG2. . . . .173 B2
Cromdale Cl NG5 . . . . . . .148 C1
Cromer Cl NG18 . . . . .102 C4
Cromer Rd NG3 . . . . .173 E7
Cromford Ave
  Carlton NG4. . . . . .174 D8
  Mansfield NG18. . . . . .102 A4
Cromford Cl
  Aldercar NG16 . . . . .143 B4
  Long Eaton NG10. . . . . . .193 A5
Cromford Rd
  Annesley Woodhouse
    NG17. . . . . .115 A1
  Langley Mill NG16 . . . . . . .143 B4
  West Bridgford NG2 . . . . . .185 F6
Cromford St DN21 . . . . . . .15 C1
Crompton Rd
  Bilsthorpe NG22 . . . . .105 F6
  Ilkeston DE7 . . . . .170 B3
  Radmanthwaite NG19 . . . . .87 D3
Crompton St
  New Houghton NG19. . . . . .86 F8
  Teversal NG17. . . . . .100 B7
Crompton View Prim Sch
  NG22. . . . . .105 F6
Cromwell Ave DE7 . . . . . . .170 A5
Cromwell Cres NG4. . . . . .163 B7
Cromwell Dr LE12 . . . . . . .205 E1
Cromwell Rd
  Aslockton NG13. . . . . .178 E3
  Beeston NG9 . . . . .183 B6
  Newark-on-T NG24 . . . . . .140 B7
Cromwell St
  Carlton NG4. . . . . .174 E7
  Eastwood NG16. . . . . .158 C8
  Gainsborough DN21 . . . . . .24 D6
  Mansfield NG18. . . . . .102 C6
  Nottingham NG7 . . . . .222 C3
Cromwell Way DN21 . . . . . .24 F3
Crookdole La NG14 . . . . . .148 F7
Crooked Billet St DN21 . . . .15 B4
Crookes Ave NG19 . . . . . . .87 A5
Crook's Ave NG19 . . . . .88 C3
Croome Cl LE11. . . . . .220 C1
Cropston Cl NG2 . . . . .185 E4
Cropton Cres NG8 . . . . . . .172 B6
Cropton Gr NG13 . . . . . . .177 C4
Cropwell Bishop Prim Sch
  NG12. . . . . .189 B6
Cropwell Bishop Rd
  NG12. . . . . .189 B6
Cropwell Butler Rd
  NG12. . . . . .189 B4
Cropwell Ct NG18 . . . . . . .102 D7
Cropwell Gdns NG12 . . . . .176 A2
Cropwell Gn NG3 . . . . . . .173 F6
Cropwell Rd
  Langar NG13 . . . . .190 C1
  Radcliffe on T NG12. . . . . .176 A2
Crosby Cl NG19 . . . . .89 A1
Crosby Rd NG2 . . . . .185 F8
Cross Comm La DN22 . . . . .33 A5
Crossdale Dr NG12 . . . . . .197 E4
Crossdale Drive Prim Sch
  NG12. . . . . .197 E4
Crossdale Wlk NG5 . . . . . .160 E8
Cross Dr
  Kirkby in A NG17 . . . . . . .115 B7
  Rainworth NG21 . . . . .104 B1
Crossfield Dr
  13 Nottingham NG5. . . . .147 A1
  Nottingham NG5 . . . . .161 A8
Crossgate Dr NG2. . . . . . .173 A1
Crosshill NG12 . . . . .188 A3
Cross Hill DN10 . . . . .12 F2
Cross Hill Cl LE12 . . . . . . .216 C3
Cross La
  Austerfield DN10. . . . . .3 C5
  Balderton NG24. . . . . .140 D1
  Blidworth NG21. . . . . .117 D6
  Collingham NG23 . . . . .112 C8
  East Bridgford NG13 . . . . . .165 D3
  Elkesley DN22 . . . . .49 F4
  Elston NG23 . . . . .154 A3
  Farndon NG24 . . . . .138 F4
  Gringley on t H DN10 . . . . .5 A1
  Harby NG23. . . . . .70 D2
  Huthwaite NG17 . . . . .100 A2
  Stanton Hill NG17 . . . . . . .100 C5
  Staunton in the Vale NG13 .169 F2
Crossland Rd NG5 . . . . . . .161 A5
Crosslands Mdw NG4 . . . .174 F4
Crossley Ave NG17 . . . . . .100 A3
Crossley Hill La S81 . . . . . .26 C4
Crossley St NG5 . . . . .161 B2
Crossman St NG5 . . . . . . .161 C2
Cross St
  Arnold NG5 . . . . .161 E8
  Barnby in t W NG24. . . . . .141 F5

Cross St *continued*
  Beeston NG9 . . . . .183 F7
  Bilsthorpe NG22 . . . . .105 F6
  Carlton, Netherfield NG4. . .175 A7
  Carlton, Thorneywood
    NG4. . . . . .174 D8
  Eastwood NG16. . . . . .144 A4
  Gainsborough DN21 . . . . . .24 D8
  Hathern LE12. . . . . .213 A1
  Langold S81. . . . . .16 E3
  Long Eaton NG10. . . . . . .193 F8
  Loughborough LE11. . . . . .220 C5
  Mansfield Woodhouse NG19 88 B2
  Morton DN21. . . . . .15 B4
  Newark-on-T NG24 . . . . . .140 B8
  Retford DN22. . . . . .40 A6
  Sandiacre NG10. . . . . .182 C6
  Sturton le S DN22 . . . . . . .32 D5
Cross The
  Carlton in L S81. . . . . .16 E3
  Cotgrave NG12 . . . . .187 E3
Crossways
  East Markham NG22 . . . . . .66 A7
  Retford DN22. . . . . .39 F8
Crossways Dr NG13 . . . . . .165 D3
Crowborough Ave NG8. . . .171 E2
Crowcroft Way NG10. . . . . .182 B2
Crow Cl NG13. . . . . .178 A4
Crow Hill NG19 . . . . .87 B5
Crow Hill Ct NG18. . . . . . .102 B8
Crow Hill Dr NG18 . . . . . .102 B8
Crow Hill La NG19 . . . . . . .88 B2
Crow Hill Rd NG4 . . . . . . .174 F7
Crow Hl Ri NG18 . . . . . . .102 B8
Crow La NG23, NG24 . . . .124 D7
Crowley Cl NG8. . . . . .171 C6
Crown Ave NG19 . . . . .103 A8
Crown Cl
  Collingham NG23 . . . . .98 A1
  Long Eaton NG10. . . . . . .193 A7
  Rainworth NG21 . . . . .118 C8
Crown Ct DN22 . . . . .32 D5
Crown Farm Way NG19. . . .103 B8
Crown St
  Mansfield NG18. . . . . .102 F6
  Newark-on-T NG24 . . . . . .139 F7
  Worksop S80 . . . . .35 E4
Crown Wy NG16 . . . . .143 B4
Crow Pk Ave NG23 . . . . . . .81 C1
Crow Pk Dr NG4 . . . . .163 E3
Crowthorne Cl NG5 . . . . . .146 E1
Crowthorne Gdns NG5 . . . .146 E1
Crowtrees Dr NG17 . . . . . .100 D1
Croxall Cl NG11. . . . . .184 E4
Croxley Gdns NG16. . . . . .159 D3
Croxton Ct NG19 . . . . .88 E3
Croydon Rd NG7 . . . . .222 A3
Crummock Cl NG9 . . . . . . .183 C8
Cuckney CE Prim Sch
  NG20. . . . . .60 A2
Cuckoo Holt S81. . . . . .35 C7
Cuckstool The NG23 . . . . . .96 F8
Cudworth Dr NG3 . . . . . . .161 F2
Cuillin Cl NG10 . . . . .182 A1
Cul-de-sac NG22 . . . . .105 F6
Cullen Cl NG24 . . . . .124 E1
Cullen's Ct NG5 . . . . .161 C2
Cullin Cl NG5 . . . . .146 F2
Cumberland Ave
  Beeston NG9 . . . . .183 D6
  Market Warsop NG20 . . . . .74 A5
Cumberland Cl
  Bircotes DN11 . . . . .9 D4
  Carlton in L S81. . . . . .25 F7
  Westwood NG16 . . . . .128 C4
Cumberland Dr NG19 . . . . .101 D7
Cumberland Pl NG1 . . . . . .223 D2
Cumbria Rd S81 . . . . .36 A5
Cundy Hill NG25 . . . . .136 B6
Cunningham Cl DN10 . . . . .19 F8
Cupar Cl NG20 . . . . .74 C6
Curie Ct NG7 . . . . .172 D2
Curlew Cl NG3 . . . . .174 C5
Curlew Wharf **5** NG7 . . .172 F2
Currie Rd NG24 . . . . .125 A2
Cursley Way NG9 . . . . . . .183 C2
Curtis Cl NG23 . . . . .98 A1
Curtis St NG15 . . . . .146 A4
Curzon Ave NG4 . . . . .174 B7
Curzon Cl NG21. . . . . .118 A8
Curzon Ct NG3. . . . . .223 F4
Curzon Dr S81 . . . . .35 F7
Curzon Gdns NG3 . . . . . . .223 F4
Curzon Pl NG3. . . . . .223 F3
Curzon St
  Carlton NG4. . . . . .175 A7
  Gainsborough DN21 . . . . . .15 C2
  Gotham NG11 . . . . .195 B1
  Long Eaton NG10. . . . . . .182 B2
  Loughborough LE11. . . . . .220 A3
  Nottingham NG3 . . . . .223 F3
Darley Ave
  Beeston NG9 . . . . .182 F3
  Carlton NG4. . . . . .162 E1
  Kirkby in A NG17 . . . . . . .115 C5
  Nottingham NG7 . . . . .172 E7
Cusworth Way S80 . . . . . . .35 D3
Cuttings Ave NG17 . . . . . .114 B8
Cuxton Cl NG8 . . . . .159 D1
Cycle Rd NG7 . . . . .222 A2
Cypress Ct NG15 . . . . .145 C5
Cyprus Ave NG9 . . . . .183 F7
Cyprus Dr NG9 . . . . .183 F7
Cyprus Rd NG3 . . . . .161 C1
Cyril Ave
  Beeston NG9 . . . . .183 E7
  Nottingham NG8 . . . . .172 D8
  Stapleford NG9 . . . . .182 D7
Cyril Rd NG2. . . . . .186 A7

D

Dabek Rise NG17 . . . . . . .115 A1
Dabell Ave NG6 . . . . .159 F8
Dadley Rd S81 . . . . .25 F7
Dadsley Rd DN11 . . . . .8 A8
Dagfa House Sch NG9. . . . .184 A7
Dagmar Gr
  Beeston NG9 . . . . .184 A6
  Nottingham NG3 . . . . .161 D1
Dahlia Ave DE55 . . . . .113 B7
Dairy La LE14 . . . . .211 F7
Daisy Cl NG12 . . . . .187 E2
Daisy Farm Rd NG16 . . . . .158 B8
Daisy Rd NG3 . . . . .162 A1
Dakeyne St NG3 . . . . .173 E5
Dalbeattie Cl NG5. . . . . . .162 B8
Dalby Sq NG8. . . . . .172 C3
Dale Ave
  Carlton NG4. . . . . .174 C7
  Long Eaton NG10. . . . . . .182 D1
  Newton DE55. . . . . .99 A3
  Nottingham NG3 . . . . .162 A2
Dalebrook Cres NG15 . . . .145 C5
Dale Cl
  Hucknall NG15. . . . . .145 C5
  Langwith NG20 . . . . .72 E8
  Retford DN22. . . . . .39 E3
  Sutton in A NG17 . . . . . . .101 A5
  West Bridgford NG2 . . . . . .186 B7
  Whaley Thorns NG20. . . . . .58 F1
Dale Cres NG24 . . . . .140 E2
Dale Farm Ave NG3 . . . . . .174 A5
Dale Gr NG2 . . . . .173 F4
Dalehead Rd NG11 . . . . . .184 D2
Dale La
  Ault Hucknall S44 . . . . . . .86 D7
  Beeston NG9 . . . . .183 E5
  Blidworth NG21. . . . . .118 B5
Dalemoor Gdns NG8 . . . . .172 B8
Dale Rd
  Carlton NG4. . . . . .174 C7
  Keyworth NG12 . . . . .197 E3
  Kimberley NG16. . . . . .158 F5
  Market Warsop NG20 . . . . .74 C5
Dales Ave NG17 . . . . . . .100 F5
Dales Cl LE12 . . . . .215 E5
Daleside NG12. . . . . .187 E2
Daleside Rd NG2. . . . . . . .174 A3
Daleside Rd E NG2, NG3. . .174 C4
Dales La DN10 . . . . .4 F4
Dale St
  Mansfield NG19 . . . . .88 B1
  Nottingham NG2 . . . . .173 E4
Dalestorth Ave NG19. . . . . .87 D1
Dalestorth Cl NG17. . . . . .101 A5
Dalestorth Gdns NG17. . . .101 A5
Dalestorth Prim Sch
  NG17. . . . . .101 A4
Dalestorth Rd NG17. . . . . .101 A5
Dalestorth St NG17. . . . . .101 A4
Dale View S81 . . . . .36 B7
Dale View Rd NG3 . . . . . . .174 B7
Dalewood Cl DE55 . . . . . . .113 A3
Dale Wy NG24 . . . . .140 F1
Dalkeith Terr **10** NG7 . . .172 F7
Dallas St NG18. . . . . .102 A6
Dallas York Rd NG9 . . . . . .184 B6
Dalley Cl NG9. . . . . .182 F7
Dalton Cl NG9 . . . . .182 E5
Daltons Cl NG16 . . . . .143 A4
Dame Flogan St NG18 . . . .102 B6
Dame La DN10 . . . . .4 B2
Dam Rd DN11 . . . . .8 A5
Damson Wlk NG3 . . . . . . .174 B8
Dane Cl NG3 . . . . .223 F4
Dane Ct NG3 . . . . .223 F4
Danes Cl NG5 . . . . .161 D8
Danes Rd DN21 . . . . .15 F1
Daneshill Gravel Pits Nature
  Reserve NG22. . . . . .19 D1
Daneshill Rd DN22 . . . . . . .20 A1
Daneswood Jun Sch
  NG17. . . . . .100 D7
Danethorpe La NG24 . . . . .126 B8
Danethorpe Vale NG5 . . . .161 C4
Daniel Cres NG18 . . . . . . .101 F7
Daniel Mews NG10 . . . . . .182 A5
Daniels Way NG15 . . . . . . .145 F4
Danners Hill NG15 . . . . . . .131 E5
Danvers Dr NG19 . . . . . . .101 E7
Darfield Ct DN11 . . . . .8 A7
Darfield Dr DE75 . . . . . . .143 A2
Darkey La NG9. . . . . .182 E5
Dark La
  Aslockton NG13. . . . . .179 A4
  Barnby in t W NG24. . . . . .142 A5
  Bingham NG13 . . . . .178 A4
  West Leake LE12 . . . . .204 F2
Darley Ave
  Beeston NG9 . . . . .182 F3
  Carlton NG4. . . . . .162 E1
  Kirkby in A NG17 . . . . . . .115 C5
  Nottingham NG7 . . . . .172 E7
Darleydale Cl NG18 . . . . . .102 D3
Darley Dr NG10 . . . . .193 A5
Darley Rd NG7 . . . . .172 E7
Darley Sq DE7 . . . . .157 E5
Darlton Dr NG5 . . . . .162 B7
Darlton Rd
  East Drayton DN22 . . . . . . .53 A1
  Tuxford NG22. . . . . .66 C4
Darlton St NG19 . . . . .101 D6
Darnal Cl NG5. . . . . .160 E7
Darnhall Cres NG8 . . . . . .171 D7
Daron Gdns **10** NG5 . . . . .161 A7

Darrel Rd DN22 . . . . .39 E5
Darricott Cl NG21 . . . . . . .118 B8
Darvel Cl **5** NG8. . . . . . .172 B6
Darwin Cl
  Elston NG23. . . . . .153 E4
  Mansfield NG18. . . . . .102 C3
  Nottingham NG5 . . . . .160 E8
Darwin Dr DN22 . . . . .42 B1
Darwin Rd NG10 . . . . .193 B5
Darwin St DN21 . . . . .24 D6
Daubeney Ave LN1. . . . . . . .57 B3
Davey Rd NG18 . . . . .102 A7
David Gr NG9. . . . . .171 E1
David La NG6 . . . . .160 D3
Davids La NG14 . . . . .165 A5
Davidson Cl NG5. . . . . . . .162 C7
Davidson Gd NG11 . . . . . .196 A7
Davidson St **5** NG2 . . . . .173 F3
David St NG17 . . . . .115 B7
Davies Ave NG17. . . . . . . .100 E3
Davies Cl NG17 . . . . .100 E3
Davies Rd NG2. . . . . .186 A7
Davis Cl NG21 . . . . .90 B4
Davis Rd NG9. . . . . .183 B3
Davy Cl NG15 . . . . .131 B2
Dawber St S81 . . . . .35 D7
Dawes Way NG7 . . . . .222 A3
Dawgates La NG19 . . . . . . .86 F1
Dawlish Cl NG15 . . . . .145 D6
Dawlish Ct NG16 . . . . .143 D3
Dawlish Dr NG5 . . . . .161 B5
Dawn Cl NG15 . . . . .131 C1
Dawn House Sch NG21. . . .103 E3
Dawn's La NG13 . . . . .179 A5
Dawn View NG9 . . . . .170 D2
Dawson Cl NG16 . . . . .144 A1
Dawver Rd NG16 . . . . .158 F6
Daybell Cl NG13 . . . . .181 B3
Daybill Cl NG25 . . . . .137 D3
Daybrook Ave **4** NG5 . . . .161 C3
Daybrook St NG5 . . . . . . .161 C3
Dayncourt Sch NG12 . . . . .176 A3
D'Ayncourt Wlk NG22 . . . .120 A6
Day St NG20 . . . . .74 B4
Deabill St NG4 . . . . .175 A6
Dead La
  Cossall NG16 . . . . .158 D1
  1 Loughborough LE11. . .220 B4
Deadwong La NG23 . . . . . .153 E1
Deakins Pl NG7 . . . . .222 A3
Deal Gdns NG6 . . . . .159 F7
Dean Ave NG3 . . . . .162 A3
Dean Cl
  Mansfield NG18. . . . . .102 C4
  Nottingham NG8 . . . . .171 D5
Deane Cl NG23 . . . . .98 A1
Dean Hole CE Prim Sch
  NG23. . . . . .109 A5
Dean Rd NG5 . . . . .161 E5
Deans Cl DN10 . . . . .6 E2
Dean's Cl NG23 . . . . .109 B5
Deanscourt NG12 . . . . . . .188 A3
Deans Croft NG9. . . . . . . .171 B1
Deansgate NG19 . . . . .87 A3
Dean St
  Langley Mill NG16 . . . . . . .143 C3
  Nottingham NG1 . . . . .223 F2
Death La DN22 . . . . .21 D6
Debdale Gate NG19 . . . . . .88 A2
Debdale Hill LE14 . . . . . .218 E4
Debdale La
  Keyworth NG12 . . . . .197 E3
  Mansfield NG19 . . . . .88 A2
Debdhill Rd DN10 . . . . .6 E2
Deben Down NG19 . . . . . . .88 D3
Deddington La NG9 . . . . . .171 C2
Deeley Cl NG16 . . . . .159 A7
Deepdale Ave NG9 . . . . . .182 D6
Deepdale Cl NG2. . . . . . . .186 C7
Deepdale Gdns NG17 . . . . .100 E4
Deepdale Pk NG17 . . . . . . .100 F4
Deepdale Rd
  Long Eaton NG10. . . . . . .193 A5
  Mansfield NG19 . . . . .88 E1
  Nottingham NG8 . . . . .171 D4
Deepdale St NG17. . . . . . .100 F4
Deepdene Cl NG8 . . . . . . .160 A2
Deepdene Way NG8 . . . . . .160 A2
Deep Furrow Ave NG4. . . . .174 D8
Deep La S45. . . . . .85 B3
Deeps La DN10 . . . . .4 B7
Deerdale La
  Bilsthorpe NG22 . . . . .105 A8
  Edwinstowe NG21 . . . . . . .91 C7
Deerleap Dr NG5. . . . . . . .161 C7
Deer Pk NG8 . . . . .171 E4
Deer Pk Dr
  Arnold NG5 . . . . .147 C1
  Nottingham NG5 . . . . .161 B8
Deers Acre LE11. . . . . .220 B6
Deetleton Cl NG16 . . . . . . .129 A3
De Ferrers Cl LE12 . . . . . . .205 E1
Delamere Cl LE11 . . . . . . .220 C4
Delamere Dr NG18 . . . . . . .102 C4
Delia Ave NG15 . . . . .131 C1
Dell Lea NG18 . . . . .103 A3
Dell The NG17 . . . . .129 F8
Dell Way NG7. . . . . .184 F2
Dellwood Cl NG4. . . . . . . .162 C2
Delta St NG7. . . . . .160 F1
Deltic Cl NG16 . . . . .159 A7
Delville Ave NG16. . . . . . . .197 E4
De Morgan Ave NG16. . . . .129 A2
Denacre Ave NG10 . . . . . . .182 F1
Denbigh Cl NG21. . . . . . . .104 C1
Denbigh Ct NG23 . . . . .98 A1
Denbury Rd NG15 . . . . . . .117 A2

Denby Dr NG18 . . . . 102 D2
Dendy Dr DN22 . . . . 53 B8
Dene Cl DN10 . . . . 20 B7
Denehurst Ave NG8 . . . . . 160 C1
Dene The S80 . . . . 35 C2
Denewood Ave NG9 . . . . . 171 C2
Denewood Cres NG8 . . . . 171 E8
Denholme Rd NG8 . . . . . . 171 D5
Denison Ave DN22 . . . . 40 A4
Denison St
  Beeston NG9 . . . . 183 E7
  Nottingham NG7 . . . . 222 B4
Denman Cl DN22 . . . . 39 D8
Denman St Central NG7 . 222 B3
Denman St E NG7 . . . . 222 B3
Denman St W NG7 . . . . . . 222 A3
Denmark Gr 1 NG3 . . . . . 173 D8
Dennett Cl NG3 . . . . 173 E6
Dennis Ave NG9 . . . . 183 E8
Dennis St
  Carlton NG4 . . . . 175 A7
  Worksop S80 . . . . 35 F2
Dennor Dr NG19 . . . . 88 E5
Denstone Rd NG3 . . . . 173 E5
Dentdale Dr NG8 . . . . 171 B4
Denton Ave NG10 . . . . 182 A6
Denton Cl
  Balderton NG24 . . . . 140 C3
  Mansfield NG19 . . . . 88 C1
Denton Dr NG2 . . . . 185 D4
Denton Gn NG8 . . . . 159 F2
Denver Ct NG9 . . . . 170 E1
Deptford Cres NG6 . . . . . 160 C5
Derby Gr 1 NG7. . . . . 222 B3
Derby Rd
  Annesley Woodhouse NG15,
    NG17. . . . . 130 B7
  Beeston NG9 . . . . 171 D1
  Eastwood NG16 . . . . 143 E2
  Hathern LE12 . . . . 212 F2
  Kegworth DE74 . . . . 203 C2
  Kirkby in A NG17 . . . . 115 D4
  Langley Mill NG16 . . . . . . 143 C3
  Long Eaton NG10 . . . . . . 193 B8
  Loughborough LE11 . . . . . 220 A5
  Mansfield NG17, NG18 . . . 116 B8
  Nottingham NG7 . . . . 222 B2
  Sandiacre NG10 . . . . 182 A5
Derbyshire Ave NG9 . . . . 170 D4
Derbyshire Cres NG8 . . . 172 A5
Derbyshire Dr NG16 . . . . 128 C4
Derbyshire La NG15 . . . . . 146 A7
Derby Sq LE11 . . . . 220 A4
Derby St
  Arnold NG5 . . . . 161 F7
  Beeston NG9 . . . . 183 F7
  Mansfield NG18 . . . . 102 C6
  Nottingham NG1 . . . . 223 D3
Dereham Dr NG5 . . . . 162 A6
Derry Dr NG5 . . . . 147 F2
Derry Hill Rd NG5 . . . . . . 147 E1
Derry La NG13 . . . . 178 B3
Derrymount Sch NG5 . . . 147 F1
Derwent Ave
  Ilkeston DE7 . . . . 157 D2
  Mansfield NG18 . . . . 103 A5
Derwent Cl
  Beeston NG9 . . . . 183 E3
  Mansfield NG18 . . . . 103 A5
  Market Warsop NG20 . . . . . 74 C5
  Rainworth NG21 . . . . 118 B8
  West Bridgford NG2 . . . . . 186 C7
  Worksop S81 . . . . 35 F6
Derwent Cres NG5 . . . . . 162 A6
Derwent Ct
  Balderton NG24 . . . . 140 D3
  Nottingham NG7 . . . . 222 C4
Derwent Dr
  Annesley Woodhouse
    NG17. . . . . 130 A8
  Hucknall NG15 . . . . 146 A4
  Selston NG16 . . . . 129 A7
Derwent St Ind Est
  NG10. . . . . 193 D6
Derwent St NG10 . . . . 193 C6
Derwent Terr 5 NG5. . . . 161 C2
Derwent Way
  Newark-on-T NG24 . . . . . 125 B2
  Nottingham NG7 . . . . 172 A4
  Nottingham NG7 . . . . 222 A2
Desborough Rd NG16 . . . 128 D7
Desford Cl NG5 . . . . 161 A4
De Vere Gdns NG5 . . . . . 162 A4
Devitt Dr NG15. . . . . 131 C1
Devon Cir NG5 . . . . 147 D1
Devon Cl
  Eastwood NG16 . . . . 144 B2
  Sandiacre NG10 . . . . 182 B5
Devon Dr
  Mansfield NG19 . . . . 101 F8
  Nottingham NG5 . . . . 161 C2
  Ruddington NG11 . . . . 196 D8
Devon La NG13 . . . . 181 B2
Devon Pk Pastures Nature
  Reserve NG24 . . . . 139 D6
Devon Rd NG4 . . . . 139 F6
Devonshire Ave
  Beeston NG9 . . . . 183 F6
  Long Eaton NG10 . . . . . . 194 A8
Devonshire Cl
  Ilkeston DE7 . . . . 157 E5
  1 Sutton in Ashfield
    NG17. . . . . 100 A2
Devonshire Cres NG5 . . . 161 B2
Devonshire Dr
  Eastwood NG16 . . . . 143 F2
  Langwith NG20 . . . . 72 F8
  Ollerton NG22 . . . . 77 A3

Devonshire Dr continued
  Stapleford NG9 . . . . 170 D2
Devonshire Dr LE11 . . . . 220 B3
Devonshire Prom NG7 . . 222 A1
Devonshire Rd
  Harworth DN11 . . . . 8 F4
  Nottingham NG5 . . . . 161 B2
  Retford DN22 . . . . 39 D6
  West Bridgford NG2 . . . . . 185 F6
Devonshire Sq 2 LE11 . . 220 B3
Devonshire St
  New Houghton NG19 . . . . . 87 A7
  Worksop S80 . . . . 35 E2
Devon St
  Ilkeston DE7 . . . . 170 A5
  Nottingham NG3 . . . . 173 F5
Dewberry La NG12 . . . . . 176 B2
DH Lawrence Birthplace Mus
  NG16. . . . . 143 F3
Dial The NG12 . . . . 187 E1
Diamond Ave
  Kirkby in A NG17 . . . . 115 C4
  Rainworth NG21 . . . . 104 C1
Dickens Cl NG16 . . . . 144 B3
Dickenson Terr DN21 . . . . 24 D7
Dickinson Way NG23 . . . 110 F3
Dickens Rd S81 . . . . 36 B3
Dickman's La LE14 . . . . . 202 B3
Dicks La NG16 . . . . 144 C3
Dickson Dr NG11 . . . . 196 D6
Didcot Dr NG8 . . . . 160 D1
Digby Ave NG3 . . . . 162 C3
Digby Ct NG7 . . . . 222 B1
Digby Hall Dr NG4 . . . . . 162 C3
Digby St
  Cossall DE7 . . . . 158 A1
  Kimberley NG16 . . . . 158 F7
Dingley Cl NG19 . . . . 88 E5
Dirca Ct NG11 . . . . 195 C8
Diseworth Gr 3 NG2 . . . 173 D1
Distillery St NG11 . . . . . . 196 C6
Division Rd NG20 . . . . 72 E4
Dixie St NG16 . . . . 128 B4
Djanogly City Acad NG7 161 A1
Dobbin Cl NG12 . . . . 189 B4
Dockholm Rd NG10 . . . . . 182 C2
Dock Rd S80 . . . . 35 E3
Doddington Hall LN6 . . . . 71 B1
Doddington La
  Claypole NG23 . . . . 156 B2
  Dry Doddington NG23 . . . 156 E5
Dodford Ct DE7 . . . . 143 A1
Dodsley Way NG21 . . . . . . 90 A4
Dog & Duck La DN21 . . . . 15 B4
Doghill La NG23 . . . . 153 B2
Dog La DN10 . . . . 10 A2
Dogwood Ave NG6 . . . . . 160 A7
Doles La
  Kirkby in A NG17 . . . . 114 C6
  Whitwell S80 . . . . 45 B7
Dolphin Ct 7 NG5 . . . . . 161 A8
Dominie Cross Rd DN22 . 39 F6
Donbas Ct NG6 . . . . 160 B4
Doncaster Ave NG10 . . . 182 B6
Doncaster Gr NG10 . . . . 182 F1
Doncaster Rd
  Bawtry DN10 . . . . 10 A8
  Carlton in L S81 . . . . 25 F7
  Langold S81 . . . . 16 F3
  Tickhill DN11 . . . . 8 A8
  Westwoodside DN9 . . . . 2 E3
Doncaster Terr 11 NG2 . 173 C1
Donington Rd NG7 . . . . . 184 E1
Donkey La NG11 . . . . 196 E3
Donner Cres DE7 . . . . . . 157 E5
Dooland Dr NG3 . . . . 161 F1
Dorchester Cl NG18 . . . . 102 D2
Dorchester Dr NG18. . . . 102 D2
Dorchester Gdns NG2 . . 185 E3
Dorchester Rd
  Annesley Woodhouse
    NG17. . . . . 115 B1
  Harworth DN11 . . . . 9 B5
  Kimberley NG16 . . . . 158 F7
Doreen Dr NG17 . . . . 100 D2
Dorewood Ct NG24 . . . . . 140 E4
Doris Rd DE7 . . . . 170 A7
Dorket Cl NG5 . . . . 148 A1
Dorket Dr NG8 . . . . 172 D3
Dorking Rd NG7 . . . . 222 B4
Dormy Cl
  Beeston NG9 . . . . 183 C7
  Mansfield Woodhouse NG19 88 E5
  Radcliffe on T NG12 . . . . . 176 B3
Dormy Ct NG6 . . . . 160 D7
Dorner Ave NG24 . . . . . . 139 D7
Dornoch Ave
  Nottingham NG5 . . . . 161 D2
  Southwell NG25 . . . . 121 F1
Dorothy Ave
  Eastwood NG16 . . . . 144 A3
  Hucknall NG15. . . . . 131 B1
  Mansfield Woodhouse NG19 88 C1
  Sandiacre NG10 . . . . 182 B5
Dorothy Dr NG19. . . . . 88 F1
Dorothy Gr 1 NG8 . . . . . 172 D6
Dorset Dr DN11 . . . . 8 F4
Dorset Gdns NG2 . . . . . . 185 C5
Dorset St NG8 . . . . 172 D5
Dorset Way NG18 . . . . . . 103 A4
Dorterry Cres DE7 . . . . . 170 A5
Dorton Ave DN21 . . . . 24 F8
Douglas Ave
  Awsworth NG16 . . . . 158 C5
  Carlton NG4 . . . . 174 E6
Douglas Cl NG12 . . . . . . 175 D4
Douglas Cres NG4 . . . . . 174 E6
Douglas Ct NG9 . . . . 183 A2

Douglas Prim Sch NG7 . . 222 B3
Douglas Rd
  Bingham NG13 . . . . 178 A4
  Long Eaton NG10 . . . . . . 182 B1
  Mansfield Woodhouse NG19 89 B2
  Nottingham NG7 . . . . 222 B3
  Sutton in A NG17 . . . . 100 D2
Douro Dr NG5 . . . . 148 B1
Dove Cl
  Bingham NG13 . . . . 177 F3
  Ollerton NG22 . . . . 77 B4
  Worksop S81 . . . . 35 E7
Dovecoat St LE12 . . . . . . 213 A1
Dovecote Cl NG13 . . . . . 165 C3
Dovecote Dr NG8 . . . . . . 171 E4
Dovecote La NG9 . . . . . . 184 A5
Dovecote Prim Sch
  NG11. . . . . 184 F3
Dovecote Rd NG16 . . . . . 144 B2
Dove Croft NG22 . . . . 77 B4
Dovedale Ave
  Long Eaton NG10 . . . . . . 193 A6
  Sutton in A NG17 . . . . 100 D1
Dovedale Cir DE7 . . . . . . 157 E5
Dovedale Cl
  Edwinstowe NG21 . . . . 76 A2
  Mansfield NG18 . . . . 102 D3
Dovedale Ct NG10 . . . . . 193 B6
Dovedale Prim Sch
  NG10. . . . . 193 A6
Dovedale Rd
  Nottingham NG3 . . . . 174 C6
  West Bridgford NG2 . . . . . 186 A5
Dove Dr NG16 . . . . 129 A7
Dove La NG10 . . . . 193 C8
Dovenby Rd NG7 . . . . 184 F2
Dover Beck Cl
  Calverton NG14 . . . . 149 A7
  Ravenshead NG15 . . . . . . 116 F2
Dover Beck Dr NG14 . . . 149 D4
Dover Bottom DN22 . . . . . 50 D3
Doveridge Ave NG4 . . . . 175 A8
Doveridge Ct NG15. . . . . 117 A3
Doveridge Rd NG4 . . . . . 175 A8
Dover St NG25 . . . . 121 E1
Dove St NG6 . . . . 160 B7
Dovey's Orch NG14 . . . . 148 D7
Downes Cl NG6 . . . . 160 A7
Downham Cl NG5 . . . . . . 162 A6
Downham Gdns NG15 . . 117 B2
Downing Cl NG6 . . . . 160 B8
Downing Gdns 7 NG6 . . 160 B8
Downing St
  Nottingham NG6 . . . . 160 B8
  South Normanton DE55 . . 113 A6
  Sutton in A NG17 . . . . 100 F3
Downs The NG11 . . . . 185 A3
Dowson Cl NG12 . . . . 176 B4
Dowson St NG3 . . . . 173 F6
Doyne Ct 2 NG2 . . . . 173 C1
Dragon St NG13 . . . . 191 B5
Dragwell DE74 . . . . 203 D2
Drakemyre Cl NG5 . . . . . 148 B1
Drake Rd NG4 . . . . 175 B6
Drake St DN21 . . . . 24 D6
Draycott Ct DE7 . . . . 157 F3
Draycott Rd NG10 . . . . . 193 A4
Draymans Ct NG7 . . . . . 160 F1
Drayton Ave NG19 . . . . . . 87 D1
Drayton St 3 NG5 . . . . . 161 C2
Drift NG13 . . . . 192 F4
Drift The
  Hucknall NG15. . . . . 131 B1
  Nottingham NG11 . . . . . . 184 E3
Drinking Pit La S80 . . . . . 46 B3
Drinsey Nook La NG23 . . . 70 C7
Drive The
  Beeston NG9 . . . . 183 E3
  Clipstone NG21 . . . . 90 A3
  Gainsborough DN21 . . . . . 24 F7
  Winthorpe NG24 . . . . 125 C6
Drive The Pk La DN22 . . . 30 A1
Drmonde Terr 7 NG3 . . . 161 C2
Dronfield Pl DE7 . . . . 157 D5
Dronley Dr NG20 . . . . 74 C7
Drove La NG24 . . . . 126 A4
Drovers Ct DN22 . . . . 39 C8
Droversdale Rd DN11 . . . . 9 C4
Drummond Ave NG4 . . . . 175 B7
Drummond Dr NG16 . . . . 159 E4
Drummond Rd DE7 . . . . . 157 E1
Drury La NG1 . . . . 8 A7
Dryden Ave NG24 . . . . . . 140 E4
Dryden Ct NG9 . . . . 170 E1
Dryden Dale S81 . . . . 36 B3
Dryden St NG1 . . . . 223 D4
Dry Pot La LE12 . . . . 212 A2
Drysdale Cl NG6 . . . . 160 B5
Duchess Gdns 8 NG6 . . 160 B8
Duchess St
  Nottingham NG6 . . . . 160 B8
  Whitwell S80 . . . . 45 A6
Ducie La DN22 . . . . 23 E3
Dudley Ct NG9 . . . . 183 A8
Dudley Doy Rd NG25 . . . 121 C1
Duesbury The DE55 . . . . 113 B4
Duffield Cl NG10 . . . . 193 A5
Duffield Ct NG5 . . . . 160 F8
Duke Cl NG6 . . . . 160 A5
Duke Cres NG16 . . . . 144 C1
Duke Pl S80 . . . . 35 E3
Dukeries Cl S81 . . . . 35 C6
Dukeries Com Coll NG22 . 77 D5
Dukeries Complex The
  NG22. . . . . 77 D5
Dukeries Cres
  Edwinstowe NG21 . . . . 76 B1
  Worksop S80 . . . . 36 C1

Dukeries Ind Est The S81 . 35 C6
Dukeries L Ctr NG22 . . . . 77 D6
Dukeries Way S81 . . . . . . 35 C6
Dukes Cl NG17 . . . . 101 C2
Duke's Dr S44 . . . . 86 A7
Duke's Pl DE7 . . . . 157 E4
Duke's Pl NG1 . . . . 223 F2
Dukes Rd LE14 . . . . 219 B6
Duke St
  Arnold NG5 . . . . 161 E7
  Hucknall NG15 . . . . 146 B7
  Huthwaite NG17 . . . . 100 A3
  Ilkeston DE7 . . . . 157 F3
  Loughborough LE11 . . . . . 220 B5
  5 Nottingham NG7 . . . . . 160 B7
  Retford DN22 . . . . 39 E6
  South Normanton DE55 . . 113 B6
  Sutton in A NG17 . . . . 100 C2
  Whitwell S80 . . . . 45 A6
Duke's Terr NG1 . . . . 10 A7
Duke's Wood Nature Reserve
  NG22. . . . . 107 A3
Duke William Mount
  NG7 . . . . 222 C2
Dulverton Vale NG8 . . . . 160 B3
Dulwich Rd NG7 . . . . 222 A3
Dumb Hall La S80 . . . . 34 B4
Dumbles The
  Lambley NG4 . . . . 163 B8
  Sutton in A NG17 . . . . 100 C1
Dunbar Cl DN21 . . . . 15 E2
Dunbar Dr NG19 . . . . 101 D5
Dunblane Rd NG11 . . . . . 196 C6
Duncan Ave NG15 . . . . . . 117 A1
Duncombe Cl NG3 . . . . . 173 E7
Duncroft Ave NG4. . . . . . 162 F1
Dundas Cl NG1 . . . . 223 E3
Dundee Dr NG19 . . . . 88 B6
Dunelm Dr NG14 . . . . 149 A7
Dunelm Dr NG17 . . . . 100 C3
Dungannon Rd NG11 . . . 195 C6
Dunham Cl
  Newton on T LN1 . . . . 55 A1
  Southwell NG25 . . . . 136 D8
Dunham on Trent CE Prim
  Sch NG22 . . . . 54 A1
Dunham Rd
  Laneham DN22 . . . . 54 A5
  Newton on T DN22, LN1 . . 54 E1
Dunholme Ave NG24 . . . 139 F7
Dunholme Cl
  Gainsborough DN21 . . . . . 24 E8
  Nottingham NG6 . . . . 160 B8
Dunholme Rd DN21 . . . . . 24 E7
Dunkery Rd NG11 . . . . . . 195 F8
Dunkirk Ind Est NG7 . . . 184 D7
Dunkirk Prim Sch NG7 . . 172 E1
Dunkirk Rd 4 NG7. . . . . 172 E1
Dunlin Wharf 2 NG2. . . . 173 A2
Dunlop Ave NG7 . . . . 222 A2
Dunn Brigg NG19 . . . . 88 D2
Dunnett Rd NG19 . . . . . . 101 E5
Dunoon Cl NG5 . . . . 146 E1
Dunoon Rd NG19. . . . . . . 101 E5
Dunsby Cl NG7. . . . . 184 E1
Dunsford Dr NG3 . . . . . . 162 C6
Dunsil Dr NG11 . . . . 185 A8
Dunsil Rd
  Eastwood NG16 . . . . 144 B4
  Pinxton NG16. . . . . 113 D2
Dunsmore Cl NG9 . . . . . . 184 B4
Dunstall Wlk DN21 . . . . . 24 F7
Dunstan Cres S80 . . . . 35 F1
Dunstan St NG4 . . . . 175 A4
Dunster Rd
  Eastwood NG16 . . . . 144 B1
  Gainsborough DN21 . . . . . 15 E2
  West Bridgford NG2 . . . . . 186 A6
Dunston Cl NG10 . . . . . . 193 F7
Dunvegan Dr NG5. . . . . . 146 F2
Dunwoody Cl NG18 . . . . . 102 F7
Durban House Heritage Ctr
  NG16. . . . . 143 F3
Durham Ave NG2 . . . . . . 173 F4
Durham Cl
  Mansfield Woodhouse
    NG19. . . . . 88 C4
  1 Nottingham NG2. . . . . 173 F4
  Worksop S81 . . . . 36 A7
Durham Cres NG6. . . . . . 160 C6
Durham Gr DN22. . . . . 30 A1
Durham St 3 DE7 . . . . . . 157 F1
Durlston Cl NG2 . . . . 185 B5
Durnford St NG7 . . . . 160 F2
Dursley Cl NG6 . . . . 160 B5
Dyce Cl NG6 . . . . 159 F7
Dykes End NG23 . . . . 112 A8
Dylan Thomas Rd NG5 . . 161 C8
Dyscarr Cl S81. . . . . 16 F3
Dyscarr Wood Nature
  Reserve S81 . . . . 16 E3

E

Eagle Cl
  Arnold NG5 . . . . 162 A7
  Beeston NG9 . . . . 183 D8
Eagle Ct NG6 . . . . 160 D7
Eagle Moor LN6 . . . . 84 F4
Eagle Pl DN22 . . . . 39 F7
Eagle Rd
  Eagle LN6 . . . . 84 B4
  North Scarle LN6 . . . . 83 E3
Eakring La LE14 . . . . 102 F7
Eakring Meadow Nature
  Reserve NG22 . . . . 93 E1

Eakring Rd
  Kneesall NG22. . . . . 93 E5
  Mansfield NG18, NG21,
    NG22. . . . . 103 D7
  Wellow NG22 . . . . 92 D8
Ealing Ave NG6 . . . . 160 D4
Eardley Rd NG5. . . . . 160 E6
Earl Cres NG4 . . . . 162 F3
Earl Dr NG16 . . . . 144 C1
Earles Ct DN22. . . . . 29 C1
Earl Howe Cres NG13 . . 190 C2
Earls Cl NG8. . . . . 171 C5
Earlsfield Dr NG5 . . . . . . 146 E1
Earls Rd LE14 . . . . 219 B6
Earlswood Dr NG12 . . . . 186 B6
Earp Ave NG24. . . . . 140 A7
Easedale Cl NG2 . . . . 186 C7
Easegill Ct NG5 . . . . 160 F8
East Acres NG12 . . . . 187 F3
Eastbourne Professional Ctr
  NG1 . . . . 101 A2
East Bridgford Rd NG13 . 165 B1
East Cir St NG1 . . . . 223 D2
East Cl NG12. . . . . 197 C2
Eastcliffe Ave NG4 . . . . . 162 D3
Eastcote Ave NG9 . . . . . . 171 B2
East Cres NG9 . . . . 184 B5
Eastcroft LN1. . . . . 57 A5
Eastcroft La NG22 . . . . . . 52 A2
Eastdale Rd NG3 . . . . 174 C6
East Dr NG7 . . . . 172 C1
East End LE14 . . . . 211 D4
Eastern Ave DN21 . . . . . . 15 F1
Eastern Dr NG24 . . . . 140 A8
Eastern Terr La NG24 . . . 140 A8
Eastfield
  North Muskham NG23 . . . 110 F2
  North Wheatley DN22 . . . . 31 E8
Eastfield Cl NG21 . . . . 89 C7
Eastfield Ct NG25 . . . . . . 136 C8
Eastfield Dr DE55 . . . . . . 113 A5
Eastfield Side NG17 . . . . 101 A4
Eastgate
  Normanton on T NG23 . . . 81 E7
  Worksop S80 . . . . 35 F3
Eastglade Prim Sch NG5 161 A8
Eastglade Rd NG5. . . . . . 161 A6
East Gr
  Bingham NG13. . . . . 177 F4
  Nottingham NG7 . . . . 173 A8
Eastham Cl NG3 . . . . 173 E6
Eastham Rd NG5. . . . . . . 162 C6
Eastholme Croft NG2. . . 174 D5
Easthorpe DE55 . . . . 136 F8
Easthorpe La NG13. . . . . 192 F4
Easthorpe Rd NG13 . . . . 181 C2
Easthorpe St NG11 . . . . . 196 C5
Easthorpe View NG13 . . 181 C2
Eastlands Jun Sch NG5,
  NG20. . . . . 74 E8
Eastlands La NG20 . . . . . . 74 E8
Eastland Terr NG20 . . . . . 74 E8
East Leake L Ctr LE12 . . 205 F2
Eastleigh Dr NG19 . . . . . . 88 B6
East Markham Prim Sch
  NG22. . . . . 65 F8
East Moor NG12 . . . . 188 A1
Eastmoor Dr NG4 . . . . . . 174 F8
East Rd LE12. . . . . 216 E4
East St
  Bingham NG13 . . . . 177 F4
  Bole DN22 . . . . 23 E3
  Gotham NG11 . . . . 195 B1
  Harworth DN11 . . . . 9 A5
  Heanor DE75 . . . . 157 A8
  Long Eaton NG10 . . . . . . 193 F8
  Nottingham NG1 . . . . 223 F3
  Retford DN22 . . . . 39 F6
  Sutton in A NG17 . . . . 101 A3
East View
  Bawtry DN10 . . . . 10 A8
  East Markham NG22 . . . . . 65 F6
  Shirebrook NG20 . . . . 72 F6
  West Bridgford NG2 . . . . . 185 D6
Eastwell St NG15. . . . . . . 146 A8
East Wlk DN22 . . . . 39 C8
Eastwold NG12 . . . . 188 A2
Eastwood Ave NG20 . . . . 74 B5
Eastwood Cl NG15 . . . . . 145 E4
Eastwood Comp Sch
  NG16. . . . . 143 E3
Eastwood Com Sports Ctr
  NG16. . . . . 143 E3
Eastwood Ct S81 . . . . 35 F8
Eastwood Inf Sch NG16 143 E3
Eastwood Jun Sch NG16 143 E2
Eastwood & Kimberley Coll
  NG16. . . . . 143 E3
Eastwood La DN10 . . . . . . 4 D3
Eastwood Rd
  Kimberley NG16 . . . . 158 C6
  Radcliffe on T NG12. . . . . 176 A3
Eastwood St NG6 . . . . . . 160 C5
Easy Par S80 . . . . 45 A5
Eather Ave NG19 . . . . 88 C4
Eaton Ave NG5. . . . . 162 A7
Eaton Cl
  Beeston NG9 . . . . 184 B6
  Farnsfield NG22. . . . . 119 F6
  Rainworth NG21 . . . . 118 A8
Eaton Ct 5 NG18 . . . . . . 103 A3
Eaton Grange Dr NG10 . 193 A6
Eatons Rd NG9 . . . . 182 D6
Eaton St NG3 . . . . 161 F2
Eaton Terr NG3 . . . . 161 F2

Eaton Wood Nature Reserve
DN22. . . . . .51 D8
Ebenezer St
Ilkeston DE7 . . . . .157 F3
Langley Mill NG16 . . . . . . .143 B3
Ebers Gr NG3 . . . . .173 C8
Ebers Rd NG3 . . . . .173 C8
Ebony Wlk NG3 . . . . .174 B8
Ebury Rd NG5. . . . . .161 B1
Eckington Terr **12** NG2 . .173 C1
Eckington Wlk NG18 . . . . . .103 B6
Eclipse Yd **3** NG18 . . . . .102 B7
Ecton Cl NG5 . . . . .146 F1
Edale Cl
Hucknall NG15. . . . . .145 C6
Long Eaton NG10. . . . . . . .193 B6
Mansfield NG18. . . . . .103 A3
Edale Ct NG17 . . . . .100 E4
Edale Rd
Mansfield NG18. . . . . .103 B6
Nottingham NG2. . . . . . . .174 A5
Edale Rise NG9 . . . . .182 E3
Edale Sq DE7 . . . . .157 E5
Eddery View NG18 . . . . . . .102 F7
Eddison Cl S81 . . . . .36 A7
Eddison Pk Ave S81. . . . . . .35 E8
Eddison Rd S81. . . . . .35 E8
Eddleston Dr NG7. . . . . . . .184 F1
Edelin Rd LE11. . . . . .220 B1
Edenbridge Ct NG8 . . . . . . .171 D2
Eden Cl NG5. . . . . .162 A6
Eden Ct DN22. . . . . .39 E3
Edenhall Gdns NG7 . . . . . . .184 F2
Eden Low NG19 . . . . .88 E3
Edern Cl NG5. . . . . .161 A7
Edern Gdns **9** NG5 . . . . .161 A7
Edgar Ave NG18 . . . . .102 C8
Edgbaston Gdns **1** NG8 .172 D8
Edgcote Way NG5. . . . . . . .161 A6
Edge Cl NG23. . . . . .110 F4
Edge Hill Ct NG10 . . . . . . .193 D4
Edgehill Dr NG24 . . . . .140 E8
Edgehill Gr NG19 . . . . .88 C2
Edge Way NG8. . . . . .159 D1
Edgewood Dr NG15 . . . . . .145 D5
Edgewood L Ctr NG15. . . . .145 D4
Edgewood Prim Sch
NG15. . . . . .145 C4
Edgewood Rd NG16 . . . . . .158 F6
Edgington Cl NG12. . . . . . .188 A1
Edginton St NG3. . . . . .173 F7
Edgware Rd NG6. . . . . .160 D7
Edinbane Cl NG5. . . . . .146 F1
Edinburgh Dr NG13 . . . . . .177 D5
Edinburgh Rd S80 . . . . . . .47 A8
Edinburgh Wlk S80 . . . . . .47 A8
Edingale Ct NG9 . . . . .171 B4
Edingley Ave
Mansfield NG19. . . . . .101 D7
Nottingham NG5 . . . . .161 C4
Edingley Hill NG22 . . . . . . .120 D4
Edingley Sq NG5. . . . . .161 B3
Edison St NG17 . . . . .114 F1
Edison Way NG5 . . . . .162 C7
Edlington Dr NG8 . . . . .171 C3
Edmond Gr NG15 . . . . .146 C7
Edmonds Cl NG5. . . . . .147 A2
Edmonton Ct NG2. . . . . . . .185 D6
Edmonton Rd NG21 . . . . . .89 E2
Edna G Olds Prim Sch
NG7. . . . . .222 B1
Ednaston Rd NG7 . . . . .172 D1
Edwald Rd NG12 . . . . .186 B3
Edwaltam Ave NG2. . . . . . .185 E7
Edwalton Cl NG12. . . . . . . .186 B3
Edwalton Ct
4 Mansfield NG18 . . . . .103 A3
Nottingham NG6 . . . . .160 E6
Edwalton Lodge Cl
NG12. . . . . .186 A3
Edwalton Prim Sch
NG12. . . . . .186 C4
Edward Ave
Newark-on-T NG24 . . . . . .139 E8
Nottingham NG8 . . . . .172 D8
Sutton in A NG17. . . . . . . .100 E4
Westwood NG16 . . . . .128 B4
Edward Cl NG15 . . . . .145 D4
Edward Rd
Eastwood NG16. . . . . .144 A2
Gainsborough DN21 . . . . . .15 D1
Long Eaton NG10. . . . . . . .193 D8
Nuthall NG16. . . . . .159 C5
West Bridgford NG2. . . . . .185 F8
Edwards Ct S80. . . . . .35 D3
Edwards La NG5 . . . . .161 C5
Edward St
Aldercar NG16. . . . . .143 B3
Kirkby in A NG17. . . . . . . .115 B6
Market Warsop NG20 . . . . .74 A5
Stapleford NG9 . . . . .182 D7
Worksop S80 . . . . .35 F4
Edwin St
Arnold NG5 . . . . .161 D6
Sutton in A NG17. . . . . . . .100 E3
Edwinstowe Dr
Nottingham NG5 . . . . .161 C4
Selston NG16. . . . . .129 B7
Eel La NG22 . . . . .79 C2
Eel Pool Rd DN10 . . . . .11 E1
Eelwood Rd NG15. . . . . . . .145 D4
Egerton Cl NG18 . . . . .103 A7
Egerton Dr NG9. . . . . .170 D2
Egerton Rd NG5 . . . . .161 E4
Egerton St NG3 . . . . .173 C7

Egerton Wlk **2** NG3. . . . .173 C7
Egham Cl NG21 . . . . .104 C1
Egling Croft NG4. . . . . .174 F4
Egmanton Rd
Laxton NG22 . . . . .79 C3
Mansfield NG18. . . . . .103 A3
Meden Vale NG20 . . . . . . .74 D7
Tuxford NG22 . . . . .65 E1
Egmont Ct **1** NG2 . . . . .173 C1
Egypt Rd NG7. . . . . .160 F1
Eider Cl NG20. . . . . .72 D3
Eighth Ave
Beeston NG9. . . . . .184 C5
Mansfield NG19. . . . . .103 A8
Eisele Cl NG6. . . . . .159 F6
Ekowe St NG7 . . . . .160 F2
Eland Rd NG20. . . . . .72 F5
Eland St NG7 . . . . .160 F1
Elder Cl NG5. . . . . .148 A1
Elder Gdns **8** NG3 . . . . .161 A8
Elder Gr NG15 . . . . .146 B4
Elder St
Kirkby in A NG17. . . . . . . .114 E6
Sutton in A NG17. . . . . . . .100 E7
Eldon Gn NG22 . . . . .65 F3
Eldon Rd NG9. . . . . .183 C1
Eldon St
Newark-on-T NG24 . . . . . .139 F7
Tuxford NG22 . . . . .65 F3
Eleanor Ave DE7. . . . . .170 A5
Eleanor Cres NG9. . . . . . . .182 F7
Electric Ave NG11. . . . . . . .185 A4
Eley Cl DE7. . . . . .157 C2
Elford Rise NG3. . . . . .173 F5
Elgar Dr NG10 . . . . .193 B5
Elgar Gdns NG3 . . . . .173 F7
Eliot Cl NG10 . . . . .193 B5
Eliot Wlk NG11. . . . . .195 C8
Elizabethan High Sch The
DN22. . . . . .39 D8
Elizabeth Cl
Gainsborough DN21 . . . . . .15 C3
Hucknall NG15. . . . . .145 E5
Elizabeth Ct DE7. . . . . .157 D1
Elizabeth Gr NG4 . . . . .162 E2
Elizabeth Rd NG24 . . . . . . .139 E5
Elkesley Prim Sch DN22. . .50 A3
Elkesley Rd NG20. . . . . . . .74 E8
Ella Bank Rd DE75 . . . . . . .143 A1
Ella Rd NG2 . . . . .173 F1
Ellastone Ave NG5. . . . . . . .161 C8
Ellerby Ave NG7 . . . . .184 E2
Ellerslie Cl NG24 . . . . .125 A1
Ellerslie Gr NG10 . . . . .182 A5
Ellesmere Bsns Pk NG5 . . .161 B2
Ellesmere Cl NG5. . . . . . . .162 B7
Ellesmere Dr NG9. . . . . . . .170 C5
Ellesmere Rd
Mansfield NG18. . . . . .102 F8
West Bridgford NG2. . . . . .185 F4
Ellington Rd NG5 . . . . .148 A2
Elliott Durham Comp Sch
NG3. . . . . .161 E2
Elliott Durham Swimming
Pool NG3. . . . . .161 E1
Elliott St NG7. . . . . .222 C3
Ellis Ave NG15 . . . . .146 B6
Ellis Cl NG10. . . . . .193 C6
Ellis Ct NG3 . . . . .223 E4
Ellis Gr NG9 . . . . .183 F5
Ellis Guilford Comp Sch
NG6. . . . . .160 C2
Ellis St NG17 . . . . .115 B5
Ellsworth Rise NG5 . . . . . . .160 F6
Ellwood Cres NG8. . . . . . . .172 A5
Elma La NG20. . . . . .59 D6
Elm Ave
Beeston, Attenborough
NG9. . . . . .183 D2
Beeston, Chilwell NG9. . . .183 E6
Bingham NG13. . . . . .178 A4
Carlton NG4. . . . . .174 F7
East Leake LE12 . . . . .205 F3
Hucknall NG15. . . . . .145 E5
Keyworth NG12 . . . . .197 F2
Long Eaton NG10. . . . . . . .193 C8
Newark-on-T NG24 . . . . . .140 B6
Nottingham NG3 . . . . .173 C7
Nuthall NG16. . . . . .159 B6
Sandiacre NG10. . . . . .182 B7
Elm Bank NG3 . . . . .173 C8
Elm Bank Dr NG3 . . . . .173 C8
Elmbridge NG5. . . . . .161 B7
Elm Cl
Keyworth NG12 . . . . .197 F2
Newark-on-T NG24 . . . . . .140 B6
Nottingham NG3 . . . . .173 C7
Pinxton NG16. . . . . .113 D2
Saxilby LN1 . . . . .57 B4
Elmcroft NG25. . . . . .134 B3
Elmdale Gdns NG8 . . . . . . .172 B8
Elm Dr NG4. . . . . .174 F7
Elm Gr
Arnold NG5 . . . . .148 A1
Church Warsop NG20 . . . . .74 A6
Elmhurst Ave
Nottingham NG3 . . . . .162 C2
South Normanton DE55. . .113 A4
Elmhurst Cl DE55 . . . . .113 A4
Elmhurst Dr NG17. . . . . . . .100 A3
Elmhurst Rd NG19 . . . . . . .88 F1
Elmore Ct NG7. . . . . .222 B4
Elmore's Mdw NG14. . . . . .152 A8
Elms Cl
Rempstone LE12 . . . . .215 D5
Ruddington NG11. . . . . . . .196 D6
Elmsfield Ave DE75 . . . . . .143 A2
Elms Gdns NG11 . . . . .196 C6

Elms Gr LE11 . . . . .220 C3
Elmsham Ave NG5 . . . . . . .146 E1
Elms Jun Sch The NG10 . . .193 C8
Elmsmere Dr S81. . . . . .17 A6
Elms Pk NG11. . . . . .196 D6
Elms Prim Sch NG3 . . . . . .173 C7
Elms Rd S80 . . . . .35 F4
Elms The
Carlton NG4. . . . . .174 F6
Watnall NG16 . . . . .158 F8
Elmsthorpe Ave NG7 . . . . .222 A2
Elmswood Gdns NG5. . . . . .161 D3
Elmton Cl S80 . . . . .58 D8
Elmton Rd S80. . . . . .58 D8
Elmtree Ave NG16. . . . . . . .128 F7
Elm Tree Ave
Mansfield Woodhouse
NG19. . . . . .88 A4
Shirebrook NG20 . . . . .72 D4
West Bridgford NG2 . . . . . .185 D2
Elmtree Cl S81 . . . . .34 F7
Elm Tree Ct S80 . . . . .35 F2
Elm Tree Dr DN10 . . . . .9 F7
Elm Tree Pl DN22 . . . . .50 B4
Elmtree Rd NG14 . . . . .148 D7
Elm Tree Rd NG17 . . . . . . .114 F6
Elm Tree Rise NG22. . . . . . .93 E5
Elm Tree St NG18 . . . . .102 C7
Elm Wlk DN22 . . . . .40 A5
Elmwood Cl DN22. . . . . . . .30 A1
Elnor St NG16 . . . . .143 C3
Elsham Wlk DN21 . . . . .24 F8
Elson St NG7 . . . . .172 F8
Elston Cl NG19. . . . . .87 D1
Elston Gdns NG11. . . . . . . .184 E4
Elston Hall NG23 . . . . .153 D4
Elston La NG23 . . . . .153 C6
Elswick Cl NG5. . . . . .161 B8
Elswick Dr NG9. . . . . .184 C4
Elterwater Dr NG2 . . . . . . .186 C6
Eltham Cl NG8 . . . . .159 F3
Eltham Dr NG8. . . . . .160 A2
Eltham Rd NG2 . . . . .186 A7
Elton Cl
Balderton NG24. . . . . .140 D3
Mansfield NG18. . . . . .103 B6
Stapleford NG9 . . . . .182 D8
Elton & Orston Sta NG13 .180 A5
Elton Rd
Mansfield NG18. . . . . .102 F6
3 Nottingham NG5. . . .161 B1
Elton Rd N NG5. . . . . .161 A1
Elton Terr NG7 . . . . .172 F7
Elvaston Cl NG18 . . . . .103 B6
Elvaston Dr NG10 . . . . .193 A4
Elvaston Rd NG8. . . . . .172 B5
Elveden Dr DE7 . . . . .157 C3
Ely Cl
Mansfield Woodhouse
NG19. . . . . .88 D4
Worksop S80 . . . . .36 A2
Emerald Cl NG19. . . . . .87 F1
Emerald Gr NG17 . . . . .115 C4
Emerys Rd NG4 . . . . .175 B8
Emma Bates Way NG21. . . .118 B6
Emmanuel Ave
Nottingham, Porchester
NG3. . . . . .162 A1
Nottingham, Rise Park
NG5. . . . . .147 A1
Emmendingen Av NG24 . . .125 B3
Emmerson Dr NG21 . . . . . .90 A5
Emneth Cl NG3 . . . . .173 F8
Empingham Cl NG9 . . . . . .183 B2
Empire St NG18 . . . . .102 D6
Empress Rd LE11. . . . . .220 D4
Emsworth Ave DN22. . . . . .29 E1
Emsworth Cl DE7. . . . . .157 D3
Ena Ave NG2 . . . . .173 F5
Enderby Cres
Gainsborough DN21 . . . . . .24 E7
Mansfield NG18. . . . . .102 F6
Enderby Gdns NG5. . . . . . .147 E1
Enderby Sq NG9 . . . . .183 F8
Endsleigh Gdns
Beeston NG9. . . . . .183 F7
West Bridgford NG12 . . . . .186 A4
Enfield St NG9. . . . . .183 E7
Engine La NG16. . . . . .144 B4
England Cres DE75. . . . . . .143 A2
English Martyrs RC Prim Sch
NG10. . . . . .182 B1
Ennerdale Cl NG2. . . . . . . .186 C7
Ennerdale Rd
Long Eaton NG10. . . . . . . .182 B2
Nottingham NG5 . . . . .161 D5
Ennismore Mews NG11. . . .185 C2
Enright Cl NG24. . . . . .139 F6
Enterprise Bsns Ctr S81. . .35 F8
Enterprise Rd NG19 . . . . . .87 D2
Enterprise Wy NG11. . . . . .118 A6
Enthorpe St **4** NG8 . . . .172 B6
Epinal Way LE11. . . . . .220 A1
Epperstone By-pass
NG14. . . . . .150 B4
Epperstone Ct **14** NG18 .103 A2
Epperstone Rd
Lowdham NG14 . . . . .150 D2
Oxton NG25. . . . . .134 C1
West Bridgford NG2 . . . . . .185 E8
Epping Way NG19. . . . . . . .103 B8
Epsom Rd NG9. . . . . .182 E3
Epsom St NG18 . . . . .102 F6
Erdington Way NG9. . . . . . .182 E3
Erewash Ct DE7 . . . . .157 D1
Erewash Dr DE7. . . . . .170 B6
Erewash Gdns NG5. . . . . . .161 A8
Erewash Gr NG9 . . . . .182 F2

Erewash Meadows Nature
Reserve
Aldercar NG16. . . . . .143 B8
Jacksdale NG16. . . . . .128 B1
Erewash Rd NG16 . . . . . . .113 E2
Erewash Sq DE7 . . . . .170 A6
Erewash St
Kirkby in A NG17 . . . . .115 A5
Long Eaton NG10. . . . . . . .193 E8
Pye Bridge DE55. . . . . . . .128 A6
Erica Dr DE55. . . . . .113 B7
Eric Ave NG15 . . . . .130 F1
Erith Cl NG8 . . . . .159 D1
Ernehale Jun & Inf Sch
NG5. . . . . .162 A6
Ernest Rd NG4 . . . . .162 B1
Erskine Rd **4** NG5 . . . . .161 B1
Esher Gr NG3 . . . . .161 C1
Eshton Rise DN10 . . . . .3 A1
Eskdale Cl NG10 . . . . .193 B5
Eskdale Ct NG2 . . . . .186 C7
Eskdale Dr
Beeston NG9. . . . . .183 B5
Nottingham NG8 . . . . .172 B8
Worksop S81 . . . . .35 E8
Eskdale Jun Sch NG9 . . . . .183 B5
Eskhouse Cl NG2. . . . . .186 C4
Essex Dr DN11 . . . . .9 D4
Essex Rd DN11. . . . . .9 D4
Essex St **2** DE7. . . . . . .157 F1
Estfeld Cl DN11. . . . . .8 A8
Estwic Ave NG16 . . . . .143 F3
Ethel Ave
Hucknall NG15. . . . . .131 C1
Nottingham NG3 . . . . .162 A1
Ethelbert Ave NG17 . . . . . .115 C1
Etheldene NG12 . . . . .189 B4
Ethel Rd NG2 . . . . .185 F7
Ethel Wainright Prim Sch
NG19. . . . . .101 F8
Etherington St DN21 . . . . . .24 D8
Eton Cl NG24 . . . . .139 F6
Eton Gr NG8 . . . . .172 B4
Eton Rd NG2. . . . . .185 E6
Eucalyptus Ave NG11. . . . .184 C1
Eugene Gdns NG2. . . . . . . .173 D2
Eugene St NG2 . . . . .223 F1
Europa Way NG2 . . . . .185 C3
Evans Ave NG17 . . . . .100 C3
Evans Rd NG6 . . . . .160 D3
Evedon Wlk NG5 . . . . .147 B1
Evelyn St
Beeston NG9. . . . . .184 B7
11 Nottingham NG2 . . .173 E4
Eversley Wlk NG5 . . . . .161 B8
Everton Prim Sch DN10 . . .11 B3
Everton Sluice La DN10 . . .11 C4
Everton St NG19 . . . . .87 C1
Evesham Cl NG19 . . . . .183 A1
Evesham Mews **7** S80 . .35 F2
Ewart Rd NG7 . . . . .173 A8
Ewe Lamb Cl NG9. . . . . . . .170 F1
Ewe Lamb La NG9. . . . . . . .170 F1
Ewell Rd NG8 . . . . .171 E5
Exbourne Rd NG8 . . . . .159 F1
Exbury Gdns NG2. . . . . . . .185 B4
Exchange Arc NG1 . . . . . . .223 E3
Exchange Rd NG2. . . . . . . .185 F4
Exchange Row **13** NG18 .102 B7
Exchange St DN22 . . . . . . .39 E7
Exchange Wlk NG1. . . . . . .223 E2
Exe Fold NG19 . . . . .88 D2
Exeter Cl
Carlton NG4. . . . . .162 F2
East Leake LE12 . . . . .205 D1
Exeter Rd
Nottingham NG7 . . . . .173 A8
West Bridgford NG2 . . . . . .185 F6
Export Dr NG17 . . . . .113 F8
Exton Rd NG5. . . . . .161 A3
Eyam Cl
Beeston NG9. . . . . .171 C2
Mansfield NG18. . . . . .103 B6
Eyre's Gdns DE7. . . . . .157 F2
Eyres La LE12. . . . . .205 A8
Eyre's La LN6 . . . . .83 E3
Eyre St NG2 . . . . .173 E4

F

Fabis Dr NG11. . . . . .184 E4
Fackley Rd NG17. . . . . .100 C6
Fackley Way NG17. . . . . . . .100 C6
Factory La
Beeston NG9. . . . . .183 E5
Ilkeston DE7 . . . . .157 E2
Factory Rd NG17. . . . . .115 A5
Factory St **2** LE11 . . . . .220 C3
Factory Yd **17** NG1. . . . .101 A4
Failsworth Cl NG11 . . . . . .184 E3
Fairbank Cres NG5. . . . . . .161 D2
Fairburn Cl NG8 . . . . .171 C4
Fairburn Wy NG16 . . . . . . .159 A7
Faircroft Ave NG10. . . . . . .182 B5
Fairdale Dr NG16 . . . . .144 B2
Fairfax Cl
Gainsborough DN21 . . . . . .24 F6
Nottingham NG7 . . . . .160 F2
Fairfield DN22 . . . . .39 E3
Fairfield Ave
Farndon NG24 . . . . .139 A5
Hilcote DE55 . . . . .99 C1
New Balderton NG24. . . . .140 C5
Fairfield Cl
Nether Langwith NG20 . . . .59 A2
Nottingham NG11 . . . . . . .185 B5
Fairfield Cres NG10 . . . . . .193 A4

Fairfield Dr
Mansfield NG18. . . . . .103 A7
Ravenshead NG15 . . . . . . .116 C3
Fairfield Prim Sch NG9. . . .182 D6
Fairfield Rd NG17 . . . . .101 B3
Fairfield Sch LE11 . . . . . . .220 B3
Fairfield St NG13 . . . . .177 E4
Fairham Ave NG11 . . . . . . .195 B1
Fairham Cl NG11. . . . . .196 B8
Fairham Com Coll NG11. . .195 F8
Fairham Dr NG8 . . . . .172 D4
Fairham Rd NG12 . . . . .197 D3
Fairhaven NG17. . . . . .115 B3
Fairholme Cl NG21 . . . . . . .89 F2
Fairholme Dr NG19 . . . . . . .87 E1
Fairisle Cl NG11 . . . . .185 A1
Fairland Cres NG2 . . . . . . .185 D4
Fairlawn Pl NG5 . . . . .161 D2
Fairlawns NG18 . . . . .103 B7
Fair Lea Cl NG10 . . . . .193 D6
Fairlie Ave NG19 . . . . .101 D5
Fairlight Way NG5 . . . . . . .161 B7
Fairmaid Gr NG7. . . . . .184 E2
Fairmead Cl NG3. . . . . .174 A8
Fairnley Rd NG8 . . . . .171 D8
Fair Vale NG23. . . . . .110 A8
Fair View NG19 . . . . .89 A2
Fairview Ave NG16 . . . . . . .128 F2
Fairview Ct NG11 . . . . .185 D2
Fairview Rd NG5 . . . . .161 E4
Fairway
Keyworth NG12 . . . . .198 A2
Newark-on-T NG24 . . . . . .139 D5
Retford DN22. . . . . .39 C4
Fairway Cres NG13. . . . . . .177 B8
Fairway Dr
Beeston NG9. . . . . .183 D6
Nottingham NG4 . . . . .174 C8
Nottingham NG6 . . . . .160 D7
Fairways Dr NG17 . . . . .114 F7
Fairways The NG19 . . . . . . .88 D6
Fairway The NG4 . . . . .162 E3
Fairweather Cl NG22 . . . . .77 F5
Falcon Cl
Eagle LN6 . . . . .84 D3
Nottingham NG7 . . . . .222 A2
Falcon Ct DE7 . . . . .157 D1
Falconers Wlk **7** NG5. . .161 C8
Falcon Gr NG7 . . . . .161 A1
Falcon St
Loughborough LE11. . . . . .220 C5
6 Nottingham NG7. . . .161 A1
Falconwood Gdns NG11 . . .184 C1
Fallow Cl
Nottingham NG7 . . . . .184 E2
Retford DN22. . . . . .29 E1
Fallow Ct S81. . . . . .36 B7
Fal Paddock NG19 . . . . . . .88 D2
Falstone Ave NG24. . . . . . .140 B6
Falston Rd NG8 . . . . .172 A7
Faraday Ave NG22 . . . . . . .66 A3
Faraday Ct NG9 . . . . .170 E1
Faraday Rd
Mansfield NG18. . . . . .102 E5
Nottingham NG7 . . . . .222 A2
Far Back La NG22 . . . . .119 F6
Far Croft Ave NG17 . . . . . .100 C3
Farfield Ave NG9. . . . . .183 E8
Farfield Gr NG9. . . . . .183 E8
Farfield Rd DE7 . . . . .170 A8
Far Holme La NG23 . . . . . .97 A8
Far La LE12. . . . . .213 D3
Farleys Gr NG15 . . . . .146 A5
Farleys La NG15 . . . . .146 A5
Farley St NG6. . . . . .160 B7
Farm Ave NG15 . . . . .145 D4
Farm Cl
East Bridgford NG13. . . . . .165 D3
Ilkeston DE7 . . . . .170 A8
Long Eaton NG10. . . . . . . .193 E5
Nottingham NG7 . . . . .184 E2
Farm Croft Rd NG19. . . . . .88 C6
Farmers Branch S81. . . . . .36 A7
Farmer St NG11. . . . . .196 E3
Farm Gr S81. . . . . .36 B7
Farmhouse Cl NG13. . . . . .181 A3
Farmilo Cres NG19. . . . . . .87 E1
Farmilo Prim Sch NG19 . . .87 C4
Farm La NG22 . . . . .65 F7
Farm Rd
Arnold NG5 . . . . .162 B7
Beeston NG9. . . . . .183 D5
Farm View DN22. . . . . .39 E3
Farm View Rd NG17. . . . . .115 C5
Farmway NG19 . . . . .88 C2
Farn'boro Sch & Tech Coll
NG11. . . . . .185 A4
Farnborough Rd NG11 . . . .185 A2
Farndale S81 . . . . .36 B7
Farndale Cl
Long Eaton NG10. . . . . . . .193 A5
Sutton in A NG17. . . . . . . .100 F5
Farndale Dr NG8 . . . . .171 B4
Farndale Rd NG17. . . . . . . .100 F5
Farndon Dr NG9 . . . . .182 F3
Farndon Gn NG8 . . . . .172 C3
Farndon Gr S81. . . . . .35 D7
Farndon Ponds Nature
Reserve NG24 . . . . .138 F6
Farndon Rd
Newark-on-T NG24,
NG23. . . . . .139 D6
Sutton in A NG17. . . . . . . .101 D1
Farndon Way NG19 . . . . . . .101 D4
Farndon Willow Holt Nature
Reserve NG24 . . . . .138 F6
Farnes Ct S81. . . . . .36 B5
Far New Cl NG10. . . . . .182 B5

Farnham Rd 1 LE11 220 B1
Farnsfield Ave NG14 164 A5
Farnsfield Ct 15 NG18 103 A2
Farnsfield Rd
Bilsthorpe NG22 105 F3
Bilsthorpe NG22 106 A4
Farnsfield St Michael Prim Sch NG22 119 F7
Farnsworth Ave NG21 103 E2
Farnsworth Cl NG16 145 A1
Farnsworth Gr NG17 99 F3
Far Pasture Cl NG12 197 E2
Farrar Cl NG24 125 C2
Far Rd NG22 67 D4
Farrendale Cl NG19 88 D1
Farriers Croft DE7 157 C3
Farriers Gn NG11 184 C2
Farringdon Cl NG8 159 D3
Farr Way NG21 118 A4
Far Rye NG8 171 F6
Far St
Bradmore NG11 196 E3
Wymeswold LE12 216 C4
Farthingate NG25 136 F8
Farthingate Cl NG25 136 F8
Farthing Ct NG10 193 B7
Farthings The LE12 213 A1
Farwells Cl NG6 160 C3
Faulconbridge Cl NG6 160 B6
Fawcett St DN21 15 C1
Fearn Chase NG4 174 E7
Fearn Cl DE72 193 A7
Fearnleigh Dr NG6 160 D2
Fearon Cl NG14 164 F5
Featherbed La S80 34 F1
Featherston Ave S80 36 B2
Featherstone Cl
Carlton NG4 162 D3
Mansfield NG18 101 D4
Feignes Ct NG12 197 E3
Feilding Way DN21 15 E1
Felen Cl NG5 161 A7
Fellbarrow Cl NG2 186 C5
Fell Croft NG24 139 A5
Felley Ave NG17 114 E1
Felley Mill La N NG16 129 C2
Felley Mill La S NG16 129 B1
Felley Priory Gdn NG16 129 C3
Fellows Rd NG9 183 E7
Fellows Yd NG12 197 E7
Fell Side NG5 162 A5
Fellside Cl NG2 186 C6
Fell Wilson St NG20 74 C4
Felly Cl NG15 145 E5
Felly Mill La S NG16 129 B1
Felstead Ct NG9 171 C1
Felton Ave NG19 88 C6
Felton Cl NG9 183 B5
Felton Rd NG2 173 D1
Fenchurch Cl NG5 147 A1
Fenimore Ct NG12 176 B3
Fen La
Balderton NG23 155 D3
Balderton NG24 141 A4
Fennel St LE11 220 B4
Fenroth Cl NG6 159 F8
Fenton Cl NG24 125 B2
Fenton Dr NG6 146 C2
Fenton Rd
Fenton NG23 142 D1
Nottingham NG5 160 F4
Fenwick Cl NG8 159 F2
Fenwick Rd NG8 159 F2
Fenwick St NG20 74 B4
Ferguson Ave NG19 88 B4
Ferguson Cl 1 NG9 183 C2
Fern Ave 7 NG5 161 B1
Fern Bank Ave NG22 64 A1
Fern Cl
Beeston NG9 183 C7
Bilsthorpe NG22 106 A5
Ravenshead NG15 117 B1
Shirebrook NG20 72 E6
Southwell NG25 121 D1
Fern Cres NG16 143 D3
Ferndale Cl
Beeston NG9 183 E2
New Ollerton NG22 77 E6
Ferndale Gr NG3 174 B6
Ferndale Rd NG3 174 B6
Ferndene Dr NG10 193 A7
Ferngill Cl 2 NG2 173 B1
Fern Lea Ave NG12 187 E2
Fernleigh Ave NG3 162 B2
Fernleigh Rise NG19 88 D1
Fern Rd NG12 189 B3
Fern St NG17 100 E4
Fernwood Cl NG19 89 A1
Fernwood Comp Sch NG8 171 D4
Fernwood Cres NG8 171 D4
Fernwood Dr NG12 175 F4
Fernwood Inf & Jun Sch NG8 171 D4
Ferny Hollow Cl NG5 160 E8
Ferous Cl NG11 195 F8
Ferrers Wlk NG3 173 E5
Ferriby Terr 13 NG2 173 C1
Ferry Farm Ctry Pk NG14 151 E1
Ferry La
Carlton-on-Trent NG23 96 F5
Everton DN10 11 C3
North Muskham NG23 110 F2
Festival Ave DN11 9 A4
Festival Dr LE11 220 A6
Festival Hall L Ctr NG17 115 A4
Festus Cl NG3 223 F4
Festus St
Carlton NG4 175 A7
Kirkby in A NG17 115 A4
Field Ave NG15 145 D4
Field Cl
Beeston NG9 183 B4
Carlton NG4 162 F2
Mansfield Woodhouse NG19 88 D5
Worksop S81 36 A7
Field Dr NG20 72 E2
Fielden Ave NG19 87 D2
Field End Cl LE12 205 C1
Fieldfare Dr S81 35 C7
Field House Cl NG8 171 D5
Fieldings The NG17 100 B2
Field La
Ault Hucknall NG19, S44 86 C6
Beeston NG9 183 B4
Blidworth NG21 117 F3
Cropwell Bishop NG12 189 A4
Morton DN21 15 A4
Woodborough NG14 149 C4
Field Maple Dr NG7 172 E8
Field Mill (Mansfield Town FC) NG18 102 B5
Field Pl NG17 114 D8
Fields Ave NG11 196 C5
Fields Dr NG13 178 F5
Fields Farm Rd NG10 193 E5
Field The DE75 157 A6
Field View
South Normanton DE55 113 A7
Sutton in A NG17 100 C1
Fieldway NG11 185 B4
Fiennes Cres NG7 222 C1
Fifth Ave
Beeston NG9 184 D6
Clipstone NG21 89 F3
Edwinstowe NG21 75 F2
Mansfield NG19 103 A8
Fiftyeights Rd DN10 1 D3
Filey St NG6 160 C8
Finch Cl NG7 184 F8
Finchley Cl NG11 184 C1
Findern Ct NG18 103 B6
Findern Gn NG3 174 A6
Fingal Cl NG7 184 E2
Fingle St DN22 32 D1
Fingleton S81 36 B6
Finkell St DN10 12 F3
Finley Way DE55 113 B4
Finningley Rd NG18 103 A3
Finsbury Ave
4 Loughborough LE11 220 C3
Nottingham NG2 173 F4
Finsbury Pk Cl NG2 185 C5
Finsbury Rd
Beeston NG9 171 C3
Nottingham NG5 147 A2
Firbank Ct NG9 183 B4
Firbeck Ave NG18 102 F5
Firbeck Cres S81 16 F3
Firbeck Prim Sch NG8 171 B4
Firbeck Rd
Arnold NG5 162 A8
Nottingham NG8 171 C4
Fir Cl
Nottingham NG6 159 F7
Shirebrook NG20 72 E6
Fircroft Ave NG8 171 F8
Fircroft Dr NG15 145 C5
Fir Dale NG12 188 A3
Firecrest Way NG6 160 D3
Firemen's Row NG17 100 E2
Firs Ave NG9 183 F7
Firsby Rd NG8 159 F2
Firs Rd NG12 186 B4
Firs St NG10 193 A4
First Ave
Beeston NG9 184 C6
Carlton, Colwick NG4 174 E5
Carlton, Gedling NG4 162 F1
Carlton, Thorneywood NG4 174 C8
Clipstone NG21 90 A3
Edwinstowe NG21 76 A2
Mansfield NG21 103 F2
Mansfield Woodhouse NG19 89 A1
Nottingham NG6 160 B7
Firs The 1 NG5 161 D3
First Holme La NG23 97 A8
Firth Cl NG5 148 C1
Firth Dr NG9 183 C2
Firth Rd DN22 39 C8
Firth Way NG6 146 A1
Fir Tree Cl NG19 89 D2
Fir View NG22 77 D5
Fisher Ave NG5 161 F5
Fisher Cl
Collingham NG23 98 B1
East Leake LE12 205 F2
Sutton in Ashfield NG17 100 D5
Fisher Ct DE7 157 F4
Fisher Gate NG1 223 F2
Fisher La
Bingham NG13 177 E4
Mansfield NG18 102 C5
Fishers St NG17 115 A1
Fisher St 4 NG7 172 F8
Fish Pond Dr NG7 223 D1
Fishpool Rd NG21 117 D3
Fiskerton Ct 6 NG18 103 A3
Fiskerton Rd
Rolleston NG23 138 B5
Southwell NG25 137 A6
Fiskerton Sta NG25 137 E4
Fitzherbert St NG20 74 C4
Five Acres NG11 185 A4
Five Fields Cl DN22 40 A4
Five Fields La DN22 40 A4
Flagholme NG12 187 F2
Flamingo Ct 5 NG2 173 A2
Flamstead Ave NG4 163 B7
Flamstead Rd DE7 157 F1
Flamsteed Rd NG8 159 D1
Flash La NG22 93 B7
Flat La S81 16 A6
Flatts La
Calverton NG14 133 E1
Westwood NG16 128 D3
Flatts The NG9 183 B5
Flawforth Ave NG11 196 D6
Flawforth La NG11 196 E7
Flaxendale NG12 188 A2
Flaxton Way NG5 160 F7
Fleam Rd NG11 184 E4
Fleeman Gr NG2 174 A1
Fleet Cl NG7 172 D6
Fleetway S81 35 E7
Fleetway Cl NG16 144 B1
Fleetwith Cl NG2 186 C5
Fleming Ave
Bottesford NG13 181 C3
Tuxford NG22 66 A3
Fleming Cl NG16 159 A8
Fleming Dr
Carlton NG4 174 C7
Newark-on-T NG24 125 B4
Woodbeck DN22 53 B8
Fleming Gdns NG11 184 C1
Fletcher Ct NG22 119 E7
Fletcher Gate NG1 223 E2
Fletcher Rd NG9 184 A7
Fletcher St NG10 193 D8
Fletcher Terr NG3 161 E2
Fletcher Way NG19 103 B8
Flewitt Gdns NG3 173 E6
Flint Ave NG19 88 F1
Flintham Dr NG5 161 C4
Flintham La NG13 166 E5
Flintham Mus NG23 153 A1
Flintham Prim Sch NG23 153 A1
Flixton Rd NG16 158 F7
Flood Rd The DN21 24 B7
Floralands Gdn Village NG4 162 E8
Floral Villas NG23 96 F7
Florence Ave NG10 182 F1
Florence Boot Cl NG9 184 B8
Florence Cres NG4 175 B8
Florence Ct DE7 157 F1
Florence Gr NG3 174 A7
Florence Rd
Carlton NG4 175 B8
Nottingham NG3 162 A1
West Bridgford NG2 186 A8
Florence St NG15 146 A5
Florence Terr DN21 24 D7
Florey Ct 1 NG7 172 E2
Florey Wlk NG11 195 C8
Florin Gdns NG10 193 A7
Floss La DN22 43 D4
Flowers Cl NG5 162 B6
Flying Horse Wlk NG1 223 E2
Foljambe Terr NG3 223 F3
Folkton Gdns NG3 161 F1
Folly Hall La LE12 209 D3
Folly La
Besthorpe NG23 98 B8
Stapleford LN6 112 F5
Folly Nook La DN22 19 A6
Fonton Hall Dr NG17 114 B8
Forbes Cl NG10 193 E5
Fordbridge La DE55 113 A7
Fordham Gn NG11 195 E8
Ford La NG23 109 A5
Ford St N NG7 161 A1
Ford St NG7 161 A1
Foredrift Cl NG11 195 A1
Forest Ave NG18 102 C5
Forest Cl
Annesley Woodhouse NG17 130 A8
Cotgrave NG12 187 E3
Rainworth NG21 104 C1
Selston NG16 129 B7
Forest Ct
Mansfield NG18 103 B7
Nottingham NG7 222 C3
Forester Cl NG9 183 C4
Forester Gr NG4 174 D8
Forester Rd NG3 174 A8
Forester St NG4 175 A7
Forest Fields Prim Sch NG7 173 A8
Forest Gdns NG15 130 B8
Forest Glade Prim Sch NG17 101 A4
Forest Gr NG7 222 C4
Forest Hill NG18 102 C2
Forest Hill Rd S81 36 A7
Forest La
Papplewick NG15 131 E3
Walesby NG22 63 E3
Worksop S80 36 C2
Forest Link NG22 105 F5
Forest Rd
Annesley Woodhouse NG17 130 A8
Bingham NG13 177 D4
Blidworth NG21 118 B5
Calverton NG14 148 D8
Clipstone NG21 89 F3
Loughborough LE11 220 A3
Mansfield NG18 102 C5
Forest Rd *continued*
Market Warsop NG20 74 D1
New Ollerton NG22 77 C4
Oxton NG25 134 B5
Sutton in A NG17 101 A5
Forest Rd E NG1 173 B7
Forest Rd W NG7 222 C4
Forest Rise NG20 74 C2
Forest St
Annesley Woodhouse NG17 130 A8
Kirkby in A NG17 115 B4
Sutton in A NG17 100 F2
Forest Town Prim Sch NG19 89 A1
Forest View
New Ollerton NG22 77 B4
Retford DN22 39 D3
Forest View Dr NG15 145 E7
Forest View Jun Sch NG22 77 D5
Forewood La DN22 42 A4
Forge Ave NG14 148 F8
Forge Cl
South Muskham NG23 124 E7
Sutton on T NG23 96 F8
Forge Hill NG9 183 D4
Forge Mill Gr NG15 146 C5
Forge The NG9 170 B5
Forman St NG1 223 E3
Forrests Yd S80 35 E2
Forrington Pl LN1 57 C3
Forster Ave NG24 139 E5
Forster St
Gainsborough DN21 15 C1
Kirkby in A NG17 114 F5
Nottingham NG7 222 A3
Forsythia Gdns NG7 172 E2
Forum Rd NG5 160 E6
Fosbrooke Dr NG10 193 D5
Fossdyke Gdns LN1 57 B3
Fosse Gr LN1 57 B3
Fosse Rd NG24, NG23 139 A4
Fossett's Ave NG16 128 F7
Fosseway 3 DN21 15 F1
Fosse Wlk NG12 188 A1
Foss Way NG13 166 B5
Foss Wy NG13 165 F2
Foster Ave NG9 183 F6
Foster Rd NG23 98 A1
Fosters Dr NG5 161 D4
Fosters La NG13 177 F4
Foster St NG18 102 C6
Foston Cl NG18 103 B6
Fothergill Ct 1 NG3 173 C7
Foundry Cl NG24 124 F2
Fountain Dale Ct 2 NG3 173 D7
Fountaindale Specl Sch NG18 116 D6
Fountain Hill DN10 13 D7
Fountain Hill Rd DN10 13 D7
Fountains Cl
Kirkby in A NG17 115 C5
West Bridgford NG2 186 B6
Four Seasons Sh Ctr NG18 102 B7
Fourth Ave
Beeston NG9 184 D6
Carlton NG4 174 B8
Clipstone NG21 89 F3
Edwinstowe NG21 76 A2
Mansfield NG19 103 A8
Rainworth NG21 103 F2
Fowler St NG3 173 D8
Foxby Hill DN21 24 E6
Foxby La DN21 24 F6
Fox Cl NG10 193 D5
Fox Covert
Carlton NG4 174 F4
3 Loughborough LE11 220 B6
Fox Covert Cl NG17 100 C1
Fox Covert La
Misterton DN10 14 A8
Nottingham NG11 184 C1
Foxcovert Plantation Nature Reserve NG14 132 F2
Fox Covert Way NG19 103 B7
Foxearth Ave NG11 185 A2
Foxes Cl NG7 222 C1
Foxglove Cl
New Balderton NG24 140 C5
Worksop S80 36 B2
Foxglove Gr NG19 88 F4
Foxglove Rd NG16 158 B8
Foxgloves The NG13 177 D3
Fox Gr NG5 160 E3
Fox Gr Ct NG6 160 E3
Foxhall Bsns Ctr NG7 173 B7
Foxhall Rd NG7 173 A8
Fox Hill NG12 187 E2
Foxhill Cl NG17 100 B3
Foxhill Ct NG4 174 E8
Foxhill Rd
Burton Joyce NG14 163 E5
Carlton NG4 174 C8
Foxhill Rd Central NG4 174 C8
Foxhill Rd E NG4 174 D8
Foxhill Rd W NG4 174 B8
Foxhills DE74 203 C1
Foxhollies Gr NG5 161 B3
Fox Mdw NG15 145 F6
Fox Rd
Nottingham NG2 173 E1
Whitwell S80 45 A6
Fox St
Annesley Woodhouse NG17 130 A8
Fox St *continued*
Sutton in A NG17 100 F3
Foxton Cl NG6 159 F8
Foxwood Cl S81 25 D1
Foxwood Found Sch & Tech Coll NG9 171 B1
Foxwood Gr NG14 148 F7
Foxwood La NG14 149 A5
Fradley Cl NG6 146 C2
Frampton Rd NG8 172 A7
Frances Gr NG15 131 B1
Frances St NG16 128 D1
Francis Chichester Wlk DN21 24 F7
Francis Gr NG6 160 E3
Francis Rd NG4 174 F8
Francis St
Mansfield NG18 102 E7
Nottingham NG7 222 C4
Francklin Rd NG14 150 D2
Franderground Dr NG17 114 E5
Frank Ave NG18 101 F5
Franklin Cl NG5 161 C8
Franklin Dr NG12 186 D1
Franklin Rd NG16 128 A4
Franklyn Gdns
Keyworth NG12 197 E4
Nottingham NG8 172 C6
Fraser Cres NG4 162 B1
Fraser Rd
Carlton NG4 162 B1
Nottingham NG2 173 D1
Fraser Sq NG4 162 B1
Fraser St NG15 130 D6
Frearson Farm Ct NG16 143 F1
Freckingham St NG1 223 F2
Freda Ave NG4 162 D2
Freda Cl NG4 162 D3
Frederick Ave
Carlton NG4 174 B7
Ilkeston DE7 170 A5
Kegworth DE74 203 C3
Kirkby in A NG17 114 D6
Frederick Gent Sch DE55 113 B5
Frederick Harrison Inf Sch NG9 182 F8
Frederick Rd NG9 182 D7
Frederick St
Long Eaton NG10 193 F7
Loughborough LE11 220 A3
Mansfield NG18 102 C6
Retford DN22 39 F6
Sutton in A NG17 100 C1
Worksop S80 35 E3
Freeby Ave NG19 88 D5
Freehold St LE11 220 C4
Freeland Cl NG9 182 F3
Freeman's La DN22 32 C5
Freemans Rd NG4 175 A8
Freemans Terr NG4 175 A8
Freemantle Wlk NG5 160 E8
Freeston Dr NG6 159 F8
Freeth St NG2 173 F2
Freiston St 5 NG7 172 E7
Fremount Dr NG8 172 A7
French St DE7 170 A6
French Terr NG20 59 A2
Fretwell St 3 NG7 172 E7
Friar La
Market Warsop NG20 74 C2
Nottingham NG1 223 D2
Friars Cl NG16 129 B7
Friars Cres NG24 139 F5
Friars Ct NG7 222 C1
Friar St
Long Eaton NG10 193 D7
8 Nottingham NG7 172 E2
Friar Wlk NG13 177 C8
Friary Cl 10 NG7 172 E2
Friary Gdns NG24 125 A1
Friary Rd 2 NG24 140 A8
Friary The NG7 172 E2
Friday La NG4 162 F1
Friend La NG21 76 B1
Frinton Rd NG8 159 E1
Frisby Ave NG10 193 E6
Fritchley Ct NG18 103 B6
Frith Gr NG19 101 E7
Frithwood La S80 58 D7
Frobisher Gdns NG5 161 D6
Frog La NG13 202 F8
Frogmore St NG1 223 E4
Front St
Arnold NG5 161 F7
Barnby in t W NG24 141 F5
East Stockwith DN21 7 D2
Morton DN21 15 B3
South Clifton NG23 68 E1
Frost Ave NG16 143 A4
Fryar Rd NG16 143 F3
Fulford Ave DN22 39 C8
Fulforth St NG1 223 E4
Fuller Cl NG18 102 B4
Fuller St NG11 196 C6
Fullwood Ave 4 DE7 157 E1
Fullwood Cl NG9 183 C4
Fullwood St 6 DE7 157 E1
Fulmar Way S81 35 C7
Fulwood Cres NG8 160 B1
Fulwood Dr NG10 193 A7
Fulwood Ind Est DE55 113 F8
Fulwood Rd N
Huthwaite NG17 99 F1
Sutton in A NG17 114 A8

Fulwood Rd S NG17 . . . . 114 A8
Fulwood Rise NG17 . . . . 114 A8
Furlong Ave NG5 . . . . 161 E8
Furlong Cl NG9 . . . . 182 D8
Furlong St NG5 . . . . 161 E8
Furnace Rd DE7 . . . . 170 B6
Furness Cl NG2 . . . . 186 A7
Furness Rd NG6 . . . . 160 C3
Furnival St S80 . . . . 36 A1
Furzebrook Rd NG4 . . . . 174 E6
Furze Gdns NG3 . . . . 173 D7
Furze The NG22 . . . . 78 C6
Fylde Cl NG9 . . . . 182 F2
Fylingdale Way NG8 . . . . 171 C4

G

Gables Farm Dr LE12 . . . 206 C1
Gable's Lea LE12 . . . . . . 213 B6
Gables The NG22 . . . . . . 106 A5
Gabor Cl NG11 . . . . 195 C8
Gabrielle Cl NG6 . . . . . . 160 D4
Gaddick View NG22 . . . . . 79 F6
Gadd St NG7 . . . . 222 B4
Gadsby Cl DE7 . . . . 170 A4
Gainas Ave DN21 . . . . 15 C2
Gainsborough Central Sta
 DN21 . . . . 24 D8
Gainsborough Cl
 Kinoulton NG12 . . . . . . 199 F2
 Long Eaton NG10 . . . . . 193 E5
 Stapleford NG9 . . . . . . 182 E6
Gainsborough Dr NG24 . . 125 B3
Gainsborough Lea Rd Sta
 DN21 . . . . 24 D5
Gainsborough Rd
 Bawtry DN10 . . . . 10 A6
 Everton DN10 . . . . 11 D2
 Girton NG23 . . . . 82 F3
 Gringley on t H DN10 . . 12 B1
 Lea DN21 . . . . 24 F2
 North Wheatley DN22 . . 22 F1
 Saundby DN22 . . . . 23 C5
 Saxilby LN1 . . . . 56 E2
 Sturton le S DN22 . . . . . 32 C6
 Winthorpe NG24 . . . . . 125 C6
Gainsborough Waterfront
 Enterprise Ctr DN21 . . . 24 C6
Gainsborough W Lindsey L
 Ctr DN21 . . . . 15 D2
Gainsford Cl NG5 . . . . . . 160 F5
Gainsford Cres NG5 . . . . 160 F5
Gaitskell Cres NG21 . . . . . 76 C1
Gaitskell Way NG24 . . . . 140 E4
Gala Way
 Nottingham NG5 . . . . . . 160 E6
 Retford DN22 . . . . 39 F5
Gale Cl NG9 . . . . 184 A7
Galena Dr NG3 . . . . 174 A7
Galen Ave DN22 . . . . 42 A1
Galen Ct **2** NG7 . . . . . . 172 E2
Galleries of Justice NG1 . 223 F2
Galley Hill Rd NG25 . . . . 122 B1
Gallows Inn Cl DE7 . . . . 170 A5
Galway Ave DN11 . . . . 9 D5
Galway Cres DN22 . . . . . 39 C8
Galway Dr DN11 . . . . 9 D5
Galway Rd
 Arnold NG5 . . . . 161 E8
 Bircotes DN11 . . . . 9 D5
 Nottingham NG7 . . . . . . 222 B1
Gamage Cl NG24 . . . . . . 140 F4
Gamble St NG7 . . . . 222 C3
Gamston CE Prim Sch
 DN22 . . . . 50 F5
Gamston Cres NG5 . . . . 161 C3
Gamston Lings Bar Rd
 NG12 . . . . 186 C3
Gamston Rd NG18 . . . . . 103 B3
Gamston Wood Nature
 Reserve DN22 . . . . 51 D6
Gant Ct DN11 . . . . 8 A8
Ganton Cl NG3 . . . . 161 F1
Garden Ave
 Carlton NG4 . . . . 174 D8
 New Houghton NG19 . . . 86 F7
 Rainworth NG21 . . . . . . 104 A1
 Shirebrook NG20 . . . . . . 72 E4
Garden City NG4 . . . . . . 174 E8
Gardendale Ave NG11 . . 184 D1
Gardenia Cres NG3 . . . . 162 B2
Gardenia Gr NG3 . . . . . . 162 B2
Garden La NG17 . . . . 101 A3
Garden Rd
 Bingham NG13 . . . . 177 D4
 Eastwood NG16 . . . . . . 144 A3
 Hucknall NG15 . . . . 145 F7
 3 Mansfield NG18 . . . 102 B6
Garden Row DE74 . . . . . 203 D3
Gardens Cl NG2 . . . . 186 A7
Garden St NG7 . . . . 222 B3
Gardiner Terr NG17 . . . . 100 D6
Gardinia Cl NG9 . . . . 183 A2
Gardner Dr NG12 . . . . . . 199 F3
Garfield Cl NG9 . . . . 170 E1
Garfield Rd NG7 . . . . 222 B3
Garfield St DN21 . . . . 15 C1
Garforth Cl NG8 . . . . 172 E8
Garibaldi Rd NG19 . . . . . 89 D2
Garibaldi Sch NG19 . . . . . 89 E2
Garners Hill NG1 . . . . . . 223 E2
Garnet Cl NG18 . . . . 102 C5
Garnet Ct NG3 . . . . 173 E5
Garnet St NG4 . . . . 174 F7

Garnon St NG18 . . . . 101 E6
Garratt Ave NG18 . . . . . . 102 C7
Garrett Gr NG11 . . . . 184 D2
Garsdale Cl NG2 . . . . 186 C6
Garsdale Dr NG11 . . . . . . 185 A3
Garside Ave NG17 . . . . . 100 D1
Garside St S80 . . . . 36 A3
Garth Ave NG17 . . . . 114 E8
Garth Rd NG18 . . . . 102 A4
Garton Cl
 Beeston NG9 . . . . 183 B5
 Nottingham NG6 . . . . . . 160 B5
Garton Rd LE11 . . . . 220 A3
Garwick Cl NG19 . . . . 89 B2
Gas St NG10 . . . . 182 C6
Gas Wlk LE14 . . . . 202 B3
Gatcombe Cl NG12 . . . . 176 A3
Gatcombe Gr NG10 . . . . 182 A3
Gateford Ave S81 . . . . . . 35 D6
Gateford Cl
 Beeston NG9 . . . . 171 C2
 Worksop S81 . . . . 35 D7
Gateford Dr S81 . . . . 35 D6
Gateford Gdns S81 . . . . . 35 D6
Gateford Glade S81 . . . . . 35 D6
Gateford Park Prim Sch
 S81 . . . . 35 D8
Gateford Rd S81, S80 . . . 35 D6
Gateford Rise S81 . . . . . . 35 D7
Gateside Rd NG2 . . . . . . 173 A1
Gatling St NG7 . . . . 222 A3
Gattlys La NG22 . . . . 77 B4
Gaul St NG6 . . . . 160 B7
Gauntley Ct **1** NG7 . . . 172 E8
Gauntley St NG7 . . . . . . 172 E8
Gautries Cl NG5 . . . . 161 A8
Gawthorne St NG7 . . . . . 161 A1
Gayhurst Gn NG6 . . . . . . 160 E5
Gayhurst Rd NG6 . . . . . . 160 E5
Gaynor Ct NG8 . . . . 172 B6
Gayrigg Ct NG9 . . . . 183 B4
Gayton Cl NG8 . . . . 171 D8
Gayton Rd DE7 . . . . 157 D1
Gaywood Cl NG11 . . . . . 195 F8
Gedling Gr NG7 . . . . 222 C4
Gedling Rd
 Arnold NG5 . . . . 162 B5
 Carlton NG4 . . . . 174 F8
Gedling Sch The NG4 . . . 162 E3
Gedling St
 Mansfield NG18 . . . . . . 102 B5
 Nottingham NG1 . . . . . . 223 F2
Gedney Ave NG3 . . . . . . 173 F8
Gelding Gr NG5 . . . . 161 F7
Gelding House Woods
 Nature Reserve NG4 . . 163 B2
Gell Rd NG9 . . . . 183 A3
George Ave
 Beeston NG9 . . . . 183 F5
 Long Eaton NG10 . . . . . 182 F1
George Dere Cl NG22 . . . 77 D6
George Rd
 Carlton NG4 . . . . 174 E7
 West Bridgford NG2 . . . 185 E7
George's La NG14 . . . . . 148 D6
George Spencer Sch & Tech
 Ctr NG9 . . . . 182 E5
George St
 Arnold NG5 . . . . 161 E6
 Gainsborough DN21 . . . 15 B2
 Hucknall NG15 . . . . 146 A8
 Langley Mill NG16 . . . . 143 B3
 Mansfield NG19 . . . . . . 101 F8
 Mansfield Woodhouse, Forest
 Town NG19 . . . . 89 A1
 Mansfield Woodhouse
 NG19 . . . . 88 D3
 Market Warsop NG20 . . 74 B4
 Market Warsop, Spion Cop
 NG20 . . . . 73 F1
 Newark-on-T NG24 . . . . 125 C1
 Nottingham NG1 . . . . . . 223 E3
 Pinxton NG16 . . . . 113 C4
 Retford DN22 . . . . 39 F5
 Sutton in A NG17 . . . . . 100 B3
 Whaley Thorns NG20 . . . 59 A2
 Worksop S80 . . . . 35 F3
George Yd **7** LE11 . . . . 220 B4
Georgia Dr NG5 . . . . 147 E2
Georgina Rd NG9 . . . . . . 183 F5
Gerrard Cl NG5 . . . . 147 A2
Gerrard Cres DE74 . . . . . 203 D1
Gervase Gdns NG11 . . . . 184 D2
Ghest Villas S81 . . . . 16 F1
Ghost House La NG9 . . . 183 B4
Gibbet Hill La DN10 . . . . . 9 F4
Gibbons Ave NG9 . . . . . . 182 D6
Gibbons Rd NG18 . . . . . . 101 F5
Gibbons St NG7 . . . . 172 E1
Gibb St NG10 . . . . 193 E7
Gibdyke DN10 . . . . 4 C3
Gibson Cres NG24 . . . . . 140 C3
Gibson Rd NG7 . . . . 173 A8
Gibson's La LE14 . . . . . . 218 C2
Gifford Gdns NG2 . . . . . . 173 B2
Gilbert Ave
 Gotham NG11 . . . . 195 B1
 Tuxford NG22 . . . . 66 A3
Gilbert Bvd NG5 . . . . 162 C7
Gilbert Gdns NG3 . . . . . . 174 A6
Gilbert Rd DN11 . . . . 9 B4
Gilbert Wy NG21 . . . . . . 118 B6
Gilcroft St
 Mansfield NG18 . . . . . . 102 C6
 Sutton in A NG17 . . . . . 100 E6
Gilead St NG6 . . . . 160 B7
Giles Ave NG2 . . . . 185 D6

Gillercomb Cl NG2 . . . . . 186 D5
Gill Gn Wlk DN22 . . . . 30 D4
Gillies The NG19 . . . . . . 101 E5
Gilliver La NG12 . . . . 187 C1
Gillot St DE75 . . . . 157 A8
Gillotts Cl NG13 . . . . 177 E5
Gill St
 Nottingham NG1 . . . . . . 223 D4
 Selston NG16 . . . . 129 A6
 Sutton in A NG17 . . . . . 100 C2
Gilmores La NG24 . . . . . 140 F1
Gilpet Ave NG3 . . . . 173 F8
Gilstrap Cl NG24 . . . . . . 140 D8
Gilstrap Ctr NG24 . . . . . 124 E1
Giltbrook Cres NG16 . . . 158 C8
Gilt Hill NG16 . . . . 158 D7
Gilthill Prim Sch NG16 . . 158 D7
Giltway NG16 . . . . 158 C7
Gimson Cl DE7 . . . . 157 C3
Gin Cl Way NG16 . . . . . . 158 C6
Gipsy La NG14 . . . . 152 B8
Girton Ct NG18 . . . . 103 B2
Girton La LN6 . . . . 83 B1
Girton Rd NG5 . . . . 161 A3
Gisburn Cl NG11 . . . . . . 185 A4
Gisburn Gr NG19 . . . . . . 103 B8
Glade Ave NG8 . . . . 172 C5
Glade Hill Prim Sch NG5 161 C8
Gladehill Rd NG5 . . . . . . 161 C7
Glade The NG11 . . . . 195 E7
Gladstone Ave
 Gotham NG11 . . . . 195 B1
 Loughborough LE11 . . . 220 B5
Gladstone Dr NG16 . . . . 143 E7
Gladstone Rd NG24 . . . . 139 F6
Gladstone St
 Beeston NG9 . . . . 183 F6
 Carlton NG4 . . . . 174 D7
 Gainsborough DN21 . . . 15 C1
 Hathern LE12 . . . . 213 A1
 Kirkby in A NG17 . . . . . 115 B5
 Langley Mill NG16 . . . . 143 C4
 Long Eaton NG10 . . . . . 193 D8
 Loughborough LE11 . . . 220 B5
 Mansfield NG18 . . . . . . 102 B5
 Mansfield Woodhouse NG19 88 C2
 Nottingham NG7 . . . . . . 173 A8
 South Normanton DE55 . 113 B6
 Worksop S80 . . . . 35 E3
Gladstone Terr
 1 Kirkby in A NG17 . . 114 F5
 Mansfield Woodhouse NG19 88 C2
Gladys St NG7 . . . . 161 A1
Glaisdale S81 . . . . 36 B7
Glaisdale Dr E NG8 . . . . 171 E6
Glaisdale Drive Ind Est
 NG8 . . . . 171 D6
Glaisdale Dr W NG8 . . . . 171 D5
Glaisdale Parkway NG8 . 171 D5
Glamis Rd
 Carlton in L S81 . . . . . . 25 E6
 Nottingham NG5 . . . . . . 161 A2
Glannis Sq NG20 . . . . 74 C6
Glanton Way NG5 . . . . . 148 A2
Glapton Prim Sch NG11 . 184 D2
Glapton Rd NG2 . . . . 173 C1
Glapton Wood Nature
 Reserve NG11 . . . . 195 D8
Glaramara Cl **1** NG2 . . 173 B1
Glasby Cl NG22 . . . . 77 B4
Glasshouse St NG1 . . . . 223 E3
Glastonbury Cl NG19 . . . 88 D4
Glaven Cl NG19 . . . . 88 D2
Glebe Ave
 Market Warsop NG20 . . . 74 C4
 Pinxton NG16 . . . . 113 D3
Glebe Cl
 North Wheatley DN22 . . 31 E8
 South Normanton DE55 . 113 A5
 Worksop S80 . . . . 35 C3
Glebe Cres DE7 . . . . 170 A2
Glebe Dr NG14 . . . . 163 D3
Glebe Farm Cl NG2 . . . . 185 C4
Glebe Farm View NG4 . . 162 F3
Glebe Jun Sch DE55 . . . 113 A5
Glebe Pk NG24 . . . . 140 C6
Glebe Rd
 Carlton NG4 . . . . 162 C2
 Nuthall NG16 . . . . 159 C6
 West Bridgford NG2 . . . 185 F7
Glebe St
 Annesley Woodhouse
 NG17 . . . . 129 F8
 Beeston NG9 . . . . 183 E6
 Hucknall NG15 . . . . 146 A8
 Loughborough LE11 . . . 220 C5
Glebe The
 Awsworth NG16 . . . . . . 158 B4
 Retford DN22 . . . . 39 D3
Glebe View NG18 . . . . . . 102 E8
Glen Ave NG16 . . . . 144 B1
Glenbrook NG12 . . . . . . 188 A3
Glenbrook Cres NG8 . . . 172 A7
Glenbrook Prim Sch
 NG8 . . . . 171 F7
Glencairn Dr NG8 . . . . . . 172 A8
Glen Cl DE55 . . . . 99 A3
Glencoe Rd NG11 . . . . . . 185 A1
Glencoyne Rd NG11 . . . . 195 E8
Glendale Cl NG4 . . . . 162 D2
Glendale Gdns NG5 . . . . 161 F7
Glendoe Gr NG13 . . . . . . 177 C4
Glendon Dr
 Hucknall NG15 . . . . 146 A5
 Nottingham NG5 . . . . . . 161 A3
Gleneagles Ct NG12 . . . 186 C3

Gleneagles Dr
 Arnold NG5 . . . . 148 B1
 Kirkby in A NG17 . . . . . 114 E7
Glen Eagles Way DN22 . . 39 D3
Glenfield Ave NG16 . . . . 158 D7
Glenfield Rd NG10 . . . . . 193 D5
Glen Helen NG4 . . . . 174 F6
Glenlivet Gdns NG7 . . . . 184 F1
Glenloch Dr NG11 . . . . . 195 F8
Glen Mooar St NG19 . . . . 89 A2
Glenmore Rd NG2 . . . . . 186 B6
Glenorchy Cres NG5 . . . 160 E8
Glen Parva Ave NG5 . . . 147 E1
Glen Rd NG14 . . . . 163 E5
Glenridding Cl NG2 . . . . 186 D5
Glensford Gdns NG5 . . . 146 E2
Glenside
 Arnold NG5 . . . . 162 B5
 Kirkby in A NG17 . . . . . 115 C5
Glenside Rd NG9 . . . . . . 171 C1
Glen St NG17 . . . . 100 E4
Glenthorn Cl S81 . . . . 34 F7
Glenstone Ct **11** NG7 . . 172 F8
Glen The NG7 . . . . 184 F2
Glentworth Rd NG7 . . . . 222 A4
Glenwood Ave NG8 . . . . 171 D3
Glinis Rd NG5 . . . . 160 F8
Glossop Ave NG18 . . . . . 103 B6
Gloucester Ave
 Beeston NG9 . . . . 183 F5
 Nottingham NG7 . . . . . . 222 A2
 Nuthall NG16 . . . . 159 F4
 Sandiacre NG10 . . . . . . 182 A4
Gloucester Rd S81 . . . . . . 36 A7
Glover Ave NG8 . . . . 171 D4
Glovers Cl NG20 . . . . 60 A3
Glovers La NG24 . . . . . . 140 D4
Go Ape! NG21 . . . . 90 D4
Goatchurch Ct **8** NG5 . 147 A1
Goathland Cl **3** NG5 . . 161 B8
Godber Rd NG15 . . . . . . 145 F5
Godfrey's Ct S80 . . . . 35 E3
Godfrey St NG4 . . . . 175 A6
Godkin Dr NG16 . . . . 143 A4
Goldcrest Cl NG13 . . . . . 178 A3
Goldcrest Rd NG6 . . . . . 160 B4
Goldcrest Rise S81 . . . . . 35 C7
Goldenholme La DN22 . . . 43 A1
Goldfinch
 Loughborough LE11 . . . 220 A3
 Mansfield NG18 . . . . . . 102 E7
Goldham Rd NG8 . . . . . . 171 D8
Goldsmith Rd
 Balderton NG24 . . . . . . 140 D5
 Worksop S81 . . . . 36 B5
Goldsmith Sq NG1 . . . . . 223 D3
Goldsmith St
 Mansfield NG18 . . . . . . 102 A4
 Nottingham NG1 . . . . . . 223 D3
Goldstraw La NG24 . . . . 140 E2
Goldswong Terr NG3 . . . 173 C7
Goldthorpe Ave S81 . . . . 16 F3
Goldthorpe Cl S81 . . . . . 16 F3
Golf Club Rd DE7 . . . . . . 170 B1
Golf Course Rd NG12 . . . 198 B2
Golf Rd NG12 . . . . 176 A3
Gomersall Cl DN22 . . . . . 40 A6
Gonalston La
 Epperstone NG14 . . . . . 150 D4
 Hoveringham NG14 . . . 151 D2
Goodacre St NG18 . . . . . 102 C7
Goodall Cres NG15 . . . . 146 C5
Goodall St **1** NG7 . . . . 172 F7
Goodhand Cres NG18 . . 101 E6
Goodliffe St **6** NG7 . . . 172 F8
Goodman Cl NG16 . . . . . 158 C8
Good Shepherd RC Prim Sch
 The NG5 . . . . 162 A5
Goodwin Cl
 Newark-on-T NG24 . . . . 140 D8
 Sandiacre NG10 . . . . . . 182 A6
Goodwin Ct NG22 . . . . . 119 F7
Goodwin Dr NG16 . . . . . 158 E6
Goodwin St NG7 . . . . . . 222 C4
Goodwood Ave NG5 . . . . 161 E8
Goodwood Dr NG9 . . . . . 182 F2
Goodwood Rd NG8 . . . . 171 D4
Goodwood Way NG18 . . 102 F7
Goosedale La NG6 . . . . . 147 A7
Goose Gate
 Cotgrave NG12 . . . . . . 187 E3
 Nottingham NG1 . . . . . . 223 F2
Goosemoor La DN22 . . . . 39 F4
Gopher Rd NG24 . . . . . . 139 F5
Gordon Ave NG18 . . . . . 102 E6
Gordonbrae NG18 . . . . . 102 C3
Gordon Cl
 Beeston NG9 . . . . 183 D2
 Farnsfield NG22 . . . . . . 119 F5
 Worksop S80 . . . . 36 B3
Gordon Cres DE55 . . . . . 113 B4
Gordondale Rd NG19 . . . 88 B1
Gordon Rd
 Burton Joyce NG14 . . . 164 A5
 5 Loughborough LE11 . 220 B6
 Nottingham NG3 . . . . . . 173 F6
 West Bridgford NG2 . . . 185 F7
Gordon Rise NG3 . . . . . . 161 E2
Gordon Sq NG2 . . . . 185 F7
Gordon St
 Gainsborough DN21 . . . 24 D6
 Ilkeston DE7 . . . . 158 A1
 Nottingham NG6 . . . . . . 160 D4
Gorman Cl NG5 . . . . 162 B7
Gorse Ave NG18 . . . . . . 103 A5
Gorse Cl
 Calverton NG14 . . . . . . 148 D7

Gorse Cl continued
 Eastwood NG16 . . . . . . 158 B8
 Long Eaton NG10 . . . . . 182 B2
Gorse Ct NG6 . . . . 160 E5
Gorse Hill NG15 . . . . 117 A1
Gorselands Ave S80 . . . . 36 C1
Gorse Rd
 Keyworth NG12 . . . . . . 197 D3
 Newark-on-T NG24 . . . . 139 F5
Gorseway NG21 . . . . 90 A3
Gorsey Rd NG3 . . . . 173 D8
Gorsy La NG25 . . . . 137 C2
Gosforth Ct NG2 . . . . . . 173 D1
Goshawk Rd DE7 . . . . . . 170 A3
Gotham La NG11 . . . . . . 206 C7
Gotham Prim Sch NG11 . 195 A1
Gotham Rd
 East Leake LE12 . . . . . . 205 E3
 Kingston-on-S NG11 . . . 204 C5
Gothic Cl NG6 . . . . 160 E4
Goverton Hill NG14 . . . . 136 F1
Goverton Sq NG6 . . . . . . 160 D5
Gowan Cl **7** NG9 . . . . 183 C2
Goyden Cl NG5 . . . . 161 A8
Grace Ave NG9 . . . . 184 B6
Grace Dr NG8 . . . . 172 D8
Gracefield La NG23 . . . . . 81 F7
Grafton Ave NG5 . . . . . . 161 E5
Grafton Cl NG17 . . . . 101 B5
Grafton Ct NG7 . . . . 222 C3
Grafton St S80 . . . . 35 E4
Graham Cl NG24 . . . . . . 140 B4
Graham St NG7 . . . . 222 B3
Grainger Ave
 Annesley Woodhouse
 NG17 . . . . 115 B1
 West Bridgford NG2 . . . 185 E3
Grainger St NG2 . . . . . . 173 E2
Graingers Terr NG15 . . . 146 B6
Grampian Dr NG5 . . . . . 147 B2
Grampian Way NG10 . . . 193 A8
Granary Cl DN21 . . . . 15 B5
Granary Ct S81 . . . . 26 A6
Granby Ave
 Mansfield NG18 . . . . . . 102 B8
 Newark-on-T NG24 . . . . 140 B6
Granby Ct NG13 . . . . 177 C5
Granby Dr
 Balderton NG24 . . . . . . 140 D3
 Bottesford NG13 . . . . . 181 A2
Granby Hill NG13 . . . . . . 191 B5
Granby La
 Plungar NG13 . . . . 191 F1
 Whatton NG13 . . . . 178 D1
Granby St
 Ilkeston DE7 . . . . 157 E2
 Loughborough LE11 . . . 220 A4
Grandfield Ave NG12 . . . 175 F4
Grandfield Cres NG12 . . 175 F4
Grange Ave
 Bawtry DN10 . . . . 9 F8
 Beeston NG9 . . . . 183 F6
 Mansfield NG18 . . . . . . 101 F5
 Misterton DN10 . . . . 14 A8
 Newark-on-T NG24 . . . . 139 E4
 Ollerton NG22 . . . . 77 B3
 Ruddington NG11 . . . . . 196 C8
Grange Cl
 Carlton in L S81 . . . . . . 26 A6
 Lambley NG4 . . . . 163 C7
 Misterton DN10 . . . . 14 A8
 Nottingham NG11 . . . . . 185 B8
Grange Cres NG4 . . . . . . 162 F3
Grange Ct
 Kirkby in A NG17 . . . . . 115 D5
 West Bridgford NG2 . . . 185 C2
Grange Dr
 Harworth DN11 . . . . 9 A5
 Long Eaton NG10 . . . . . 193 F8
 Misterton DN10 . . . . 14 A8
Grange Farm Cl NG9 . . . 183 A1
Grange La NG24 . . . . . . 155 A4
Grangelea Gdns NG9 . . . 183 B8
Grange Pk
 Cropwell Butler NG12 . . 189 A7
 Gainsborough DN21 . . . 15 B5
 West Bridgford NG2 . . . 186 C5
Grange Prim Sch NG10 . 193 F8
Granger Ct **4** LE11 . . . 220 A4
Grange Rd
 Arnold NG5 . . . . 161 E4
 Blidworth NG21 . . . . . . 118 B5
 Long Eaton NG10 . . . . . 193 F8
 Nottingham NG6 . . . . . . 160 D3
 Retford DN22 . . . . 39 E3
 West Bridgford NG2 . . . 186 A4
Grange The
 North Muskham NG23 . . 110 F3
 Retford DN22 . . . . 39 E3
 South Normanton DE55 . 113 A4
Grange View
 Eastwood NG16 . . . . . . 143 F3
 Harworth DN11 . . . . 9 A5
Grange View Rd NG4 . . . 163 A2
Grange Wlk DN10 . . . . 7 A1
Grangewood Ct NG8 . . . 171 C3
Grangewood Rd
 3 Kirkby in A NG17 . . 114 F7
 Nottingham NG8 . . . . . . 171 C3
Grannis Dr NG8 . . . . 172 A8
Grantham Cl NG16 . . . . . 158 C7
Grantham Rd
 Bingham NG13 . . . . 178 B3
 Bottesford NG13 . . . . . 181 D2
 Radcliffe on T NG4 . . . . 175 F2
Grantleigh Cl NG8 . . . . . 171 C6
Granton Ave NG11 . . . . . 195 F8
Granton Rise NG19 . . . . 101 D5

Grant St NG7 . . . . 222 B3
Granville Ave NG10 . . . 182 D1
Granville Cres NG12 . . . . 175 E2
Granville Ct 4 NG3 . . . 173 F6
Granville Gr 4 NG3 . . . 173 F5
Granville St LE11 . . . . . . 220 A4
Grasmere Cl
  Gainsborough DN21 . . . . 15 E2
  Hucknall NG15 . . . . 145 F8
Grasmere Rd
  Beeston NG9 . . . . 183 D8
  Long Eaton NG10 . . . . . 182 B2
  Worksop S81 . . . . 35 F7
Grasmere St NG10 . . . . . 182 C5
Grassingdale Cl NG4 . . . 162 D2
Grassington Rd NG8 . . . 172 D7
Grassmere NG12 . . . . . . 188 A3
Grass St DE7 . . . . 157 E3
Grassthorpe Rd NG23 . . . 81 E2
Grassy La NG9 . . . . 184 A5
Gratton Ct 1 NG17 . . . . 114 F7
Gravelholes La DN10 . . . . 6 E1
Gravel La NG22 . . . . 79 D7
Gravelly Hollow NG14 . . 133 A1
Gravelly La NG25 . . . . . . 137 E3
Gravel Pit La DE7 . . . . . . 50 F1
Graveney Gdns NG5 . . . . 162 C6
Graves Moor La S81 . . . . 18 E2
Gray Fallow DE55 . . . . . 113 B4
Gray La NG22 . . . . 120 E1
Graylands Rd NG8 . . . . . 171 E6
Grays Dr NG15 . . . . 132 B6
Grayson Ms NG9 . . . . . . 183 B2
Gray St LE11 . . . . 220 B2
Graystones Cl NG2 . . . . . 186 C5
Grazingfield NG11 . . . . . 185 A4
Greasley Ave NG16 . . . . 144 C2
Greasley Beauvale DH
  Lawrence Inf Sch
  NG16 . . . . 144 B3
Greasley Beauvale Jun Sch
  NG16 . . . . 144 B2
Greasley Ct NG18 . . . . . 103 B3
Greasley St NG6 . . . . . . 160 B7
Great Central Rd
  Loughborough LE11 . . . . 220 C3
  Mansfield NG18 . . . . . . 102 C6
Great Central Rly LE11 . . 220 C2
Great Central Sta LE11 . . 220 C3
Great Freeman St NG3 . . 223 E4
Great Hoggett Dr NG9 . . 183 B6
Great La NG22 . . . . 65 F7
Great Northern Cl The
  NG2 . . . . 223 F1
Great Northern Rd NG16 143 D2
Great Northern Way
  NG4 . . . . 175 B6
Great N Rd
  Balderton NG23, NG24 . . . 155 F5
  Barnby Moor DN22 . . . . 28 C5
  Bircotes DN10 . . . . 9 F5
  Carlton-on-T NG23 . . . . 96 F6
  Claypole NG24 . . . . 155 F7
  Eaton DN22 . . . . 40 A2
  Gamston DN22 . . . . 51 A4
  North Muskham NG23 . . 110 F5
  Ranskill DN22 . . . . 19 B3
  Scrooby DN10 . . . . 10 A2
  South Muskham NG23,
    NG24 . . . . 124 D5
  West Markham NG22 . . . 65 C6
  Weston NG23 . . . . 81 C3
Greaves Ave LE14 . . . . . 219 C6
Greaves Cl
  Arnold NG5 . . . . 162 B5
  Newark-on-T NG24 . . . . 140 D8
  Nottingham NG8 . . . . . . 159 D1
Greaves La NG22 . . . . . . 120 B3
Grebe Cl NG24 . . . . 140 C5
Greek St NG7 . . . . 222 C3
Greenacre
  Burton Joyce NG14 . . . . 163 E5
  Mansfield NG18 . . . . . . 102 E6
  Stanton Hill NG17 . . . . 100 C5
Green Acre
  Nottingham NG8 . . . . . . 171 B5
  West Bridgford NG2 . . . 186 B4
Greenacre Ave S81 . . . . . 36 A6
Greenacre Rd S81 . . . . . 36 A6
Greenacres NG17 . . . . . . 115 B2
Greenacres Cl NG16 . . . . 144 C2
Greenacres Dr DE55 . . . 113 B6
Green Ap NG4 . . . . 174 C8
Green Ave NG4 . . . . 175 A7
Greenbank NG4 . . . . 174 D6
Green Bank NG21 . . . . . 118 C8
Greenbank Dr NG17 . . . . 100 E5
Greenburn Cl NG2 . . . . . 186 D6
Green Cl
  Blidworth NG21 . . . . . . 118 A4
  Hucknall NG15 . . . . . . 146 C5
  Keyworth NG12 . . . . . . 197 F4
  Newton DE55 . . . . 99 A3
Greenclose La 9 LE11 . . 220 A4
Green Cres NG16 . . . . . . 128 F6
Greencroft NG11 . . . . . . 184 F2
Greendale Ave NG21 . . . . 76 A3
Greendale Cl
  Market Warsop NG20 . . . 74 A4
  Stanton Hill NG17 . . . . 100 C6
Greendale Cres NG21 . . . 90 B4
Greendale Gdns NG8 . . . 172 B8
Greendale Rd
  Arnold NG5 . . . . 161 F6
  Nottingham NG3 . . . . . . 174 C6
Green Dr NG25 . . . . 137 F3
Green Farm Rd NG16 . . . 128 D6
Greenfield Ave S80 . . . . . 45 C6

Greenfield Cl
  Edwinstowe NG21 . . . . . 91 B8
  Mansfield Woodhouse NG19 89 B3
Greenfield Com Prim Sch
  NG2 . . . . 173 D1
Greenfield Gr NG4 . . . . . 174 C8
Greenfields NG16 . . . . . . 143 A4
Greenfields Cres NG12 . . 77 C4
Greenfields Dr NG12 . . . 187 F2
Greenfield St NG7 . . . . . 172 D1
Greenfield Way 2 S81 . . . 25 F7
Greenfinch Dale S81 . . . . 35 C7
Greenford Ct NG16 . . . . 159 E3
Greengate NG23 . . . . . . 153 A4
Greengate Rd DN22 . . . . 53 B4
Greengates Ave NG3 . . . 161 F3
Green Hill LE12 . . . . 213 A1
Greenhill Cres NG4 . . . . 174 E6
Greenhill La NG17 . . . . . 129 F8
Greenhill Rd NG4 . . . . . 174 E6
Greenhill Rise NG4 . . . . 174 E7
Green Hill Rise LE12 . . . 213 A1
Greenhills Ave NG16 . . . 144 A4
Greenhills Rd NG16 . . . . 143 F3
Greenholme Cl NG17 . . . 115 A4
Greenholme Pk NG19 . . . 88 E6
Greenholme Sch NG7 . . . 222 A1
Green Inf Sch The DE55 . 113 A7
Green La
  Babworth DN22 . . . . . . 38 E5
  Bathley NG23 . . . . 110 B2
  Bottesford NG13 . . . . . 181 C1
  Collingham NG23 . . . . . 112 B7
  Darlton NG22 . . . . 67 C4
  Dry Doddington NG23 . . 156 E2
  Eagle LN6 . . . . 84 F4
  Granby NG13 . . . . 191 B5
  Harby LE14 . . . . 202 C2
  Hodthorpe S80 . . . . 45 C5
  Ilkeston DE7 . . . . 170 A7
  Lambley NG4 . . . . 149 B1
  Laxton NG22 . . . . 79 D1
  Lea DN21 . . . . 24 F1
  Mansfield, Moorhaigh NG19 87 A2
  Mansfield NG18 . . . . . . 102 C3
  Nottingham NG7 . . . . . . 184 E1
  Pleasley S44 . . . . 86 D8
  Ranskill DN10 . . . . 18 F8
  South Leverton DN22 . . . 42 D6
  Upper Broughton LE14 . . 210 A4
  Walesby NG22 . . . . 64 A2
Greenland Cres NG9 . . . 183 C4
Greenland Rd NG17 . . . . 100 E7
Green Leys NG2 . . . . 185 C4
Green Mile La DN22 . . . . 38 E3
Green Platt NG12 . . . . . . 187 E3
Green Rd DN10 . . . . 13 A2
Greens Ct DE7 . . . . 157 D1
Green's Farm La NG4 . . . 163 A2
Greensfields NG17 . . . . . 101 A5
Greenside Ave DN22 . . . . 42 F2
Greenside Cl NG10 . . . . . 193 E2
Greens La NG16 . . . . . . 159 A6
Greensquare Rd NG16 . . 113 E2
Green St
  Barton in F NG11 . . . . . 195 A7
  Nottingham NG2 . . . . . . 173 D1
Green The
  Barkestone-le-V NG13 . . . 192 B2
  Beeston NG9 . . . . 183 E4
  Bilsthorpe NG22 . . . . . 105 F7
  Carlton in L S81 . . . . . 26 A6
  Coddington NG24 . . . . . 126 B2
  Collingham NG23 . . . . . 111 F7
  East Leake LE12 . . . . . 205 E1
  Elston NG23 . . . . 153 A4
  Gainsborough DN21 . . . . 24 F7
  Glapwell S44 . . . . 86 B8
  Hardstoft S45 . . . . 85 A4
  Harworth DN11 . . . . 8 E4
  Hathern LE12 . . . . 213 A1
  Hose LE14 . . . . 211 F7
  Huthwaite NG17 . . . . . 99 F1
  Kingston-on-S LE12 . . . 204 A4
  Kirklington NG22 . . . . . 120 F8
  Long Whatton LE12 . . . 212 C3
  Lowdham NG14 . . . . . . 149 F2
  Mansfield Woodhouse NG19 88 A3
  Orston NG13 . . . . 179 F7
  Radcliffe on T NG12 . . . 175 E3
Greentrees Ct NG17 . . . . 100 D1
Greenvale NG12 . . . . . . 120 A6
Greenview Cl NG19 . . . . . 89 B3
Greenway
  Carlton in L S81 . . . . . 26 A6
  Clipstone NG19 . . . . . . 89 D3
  Newark-on-T NG24 . . . . 139 E6
  Retford DN22 . . . . 39 D3
Greenway Cl NG12 . . . . . 175 E3
Greenwich Ave NG6 . . . 160 C4
Greenwich Pk Cl NG2 . . . 185 C5
Green Wlk NG13 . . . . . . 178 F4
Greenwood Ave
  Edwinstowe NG21 . . . . . 76 B2
  Harworth DN11 . . . . 8 F5
  Hucknall NG15 . . . . . . 145 F8
  Huthwaite NG17 . . . . . 99 F2
  Ilkeston DE7 . . . . 170 A4
  Mansfield Woodhouse NG19 88 B4
  Nottingham NG3 . . . . . . 174 D5
Greenwood Cl
  Carlton in L S81 . . . . . 25 D1
  Farnsfield NG22 . . . . . . 120 A6
  Worksop S80 . . . . 35 D8
Greenwood Cotts NG18 . . 102 F6
Greenwood Craft Ctr
Greenwood Cres
  Boughton NG22 . . . . . . 77 E5
  Carlton NG4 . . . . 174 E6
Greenwood Dale Tech Sch
  NG2 . . . . 174 A4
Greenwood Dr NG17 . . . 114 F5
Greenwood Gdns NG11 . . 196 D6
Greenwood Inf Sch NG2 . 174 A5
Greenwood Jun Sch
  NG2 . . . . 174 A4
Greenwood Prim Sch
  NG17 . . . . 114 E6
Greenwood Rd NG3 . . . . 174 C5
Greenwood Vale NG15 . . 145 F8
Greer La S44 . . . . 86 D8
Greet Park Cl NG25 . . . . 121 F1
Greetwell Cl 1 NG8 . . . . 172 A6
Gregory Ave
  Aldercar NG16 . . . . 143 A4
  Nottingham, New Lenton
    NG7 . . . . 222 B1
  Nottingham, Portchester
    NG3 . . . . 162 A2
Gregory Bvd NG7 . . . . . 173 A7
Gregory Cl NG9 . . . . 182 F8
Gregory Cres DN11 . . . . . 8 E4
Gregory Ct
  Beeston NG9 . . . . 183 B4
  Nottingham NG7 . . . . . . 222 A1
Gregory Gdns NG22 . . . . 119 F5
Gregory St
  9 Ilkeston DE7 . . . . . . 157 E1
  6 Loughborough LE11 . . 220 B3
  Nottingham NG7 . . . . . . 172 C2
Gregson Gdns NG9 . . . . 183 B1
Gregson Rd NG9 . . . . . . 183 B2
Grendon Way NG17 . . . . 101 B5
Grenville Dr
  Ilkeston DE7 . . . . 157 F3
  Stapleford NG9 . . . . . . 182 E8
Grenville Rd NG9 . . . . . . 184 B4
Grenville Rise NG5 . . . . 147 F1
Gresham Cl
  Newark-on-T NG24 . . . . 140 E8
  West Bridgford NG2 . . . 185 C7
Gresham Gdns
  Arnold NG5 . . . . 162 A5
  West Bridgford NG2 . . . 185 D7
Gresley Ave DN10 . . . . . 10 A8
Gresley Dr NG2 . . . . 173 F3
Gresley Rd
  11 Ilkeston DE7 . . . . . . 157 F1
  Retford DN22 . . . . 39 D5
Greta N Rd NG23 . . . . . . 96 F3
Gretton Cl NG23 . . . . . . 156 C6
Gretton Rd NG3 . . . . . . 162 A4
Greyfriar Gate NG1 . . . . 223 E1
Greyhound St NG1 . . . . . 223 E2
Greys Rd NG5 . . . . 161 F4
Grey St
  Eastwood NG16 . . . . . . 144 A1
  Gainsborough DN21 . . . . 15 B2
  Kirkby in A NG17 . . . . . 114 D5
Greystoke Dr NG8 . . . . . 171 C7
Greystones Rd DN21 . . . 15 B3
Greythorn Dr NG2 . . . . . 185 D4
Greythorn Prim Sch
  NG2 . . . . 185 D5
Griceson Cl NG22 . . . . . 77 B2
Grierson Ave NG5 . . . . . 161 B8
Griffs Hollow NG4 . . . . . 174 E7
Grimesmoor Rd NG14 . . 149 A8
Grimsby Terr NG3 . . . . . 223 E4
Grimston Rd NG7 . . . . . 222 A4
Grindon Cres NG6 . . . . . 146 C2
Gringley Rd
  Clayworth DN22 . . . . . . 21 E6
  Misterton DN10 . . . . . . 6 E1
  Walkeringham DN10 . . . 13 E4
Grinsbrook NG7 . . . . . . 222 A2
Gripps Comm NG12 . . . . 187 F1
Grisedale Ct NG9 . . . . . 183 A4
Gritley Mews NG2 . . . . . 173 B2
Grives La NG17 . . . . 115 B2
Grizedale Cl NG19 . . . . . 103 A8
Grizedale Gr NG13 . . . . 177 B4
Grizedale Rd NG3 . . . . . 103 A8
Grosvenor Ave
  Long Eaton NG10 . . . . . 193 A4
  Nottingham NG3 . . . . . . 161 C1
  Sutton in A NG17 . . . . . 100 D2
Grosvenor Cl NG12 . . . . 176 D3
Grosvenor Rd
  Bircotes DN11 . . . . 9 B4
  Eastwood NG16 . . . . . . 143 F2
  New Balderton NG24 . . . 140 B4
Grosvenor Sch NG16 . . . 186 A4
Grouville Dr NG5 . . . . . . 162 A5
Grove Ave
  Beeston NG9 . . . . 183 E6
  Nottingham NG7 . . . . . . 222 C4
Grove Cl NG14 . . . . 163 F5
Grove Coach Rd DN22 . . 40 B4
Grove La DN22 . . . . 40 B6
Grove Mews NG16 . . . . . 143 E1
Grove Pk DN10 . . . . 6 F1
Grover Ave NG3 . . . . 162 A3
Grove Rd
  Church Warsop NG20 . . . 74 A6
  Grove DN22 . . . . 41 C6
  Nottingham NG7 . . . . . . 222 B1
  Retford DN22 . . . . 40 C3
Grove Sch The NG24 . . . 140 C5
Groveside Cres NG11 . . . 184 C3
Grove Sports Ctr NG24 . . 140 C5
Grove St
  Beeston NG9 . . . . 184 A5

Grove St continued
  6 Mansfield NG18 . . . . . 102 B6
  Mansfield Woodhouse NG19 88 B3
  New Balderton NG24 . . . 140 B5
  Retford DN22 . . . . 39 F7
Grove The
  Beckingham DN10 . . . . . 14 B1
  Calverton NG14 . . . . . . 149 A7
  Newton on T LN1 . . . . . 55 A1
  Nottingham NG5, Carrington
    NG5 . . . . 161 B2
  Nottingham NG7 . . . . . . 222 B4
Groveview Rd NG24 . . . . 140 C5
Grove Way NG19 . . . . . . 88 B3
Grove Wood Rd DN10 . . . 6 F1
Grove Wood Terr DN10 . . 6 F1
Grundy Ave LE16 . . . . . . 128 D2
Grundy Nook S80 . . . . . . 45 A5
Grundy St NG7 . . . . 172 E7
Guildford Ave NG19 . . . . 88 C6
Guildhall St NG24 . . . . . 140 A8
Guinea Cl NG10 . . . . . . 193 A7
Gunn Cl NG6 . . . . 160 A7
Gunnersbury Way NG8 . . 159 E3
Gunthorpe CE Prim Sch
  NG14 . . . . 165 A5
Gunthorpe Cl NG5 . . . . . 161 B3
Gunthorpe Ct NG18 . . . . 103 B3
Gunthorpe Dr NG5 . . . . . 161 B3
Gunthorpe Rd
  Carlton NG4 . . . . 162 D3
  Lowdham NG14 . . . . . . 164 E8
  West Stockwith DN9 . . . . 7 E8
Gutersloh Ct NG9 . . . . . 182 F8
Guy Cl NG9 . . . . 182 E6
Guylers Hill Dr NG21 . . . 89 F2
Gwenbrook Ave NG9 . . . 183 B5
Gwenbrook Rd NG9 . . . . 183 B5
Gwndy Gdns 3 NG5 . . . . 161 A7
Gypsum Way NG11 . . . . 205 A7

H

Habblesthorpe Cl DN22 . . 32 E1
Habblesthorpe Rd DN22 . . 32 E1
Hackers Cl NG13 . . . . . . 165 C3
Hackworth Cl NG16 . . . . 144 B3
Hadbury Rd NG5 . . . . . . 160 F3
Hadden Ct NG8 . . . . 171 D5
Hadden Pk High Sch
  NG8 . . . . 172 A4
Hadderley Wlk NG3 . . . . 223 F4
Haddon Cl
  Carlton NG4 . . . . 162 D2
  Hucknall NG15 . . . . . . 146 A6
  Selston NG16 . . . . 129 B7
Haddon Cres NG9 . . . . . 183 C2
Haddon Dr NG24 . . . . . . 140 D3
Haddon Nurseries DE7 . . 157 E3
Haddon Pl NG20 . . . . . . 72 D7
Haddon Prim Sch NG4 . . 162 D2
Haddon Rd
  Mansfield NG18 . . . . . . 102 B8
  Ravenshead NG15 . . . . 117 A3
  Retford DN22 . . . . 40 B4
  West Bridgford NG2 . . . 185 F6
Haddon St
  Ilkeston DE7 . . . . 157 E3
  Nottingham NG5 . . . . . . 161 B2
  Sutton in A NG17 . . . . . 100 E4
  Tibshelf DE55 . . . . 99 A6
Haddon Way NG12 . . . . . 176 A4
Hades La LE12 . . . . 217 D5
Hadfield Wlk NG18 . . . . 103 B6
Hadleigh Cl NG9 . . . . . . 182 E2
Hadley St DE7 . . . . 170 A5
Hadrian Gdns NG5 . . . . . 147 A2
Hadstock Cl NG10 . . . . . 182 B4
Hagg La
  Bawtry DN10 . . . . 10 E8
  Egmanton NG22 . . . . . . 80 A5
  Epperstone NG14 . . . . . 150 B5
Haggonfields Prim Sch
  S80 . . . . 35 A4
Hagley Cl NG3 . . . . 174 A6
Haileybury Cres NG2 . . . 185 F5
Haileybury Rd NG2 . . . . 185 F5
Hainton Cl DN21 . . . . . . 24 E7
Haise Ct NG6 . . . . 159 F5
Halam CE Prim Sch
  NG22 . . . . 120 F2
Halam Cl NG19 . . . . 101 D7
Halam Hill NG22 . . . . . . 121 A1
Halberton Dr NG2 . . . . . 185 D4
Haldane St DN21 . . . . . . 15 B1
Hales Cl NG12 . . . . 187 E3
Haley Cl NG16 . . . . 158 D6
Halfmoon Dr NG17 . . . . 115 B3
Halifax Ct NG8 . . . . 159 D2
Halifax Dr S81 . . . . 35 E8
Halifax Pl NG1 . . . . 223 E2
Hallam Fields Rd DE7 . . . 170 B4
Hallam Rd
  Beeston NG9 . . . . 183 F6
  Nottingham NG3 . . . . . . 162 A2
Hallams La NG9 . . . . . . 183 D5
Hallam's La NG17 . . . . . 161 F7
Hallamway NG18 . . . . . . 88 C1
Hall Barn La NG19 . . . . . 101 D8
Hall Cl
  Radcliffe on T NG12 . . . 175 E3
  Rainworth NG21 . . . . . 118 B8
Hall Cl The NG22 . . . . . . 66 A7
Hall Croft NG9 . . . . 183 F5
Hallcroft Ave DN22 . . . . 39 E8
Hallcroft Ind Est DN22 . . 29 D2
Hallcroft Inf Sch DN22 . . 29 C1

Hallcroft Rd DN22 . . . . . 29 D2
Hall Dr
  Beeston NG9 . . . . 183 D5
  Clayworth DN22 . . . . . . 21 D5
  Cropwell Bishop NG12 . . 189 A4
  Gotham NG11 . . . . 195 A1
  Nottingham NG8 . . . . . . 171 E3
  Sandiacre NG10 . . . . . . 182 B6
  Worksop S80 . . . . 35 D2
Hallfield Rd DE55 . . . . . . 99 A3
Hallfields NG12 . . . . 186 B3
Hall Gdns
  Beeston NG9 . . . . 183 B7
  East Leake LE12 . . . . . 214 F8
Hall Grounds NG12 . . . . 200 C7
Hall Grounds Dr NG12 . . 200 C8
Halliday Cl S80 . . . . 35 D3
Hallifax Ave NG20 . . . . . 74 B7
Halliwell Cl NG24 . . . . . 125 B4
Hall La
  Brinsley NG16 . . . . 143 D6
  Colston Bassett NG12 . . 200 C6
  East Markham NG22 . . . 66 A7
  Kinoulton NG12 . . . . . . 200 A3
  Newton DE55 . . . . 99 A3
Halloughton Rd NG25 . . . 136 D7
Hallowell Dr NG8 . . . . . 171 F5
Hall Rd NG16 . . . . 143 C4
Halls Brook LE12 . . . . . . 205 E2
Halls La NG16 . . . . 158 A8
Halls Rd NG9 . . . . 182 D6
Hall's Rd DN10 . . . . 13 A3
Hall St
  Mansfield NG18 . . . . . . 102 E6
  Nottingham NG5 . . . . . . 161 D3
  Sutton in A NG17 . . . . . 100 E6
Hallum Ct DE7 . . . . 157 F3
Hall View
  Mattersey DN10 . . . . . . 20 B7
  Worksop S80 . . . . 35 D2
Hall View Dr NG8 . . . . . 171 D6
Halstead Cl
  Beeston NG9 . . . . 183 C4
  Mansfield Woodhouse NG19 88 F2
  Nottingham NG8 . . . . . . 160 B3
Haltham Gn 2 DN21 . . . . 24 F8
Haltham Wlk NG11 . . . . 195 D8
Hamble Cl NG19 . . . . . . 88 D3
Hambledon Dr NG8 . . . . 172 B5
Hambleton Cl NG10 . . . . 182 A1
Hambleton Ct S81 . . . . . 25 E7
Hambling Cl NG6 . . . . . . 160 A7
Hamilton Cl
  Arnold NG5 . . . . 148 C1
  Beeston NG9 . . . . 182 F2
Hamilton Dr
  Market Warsop NG20 . . . 74 A4
  Nottingham NG7 . . . . . . 223 D1
  Radcliffe on T NG12 . . . 175 F4
Hamilton Gdns 11 NG5 . . 161 B1
Hamilton Rd
  Long Eaton NG10 . . . . . 182 D1
  Nottingham NG5 . . . . . . 173 B8
  Sutton in A NG17 . . . . . 101 C2
Hamilton St
  Mansfield NG18 . . . . . . 102 E6
  Worksop S81 . . . . 35 E6
Hamlet La DE55 . . . . . . 113 A5
Hamlet The DE55 . . . . . 113 A5
Hammersmith Cl
  Nuthall NG16 . . . . 159 E4
  Radcliffe on T NG12 . . . 176 D2
Hammerwater Dr NG20 . . 74 A3
Hammond Gr NG17 . . . . 115 B2
Hampden Gr NG9 . . . . . 183 E6
Hampdens Cl NG24 . . . . 125 E2
Hampden St
  Eastwood NG16 . . . . . . 158 B8
  Kirkby in A NG17 . . . . . 114 F5
  Nottingham NG1 . . . . . . 223 D3
Hampshire Ct NG16 . . . . 128 B4
Hampshire Dr NG10 . . . . 182 B5
Hampstead Rd NG3 . . . . 161 E1
Hampton Cl NG9 . . . . . . 182 E3
Hampton Rd NG2 . . . . . 185 E6
Hanbury Ct NG18 . . . . . 103 B6
Handel House Sch DN21 . 15 D1
Handel St NG3 . . . . 173 E5
Handley Arc 5 NG18 . . . 102 B7
Handley Ct NG24 . . . . . . 124 F1
Hand's Rd DE75 . . . . . . 143 A1
Hand's Wlk NG13 . . . . . 181 A2
Hanford Way LE11 . . . . . 220 B5
Hangar Hill S80 . . . . 45 A6
Hankin Ave NG16 . . . . . 129 A2
Hankin St NG15 . . . . . . 146 C6
Hanley Ave NG9 . . . . . . 183 B8
Hanley St NG1 . . . . 223 D3
Hannah Cres NG11 . . . . 185 B7
Hannam's Yd DN22 . . . . 39 D7
Hanover Ct NG8 . . . . . . 171 D6
Hanslope Cres NG8 . . . . 171 D7
Hanson Cres NG15 . . . . 146 A4
Hanstubbin Rd NG16 . . . 128 C6
Hanworth Gdns NG5 . . . 161 D8
Harberton Cl NG5 . . . . . 147 E1
Harby Ave
  Mansfield Woodhouse
    NG19 . . . . 88 D5
  Sutton in A NG17 . . . . . 101 C1
Harby Cl NG24 . . . . 140 D3
Harby Dr NG8 . . . . 172 C4
Harby La
  Colston Bassett NG12 . . 200 F6
  Hose LE14 . . . . 211 F7

Harby La continued
  Plungar LE14 . . . . **202** F3
Harby Rd NG13 . . . . **190** D1
Harcourt Cl DE7 . . . . . . **157** D1
Harcourt Cres NG16 . . . **159** F3
Harcourt Pl DN22 . . . . . . **40** A4
Harcourt Rd NG7 . . . . . **173** A8
Harcourt St
  Beeston NG9 . . . . **183** E6
  Kirkby in A NG17 . . . . . **115** A5
  Mansfield NG18 . . . . . . **102** D6
  Newark-on-T NG24 . . . . **140** B7
Harcourt Terr NG3 . . . . **223** F3
Harden Cl NG11 . . . . . . **195** C8
Hardie Ave DE55 . . . . . **113** A6
Hardigate Rd NG12. . . . **189** A8
Hardstaff Cl
  Annesley Woodhouse
  NG17 . . . . **114** E1
  Retford DN22 . . . . **29** C1
Hardstaff Rd NG2 . . . . . **174** A4
Hardwick Ave
  Mansfield NG21 . . . . . . **103** F1
  Newark-on-T NG24 . . . . **139** F7
  Shirebrook NG20 . . . . . . **72** E4
  Sutton in A NG17 . . . . . **101** A6
Hardwick Cl
  Saxilby LN1 . . . . **56** F4
  Sutton in A NG17 . . . . . **101** A6
Hardwick Cres S80 . . . . **36** B2
Hardwick Ct DN11 . . . . . . **9** B5
Hardwick Dr
  Ollerton NG22 . . . . **77** A3
  Selston NG16 . . . . **129** B7
Hardwicke Rd NG9 . . . . **183** C3
Hardwick Gr
  Nottingham NG7 . . . . . . **222** B2
  West Bridgford NG2 . . . **173** F1
Hardwick Hall S44 . . . . . **85** E4
Hardwick Hall Ctry Pk
  S44 . . . . **85** F5
Hardwick La NG17 . . . . **100** F2
Hardwick Old Hall S44 . . **85** E4
Hardwick Pk Nature Wlk
  S44 . . . . **85** C4
Hardwick Rd
  1 Nottingham, Carrington
  NG5 . . . . **161** C3
  Nottingham, The Park NG7 **222** C1
Hardwick Rd E S80 . . . . **36** B2
Hardwick Rd W S80 . . . . **36** B2
Hardwick St
  Langwith NG20 . . . . **72** F8
  Mansfield NG18 . . . . . . **102** D7
  Shirebrook NG20 . . . . . . **73** A4
  Sutton in A NG17 . . . . . **100** F2
  Tibshelf DE55 . . . . **99** A7
Hardwick View NG17 . . . **101** A6
Hardwood Cl
  1 Nottingham NG6. . . . **159** F7
  Nottingham NG6 . . . . . . **159** F7
Hardy Barn DE75 . . . . . **157** A7
Hardy Cl
  Kimberley NG16 . . . . . . **158** F7
  Long Eaton NG10 . . . . . **193** D6
Hardy Pl NG18 . . . . **101** F6
Hardys Cl NG12 . . . . . . **189** B4
Hardy's Dr NG4 . . . . . . **162** F1
Hardy St
  Kimberley NG16 . . . . . . **158** F7
  Nottingham NG7 . . . . . . **222** C4
  Worksop S80 . . . . **35** E3
Harefield LE12 . . . . **205** E3
Hareholme St NG18 . . . . **102** A8
Harewood Ave
  Newark-on-T NG24 . . . . **139** F7
  Nottingham NG6 . . . . . . **160** D5
  Retford DN22 . . . . **39** C5
Harewood Cl
  Radcliffe on T NG12 . . . **176** A3
  Sandiacre NG10. . . . . . **182** B4
Harewood Ct DN11 . . . . . . **9** B5
Harewood Dr DN10 . . . . **10** A8
Harewood Rd S81 . . . . . **35** F7
Hargon La NG24 . . . . . . **125** D6
Harkstead Rd NG5 . . . . **147** B1
Harlaxton Dr
  Long Eaton NG10 . . . . . **194** A8
  Nottingham NG7 . . . . . . **222** B2
Harlaxton Wlk NG3 . . . . **223** E4
Harlech Cl DE7 . . . . **157** C3
Harlech Rise NG9 . . . . . **183** B4
Harlequin Cl NG12 . . . . **176** B3
Harlequin Ct NG16 . . . . **143** D3
Harles Acres LE14 . . . . **210** C6
Harley Cl S80 . . . . **46** E8
Harley Gall The S80 . . . . **45** E1
Harley St NG2 . . . . **222** B1
Harlow Ave NG18 . . . . . **102** C3
Harlow Cl
  Mansfield Woodhouse
  NG19 . . . . **88** C6
  Sutton in A NG17 . . . . . **100** F6
Harlow Gr NG4 . . . . **162** E2
Harlow St NG21 . . . . . . **118** B5
Harmston Rise NG5 . . . . **160** F4
Harold Ave NG16 . . . . . **143** B4
Harold St NG2 . . . . **173** E4
Harpenden Sq NG8 . . . . **160** B3
Harpham Rd DN21 . . . . . **44** B8
Harpole Wlk NG5 . . . . . **147** F2
Harrier Gr NG15 . . . . . . **145** E4
Harriers Gr NG17 . . . . . **101** B4
Harriett St NG9 . . . . . . **182** D7
Harrimans La NG7 . . . . **184** E8

Harrington Cl NG4 . . . . **163** B1
Harrington Dr NG7 . . . . **222** B2
Harrington Jun Sch
  NG10. . . . . **182** B1
Harrington St
  Long Eaton NG10. . . . . **193** B5
  Mansfield NG18. . . . . . **102** A6
  Worksop S80 . . . . **35** D2
Harris Cl NG8 . . . . **171** F5
Harrison Ct NG13 . . . . . **177** C4
Harrison Dr S81 . . . . . . **16** E3
Harrison Rd
  Mansfield NG18 . . . . . . **101** E6
  Stapleford NG9 . . . . . . **182** D8
Harrison's Plantation Nature
  Reserve NG8 . . . . . . **171** F5
Harris Rd NG9 . . . . **183** D6
Harrogate Rd NG3 . . . . **174** C5
Harrogate St NG4 . . . . . **174** F7
Harrop White Rd NG19 . **101** F8
Harrow Cl
  Gainsborough DN21 . . . . **15** F2
  Rainworth NG21 . . . . . . **118** A8
Harrow Dr DE7 . . . . **170** A4
Harrow Gdns NG8. . . . . **172** C4
Harrow La NG22 . . . . . . **77** F5
Harrow Rd
  Hucknall NG15. . . . . . . **145** D5
  Nottingham NG8 . . . . . . **172** B4
  West Bridgford NG2 . . . **185** E5
Harstoft Ave S81. . . . . . **35** F5
Hart Ave NG10 . . . . **182** A5
Hartcroft Rd NG5 . . . . . **161** B6
Hartford Cl 2 NG2. . . . **173** D2
Harthill Cl 10 NG9. . . . . **183** C2
Hartill Dr NG19 . . . . **101** D5
Hartington Ave
  Carlton NG4. . . . . **162** D1
  Hucknall NG15. . . . . . . **145** C6
Hartington Ct NG18 . . . . **103** B6
Hartington Dr
  Selston NG16. . . . . **129** A7
  Sutton in A NG17 . . . . . **101** A4
Hartington Pl DE7 . . . . **157** E5
Hartington Rd NG5. . . . . **161** C3
Hartington St NG20 . . . . **72** F8
Hartland Rd S80 . . . . . . **35** E2
Hartley Ct NG7. . . . . . . **222** B4
Hartley Dr NG9 . . . . . . **184** B6
Hartley Rd
  Kirkby in A NG17 . . . . . **114** F5
  Nottingham NG7 . . . . . . **222** B4
Hartness Rd NG11. . . . . **184** C1
Hartside Cl NG2 . . . . . . **186** C7
Hartside Gdns 1 NG10. **193** A8
Hart St NG7 . . . . **222** B1
Hartwell St NG3 . . . . . . **223** F4
Hartwood Dr NG9 . . . . . **170** D1
Harvest Cl
  Bingham NG13. . . . . . . **177** D4
  Carlton in L S81. . . . . . . **25** F7
  Nottingham NG5 . . . . . . **160** F8
  Worksop S81 . . . . **36** B7
Harvest Dr NG24 . . . . . **125** C4
Harvey Cl NG11 . . . . . . **196** D5
Harvey Croft NG9 . . . . . **170** C4
Harvey Ct 3 NG7 . . . . **172** E2
Harvey Hadden Sports Ctr
  NG8. . . . . **171** F7
Harvey Rd
  Mansfield NG18 . . . . . . **102** E5
  Nottingham, Bilborough
  NG8. . . . . **171** F7
  Nottingham, Dunkirk NG7 **172** E2
Harvey's Field NG25 . . . **136** E8
Harwell Sluice La DN10 . **11** D3
Harwich Cl NG6 . . . . . . **160** A8
Harwill Cres NG8 . . . . . **160** B2
Harwood Cl
  Arnold NG5 . . . . **162** B8
  Sutton in A NG17 . . . . . **101** A4
Harwood Pl NG17 . . . . . **101** A4
Harworth Ave S81 . . . . . **18** A6
Harworth CE Prim Sch
  DN11. . . . . **9** A4
Harworth Cl NG19. . . . . **101** D6
Haslam St NG7 . . . . . . **223** D1
Haslehurst Gdns S80 . . . **35** E2
Haslemere Gdns NG15 . **116** F2
Haslemere Rd
  Long Eaton NG10 . . . . . **193** B8
  Nottingham NG8 . . . . . . **172** D8
Hassock La N DE75. . . . **157** B7
Hassock La S DE75. . . . **157** C6
Hassocks La NG9 . . . . . **184** B7
Hassop Wlk NG18 . . . . . **103** B6
Hastings St
  Carlton NG4. . . . . **174** C7
  6 Loughborough LE11 . **220** A4
Haswell Rd NG6 . . . . . . **160** B5
Hatchet's La NG24 . . . . **125** A3
Hatfield Ave
  Meden Vale NG20 . . . . . **74** F8
  Sandiacre NG10. . . . . . **182** B4
Hatfield Cl NG21 . . . . . . **104** B1
Hatfield Dr NG2. . . . . . . **185** C4
Hatfield Rd NG3 . . . . . . **161** C1
Hatfield St DN22 . . . . . . **40** A6
Hather Cl DN22 . . . . **51** A5
Hatherleigh Cl NG3 . . . . **162** C6
Hathern Cl NG10 . . . . . . **193** D5
Hathern Gn NG9 . . . . . . **184** A8
Hathern Rd LE12 . . . . . . **212** D2
Hathern Turn LE12 . . . . **212** F2
Hathernware Ind Est
  LE12 . . . . **213** D5
Hathersage Ave NG10 . . **193** A5

Hathersage Rise NG15 . **117** A3
Hathersage Way NG17 . **100** E4
Hathersage Wlk NG18 . . **103** B6
Hatley Cl 7 NG2. . . . . . **173** B1
Hatton Cl NG5 . . . . **147** A2
Hatton Crofts NG10. . . . **193** C6
Hatton Ct NG18 . . . . . . **103** B6
Hatton Gdns
  Newark-on-T NG24 . . . . **140** B8
  Nuthall NG8 . . . . **159** E3
Haughgate Hill DN22. . . . **22** B1
Havelock Gdns NG3 . . . **223** F4
Haven Cl
  Clipstone NG21 . . . . **89** F3
  Sutton in A NG17. . . . . . **100** D3
  West Bridgford NG2 . . . **185** D5
Havenden Gdns 2 NG7 . **172** F7
Haven Hill S81. . . . . **16** D6
Havenwood Rise NG11 . **195** D8
Haverhill Cres NG5. . . . . **146** D1
Hawarden Terr 9 NG7 . . **172** F7
Hawbush Rd NG23 . . . . . **81** A6
Hawkesworth Ave NG19 . **89** B1
Hawkhill Cl NG22 . . . . . . **77** A3
Hawkhurst Dr NG8 . . . . **171** D2
Hawking La S44 . . . . **85** A7
Hawkins Ct DE7. . . . . . . **157** F4
Hawk Ridge Gdns 1
  NG3. . . . . **173** E5
Hawkshead Cl NG2. . . . **186** D5
Hawksley Gdns NG11. . . **184** C2
Hawksley Rd 14 NG7 . . **172** F7
Hawkswood Cl NG9 . . . . **183** B4
Hawksworth Ave NG5 . . **161** D4
Hawksworth Rd
  Hawksworth NG13. . . . . **167** B3
  Scarrington NG13 . . . . . **178** F8
  Syerston NG23. . . . . . . **153** B3
  West Bridgford NG2 . . . **173** F1
Hawksworth St
  Gainsborough DN21 . . . . **24** D8
  10 Nottingham NG3. . . . **173** E5
Hawley Cl LE12 . . . . **205** F1
Hawson Way S81 . . . . . . **35** C7
Hawthorn Ave
  Gainsborough DN21 . . . . **15** D1
  Glapwell S44 . . . . **86** B8
  Hucknall NG15. . . . . . . **145** F7
  Stapleford NG9 . . . . . . **182** D6
Hawthorn Cl
  Beckingham DN10 . . . . . **23** B8
  Keyworth NG12. . . . . . . **197** E5
  New Ollerton NG22 . . . . **77** D5
  5 Nottingham NG2. . . . **173** B1
  Old Dalby LE14 . . . . . . **218** E4
  West Bridgford NG2 . . . **186** B4
Hawthorn Cres
  Arnold NG5 . . . . **148** A1
  4 Kirkby in A NG17 . . . **114** F6
  Kirkby in A NG17 . . . . . **115** A6
Hawthorn Ct 6 NG2 . . . **173** B1
Hawthorn Dr NG22 . . . . . **77** D5
Hawthorne Ave
  Hathern LE12. . . . . **213** A1
  Long Eaton NG10 . . . . . **193** C6
  Shirebrook NG20 . . . . . . **72** D4
  Tibshelf DE55 . . . . **99** B8
Hawthorne Cl
  North Leverton with
  Habblesthorpe DN22 . . **42** D8
  Stanton Hill NG17 . . . . . **100** B6
  Woodborough NG14 . . . **149** C4
Hawthorne Cres NG24 . . **139** A4
Hawthorne Gr NG9 . . . . **184** B6
Hawthorne Prim Sch
  NG6. . . . . **146** E4
Hawthorne Rd NG16 . . . **113** D3
Hawthorne Rise NG16 . . **158** B4
Hawthorne Way NG21 . . **91** B8
Hawthorn Gr DN21 . . . . . **15** D1
Hawthorn Prim Sch
  NG6. . . . . **146** E4
Hawthorns The
  Kirkby in Ashfield NG17. . **114** F6
  Market Warsop NG20 . . . **74** A4
  Walesby NG22 . . . . **64** A2
Hawthorn Way S81 . . . . **25** E7
Hawton Cl
  Gainsborough DN21 . . . . **15** E2
  Mansfield NG19. . . . . . . **87** F1
Hawton Cres NG8. . . . . **172** C3
Hawton La NG24 . . . . . . **140** B4
Hawton Rd NG24 . . . . . **139** E5
Hawton Spinney NG8. . . **172** C4
Hawtonville Jun Sch
  NG24. . . . . **139** F6
Haxey Gate Rd DN10 . . . . **6** F5
Haxey Rd DN10 . . . . **6** F4
Haycroft Cl NG19 . . . . . . **88** E5
Haycroft Way NG13 . . . . **165** C2
Hayden La NG15 . . . . . . **131** B1
Haydn Ave NG5 . . . . . . **161** B2
Haydn Prim Sch NG5. . . **161** C2
Haydn Rd NG5. . . . . **161** B2
Haydock Cl NG16 . . . . . **158** E7
Hayes Cl NG16 . . . . **113** C3
Hayes Rd NG12 . . . . . . **197** E3
Hayles Cl NG5 . . . . **161** B6
Hayling Cl DE7. . . . . **157** C3
Hayling Dr NG8 . . . . **160** D1
Haynes Ave NG9 . . . . . **170** C5
Haynes Cl
  Nottingham NG11 . . . . . **184** F3
  Tuxford NG22 . . . . **66** A3
Hays Cl DE7 . . . . **157** D2
Hayside Ave NG10 . . . . **140** B3
Hayward Ave LE11 . . . . **220** C2
Haywood Ave NG21 . . . **118** A5
Haywood Ct 2 NG2. . . . **173** E4

Haywood Oaks La NG21 . **118** C3
Haywood Rd NG3 . . . . . **162** A3
Haywood Sch NG5 . . . . **161** C5
Haywood St NG2. . . . . . **173** E4
Hazelas Dr NG14 . . . . . **165** A5
Hazel Bank NG18 . . . . . **102** E8
Hazelbank Ave NG3 . . . . **161** F1
Hazelby Rd S80 . . . . **58** E8
Hazel Cl NG13 . . . . **178** A4
Hazel Cres NG20 . . . . . . **72** D4
Hazel Dr NG16 . . . . **159** B6
Hazelford Way NG15 . . . **130** D7
Hazel Gr
  Edwinstowe NG21 . . . . . **76** B1
  Hucknall NG15. . . . . . . **146** A5
  Kirkby in A NG17 . . . . . **115** C5
  Mansfield Woodhouse NG19 **88** B5
  New Balderton NG24. . . **140** C5
  Nottingham NG3 . . . . . . **162** A4
  South Normanton DE55. . **113** B5
Hazel Hill Cres NG5 . . . . **161** B8
Hazelhurst Gdns 3 NG6 . **160** B7
Hazel Hurst Prep Sch
  NG3. . . . . **162** A3
Hazel Mdws NG15 . . . . . **146** A5
Hazelmere Gr NG7 . . . . **222** A2
Hazel Rd NG7 . . . . **222** D5
Hazel St
  Nottingham NG6 . . . . . . **160** B8
  Sutton in A NG17 . . . . . **100** D7
Hazel Way NG15 . . . . . . **131** B2
Hazelwood NG12. . . . . . **188** A3
Hazelwood Cl
  Eastwood NG16 . . . . . . **144** B2
  Mansfield Woodhouse NG19 **89** B2
Hazelwood Dr NG15. . . . **145** C6
Hazelwood Gr S80 . . . . . **35** C2
Hazelwood La DN22 . . . . **41** E1
Hazelwood Rd NG7 . . . . **172** E7
Headingley Gdns 3
  NG8. . . . . **172** D8
Headland Ave DN22 . . . . **50** A3
Headstead Bank DN22. . . **43** D6
Head Stocks The NG17 . **100** A1
Heafield Dr DE74 . . . . . **203** D2
Healdswood Inf Sch
  NG17. . . . . **100** D6
Healdswood St NG17. . . **100** D7
Healey Cl
  Collingham NG23 . . . . . **112** A8
  Nottingham NG2 . . . . . . **173** C2
Heanor Rd DE7 . . . . **157** D3
Heanor Wlk NG18 . . . . . **103** B6
Heapham Cres DN21 . . . . **24** F8
Heapham Rd 3 DN21 . . . **24** F8
Heard Cres NG9 . . . . . . **183** F8
Heath Ave NG18 . . . . . . **103** B7
Heathcoat St
  12 Loughborough LE11 . . **220** A4
  Nottingham NG1 . . . . . . **223** F3
Heathcote Pl NG17. . . . **101** A1
Heather Cl
  Eastwood NG16 . . . . . . **144** C2
  10 Kirkby in A NG17 . . . **114** F7
  Mansfield NG18 . . . . . . **102** A6
  Nottingham NG3 . . . . . . **173** D7
  South Normanton DE55. . **113** A3
Heather Croft NG2 . . . . **185** C4
Heather Ct DE75 . . . . . . **143** B1
Heather La NG15. . . . . . **132** B8
Heatherley Dr
  Mansfield NG19. . . . . . . **88** E1
  Nottingham NG6 . . . . . . **160** F4
Heatherley Prim Sch
  NG19. . . . . **88** E1
Heather Rd NG4 . . . . . . **162** D1
Heather Rise NG9 . . . . . **171** E1
Heathers The NG22 . . . . **77** F5
Heathervale NG2. . . . . . **185** B6
Heather Way NG18 . . . . **103** A6
Heathfield Ave DE7 . . . . **170** A8
Heathfield Ct 12 NG17 . **114** E7
Heathfield Gdns
  Retford DN22. . . . . **39** E8
  Tibshelf DE55 . . . . **99** A7
Heathfield Gr NG9 . . . . . **183** C3
Heathfield Prim Sch
  NG5. . . . . **160** F3
Heathfield Rd NG5 . . . . **160** F4
Heathfield Wy NG18. . . . **102** D5
Heath Gdns DE72 . . . . . **193** A8
Heathland Cl NG18. . . . . **103** A6
Heathlands Prim Sch
  NG21. . . . . **103** D3
Heathrington Gdns 9
  NG5 . . . . **147** A1
Heath The NG16 . . . . . . **158** B8
Heaton Cl
  Newark-on-T NG24 . . . . **140** D8
  Nottingham NG3 . . . . . . **161** F1
Heaton St DN21. . . . . . . **24** D8
Heavenside LE12 . . . . . . **205** E3
Heavytrees Ave NG15 . . **117** A1
Hecadeck La LE14 . . . . **219** C8
Heckdyke La DN10 . . . . . . **7** E5
Heckington Dr NG8 . . . . **172** B5
Heddington Gdns 1
  NG5 . . . . **161** D8
Heddon Bar NG19. . . . . . **88** E3
Hedgerow Cl NG17. . . . . **100** C1
Hedges Dr DE7 . . . . **170** A5
Hedley St NG7 . . . . **173** A8
Hedley Villas 5 NG7. . . **161** A1
Helenship La DN22 . . . . . **54** B7
Hellebore Cl NG5 . . . . . **160** E7
Helm Cl NG6. . . . . **159** F7

Helmsdale Cl
  Arnold NG5 . . . . **148** B1
  Mansfield NG19. . . . . . . **101** E5
Helmsdale Gdns NG5. . . **146** F1
Helmsley Rd NG21 . . . . **103** E3
Helston Dr NG8 . . . . **159** E1
Helvellyn Cl 7 NG2 . . . **173** C2
Helvellyn Way NG10. . . . **182** B2
Hemingway Cl
  Carlton NG4. . . . . **174** C7
  Eastwood NG16 . . . . . . **144** C1
Hemlock Ave
  Long Eaton NG10. . . . . **182** D1
  Stapleford NG9 . . . . . . **182** E8
Hemlock Gdns NG6 . . . . **159** F6
Hemmingfield Cl S81 . . . **35** F8
Hemmingfield Cres S81 . **35** F7
Hemmingfield Rd S81. . . **36** A7
Hemmingfield Way S81 . **36** A8
Hemplands La NG23. . . . **96** E8
Hemplands The NG23 . . **98** A1
Hempshill Hall Prim Sch
  NG6. . . . . **159** F5
Hempshill La NG6. . . . . **160** A6
Hemsby Gdns 5 NG6 . . **160** B8
Hemscott Cl NG6 . . . . . **159** F8
Hemsley Dr NG16 . . . . . **143** D3
Hemswell Cl NG3 . . . . . **174** A5
Hendon Rise NG3 . . . . . **173** F8
Hendre Gdns 1 NG5. . . **161** A7
Henley Cl NG4 . . . . **175** A6
Henley Ct DN21 . . . . **15** C2
Henley Gdns NG9 . . . . . **170** E1
Henley Rise NG5 . . . . . . **161** A3
Hennessey Cl 11 NG9. . . **183** C2
Henning Gdns 13 NG5 . . **161** A8
Henning La NG17 . . . . . **100** B1
Hennymoor Cl S80 . . . . . **45** A5
Hennymoor La S80. . . . . **45** C2
Henrietta St NG6. . . . . . **160** C6
Henry Ave NG19 . . . . . . **88** B5
Henry Ct NG2. . . . . **173** C2
Henry Mellish Comp Sch
  NG6. . . . . **160** D5
Henry Rd
  Beeston NG9 . . . . **184** A6
  Nottingham NG7 . . . . . . **222** A1
  West Bridgford NG2 . . . **185** E8
Henry St
  Arnold NG5 . . . . **147** E2
  Hucknall NG15. . . . . . . **146** B6
  6 Nottingham NG2. . . . **173** E4
  Sutton in A NG17. . . . . . **100** F1
Henry Whipple Inf Sch
  NG5. . . . . **160** F6
Henry Whipple Jun Sch
  NG5. . . . . **160** F6
Henshaw Pl DE7 . . . . . . **157** E4
Henson Cl NG12 . . . . . . **176** E3
Henson La NG12 . . . . . . **176** E2
Henson's Sq NG9. . . . . . **183** B8
Henton Cl NG24. . . . . . . **125** E2
Henton Rd NG21 . . . . . . **76** C1
Hepple Dr NG6 . . . . **159** F7
Herald Cl NG9 . . . . **184** B7
Herbert Rd
  Annesley Woodhouse
  NG17. . . . . **115** B1
  Nottingham NG5 . . . . . . **161** B1
Herbert St
  Loughborough LE11 . . . . **220** B5
  Mansfield NG18. . . . . . . **102** A6
Hercules Dr NG24 . . . . . **140** B7
Hereford Ave
  Mansfield Woodhouse
  NG19. . . . . **88** C6
  Ollerton NG22 . . . . **77** A2
Hereford Cl S81 . . . . **36** A6
Hereford Rd
  Arnold NG5 . . . . **161** E5
  Carlton NG4. . . . . **162** F2
  Nottingham NG3 . . . . . . **174** B5
  Ravenshead NG15. . . . . **117** A3
Herewood Cl NG20 . . . . **72** C4
Hermes Cl DN10 . . . . **9** B8
Hermitage Ave NG18 . . . **101** F5
Hermitage La NG18 . . . . **101** E4
Hermitage Sq 1 NG2 . . **173** E3
Hermitage Way NG18 . . . **101** E4
Hermitage Wlk NG7. . . . **222** C1
Hermon St NG7 . . . . . . **222** C3
Herne St NG17 . . . . **101** A4
Heron Dr NG7 . . . . **222** A2
Heron Glade S81. . . . . . . **35** C7
Herons Ct NG2. . . . . . . **186** C4
Heron Way
  Mansfield NG19. . . . . . . **87** C1
  New Balderton NG24. . . **140** C5
Heron Wharf 2 NG7 . . . **172** F2
Herrick Rd LE11 . . . . . . **220** A2
Herril Ings DN11. . . . . . . **8** B8
Herriot Gr DN11 . . . . **9** A4
Herrods View NG17 . . . . **100** C6
Hervey Gn NG7 . . . . . . **184** E2
Heskey Cl NG3 . . . . **223** E4
Heskey Wlk NG3 . . . . . . **223** E4
Heslington Ave NG8. . . . **172** E8
Heslop Ct S80 . . . . **35** D3
Hethbeth Ct 5 NG2. . . . **173** C2
Hethersett Gdns 4 NG6. **160** B8
Hetley Rd NG9 . . . . **183** F8
Hett's La NG20. . . . . **74** B5
Hetts Lane Inf Sch NG20 . **74** B5
Hewett St NG20. . . . . . . **73** D5
Hewson's La NG23 . . . . **112** A5
Hexham Ave DE7. . . . . . **170** A4
Hexham Cl
  Mansfield NG18. . . . . . . **102** F5

Hexham Cl *continued*
West Bridgford NG2 . . . . . 186 A6
Hexham Gdns 1 NG5 . . . 147 A1
Heyes The NG15 . . . . 117 A1
Heyford Ct DE75 . . . . 143 A1
Heymann Prim Sch NG2 185 D4
Hey St NG10 . . . . 193 C4
Heyward St NG18 . . . . 102 D7
Heywood Cl NG25 . . . . 121 F1
Heywood St NG18 . . . . 102 D7
Hibbert Cres NG17 . . . . . . 101 A3
Hibbert Rd NG18 . . . . 102 D7
Hickings La NG9 . . . . 182 E8
Hickling Ct NG18 . . . . 102 D7
Hickling La LE14 . . . . 211 A4
Hickling Rd
Kinoulton NG12 . . . . 200 B2
Nottingham NG3 . . . . 162 A2
Hickling Way NG12 . . . . . . 188 A1
Hickman Cres DN21 . . . . . . 15 C4
Hickman Ct DN21 . . . . 24 E8
Hickman St DN21 . . . . 24 D8
Hickory Cl 8 NG17 . . . . . . 114 F7
Hickton Dr NG9 . . . . 183 B1
Hide Hill View NG12 . . . . . 186 D1
Highbank Dr NG11 . . . . . . 195 E7
Highbank Prim Sch
NG11 . . . . 195 D7
Highbury Ave NG6 . . . . . . 160 D5
Highbury Cl NG8 . . . . 159 E3
Highbury Hospl NG6 . . . . . . 160 C5
Highbury Rd
Keyworth NG12 . . . . 197 E4
Nottingham NG6 . . . . 160 C6
Highbury Wlk NG6 . . . . . . 160 C6
High Church St NG7 . . . . . 161 A1
High Church Street 1
NG7 . . . . 173 A8
High Cl NG17 . . . . 115 B1
Highclere Dr NG4 . . . . 174 F8
Highcliffe Ave NG20 . . . . . . 72 D4
Highcliffe Rd NG3 . . . . 174 A5
High Common La
Austerfield DN10 . . . . 3 A6
Tickhill DN11 . . . . 9 A8
High Cres NG17 . . . . 115 B1
Highcroft NG3 . . . . 161 F4
Highcroft Cl NG10 . . . . . . 193 E5
Highcroft Dr NG8 . . . . 171 B5
High Cross NG14 . . . . 136 E2
Highcross Ct NG7 . . . . 222 B4
Highcross Hill NG25,
NG14 . . . . 136 D3
High Cross St NG1 . . . . . . 223 F3
Highfield DN22 . . . . 29 C1
Highfield Ave
Kirkby in A NG17 . . . . 114 E6
Mansfield NG19 . . . . 88 B1
Shirebrook NG20 . . . . 72 D6
Highfield Cl
Gainsborough DN21 . . . . . . 15 E1
Mansfield NG19 . . . . 88 B1
Ravenshead NG15 . . . . 117 A2
Highfield Ct NG9 . . . . 183 F6
Highfield Dr
Bilsthorpe NG22 . . . . 105 F4
Carlton NG4 . . . . 174 B8
Nuthall NG16 . . . . 159 F4
South Normanton DE55 . . . 113 B5
Stapleford LN6 . . . . 127 A4
Highfield Gr
Carlton in L S81 . . . . 26 B5
West Bridgford NG2 . . . . . . 185 F7
Highfield La S80 . . . . 36 C1
High Field La DN10 . . . . 3 B3
Highfield Prim Sch
Cotgrave NG12 . . . . 187 F3
Long Eaton NG10 . . . . 182 C2
Highfield Rd
Bawtry DN10 . . . . 10 B8
Beeston NG9 . . . . 183 A3
Clipstone NG21 . . . . 90 A4
Keyworth NG12 . . . . 197 E4
Nottingham NG7 . . . . 172 D1
Nuthall NG16 . . . . 159 E4
Saxilby LN1 . . . . 57 A4
Sutton in A NG17 . . . . 100 C3
West Bridgford NG2 . . . . . 185 F7
Highfields Ct NG15 . . . . . . 146 A6
Highfields Dr NG22 . . . . . 106 A4
Highfields Sch NG24 . . . . 140 C6
Highfield St NG10 . . . . . . 182 C1
Highfield Terr 8 NG18 . . 102 B6
Highfield Villas S81 . . . . . . 25 F8
Highfield Way NG18 . . . . . 102 A5
Highgate Cl NG4 . . . . 162 C2
Highgate Dr DE7 . . . . 157 C3
Highgate La NG13 . . . . 202 F8
High Gr NG19 . . . . 88 E1
High Grounds Rd S80 . . . . 35 C4
High Grounds Way S80 . . . 35 B4
Highgrove Ave NG9 . . . . . 183 D6
Highgrove Gdns NG12 . . . 186 A4
High Hazles Cl NG4 . . . . . 162 E3
High Hazles Dr NG17 . . . . 100 A2
High Hoe Ct S80 . . . . 36 A3
High Hoe Dr S80 . . . . 36 A3
High Hoe Rd S80 . . . . 36 B3
High Holborn DE7 . . . . 157 E3
High Hurst NG14 . . . . 148 E7
High La Central DE7 . . . . 157 A1
High La E DE7 . . . . 157 A1
Highland Cl NG19 . . . . 88 D3
Highland Gr S81 . . . . 36 A5
Highland Rd NG18 . . . . 102 E2
High Leys Dr NG15 . . . . . . 116 C3
High Leys Rd NG15 . . . . . . 145 F5
High Mdw
Bawtry DN10 . . . . 9 F7
Hathern LE12 . . . . 213 A1
Tollerton NG12 . . . . 186 D1
High Oakham Dr NG18 . . 102 B3
High Oakham Hill NG18 . 102 A4
High Oakham Prim Sch
NG18 . . . . 102 B3
High Oakham Rd NG18 . . 102 B4
High Pavement
Nottingham NG1 . . . . 223 F2
Sutton in A NG17 . . . . 100 E2
High Pavement Sixth Form
Coll NG1 . . . . 223 D3
High Pk Cotts NG16 . . . . . 144 D6
High Rd
Beeston, Chilwell NG9 . . . . 183 D4
Beeston NG9 . . . . 184 A7
Beeston, Toton NG9 . . . . . . 183 A1
Carlton in L S81 . . . . 26 A5
High Ridge NG19 . . . . 88 F2
High St Ave NG5 . . . . 161 E7
High St Pl NG1 . . . . 223 E2
High Spania NG16 . . . . 158 F7
High St
Arnold NG5 . . . . 161 E7
Bawtry DN10 . . . . 10 A7
Beckingham DN10 . . . . 23 B8
Blyth S81 . . . . 18 B2
Bottesford NG13 . . . . 181 A2
Brinsley NG16 . . . . 128 E1
Collingham NG23 . . . . 112 A8
Eagle LN6 . . . . 84 D3
East Markham NG22 . . . . . . 65 F7
Edwinstowe NG21 . . . . 76 B1
Elkesley DN22 . . . . 50 B4
Everton DN10 . . . . 11 C3
Gainsborough DN21 . . . . . . 24 D7
Girton NG23 . . . . 82 F1
Gringley on t H DN10 . . . . . 12 F2
Harby NG23 . . . . 70 E2
Hucknall NG15 . . . . 146 B7
Huthwaite NG17 . . . . 100 A3
Kegworth DE74 . . . . 203 C2
Kimberley NG16 . . . . 158 F6
Laxton NG22 . . . . 79 B3
Long Eaton NG10 . . . . 193 E8
Loughborough LE11 . . . . . . 220 B4
Mansfield Woodhouse NG19 88 C3
Market Warsop NG20 . . . . . 74 B4
Marton DN21 . . . . 44 C7
Misson DN10 . . . . 4 B2
Misterton DN10 . . . . 6 F2
Newton on T LN1 . . . . 55 A1
North Scarle LN6 . . . . 83 D2
Nottingham NG1 . . . . 223 E2
Orston NG13 . . . . 179 F7
Pleasleyhill NG19 . . . . 87 B5
Retford DN22 . . . . 39 E3
Ruddington NG11 . . . . 196 C7
Saxilby LN1 . . . . 57 A3
South Leverton DN22 . . . . . 42 C6
South Normanton DE55 . . . 113 A6
Stanton Hill NG17 . . . . 100 C6
Stapleford NG9 . . . . 182 E7
Staunton in t V NG13 . . . . . 169 B4
Sutton in A NG17 . . . . 100 E2
Sutton on T NG23 . . . . 96 F8
Tibshelf DE55 . . . . 99 A7
Walkeringham DN10 . . . . . . 13 F6
High Tor NG17 . . . . 100 E7
Highurst St NG7 . . . . 222 C3
High View Ave NG12 . . . . 198 A3
High View Rd DE55 . . . . . . 113 C7
High View Rd Ind Units
DE55 . . . . 113 C7
Highwood Ave NG8 . . . . . . 171 F8
Highwood Player Inf Sch
NG8 . . . . 171 F8
Highwood Player Jun Sch
NG8 . . . . 171 E8
Highwray Gr NG11 . . . . . . 184 D1
Hilary Cl NG8 . . . . 171 D3
Hilcot Dr NG8 . . . . 160 C1
Hilcote La DE55 . . . . 99 A1
Hilcote St DE55 . . . . 113 A6
Hillary Way NG24 . . . . 140 E4
Hillbeck Cres NG8 . . . . . . 171 C4
Hill Cl
Eastwood NG16 . . . . 144 C1
West Bridgford NG2 . . . . . 186 B6
Hill Cres
Gainsborough DN21 . . . . . . 15 F1
Sutton in A NG17 . . . . 101 B4
Hillcrest NG25 . . . . 136 D8
Hill Crest NG20 . . . . 72 D3
Hillcrest Ave DE55 . . . . . . 113 A4
Hillcrest Cl NG16 . . . . 159 A6
Hillcrest Dr NG15 . . . . 145 D6
Hillcrest Gdns NG14 . . . . . 163 E5
Hill Crest Gr NG5 . . . . 161 B3
Hillcrest Mews DN22 . . . . . 40 A7
Hillcrest Rd NG12 . . . . 197 E4
Hillcrest View NG4 . . . . . . 162 B1
Hill Dr NG13 . . . . 177 D5
Hill Farm Cl NG12 . . . . 186 D1
Hill Farm Ct NG12 . . . . 186 A2
Hillfield Gdns NG5 . . . . . . 146 E1
Hillfield Rd NG9 . . . . 170 F1
Hill Fields DE55 . . . . 113 A3
Hillgrove Gdns 14 NG5 . . 161 A8
Hilliers Ct NG5 . . . . 160 F8
Hillington Rise NG5 . . . . . 161 C7
Hillmoor St NG19 . . . . 87 C3
Hillocks Prim Sch NG17 . 101 B3
Hill Rd
Beeston NG9 . . . . 183 B2
Bestwood Village NG6 . . . . 146 E4
Hill Rd *continued*
Gotham NG11 . . . . 205 B7
Harworth DN11 . . . . 8 F3
Orston NG13 . . . . 180 A6
Hill Rise NG9 . . . . 170 C4
Hillsborough Ave NG17 . . 114 D8
Hillsborough Way NG17 . 114 D8
Hillsford Cl NG8 . . . . 172 A5
Hillside
Beckingham LN5 . . . . 142 C8
Kegworth DE74 . . . . 203 D1
Langley Mill NG16 . . . . 143 A3
Marton DN21 . . . . 44 C8
Tuxford NG22 . . . . 66 B3
Hill Side NG7 . . . . 172 D3
Hillside Ave
Misterton DN10 . . . . 7 A2
Nottingham NG3 . . . . 162 A4
Hillside Cres
Beeston NG9 . . . . 183 E8
Worksop S81 . . . . 35 F5
Hillside Dr
Burton Joyce NG14 . . . . . . 163 F5
Long Eaton NG10 . . . . 193 B8
Southwell NG25 . . . . 136 D8
Hillside Gr NG10 . . . . 182 A6
Hillside Rd
Beeston, Bramcote NG9 . . 183 D8
Beeston, Chilwell NG9 . . . . 183 B3
Blidworth NG21 . . . . 118 A4
Radcliffe on T NG12 . . . . . . 176 A3
Hillside Wlk NG21 . . . . 118 A4
Hills Rd NG5 . . . . 161 F4
Hill St
Pleasleyhill NG19 . . . . 87 B5
Retford DN22 . . . . 39 E4
Worksop S80 . . . . 35 E2
Hillsway NG20 . . . . 72 D3
Hillsway Cres NG18 . . . . . 102 A4
Hill Syke NG14 . . . . 150 A2
Hill The NG17 . . . . 114 E5
Hill Top NG13 . . . . 180 A6
Hill Top Ave NG20 . . . . 72 E4
Hilltop Cl LN6 . . . . 84 D3
Hill Top Ct DN11 . . . . 9 A4
Hilltop Rd NG16 . . . . 113 C3
Hill Top View NG17 . . . . . 100 C1
Hillview Ave NG3 . . . . 161 D2
Hillview Cres DN22 . . . . . . 30 E4
Hillview Ct NG19 . . . . 88 D4
Hillview Rd
Carlton NG4 . . . . 162 A1
Retford DN22 . . . . 39 E3
Hill View Rd
Beeston NG9 . . . . 183 A2
Kirkby in A NG17 . . . . 115 C5
Hill Vue Ave NG24 . . . . 140 B8
Hill Vue Gdns NG24 . . . . . 140 B8
Hillwood Cl S80 . . . . 35 B2
Hilton Cres NG2 . . . . 186 B5
Hilton Ct NG2 . . . . 186 B5
Hilton Rd NG3 . . . . 162 A3
Hinchin Brook NG7 . . . . . 222 A2
Hindlow Ct NG18 . . . . 103 B6
Hind St DN22 . . . . 40 A6
Hine Ave NG24 . . . . 140 E8
Hinsley Cl NG5 . . . . 162 B8
Hirst Cres NG8 . . . . 171 E4
Hirst Rd DN22 . . . . 40 A8
Hives La LN6 . . . . 83 D3
Hobart Cl NG2 . . . . 173 C1
Hobart Dr NG9 . . . . 170 F1
Hobhouse Rd NG19 . . . . . . 87 D2
Hobsic Cl NG16 . . . . 143 D8
Hobsic La NG16 . . . . 128 E8
Hobson's Acre NG14 . . . . . 165 A5
Hockerton Hts NG23 . . . . 122 B6
Hockerton Rd NG25,
NG23 . . . . 122 F2
Hockerwood NG11 . . . . 184 E4
Hockerwood La NG23 . . . 122 C2
Hockley NG1 . . . . 223 F2
Hockley Pl NG17 . . . . 114 E4
Hodgkin Cl NG11 . . . . 184 C1
Hodgkinson Rd NG17 . . . . 115 B4
Hodgkinson St NG4 . . . . . . 175 A6
Hodmire La S44 . . . . 85 E7
Hodsock La S81 . . . . 26 B7
Hodsock Priory Gdns S81 26 E7
Hodthorpe Prim Sch S80 . 45 C5
Hoefield Cres NG6 . . . . 160 A6
Hoe La NG12 . . . . 189 A6
Hoe Nook NG12 . . . . 189 A4
Hoe View Rd NG12 . . . . . . 189 A4
Hoewood Rd NG6 . . . . 160 A8
Hogan Gdns NG5 . . . . 147 A1
Hogarth Cl NG9 . . . . 182 E6
Hogarth Prim Sch NG3 . . 174 A7
Hogarth St NG3 . . . . 173 F6
Hoggetts Cl NG9 . . . . 183 B5
Hogg La NG12 . . . . 175 E3
Hoggs Field NG16 . . . . 143 F2
Holbeck La S80 . . . . 59 D8
Holbeck Rd
Hucknall NG15 . . . . 131 B1
Nottingham NG8 . . . . 172 D6
Holbeck Way NG21 . . . . . . 104 B1
Holbein Cl LE11 . . . . 220 C4
Holborn Ave NG2 . . . . 173 F4
Holborn Cl NG16 . . . . 159 D3
Holborn Pl NG6 . . . . 160 C7
Holbrook Cl NG19 . . . . 87 A5
Holbrook Ct
Mansfield NG18 . . . . 103 B6
Nottingham NG11 . . . . 195 E8
Holbrook St DE75 . . . . 143 A2
Holby Cl NG5 . . . . 160 F8
Holcombe Cl NG8 . . . . 160 B2
Holdale Rd NG3 . . . . 174 B6
Holdenby Cl DN22 . . . . 40 A8
Holden Cres
Newark-on-T NG24 . . . . 139 F6
Nuthall NG16 . . . . 159 C6
Holden Gdns NG9 . . . . 182 E6
Holden Rd NG9 . . . . 183 E7
Holden St
Mansfield NG18 . . . . 102 A6
Nottingham NG7 . . . . 222 C3
Holderness Cl DN11 . . . . 9 A4
Holding S81 . . . . 36 B5
Holds La DN22 . . . . 19 B2
Holgate NG11 . . . . 184 C2
Holgate Rd NG2 . . . . 173 C1
Holgate Sch NG15 . . . . 145 E6
Holgate Wlk NG15 . . . . 145 E6
Holkham Ave NG9 . . . . 183 C5
Holkham Cl
Arnold NG5 . . . . 162 A6
Shipley DE7 . . . . 157 C3
Holland Cl NG11 . . . . 195 B1
Holland Cres NG16 . . . . . . 129 B7
Holland Mdw NG10 . . . . . . 193 D5
Holland St NG7 . . . . 172 F7
Holles Cl NG22 . . . . 77 E5
Holles Cres NG7 . . . . 222 C1
Holles St S80 . . . . 35 F2
Hollies Ave NG24 . . . . 125 B4
Hollies Dr NG12 . . . . 186 A4
Hollies The
Eastwood NG16 . . . . 143 F2
Rainworth NG21 . . . . 104 B1
Ravenshead NG15 . . . . 116 F1
Sandiacre NG10 . . . . 182 A5
Hollington Rd NG8 . . . . . . 172 B6
Hollington Way NG18 . . . . 103 B7
Hollingwell Dr 4 NG18 . . 103 B7
Hollingworth Ave NG10 . 182 B3
Hollins The NG14 . . . . 149 A8
Hollinwell Ave NG8 . . . . . 172 C5
Hollinwell Cl 9 NG17 . . . 114 E7
Hollinwell Ct NG12 . . . . . . 186 B3
Hollinwood Lane NG14 . . 148 C8
Hollis Mdw LE12 . . . . 205 E3
Hollis St NG7 . . . . 161 A1
Holloway Cl NG13 . . . . 165 D3
Hollowdyke La NG24 . . . . 140 F3
Hollowgate La NG23 . . . . . 68 B1
Hollows The
Long Eaton NG10 . . . . 194 A8
Maplebeck NG22 . . . . 108 A7
Nottingham NG11 . . . . 185 A4
Thurgarton NG14 . . . . 151 C7
Hollow Stone NG1 . . . . . . 223 F2
Holly Ave
Carlton NG4 . . . . 174 D8
Nottingham, Wilford NG11 185 B8
Hollyberry Croft NG17 . . . 100 D1
Hollybrook Gr NG16 . . . . . 159 B7
Holly Bush Cl DN22 . . . . . . 50 B4
Holly Cl
Bingham NG13 . . . . 178 A4
Hucknall NG15 . . . . 146 B5
Hollycroft NG2 . . . . 186 A4
Holly Ct
Beeston NG9 . . . . 183 C8
Harworth DN11 . . . . 8 E4
Mansfield NG19 . . . . 88 E1
Retford DN22 . . . . 39 F6
Rolleston NG23 . . . . 138 A5
Hollydale Rd NG3 . . . . 174 B6
Hollydene Cl NG15 . . . . . . 145 C5
Hollydene Cres NG6 . . . . . 160 B4
Holly Dr NG19 . . . . 89 A1
Holly Farm Ct NG16 . . . . . 144 C1
Hollygate Ind Pk NG12 . . 188 A4
Hollygate La NG12 . . . . . . 188 B5
Holly Gdns NG3 . . . . 173 F7
Hollygirt Sch NG3 . . . . 173 C7
Holly Gr NG17 . . . . 114 F6
Holly Hill Prim Sch
NG16 . . . . 129 A7
Holly Hill Rd NG16 . . . . . . 129 A6
Hollyhouse Dr DE55 . . . . . 113 B6
Holly La NG9 . . . . 183 E5
Hollymount 1 DN22 . . . . . . 40 A6
Holly Prim Sch NG19 . . . . . 89 A1
Holly Rd
Mansfield Woodhouse
NG19 . . . . 89 A2
Retford DN22 . . . . 39 F6
Watnall NG16 . . . . 159 A7
Holly Rise NG22 . . . . 77 D5
Hollythorpe Pl NG15 . . . . 145 C5
Hollytree Cl LE12 . . . . 215 C2
Hollytree La LE14 . . . . 211 C3
Hollywell Prim Sch
NG16 . . . . 158 F7
Holme Ave LE12 . . . . 205 E3
Holme Cl
Ilkeston DE7 . . . . 157 D2
Woodborough NG14 . . . . . . 149 D4
Holmecroft Ave NG17 . . . 100 F5
Holmefield NG24 . . . . 139 A4
Holmefield Cres DE7 . . . . 170 A8
Holmefield Rd S80 . . . . 45 A6
Holmefield Wlk NG18 . . . 103 B6
Holme Gr NG2 . . . . 174 B2
Holme La
Egmanton NG22 . . . . 79 E6
Halam NG22 . . . . 120 F3
Langford NG23 . . . . 111 E3
Normanton on T NG23 . . . . . 82 B5
Radcliffe on T NG12 . . . . . . 175 C3
Rockley DN22 . . . . 51 C2
Winthorpe NG24 . . . . 125 D7
Holme Pierrepont Ctry Pk
NG12 . . . . 174 F3
Holme Pierrepont Hall
NG12 . . . . 175 B3
Holme Pit Nature Reserve
NG11 . . . . 184 C3
Holme Rd
Bingham NG13 . . . . 178 A4
West Bridgford NG2 . . . . . 174 A1
Holmes Cl NG16 . . . . 143 A3
Holmesfield Dr DE75 . . . . 157 A7
Holmes Rd DN22 . . . . 39 F7
Holme St NG2 . . . . 173 E2
Holme The NG25 . . . . 136 B7
Holme Way S81 . . . . 25 D1
Holme Wlk DN21 . . . . 15 F1
Holmewood Cres NG5 . . . 161 B6
Holmewood Dr NG16 . . . . 158 B8
Holmfield Cl S81 . . . . 36 A5
Holmfield Rd NG9 . . . . 183 C3
Holmhurst Cl S81 . . . . 35 E5
Holmsfield NG12 . . . . 197 E2
Holmwood Rd NG21 . . . . . 104 C1
Holocaust Ctr The NG22 . . 78 E3
Holroyd Ave NG2 . . . . 173 F4
Holt Dr 1 LE11 . . . . 220 A1
Holt Gr NG14 . . . . 148 F7
Holt The
Gainsborough DN21 . . . . . . 15 F1
Newark-on-T NG24 . . . . . . 139 D6
Holwood Ct NG6 . . . . 160 A6
Holy Cross RC Prim Sch
NG15 . . . . 131 B1
Holy Family RC Prim Sch
S80 . . . . 47 A8
Holyoake Rd NG3 . . . . 162 C3
Holyrood Ct NG9 . . . . 171 C1
Holy Trinity Inf Sch
NG25 . . . . 136 D7
Holy Trinity RC Prim Sch
NG24 . . . . 139 E7
Holywell Rd DE7 . . . . 157 C3
Home Cl NG5 . . . . 161 D8
Homecroft Dr NG16 . . . . . 128 E7
Home Croft The NG9 . . . . 183 B7
Home Farm Cl
Gotham NG11 . . . . 195 A1
Laughterton LN1 . . . . 55 B4
Newark-on-T NG24 . . . . . . 124 A4
Homefarm La NG23 . . . . . . 70 A6
Homefield Ave NG5 . . . . . 148 A1
Homefield Croft DN10 . . . 10 A2
Homefield Rd NG8 . . . . . . 172 D7
Home Fm Ct NG16 . . . . . . 128 D6
Homelands The NG17 . . . 100 F1
Home Mdws DN11 . . . . 8 A6
Home Pastures LE14 . . . . 211 F7
Homestead NG16 . . . . 143 A4
Homesteads The NG20 . . . 74 B4
Homewood Dr NG17 . . . . 114 E7
Honeycroft Ct DE55 . . . . . 113 B4
Honeyknab La NG25 . . . . . 134 D5
Honeys La NG23 . . . . 139 B1
Honeysuckle Cl
New Balderton NG24 . . . . . 140 C4
4 Nottingham NG8 . . . . . . 159 E1
Honeysuckle Gr
Bingham NG13 . . . . 177 D3
Nottingham NG6 . . . . 160 B4
Honeywood Dr NG3 . . . . . 174 A7
Honeywood Wlk NG3 . . . . 174 A7
Honing Dr NG25 . . . . 136 D8
Honingham Cl NG5 . . . . . . 162 A6
Honingham Rd DE7 . . . . . 157 C3
Honister Cl
Mansfield NG18 . . . . 102 C4
Nottingham NG11 . . . . 195 D7
West Bridgford NG2 . . . . . 186 C7
Honister Ct NG18 . . . . 102 C4
Honiton Cl NG9 . . . . 183 A2
Honiton Rd NG8 . . . . 159 E1
Hood St NG5 . . . . 161 D2
Hook Cl 9 NG9 . . . . 183 C2
Hooley Cl NG10 . . . . 193 B6
Hooley Pl 3 NG5 . . . . 161 D3
Hooley St NG16 . . . . 128 F6
Hoopers Cl NG13 . . . . 181 A2
Hoopers Wlk 6 NG2 . . . . . 173 C2
Hooton Rd NG4 . . . . 174 C7
Hooton St NG3 . . . . 173 F5
Hope Cl NG2 . . . . 173 B2
Hopedale Cl NG7 . . . . 222 A3
Hope Dr NG7 . . . . 223 D1
Hope St
Beeston NG9 . . . . 183 E7
Mansfield NG18 . . . . 102 D6
Hopewell Cl NG12 . . . . 176 A4
Hopewell Wlk DE7 . . . . . . 157 F5
Hopkiln La NG25 . . . . 121 C1
Hopkins Ct NG16 . . . . 143 F3
Hopyard La
Egmanton NG22 . . . . 79 E8
Normanton on T NG23 . . . . . 82 A6
Horace Ave NG9 . . . . 182 D6
Hornbeam Cl DE7 . . . . 170 B7
Hornbeam Gdns NG6 . . . . 159 F7
Hornbuckle Ct NG7 . . . . . 222 B3
Hornchurch Rd NG8 . . . . . 171 D8
Hornsby Wlk NG5 . . . . 160 E8
Horridge St DE7 . . . . 157 F4
Horsecroft Cl DE7 . . . . . . 157 C2
Horsendale Ave NG16 . . . 159 F4
Horsendale Prim Sch
NG16 . . . . 159 E3
Horsewells St DN10 . . . . . . 12 F2

Horsham Dr NG5....... 160 F8
Horsley Cres NG16..... 143 A3
Hose CE Prim Sch LE14 . 211 F7
Hose La
  Colston Bassett LE14..... 201 A3
  Harby LE14........ 202 A1
  Hose LE14........ 211 F5
Hoselett Field Rd NG10. 193 E6
Hosiery St NG17........ 115 A5
Hospital Rd DN22....... 39 E7
Hotchkin Ave LN1....... 57 C3
Hoten Rd **7** NG2....... 173 F3
Hoton Rd LE12........ 216 B3
Hotspur Cl NG6....... 160 E5
Hotspur Rd DN21....... 15 C5
Houfton Rd NG18....... 102 E8
Hougham Rd NG23....... 156 F5
Houghton Ave DE7....... 157 C3
Houghton Cl NG16....... 159 E4
Houldsworth Rise NG5... 147 E2
Hound Rd NG2........ 185 E8
Hounsfield Cl NG24....... 140 E8
Hounsfield Way NG23.... 96 F8
Houseman Gdns NG2.... 173 C2
Houston Cl NG5........ 146 E1
Hove Rd NG5........ 160 E5
Hoveringham Rd NG14 . 165 C8
Howard Cl NG10....... 182 E1
Howard Rd
  Bircotes DN11......... 9 C4
  Mansfield NG19........ 101 F8
Howard's Gdns NG24.... 140 C4
Howard St
  Loughborough LE11..... 220 B5
  Nottingham NG1....... 223 E3
  Sutton in A NG17....... 100 F4
  Worksop S80....... 36 B2
Howbeck La DN22....... 30 E4
Howbeck Rd NG18....... 162 B8
Howden Rd NG6........ 146 C1
Howell-Jones Rd NG9.. 183 B3
Howells Cl NG5........ 161 C8
Howe Rd LE11........ 220 B1
Howes Ct NG24....... 140 A8
Howick Dr NG6........ 159 F8
Howitts Rd NG13....... 181 A1
Howitt St
  Heanor DE75......... 143 A2
  Long Eaton NG10....... 193 E7
Hoylake Cl NG8........ 88 E6
Hoylake Cres NG8....... 171 D7
Hoyland Ave NG7....... 172 E2
Hubert St NG7........ 222 B4
Huckerby Rd DE7....... 157 C2
Huckerbys Field NG4... 162 C1
Hucklow Ct NG18....... 103 B6
Hucknall Annie Holgate Jun
  Sch NG15........ 145 F6
Hucknall Cl NG8........ 159 D2
Hucknall Cres NG4....... 162 E2
Hucknall Ind Pk NG15... 145 E4
Hucknall La NG6........ 146 D2
Hucknall L Ctr NG15... 146 B8
Hucknall Rd
  Newstead NG15....... 130 D5
  Nottingham NG6....... 160 E6
  Hucknall Sta NG15... 146 C7
Huddlestones Wharf
  NG24........ 139 E8
Hudson St
  Loughborough LE11..... 220 C4
  Nottingham NG3....... 173 F6
Hudson Wy NG12....... 176 B4
Hufton's Cl DE7....... 157 A7
Hufton's Dr DE75....... 157 A7
Hugessen Ave NG15... 146 C8
Hugget Gdns **4** NG5... 161 A8
Humber Cl NG2........ 173 C2
Humber La NG23....... 153 B8
Humber Rd
  Beeston NG9........ 184 A7
  Long Eaton NG10....... 182 C1
Humber Rd S NG9....... 184 B6
Humber St
  Retford DN22........ 40 A6
  Worksop S80....... 35 E4
Humberston Rd NG8... 171 C3
Hume St LE11........ 220 C4
Humphrey Cl LE11....... 220 B2
Humphries Gdns S80.... 35 E1
Hundred Acre La S81.... 26 C3
Hundred Acres La NG24. 140 D1
Hundreds La DN10....... 5 B2
Hungary La LE12....... 213 C7
Hungerhill Rd NG3....... 173 D7
Hungerton St NG7....... 222 B1
Hunston Cl NG8........ 172 A7
Hunt Cl NG12........ 175 F3
Hunter Rd NG5........ 162 C6
Hunters Chase NG19.... 88 B2
Hunters Cl NG11....... 185 A6
Hunters Ct NG17....... 114 E5
Hunter's Dr DN10....... 12 E2
Huntingdon Dr NG7.... 223 D2
Huntingdon Prim Sch
  NG3........ 223 E4
Huntingdon St NG1....... 223 E3
Huntingdon Way NG9... 182 F2
Huntingdon Wlk NG10. 182 B5
Huntly Cl
  Mansfield NG19....... 101 D5
  Nottingham NG7....... 184 F1
Hunt's Hill NG16....... 144 A7
Huntsman Pl DN22....... 19 B2

Hurcomb St NG3....... 173 F7
Hurst Cl NG21....... 103 F1
Hurts Croft NG9....... 183 D4
Hurt's Yd NG1....... 223 E2
Huss's La NG10....... 193 F7
Hutchinson Gn NG3.... 223 F4
Hutchinson Rd NG24... 140 E8
Huthwaite La DE55....... 99 C2
Huthwaite L Ctr NG17... 99 F3
Huthwaite Rd NG17.... 100 C2
Hutton Cl NG9........ 171 D1
Hutton St NG2........ 173 F3
Huxley Cl NG8........ 171 D7
Hyde Cl NG11....... 184 F4
Hyde Pk Cl NG2....... 185 C5
Hyson Cl **10** NG7....... 172 F8
Hyson St **12** NG7....... 172 F7

I
Ian Gr NG4........ 174 F8
IBTE Mus of
  Telecommunications
  S81........ 35 F2
Idle Bank DN9......... 2 D5
Idle Ct DN10........ 10 A7
Idle View DN22....... 29 F1
Idlewells Sh Ctr NG17... 100 E2
Ilam Sq DE7........ 157 E5
Ilford Cl DE7....... 157 D3
Ilion St NG19....... 87 F2
Ilkeston Com Hospl DE7 157 D4
Ilkeston Rd
  Sandiacre NG10....... 182 C8
  Stapleford NG9....... 170 F2
  Trowell NG9........ 170 C5
ILS Nottingham NG5... 173 B8
Imperial Ave
  Beeston NG9........ 183 E6
  Carlton NG4....... 162 E1
Imperial Rd
  Beeston NG9........ 183 E6
  Nottingham NG6....... 160 D6
Inchwood Cl NG9....... 182 F2
Incinerator Rd NG2.... 173 E2
Independent St NG7.... 222 B4
Industrial Mus & Yd Gall
  NG8........ 172 A3
Infield La
  Cuckney NG20......... 60 B5
  North Leverton w H DN22.. 32 E1
  Weston NG23........ 81 B3
Ingamells Dr LN1....... 57 C3
Ingham Gr NG7....... 222 A1
Ingham Rd
  Bawtry DN10......... 9 F8
  Long Eaton NG10....... 182 C2
Ingleborough Gdns **6**
  NG10........ 193 A8
Ingleby Cl
  Cotgrave NG12....... 187 E2
  Nottingham NG8....... 171 B4
Ingleby Medieval Village of
  LN1........ 57 A8
Inglefield Rd DE7....... 170 A6
Inglemere Cl S81....... 36 A5
Inglewood Cl NG24.... 140 D2
Inglewood Rd NG7.... 184 E1
Ingram Rd NG6....... 160 D6
Ingrams La NG23....... 82 A3
Ingram Terr NG6....... 160 C6
Ings Rd DN10....... 12 E6
Inham Cir NG9....... 183 C6
Inham Cl NG9....... 183 A5
Inham Fields Cl NG14.. 165 A5
Inham Rd NG9....... 183 B5
Inholms Gdns NG23.... 152 F2
Inholms Rd NG23....... 152 F2
Inkerman Rd NG16.... 128 F5
Inkerman St NG16.... 128 F5
Innes Rd NG4....... 174 C7
Institute St NG17....... 100 C6
Instow Rise NG3....... 223 F4
Intake Ave NG18....... 101 F5
Intake Farm Prim Sch
  NG19........ 101 E7
Intake Rd
  Clipstone NG21....... 90 A3
  Keyworth NG12....... 197 D3
Iona Cl DN21....... 15 E2
Iona Dr NG9........ 170 D2
Iona Gdns NG5....... 147 A1
Iona Sch NG3....... 174 A5
Ipswich Cir NG3....... 174 A5
Ireland Ave NG9....... 184 A5
Ireland Cl NG9....... 184 A5
Iremonger Rd NG2.... 173 D2
Irene Terr NG7....... 160 F2
Ireton Ave **6** NG24... 140 E8
Ireton Gr NG9....... 183 D2
Ireton St
  Beeston NG9........ 183 E6
  Nottingham NG7....... 222 C3
Irving La NG22....... 120 A5
Irwin Dr NG6........ 160 A6
Isaac's La NG9....... 182 D7
Isabella St NG7....... 223 E1
Island Bsns Quarter NG1 223 F1
Islay Cl
  Arnold NG5........ 147 F1
  Stapleford NG9....... 170 D3
Ivatt Cl DN10....... 10 A8
Ivatt Dr NG2........ 173 F3
Iveagh Cl NG20....... 74 C5
Ives Cl NG2........ 185 C4
Ivies The NG24....... 139 C6
Ivy Cl NG16....... 144 F1

Ivy Gr
  Carlton NG4........ 174 D7
  Kirkby in A NG17....... 114 F6
  Nottingham NG7....... 173 A8
Ivy La NG16....... 143 E2
Ivy Lodge La S81........ 16 B3
Ivy Row NG13....... 179 B3

J
Jacklin Gdns NG5....... 147 A1
Jacksdale Nature Reserve
  NG16........ 128 B3
Jacksdale Prim Sch
  NG16........ 128 B3
Jackson Ave
  8 Ilkeston DE7....... 157 E1
  Sandiacre NG10....... 182 A6
Jackson Terr NG20.... 74 E8
James' Murray Mews
  NG18........ 102 C7
James Peacock Inf Sch
  NG11........ 196 B7
James St
  Annesley Woodhouse
    NG17........ 115 A1
  Arnold NG5........ 161 E8
  Kimberley NG16....... 158 F6
  Worksop S81........ 35 E5
James William Turner Ave
  NG17........ 100 E1
Jamia Al Hudaa Ind Sch
  NG3........ 173 C8
Jamia Al-Karam DN22 ... 40 A1
Japan Rd DN21....... 15 B1
Japonica Dr NG6....... 160 B4
Jardine S81........ 36 B6
Jardines The NG9....... 171 C1
Jarrow Gdns NG5....... 146 F2
Jarvis Ave NG3....... 174 B4
Jasmin Cl NG20....... 72 D6
Jasmine Cl
  Beeston NG9........ 171 D1
  5 Nottingham, Broxtowe
    NG8........ 159 E1
  Nottingham, Glapton NG11 184 C1
Jasmine Dr DE55....... 99 B7
Jasmine Rd NG5....... 160 E3
Jasper Cl NG12....... 175 E2
Jayne Cl
  Carlton NG4........ 163 A2
  Nottingham NG8....... 171 E5
Jay's Cl NG13....... 181 A1
Jedburgh Cl NG3....... 223 F4
Jedburgh Wlk NG3.... 223 F4
Jeffares Cl DE7....... 203 C3
Jeffries Prim Sch NG17. 114 F5
Jellicoe St NG20....... 59 A2
Jenford St NG18....... 101 E6
Jenkins Ave NG19....... 101 D7
Jenned Rd NG5....... 148 A2
Jenner St **14** NG5....... 161 B1
Jenness Ave NG5....... 146 E1
Jennison St
  Mansfield NG19....... 88 A1
  Nottingham NG6....... 160 C7
Jenny Beckett's La NG18 102 F4
Jenny Burton Way NG15. 146 C5
Jensen Way NG5....... 161 B1
Jephson Rd NG17....... 114 F6
Jericho La NG13....... 192 A3
Jericho Rd NG24....... 140 D2
Jermyn Dr NG5....... 147 A1
Jersey Gdns NG3....... 173 E6
Jersey St NG24....... 139 F5
Jerusalem LN6....... 71 F2
Jerusalem Rd LN6....... 71 F3
Jervis Ct DE7....... 157 F3
Jesmond Rd NG6....... 160 D6
Jesse Boot Prim Sch
  NG3........ 174 B5
Jesse Gray Prim Sch
  NG2........ 185 E4
Jessop Cl NG24....... 125 C1
Jessop's La NG4....... 162 E1
Jessop Way NG24....... 125 C1
Job La DN10........ 20 B7
Job's La LN6........ 84 F2
Jockey La DN22....... 50 A5
John Barrow Cl NG21... 118 C8
John Blow Prim Sch
  NG23........ 112 A8
John Carroll Ct **2** NG3. 173 F6
John Carroll L Ctr NG7. 222 B3
John Clifford Prim Sch
  NG9........ 184 A6
John Coupland Hospl
  DN21........ 15 B3
John Davies Prim Sch
  NG17........ 99 F4
John Gold Av NG24.... 140 B7
John Hunt Inf Sch NG24 140 C4
John Hunt Jun Sch
  NG24........ 140 C4
John King Workshop Mus
  NG16........ 113 D3
John Pope Way NG24... 125 B4
Johnson Ave NG15....... 146 B5
Johnson Dr NG18....... 102 C3
Johnson Rd NG7....... 222 A2
Johns Rd NG12....... 176 B3
John St
  Ilkeston DE7........ 157 F1
  Nottingham NG7....... 160 F1
  Sutton in A NG17....... 100 F4
  Worksop S80....... 35 E3
John T Rice Inf Sch NG19. 89 E3

John Wright Cl NG5.... 146 D1
Joseph Whitaker Sch
  NG21........ 117 F8
Joyce Ave
  Beeston NG9........ 182 E3
  Nottingham NG5....... 161 D5
Joyce Cl NG5....... 161 D4
Jubilee Ave NG9....... 184 B8
Jubilee Cl DN10......... 4 B3
Jubilee Dr LE11....... 220 A6
Jubilee Rd
  Arnold NG5........ 161 E6
  Retford DN22........ 39 D5
  Sutton in A NG17....... 100 E3
Jubilee St
  Kimberley NG16....... 158 E7
  Newark-on-T NG24.... 140 A7
  3 Nottingham NG2.... 173 F4
Jubilee Way N NG18... 103 C6
Jubilee Way S NG18... 103 B4
Judges St LE11....... 220 C3
Judson Ave NG9....... 182 F6
Julian Cl DE7....... 170 A6
Julian La NG12....... 164 C1
Julian Rd NG2....... 174 B1
Julias Wy NG17....... 115 B8
Julie Ave DE75....... 143 A1
Jumelles Dr NG14....... 148 D7
Junction Rd
  Long Eaton NG10....... 194 A6
  Sutton in A NG17....... 101 B2
Juniper Cl
  Bilsthorpe NG22....... 106 A5
  Nottingham NG11....... 184 C1
Juniper Ct NG16....... 158 C8
Juniper Gdns NG13.... 178 A4

K
Kansington Ct **5** NG5 . 161 C3
Kappler Cl NG4....... 175 A7
Karen Rise NG5....... 148 A1
Katherine Dr NG9....... 182 F4
Kaye Rd NG19....... 101 D7
Kayes Wlk NG1....... 223 F2
Keats Ave NG17....... 100 B3
Keats Cl
  Arnold NG5........ 161 D7
  Long Eaton NG10....... 193 B5
  Nuthall NG16....... 159 B6
Keats Cres S81....... 36 B4
Keats Dr NG15....... 145 D6
Keats Rd NG24....... 140 D5
Kedleston Cl
  Beeston NG9........ 183 C5
  Long Eaton NG10....... 193 A5
Kedleston Dr DE7....... 157 D3
Kedleston Cl NG17....... 99 F2
Kedleston Rd S81....... 35 F6
Keel Dr NG13....... 181 A2
Keeling Cl NG16....... 144 B1
Keepers Cl NG6....... 146 E4
Keep The LE12....... 205 F1
Kegworth La DE74....... 212 C5
Kegworth Mus DE74... 203 C2
Kegworth Rd
  Gotham NG11....... 195 A1
  Kingston-on-S NG11... 204 E8
  Ratcliffe on S NG11... 203 F5
Keighton Hill NG7....... 172 C1
Keilder Dr NG13....... 177 C4
Kelfield Cl NG6....... 160 E5
Kelham Gn NG3....... 173 F6
Kelham La NG24....... 124 D3
Kelham Rd
  Mansfield NG19....... 101 E7
  Newark-on-T NG24.... 124 E1
Kelham Way NG16....... 143 E3
Keller Ct DN22....... 53 B8
Kelling Cl NG5....... 161 A6
Kelly Wlk NG2....... 185 B7
Kelsey Cl NG9....... 183 E3
Kelso Gdns NG2....... 173 B2
Kelstedge Dr NG18.... 103 B6
Kelstern Cl
  Mansfield NG18....... 103 A7
  Nottingham NG8....... 160 C3
Kelvedon Gdns NG3.... 173 E6
Kelvin Cl NG9....... 182 C5
Kelvin Rd
  Clipstone NG19....... 89 D3
  Nottingham NG3....... 174 A7
Kemmel Rd NG6....... 160 D5
Kempsey Cl NG5....... 160 E8
Kempson St NG11....... 196 C6
Kempton Cl NG16....... 158 E7
Kempton Dr NG5....... 148 A1
Kempton Rd NG18....... 102 F7
Kendal Cl
  Annesley Woodhouse
    NG17........ 130 A8
  Hucknall NG15....... 145 F8
  Worksop S81........ 35 E8
Kendal Ct NG2....... 186 B8
Kendale Dr NG9....... 183 D8
Kendale Ct NG3....... 161 F1
Kendal Rd NG12....... 189 A4
Kenia Cl NG4....... 174 D8
Kenilworth Ave NG17... 101 B4
Kenilworth Cl
  Saxilby LN1........ 57 A4
  Worksop S80....... 36 A1
Kenilworth Ct
  Beeston NG9........ 184 A7
  Nottingham NG7....... 223 D1
Kenilworth Dr S81....... 25 F6

Kenilworth Rd
  Beeston NG9........ 184 A8
  Nottingham NG7....... 223 D1
Kenley Cl S81........ 35 D8
Kenmare Cres DN21.... 24 F6
Ken Martin Swimming Ctr
  NG6........ 146 C1
Kenmore Cl NG19....... 101 E5
Kenmore Gdns NG3.... 223 F4
Kennack Cl DE55....... 113 C6
Kennedy Ave
  Long Eaton NG10....... 193 C5
  Mansfield Woodhouse
    NG19........ 88 D4
Kennedy Cl NG5....... 161 E7
Kennedy Ct
  Walesby NG22....... 64 A2
  Worksop S81........ 36 A4
Kennedy Dr NG9....... 170 E1
Kennedy Rise NG22.... 64 A2
Kennedy Wlk NG24.... 140 E4
Kennel Dr NG22....... 28 C5
Kennel La NG6....... 71 C1
Kenneth Rd NG5....... 147 F2
Kennel Paddock NG19... 88 D3
Kennington Rd NG8.... 172 D5
Kenrick Rd NG3....... 162 A2
Kenrick St NG4....... 175 A7
Kensington Cl
  Beeston NG9........ 183 A1
  Mansfield Woodhouse NG19 88 E3
  Sutton in A NG17....... 100 E2
Kensington Gdns
  Carlton NG4........ 174 E7
  Ilkeston DE7....... 170 A7
Kensington Pk Cl NG2.. 185 C5
Kensington Rd NG10... 182 A4
Kenslow Ave **10** NG7.. 172 E7
Kent Ave
  Beeston NG9........ 183 F4
  Westwood NG16....... 128 B4
Kent Cl S81........ 36 A6
Kentmere Cl NG2....... 186 C7
Kenton Ave NG16....... 159 D3
Kenton Ct **6** NG2.... 173 D1
Kent Rd
  Eastwood NG16....... 158 C8
  Nottingham NG3....... 162 A4
Kent St NG1........ 223 F3
Kentwood Rd NG2....... 173 F4
Kenyon Rd NG7....... 172 D3
Keppel Ct DE7....... 157 F3
Kersall Dr NG6....... 160 D5
Kersall Dr NG6....... 160 D5
Kersall Gdns NG15....... 146 B7
Kestral Dr NG13....... 177 F3
Kestral Rd NG18....... 101 E4
Kestrel Cl NG4....... 162 B1
Kestrel Dr NG21....... 118 B8
Kestrel Mews S81....... 35 C7
Kestrel Rise LN6....... 84 D2
Keswick Cl
  Beeston NG9........ 183 D8
  West Bridgford NG2... 186 C7
Keswick Ct
  Long Eaton NG10....... 182 B2
  3 Nottingham NG2.... 173 E4
Keswick St NG2....... 173 E4
Ketlock Hill La DN22.... 32 C1
Kettlethorpe Rd LN1.... 55 D5
Kett St NG6........ 160 B6
Keverne Cl NG8....... 160 C2
Kevin Rd NG8....... 171 D2
Kew Cl NG11....... 185 C3
Kew Cres DE75....... 143 B1
Kew Gdns
  New Balderton NG24... 140 B4
  Nuthall NG8........ 159 E3
Kexby Wlk DN21....... 24 F7
Keyes Cl DN10....... 19 F8
Keyes Ct DN10....... 19 F8
Keyes Rise DN10....... 19 F8
Keys Cl NG6....... 160 A7
Key St NG3....... 173 F5
Keyworth Cl NG19....... 101 E7
Keyworth Dr NG19....... 89 C1
Keyworth L Ctr NG12... 197 F2
Keyworth Mdw Nature
  Reserve NG12....... 207 E6
Keyworth Prim Sch
  NG12........ 197 E3
Keyworth Rd
  Carlton NG4........ 162 D3
  Widmerpool NG12.... 208 C5
  Wysall NG12....... 207 C5
Kibworth Cl NG5....... 160 F4
Kiddier Ave NG5....... 162 B7
Kid La S81........ 16 A5
Kighill La NG15....... 132 B7
Kilbourne Rd NG5....... 148 B1
Kilbourne St NG3....... 223 E4
Kilburn Cl NG9....... 171 B2
Kilby Ave NG3....... 174 A6
Kildare Rd NG3....... 173 F8
Kildonan Cl NG8....... 159 D2
Killerton Gn NG11....... 195 F3
Killerton Pk Dr NG11... 185 B4
Killisick Jun Sch NG5... 162 B8
Killisick Rd NG5....... 162 B8
Kilnbrook Ave NG5....... 148 B1
Kilnwood Cl NG3....... 174 A1
Kilsby Rd NG7....... 184 F2
Kilton Ave NG18....... 103 B7
Kilton Cl S81........ 36 A4
Kilton Cres S81....... 36 B4
Kilton Glade S81....... 36 B4
Kilton Hill S81....... 36 A5

Kilton Rd S80............ 36 A3
Kilton Terr S80............ 36 A3
Kilverston Rd NG10........182 A6
Kilverton Cl NG8.........172 C4
Kilvington Rd NG5........162 B7
Kimber Cl NG8...........171 D6
Kimberley Cl NG16.........158 F5
Kimberley Comp Sch
NG16.................159 A6
Kimberley L Ctr NG16....159 A6
Kimberley Prim Sch
NG16.................158 F6
Kimberley Rd
Nottingham NG2.........174 A4
Nuthall NG16............159 C5
Kimbolton Ave NG7.........222 B2
Kindlewood Dr NG9........183 B1
King Charles St NG1......223 D2
King Edward Ave NG18....102 B4
King Edward Gdns NG10..182 B6
King Edward Prim Sch
NG18.................102 C6
King Edward Rd LE11.....220 C3
King Edward St
Hucknall NG15..........146 A6
Nottingham NG1.........223 E3
Sandiacre NG10.........182 B6
Shirebrook NG20..........72 F4
King Edward's Terr DN22..39 F6
King Edwin Prim Sch
NG21..................75 F1
Kingerby Cl DN21.........24 E7
Kingfield Cl NG21.......118 B8
Kingfisher Cl
New Balderton NG24......140 C5
Nottingham NG6.........160 D4
Kingfisher Ct
Beeston NG9............184 B5
2 Loughborough LE11....220 A2
Kingfisher Rd NG19........87 D1
Kingfishers Ct NG2......186 C4
Kingfisher Way 1 LE11..220 A2
Kingfisher Wharf
4 Nottingham NG7......172 F2
1 Nottingham NG7......173 A2
Kingfisher Wlk S81.......35 C7
King George Ave LE11....220 D2
King George Rd LE11.....220 D2
King George V Ave NG18..102 E5
King Johns Arc NG1......223 E2
King John's Rd NG21......90 A4
Kinglake Pl NG2.........173 C2
King Rd NG20............74 A4
Kingrove Ave NG9........183 D6
King St E DN21..........24 D7
Kings Ave NG4...........162 E2
Kingsbridge Ave NG3.....162 C6
Kingsbridge Way NG9.....183 C6
Kingsbury Dr NG8........172 A8
Kings Ct NG25...........121 E1
Kingsdale S81...........36 B8
Kingsdale Cl NG10.......193 A5
Kingsdown Mount NG8....171 E2
Kings Dr NG16...........143 E7
Kingsford Ave NG7.......222 A4
Kingshaugh Camp (Ancient
Mon) NG22.............66 F8
Kingsley Ave NG19........88 D5
Kingsley Cl NG19.........88 D4
Kingsley Cres NG10......193 B4
Kingsley Ct NG19.........88 D5
Kingsley Dr NG4.........175 A7
Kingsley Rd NG2.........174 A3
Kingsley St NG15........115 B4
Kings Lodge Dr NG18....101 E4
King's Marina NG24......124 F2
King's Mdw Rd NG2......173 A2
Kingsmead DN22..........39 D3
Kingsmead Ave NG9......170 D2
Kingsmeadow NG21......118 C4
King's Mill NG17........101 C5
King's Mill Ctr Hospl
NG17.................101 C5
Kings Mill La NG18......101 D4
Kings Mill Rd E NG17,
NG19.................114 E8
Kings Mill Way NG18....101 E4
Kings Moor NG5.........160 E7
Kingsnorth Cl NG24.....140 A8
King's Pl NG1...........223 F2
Kings Rd
Long Clawson LE14......211 C2
Sandiacre NG10.........182 B6
King's Rd NG24..........124 F1
Kings Sch The NG2.......173 D1
Kings Stand NG18........102 E4
King St
Beeston NG9............184 A6
Eastwood NG16..........143 F2
Gainsborough DN21......24 D7
Hodthorpe S80..........45 C6
Huthwaite NG17.........100 B3
Ilkeston DE7...........157 F1
Kirkby in A NG17.......115 A4
Long Eaton NG10........193 D8
Loughborough LE11......220 C3
Mansfield NG18.........102 D7
Mansfield Woodhouse
NG19..................88 D2
Nether Broughton LE14...219 D8
Newark-on-T NG24.......139 E7
Nottingham NG1.........223 E3
Pinxton NG16...........113 D4
South Normanton DE55...113 A5
Southwell NG25.........121 E1
Sutton in A NG17.......100 E2
Tibshelf DE55...........99 A7
Warsop Vale NG20........73 D5

King St continued
Worksop S80............35 E2
Kingsthorpe Cl
Mansfield NG19..........88 E1
Nottingham NG3.........161 F1
Kingston Ave DE7........170 A4
Kingston Cl S80.........47 C8
Kingston Ct
Kingston-on-S NG11.....204 D5
14 Nottingham NG2.....173 E4
Kingston Dr
Cotgrave NG12..........187 F1
Ollerton NG22...........77 A3
Kingston La DE74........203 F3
Kingston Pk Prim Sch
S81..................25 F6
Kingston Rd
Carlton in L S81........25 E6
Mansfield NG18.........102 D7
West Bridgford NG2.....185 E6
Worksop S80............47 B8
Kingsway
Ilkeston DE7...........170 A6
Kirkby in A NG17.......115 B3
Mansfield Woodhouse NG19.89 A1
New Balderton NG24.....140 C3
Radcliffe on T NG12....175 E2
Worksop S81............36 A4
Kingsway Rd NG15.......145 E4
Kingsway Ave NG22.......77 D6
Kingsway Gdns NG15.....145 E4
Kingsway Prim Sch
NG17.................115 B3
Kingsway Rd NG15.......145 E4
Kingswell Rd NG5.......161 F6
Kings Wlk NG18.........102 E4
Kingswood Cl S81........16 A5
Kingswood Dr NG17......114 F6
Kingswood Rd
Nottingham NG8........172 B5
West Bridgford NG2.....185 D5
Kinlet Rd NG5..........161 A6
Kinoulton La
Kinoulton NG12.........209 B8
Kinoulton, Owthorpe NG12 199 F4
Kinoulton Prim Sch
NG12.................199 E1
Kinoulton Rd NG12......188 F2
Kinsdale Wlk NG11......184 E3
Kipling Cl
Nottingham NG11.......195 C8
Worksop S81............36 B5
Kipling St 6 NG18......102 A7
Kipps St NG1...........223 F3
Kirby Cl
Blidworth NG21.........118 A4
Eastwood NG16..........144 A3
Kirby Dr DE74..........203 C1
Kirby Rd NG16..........144 A3
Kirk Ave DE74..........203 D2
Kirkbride Ct NG9.......183 B4
Kirkby Cl NG25.........121 E2
Kirkby Folly Rd NG17...101 B1
Kirkby Gdns NG2........173 D2
Kirkby House Dr NG17...114 E5
Kirkby-in-Ashfield Sta
NG17.................115 A5
Kirkby La NG16.........114 B4
Kirkby Mill View NG17..114 E5
Kirkby Rd
Ravenshead NG15........116 C3
Sutton in A NG17.......100 E1
Kirkby Woodhouse Prim Sch
NG17.................114 E1
Kirk Cl NG9............183 D4
Kirkdale Cl NG8........171 B4
Kirkdale Gdns NG10.....193 B6
Kirkdale Rd
Long Eaton NG10........193 B6
Nottingham NG3.........174 B6
Kirk Dr NG22............77 E6
Kirke Cl NG22...........66 B7
Kirke St NG22...........39 F7
Kirkewhite Ave NG10....193 D7
Kirkfell Cl NG2........186 C5
Kirk Gate NG24.........124 F1
Kirkham Dr NG9.........182 F2
Kirkhill NG13..........177 E5
Kirk Hill NG13.........165 B2
Kirk La NG11...........196 C7
Kirkland Ave NG18......101 F6
Kirkland Cl NG17.......115 B8
Kirkland Dr NG9........183 C2
Kirkley Gdns NG5.......162 A8
Kirk Ley Rd LE12.......214 D8
Kirklington Prim Sch
NG22.................120 E7
Kirklington Rd
Bilsthorpe NG22........105 D2
Eakring NG22...........106 E8
Rainworth NG21, NG22..104 C1
Southwell NG25.........121 D1
Kirkpatrick Dr S81......35 C7
Kirk Rd NG3............162 A2
Kirk's Bldgs NG4.......174 D7
Kirkstead Cl NG16......113 D3
Kirkstead Gdns 7 NG7..172 F7
Kirkstead Jun Sch NG16 113 D3
Kirkstead Rd NG16......113 D3
Kirkstead St 6 NG7.....172 F7
Kirkstone Ct NG10......182 B2
Kirkstone Dr NG2.......186 C7
Kirk White Ct NG2......173 D2
Kirtle Rd NG8..........172 B8
Kirtley Dr NG2.........173 A2
Kirton Ave NG10........193 D7

Kirton Cl
Balderton NG24.........140 D2
Mansfield NG19.........101 D7
Meden Vale NG20.........74 E8
Kirton Ct NG22..........78 B6
Kirton Pk NG22..........78 C6
Kirton Rd NG22..........79 D6
Kirton Wood Nature Reserve
NG22..................78 F5
Kitchener Dr NG18......102 C6
Kitchener Gdns NG18.....35 E8
Kitchener Terr NG20.....59 A2
Kitson Ave NG16........128 C4
Kittiwake Mews NG7.....222 A4
Kiwi Cl NG15...........145 D5
Knapp Ave NG16.........143 F1
Knaton Rd S81...........25 E7
Kneesall Cl NG22........74 D7
Kneesall Gr NG15.......146 B7
Kneeton Cl
Carlton NG4............162 D4
Nottingham NG5.........161 C4
Kneeton Rd NG13........165 E5
Kneeton Vale NG5.......161 C4
Knighton Av NG7........172 E6
Knighton Ave NG7.......222 A4
Knighton Rd NG5........161 D5
Knightsbridge Dr
Nuthall NG16...........159 E3
West Bridgford NG2.....185 C4
Knightsbridge Gdns
NG15.................130 F1
Knights Cl
Nottingham NG5.........160 F8
West Bridgford NG2.....185 C3
Knight's Cl NG13.......166 E4
Knight's Ct NG24.......140 A8
Knight St NG4..........175 A6
Knipton Cl NG24........140 D3
Knole Rd NG8...........171 E5
Knoll Ave NG15.........145 D5
Knoll The
Mansfield NG18.........101 E6
Shirebrook NG20.........72 E6
Knott End S81...........16 E3
Knott's Ct NG24........140 D4
Knowle Hill NG16.......159 A5
Knowle La NG16.........159 A5
Knowle Pk NG16.........159 A5
Knowles Wlk 3 NG5.....161 D8
Krebs Cl NG11..........184 C1
Kyle View NG5..........147 A1
Kyme St NG7............222 B3
Kynance Cl DE55........113 C6
Kynance Gdns NG11......185 B5

L

Labray Rd NG14.........148 E8
Laburnum Cl NG24.......140 C5
Laburnum Ave
Gainsborough DN21......15 D2
Keyworth NG12..........198 A2
Kirkby in A NG17.......114 D3
Shirebrook NG20.........72 E5
Laburnum Cl
Hathern LE12...........213 A1
Sandiacre NG10.........182 B7
South Normanton DE55...113 B7
Worksop S80.............35 D1
Laburnum Gr
Beeston NG9............184 B5
Hucknall NG15..........146 B5
Mansfield Woodhouse NG19 88 A4
Laburnum Rd S81.........16 F4
Laburnum St NG3........173 D2
Laceby Cl NG19..........88 E4
Lace Ctr The NG1.......223 D2
Lace Market Theatre The
NG1..................223 E2
Lace Mkt Ctr The NG1...223 E2
Lace Rd NG9............183 F7
Lace St NG7............172 D1
Lace Wy NG1............173 E3
Lacey Ave NG15.........146 A5
Lacey Cl DE7...........157 C3
Lacey Fields Rd DE75...143 B1
Lacey Gn NG24..........140 E3
Ladbrooke Cres NG6.....160 C3
Ladybank Rise NG5......162 C8
Lady Bay Ave NG2.......173 F1
Lady Bay Bridge NG2....173 F1
Lady Bay Prim Sch NG2..174 A1
Lady Bay Rd NG2........174 A1
Lady Bay Ret Pk NG2....173 E3
Ladybridge Cl NG9......183 E3
Ladybrook La NG18......101 F7
Ladybrook Pl NG19......101 E7
Ladybrook Primary Sch
NG19.................101 D8
Ladybrook Prim Sch
NG19.................101 D8
Ladycroft Ave NG15.....146 A7
Ladycross Inf Sch NG10.182 B6
Ladylea Cl NG18.........35 B2
Ladylea Rd NG10........193 A4
Lady Lee Quarry Nature
Reserve S80............35 A4
Ladysmith Rd NG2.......174 A4
Ladysmock Gdns NG2....173 D2
Lady Well La DN22.......52 B8
Lake Ave NG16..........101 E7
Lake Farm Rd NG21......103 F1
Lakeland Ave NG15......146 C5
Lakeside Arts Ctr NG7..172 D1

Lakeside Ave NG10......193 C4
Lakeside Cres NG10.....193 C5
Lakeside Inf Sch NG10..193 B4
Lakeside View NG17.....101 B4
Lake St NG7............222 B4
Lake View Dr NG17......129 F6
Lakeview Prim Sch
NG21.................103 F1
Lakeview Sixth Form Coll
NG9..................183 D3
Lamartine Cl NG3.......223 F3
Lamartine St NG3.......223 F3
Lamb Cl NG24...........139 C7
Lamb Cl Dr NG16........144 B4
Lambcroft Rd NG16.....113 D4
Lambert Ct NG9.........184 B7
Lambert Gdns NG8......172 C8
Lambert St NG7.........172 E7
Lambeth Rd NG5........147 A2
Lambie Cl NG8..........172 C5
Lamb La S81............16 C5
Lambley Ave
Mansfield NG18.........102 F5
Nottingham NG3.........162 B3
Lambley Bridle Rd NG14 163 D6
Lambley La
Burton Joyce NG14.....163 E5
Carlton NG4............162 F3
Lambley Prim Sch NG4..163 B7
Lambley Rd NG14........150 B1
Lambourne Cres NG14...150 F1
Lambourne Dr NG8......172 A5
Lambourne Gdns NG5....162 A5
Lambton Cl DE7.........157 E3
Lamcote Gdns NG12.....175 E3
Lamcote Gr NG2.........173 D1
Lamcote Mews NG4......175 E3
Lamcote St NG2.........173 D1
Laming Gap La NG12....198 E5
Lamins La NG5..........147 D4
Lammas Cl NG17........100 E2
Lammas Gdns
East Bridgford NG13....165 D4
Nottingham NG2........173 D2
Lammas La NG13........165 D4
Lammas Rd NG17........100 E2
Lammas Sch The NG17...100 E3
Lamond Cl NG19........101 E5
Lamorna Gr NG11.......185 B6
Lamplands NG12........187 E3
Lamp Wood Cl NG14.....148 E7
Lanark Cl NG8..........172 C3
Lancaster Ave
Sandiacre NG10........182 A4
Stapleford NG9.........182 E7
Lancaster Cl DN11.......8 B7
Lancaster Dr DN10.......9 F8
Lancaster Rd
Bestwood Village NG6..146 E4
Gringley on t H DN10...22 A8
Hucknall NG15.........145 D4
Newark-on-T NG24......125 E2
Nottingham NG3........174 B7
Lancaster Way NG8.....159 D2
Lancaster Wlk S81......35 E8
Lancastrian Way S81....36 A6
Lancelot Dr NG16.......145 A1
Lancelyn Gdns NG2.....185 E4
Lancster Cres DN11......8 B7
Landa Gr NG22..........66 A3
Landcroft Cres NG5.....161 A6
Landmere Cl DE7.......157 C3
Landmere Gdns NG3....161 F1
Landmere La
West Bridgford NG11...185 C3
West Bridgford NG11,
NG12.................185 E1
Landsdowne Ct DN22....39 D4
Landsdowne Rd NG5.....160 E4
Landsdown Gr NG10.....182 F1
Landseer Cl
Nottingham NG7........222 A4
Southwell NG25........136 C8
Landseer Rd NG25......136 C8
Lane End NG17.........115 A5
Laneham Ave NG5.......162 A7
Laneham Rd
Dunham on T NG22......54 A2
Stokeham DN22..........53 D6
Laneham St DN22........43 A1
Lanercost Mews 3 S80..36 E7
Laneside Ave NG9......182 E2
Lane The
Awsworth NG16.........158 C4
Cotham NG23...........154 F3
Laneward Cl DE7.......157 D4
Langar Cl NG5..........161 C4
Langar Industrial Estate
NG13.................201 E6
Langar La
Colston Bassett NG12..200 F8
Harby LE14............202 A4
Langar Pl NG19.........103 B8
Langar Rd NG13........177 E4
Langdale Cl NG24.......139 E4
Langdale Dr
Long Eaton NG10.......193 A6
Tickhill DN11...........8 B8
Langdale Gr NG13.......177 B4
Langdale Rd
Nottingham NG3........174 C5
Worksop S81.............35 F7
Langdon Cl NG10.......182 A1
Langdown Cl NG6.......160 A8
Langford La NG23......111 A3

Kil–Lau **243**

Langford Rd
Arnold NG5............162 B7
Mansfield NG19.........101 D6
Langford St NG17.......100 E3
Langham Ave NG3.......174 A6
Langham Dr NG14.......163 F5
Langham Pl NG18.......101 F7
Langley Ave
Arnold NG5............161 F6
Ilkeston DE7...........157 D5
Langley Cl NG19........87 E1
Langley Dr DE7........203 C2
Langley Mill Business Park
NG16.................143 B2
Langley Mill CE Inf Sch
NG16.................143 B3
Langley Mill Jun Sch
NG16.................143 A4
Langley Mill Sta NG16..143 B2
Langley Pk NG16.......143 B3
Langley St 1 S80.......35 F2
Langold Ctry Pk S81.....16 E2
Langold Dyscarr Com Sch
S81..................16 D3
Langstrath Dr NG2......186 C4
Langstrath Rd NG7......184 E1
Langton Ave NG17......114 C6
Langton Cl NG4.........174 E6
Langton Hollow NG16...128 D6
Langton Rd NG17.......100 E2
Langtree Gdns NG13....177 F5
Langtry Gr NG7.........161 A1
Langwell Dr NG19.......89 C2
Langwith Bassett Prim Sch
NG20..................72 E7
Langwith Dr NG20........58 F1
Langwith Maltings NG20.72 F8
Langwith Rd
Cuckney NG20...........60 A2
Shirebrook NG20.........72 F5
Langwith-Whaley Thorns Sta
NG20..................58 F2
Lansbury Ave NG22......77 C6
Lansbury Dr
Bilsthorpe NG22........105 F7
South Normanton DE55..113 A6
Lansbury Gdns NG18....102 E8
Lansbury Rd
Bilsthorpe NG22........105 E2
Edwinstowe NG21........76 B2
New Balderton NG24....140 C4
Sutton in A NG17.......100 F1
Lansdall Ave DN21.......24 E3
Lansdown Cl NG9.......183 B4
Lansdowne Ave NG18...102 C4
Lansdowne Dr
Loughborough LE11.....220 A1
West Bridgford NG2....185 D4
Lansic La NG14.........151 C1
Lansing Cl NG11.......195 C8
Lantern La LE12........205 F2
Lanthwaite Cl NG7......184 F1
Lanthwaite Rd NG7......184 F1
Lapford Cl NG3.........162 D6
Larch Ave
Mansfield Woodhouse
NG19..................88 B5
Shirebrook NG20.........72 D4
Larch Cl
Bingham NG13..........178 A4
Hucknall NG15..........146 B5
Nottingham NG5.........161 C8
Larch Cres
Beeston NG9............183 D7
Eastwood NG16.........143 E2
Larch Ct DN21...........15 E2
Larchdale Cl DE55......113 A4
Larchdene Ave NG8......171 D3
Larch Dr NG10..........182 B7
Larch Gdns NG6.........160 A2
Larch Rd NG22...........77 D5
Larch Way NG12........198 A2
Largs Cl NG5...........146 E1
Lark Cl NG9............183 A5
Larkdale St NG7........222 C4
Larkfield Ave NG17.....114 E1
Larkfield Rd NG16......159 B6
Larkfields Inf Sch NG16 159 B5
Larkfields Jun Sch NG16 159 B5
Larkhall Pl NG18.......101 E5
Larklands Ave DE7......170 A7
Lark Spinney S81........35 C6
Larkspur Ave NG5......147 E2
Larkspur Cl
Mansfield NG19.........88 D2
South Normanton DE55..113 A4
Larpit Gn S80...........45 A5
Larwood S81............36 B5
Larwood Cres NG17.....114 F1
Larwood Gr NG5........161 C4
Lascelles Ave NG4......162 D2
Latham St NG6.........160 B7
Lathkill Ave DE7.......157 E5
Lathkill Cl NG6........160 B7
Lathkilldale Cres NG10.193 A5
Lathkill Dr NG16.......128 C4
Latimer Cl NG6........160 C6
Latimer Dr NG9........171 B3
Latimer Way NG22......77 C4
Laughton Ave NG2......185 C4
Laughton Cres NG15....145 E4
Laughton Rd DN21.......15 C7
Launceston Cres NG11..185 A4
Launder St
Nottingham NG2........173 C2

Launder St continued
Orston NG13 . . . . **179** F7
Launds Ave NG16 . . . . **128** D7
Laurel Ave
Church Warsop NG20 . . . . **74** A7
Keyworth NG12 . . . . **197** F2
Mansfield NG18 . . . . **102** C5
Mansfield Woodhouse NG19 **89** A1
Misterton DN10 . . . . **6** E3
Laurel Cl
Gainsborough DN21 . . . . . . **15** E2
Shirebrook NG20 . . . . **72** D6
Wysall NG12 . . . . **207** C3
Laurel Cres
Long Eaton NG10 . . . . **193** C6
Nuthall NG16 . . . . **159** B6
Laurel Gr
Kirkby in A NG17 . . . . **115** C5
South Normanton DE55 . . **113** A4
Laurel Rd NG4 . . . . **174** C8
Laurie Ave NG7 . . . . **173** A8
Laurie Cl 4 NG7 . . . . **173** A8
Lauriston Dr NG6 . . . . . . **160** D4
Lavender Cl
2 Nottingham NG8 . . . . . **159** E1
Tibshelf DE55 . . . . **99** B7
Lavender Cres NG4 . . . . **162** D1
Lavender Gdns DE75 . . . **143** B1
Lavender Gr NG9 . . . . . . **184** B5
Lavender Wlk NG3 . . . . . **173** D7
Lavenham Mews 8 S80 . . **35** F2
Laver Cl NG17 . . . . **162** B7
Laverick Rd NG16 . . . . . . **128** A4
Lawdon Rd NG5 . . . . **148** A1
Lawley Ave NG9 . . . . **172** A1
Lawn Ave NG17 . . . . **100** F2
Lawn La
Old Dalby LE14 . . . . **218** E2
Sutton in A NG17 . . . . **100** E1
Lawn Mill Rd NG16 . . . . . **158** E7
Lawn Rd
Carlton in L S81 . . . . **25** E8
Sutton in A NG17 . . . . **101** B3
Lawns Rd NG17 . . . . **129** F8
Lawns The
Collingham NG23 . . . . **98** B1
Whatton NG13 . . . . **179** A3
Lawnwood Ave DN22 . . . . **50** A3
Lawnwood La DN22 . . . . . **50** A3
Lawrence Ave
Awsworth NG16 . . . . **158** C4
Carlton NG4 . . . . **174** E5
Eastwood NG16 . . . . **143** F2
Kirkby in A NG17 . . . . **114** E5
Mansfield Woodhouse NG19 **88** B4
Lawrence Cl NG12 . . . . . **187** F3
Lawrence Cres NG17 . . . **101** B4
Lawrence Dr NG16 . . . . . **143** D8
Lawrence Pk NG16 . . . . . **129** B3
Lawrence Pl NG24 . . . . . . **125** A1
Lawrence St
Long Eaton NG10 . . . . **193** D8
Newark-on-T NG24 . . . . . . **125** A1
Sandiacre NG10 . . . . **182** B7
Stapleford NG9 . . . . **182** D6
Lawrence Way 6 NG2 . . **173** A2
Lawson Ave NG10 . . . . . . **193** E7
Lawson Cl DN22 . . . . **50** F2
Lawson Sq S81 . . . . **18** B2
Lawson St NG7 . . . . **222** C4
Lawton Dr NG6 . . . . **146** C1
Laxton Ave
Nottingham NG6 . . . . **160** D5
Sutton in A NG17 . . . . **101** C1
Laxton Dr
Hucknall NG15 . . . . **145** E6
Meden Vale NG20 . . . . **74** D8
Laxton Heritage Mus
NG22 . . . . **79** B3
Laxton Rd NG22 . . . . **79** D4
Laxton Visitors Ctr NG22 . **79** C3
Laycock Ave DN10 . . . . . . **12** E2
Layton Ave NG18 . . . . . . **102** A7
Layton Burroughs 11
NG18 . . . . **102** A7
Leabrook Cl NG11 . . . . . . **184** C3
Leabrook Gdns NG15 . . . **146** C8
Leabrooks Ave
Mansfield Woodhouse
NG19 . . . . **88** D5
Sutton in A NG17 . . . . **101** C1
Leach Cl NG22 . . . . **54** C1
Leachcroft Hill NG25 . . . **136** B8
Leach Wy NG21 . . . . **118** B6
Lea Cl NG15 . . . . **117** B2
Leacroft Rd NG8 . . . . **172** D8
Lea Ct S80 . . . . **35** C2
Leadale Ave NG15 . . . . . . **146** C8
Leadale Cres NG19 . . . . . . **88** E5
Lead Hill S80 . . . . **35** E2
Leaf Cl NG15 . . . . **131** B1
Leafe Cl NG9 . . . . **183** C2
Leafield DE72 . . . . **39** D8
Leafield Gn NG7 . . . . **184** E2
Leahurst Gdns NG2 . . . . . **186** B6
Leahurst Rd NG2 . . . . **186** B5
Leake La LE12 . . . . **214** D3
Leake Rd
Costock LE12 . . . . **206** B1
Gotham NG11 . . . . **205** C6
Lea La NG16 . . . . **128** F6
Leam Glen NG19 . . . . **88** D2
Leamington Dr
Beeston NG9 . . . . **183** C4
South Normanton DE55 . . **113** B5

Leamington Dr continued
Sutton in A NG17 . . . . **114** E8
Leamington Hall NG17 . . **100** E1
Leamington Prim Sch
NG17. . . . . **114** F8
Leander Cl NG11 . . . . **185** B6

Lea Rd
Gainsborough DN21 . . . . . . **24** E5
Market Warsop NG20 . . . . . **74** C3
Ravenshead NG15 . . . . . . **117** B2
Lea Rd W DN21 . . . . **24** D5
Leas Ave NG19 . . . . **87** A5
Leas Park Jun Sch NG19 . **88** C4
Leas Rd NG19 . . . . **88** D4
Leas The NG4 . . . . **164** B5
Leatherlands DE74 . . . . . **203** D3
Lea Vale NG19 . . . . **113** A4
Leaway The NG20 . . . . **72** D3
Le Brun Sq S81 . . . . **25** E7
Lechlade Rd NG5 . . . . **161** A6
Ledbury Vale NG8 . . . . . . **172** B8
Leech Cl NG16 . . . . **158** B7
Leeks Rd NG25 . . . . **121** E1
Lee La DE75 . . . . **143** B1
Leeming Cl NG20 . . . . **74** C5
Leeming La NG19, NG20 . . **88** C4
Leeming La N NG19 . . . . . . **88** E5
Leeming La S NG19 . . . . . . **88** C2
Leeming Pk NG19 . . . . **88** C3
Leeming St NG18 . . . . . . **102** B7
Leen Cl
Bestwood Village NG6 . . . **146** F4
Hucknall NG15 . . . . **146** C8
Leen Ct NG22 . . . . **78** A4
Leen Dr
Hucknall NG15 . . . . **131** B1
Nottingham NG6 . . . . **146** C1
Leen Gate NG7 . . . . **172** E2
Leen Mills La NG15 . . . . . **131** A1
Leen Mills Prim Sch
NG15 . . . . **146** B8
Leen Pl NG7 . . . . **222** A3
Leen Valley Dr NG20 . . . . **72** E3
Leen Valley Way NG15 . . **146** C5
Lee Rd
Burton Joyce NG14 . . . . . **164** A5
Calverton NG14 . . . . **148** D8
Lees Ave NG19 . . . . **101** D7
Lees Barn Rd NG12 . . . . . **175** D2
Lees Hill St NG2 . . . . **173** E4
Lees La DE55 . . . . **113** A6
Lees Rd NG3 . . . . **162** A2
Leeway Cl NG21 . . . . **103** E2
Leeway Rd
Mansfield NG21 . . . . **103** E2
Southwell NG25 . . . . **121** D1
Legion Dr NG17 . . . . **100** D6
Leicester Cres S81 . . . . . . **35** E7
Leicester Rd LE11 . . . . . . **220** C2
Leicester St NG10 . . . . . . **193** E6
Leigh Cl NG2 . . . . **185** C6
Leigh Rd NG9 . . . . **182** F3
Leighton St NG3 . . . . **173** F6
Leiston Gdns NG5 . . . . . . **161** A8
Leivers Ave NG5 . . . . **161** F8
Leivers Cl LE12 . . . . **205** E1
Lema Cl NG6 . . . . **160** D7
Lemont Rd NG19 . . . . **89** D2
Lemyngton St LE11 . . . . . **220** B4
Lendrum Ct NG14 . . . . . . **163** F4
Lennox St NG1 . . . . **223** F3
Lenton Ave
Nottingham NG7 . . . . **222** C1
Tollerton NG12 . . . . **186** C1
Lenton Bvd NG7 . . . . **222** B2
Lenton Cir NG12 . . . . **186** C1
Lenton Ct NG7 . . . . **222** B2
Lenton Hall Dr NG7 . . . . **172** C1
Lenton Ind Est E NG7 . . . **184** F8
Lenton Ind Est W NG7 . . **184** F8
Lenton La NG7 . . . . **184** F8
Lenton Manor NG7 . . . . . **222** A1
Lenton Prim Sch NG7 . . . **222** B1
Lenton Rd NG7 . . . . **223** D2
Lenton St NG10 . . . . **182** C7
Leonard Ave NG5 . . . . . . **161** B2
Leonard Cheshire Cl
DE75 . . . . **143** B1
Leonard St NG6 . . . . **160** B5
Leopold St
Long Eaton NG10 . . . . **193** D8
Loughborough LE11 . . . . . **220** A5
Sutton in A NG17 . . . . **100** E1
Le Page Ct NG8 . . . . **172** A7
Leroy Wallace Ave NG7 . **222** B4
Lerwick Cl NG11 . . . . **185** A1
Leslie Ave
Beeston NG9 . . . . **183** F5
Kimberley NG16 . . . . **158** F5
6 Nottingham NG7 . . . . . **173** A8
Leslie Gr NG14 . . . . **148** F7
Leslie Rd NG7 . . . . **173** A8
Letchworth Cres NG9 . . . **183** C4
Letcombe Rd NG11 . . . . . **184** E3
Letwell Ave S81 . . . . **16** A2
Levellers Way NG24 . . . . **140** E8
Levels La
Blaxton DN9 . . . . **1** A8
Misson DN10 . . . . **4** B6
Levens Cl NG2 . . . . **186** C5
Leverton Gn NG7 . . . . . . **184** E2
Leverton Rd
Mansfield NG19 . . . . **101** E7
Retford DN22 . . . . **40** C7
Sturton le S DN22 . . . . **32** D4
Leverton Wlk NG5 . . . . . **162** A8

Levick Ct 2 NG2 . . . . . . **173** C2
Lewcote La DE7 . . . . **157** A1
Lewindon Ct NG5 . . . . . . **161** E4
Lewis Cl NG3 . . . . **223** F4
Lewis St DN21 . . . . **24** D8
Lexington Ct NG22 . . . . . . **65** F2
Lexington Gdns
Nottingham NG5 . . . . **161** D4
Tuxford NG22 . . . . **65** F2
Leybourne Dr NG5 . . . . . **160** E6
Ley Croft NG19 . . . . **88** D5
Ley La
East Drayton DN22 . . . . **53** D3
Mansfield Woodhouse
NG19. . . . . **88** D4
Leyland Cl NG9 . . . . **182** F2
Leys La DN10 . . . . **12** E2
Leys Rd NG11 . . . . **196** C6
Ley St NG4 . . . . **175** A7
Leys The
Lowdham NG14 . . . . **150** D2
Normanton-on-t-W NG12 . **197** F7
Nottingham NG11 . . . . . . **184** D1
Leyton Ave NG17 . . . . . . **101** A5
Leyton Cres NG9 . . . . **184** B5
Liber Cl NG18 . . . . **102** F8
Library Rd NG7 . . . . **172** C1
Lichfield Ave NG18 . . . . . **102** C2
Lichfield Cl
Beeston NG9 . . . . **182** E3
Mansfield NG18 . . . . **102** C2
Worksop S81 . . . . **36** A7
Lichfield La NG18 . . . . . . **102** D3
Lichfield Rd NG2 . . . . **174** A4
Lichfield Wlk S81 . . . . **25** E7
Liddell Gr NG8 . . . . **171** F4
Liddington St NG7 . . . . . **160** F1
Lidget La DN22 . . . . **40** A8
Lifton Ave DN22 . . . . **29** E1
Lightfoot Cl NG24 . . . . . . **140** E8
Lilac Ave NG4 . . . . **174** C8
Lilac Cl
Keyworth NG12 . . . . **198** A2
Newark-on-T NG24 . . . . . . **139** F4
7 Nottingham NG8 . . . . . **159** E1
Lilac Cres NG9 . . . . **184** B5
Lilac Gr
Bawtry DN10 . . . . **9** F7
Beeston NG9 . . . . **184** B5
Carlton in L S81 . . . . **25** E7
Clipstone NG19 . . . . **89** D2
Glapwell S44 . . . . **86** B8
Market Warsop NG20 . . . . . **73** F7
Shirebrook NG20 . . . . **72** E5
South Normanton DE55 . . **113** A4
Lilac Mews DE7 . . . . **157** D3
Lilac Rd NG15 . . . . **146** B5
Lilburne Cl NG24 . . . . **140** E8
Lillee Ct S81 . . . . **36** B5
Lilleker Rise NG5 . . . . . . **147** E1
Lilley Cl NG16 . . . . **128** E6
Lillington Rd NG6 . . . . . . **160** B7
Lily Ave NG4 . . . . **175** A7
Lily Gr NG9 . . . . **184** B5
Limb Cres NG17 . . . . **100** F1
Lime Ave
Firbeck S81 . . . . **16** A6
Huthwaite NG17 . . . . **100** A3
Langley Mill NG16 . . . . . . **143** C2
Loughborough LE11 . . . . . **220** C3
Sutton in A NG17 . . . . **100** F4
Lime Cl
Nuthall NG16 . . . . **159** A6
Pinxton NG16 . . . . **113** D3
Radcliffe on T NG12 . . . . . **175** F3
Lime Cres NG20 . . . . **73** F7
Lime Gr
Bottesford NG13 . . . . **181** A2
Long Eaton NG10 . . . . **193** D8
Mansfield Woodhouse NG19 **89** C1
Newark-on-T NG24 . . . . . . **139** F7
Retford DN22 . . . . **39** D7
Sandiacre NG10 . . . . **182** B6
South Normanton DE55 . . **113** A5
Stapleford NG9 . . . . **182** D5
Lime Gr Ave NG9 . . . . **183** E5
Limehurst Ave LE11 . . . . **220** A5
Limehurst High Sch
LE11 . . . . **220** A5
Limekiln Ct NG6 . . . . **160** A8
Lime Kiln Pl NG18 . . . . . . **102** B6
Lime La NG5 . . . . **147** F4
Limes Ave NG20 . . . . **59** A2
Limes Cres NG20 . . . . **72** D5
Limes Ct NG17 . . . . **101** C1
Lime St
Kirkby in A NG17 . . . . **115** A5
Nottingham NG6 . . . . **160** B7
Sutton in A NG17 . . . . **101** A3
Limes The DN10 . . . . **14** B1
Limestone Ri NG19 . . . . . **102** A8
Limestone Rise NG19 . . . . **88** A1
Limestone Terr NG19 . . . . **88** B4
Lime Terr NG17 **2** NG6 . . **172** E7
Lime Terr NG10 . . . . **193** D8
Limetree Ave S80 . . . . **48** C6
Lime Tree Ave
Carlton in L S81 . . . . **25** E7
Gainsborough DN21 . . . . . . **15** D1
Glapwell S44 . . . . **86** B8
Kirkby in A NG17 . . . . **114** F5
Mansfield Woodhouse NG19 **88** A5
Nottingham NG8 . . . . **160** C3
Retford DN22. . . . . **39** D7
Sutton in A NG17 . . . . **100** D6
Limetree Cl NG12 . . . . . . **197** F2
Lime Tree Cl
Collingham NG23 . . . . **112** A8
New Ollerton NG22 . . . . . . **77** D5

Lime Tree Cres DN10 . . . . . **9** F7
Lime Tree Ct NG9 . . . . . . **172** A1
Lime Tree Dr NG18 . . . . . **116** E7
Lime Tree Gdns NG14 . . . **150** E1
Limetree Gr 5 LE11 . . . . **220** C3
Lime Tree Pl
Mansfield NG18 . . . . **102** C6
Rainworth NG21 . . . . **104** C1
Lime Tree Rd
Elkesley DN22 . . . . **50** B3
Hucknall NG15 . . . . **146** B4
New Ollerton NG22 . . . . . . **77** C5
Limmen Gdns NG3 . . . . . **173** E6
Limpenny St NG7 . . . . . . **222** C4
Linby Ave
Hucknall NG15 . . . . **146** B7
Mansfield NG19 . . . . **101** D6
Linby Cl
Carlton NG4 . . . . **162** E2
Nottingham NG5 . . . . **161** C8
Linby Cum Papplewick CE
Prim Sch NG15 . . . . . . **131** B3
Linby Dr NG8 . . . . **159** D2
Linby Gr NG15 . . . . **146** B7
Linby La NG15 . . . . **131** C3
Linby Rd NG15 . . . . **146** B8
Linby Wlk NG15 . . . . **146** A8
Lincoln Ave NG10 . . . . . . **182** A4
Lincoln Cir NG7 . . . . **222** C2
Lincoln Cl
Stapleford NG9 . . . . **170** E1
Tibshelf DE55 . . . . **99** A6
Lincoln Coll DN21 . . . . **15** C1
Lincoln Dr NG19 . . . . **88** D4
Lincoln Gr NG12 . . . . **175** F3
Lincoln Rd
East Markham NG22 . . . . . . **66** A7
Fenton LN1 . . . . **55** D6
Newark-on-T NG24 . . . . . . **125** B3
Saxilby LN1 . . . . **57** D3
Tuxford NG22 . . . . **66** A3
Lincoln Rd Bridge NG24 . **125** A2
Lincoln St
Gainsborough DN21 . . . . . . **15** C1
Newark-on-T NG24 . . . . . . **125** A2
Nottingham NG1 . . . . **223** E2
Nottingham, Old Basford
NG6. . . . . **160** E3
Tibshelf DE55 . . . . **99** A6
Worksop S80 . . . . **36** A1
Lincoln View S80 . . . . **36** A2
Lindale Cl NG2 . . . . **186** C6
Lindbergh Cl S80 . . . . **35** C2
Lindbridge Rd NG8 . . . . . **159** F2
Lind Cl NG21 . . . . **103** F1
Linden Ave
New Balderton NG24 . . . . . **140** B5
Nottingham NG11 . . . . . . **184** C1
Tuxford NG22 . . . . **66** A2
Linden Gr
Beeston NG9 . . . . **184** A5
Carlton NG4 . . . . **163** B1
Kirkby in A NG17 . . . . **114** D6
Sandiacre NG10 . . . . **182** A7
Shirebrook NG20 . . . . **72** F4
Stapleford NG9 . . . . **182** E6
Linden Pl NG5 . . . . **162** C6
Linden Rd
Mansfield NG18 . . . . **102** F8
Linden St
Mansfield NG19 . . . . **88** A1
Nottingham NG3 . . . . **173** D7
Shirebrook NG20 . . . . **72** F4
Linden Terr DN21 . . . . **24** D7
Lindfield Cl NG8 . . . . **160** A2
Lindfield Rd NG8 . . . . **159** F2
Lindholme Way NG17 . . . **100** F5
Lindhurst La NG18 . . . . . . **102** F4
Lindisfarne Gdns 6
NG5 . . . . **147** A1
Lindley's La NG17 . . . . . . **115** A3
Lindley St
Eastwood NG16 . . . . **144** B4
Mansfield NG18 . . . . **102** A7
Selston NG16 . . . . **128** D6
Lindley Terr 2 NG7 . . . . **172** E7
Lindrick DN11 . . . . **8** A6
Lindrick Cl
Carlton in L S81 . . . . **25** F7
Mansfield Woodhouse
NG19. . . . . **88** D6
West Bridgford NG2 . . . . . **186** C4
Worksop S80 . . . . **35** F5
Lindrick Ct DN22 . . . . **39** D2
Lindrick La DN11 . . . . **8** A6
Lindrick Rd NG17 . . . . . . **114** F7
Lindsay Ave
Annesley Woodhouse
NG17. . . . . **115** B1
Newark-on-T NG24 . . . . . . **139** F4
Lindsay Cl NG18 . . . . **102** A6
Lindsay Dr NG18 . . . . **103** A3
Lindsey Rd DN11 . . . . **9** A5
Lindum Gr 3 NG2 . . . . . . **173** F3
Lindum Mews NG24 . . . . **140** A8
Lindum Rd NG6 . . . . **160** D3
Lindum St 3 NG24 . . . . . **140** A8
Lindwall Cl S81 . . . . **36** B5
Linecroft La DN10 . . . . **14** C7
Linette Cl NG5 . . . . **161** A2
Linford NG9 . . . . **171** B3
Ling Beeches DN22 . . . . . . **39** D4
Ling Cres NG11 . . . . **196** C8

Lingdale Cl LE11 . . . . **220** B1
Lingfield Cl NG18 . . . . . . **102** F5
Lingfield Ct NG8 . . . . **171** D3
Lingford NG12 . . . . **188** A3
Lingford St NG15 . . . . . . **146** B6
Lingforest Cl NG18 . . . . . **103** A5
Lingforest Ct 3 NG18 . . . **103** A5
Lingforest Rd NG18 . . . . . **103** A5
Ling Rd LE11 . . . . **220** B1
Lings Bar Hospl NG2 . . . **186** D6
Lings La NG12 . . . . **207** F2
Lings View NG20 . . . . **74** C3
Lingwood Gr NG18 . . . . . **103** A7
Lingwood La NG14 . . . . . **149** B3
Linkin Rd NG9 . . . . **183** C6
Linkmel Cl NG2 . . . . **173** A1
Linkmell Cl NG2 . . . . **186** C6
Linkmel Rd NG16 . . . . **143** C3
Linksfield Ct NG11 . . . . . **185** C2
Links The NG18 . . . . **103** B6
Linley Cl NG23 . . . . **112** A8
Linnell St NG3 . . . . **173** F6
Linnets Dr NG18 . . . . **102** E7
Linnets The S81 . . . . **35** D7
Linsdale Cl NG8 . . . . **171** B5
Linsdale Gdns NG4 . . . . . **162** D4
Lintin Ave NG21 . . . . **75** F2
Linton Cl
Farndon NG24 . . . . **139** B5
Mansfield NG18 . . . . **103** B6
Linton Dr NG22 . . . . **77** F5
Linton Rise NG3 . . . . **174** A6
Linwood Cl DN21 . . . . **24** F7
Linwood Cres
Eastwood NG16 . . . . **144** A1
Ravenshead NG15 . . . . . . **116** F3
Linwood Ct NG19 . . . . **88** E4
Lion Cl NG8 . . . . **160** C2
Liquorice La S81 . . . . **26** B4
Lisle St 1 LE11 . . . . **220** A5
Lismore Cl NG7 . . . . **222** A3
Lismore Ct NG19 . . . . **101** D5
Lissington Rd DN21 . . . . . . **24** E7
Lister Ct 4 NG7 . . . . **172** E2
Lister Gate NG1 . . . . **223** E2
Lister Rd NG7 . . . . **172** E2
Listowel Cres NG11 . . . . . **195** E8
Litchen Cl DE7 . . . . **157** F2
Litchfield Cl NG10 . . . . . . **194** A7
Litchfield Rise NG5 . . . . . **147** E2
Little Acre NG19 . . . . **88** E5
Little Barn Ct NG18 . . . . . **102** F6
Little Barn Gdns NG18 . . **102** F5
Little Barn La NG18 . . . . . **102** F6
Little Belt The DN21. . . . . . **15** D3
Littleborough Rd DN22. . . . **33** B3
Little Breck DE55 . . . . **113** A4
Little Carter La NG18 . . . **102** E7
Little Debdale La NG19 . . . **87** F1
Littlegreen Rd NG5 . . . . . **161** F5
Little Hallam La DE7 . . . . **170** A6
Little Hayes NG2 . . . . **185** C4
Little Holland Gd NG16 . . **159** B7
Little Hollies NG19 . . . . . . **89** A2
Little John Ave NG20 . . . . **74** C2
Little John Cl NG22 . . . . . . **77** D6
Little John Dr NG21 . . . . . **104** A1
Little John Wlk 1 NG3 . . **173** D7
Little La
Blyth S81 . . . . **18** B3
Calverton NG14 . . . . **148** D7
Collingham NG23 . . . . **111** F7
Edingley NG22 . . . . **120** D3
Gringley on t H DN10 . . . . . **12** F2
Huthwaite NG17 . . . . **99** E2
Kimberley NG16 . . . . **158** F5
Pleasleyhill NG19 . . . . **87** B5
Shirebrook NG20 . . . . **72** D3
Thorpe Salvin S80 . . . . **34** B6
Tollerton NG12 . . . . **186** E3
Little Lunnon NG11 . . . . . **194** E6
Little Mdw NG12 . . . . **188** A2
Littlemoor La NG11 . . . . . **196** E3
Little Moor La LE11 . . . . . **220** C4
Little Oak Ave NG17 . . . . **130** A7
Little Oak Dr NG17 . . . . . **129** F7
Little Oakwood Dr NG5 . . **146** D2
Littleover Ave NG18 . . . . **103** B6
Little Ox NG4 . . . . **174** F4
Little Ricket La NG15 . . . **116** D3
Little Tennis St S NG2 . . . **174** A3
Little Tennis St NG2 . . . . **174** A3
Little Top La DN22 . . . . . . **20** C1
Little Wlk DN21 . . . . **7** D1
Littlewood Gdns NG8 . . . **171** C5
Littlewood La NG19 . . . . . . **88** A6
Littleworth NG18 . . . . **102** C5
Litton Ave NG17 . . . . **101** A4
Litton Cl
Arnold NG5 . . . . **161** E4
Ilkeston DE7 . . . . **157** E4
Ravenshead NG15 . . . . . . **117** A3
Littondale S81 . . . . **36** A7
Litton Rd NG19 . . . . **88** E3
Liverpool St NG3 . . . . **173** E5
Livingstone St NG15 . . . . **130** E6
Llanberis Gr NG8 . . . . **160** C2
Lloyd St NG5 . . . . **161** C2
Loach Ct NG8 . . . . **172** C5
Lobelia Cl NG3 . . . . **173** D7
Lockerbie St NG4 . . . . . . **174** F6
Lock La
Long Eaton NG10 . . . . **193** C4
Sandiacre NG10 . . . . **182** C4
Locksley La NG11 . . . . . . **184** C4
Lockwood Cl
Beeston NG9 . . . . **184** C4
16 Nottingham NG5 . . . . . **147** A1

Lockwood Dr DN22 39 D3
Lodge Cl
Arnold NG5 147 E2
Nottingham NG8 172 D8
Lodge Farm La NG5 147 E1
Lodgefield La NG14 151 E2
Lodge La
Elston NG23 153 C5
Kirkby in A NG17 115 D4
Screveton NG13 166 D5
Tuxford NG22 66 A1
Lodge Rd
Eastwood NG16 158 A8
Long Eaton NG10 193 D5
Lodgewood Cl NG6 160 A6
Lodore Cl NG2 186 C6
Lodore Rd S81 35 F7
Logan St NG6 160 D6
Lois Ave NG7 222 B1
Lombard Cl NG7 222 B2
Lombard St
Newark-on-T NG24 139 F8
Orston NG13 180 A6
Lonan Cl NG19 89 A2
London La
Willoughby-on-t-W LE12 217 D7
Wymeswold LE12 216 B3
London Rd
Kegworth DE74 203 D1
Newark-on-T NG24 140 C5
Nottingham NG2 173 D2
Retford DN22 40 A3
Longacre NG5 161 F4
Long Acre NG15 145 D7
Longbeck Ave NG3 162 A1
Long Brecks La S81 18 C1
Long Clawson CE Prim Sch LE14 211 D3
Longcliff Cl LE14 218 E4
Longcliff Hill LE14 218 E4
Longcroft View S80 45 A6
Longdale NG19 88 E1
Longdale Ave NG15 117 A1
Longdale Craft Ctr & Mus NG15 132 D6
Longdale La
Calverton NG21 133 B5
Ravenshead NG15 132 C6
Longdale Rd NG5 161 D6
Longden Cl NG9 170 F2
Longden St 5 NG3 173 E5
Longden Terr
Market Warsop NG20 74 B4
Stanton Hill NG17 100 D6
Long Eaton Sch The NG10 193 D7
Long Eaton Sta NG10 193 C5
Longfellow Dr
Balderton NG24 140 D5
Worksop S81 36 B4
Longfellows Cl NG5 161 B8
Longfield La DE7 170 A5
Longford Cres NG6 146 C2
Longford Wlk NG18 103 B6
Longhedge La
Bottesford NG13 180 F3
Flawborough NG13, NG23 168 A2
Orston NG13 180 E7
Pleasley NG19 86 E6
Sibthorpe NG13 167 E5
Longhill Rise NG17 114 F1
Long Hill Rise NG15 145 F6
Longholme Rd DN22 40 B8
Longhurst S81 36 B5
Longhurst View S80 45 A5
Long La
Barkestone-le-V NG13 192 F1
Barnby in t W NG24 141 F7
Beeston NG9 183 E3
Carlton in L S81 25 F6
East Drayton DN22 53 C3
Farndon NG24 139 B5
Hickling LE14 210 C6
Kegworth DE74 203 D5
Shipley DE75 157 D6
Shirebrook NG20 72 E3
Stathern LE14 202 F4
Watnall NG16 145 A1
Longland La NG22 119 D4
Longlands Cl NG9 184 B4
Longlands Dr NG2 186 D5
Longlands Rd NG9 184 B4
Longleat Cres NG9 183 C5
Long Mdw
Farnsfield NG22 120 A6
Mansfield Woodhouse NG19 88 D5
Long Mdw Hill NG14 150 A2
Long Mdws DN10 11 B3
Longmead Cl NG5 161 C6
Longmead Dr
Fiskerton NG25 137 E3
Nottingham NG5 161 C6
Longmoor Ave NG14 164 E8
Longmoor Gdns NG10 182 B2
Longmoor La
Long Eaton NG10 182 A2
Scarrington NG13 179 B8
Longmoor Prim Sch NG10 182 C3
Longmoor Rd NG10 182 B2
Longnor Wlk NG18 103 B6
Longore Sq NG8 172 D4
Longridge Rd NG5 161 F4
Long Row
Kingston-on-S LE12 204 A4
Newark-on-T NG24 140 B8
Nottingham NG1 223 E2
Long Row W NG1 223 E2
Longshaw Rd NG18 103 B6
Longster La NG20 73 C3
Longstone Way NG19 101 D6
Long Stoop Way NG19 103 B7
Longue Dr NG14 148 D7
Longwall Ave NG2 173 A1
Longwest Croft NG14 148 C7
Long Whatton CE Prim Sch LE12 212 C3
Longwood Com Inf Sch NG16 113 C1
Longwood Ct NG5 160 F8
Longwood Dr NG17 100 E1
Longwood Rd NG16 113 E2
Lonscale Cl NG2 186 C5
Lonsdale Dr NG9 182 E1
Lonsdale Rd NG7 222 A4
Lord Haddon Rd DE7 157 E1
Lord Nelson St NG2 173 F4
Lordship La NG13 180 A6
Lord St
Gainsborough DN21 24 C8
Mansfield NG18 102 B5
Nottingham NG2 173 E4
Lorimer Ave NG4 162 F2
Lorne Cl 5 NG3 173 C7
Lorne Gr NG12 175 F3
Lorne Wlk 6 NG3 173 C7
Lortas Rd NG5 160 F2
Loscoe Gdns 2 NG5 161 B1
Loscoe Mount Rd NG5 161 C2
Loscoe Rd NG5 161 C1
Lothian Rd NG12 186 C1
Lothmore Ct 1 NG2 173 B2
Lotus Cl NG3 173 E7
Loughbon NG13 180 A7
Loughborough Ave NG2 173 F4
Loughborough Carillon Twr & War Meml LE11 220 B3
Loughborough CE Prim Sch LE11 220 A3
Loughborough General Hospl LE11 220 B4
Loughborough Gram Sch LE11 220 B2
Loughborough High Sch LE11 220 B3
Loughborough Rd
Bradmore NG11 196 E5
Bunny NG11 206 E8
East Leake LE12 214 F7
Hathern LE12 213 A1
Hoton LE12 215 C1
Loughborough LE11 220 D1
Rempstone LE12 215 D5
West Bridgford NG12 185 E5
Loughborough Sta LE11 220 C5
Loughborough Uni 4 LE11 220 A3
Loughborugh Rd LE12 220 F6
Loughrigg Cl 3 NG2 173 B1
Louis Ave NG9 183 E7
Louise Ave NG4 175 A8
Lound House Cl NG17 100 F5
Lound House Rd NG17 100 F5
Lound Low Rd DN22 29 D7
Louwil Ave NG19 88 E5
Loveden Cl NG24 140 D3
Love La DN21 15 C1
Lovell Cl NG6 159 F5
Lover's La NG24 125 A1
Lovers Lane Prim Sch NG24 125 A1
Lowater St NG4 174 B7
Low Comm DN11 8 D4
Lowcroft NG5 161 F4
Lowdam Rd NG14 150 A5
Lowdham CE Prim Sch NG14 150 D2
Lowdham La NG14 149 E4
Lowdham Rd
Carlton NG4 162 C3
Gunthorpe NG14 164 E7
Lowdham St 8 NG3 173 E5
Lowdham Sta NG14 164 E8
Lower Bagthorpe NG16 128 F3
Lower Beauvale NG16 144 A3
Lower Bloomsgrove Rd DE7 157 F2
Lower Brook St NG10 193 E7
Lower Cambridge St LE11 220 B5
Lower Canaan NG11 196 D8
Lower Chapel St 9 DE7 157 F1
Lower Clara Mount Rd DE75 143 A1
Lower Ct NG9 184 B7
Lower Dunstead Rd NG16 143 A3
Lower Eldon St 12 NG2 173 E4
Lower Gladstone St 3 LE11 220 B5
Lower Granby St DE7 157 F2
Lower Kirklington Rd NG25 121 D2
Lower Maples DE75 157 A7
Lower Middleton St DE7 158 A1
Lower Oakham Way NG18 101 F3
Lower Orch St NG9 182 D7
Lower Parliament St NG1 223 F2
Lower Pasture La DN22 31 E8
Lower Pk St NG9 182 C5
Lower Rd NG9 184 B7
Lower Regent St NG9 184 A6
Loweswater Ct NG2 186 C7
Lowes Wong NG25 136 D8
Lowes Wong Inf & Jun Sch NG25 121 D1
Lowfield DN22 29 D1
Lowfield Cl DN22 19 C4
Lowfield La NG24 140 C2
Low Field La DN10 3 C1
Low Holland La DN22 32 E4
Lowlands Dr NG12 197 F4
Low Moor Rd NG17 115 B6
Lowmoor Rd Ind Est NG17 115 B7
Low Pavement NG1 223 E2
Low Rd
Besthorpe NG23 97 F6
Scrooby DN10 10 A2
Sutton in A NG17 100 F7
Low's La DE7 170 B2
Low St
Beckingham DN10 14 C1
Carlton in L S81 26 A5
Collingham NG23 111 F8
East Drayton DN22 53 B3
East Markham NG22 66 A6
Elston NG23 153 D5
Gringley on t H DN10 12 F2
Harby NG23 70 D2
North Wheatley DN22 31 D8
Sutton in A NG17 100 E2
Torworth DN22 19 B2
Lowther Sq S81 25 E7
Lowther Way LE11 220 B1
Lowtown Cl S80 36 A2
Lowtown St S80 36 A2
Lowtown View S80 36 A2
Low Wood La LN6 98 F7
Low Wood Rd NG6 159 F6
Loxley Dr NG18 103 A3
Lucerne Cl NG11 185 B6
Lucknow Ave NG3 161 D1
Lucknow Ct NG3 173 D8
Lucknow Dr
Mansfield NG17, NG18 101 E5
Nottingham NG3 161 D1
Sutton in A NG17, NG18 101 B3
Lucknow Rd NG3 173 D8
Ludborough Wlk NG19 88 E4
Ludford Cres DN21 24 E7
Ludford Rd NG6 160 C8
Ludgate Cl NG5 147 A2
Ludgate Dr NG13 165 D2
Ludham Ave NG6 160 B8
Ludlam Ave NG16 158 A7
Ludlow Cl NG9 171 D1
Ludlow Hill Rd NG2 185 F5
Lulworth Cl NG2 185 C5
Lulworth Ct NG16 158 F7
Lumley Dr DN11 8 B7
Lune Cl NG9 183 E3
Lune Mdw NG19 88 E3
Lunn La NG23 111 F7
Lupin Cl NG3 173 D7
Luther Ave NG17 100 E2
Luther Cl NG3 173 E7
Luton Cl NG8 160 D1
Lutterell Ct NG2 185 D5
Lutterell Way NG2 186 C5
Lybster Mews 6 NG2 173 B2
Lydia Gdns NG16 143 E1
Lydney Pk NG2 185 C5
Lyle Cl NG16 158 E7
Lyme Pk NG2 185 B5
Lymington Gdns NG3 174 A6
Lymington Rd NG19 101 D6
Lymn Ave NG4 162 F2
Lyncombe Ct DN22 39 D4
Lyncombe Gdns NG12 197 F3
Lyndale Rd NG9 183 A8
Lynd Cl NG16 129 B7
Lynden Ave NG10 193 D6
Lyndhurst Ave NG21 118 B5
Lyndhurst Gdns NG2 185 D4
Lyndhurst Rd NG2 173 F4
Lynds Cl NG21 76 B2
Lyngs The NG13 165 D2
Lynmouth Cres NG7 172 E7
Lynmouth Dr DE7 157 D3
Lynncroft NG16 144 A3
Lynncroft Prim Sch NG16 144 A3
Lynnes Cl NG21 118 A4
Lynstead Dr NG15 145 C5
Lynton Gdns NG5 162 A8
Lynton Rd NG9 183 C6
Lyons Cl NG11 196 B8
Lytham Dr NG12 186 C3
Lytham Gdns NG5 147 A1
Lytham Rd NG17 114 E7
Lythe Cl NG11 185 A5
Lytton Cl NG3 173 E5

M

Mabel Ave NG17 101 A1
Mabel Gr NG2 186 A8
Mabel St NG2 173 D2
Mable St S80 35 A4
McArthur Glen Designer Outlet NG17 113 E6
MacAulay Cl
Balderton NG24 140 D5
Worksop S81 36 C4
MacAulay Dr NG24 140 D5
MacAulay Gr NG16 159 B6
McClelland Av NG6 147 B5
Machin Gr S81 35 C7
Machins La NG12 186 A3
McIntosh Rd NG4 162 D3
Mackinley Ave NG9 170 E1
Mackleys La NG23 110 F2
Mackworth Ct NG18 103 B5
MacLaren Gdns NG11 196 D5
Maclean Rd NG4 174 C7
Macmillan Cl NG3 161 F2
MacPhail Cres LN1 57 C3
Madford Ret Pk NG5 161 D6
Madison Dr DN10 9 F6
Madryn Wlk 7 NG5 161 A7
Mafeking St NG2 174 A4
Magdala Rd NG3 173 C8
Magdalen Dr NG13 165 D3
Magdalene View NG24 140 B8
Magdalene Way NG15 146 A7
Mag La NG20 58 D5
Magna Cl NG14 150 E1
Magnolia Cl 3 NG8 159 E1
Magnolia Ct NG9 171 D1
Magnolia Gr NG15 146 B4
Magnums Com Sports Ctr NG24 140 A6
Magnus CE Sch NG24 140 A6
Magnus Rd NG5 161 C3
Magnus St NG24 140 A8
Magpie Cl S81 35 C7
Magpie La DN22 32 E1
Magson St NG3 173 E5
Maida La NG22 77 B4
Maiden La NG1 223 F2
Maidens Dale NG5 161 D8
Maid Marian Ave NG16 129 B6
Maid Marian Way NG1 223 E2
Maid Marion Ave NG22 106 A4
Maid Marion Way NG22 77 D6
Maid Marrion Dr NG21 76 C2
Maidstone Dr NG8 171 D2
Main Ave NG19 103 A8
Main La NG12 164 C1
Main Rd
Annesley Woodhouse NG17 114 E1
Barnstone NG13 190 E3
Beeston NG9 184 C5
Boughton NG22 77 E5
Carlton NG4 163 A1
Cotgrave NG12 187 E4
Kelham NG23 124 A4
Nether Langwith NG20 59 A1
Nottingham NG11 185 B7
Old Dalby LE14 218 E4
Plumtree NG12 197 E7
Pye Bridge DE55 128 A6
Radcliffe on T NG12 175 E3
Radcliffe on T, Shelford NG12 176 C8
Ravenshead NG15 117 B3
Selston NG16 128 F2
Upton NG23 122 E2
Watnall NG16 159 A7
Westwood NG16 128 B3
Mainside Cres NG16 129 A1
Main St
Annesley Woodhouse NG17 129 F8
Aslockton NG13 179 A5
Awsworth NG16 158 C5
Balderton NG24 140 E4
Bathley NG23 110 B3
Bleasby NG14 152 B7
Blidworth NG21 117 F4
Bothamsall DN22 63 E7
Bradmore NG11 196 E3
Brinsley NG16 128 D1
Bunny NG11 206 E8
Burton Joyce NG14 163 F4
Calverton NG14 148 F7
Carlton-on-Trent NG23 96 F4
Caunton NG23 109 B5
Clarborough DN22 30 D6
Claypole NG23 156 C6
Coddington NG24 126 B2
Costock LE12 206 C1
Cromwell NG23 110 F8
Cropwell Butler NG12 189 A7
Doddington LN6 71 C1
Dry Doddington NG23 156 E2
Eakring NG22 92 E1
East Bridgford NG13 165 C2
East Leake LE12 205 E1
Eastwood, Beauvale NG16 144 C2
Eastwood NG16 143 F1
Edingley NG22 120 C4
Egmanton NG22 79 F6
Farndon NG24 139 A4
Farnsfield NG22 119 F6
Fenton NG23 142 D2
Fiskerton NG25 137 F3
Flintham NG13 167 A8
Granby NG13 191 B5
Gunthorpe NG14 165 A5
Harby LE14 202 A3
Harworth DN11 8 E4
Hickling LE14 210 C6
Hoveringham NG14 151 D2
Huthwaite NG17 99 F3
Keyworth NG12 197 E2
Kimberley NG16 158 F6
Kinoulton NG12 199 E2
Kirton NG22 78 B6
Lambley NG4 163 C7
Laneham DN22 54 A5
Langar NG13 190 C2
Laxton NG22 79 C2
Linby NG15 131 B3
Long Eaton NG10 193 E7
Long Whatton LE12 212 B3
Main St *continued*
Lowdham NG14 150 D2
Mattersey DN10 20 B7
Morton NG25 137 D3
Newton DE55 99 A4
Normanton on S LE12 213 D3
North Leverton w H DN22 32 D1
North Muskham NG23 110 F2
Nottingham NG6 160 C7
Oldcotes S81 16 F5
Ollerton NG22 77 A3
Ossington NG23 95 D6
Oxton NG25 134 B3
Papplewick NG15 131 E5
Redmile NG13 192 F3
Scarrington NG13 178 E8
Shirebrook NG20 72 E3
Sibthorpe NG23 167 E8
South Muskham NG23 124 D7
South Normanton DE55 113 B6
Stanford on S LE12 214 C1
Strelley NG16 159 A1
Sutton Bonington LE12 213 B7
Sutton on T NG23 96 F7
Torksey LN1 44 B2
Walesby NG22 64 A2
West Bridgford NG2 186 C7
West Leake LE12 204 F1
Weston NG23 81 A4
West Stockwith DN10 7 E2
Whaley Thorns S44 59 A2
Whatton NG13 179 B3
Willoughby-on-t-W LE12 217 D7
Woodborough NG14 149 C4
Wysall NG12 207 C3
Zouch LE12 213 B3
Maitland Ave NG5 161 F4
Maitland Rd NG5 161 F4
Majestic Theatre DN22 39 E7
Major St NG1 223 E3
Making It! NG18 102 C6
Malbon Cl NG3 173 F8
Malcolm Cl NG3 173 C7
Maldon Cl NG9 183 B4
Malham Cl DN10 9 F8
Malin Cl NG5 162 B8
Malin Hill NG1 223 F2
Malkin Ave NG12 176 A4
Mallam Rd NG22 77 D6
Mallard Cl
Bingham NG13 178 A3
Nottingham NG6 160 F4
Shirebrook NG20 72 D3
Mallard Ct NG9 184 A5
Mallard Gn NG24 140 C5
Mallard Rd NG4 175 B6
Mallards The S81 35 C7
Mallatratt Pl NG19 88 B4
Mallow Way NG13 177 C4
Malmesbury Rd NG3 162 A4
Malpas Ave DN21 15 D1
Maltby Cl NG8 160 B2
Maltby Rd
Mansfield NG18 102 E6
Nottingham NG3 162 A4
Oldcotes S81 16 E6
Malt Cotts NG7 160 F1
Malthouse Cl NG16 143 F1
Malthouse Rd
Ilkeston DE7 170 A4
Whitwell S80 45 A6
Malting Cl NG11 196 C6
Maltings The
Blyth S81 18 B3
Cropwell Bishop NG12 189 A4
Maltkiln Cl NG22 77 C2
Maltkiln La NG24 125 A2
Maltkiln Rd LN1 55 D6
Maltkins The DN22 42 C8
Maltmill La NG1 223 E2
Malton Rd NG5 160 F2
Malt St NG11 195 B1
Maltsters The NG24 139 C6
Malvern Cl NG3 161 E1
Malvern Cres NG2 185 F5
Malvern Gdns 3 NG10 193 A8
Malvern Rd
Nottingham NG3 161 E1
West Bridgford NG2 185 E5
Manby Ct NG20 74 D8
Manchester St NG10 193 D6
Mandalay St NG6 160 D4
Mandeen Gr NG18 103 A4
Manesty Cres NG11 195 E7
Mangham La DN11 8 A8
Manifold Dr NG16 129 A7
Manifold Gdns NG2 173 C2
Manitoba Way NG16 128 F7
Manly Cl NG5 160 E8
Manners Ave DE7 157 D1
Manners Ind Est DE7 157 F2
Manners Rd
Balderton NG24 140 D3
Ilkeston DE7 157 E1
Newark-on-T NG24 124 E1
Manners St DE7 170 A6
Manners Sutton Prim Sch NG23 123 F2
Manning Comp Sch NG8 172 B8
Manning St NG3 173 D7
Manning View DE7 157 F2
Mannion Cres NG10 193 B5
Manns Leys NG12 187 E2
Mann St 5 NG7 172 F8

Manor Ave
Beeston NG9 . . . . 183 F5
17 Nottingham NG2. . . 173 E4
Stapleford NG9 . . . . 182 D8
Manor Cl
Bleasby NG14 . . . . 152 A8
Boughton NG22 . . . . 77 F6
Costock LE12 . . . . 206 C1
Eagle LN6 . . . . 84 D3
Gamston DN22 . . . . 50 F5
Long Whatton LE12 . . . . 212 B3
Misson DN10 . . . . 4 C3
Newton DE55 . . . . 99 A3
Oxton NG25 . . . . 134 B3
Southwell NG25 . . . . 121 E1
Walesby NG22 . . . . 64 A2
West Bridgford NG12 . . . 186 B3
Worksop S80 . . . . 35 C2
Manor Cres
Carlton NG4 . . . . 174 F8
Kirkby in A NG17 . . . . . . 115 B3
Manor Croft NG6 . . . . . 160 E3
Manor Ct
Beeston NG9 . . . . 183 B7
Carlton NG4 . . . . 174 F7
Church Warsop NG20 . . . 74 C6
Wymeswold LE12 . . . . . . 216 D4
Manor Dr NG25 . . . . . . 137 D3
Manor Farm Animal Ctr &
Donkey Sanctuary
LE12 . . . . 214 F8
Manor Farm Cl
Bradmore NG11 . . . . 196 E3
Rolleston NG23 . . . . 138 A6
Manor Farm La NG7 . . . 184 E2
Manor Farm Mdw LE12 . 205 E1
Manor Farm Rise DN22 . 32 C1
Manor Gn Wlk NG4 . . . . 174 F8
Manor Gr S80 . . . . 35 C2
Manor House Cl NG14 . . 150 D2
Manor House Ct NG17 . . 114 D4
Manor House Dr
North Muskham NG23 . . . 110 F3
Wysall NG12 . . . . 207 C3
Manor House La NG23 . . 156 D2
Manor House Rd NG10 . . 193 F6
Manor La
Broadholme LN6 . . . . 71 A8
Shelford NG12 . . . . 164 C2
Whatton NG13 . . . . 179 A1
Manor Pk NG11 . . . . . . 196 C7
Manor Pk Inf Sch NG14 . 148 E8
Manor Rd
Barton in F NG11 . . . . . . 194 E6
Bingham NG13 . . . . 177 F4
Bottesford NG13 . . . . 181 C2
Calverton NG14 . . . . 148 E7
Carlton NG4 . . . . 174 F8
Caunton NG23 . . . . 109 A4
Church Warsop NG20 . . . 74 C6
Collingham NG23 . . . . . . 112 A8
East Leake LE12 . . . . 205 F3
Eastwood NG16 . . . . 143 F1
Ilkeston DE7 . . . . 157 E1
Keyworth NG12 . . . . 197 E3
Mansfield Woodhouse NG19 88 A4
Morton DN21 . . . . 15 B4
Saxilby LN1 . . . . 57 A4
Scrooby DN10 . . . . 10 A2
Sutton in A NG17 . . . . . . 100 E7
Manor Rise NG13 . . . . . 165 C4
Manor Sch The NG19 . . . 88 C5
Manor St
Nottingham NG2 . . . . 173 E4
Sutton in A NG17 . . . . . . 100 E2
Manorwood Rd NG12 . . . 187 F2
Manse Ave S80 . . . . 58 D8
Manse Cl S80 . . . . 58 D8
Mansell Cl NG16 . . . . . . 144 B1
Mansey Common Nature
Reserve NG22 . . . . 107 A6
Mansfield Bsns Ctr NG19 . 88 B1
Mansfield Com Hospl
NG18 . . . . 102 A6
Mansfield Ct **7** NG5 . . . 173 B8
Mansfield Gr NG1 . . . . . . 223 D4
Mansfield La
Calverton NG14 . . . . 148 F7
Sutton in A NG17 . . . . . . 101 A7
Mansfield L Ctr NG19 . . . 102 A8
Mansfield L Pk NG18 . . . 102 B5
Mansfield Mus NG18 . . . 102 C7
Mansfield Prep Sch The
NG19 . . . . 88 C3
Mansfield Rd
Annesley NG15 . . . . 130 A6
Arnold NG5, NG15 . . . . . 147 D6
Babworth DN22 . . . . 38 D3
Blidworth NG21 . . . . 118 A5
Brinsley NG16 . . . . 143 F4
Clipstone NG21 . . . . 90 B5
Cuckney NG20 . . . . 60 B3
Dalesnorth NG17 . . . . . . 101 D4
Edingley NG22 . . . . 120 C5
Edwinstowe NG21 . . . . . 75 E2
Farnsfield NG22 . . . . 119 C7
Glapwell S44 . . . . 86 D8
Heanor DE75 . . . . 143 A2
Mansfield Woodhouse NG19 88 C2
Market Warsop NG20 . . . 73 F1
Nottingham NG5 . . . . 161 D4
Ollerton NG22 . . . . 76 F3
Ravenshead NG15 . . . . . 116 F1
Selston, Friezeland NG16 . 129 C4
Selston NG16 . . . . 128 F7

Mansfield Rd continued
South Normanton DE55 . . 113 D6
Sutton in A, Skegby NG17 . 100 E6
Sutton in A, Sutton Forest Side
NG17 . . . . 101 B4
Tibshelf DE55 . . . . 99 B7
Worksop S80 . . . . 46 A8
Mansfield St NG5 . . . . . . 161 C2
Mansfield Town Sta
NG18 . . . . 102 B6
Mansfield Woodhouse Sta
NG19 . . . . 88 B3
Manston Way S81 . . . . . . 35 C8
Manthorpe Cres NG5 . . . 161 F3
Manthorpe House NG24 . 140 E4
Manthorpe Way NG24 . . 140 E4
Manton Cl NG21 . . . . . . 118 B8
Manton Cres
Beeston NG9 . . . . 184 A8
Worksop S80 . . . . 36 B1
Manton Dale S80 . . . . . . 36 B1
Manton Villas S80 . . . . . 36 C1
Manton Wood Enterprise
Zone S81 . . . . 36 F1
Manvers Cres NG21 . . . . 75 D3
Manvers Ct
Market Warsop NG20 . . . 73 A4
9 Nottingham NG2 . . . . . 173 E4
Manvers Gr NG12 . . . . . 175 F3
Manvers Rd
Retford DN22 . . . . 39 D5
West Bridgford NG2 . . . . 185 F6
Manvers St
Carlton NG4 . . . . 175 A4
Mansfield NG18 . . . . 102 A7
Mansfield Woodhouse NG19 88 A3
Market Warsop NG20 . . . 74 B3
Nottingham NG2 . . . . 173 E4
Shirebrook NG20 . . . . . . 73 A4
Worksop S80 . . . . 35 E3
Manvers View NG22 . . . . 77 E6
Manville Cl
Beeston NG9 . . . . 171 B3
Nottingham NG8 . . . . 172 C6
Maori Ave NG15 . . . . . . 145 D5
Maple Ave
Beeston NG9 . . . . 184 B5
Sandiacre NG10 . . . . 182 B7
Maplebeck Ave NG20 . . . 74 D8
Maplebeck Rd
Arnold NG5 . . . . 162 A7
Caunton NG23 . . . . 108 E6
Maple Cl
East Leake LE12 . . . . 214 D8
Gainsborough DN21 . . . . 15 B3
Keyworth NG12 . . . . 198 A2
Mansfield NG18 . . . . 88 E1
Radcliffe on T NG12 . . . . 175 F2
Tuxford NG22 . . . . 66 A2
Maple Cres NG17 . . . . . . 114 F6
Maple Ct **4** DN21 . . . . . 15 F1
Mapledene Cres NG8 . . . 171 C3
Maple Dr
Carlton NG4 . . . . 163 B2
Elkesley DN22 . . . . 50 B3
Hucknall NG15 . . . . 145 E5
Nuthall NG16 . . . . 159 C6
Ravenshead NG18 . . . . . 116 D7
South Normanton DE55 . . 113 B4
Worksop S81 . . . . 36 A7
Maple Gr
Bawtry DN10 . . . . 9 F7
Glapwell S44 . . . . 86 B8
Newark-on-T NG24 . . . . . 139 F4
Maples St **15** NG7 . . . . . 172 F7
Maplestead Ave NG11 . . 185 B6
Mapletoft Ave NG19 . . . . 88 A5
Mapleton Way NG17 . . . 101 A4
Mapletree Cl NG5 . . . . . 161 B7
Maple Wy NG16 . . . . 128 F7
Mapperley Cres NG3 . . . 161 E2
Mapperley Hall Dr NG3 . 161 D2
Mapperley Orch NG5 . . . 162 C7
Mapperley Pk Dr **1** NG3 . 173 C8
Mapperley Plains NG3 . . 162 C6
Mapperley Plains Prim Sch
NG3 . . . . 162 B3
Mapperley Rd NG3 . . . . . 173 C7
Mapperley Rise NG3 . . . 161 E2
Mapperley St NG5 . . . . . 161 C2
Mapplewells Cres NG17 . 100 B1
Mapplewells Prim Sch
NG17 . . . . 100 B1
Mapplewells Rd NG17 . . 100 C1
March Cl NG5 . . . . 160 E7
Marches Cl NG15 . . . . . . 145 E4
Marchwood Cl NG8 . . . . 172 D5
Mardale Cl NG2 . . . . 186 C6
Mardling Av NG5 . . . . . . 161 A5
Margaret Ave
Long Eaton NG10 . . . . . . 182 F1
Sandiacre NG10 . . . . 182 B4
Margaret Cres NG4 . . . . 162 E2
Margaret Pl NG13 . . . . . . 177 D5
Margaret's Ct NG9 . . . . . 183 A8
Marham Cl NG2 . . . . 173 E3
Marhill Rd NG4 . . . . 174 F7
Marie Gdns NG15 . . . . . 146 A5
Marina Ave NG9 . . . . 183 F5
Mariner Ct NG6 . . . . 160 A6
Marion Ave
Hucknall NG15 . . . . 131 C1
Kirkby in A NG17 . . . . . . 115 B2
Marion Murdoch Ct NG4 . 162 E2
Maris Cl NG11 . . . . 184 C2
Maris Dr NG14 . . . . 163 E3
Marjorie St S80 . . . . 35 A4

Market Cl
Shirebrook NG20 . . . . . . 72 F3
South Normanton DE55 . . 113 A6
Market House Pl **12**
NG18 . . . . 102 B7
Market Pl
Bingham NG13 . . . . 177 E4
Gainsborough DN21 . . . . 24 C8
Hucknall NG15 . . . . 146 A7
Huthwaite NG17 . . . . 99 F3
Kegworth DF74 . . . . 203 D2
Long Eaton NG10 . . . . . . 193 E8
Loughborough LE11 . . . . 220 B4
9 Mansfield NG18 . . . . . 102 B7
Mansfield Woodhouse NG19 88 C3
Nottingham NG6 . . . . 160 B7
Ollerton NG22 . . . . 77 A3
Retford DN22 . . . . 39 F7
South Normanton DE55 . . 113 A6
Southwell NG25 . . . . 136 E8
Stanton Hill NG17 . . . . . . 100 E2
Tickhill DN11 . . . . 8 A7
Tuxford NG22 . . . . 65 F3
Worksop S80 . . . . 35 F2
Market Pl The NG5 . . . . 161 F7
Market Side **9** NG6 . . . . 160 B7
Market St
Bingham NG13 . . . . 177 E4
Bottesford NG13 . . . . 181 B2
Gainsborough DN21 . . . . 24 D8
Huthwaite NG17 . . . . 99 F3
Loughborough LE11 . . . . 220 A4
Nottingham NG1 . . . . 223 E2
Shirebrook NG20 . . . . . . 72 F4
South Normanton DE55 . . 113 A5
Sutton in A NG17 . . . . . . 100 E2
Worksop S80 . . . . 35 F3
Markham Ave NG24 . . . . 125 B3
Markham Cl NG22 . . . . . 77 B4
Markham Cres NG5 . . . . 161 C4
Markham Pl NG19 . . . . . 101 D7
Markham Rd
Beeston NG9 . . . . 171 D1
Langold S81 . . . . 16 E3
Tuxford NG22 . . . . 65 F4
Markham St NG15 . . . . . 130 D6
Markhams The NG22 . . . 77 B4
Mark La NG22 . . . . 65 F4
Markland La NG20 . . . . . 58 A8
Marklew Cl NG21 . . . . . . 118 A5
Mark St NG10 . . . . 182 C5
Markwick Cl NG24 . . . . . 140 D8
Marlborough Cl
Newark-on-T NG24 . . . . . 139 D5
Worksop S81 . . . . 35 D5
Marlborough Ct NG24 . . . 139 D6
Marlborough Rd
Arnold NG5 . . . . 161 E4
Beeston NG9 . . . . 183 F7
Kirkby in A NG17 . . . . . . 115 B5
Long Eaton NG10 . . . . . . 182 F1
Mansfield NG19 . . . . 87 F1
Marlborough St
Gainsborough DN21 . . . . 24 D7
2 Nottingham NG7 . . . . . 172 E1
Marldon Cl NG8 . . . . 171 C5
Marle Pit Hill LE12 . . . . . 213 A8
Marlock Cl NG25 . . . . . . 137 E3
Marlow Ave NG6 . . . . . . 160 E2
Marlowe Dr NG24 . . . . . . 140 D4
Marlowe Gdns S81 . . . . . 36 B4
Marlow Rd DN21 . . . . . . 15 E2
Marl Rd NG12 . . . . 176 B3
Marlwood NG12 . . . . 188 A2
Marly Bank NG18 . . . . . . 102 E5
Marmion Rd NG3 . . . . . . 174 A6
Marnham Dr NG3 . . . . . . 161 E1
Marnham Rd NG22 . . . . . 66 D2
Marples Ave NG19 . . . . . 88 E5
Marple Sq NG3 . . . . 173 C7
Marquis Ave NG24 . . . . . 140 D3
Marquis Gdns DN22 . . . . 40 A4
Marquis Rd LE14 . . . . . . 219 B6
Marriotts La NG21 . . . . . 117 F4
Marriott Ave
Beeston NG9 . . . . 183 A5
Mansfield NG18 . . . . 101 F7
Marriott Cl NG9 . . . . 183 A5
Marrison Way NG25 . . . . 121 F1
Marsant Cl **1** NG8 . . . . . 172 C5
Marshall Ave NG17 . . . . 115 C4
Marshall Ct NG24 . . . . . . 140 E4
Marshall Dr NG9 . . . . . . 183 A8
Marshall Farm Cl NG13 . 192 B2
Marshall Hill Dr NG3 . . . 162 B2
Marshall Rd
Cropwell Bishop NG12 . . . 189 A4
Nottingham NG3 . . . . 162 A1
Marshall St
Heanor DE75 . . . . 143 A2
Nottingham NG5 . . . . 161 C2
Marshall Terr NG17 . . . . 100 D6
Marsh La
Farndon NG24 . . . . 139 A5
Laughterton LN1 . . . . . . 55 A4
Misterton DN10 . . . . 7 B1
North Leverton w H DN22 . 33 D1
North Muskham NG23 . . . 110 F4
Saundby DN22 . . . . 23 D5
Marsh Rd DN10 . . . . 14 C5
Marsh's Paddock LE14 . . 210 C6
Marston Ave NG20 . . . . . 74 D8
Marston Rd NG24 . . . . . . 140 C3
Marston Moor Rd NG24 . 140 E8
Marston Rd NG3 . . . . . . 174 B7
Martin Cl NG6 . . . . 160 A8
Martin Ct NG6 . . . . 160 A8

Martindale Cl NG2 . . . . . 186 C7
Martin La DN10 . . . . 9 F8
Martinmass Cl NG7 . . . . 222 A1
Martins Hill NG4 . . . . . . 174 E7
Martin's Pond Nature
Reserve NG8 . . . . 171 E5
Martlet Way S80 . . . . . . 47 E8
Marton Rd
Beeston NG9 . . . . 183 C3
Newark-on-T NG24 . . . . . 140 B6
Nottingham NG6 . . . . 146 C1
Martyn Ave NG17 . . . . . 100 F1
Marvin Rd NG9 . . . . 183 F6
Marwood Cres NG4 . . . . 162 C2
Marwood Rd NG4 . . . . . . 162 C2
Maryfield Cl DN22 . . . . . 29 E1
Maryland Ct NG9 . . . . . . 170 E1
Mary Rd NG16 . . . . 144 B1
Marys Cl LE12 . . . . 216 C3
Mary St
Kirkby in A NG17 . . . . . . 115 B6
Rhodesia S80 . . . . 35 B4
Whaley Thorns NG20 . . . . 59 A2
Masefield Cres NG24 . . . 140 D4
Masefield Pl S81 . . . . 36 B4
Masonic Pl NG1 . . . . 223 D3
Mason Rd DE7 . . . . 157 D2
Mason St NG17 . . . . 101 B4
Massey Cl NG14 . . . . 163 E3
Massey Gdns **1** NG3 . . . 173 E6
Massey St NG24 . . . . 140 B8
Masson Ct **7** NG5 . . . . . 147 A1
Mather Rd NG24 . . . . . . 124 F1
Matlock Ave NG18 . . . . . 102 A5
Matlock Ct NG1 . . . . 223 E3
Matlock St NG4 . . . . 174 F7
Mattersey Ct NG19 . . . . 88 B1
Mattersey Prim Sch DN10 . 20 B7
Mattersey Rd
Everton DN10 . . . . 11 C1
Lound DN22 . . . . 20 B2
Ranskill DN22 . . . . 19 D6
Matthew Holland Sch The
NG16 . . . . 128 F7
Matthews Ct NG9 . . . . . . 170 F2
Mattingly Rd NG6 . . . . . 160 A5
Mattley Ave NG17 . . . . . 115 A1
Maud St NG7 . . . . 161 A1
Maun Ave
Kirkby in A NG17 . . . . . . 115 B7
Nottingham NG7 . . . . 172 D6
Maun Cl
Mansfield NG18 . . . . 101 F4
Retford DN22 . . . . 39 F5
Maun Cres NG22 . . . . . . 77 C5
Maundale Ave NG17 . . . . 101 B4
Maun Gn NG24 . . . . 125 B2
Maun Inf Sch NG22 . . . . 77 B5
Maunleigh NG19 . . . . . . 88 E1
Maunside NG18 . . . . 101 F4
Maunside Ave NG17 . . . . 101 B1
Maun Valley Ind Pk
NG17 . . . . 101 C2
Maun Way
Mansfield NG18 . . . . 101 F4
Wellow NG22 . . . . 78 A4
Maurice Dr NG3 . . . . 161 E2
Mavis Ave NG15 . . . . 117 A2
Mawkin La NG16 . . . . . . 113 F5
Maws La NG16 . . . . 158 E7
Maxtoke Rd NG7 . . . . . . 222 C1
Maxwell Cl NG7 . . . . 222 B1
May Ave NG8 . . . . 171 E4
Maycroft Gdns NG3 . . . . 174 A7
May Ct **6** NG5 . . . . 161 B1
Maydene Cl NG11 . . . . . . 184 D1
Mayes Rise NG6 . . . . 146 E4
Mayfair NG12 . . . . 176 D3
Mayfair Ave NG18 . . . . . 102 D5
Mayfair Ct DN11 . . . . 8 F4
Mayfair Ct NG7 . . . . 160 F1
Mayfair Gdns NG5 . . . . . 160 F5
Mayfair Rd NG22 . . . . . . 66 A2
Mayfield Ave
Burton Joyce NG14 . . . . . 163 F5
Gainsborough DN21 . . . . 15 B3
Mayfield Cl NG18 . . . . . . 103 B5
Mayfield Ct NG2 . . . . 173 C2
Mayfield Dr
Loughborough LE11 . . . . 220 A2
Stapleford NG9 . . . . 170 F2
Mayfield Gr NG10 . . . . . . 182 E1
Mayfield Pl NG17 . . . . . . 100 D2
Mayfield Rd NG4 . . . . . . 174 B7
Mayfield St NG17 . . . . . . 114 D3
Mayfield Terr NG20 . . . . 74 B3
Mayflower Ave DN10 . . . . 10 A2
Mayflower Cl
Bawtry DN10 . . . . 10 A8
Gainsborough DN21 . . . . 24 E4
West Bridgford NG2 . . . . 186 A7
Mayflower Ct NG20 . . . . 72 E4
Mayflower Jun & Inf Sch
DN10 . . . . 10 B8
Mayflower Rd NG16 . . . . 158 B8
Mayhall Ave NG19 . . . . . 88 A4
May Hill NG25 . . . . 136 C8
Mayland Ct NG18 . . . . . . 171 C6
May Lodge Dr NG22 . . . . 91 E6
Mayo Rd NG5 . . . . 161 B1
Maypole NG11 . . . . 184 E3
Maypole Ct NG22 . . . . . . 92 E8
Maypole Rd NG22 . . . . . . 92 E8
Maypole Yd NG1 . . . . . . 223 E3
May S DE7 . . . . 157 D3
Mays Ave NG4 . . . . 174 D6
Mays Cl NG4 . . . . 174 C6
Mays La LN1 . . . . 57 C3

May St DE7 . . . . 157 E4
Maythorn Cl NG11 . . . . . 185 C3
Maythorne Cl NG24 . . . . 140 C5
Maythorne Wlk **1** NG5 . . 161 C2
Maythorn Gr NG21 . . . . . 76 B3
Meade Dr S81 . . . . 36 A7
Meadow Ave
Loughborough LE11 . . . . 220 B6
Mansfield NG18 . . . . 102 C5
Meadow Bank
Mansfield Woodhouse
NG19 . . . . 88 E6
South Normanton DE55 . . 113 A7
Meadowbank Day Hospl
NG2 . . . . 173 E1
Meadowbank Way NG16 . 143 D3
Meadow Cl
Aslockton NG13 . . . . 179 A5
Eastwood NG16 . . . . 143 F4
Farnsfield NG22 . . . . 120 A6
Hucknall NG15 . . . . 145 D5
2 Kirkby in A NG17 . . . . . 114 E6
North Muskham NG23 . . . 110 F1
Nottingham NG2 . . . . 173 E1
Retford DN22 . . . . 29 E1
Tibshelf DE55 . . . . 99 B7
Meadow Cotts
Carlton NG4 . . . . 174 F7
Mansfield Woodhouse NG19 88 C3
Meadow Ct
Nottingham NG2 . . . . 173 F2
South Normanton DE55 . . 113 A4
Meadow Dr
Keyworth NG12 . . . . 198 A3
Misterton DN10 . . . . 6 F2
Sutton in A NG17 . . . . . . 100 C3
Tickhill DN11 . . . . 8 C7
Worksop S80 . . . . 35 C2
Meadow End
Gotham NG11 . . . . 195 B1
Radcliffe on T NG12 . . . . 176 C3
Meadow Farm View
NG17 . . . . 114 E5
Meadow Gdns
Beeston NG9 . . . . 183 E4
Heanor DE75 . . . . 143 B1
Meadow Gr
Bilsthorpe NG22 . . . . 106 A4
Newton DE55 . . . . 99 A3
Nottingham NG2 . . . . 173 E2
Meadow La
Beeston NG9 . . . . 183 E4
Bothamsall DN22 . . . . . . 63 E7
Burton Joyce NG14 . . . . . 163 F4
Girton NG23 . . . . 82 F4
Long Eaton NG10 . . . . . . 193 E4
Loughborough LE11 . . . . 220 B7
North Scarle LN6 . . . . . . 83 F2
2 Nottingham NG2 . . . . . 173 F3
Shirebrook NG20 . . . . . . 72 D2
South Normanton DE55 . . 113 A7
Weston NG23 . . . . 81 B4
Meadow La Ind Est LE11 . 220 B6
Meadow Lane Inf Sch
NG9 . . . . 183 E4
Meadow La (Notts Cty FC)
NG2 . . . . 173 E2
Meadow Pl NG20 . . . . . . 74 A4
Meadow Rd
Awsworth NG16 . . . . 158 C5
Beeston NG9 . . . . 184 B4
Blidworth NG21 . . . . 118 A5
Carlton NG4 . . . . 174 F7
New Balderton NG24 . . . . 140 C4
Worksop S80 . . . . 35 C2
Meadow Rise
Nottingham NG6 . . . . 159 F6
Saxilby LN1 . . . . 57 B4
Meadows Ed Ctr NG2 . . . 173 D1
Meadows La LE14 . . . . . . 201 D1
Meadow St DE7 . . . . 157 F1
Meadows The
Beckingham DN10 . . . . . . 23 B8
Farndon NG24 . . . . 139 A5
South Wheatley DN22 . . . 31 E8
Woodborough NG14 . . . . 149 B4
Meadows Way NG2 . . . . . 173 C2
Meadowsweet Hill NG13 . 177 C4
Meadow The DN22 . . . . . 39 F8
Meadowvale Cres NG7 . . 184 E1
Meadow View NG25 . . . . 121 F1
Meadow Way
Harworth DN11 . . . . 8 F5
Kinoulton NG12 . . . . 199 F2
Mead Way NG24 . . . . 140 C3
Medawar Cl NG11 . . . . . . 184 C1
Meden Ave
Market Warsop NG20 . . . 74 C5
New Houghton NG19 . . . . 86 F7
Meden Bank
Bothamsall DN22 . . . . . . 63 F7
Pleasleyhill NG19 . . . . . . 87 B5
Stanton Hill NG17 . . . . . . 100 C6
Meden Cl
Nottingham NG11 . . . . . . 184 E3
Pleasleyhill NG19 . . . . . . 87 B5
Meden Cres NG17 . . . . . . 100 C4
Meden Gdns NG7 . . . . . . 172 D7
Meden Glen NG20 . . . . . . 74 C5
Meden Rd
Mansfield Woodhouse
NG19 . . . . 88 D4
Wellow NG22 . . . . 78 A4
Meden Sch & Tech Coll The
NG20 . . . . 74 B5
Meden Sports Ctr NG20 . 74 B5
Meden Sq NG19 . . . . 87 B5
Meden Way DN22 . . . . . . 39 F5

Med–Mos 247

Medina Dr NG12 186 E1
Medway DN22 29 D1
Medway Cl NG9 183 C5
Meeks Rd NG5 162 B8
Meering Ave NG24 125 B4
Meering Cl NG23 98 A1
Meerings The NG23 81 E1
Meer Rd NG9 183 A5
Meeting House Cl LE12 205 F1
Meetinghouse La DN22 42 B6
Melbourne Ct
Mansfield NG18 103 B6
Nottingham NG8 160 C1
Melbourne Gr DN11 8 F4
Melbourne Rd
Nottingham NG8 160 C1
Stapleford NG9 170 E1
West Bridgford NG2 174 A1
Melbourne St
Mansfield Woodhouse NG19 88 C6
Selston NG16 129 B6
Melbury Prim Sch NG8 171 D8
Melbury Rd
Nottingham, Bilborough NG8 171 D8
Nottingham, Woodthorpe NG3 162 A4
Meldreth Rd NG8 171 E6
Meldrum Cres NG24 139 E5
Meldrum Dr DN21 24 E5
Melford Hall Dr NG2 185 C4
Melford Rd NG8 171 D8
Melksham Rd NG5 161 C8
Mellbreak Cl NG2 186 C6
Mellers Prim Sch NG7 222 B3
Mellish Rd S81 16 E2
Mellors Rd
Arnold NG5 147 F1
Mansfield NG19 101 D8
West Bridgford NG2 185 F6
Melrose Ave
Beeston NG9 184 A5
Mansfield NG18 102 D5
3 Nottingham NG5 161 C3
Melrose Gdns NG2 185 C4
Melrose Rd DN21 15 C2
Melrose St NG5 161 C2
Melrose Wlk 2 S80 35 F2
Melton Ct NG10 182 A5
Melton Gdns NG12 186 B4
Melton Gr NG2 185 E7
Melton La LE12 204 C2
Melton Rd
East Leake LE12 214 E5
Long Clawson LE14 211 B1
Plumtree NG12 197 E8
Rempstone LE12 215 C6
Stanton-on-t-W NG12 198 D4
Upper Broughton LE14 210 A1
West Bridgford NG12 186 A3
Widmerpool NG12, LE12 209 C4
Melton Way NG18 101 E4
Melville Ct 3 NG3 173 C8
Melville Gdns NG3 173 E6
Melville St NG1 223 E1
Melvyn Dr NG13 177 E4
Memorial Ave S80 35 F2
Mendip Cl
Long Eaton NG10 182 A1
Mansfield NG18 102 E4
Mendip Ct
Carlton in L S81 25 E7
Nottingham NG5 160 F8
Mensing Ave NG12 187 E3
Mercer Rd DN21 15 B2
Merchant St
Nottingham NG6 160 B8
Shirebrook NG20 73 A4
Mercia Ave NG12 189 A4
Mercia Cl S81 36 A7
Mercia Rd NG24 139 F5
Mercury Cl NG6 160 E5
Mere Ave NG14 148 F7
Mere Cl NG14 148 F7
Meredith Cl NG2 173 B1
Meredith Ct NG9 170 E2
Meregill Cl NG5 146 F1
Merevale Ave NG11 184 F4
Merevale Cl NG14 150 E1
Mere Way NG11 196 D5
Meriac Cl NG5 160 F8
Meriden Ave NG9 184 A8
Meridian Cl DE7 157 E4
Meridian Ct NG5 161 A2
Merlin Cl NG7 184 E2
Merlin Dr NG15 145 E4
Merlin Way DE7 170 A3
Merrick Dr S81 36 C3
Merrivale Ct NG3 173 C8
Merryvale Dr NG19 101 D6
Merryweather Cl
Edwinstowe NG21 91 C8
Southwell NG25 121 E2
Mersey St NG6 160 B7
Merton Ave DN22 29 E1
Merton Cl NG5 148 B1
Merton Ct NG9 170 E1
Metcalf Cl NG22 105 F7
Metcalfe Cl NG25 136 F8
Metcalf Rd NG16 144 B3
Methuen St NG18 102 E6
Metro Ave DE55 99 A3
Mettham St NG7 222 B1
Mews La NG14 148 E8
Mews The S81 18 A3
Meynell Gr 7 NG7 161 A1
Meynell Rd NG10 193 D5
Meyrick Rd NG24 125 A1
Miall Ct NG7 222 A3
Michaels Vw St NG16 129 A5
Micklebarrow Cl NG25 136 C8
Mickleborough Ave NG3 174 A8
Mickleborough Way
NG2 185 C3
Mickledale Cl NG22 105 E7
Mickledale La NG22 105 E6
Mickleden Cl 9 NG2 173 B2
Mickledon Cl 1 NG10 193 B8
Middle Ave NG4 174 C8
Middlebeck Ave NG5 162 C8
Middlebeck Dr NG5 162 C8
Middlebridge Rd DN10 12 E4
Middlebrook Rd NG16 129 B4
Middledale Rd NG4 174 C6
Middlefell Way NG11 184 D1
Middlefield La DN21 24 E7
Middlefield Rd DN22 31 E8
Middle Furlong Gdns 5
NG2 173 B2
Middle Furlong Mews 4
NG2 173 B2
Middle Gate NG24 139 F8
Middlegate Field Dr S80 45 A5
Middle Hill NG1 223 E2
Middle Holme La NG23 97 A8
Middle La
Beeston NG9 183 E5
Morton NG25 137 D3
Nether Broughton LE14 219 D8
Middle Pavement NG1 223 E2
Middle St
Barkestone-le-V NG13 192 C2
Beeston NG9 184 A6
Hose LE14 211 F7
Misson DN10 4 C2
Middleton Bvd NG8 172 C3
Middleton Cl NG16 159 C6
Middleton Cres NG9 171 E1
Middleton Ct
Mansfield NG18 103 B6
New Ollerton NG22 77 C5
Middleton Pl LE11 220 A2
Middleton Prim Sch
NG8 172 C4
Middleton Rd
Clipstone NG21 89 F4
Ilkeston DE7 170 A5
Mansfield Woodhouse NG19 88 C5
Newark-on-T NG24 125 C3
Middleton St
Awsworth NG16 158 C4
Beeston NG9 183 F7
Cossall DE7 158 A1
Nottingham NG7 222 A3
Middle Wood La DN10 4 C6
Midfield Rd NG17 115 B1
Midhurst Cl NG9 183 C4
Midhurst Way NG7 184 E2
Midlame Gdns NG6 159 F7
Midland Ave
Carlton NG4 175 A7
Nottingham NG7 222 A1
Stapleford NG9 182 C5
Midland Cres NG4 174 F7
Midland Ct NG7 172 D5
Midland Gr NG4 175 A8
Midland Rd
Carlton NG4 174 F7
Eastwood NG16 143 F2
Sutton in A NG17 101 B2
Midland St NG10 193 E8
Midland Wy NG18 102 B5
Midway The NG7 184 E7
Midworth St NG18 102 B6
Mikado Rd NG10 193 C5
Mike Powers Pottery
NG11 196 C7
Milburn Gr NG13 177 C4
Mildenhall Cres NG5 161 C8
Mile End Rd NG4 174 E5
Miles Yd LE11 220 B3
Milford Ave NG10 182 B3
Milford Cl NG6 160 A8
Milford Cres NG19 101 D7
Milford Ct NG5 161 D6
Milford Dr
Ilkeston DE7 157 D3
Nottingham NG3 174 C7
Milford Prim Sch NG11 195 E8
Millash La S80 45 B4
Millbank DE75 157 A8
Millbank Cl DE7 157 D3
Millbaulk La NG22 93 E7
Mill Baulk Rd DN10 14 A6
Millbeck Ave NG8 171 C3
Millbeck Cl NG2 186 C6
Millbrook Dr NG4 162 C1
Mill Cl
Huthwaite NG17 100 A3
North Leverton w H DN22 32 C1
Sutton on T NG23 96 F8
Mill Cl The NG8 160 E3
Mill Cres
Arnold NG5 161 E8
Whitwell S80 45 A6
Mill Croft NG17 100 E1
Milldale Cl NG11 184 C2
Milldale Ct NG18 103 A5
Milldale Rd
Farnsfield NG22 120 A6
Long Eaton NG10 193 B6
Milldale Wlk NG17 100 E4
Millennium Way E NG6 160 A4
Millennium Way W NG6 160 A4
Miller Hives Cl NG12 187 E3
Millers Bridge NG12 187 E2
Millers Cl NG12 164 C1
Millers Ct
Clarborough DN22 30 E4
Nottingham NG7 222 A4
Millersdale Ave
Ilkeston DE7 157 E5
Mansfield NG18 101 E4
Millers Gn 7 NG2 174 A4
Miller's La LE12 206 C1
Millers Way
Kirkby in Ashfield NG17 115 A5
Retford DN22 39 C8
Millers Wy NG17 101 D5
Millfield Ave LN1 57 B4
Millfield Cl
Ilkeston DE7 157 C3
Retford DN22 39 E3
Mill Field Cl
Burton Joyce NG14 163 E3
Harby NG23 70 D2
Millfield Rd
Ilkeston DE7 170 A8
Kimberley NG16 158 E7
South Leverton DN22 42 A6
Millfield View S80 35 C2
Mill Gate
East Bridgford NG13 165 C3
Newark-on-T NG24 139 E8
Millgate Mus NG24 139 E8
Mill Gdns S80 35 D2
Mill Gn NG24 140 B8
Mill Heyes NG13 165 D3
Mill Hill DN10 12 D2
Mill Hill Rd NG13 177 D3
Mill Holme DE55 113 B4
Millicent Gr NG2 185 F8
Millicent Rd NG2 185 E8
Millidge Cl NG5 160 F5
Millingdon Ave NG16 159 D3
Mill La
Annesley Woodhouse
NG17 114 E2
Arnold NG5 161 E8
Caunton NG23 109 A5
Cossall NG16 158 C1
Cotgrave NG12 187 E4
Eagle LN6 84 E4
East Leake LE12 214 F8
Edwinstowe NG21 76 A1
Hickling LE14 210 C7
Huthwaite NG17 100 A2
Kegworth DE74 203 D2
Lambley NG4 163 B7
Long Clawson LE14 211 D3
Long Whatton LE12 212 D4
Loughborough LE11 220 C5
Morton DN21 15 C5
Newark-on-T NG24 139 E8
Normanton on T NG23 81 D7
North Clifton NG23 68 F5
North Leverton w H DN22 42 B8
North Muskham NG23 110 F1
Orston NG13 180 A7
Pinxton NG16 113 D2
Rockley DN22 51 A2
Sandiacre NG10 182 C6
Saxilby LN1 57 B4
Scarrington NG13 178 F7
Scrooby DN10 10 A3
South Leverton DN22 42 D7
Stainsby S44 85 C8
Upton NG23 137 E8
Walesby NG22 63 F2
Walkeringham DN10 13 F4
Whitwell S80 45 A6
Willoughby-on-t-W LE12 217 D8
Mill Lakes NG6 146 B2
Millman Way DN22 29 C1
Mill Mdw View S81 18 B3
Mill Pk NG25 121 F1
Mill Rd
Eastwood NG16 144 B3
Elston NG23 153 E4
Heanor DE75 157 A8
Stapleford NG9 182 D8
Mills Dr NG24 139 C6
Mill St
Ilkeston DE7 157 E2
Mansfield NG18 102 D6
Nottingham NG6 160 D3
Retford DN22 39 F6
Sutton in A NG17 100 E2
Worksop S80 35 E4
Millstone Cl NG18 102 E4
Millview Cl 6 NG2 173 F4
Millview Ct 13 NG2 173 E4
Millway NG19 88 D1
Mill Wlk S80 45 A6
Mill Yd
Beeston NG9 183 F6
Hucknall NG15 146 A7
Milne Ave DN11 9 C4
Milne Dr DN11 9 D4
Milne Gr DN11 9 C4
Milnercroft DN22 29 D1
Milnercroft Gn DN22 29 D1
Milne Rd DN11 9 D4
Milner Fields NG22 92 E8
Milner Rd
Long Eaton NG10 193 D8
Nottingham NG5 161 C2
Milner St
Newark-on-T NG24 140 A7
Sutton in A NG17 101 A6
Milnhay Rd NG16 143 C2
Milton Ave DE7 157 E4
Milton Cl NG17 101 B4
Milton Cres
Beeston NG9 183 C2
Ravenshead NG15 117 A2
Milton Ct NG5 162 B7
Milton Dr
Ravenshead NG15 117 A2
Worksop S81 36 B4
Milton Rd
Gainsborough DN21 15 E2
Ilkeston DE7 157 F4
West Markham NG22 65 B6
Milton Rise NG15 145 C5
Milton St
Ilkeston DE7 157 F4
Kirkby in A NG17 115 B5
Long Eaton NG10 193 D7
Mansfield NG18 102 A7
New Balderton NG24 140 C6
Nottingham NG1 223 E3
Milton Wlk S81 36 B4
Milverton Rd NG5 161 C8
Mimosa Cl NG11 184 C1
Minerva St NG6 160 B8
Minster Cl
Hucknall NG15 146 B8
Kirkby in A NG17 114 F6
Minster Gdns NG16 144 B1
Minster Rd DN10 6 E2
Minster Sch The NG25 136 E7
Minstrel Av NG5 161 A2
Minstrel Cl NG15 146 A5
Mint Cl NG10 193 A7
Minton Pastures 3 NG19 89 A1
Minver Cres NG8 160 B2
Mirberry Mews NG7 222 A1
Mire La DN22 28 F6
Misk Hollows NG15 145 E8
Misk View NG16 144 B2
Mission Carr Nature Reserve
DN9 5 A7
Misson Bank DN9 1 F4
Misson Prim Sch DN10 4 B3
Misterton Cres NG15 116 F1
Misterton Ct NG19 88 B1
Misterton Prim Sch DN10 13 F8
Mitchell Ave NG16 143 A4
Mitchell Cl
Nottingham NG6 160 A6
Worksop S81 35 E8
Mitchell St NG10 193 E7
Mitchell Terr DE7 170 A5
M Lark Cl NG17 100 D1
Mob La LE12 217 D7
Model Village S80 58 E8
Model Village Prim Sch
NG20 72 E3
Moffat Cl NG3 173 F7
Moira St LE11 220 B3
Mollington Sq NG6 160 B3
Monarch Way LE11 220 A6
Mona Rd NG2 174 A1
Mona St NG9 184 B6
Monckton Dr NG25 121 E1
Monckton Rd
Bircotes DN11 9 C4
Retford DN22 39 C8
Monks Cl DE7 170 A8
Monk's La NG11 195 A1
Monks Mdw LE12 205 F2
Monksway NG11 185 A4
Monks Way S81 34 F7
Monkton Cl DE7 157 C3
Monkton Dr NG8 171 E7
Monkwood Cl NG23 98 B1
Monmouth Cl NG8 171 B4
Monmouth Rd S81 36 A6
Monroe Wlk 11 NG5 161 A7
Monsaldale Cl NG10 193 B6
Monsall Ave DE7 157 E5
Monsall St NG7 160 F1
Monsell Dr NG5 147 E1
Montague Rd NG15 146 A8
Montague St
Beeston NG9 183 E7
Mansfield NG18 102 E6
Nottingham NG6 160 C7
Montfort Cres NG5 161 D4
Montfort St NG7 222 C3
Montgomery Cl 8 NG9 183 C2
Montgomery Rd NG24 140 A5
Montgomery St NG7 222 C4
Montpelier Rd NG7 172 E1
Montrose S81 36 B5
Montrose Ct NG9 170 E1
Montrose Sq NG19 88 B6
Montys Mdw S81 35 D8
Monyash Cl DE7 157 E3
Moor Bridge NG6 146 D1
Moorbridge Cotts NG6 146 D2
Moorbridge Ct NG13 177 E5
Moorbridge La NG9 170 D1
Moorbridge Rd NG13 177 E5
Moorbridge Rd E NG13 177 E5
Moore Ave DE74 203 D3
Moore Cl
Claypole NG23 156 D6
East Leake LE12 205 F2
West Bridgford NG2 174 B1
Moore Gate NG9 184 A6
Moore Rd NG3 162 A2
Moores Ave NG10 182 C7
Moore St NG6 160 C5
Moor Farm Inn La NG9 171 A2
Moorfield Cres NG10 182 B5
Moorfield Ct NG9 170 E1
Moorfield La NG20 58 F4
Moorfield Pl NG20 74 C5
Moorfields Ave NG16 143 F3
Moorgate Ave NG19 86 F7
Moorgate Pk DN22 39 F8
Moorgate St NG7 222 C3
Moorgreen NG16 144 C3
Moorgreen Dr NG8 159 D2
Moorhaigh La NG19 87 A3
Moorhouse Rd
Egmanton NG22 80 C4
Nottingham NG8 171 E6
Moorings The 3 NG7 172 F2
Moor La
Aslockton NG13 178 D5
Beeston NG9 171 B2
Besthorpe NG23 98 C6
Bingham NG13 177 E5
Blyth S81 18 D2
Bunny NG11 206 E8
Calverton NG14 149 D6
Dry Doddington NG23 169 E6
Elston NG23 154 B5
Gotham NG11 205 C8
Loughborough LE11 220 C3
Mansfield NG18 101 F6
Morton NG25 137 C3
Normanton on S LE12 213 C4
North Clifton NG23 69 B4
Ruddington NG11 196 C6
South Clifton NG23 69 D3
Stathern NG13 202 F5
Syerston NG23 153 C3
Upper Langwith S44 72 A8
Moorland Ave
Stapleford NG9 182 D6
Walkeringham DN10 13 F6
Moorland Cl
Sutton in A NG17 101 A6
Walkeringham DN10 13 F6
Moorlands Cl NG10 182 B2
Moorland Way NG18 103 A6
Moorland Wlk DN10 13 F6
Moor Rd
Bestwood Village NG6 146 E6
Brinsley NG16 143 E8
Calverton NG14 149 A7
Collingham NG23 98 B1
Nottingham NG8 159 D1
Moorsholm Dr NG8 171 D4
Moor St
Carlton NG4 175 A7
Mansfield NG18 102 A6
Moor The NG16 143 D8
Moor Top Rd DN11 8 F5
Moor View NG11 206 E8
Moray Ct NG16 158 F7
Moray Sq NG19 101 D5
Morden Cl NG8 171 D8
Morden Rd NG16 158 C8
Moreland Ct
Carlton NG4 174 C7
10 Nottingham NG2 173 F3
Moreland Pl 11 NG2 173 F3
Moreland St NG2 173 F3
Morello Ave NG4 174 F7
Moreton Rd NG11 195 E7
Morgan Mews NG7 184 D2
Morgans Cl NG24 126 B2
Morkinshire Cres NG12 187 F4
Morkinshire La NG12 187 E4
Morley Ave
Nottingham NG3 161 E2
Retford DN22 29 C1
Morley Cl NG18 103 B5
Morley Ct 5 NG2 173 E4
Morley Dr DE7 157 D3
Morley Rd NG3 162 A1
Morley's Cl NG14 150 E1
Morley St
Arnold NG5 161 D6
Gainsborough DN21 24 C8
Kirkby in A NG17 115 B4
Loughborough LE11 220 C5
Stanton Hill NG17 100 C6
Sutton in A NG17 100 F3
Mornington Cl NG10 182 C6
Mornington Cres NG8 159 D3
Mornington Prim Sch
NG16 159 D4
Morrell Bank NG5 160 F6
Morris Ave NG9 183 B1
Morris Cl LE11 220 C4
Morris Rd NG8 159 D1
Morris St NG4 175 A7
Morton Cl
Mansfield NG18 103 B6
Morton DN21 15 B4
Radcliffe on T NG12 176 C3
Morton Gdns NG12 176 C3
Morton Gr S81 35 E8
Morton Hall Gdns DN22 38 A5
Morton Rd DN21 15 C3
Morton St NG19 87 E1
Morton Terr DN21 15 C2
Morton Trentside Prim Sch
DN21 15 A4
Morval Rd NG8 171 E6
Morven Ave
Hucknall NG15 146 B6
Mansfield Woodhouse NG19 88 B2
Sutton in A NG17 100 E2
Morven Park Prim Sch
NG17 115 B5
Morven Rd NG17 115 B5
Morven St S80 58 F8
Morven Terr NG20 74 B3
Mosborough Rd NG17 100 A1

Moseley Rd NG15 .... 130 C8
Moses View S81 .... 34 F7
Mosgrove Cl S81......... 35 C7
Mosley St
Hucknall NG15.......... 146 A6
Nottingham NG7 .... 172 F8
Moss Cl
Arnold NG5 .... 147 C1
East Bridgford NG13..... 165 D3
Mosscroft Ave NG11 .... 184 D1
Mossdale S81 .... 36 A8
Mossdale Rd
Mansfield NG18......... 102 E8
Nottingham NG5 .... 161 C5
Moss Dr NG9 .... 183 B7
Moss Rd NG15 .... 145 F7
Moss Rise NG3.......... 162 B2
Moss Side NG11 .... 185 A3
Mosswood Cres NG5 .... 161 B7
Mottram Rd NG9........ 183 C6
Moulton Cres NG24 ..... 140 C3
Mount Ave S81 .... 35 E5
Mountbatten Ct DE7 .... 157 F3
Mountbatten Gr NG4.... 162 E2
Mountbatten Way NG9 .. 183 C2
Mount CE Prim Sch
NG24.................. 125 A1
Mount Cl DN11 ....8 F5
Mount Cres
Market Warsop NG20 ..... 74 C3
South Normanton DE55... 113 A3
Mount Ct NG24 .... 140 D4
Mountfield Ave NG10.... 182 B4
Mountfield Dr NG5...... 161 A7
Mountford House Sch
NG5................... 161 C1
Mount Hooton Rd NG7 .. 222 C4
Mount Hooton St NG7 .. 173 A7
Mount La NG24 .... 140 A8
Mount Milner NG18 ..... 102 D6
Mount Pleasant
Carlton NG4............ 174 E7
Ilkeston DE7 .... 157 E4
Keyworth NG12 .... 198 A2
Lowdham NG14 .... 150 D2
2 Mansfield NG18....... 102 A7
Nottingham NG6 .... 160 E2
Radcliffe on T NG12...... 175 E3
Retford DN22............ 39 F7
Sutton in A NG17........ 100 F4
Mount Rd NG24......... 140 C4
Mountsorrel Dr NG2 .... 186 B6
Mount St
Nottingham, New Basford
NG7................... 160 F1
Nottingham NG1 .... 223 D2
Stapleford NG9 .... 182 E7
Mount The
Arnold NG5 .... 147 D1
Bestwood Village NG6.... 146 E4
Clipstone NG19 .... 89 D3
Nottingham, Broxtowe
NG8................... 159 E1
Nottingham, Portchester
NG3................... 162 C2
Stapleford NG9 .... 182 D6
Mount Vernon Pk DN22 .. 40 A4
Mount View Cl NG18 .... 102 D6
Mowbray Ct NG3........ 223 F3
Mowbray Gdns NG2...... 185 F5
Mowbray Rise NG5...... 161 F8
Mowbray Str DN21 .... 15 C2
Mowlands Cl NG17...... 101 B2
Moyra Dr NG5 .... 161 C7
Mozart Cl NG7 .... 222 A3
Mr Straw's House S80.... 36 A5
Muir Ave NG12.......... 197 D8
Muirfield S81............ 36 B6
Muirfield Cl 8 NG17 .... 114 E7
Muirfield Rd NG5 .... 147 A1
Muirfield Way NG19...... 88 E6
Mulberry Cl NG2........ 185 B5
Mulberry Cres S81 .... 25 F7
Mulberry Gdns 1 NG6 .. 160 A8
Mulberry Gr NG15....... 146 B4
Mumby Cl NG24......... 125 A1
Mundella Rd NG2 .... 173 D1
Mundy St DE7 .... 157 E2
Munford Circ NG6 ...... 160 B3
Munks Ave NG15........ 145 F7
Murby Cres NG6 .... 160 B8
Murden Way NG9 .... 184 B6
Muriel Rd NG9.......... 183 F7
Muriel St NG6 .... 160 B7
Murray Cl NG5.......... 160 F5
Murray St NG18......... 102 B5
Muschamp Terr NG20 .... 74 B3
Mushill La LE12 .... 216 D5
Muskham Ave DE7 ...... 157 F3
Muskham Ct NG19 .... 88 B1
Muskham La NG23 ...... 110 C2
Muskham Prim Sch
NG23.................. 110 F2
Muskham St NG2 .... 173 D1
Musters Cres NG2....... 185 F5
Musters Croft NG4 ...... 174 F4
Musters Rd
Bingham NG13.......... 177 D4
Langar NG13........... 190 D2
Newstead NG15......... 130 D6
Ruddington NG11........ 196 C6
West Bridgford NG2 ..... 185 E5
Musters St NG20 .... 73 A4
Musters Wlk 4 NG6 .... 160 A7
Muston Cl NG3 .... 161 F1
Muston La NG13 .... 181 D1
Mutton La DN10 .... 23 A8
Muttonshire Hill DN22.... 50 F5
Mynd The NG19.......... 88 E5
Myrtle Ave
Long Eaton NG10........ 193 C6
1 Nottingham NG7...... 173 B8
Stapleford NG9 .... 182 E6
Myrtle Cl NG20 .... 72 D6
Myrtle Gr NG9 .... 184 A7
Myrtle Rd NG4.......... 174 C8
Myrtle St DN22 .... 39 D6
Myrtus Cl NG11 .... 184 C2
Mytholme Cl NG10 ...... 182 C2

N

Nabbs La NG15 .... 145 E5
Naburn Ct 4 NG8....... 172 D8
Nairn Cl
Arnold NG5 .... 148 B1
Farnsfield NG22......... 119 F5
Nairn Mews NG4........ 174 E7
Nan Sampson Bank DN9... 1 D8
Nansen St NG6 .... 160 C6
Naomi Cres NG6 .... 146 C1
Naomi Ct NG6 .... 146 C1
Narrow La
Bawtry DN10............ 10 B8
Greasley NG16 .... 145 A4
Hathern LE12........... 213 A1
Wymeswold LE12........ 217 B2
Naseby Cl NG5.......... 160 F4
Naseby Dr NG10 .... 193 E4
Naseby Rd NG24 .... 140 E8
Nash Cl S81 .... 36 C4
Nathaniel Rd NG10...... 193 F7
Nathans La NG12........ 187 A7
National CE Inf Sch
NG15.................. 146 A8
National Jun Sch 1
NG15.................. 146 A8
National Sch The NG15 .. 130 F1
National Water Sports Ctr
NG12.................. 174 F3
Naturescape Wild Flower
Farm NG13 .... 190 E1
Navenby Wlk NG7....... 184 E2
Navigation Way LE11.... 220 A5
Navigation Yd NG24..... 139 F8
Naworth Cl NG6 .... 160 E5
Naylor Ave
Gotham NG11 .... 195 B1
Loughborough LE11...... 220 D2
Neal Ct NG16 .... 143 A3
Neale St NG10 .... 193 E7
Near Mdw NG10 .... 193 E5
Nearsby Dr NG2 .... 186 B6
Needham Rd NG5........ 162 A8
Needham St NG13 ...... 177 E4
Needwood Ave NG9...... 170 D2
Neeps Croft NG14....... 150 A6
Negus Ct NG4 .... 163 B6
Neighwood Cl NG9...... 182 E2
Nell Gwyn Cres NG5..... 147 C1
Nelper Cres DE7........ 170 A5
Nelson La NG23......... 110 F2
Nelson Rd
Arnold NG5 .... 161 E7
Beeston NG9 .... 184 A4
New Balderton NG24..... 140 B4
Nottingham NG6 .... 160 C7
Nelson St
Gainsborough DN21 ...... 15 C2
Ilkeston DE7 .... 157 F3
Long Eaton NG10........ 193 D6
Nottingham NG1 .... 223 F2
Retford DN22............ 39 F6
Nene Cl NG15........... 145 E3
Nene Wlk S81 .... 35 E7
Nesbitt St NG17......... 100 F1
Nesfield Ct DE7......... 157 E1
Nesfield Rd DE7 .... 157 E1
Neston Dr NG6.......... 160 C4
Nether Cl
Eastwood NG16......... 143 F4
Nottingham NG3 .... 174 A6
Nethercross Dr NG20..... 74 C5
Nether Ct NG22 .... 120 A6
Netherfield Inf Sch NG20. 74 D8
Netherfield La
Church Warsop NG20 ..... 74 D7
Market Warsop NG20 ..... 61 C1
Netherfield Prim Sch
NG4................... 175 A7
Netherfield Rd
Long Eaton NG10........ 193 C4
Sandiacre NG10......... 182 B4
Netherfield Sta NG4 ..... 174 F6
Nethergate NG11 .... 184 C2
Nethergate Specl Sch
NG11.................. 185 A1
Nether Pasture NG4..... 175 B6
Nether St
Beeston NG9 .... 184 A6
Harby LE14 .... 202 A3
Nether Thorpe Rd S80 ... 34 A5
Netherton Pl S80 .... 36 A1
Netherton Rd S80......... 47 A7
Nettlecliff Wlk NG5 ..... 160 E8
Nettle Croft DN11.......... 8 C7
Nettleworth Inf Sch NG19 88 C4
Neville Dr NG12......... 200 A2
Neville Rd NG14 .... 148 F6
Neville Sadler Ct NG9 ... 184 B7
Newall Dr
Beeston NG9 .... 183 C2
Newall Dr *continued*
Everton DN10 .... 11 A1
Newark Air Mus NG24... 126 A5
Newark Ave 16 NG2..... 173 E4
Newark Castle NG24 .... 139 F8
Newark Castle Sta NG24 124 F1
Newark Cl NG18 .... 102 F2
Newark Cres NG2....... 173 E4
Newark Ct NG5 .... 160 F5
Newark Dr NG18 .... 102 F2
Newark High Sch The
NG24.................. 139 F7
Newark Hospl NG24..... 140 A6
Newark Mus & Tudor Hall
NG24.................. 140 A8
Newark North Gate Sta
NG24.................. 125 B1
Newark Rd
Barnby in t W NG24...... 141 D6
Caunton NG23.......... 109 B4
Coddington NG24........ 125 F1
Collingham LN6 .... 112 F3
Eakring NG22............ 92 F1
Kirklington NG22 .... 120 F8
Laughterton LN1 .... 55 B7
Ollerton NG22 .... 77 A3
Southwell NG25......... 121 F1
Stapleford LN6.......... 127 C8
Sutton in A NG17........ 101 C1
Tuxford NG22............ 65 F2
Wellow NG22............. 77 D2
Newark & Sherwood Coll
Blidworth NG21......... 118 A6
Edwinstowe NG21......... 76 B2
Newark-on-Trent NG24 .. 140 A8
Rainworth NG21 .... 104 B2
Newark St NG2 .... 173 E4
Newark Way NG18 ...... 103 A2
Newbarn Cl NG20 .... 72 D2
Newberry Cl NG12 ...... 189 A4
Newbery Ave NG10...... 193 F6
Newbery Cl NG21 .... 76 A3
Newbold Way NG12...... 199 F2
Newbound La NG17 ...... 86 C2
Newboundmill La NG19 .. 87 A4
New Brickyard La DE74.. 203 D1
Newbury Cl NG3 .... 162 A4
Newbury Ct 3 NG5 ..... 173 B8
Newbury Dr NG16....... 159 D3
Newbury Mews 5 S80 ... 35 F2
Newbury Rd
Balderton NG24......... 140 E8
Newark-on-T NG24 ...... 125 E1
Newcastle Ave
Beeston NG9 .... 183 F6
Carlton NG4............ 162 E1
Newark-on-T NG24 ...... 140 A6
Worksop S80............. 35 E1
Newcastle Cir NG7...... 222 C2
Newcastle Dr NG7 ...... 222 C3
Newcastle Farm Dr NG8. 160 C1
Newcastle St
Huthwaite NG17 .... 100 A3
4 Mansfield NG18 ...... 102 A7
Mansfield Woodhouse NG19 88 B3
Market Warsop NG20 ..... 74 B4
Nottingham, Bulwell NG6 . 160 C8
Nottingham NG1 .... 223 E3
Tuxford NG22............ 65 F2
Worksop S80............. 35 F2
New Cl
Blidworth NG21......... 118 A5
Kirkby in A NG17 .... 115 A5
New Coll Nottingham
Hucknall NG15.......... 146 B7
Nottingham NG1 .... 223 E4
Nottingham NG5 .... 173 B8
Newcombe Dr NG5....... 162 C7
New Cotts NG20 .... 59 F3
New Cross St NG17 ..... 100 F4
New Cswy NG13 .... 192 C2
New Derby Rd NG16..... 143 C3
Newdigate Rd NG16..... 159 A7
Newdigate St
Ilkeston DE7 .... 170 A6
Kimberley NG16......... 159 A6
Nottingham NG7 .... 222 C3
Newdigate Villas NG7 ... 222 C3
New Eaton Rd NG9...... 182 E5
New England Way NG19.. 87 C3
New Fall St NG17 .... 99 F3
New Farm La NG16...... 159 C6
Newfield La NG23........ 167 E6
Newfield Rd NG5 .... 161 A3
Newgate Cl NG4 .... 174 E7
Newgate Ct NG7 .... 222 B2
Newgate La NG18 .... 102 D7
Newgate Lane Prim Sch
NG18.................. 102 C7
Newgate St
Bingham NG13.......... 177 E5
Worksop S80............. 35 F2
Newhall Gr NG2 .... 173 F1
Newhall La NG22........ 120 C2
Newham Cl DE75........ 143 A1
Newhaven Ave NG19 ..... 88 B3
New Hill
Farnsfield NG22......... 119 F6
Walesby NG22............ 64 A2
New Holles Ct S80 .... 35 F2
Newholm Dr NG11 ...... 185 A4
New Hucknall Way 2
NG17.................. 100 A1
Newings La DN22 .... 42 F8
Newington Rd DN10....... 10 C8
New Inn Wlk DN22 .... 39 F5
New King St LE11 .... 220 C3
New La
Aslockton NG13......... 178 E6
Blidworth NG21......... 117 E5
Girton NG23............. 83 B4
Hilcote DE55 .... 99 C2
Stanton Hill NG17 .... 100 D6
Newland Cl
Beeston NG9 .... 183 A2
Nottingham NG8 .... 172 C5
Newlands
Gainsborough DN21 ...... 15 E1
Retford DN22............ 39 D4
Newlands Ave NG22...... 77 E5
Newlands Cl NG2 .... 186 C4
Newlands Cres DE55 ..... 99 A3
Newlands Dr
Carlton NG4............ 162 F1
Clipstone NG19 .... 89 D2
Newlands Jun Sch NG19 . 89 E3
Newlands Rd
Clipstone NG19 .... 89 C1
Mansfield NG19......... 103 B8
New Linden St NG20 ..... 73 A4
New Line Rd NG17 ...... 114 E5
Newlyn Dr NG8 .... 172 D8
Newlyn Gdns NG8....... 172 D8
Newmanleys Rd NG16... 157 E8
Newmanleys Rd S NG16 . 157 E8
Newman Rd NG14........ 148 E8
New Manton Prim S80 ... 36 B1
Newmarket Rd NG6 ..... 160 B6
Newmarket St NG18..... 102 E6
Newmarket Way NG9 ... 182 F1
New Mill La NG19......... 88 E3
Newnham Rd NG24 ..... 125 A2
New Pl DN22 .... 40 A7
Newport Cres NG19 ...... 87 E1
Newport Dr NG8 .... 160 D1
Newquay Ave 1 NG7.... 172 E7
New Rd
Barton in F NG11........ 194 F6
Bilsthorpe NG22 .... 105 E6
Blidworth NG21......... 118 A5
Colston Bassett NG12.... 189 D2
Firbeck S81 .... 16 A6
Greasley NG16 .... 144 E6
Hawksworth NG13....... 167 C3
Morton NG25........... 137 C5
Nottingham NG7 .... 172 D6
Oxton NG25............ 134 B3
Radcliffe on T NG12...... 175 F3
Stapleford NG9 .... 170 D1
Staunton in t V NG13..... 169 D3
Tickhill DN11 .... 8 A7
Treswell DN22............ 42 C3
New Rose Prim Sch
NG19.................. 101 D8
New Row
Carlton NG4............ 174 D7
Westwood NG16 .... 128 A5
New Scott St NG20....... 59 A2
New St
Gainsborough DN21 ...... 15 C1
Hilcote DE55 .... 113 C8
Huthwaite NG17 .... 99 F3
Kegworth DE74 .... 203 E3
Kirkby in A NG17 .... 115 B4
Long Eaton NG10........ 193 E8
Loughborough LE11...... 220 A3
Newark-on-T NG24 ...... 140 A8
Newton DE55............. 99 A4
15 Nottingham NG5...... 161 B1
Retford DN22............ 39 F6
South Normanton DE55... 113 A7
Sutton in A NG17........ 100 E2
Newstead Abbey & Gdns
NG15.................. 131 C8
Newstead Ave
Newark-on-T NG24 ...... 125 A1
Nottingham NG3 .... 162 C2
Radcliffe on T NG12...... 176 A4
Newstead Cl
Kirkby in A NG17 .... 115 C5
Selston NG16............ 129 B7
Newstead Dr NG2........ 186 B7
Newstead Gr
Bingham NG13.......... 177 C4
Nottingham NG1 .... 223 D4
Newstead Ind Est NG5 .. 162 A7
Newstead Prim Sch
NG15.................. 130 D6
Newstead Rd
Long Eaton NG10........ 182 C3
Newstead NG15......... 130 D7
Newstead Rd S DE7 ..... 157 D3
Newstead St
Mansfield NG19......... 101 D7
6 Nottingham NG5...... 161 C3
Newstead Sta NG15 ..... 130 E6
Newstead Terr NG15 .... 146 A8
Newstead Way NG8 ..... 159 D2
New Terr
Pleasley NG19 .... 86 F5
Sandiacre NG10......... 182 B6
Newthorpe Comm NG16. 144 A1
Newthorpe St NG2 ...... 173 D2
Newton Ave
Bingham NG13.......... 177 D4
Radcliffe on T NG12...... 176 A4
Newton Cl
Arnold NG5 .... 162 B6
1 Gainsborough DN21.... 24 F8
Lowdham NG14 .... 150 E1
Worksop S81............. 35 C7
Newtondale Ave NG19.... 88 E1
Newtondale Cl NG8 ..... 160 C1
Newton Dr
Stapleford NG9 .... 182 E6
Newton Dr *continued*
West Bridgford NG2 ..... 185 C4
Newton Gdns NG13 ..... 177 C6
Newton Prim Sch DE55... 99 A3
Newton Rd
Carlton NG4............ 162 E3
Newton DE55............. 99 A4
Newton's La NG16....... 158 B4
Newton St
Beeston NG9 .... 183 E6
Mansfield NG18......... 102 C6
Newark-on-T NG24 ...... 140 A7
Nottingham NG7 .... 172 E1
Retford DN22............ 39 F4
Newtonwood La DE55.... 99 C5
New Tythe St NG10 ..... 193 F7
New Vale Rd NG4 .... 174 E5
Nicholas Pl NG22 .... 66 A3
Nicholas Rd NG9......... 171 D1
Nicholson's Row NG20 ... 72 F3
Nicholson St NG24 ...... 140 A7
Nicker Hill NG12 .... 198 A3
Nicklaus Ct 5 NG5...... 161 A8
Nidderdale NG8 .... 171 C4
Nidderdale Cl NG8...... 171 C3
Nightingale Ave
Hathern LE12........... 213 A1
Pleasley NG19........... 87 A4
Nightingale Cl
Balderton NG24......... 140 E4
Nuthall NG16........... 159 D6
Nightingale Cres NG16 .. 129 B6
Nightingale Dr NG19 ..... 87 E1
Nightingale Gr S81....... 35 D7
Nightingale Way
Bingham NG13.......... 178 A3
Woodbeck DN22 .... 53 B8
Nile St NG1 .... 223 F3
Nilsson Rd NG9 .... 183 B3
Nimbus Wy NG16 .... 159 A7
Nine Acre Gdns NG6 .... 159 F8
Nine Acres DE74 .... 203 C2
Nine Scores La DN9........ 1 E7
Ninth Ave NG19 .... 103 A8
Nixon Rise NG15 .... 145 D5
Nixon Walk LE12........ 205 E2
Noble La NG13.......... 179 A5
Noburn Cres NG6 .... 160 F3
Noel St
Gainsborough DN21 ...... 15 C2
Kimberley NG16......... 159 A6
Mansfield NG18......... 102 A7
Nottingham NG7 .... 172 F8
Nookin NG22 .... 66 B6
Nook The
Beeston, Chilwell NG9.... 183 E4
Beeston NG9 .... 184 A7
Calverton NG14......... 148 F7
East Leake LE12 .... 205 E1
Nottingham NG8 .... 171 E4
Shirebrook NG20.......... 72 D3
Norbett Cl NG9 .... 183 C3
Norbett Ct NG5 .... 148 A1
Norbett Rd NG5......... 148 A1
Norbreck Cl NG8........ 160 B3
Norbury Dr NG18 .... 102 E4
Norbury Way NG10...... 182 A6
Nordean Rd NG5........ 162 A5
Norfolk Ave
Beeston NG9 .... 183 A1
Bircotes DN11 .... 9 D4
Norfolk Cl
Hucknall NG15.......... 145 D5
Market Warsop NG20 ..... 74 A4
Norfolk Ct NG19 .... 88 E5
Norfolk Dr
Bircotes DN11 .... 9 C4
Mansfield NG18......... 102 B8
Norfolk Gr DN11 .... 9 C4
Norfolk Pl
Arnold NG5 .... 162 B5
Nottingham NG1 .... 223 E3
Norfolk Rd
Bircotes DN11 .... 9 C4
Long Eaton NG10........ 182 F1
Norfolk St S80 .... 35 E2
Norfolk Wlk NG10....... 182 B5
Norland Cl NG3 .... 173 E7
Norman Ave
Newark-on-T NG24 ...... 125 B4
Sutton in A NG17........ 101 A1
Normanby Rd NG8 ...... 171 C3
Norman Cl
Beeston NG9 .... 183 C6
Nottingham NG1 .... 173 C6
Nottingham NG3 .... 223 E4
Norman Cres DE7........ 157 E3
Norman Dr
Eastwood NG16......... 144 B2
Hucknall NG15.......... 145 E4
Norman Rd NG3 .... 174 A8
Norman St
Carlton NG4............ 175 A6
Ilkeston DE7 .... 157 E3
Kimberley NG16......... 158 F7
Normanton Cl NG21 ...... 75 F3
Normanton Dr
Loughborough LE11...... 220 B6
Mansfield NG18......... 102 E7
Normanton La
Bottesford NG13 .... 181 B5
Keyworth NG12 .... 197 F4
Stanford on S LE12 ...... 214 B1
Normanton on Soar Prim Sch
LE12.................. 213 D3
Normanton Rd
Newark-on-T NG24 ...... 125 D1
Southwell NG25......... 121 F2

Nornay Cl S81 . . . . 18 A4
Northall Ave NG6 . . . . . . 160 B6
Northampton St **2** NG3 . 173 E6
North Ave
  Bawtry DN10 . . . . 10 A8
  Rainworth NG21 . . . . 104 A1
  Sandiacre NG10 . . . . 182 B6
North Carr Rd DN10 . . . . . . 7 C3
North Church St NG1 . . 223 E3
North Cir St NG1 . . . . . . 223 D2
Northcliffe Ave NG3 . . . 162 B2
North Clifton Prim Sch
  NG23 . . . . 68 E3
Northcote St NG10 . . . . 193 E6
Northcote Way NG6 . . . 160 C5
North County Prim Sch
  DN21 . . . . 15 B2
North Cres
  Bottesford NG13 . . . . 181 A2
  Clipstone NG21 . . . . 90 A3
Northcroft LN1 . . . . 57 A5
Northdale Rd NG3 . . . . . 174 B7
Northdown Dr NG3 . . . . 183 C4
Northdown Rd NG8 . . . . 172 D6
North Dr
  Beeston NG9 . . . . 183 E6
  Bilsthorpe NG22 . . . . 105 F7
North End NG24 . . . . . . 138 F5
Northern Ct NG6 . . . . . . 160 D4
Northern Dr NG9 . . . . . . 170 D3
Northern Rd NG24 . . . . 125 B1
Northern Rd Ind Est
  NG24 . . . . 125 B1
Northern View NG17 . . . 100 F3
Northfield Ave
  Ilkeston DE7 . . . . 157 E2
  Long Eaton NG10 . . . . . . 193 A4
  Mansfield Woodhouse NG19 88 A4
  Radcliffe on T NG12 . . . . 176 C3
Northfield Cres NG9 . . . 183 A4
Northfield Dr NG18 . . . . 102 E6
Northfield La
  Mansfield Woodhouse
    NG19 . . . . 88 A5
  Treswell DN22 . . . . 42 B4
Northfield Pk NG19 . . . . . 88 B5
Northfield Prim Sch NG19 88 B5
Northfield Rd
  Beeston NG9 . . . . 183 A4
  North Leverton w H DN22 . . 33 B1
Northfields NG10 . . . . . . 193 B4
Northfields Cl NG17 . . . 100 E3
Northfields Way LE12 . . 205 E3
Northfold Way DN22 . . . 39 D8
North Gate
  Newark-on-T NG24 . . . . . 125 A2
  Nottingham NG7 . . . . 160 F1
  Tickhill DN11 . . . . 8 A8
Northgate Bsns Ctr
  NG24 . . . . 124 F1
North Gate Pl NG7 . . . . 160 F1
Northgate Prim Sch NG7 160 F1
Northgate Ret Pk NG24 . 125 A2
Northgate St 4 DE7 . . . 157 F1
North Gn
  Calverton NG14 . . . . 133 D1
  East Drayton DN22 . . . . . . 53 B3
North Hill Ave NG15 . . . 145 F7
North Hill Cres NG15 . . 145 F7
North Leverton CE Prim Sch
  DN22 . . . . 32 D1
North Leverton Windmill
  DN22 . . . . 32 B1
North Leys Rd DN22 . . . 43 C8
North Marsh Rd DN21 . . 15 C2
North Moor Dr DN10 . . . 13 F6
North Moor Rd DN10 . . . 13 F6
North Par DN21 . . . . 24 F7
North Pk NG18 . . . . 102 E3
North Rd
  Long Eaton NG10 . . . . . . 193 C6
  Loughborough LE11 . . . . 220 B6
  Nottingham NG7 . . . . 222 B2
  Retford DN22 . . . . 29 B2
  Ruddington NG11 . . . . . . 196 B8
  West Bridgford NG2 . . . . 185 E7
Northrowe NG17 . . . . . . 129 E8
North Scaffold La NG23 112 B2
North Scarle Rd NG23 . . 98 E7
North Sherwood St NG1 . 223 E4
Northside La DN22 . . . . . 32 F1
Northside Wlk NG5 . . . . 147 F2
North St
  Beeston NG9 . . . . 183 E6
  Eastwood NG16 . . . . 144 C2
  Gainsborough DN21 . . . . . 15 C1
  Huthwaite NG17 . . . . 100 A3
  7 Ilkeston DE7 . . . . 157 F1
  Kimberley NG16 . . . . 159 A5
  Kirkby in A NG17 . . . . . . 115 B2
  Langley Mill NG16 . . . . . 143 B3
  Morton DN21 . . . . 15 B4
  4 Nottingham NG2 . . . . 173 E4
  Pinxton NG16 . . . . 113 D3
  South Normanton DE55 . . 113 A5
  Sturton le S DN22 . . . . . . 32 D6
  Warsop Vale NG20 . . . . . . 73 D4
  Whaley Thorns NG20 . . . . 59 A2
Northumberland Ave S81 . 25 E8
Northumberland Cl NG3 . 223 F4
Northumbria Cl S81 . . . . 36 B6

Northumbria Dr DN22 . . . 39 D5
North Warren Rd DN21 . . 15 B2
North Way S81 . . . . 25 F7
North Wheatley CE Prim Sch
  DN22 . . . . 31 E8
North Wlk DN22 . . . . 39 C8
Northwold Ave NG2 . . . . 185 D6
Northwood S81 . . . . 36 A6
Northwood Ave NG17 . . 160 D4
Northwood Cres NG5 . . 161 C6
Northwood Rd NG5 . . . . 161 C6
Northwood St NG9 . . . . 182 D8
Norton La NG20 . . . . 60 B3
Norton Rd LN6 . . . . 127 E8
Norton St NG7 . . . . 222 B3
Norwell CE Prim Sch
  NG23 . . . . 110 A8
Norwell Ct NG19 . . . . . . 88 B1
Norwell La
  Brough NG23 . . . . 112 C1
  Cromwell NG23 . . . . 110 D8
Norwell Rd NG23 . . . . . . 109 C5
Norwich Cl NG19 . . . . . . 88 D5
Norwich Gdns NG6 . . . . 146 B1
Norwood Cl NG17 . . . . . 100 B3
Norwood Gdns NG25 . . 121 E2
Norwood Rd NG7 . . . . . . 222 A3
Nostell Mews 6 S80 . . . 35 F2
Notintone St NG2 . . . . . 173 E4
Nottingham Airport
  NG12 . . . . 186 F5
Nottingham Arts Theatre
  NG1 . . . . 223 F2
Nottingham Bluecoat Sch
  NG8 . . . . 172 C8
Nottingham Canal Nature
  Reserve NG9 . . . . 170 C7
Nottingham Castle (site of)
  NG7 . . . . 223 D2
Nottingham Cath NG1 . . 223 D2
Nottingham City Hospl
  NG5 . . . . 161 A4
Nottingham Com Coll
  NG3 . . . . 173 E5
Nottingham Emmanuel Sch
  The NG11 . . . . 185 C8
Nottingham High Jun Sch
  NG7 . . . . 223 D4
Nottingham High Sch
  NG7 . . . . 223 D4
Nottingham High Sch for
  Girls NG1 . . . . 223 D4
Nottingham Ice Ctr & Arena
  NG1 . . . . 223 F2
Nottingham La LE14 . . . 218 C5
Nottingham Nuffield Hospl
  The NG5 . . . . 161 D4
Nottingham Playhouse
  NG1 . . . . 223 D2
Nottingham Racecourse
  NG2 . . . . 174 B3
Nottingham Rd
  Arnold NG5 . . . . 161 E6
  Beeston NG9 . . . . 183 B1
  Bingham NG13 . . . . 177 D4
  Bottesford NG13 . . . . . . 180 E2
  Burton Joyce NG14 . . . . 163 D3
  Costock LE12 . . . . 206 D2
  Cropwell Bishop NG12 . . 189 B7
  Eastwood, Giltbrook NG16 158 C8
  Eastwood NG16 . . . . 144 A2
  Gotham NG11 . . . . 195 B4
  Gunthorpe NG14 . . . . . . 164 B6
  Hucknall NG15 . . . . 146 C4
  Ilkeston DE7 . . . . 170 A6
  Kegworth DE74 . . . . 203 D2
  Keyworth NG12 . . . . 197 E3
  Kimberley NG16 . . . . 159 A5
  Kirkby in A NG17 . . . . . . 115 B2
  Long Eaton NG10 . . . . . . 193 E8
  Loughborough LE11 . . . . 220 D6
  Mansfield NG18 . . . . 102 C3
  Nether Broughton LE14 . . 219 E7
  Nottingham, New Basford
    NG7 . . . . 160 F1
  Nuthall NG16 . . . . 159 F4
  Oxton NG25 . . . . 134 A2
  Radcliffe on T NG12 . . . . 175 D2
  Ravenshead NG15 . . . . . 116 B3
  Selston NG16 . . . . 129 A6
  Southwell NG25 . . . . 136 D6
  Stapleford NG9 . . . . 182 E7
  Thurgarton NG14 . . . . . . 151 C6
  Trowell NG9 . . . . 170 E5
  Woodborough NG14 . . . . 148 E2
Nottingham Rd E NG16 . 144 B1
Nottingham Science & Tech
  Pk NG2 . . . . 172 D4
Nottingham Sta NG2 . . . 223 F1
Nottingham S & Wilford Ind
  Est NG2 . . . . 185 B4
Nottingham Transport Her
  Ctr NG11 . . . . 196 C5
Nottingham Trent Univ The
  Clifton NG11 . . . . 184 D3
  Nottingham NG1 . . . . . . 223 D3
  Southwell NG25 . . . . 136 D5
Nuart Rd NG9 . . . . 183 F7
Nugent Gdn NG3 . . . . . 173 E6
Nugent Gdns 4 NG3 . . . 173 E6
Nuncar Ct NG17 . . . . . . 115 A1
Nuncargate Rd NG17 . . 115 A1
Nunn Brook La NG17 . . . 99 E1
Nunn Brook Rise NG17 . . 99 E2
Nunn Cl NG17 . . . . 99 E1
Nurseries The NG16 . . . 144 A4
Nursery Ave
  Beeston NG9 . . . . 183 C5

Nursery Ave *continued*
  Farndon NG24 . . . . 139 A5
  Sutton in A NG17 . . . . . . 100 C2
Nursery Cl
  Hucknall NG15 . . . . 146 A4
  Radcliffe on T NG12 . . . . 176 B3
  Saxilby LN1 . . . . 57 B4
Nursery Ct
  Mansfield NG18 . . . . 102 C8
  Newark-on-T NG24 . . . . 125 A1
Nursery Dr NG4 . . . . . . 174 D8
Nursery End NG25 . . . . 121 D1
Nursery Gdns DE55 . . . 113 C4
Nursery La
  Morton DN21 . . . . 15 A5
  Nottingham NG6 . . . . . . 160 E4
  Sutton on T NG23 . . . . . . 96 F8
Nursery Rd
  Arnold NG5 . . . . 162 A7
  Bingham NG13 . . . . 178 B4
  Radcliffe on T NG12 . . . . 176 B3
Nursery St NG18 . . . . . . 102 C8
Nursery Vale DN21 . . . . . 15 B5
Nursury Gdns NG14 . . . 150 D2
Nuthall Gdns NG8 . . . . . 172 D8
Nuthall Rd NG8 . . . . 160 C2
Nuthatch Cres S81 . . . . . 25 D1
Nutkin Cl 4 LE11 . . . . . 220 A2

O

Oak Acres NG9 . . . . 183 A5
Oak Ave
  Aldercar NG16 . . . . 143 B5
  Bingham NG13 . . . . 178 A4
  Blidworth NG21 . . . . 118 B4
  Farndon NG24 . . . . 139 A4
  Mansfield NG18 . . . . 102 C8
  New Ollerton NG22 . . . . . 77 D4
  Radcliffe on T NG12 . . . . 175 E4
  Rainworth NG21 . . . . 104 C1
  Sandiacre NG10 . . . . 182 A7
  Shirebrook NG20 . . . . 72 D4
Oak Bank Cl NG18 . . . . . 102 B8
Oak Cl
  Pinxton NG16 . . . . 113 C3
  Worksop S81 . . . . 35 E1
Oak Cres LE12 . . . . 214 D8
Oakdale Dr NG9 . . . . . . 183 C4
Oakdale Rd
  Arnold NG5 . . . . 162 B8
  Carlton NG3 . . . . 174 C6
  Mansfield NG18 . . . . 101 F7
  Retford DN22 . . . . 39 E8
  South Normanton DE55 . . 113 A4
Oak Dr
  Eastwood NG16 . . . . 143 E2
  Mansfield Woodhouse NG19 88 E2
  New Balderton NG24 . . . . 140 C4
  Nuthall NG16 . . . . 159 B6
Oakenhall Ave NG15 . . . 146 C7
Oakfield LN1 . . . . 57 A3
Oakfield Ave
  Market Warsop NG20 . . . . 74 B3
  Sutton in A NG17 . . . . . . 114 E8
Oakfield Cl
  Mansfield NG18 . . . . 102 F2
  Nottingham NG8 . . . . . . 171 C3
Oakfield Dr NG10 . . . . . 182 B3
Oakfield La NG20 . . . . . . 74 B2
Oakfield Rd
  Hucknall NG15 . . . . 146 B6
  Nottingham NG8 . . . . . . 171 C3
  Stapleford NG9 . . . . 182 D7
Oakfields Rd NG2 . . . . . 174 A1
Oak Flatt NG9 . . . . 183 A5
Oakford Cl NG8 . . . . 160 A2
Oak Gr NG15 . . . . 146 A4
Oakham Bsns Pk NG18 . 101 F3
Oakham Cl
  Mansfield NG18 . . . . 102 B4
  Nottingham NG5 . . . . . . 160 F7
Oakham Way DE7 . . . . . 157 D3
Oakholme Ave S81 . . . . . 35 F5
Oakholme Rise S81 . . . . . 35 F6
Oakington Cl NG5 . . . . . 161 B5
Oakland Ave
  Huthwaite NG17 . . . . 99 F2
  Long Eaton NG10 . . . . . . 193 C5
Oakland Ct NG9 . . . . . . 171 A1
Oakland Gr NG14 . . . . . 148 F7
Oakland Rd NG18 . . . . . 102 F8
Oaklands NG23 . . . . 112 A8
Oaklands Ave DE75 . . . . 143 A2
Oaklands Dr DN11 . . . . . . 8 D2
Oaklands La DN22 . . . . . 40 A5
Oakland St 6 NG7 . . . . 172 E7
Oaklands The DE55 . . . . 113 A4
Oakland Terr NG10 . . . . 193 C5
Oakleaf Cres NG17 . . . . 100 C1
Oakleigh Ave
  Mansfield Woodhouse
    NG19 . . . . 88 E4
  Nottingham NG3 . . . . . . 162 C2
Oakleigh St NG6 . . . . . . 160 D4
Oakley Dr LE12 . . . . 212 D2
Oakley Mews NG6 . . . . 159 F6
Oakley's Rd NG10 . . . . . 193 E7
Oakley's Rd W NG10 . . . 193 D6
Oak Lodge Dr NG16 . . . 158 F7
Oakmead Ave NG8 . . . . 171 F8
Oakmere Cl NG2 . . . . . . 186 C4
Oakridge Cl NG19 . . . . . . 88 F1
Oak Rise NG22 . . . . 105 C4
Oaks Ave S80 . . . . 58 C8

Oaks Cl DN22 . . . . 19 B5
Oaks Ind Est LE11 . . . . . 220 A6
Oaks La
  Oxton NG25 . . . . 133 F7
  Walkeringham DN10 . . . . . 13 E3
Oak St
  Kirkby in A NG17 . . . . . . 115 B5
  Nottingham NG5 . . . . . . 161 B1
  Sutton in A NG17 . . . . . . 100 D7
Oaks The
  Mansfield NG18 . . . . 102 C3
  Newark-on-T NG24 . . . . 140 E4
Oak Tree NG14 . . . . 152 A8
Oaktree Ave DN21 . . . . . 15 F2
Oak Tree Ave
  Edwinstowe NG21 . . . . . . 76 A2
  Glapwell S44 . . . . 86 B8
  Radcliffe on T NG12 . . . . 175 F4
Oak Tree Bsns Pk NG18 . 103 B4
Oak Tree Cl
  Hucknall NG15 . . . . 145 D4
  Mansfield NG18 . . . . 103 B7
  West Bridgford NG2 . . . . 186 A8
Oak Tree Cres NG19 . . . . 88 B4
Oaktree Dr NG22 . . . . . . 106 A4
Oak Tree Dr NG4 . . . . . . 163 A2
Oak Tree La NG18 . . . . . 103 A6
Oak Tree La L Ctr NG18 . 103 B5
Oak Tree Prim Sch
  NG18 . . . . 103 C6
Oaktree Rd DE55 . . . . . . 99 C1
Oak Tree Rd
  Bawtry DN10 . . . . 9 F7
  Sutton in A NG17 . . . . . . 101 A4
Oak Tree Rise S81 . . . . . 25 E7
Oak View Rise NG18 . . . 116 D7
Oakwood Dr
  Nottingham NG8 . . . . . . 172 C7
  Ravenshead NG15 . . . . . 117 A1
Oakwood Gr NG21 . . . . . 91 B8
Oakwood Mews S80 . . . . 35 C3
Oakwood Rd NG18 . . . . 103 B4
Oatfield La NG12 . . . . . . 176 D6
Oban Rd NG9 . . . . 183 C6
Observatory Way NG17 . 115 B8
Occupation La
  Edwinstowe NG21 . . . . . . 76 B1
  Kirkby in A NG17 . . . . . . 114 F6
  Rolleston NG25 . . . . 137 E5
  Willoughby-on-t-W LE12 . . 217 E6
Occupation Rd
  Hucknall NG15 . . . . 146 A5
  New Houghton NG19 . . . . 86 F7
  Nottingham NG6 . . . . . . 160 B5
Ochbrook Ct DE7 . . . . . 157 F3
Ockerby St NG6 . . . . . . 160 C6
Oddicroft La NG17 . . . . 101 A1
Odesa Dr NG6 . . . . 160 B4
Ogdon Ct NG3 . . . . 173 F6
Ogle Dr
  Nottingham NG1 . . . . . . 173 B3
  Nottingham NG7 . . . . . . 223 D1
Ogle St NG15 . . . . 146 A7
Oldacres NG14 . . . . 149 D4
Old Basford Prim Sch
  NG6 . . . . 160 D3
Old Bell La NG23 . . . . . . 96 F4
Old Blyth Rd DN22 . . . . . 38 A6
Old Bowling Gn The S81 . 35 B4
Old Brickyard NG3 . . . . 174 A7
Old Chapel Cl NG17 . . . 114 E5
Old Chapel La
  Elston NG23 . . . . 153 E5
  Selston NG16 . . . . 129 A3
Old Church St 9 NG7 . . 172 E2
Old Coach Rd
  Nottingham NG8 . . . . . . 171 F5
  Nottingham NG8 . . . . . . 171 F6
  Worksop S80 . . . . 47 E7
Old Ctyd The DN21 . . . . 44 C8
Old Dalby CE Sch LE14 . 218 E5
Old Dalby La LE14 . . . . . 219 D6
Old Derby Rd NG16 . . . . 143 D3
Old Dr NG9 . . . . 183 E8
Old Engine Yd The LE12 . 215 E5
Old Epperstone Rd NG14 150 B4
Oldershaw Ave DE74 . . . 203 C2
Oldershaw Rd LE12 . . . . 205 F1
Old Farm Rd NG5 . . . . . 160 F8
Old Forge Cl LE12 . . . . . 213 A1
Old Forge La NG13 . . . . 191 C5
Old Forge Rd DN10 . . . . . 6 E2
Old Gateford Rd S81 . . . . 35 C8
Old Grantham Rd NG13 . 179 A3
Old Great N Rd NG23 . . . 96 E8
Old Hall Cl
  Calverton NG14 . . . . 148 E7
  Farndon NG24 . . . . 138 F4
  Market Warsop NG20 . . . . 74 C5
Old Hall Dr
  Nottingham NG3 . . . . . . 161 D2
  Widmerpool NG12 . . . . . 208 C5
Old Hall Gdns NG24 . . . 125 F2
Old Hall La
  East Markham NG22 . . . . . 65 F7
  Norwell NG23 . . . . 110 B8
Old Hall The DN21 . . . . . 15 C1
Oldknow St NG7 . . . . . . 172 F7
Old La NG17 . . . . 185 D1
Old La The NG14 . . . . . . 150 D7
Old Lenton Cl NG12 . . . 189 A4
Old Lenton St NG1 . . . . 223 F2
Old Liby Arts Ctr The
  NG18 . . . . 102 B7
Old London Rd
  Babworth DN22 . . . . 49 F8
  Barnby Moor DN22 . . . . . 28 C3

Old London Rd *continued*
  West Drayton DN22 . . . . . 50 F2
Old Main Rd
  Bulcote NG14 . . . . 164 B5
  Costock LE12 . . . . 206 D1
Old Manor Cl NG14 . . . . 149 D4
Old Manor Rd NG19 . . . . 88 B3
Old Melton Rd NG12 . . . 197 F7
Old Mill Cl
  Beeston NG9 . . . . 183 A2
  Bestwood Village NG6 . . 146 D3
  Nottingham NG7 . . . . . . 222 B3
Old Mill Cres NG24 . . . . 140 B8
Old Mill Ct NG13 . . . . . . 177 F5
Old Mill La
  Cuckney NG20 . . . . 60 B3
  Mansfield NG19 . . . . 88 E1
Old Mkt Pl
  Mansfield NG18 . . . . 102 B7
  South Normanton DE55 . . 113 A6
Old Mkt Sq NG1 . . . . . . 223 E2
Old Newark Rd NG18 . . . 102 E2
Oldoak Rd NG11 . . . . . . 185 A2
Old Parsonage La LE12 . 215 C1
Old Pk Cl NG11 . . . . 203 F6
Old Pk The NG12 . . . . . . 187 F4
Old Post Office St DN10 . 11 C3
Old Rd NG17 . . . . 100 F7
Old Rectory Cl LE12 . . . 205 E1
Old Rectory Mus & Wildlife
  Gdn LE11 . . . . 220 B4
Old Rufford Rd
  Bilsthorpe NG22 . . . . 105 C4
  Calverton NG14 . . . . 133 C6
  Edwinstowe NG22 . . . . . . 91 D4
  Farnsfield NG22 . . . . 119 B5
  Ollerton NG22 . . . . 77 A3
Old Sch Cl NG11 . . . . . . 195 E8
Old Sch House Cl NG12 . 189 B7
Old Sch La NG19 . . . . 87 A5
Old Showfields NG15 . . . 15 D2
Old Sookholme La NG20 . 74 A4
Old St NG1 . . . . 223 E3
Old Sta Yd NG13 . . . . . . 181 C3
Old Storth La DE55 . . . . 113 B4
Old Tannery Dr NG14 . . 150 E1
Old Terr NG19 . . . . 86 F4
Old Tollerton Rd NG2 . . 186 C7
Old Trent Rd DN10 . . . . . 14 F1
Old Way LE12 . . . . 213 A1
Olga Ct NG3 . . . . 173 F6
Olga Rd NG3 . . . . 173 F6
Olive Ave
  Long Eaton NG10 . . . . . . 182 E1
  Shirebrook NG20 . . . . 72 D6
Olive Ct NG17 . . . . 100 F4
Olive Gr
  Burton Joyce NG14 . . . . 163 F5
  Mansfield NG19 . . . . 103 A8
Oliver Cl
  Heanor DE75 . . . . 143 B2
  Nottingham NG7 . . . . . . 222 C4
Oliver Ct NG24 . . . . 140 B8
Oliver Quibell Inf Sch
  NG24 . . . . 140 A5
Oliver Rd LE11 . . . . 220 B2
Oliver St NG7 . . . . 222 C3
Ollerton Prim Sch NG22 . 77 D5
Ollerton Rd
  Arnold NG5 . . . . 147 E6
  Calverton NG14 . . . . 132 F2
  Edwinstowe NG21 . . . . . . 76 D3
  Farnsfield NG22 . . . . 119 A1
  Gamston DN22 . . . . 50 E5
  Kelham NG23 . . . . 124 A5
  Kirton NG22 . . . . 78 F8
  Ollerton NG22 . . . . 77 A4
  Retford DN22 . . . . 39 E4
  South Muskham NG23 . . 124 B7
  Tuxford NG22 . . . . 65 C2
  Worksop S80 . . . . 47 B4
Ollerton Water Mill NG22 77 A3
Olton Ave NG9 . . . . 171 F1
Olympus Ct NG15 . . . . . 145 D3
Omberley Ave NG17 . . . 101 B6
Onchan Ave NG4 . . . . . . 174 E6
Ontario Dr NG16 . . . . . . 129 A7
Opal Cl
  Mansfield NG18 . . . . 102 E4
  Rainworth NG21 . . . . 104 C1
Orange Cl NG20 . . . . 72 E6
Orange Croft DN11 . . . . . 8 B8
Orange Gdns NG2 . . . . . 173 D2
Orby Cl NG3 . . . . 173 F6
Orby Wlk NG3 . . . . 173 F6
Orchard Ave
  Bingham NG13 . . . . 177 D4
  Carlton NG4 . . . . 174 E7
  North Leverton w H DN22 . 42 D8
Orchard Bsns Pk
  Ilkeston DE7 . . . . 157 D1
  Sandiacre NG10 . . . . 182 C6
Orchard Cl
  Barkestone-le-Vale
    NG13 . . . . 192 B2
  Barnstone NG13 . . . . . . 190 F3
  Bleasby NG14 . . . . 152 A8
  Burton Joyce NG14 . . . . 163 F5
  East Bridgford NG13 . . . 165 D3
  East Leake LE12 . . . . . . 214 D8
  Gunthorpe NG14 . . . . . . 165 A5
  Mansfield NG18 . . . . 102 C2
  Morton DN21 . . . . 15 B4
  North Leverton w H DN22 . 42 D8
  Radcliffe on T NG12 . . . . 175 E3

Orchard Cl *continued*
Shirebrook NG20 . . . . **72** E5
South Muskham NG23 . . **124** E7
Southwell NG25 . . . . **121** D2
Sutton Bonington LE12 . . **213** C5
Tollerton NG12 . . . . **186** D1
Orchard Cres
Beeston NG9 . . . . **183** C5
Glapwell S44 . . . . **86** B8
Tuxford NG22 . . . . **65** F2
Orchard Ct
Carlton NG4 . . . . **174** E7
Gedling NG4 . . . . **162** D2
Hucknall NG15 . . . . **146** A6
Langley Mill NG16 . . . . . . **143** B3
Nottingham NG8 . . . . **172** E8
Orchard Dr NG14 . . . . **149** A7
Orchard Gr
Arnold NG5 . . . . **161** C6
Misterton NG10 . . . . **14** A8
Orchard La LN1 . . . . **57** A4
Orchard Leigh DN22 . . . . . . **39** D4
Orchard Pk NG24 . . . . **125** F2
Orchard Prim Sch NG17 . **114** E5
Orchard Rd NG17 . . . . **114** E5
Orchard Rise NG4 . . . . **163** C7
Orchard Sch DN22 . . . . **42** C7
Orchard Specl Sch NG24 **125** A1
Orchard St
Eastwood NG16 . . . . **144** A1
Gotham NG11 . . . . **195** B1
Hucknall NG15 . . . . **146** A6
Kimberley NG16 . . . . **158** F6
Langley Mill NG16 . . . . . . **143** B3
Long Eaton NG10 . . . . . . **193** E7
10 Loughborough LE11 . . **220** A4
Mansfield NG19 . . . . **88** B1
Stapleford NG9 . . . . **182** D7
Orchards The
Carlton NG4 . . . . **163** A1
Lowdham NG14 . . . . **164** E8
Oxton NG25 . . . . **134** C4
Westwood NG16 . . . . **128** B4
Orchard The
Elston NG23 . . . . **153** E4
Sutton in A NG17 . . . . **101** B1
Orchard View NG19 . . . . . **88** B3
Orchard Way
Balderton NG24 . . . . **140** D3
Sandiacre NG10 . . . . **182** A3
Sutton in A NG17 . . . . **114** C8
Wymeswold LE12 . . . . . . **216** D3
Orchard Wlk NG17 . . . . . . **114** E5
Orchid Cl
4 Kirkby in A NG17 . . . . **114** F7
New Balderton NG24 . . . . **140** B5
West Bridgford NG11 . . . . **185** C4
Orchid Dr
Farndon NG24 . . . . **139** B6
Sutton in A NG17 . . . . **101** B1
Orchid Way NG20 . . . . **72** D3
Ordsall Pk Cl DN22 . . . . . . **39** D6
Ordsall Pk Dr DN22 . . . . . . **39** D6
Ordsall Pk Rd DN22 . . . . . . **39** D6
Ordsall Prim Sch DN22 . . **39** D4
Ordsall Rd DN22 . . . . **39** C5
Orford Ave
Nottingham NG11 . . . . . . **184** F4
Radcliffe on T NG12 . . . . **175** F2
Orion Cl NG8 . . . . **171** E7
Orion Dr NG8 . . . . **171** E7
Orlando Dr NG4 . . . . **174** F8
Orlock Wlk NG5 . . . . **161** B5
Ormonde St NG16 . . . . . . **143** F4
Ormonde Terr
Aldercar NG16 . . . . **143** B4
Nottingham NG5 . . . . **161** C2
Ornsay Cl NG5 . . . . **146** E1
Orpean Way NG9 . . . . **182** E2
Orston Ave
Arnold NG5 . . . . **162** A1
Newark-on-T NG24 . . . . . **139** E6
Orston Dr NG8 . . . . **172** D4
Orston Gn NG8 . . . . **172** D3
Orston La NG13 . . . . **180** F3
Orston Prim Sch NG13 . . **180** A7
Orston Rd E NG2 . . . . **173** F1
Orston Rd W NG2 . . . . **173** E1
Orton Ave NG9 . . . . **183** C6
Ortzen St NG7 . . . . **222** B4
Orville Rd NG5 . . . . **160** E5
Osberne Wy NG17 . . . . **89** F2
Osberton Rd DN22 . . . . **39** F6
Osberton View S81 . . . . . . **36** B5
Osborne Ave 2 NG5 . . . . **161** C3
Osborne Cl NG10 . . . . **182** B4
Osborne Gr NG5 . . . . **161** C3
Osborne St NG7 . . . . **222** A4
Osbourne Cl NG16 . . . . . . **159** B7
Osbourne St NG17 . . . . . . **129** F8
Osgood Rd NG5 . . . . **162** C5
Osier Dr NG15 . . . . **130** A6
Osier Fields LE12 . . . . **205** F2
Osier Rd NG2 . . . . **173** B1
Osiers The
Kegworth DE74 . . . . **203** D2
Newark-on-T NG24 . . . . . **139** C6
Osman Cl NG2 . . . . **173** B1
Osmanthorpe Nature Reserve
NG22 . . . . **120** F6
Osmaston St
Nottingham NG7 . . . . **222** A4
Sandiacre NG10 . . . . **182** C5
Osprey Cl NG11 . . . . **184** C1

Ossington Cl
Meden Vale NG20 . . . . **74** D8
Nottingham NG1 . . . . **223** E4
Ossington Rd NG22 . . . . . . **93** E5
Ossington St NG7 . . . . . . **222** B4
Ossington Way NG24 . . . . **124** F1
Oster Fen La NG23 . . . . . . **156** F7
Osterley Gr NG8 . . . . **159** D2
Otter Ave LN1 . . . . **57** A4
Otter Way NG19 . . . . **87** D1
Oulton Cl NG5 . . . . **161** F6
Oundle Dr
Ilkeston DE7 . . . . **170** A7
Mansfield NG19 . . . . **87** D1
Nottingham NG8 . . . . **172** C3
Our Lady of Perpetual
Succour Prim Sch NG6 **160** D6
Our Ladys Convent Sch
LE11 . . . . **220** B2
Oursham St NG17 . . . . . . **100** F2
Ousebridge Cres NG4 . . . **175** A8
Ouse Bridge Dr NG4 . . . . **175** A8
Outgang La
Mansfield Woodhouse
NG19 . . . . **88** D4
Pleasley NG19 . . . . **87** C6
Treswell DN22 . . . . **42** F4
Outram St NG17 . . . . **100** F3
Oval Gdns 2 NG8 . . . . **172** D8
Oval The
Retford DN22 . . . . **39** D4
Sutton in A NG17 . . . . . . **100** D4
Tickhill DN11 . . . . **8** B8
Overdale Ave NG17 . . . . . **100** E7
Overdale Cl NG10 . . . . . . **193** A6
Overdale Rd NG6 . . . . **160** C3
Overend Rd S80 . . . . **35** F4
Overmoor View DE55 . . . . **99** B7
Overstone Cl NG17 . . . . . **100** F5
Overstrand Cl NG5 . . . . . . **161** F6
Owday La S81 . . . . **25** D3
Owen Ave NG10 . . . . **194** A6
Owlston Cl NG16 . . . . **143** F3
Owlsthorpe Cl NG5 . . . . . **161** A8
Owston Rd DN10 . . . . **7** C4
Owston Ferry Rd DN9 . . . . . **7** D7
Owthorpe Gr NG5 . . . . **161** B2
Owthorpe La NG12 . . . . . . **199** F3
Owthorpe Rd
Colston Bassett NG12 . . . **200** B7
Cotgrave NG12 . . . . **187** F2
Oxborough Rd NG5 . . . . . . **161** C7
Oxbow Cl NG2 . . . . **173** C1
Oxbury Rd NG16 . . . . **158** F8
Oxclose La
Mansfield Woodhouse
NG19 . . . . **88** A3
Nottingham NG5 . . . . **161** C6
Radmanthwaite NG19 . . . **87** D3
Oxcroft La NG20 . . . . **58** A8
Oxengate NG5 . . . . **161** C6
Oxford Cl NG21 . . . . **118** A8
Oxford Dr DN11 . . . . **8** F5
Oxford Rd
Carlton in L S81 . . . . **25** F6
West Bridgford NG2 . . . . . **186** A7
Oxford St
Carlton NG4 . . . . **174** E8
Eastwood NG16 . . . . **143** F4
Kirkby in A NG17 . . . . . . **115** B4
Long Eaton NG10 . . . . . . **193** D8
Loughborough LE11 . . . . **220** A4
Mansfield Woodhouse NG19 **88** C1
Nottingham NG1 . . . . **223** D2
Sutton in A NG17 . . . . . . **100** D2
Oxpasture La NG20 . . . . . . **58** B6
Oxton Ave NG5 . . . . **161** C4
Oxton By-Pass NG25 . . . . **134** A4
Oxton Cl
Mansfield NG19 . . . . **101** E7
Retford DN22 . . . . **39** E3
Oxton Hill NG15 . . . . **134** E4
Oxton Rd
Calverton NG14 . . . . **133** D1
Southwell NG25 . . . . **135** C6
Ozier Holt
Carlton NG4 . . . . **174** E4
Long Eaton NG10 . . . . . . **193** C6

P

Packe St LE11 . . . . **220** A4
Pack Horse La 5 LE11 . . **220** B4
Packington Hill DE74 . . . . **203** C2
Packman Dr NG11 . . . . **196** D8
Paddington Ms NG3 . . . . . **174** A7
Paddocks Cl
Elston NG23 . . . . **153** D4
Pinxton NG16 . . . . **113** C4
Paddocks The
Beckingham DN10 . . . . **14** B1
Bottesford NG13 . . . . **181** A2
Elston NG23 . . . . **153** E4
Hockerton NG25 . . . . **122** B6
Lound DN22 . . . . **20** C2
Mansfield Woodhouse NG19 **88** C8
Marton DN21 . . . . **44** C8
Newark-on-T NG24 . . . . . **140** B7
Newton on T LN1 . . . . **55** A1
Sandiacre NG10 . . . . **182** A5
Stapleford LN6 . . . . **127** E8

Paddocks The *continued*
Sutton Bonington LE12 . . **213** B6
West Bridgford NG12 . . . . **186** B3
Worksop S81 . . . . **36** B7
Paddocks View NG10 . . . . **193** A8
Paddock The
Beeston NG9 . . . . **183** D2
Bingham NG13 . . . . **177** E4
Collingham NG23 . . . . . . **112** A7
Gunthorpe NG13, NG14 . . **164** F5
Kirkby in A NG17 . . . . . . **114** F4
Retford DN22 . . . . **40** A4
Stanton Hill NG17 . . . . . . **100** C5
Tickhill DN11 . . . . **8** B8
Paddy's La LE14 . . . . **218** A1
Padge Rd NG9 . . . . **184** B6
Padgham Ct 11 NG5 . . . . **161** A8
Padley Hill NG18 . . . . **102** A6
Padleys La NG14 . . . . **163** E5
Padstow Cl NG18 . . . . **103** B2
Padstow Rd NG5 . . . . **160** F6
Pagdin Dr DN11 . . . . **8** E1
Paget Cres NG11 . . . . **196** C8
Paget St 3 LE11 . . . . **220** A5
Paignton Cl NG8 . . . . **160** B2
Paisley Gr NG9 . . . . **183** C1
Palace Theatre NG18 . . . . **140** A8
Palace View NG25 . . . . . . **136** F8
Palatine St
Nottingham NG1 . . . . **173** B3
Nottingham NG7 . . . . **223** D1
Paling Cres NG17 . . . . **100** E3
Palin Gdns NG12 . . . . **176** A3
Palin St NG7 . . . . **222** B4
Palm Ct Ind Ctr NG7 . . . . **160** F1
Palmer Ave NG15 . . . . **146** A8
Palmer Cres NG4 . . . . **174** D7
Palmer Dr NG9 . . . . **182** D5
Palmer Rd
Retford DN22 . . . . **30** A1
Sutton on T NG23 . . . . **96** F8
Palmers Ct 5 NG25 . . . . **136** F8
Palmerston Gdns NG3 . . . **223** E4
Palmerston St
Selston NG16 . . . . **128** F2
Westwood NG16 . . . . **128** C4
Palm St NG7 . . . . **160** F1
Palmwood Cl NG6 . . . . . . **160** C5
Palm Wood Ct NG6 . . . . . **160** C6
Paper Mill La DN11 . . . . **8** C8
Papplewick Grange
NG15 . . . . **131** D1
Papplewick Hall & Gdns
NG15 . . . . **131** D4
Papplewick La NG15 . . . . **146** C8
Papplewick Ppg Sta
NG15 . . . . **132** E5
Paradise La LE14 . . . . **218** F4
Parfitt Dr NG22 . . . . **120** A5
Park Ave
Annesley Woodhouse
NG17 . . . . **130** B8
Arnold NG5 . . . . **161** E5
Awsworth NG16 . . . . **158** B5
Blidworth NG21 . . . . **118** B5
Burton Joyce NG14 . . . . . **163** E4
Carlton NG4 . . . . **174** F8
Eastwood NG16 . . . . **143** E3
Hucknall NG15 . . . . **145** F7
Keyworth NG12 . . . . **197** F4
Kimberley NG16 . . . . **159** A4
Loughborough LE11 . . . . **220** B1
Mansfield NG18 . . . . **102** C8
Mansfield Woodhouse NG19 **88** C1
Misterton DN10 . . . . **6** E3
Nottingham NG3 . . . . **173** C7
Shirebrook NG20 . . . . **72** E4
West Bridgford NG2 . . . . . **185** F8
Woodborough NG14 . . . . **149** B4
Park Ave E NG12 . . . . **197** D3
Park Ave W NG12 . . . . **197** D3
Park Chase NG6 . . . . **160** B5
Park Cl
Lea DN21 . . . . **24** F1
Nottingham NG3 . . . . **161** E2
Pinxton NG16 . . . . **113** C2
Park Cres
Eastwood NG16 . . . . **143** F4
Ilkeston DE7 . . . . **170** A8
Newark-on-T NG24 . . . . . **125** B4
Nottingham NG8 . . . . **171** C4
Retford DN22 . . . . **40** A8
Parkcroft Rd NG2 . . . . **185** F6
Park Ct
Loughborough LE11 . . . . **220** B2
Mansfield NG18 . . . . **102** C8
Parkdale Prim Sch NG4 . **174** D6
Parkdale Rd NG3 . . . . **174** C6
Park Dr
Blyth S81 . . . . **18** A3
Hucknall NG15 . . . . **146** B6
Nottingham NG7 . . . . **222** C2
Sandiacre NG10 . . . . **182** A3
Parker Cl NG5 . . . . **162** C8
Parker's La NG19 . . . . **88** C3
Parker St
Hucknall NG15 . . . . **146** B7
Newark-on-T NG24 . . . . . **140** A8
Parkes Cl NG24 . . . . **126** B2
Park Farm Cotts LN1 . . . . **55** F1
Park Gate NG15 . . . . **131** B1
Park Gdn NG17 . . . . **100** A3
Park Hall Gdns NG19 . . . . **88** C5
Park Hall Rd NG19 . . . . **88** C5
Parkham Rd NG16 . . . . . . **158** F7
Park Hill NG16 . . . . **158** B5
Park Hill Dr S81 . . . . **16** A5
Park House Gates NG3 . . **161** D1

Park Hts NG7 . . . . **222** C1
Parkin Cl NG12 . . . . **189** A4
Park La
Elkesley DN22 . . . . **50** C3
Holbeck NG20 . . . . **59** C6
Kirkby in A NG17 . . . . . . **114** C2
Lambley NG4 . . . . **163** E8
Mansfield NG18 . . . . **102** B5
Nottingham NG6 . . . . **160** E4
Owthorpe NG12 . . . . **199** E7
Pinxton NG16 . . . . **113** C2
Retford DN22 . . . . **40** A8
Southwell NG25 . . . . **136** D6
Sutton Bonington LE12 . . **213** C5
Parkland Cl
Mansfield NG18 . . . . **102** E2
Nottingham NG11 . . . . . . **184** D3
Parklands Adult Ctr
NG10 . . . . **193** D8
Parklands Cl
Coddington NG24 . . . . . . **125** F2
1 Nottingham NG5 . . . . **147** B1
Parklands Dr 2 LE11 . . . **220** A1
Parklands Inf Sch NG10 . **182** B1
Park Mews
Mansfield Woodhouse
NG19 . . . . **88** C4
Nottingham NG3 . . . . **173** C8
Retford DN22 . . . . **40** A8
Park Pl S80 . . . . **35** F1
Park Ravine NG7 . . . . **222** C1
Park Rd
Arnold NG5 . . . . **161** E5
Barnstone NG13 . . . . **190** E3
Bawtry DN10 . . . . **9** F7
Beeston, Bramcote NG9 . **183** A8
Beeston, Chilwell NG9 . . . **183** E6
Bestwood Village NG6 . . **146** E4
Calverton NG14 . . . . **148** E7
Carlton NG4 . . . . **174** F7
Hucknall NG15 . . . . **145** F7
Ilkeston DE7 . . . . **170** A/
Keyworth NG12 . . . . **197** F5
Loughborough LE11 . . . . **220** B2
Mansfield Woodhouse NG19 **88** B3
Nottingham NG7 . . . . **222** B1
Radcliffe on T NG12 . . . . **175** F4
Shirebrook NG20 . . . . **72** C5
Park Rd E NG14 . . . . **149** A7
Park Rd N NG9 . . . . **183** E6
Park Row NG1 . . . . **223** D2
Parkside
Huthwaite NG17 . . . . **100** A3
Keyworth NG12 . . . . **197** F4
Nottingham NG8 . . . . **171** E2
Parkside Ave NG10 . . . . . **193** B8
Parkside Dr NG10 . . . . . . **193** B8
Parkside Gdns NG8 . . . . . **171** E2
Parkside Rd NG21 . . . . **75** F2
Parkside Rise NG12 . . . . . **197** F2
Park Springs Rd DN21 . . . **24** F6
Park St
Beeston NG9 . . . . **183** E6
Kirkby in A NG17 . . . . . . **114** F5
Long Eaton NG10 . . . . . . **182** C1
Loughborough LE11 . . . . **220** B3
Mansfield Woodhouse NG19 **88** B3
Nottingham NG7 . . . . **222** B2
Stapleford NG9 . . . . **182** C5
Sutton in A NG17 . . . . . . **100** F3
Parkstone Ave NG21 . . . . **103** F2
Parkstone Cl NG2 . . . . **185** C5
Park Terr
Keyworth NG12 . . . . **197** F5
Nottingham NG1 . . . . **223** D2
Park The
Cotgrave NG12 . . . . **187** F4
Mansfield NG18 . . . . **102** C8
Newark-on-T NG24 . . . . . **140** A7
North Muskham NG23 . . . **110** F3
Park Valley NG7 . . . . **223** D2
Park View
Beeston NG9 . . . . **183** D6
Nottingham NG3 . . . . **161** E2
Pleasley NG19 . . . . **87** A5
Parkview Rd NG5 . . . . **161** A7
Park View Way NG18 . . . . **102** C5
Parkway
Clipstone NG19 . . . . **89** D3
Newark-on-T NG24 . . . . . **139** E6
Sutton in A NG17 . . . . . . **100** B3
Whitwell S80 . . . . **45** A6
Parkway Ct NG8 . . . . **171** D5
Parkwood Cres NG5 . . . . . **161** E3
Parkwood Ct NG6 . . . . **160** E5
Parkyn Rd NG5 . . . . **161** D6
Parkyns Piece LE12 . . . . . **205** E2
Parkyns St NG11 . . . . **196** C6
Parliament Ct NG24 . . . . **139** E8
Parliament Rd NG19 . . . . **101** E8
Parliament St
Newark-on-T NG24 . . . . . **139** E7
Sutton in A NG17 . . . . . . **100** F2
Parliament Terr NG1 . . . . **223** D3
Parliament Wlk NG24 . . . **139** E8
Parnell St DN21 . . . . **24** C8
Parnham's Cl LE14 . . . . . . **219** C8
Parr Gate NG9 . . . . **183** A5
Parr La NG4 . . . . **150** A5
Parrs The NG9 . . . . **184** B6
Parry Ct 5 NG3 . . . . **174** A6
Parry Way NG5 . . . . **162** B8
Parsons Mdw NG4 . . . . . . **174** F4
Parthenon Cl NG19 . . . . . . **86** F5
Partridge Cl NG21 . . . . . . **118** B8
Paschall Rd NG17 . . . . . . **115** B1
Pasteur Ct 5 NG7 . . . . . . **172** E2

Pasture Cl
Carlton in L S81 . . . . **26** A7
Carlton NG2 . . . . **174** E4
Stanton Hill NG17 . . . . . . **100** C5
Worksop S80 . . . . **35** C2
Pasture Farm & Victorian
Carriages Mus NG22 . . . . **78** B7
Pasture La
Hathern LE12 . . . . **213** B2
Hilcote DE55 . . . . **99** C1
Hose LE14 . . . . **211** F6
Long Eaton NG10 . . . . . . **194** A5
Ruddington NG11 . . . . . . **196** A7
Sutton Bonington LE12 . . **213** A6
Pasture Rd
Gainsborough DN21 . . . . . **24** F8
Stapleford NG9 . . . . **170** D1
Pastures Ave NG11 . . . . . . **195** D7
Pastures The
Bawtry DN10 . . . . **10** A6
Calverton NG14 . . . . **148** D7
Eastwood NG16 . . . . **158** B8
Mansfield Woodhouse NG19 **88** B3
Rampton DN22 . . . . **43** A1
Tuxford NG22 . . . . **65** E2
Pasture View NG14 . . . . . **165** A5
Patchills The NG18 . . . . . **102** F7
Patchings Art Ctr NG14 . . **148** A8
Pateley Rd NG3 . . . . **162** A4
Paton Rd NG5 . . . . **160** E5
Patricia Dr NG5 . . . . **148** A1
Patrick Rd NG2 . . . . **185** E8
Patriot Cl NG16 . . . . **159** A7
Patterdale Cl NG2 . . . . . . **186** C6
Patterdale Rd NG5 . . . . . . **161** F5
Patterson Pl NG18 . . . . . . **102** D7
Patterson Rd 13 NG7 . . . **172** F7
Paul Ave NG18 . . . . **103** A6
Paulson's Dr NG18 . . . . . . **102** B7
Pavilion Cl
Market Warsop NG20 . . . . **74** B4
2 Nottingham NG2 . . . . **173** D1
Pavilion Ct NG14 . . . . **164** E8
Pavilion Gdns
New Houghton NG19 . . . . **86** F8
Sutton in A NG17 . . . . . . **101** A6
Pavilion Rd
Ilkeston DE7 . . . . **157** F6
Kirkby in Ashfield NG17 . . **115** B6
Nottingham NG5 . . . . **147** B1
West Bridgford NG2 . . . . . **173** E1
Pavillion Way LE11 . . . . . . **220** A7
Paviour Rd NG5 . . . . **160** F5
Paxton Gdns NG3 . . . . **173** E5
Paxtons Ct NG24 . . . . **124** F1
Payne Rd NG9 . . . . **183** B3
Peach Ave
Selston NG16 . . . . **128** F6
South Normanton DE55 . . **113** B7
Peache Way NG9 . . . . **183** C7
Peachey St NG1 . . . . **223** E3
Peacock Cl
Gunthorpe NG14 . . . . **165** A4
Ruddington NG11 . . . . . . **196** B6
Peacock Cres NG7 . . . . . . **184** C2
Peacock Dr NG21 . . . . **118** C8
Peacock Pl DE7 . . . . **157** D4
Peacock St 2 NG18 . . . . . **102** B6
Peafield La NG19 . . . . **88** E4
Peafield Lane Prim Sch
NG19 . . . . **88** F4
Peakdale Cl NG10 . . . . . . **193** A6
Peake's Croft DN10 . . . . . . **10** A7
Peak Hill Cl S81 . . . . **25** D1
Peak The NG20 . . . . **72** E3
Pearce Dr NG8 . . . . **172** B7
Pearl Ave NG17 . . . . **115** B3
Pearl Cl NG21 . . . . **104** C1
Pearmain Dr NG3 . . . . **173** F7
Pearson Ave NG9 . . . . **183** B5
Pearson Cl NG9 . . . . **183** B5
Pearson St
Carlton NG4 . . . . **175** A6
Nottingham NG7 . . . . **160** F2
Pear Tree Cl DN22 . . . . **30** D4
Pear Tree Ct NG6 . . . . **160** E4
Pear Tree Dr NG20 . . . . . . **72** E6
Peartree La NG17 . . . . **86** B2
Peartree Orch NG11 . . . . . **196** C7
Peary Cl NG5 . . . . **160** F6
Peas Hill Rd NG3 . . . . **223** F4
Peatfield Rd NG9 . . . . **170** D1
Peck La NG1 . . . . **223** E2
Pecks Hill NG18 . . . . **102** E7
Pedmore Valley NG5 . . . . **161** A7
Peebles Rd NG24 . . . . **139** D5
Peel Ave
Retford DN22 . . . . **40** B3
Tuxford NG22 . . . . **65** F2
Peel Cres NG19 . . . . **87** D2
Peel Dr LE11 . . . . **220** C4
Peel Rd NG19 . . . . **101** E8
Peel St
Langley Mill NG16 . . . . . . **143** B3
Long Eaton NG10 . . . . . . **193** E8
Nottingham NG1 . . . . **223** D4
South Normanton DE55 . . **113** B6
Sutton in A NG17 . . . . . . **101** A3
Peets Dr NG23 . . . . **110** F2
Pelham Ave
Ilkeston DE7 . . . . **157** E1
Nottingham NG5 . . . . **173** B8
Pelham Cl NG24 . . . . **139** F8
Pelham Cres
Beeston NG9 . . . . **184** B7
Nottingham NG7 . . . . **222** B2
Pelham Ct 4 NG5 . . . . . . **173** B8
Pelham Gdns NG24 . . . . . **139** F8

Pelham Rd
Kirkby in A NG17 . . . . 115 A6
Nottingham NG5 . . . . 173 B8
Retford DN22 . . . . 39 D6
Pelham St
Mansfield NG18 . . . . 102 C7
Newark-on-T NG24 . . . . . 139 F8
Nottingham NG1 . . . . 223 E2
Sutton in A NG17 . . . . 100 D2
Worksop S80 . . . . 36 A1
Pelham Way NG19 . . . . 89 D3
Pemberley Ch NG17 . . . . . 100 D1
Pemberton St NG1 . . . . . . 223 F2
Pemberton The DE55 . . . . 113 B4
Pembleton Dr NG19 . . . . . . 87 D1
Pembrey Cl NG9 . . . . 170 D2
Pembridge Cl NG6 . . . . . . 160 D2
Pembroke Cres NG24 . . . 125 C3
Pembroke Dr
Carlton in L S81 . . . . 25 E6
Nottingham NG3 . . . . 161 C1
Pembroke Rd S81 . . . . 34 F7
Pembury Rd NG8 . . . . 171 E5
Penarth Gdns NG5 . . . . . . 161 E3
Penarth Rise NG5 . . . . 161 E3
Pen Cl DE55 . . . . 99 A3
Pendean Cl DN21 . . . . 15 E2
Pendennis Cl NG4 . . . . . . 163 B1
Pendine Cl
Arnold NG5 . . . . 147 D1
South Normanton DE55 . . 113 C6
Pendle Cres NG3 . . . . 161 F1
Pendock La NG12 . . . . 197 A2
Penfold Cl LE12 . . . . 213 A1
Penhale Dr NG15 . . . . 145 C5
Penhurst Cl NG11 . . . . 185 A4
Pen La NG12 . . . . 208 D4
Penllech Cl NG5 . . . . 161 A7
Penllech Wlk 4 NG5 . . . . 161 A7
Pennant Rd NG6 . . . . 160 D2
Pennard Wlk NG11 . . . . . . 195 D8
Penn Ave NG7 . . . . 222 A1
Pennhome Ave 8 NG5 . . 161 C2
Penniment La NG19 . . . . . . 87 B2
Pennine Cl
Huthwaite NG17 . . . . 99 E4
Long Eaton, Breaston
NG10 . . . . 182 A1
Long Eaton, New Sawley
NG10 . . . . 193 D4
Mansfield Woodhouse NG19 88 C4
Newton DE55 . . . . 99 A3
Nottingham NG5 . . . . 147 B1
Pennine Dr
Kirkby in A NG17 . . . . 114 D4
Selston NG16 . . . . 128 F7
Pennington Wlk DN22 . . . . 40 A6
Penn La LE14 . . . . 202 F4
Penn Moor Cl NG10 . . . . . 193 A6
Penn St NG17 . . . . 100 F3
Pennyfields Bvd NG10 . . . 193 A7
Pennyfoot St NG1 . . . . . . 173 E4
Penny Gn S80 . . . . 45 A5
Penrhyn Cl NG3 . . . . 223 F4
Penrhyn Cres NG9 . . . . . . 183 B4
Penrith Ave NG12 . . . . . . 176 A4
Penrith Cres NG8 . . . . 160 C2
Penrith Pl NG19 . . . . 101 D8
Penshore Cl NG11 . . . . . . 184 D1
Penswick Gr NG24 . . . . . . 125 F2
Pentland Cl NG19 . . . . . . 101 D5
Pentland Dr
Carlton in L S81 . . . . 25 E7
Nottingham NG5 . . . . 147 B2
Pentland Gdns NG10 . . . . 182 A1
Pentrich Wlk NG18 . . . . . 103 B5
Pentwood Ave NG5 . . . . . 147 F2
Penzance Pl NG18 . . . . . . 103 B7
Peoples Coll The Nottingham
NG1 . . . . 223 E1
Peppercorn Gdns NG8 . . 172 C5
Pepper Rd NG14 . . . . 148 E8
Peppers Dr DE74 . . . . 203 B2
Pepper St
Nottingham NG1 . . . . 223 E2
Sutton in A NG17 . . . . 101 B2
Percival Cl NG17 . . . . 100 E3
Percival Cres NG17 . . . . . 100 E3
Percival Rd NG5 . . . . 161 C2
Percival St S81 . . . . 35 E5
Percy St
Eastwood NG16 . . . . 144 A2
Nottingham NG6 . . . . 160 D3
Sutton in A NG17 . . . . 100 D2
Peregrine Cl NG7 . . . . . . 222 A2
Peregrine Ct S81 . . . . 35 C7
Perivale Cl NG16 . . . . 159 D3
Perkin's La LE14 . . . . 219 A1
Perlethorpe Ave
Carlton NG4 . . . . 162 A4
Mansfield NG19 . . . . 88 A1
18 Nottingham NG1 . . . . 173 E4
Perlethorpe Cl
Carlton NG4 . . . . 162 A4
Edwinstowe NG21 . . . . . . 75 F3
Perlethorpe Cres NG4 . . 162 E2
Perlethorpe Dr
Carlton NG4 . . . . 162 A4
Hucknall NG15 . . . . 146 B7
Perlethorpe Ave NG20 . . 74 D8
Perry Gdns NG5 . . . . 161 B3
Perry Gr
Bingham NG13 . . . . 177 F4
Loughborough LE11 . . . . . 220 C1
Perry Rd NG5 . . . . 161 B3
Perth Cl NG19 . . . . 88 C5
Perth Dr NG9 . . . . 170 F1
Perth St NG1 . . . . 223 E3

Peterborough Rd NG23 . . 98 B1
Peter Donnelly Ctr The
NG18 . . . . 102 E4
Peters Cl
Arnold NG5 . . . . 162 C6
Eastwood NG16 . . . . 144 C2
Petersfield Cl
Mansfield NG19 . . . . 101 C8
Nottingham NG5 . . . . 160 F7
Petersgate NG10 . . . . 182 A1
Petersgate Cl NG10 . . . . 182 A1
Petersham Mews NG7 . . 222 B1
Petersham Rd NG10 . . . . 182 A1
Petersmiths Cl NG22 . . . . 77 C6
Petersmiths Cres NG22 . . 77 C6
Petersmiths Dr NG22 . . . . 77 C6
Petworth Ave NG9 . . . . . 182 F3
Petworth Dr NG5 . . . . . . 160 F4
Peveril Cres NG10 . . . . . . 193 A5
Peveril Dr
Ilkeston DE7 . . . . 157 D2
Nottingham NG7 . . . . 223 D1
Sutton in A NG17 . . . . 100 C2
West Bridgford NG2 . . . . 185 E3
Peveril Mews NG7 . . . . . . 222 C1
Peveril Rd NG9 . . . . 184 A7
Peveril St
Hucknall NG15 . . . . 146 A8
Nottingham NG7 . . . . 222 B4
Pharaoh Ct NG8 . . . . 159 D2
Pheasant Hill NG19 . . . . . . 88 A1
Philip Ave
Eastwood NG16 . . . . 144 A1
Kirkby in A NG17 . . . . 115 B2
Nuthall NG16 . . . . 159 C6
Philip Cl NG21 . . . . 118 C8
Philip Gr NG4 . . . . 162 E2
Philip Rd NG24 . . . . 139 E5
Phoenix Ave NG4 . . . . . . 162 E2
Phoenix Cl NG2 . . . . 173 B2
Phoenix Ct
Eastwood NG16 . . . . 144 A1
Nottingham NG7 . . . . 184 F8
Phoenix Ctr NG6 . . . . . . 160 A4
Phoenix Inf Sch 1 NG4 . 162 E1
Phoenix St NG17 . . . . . . 101 B4
Phyllis Cl NG15 . . . . 130 F1
Phyllis Gr NG10 . . . . 193 F7
Piccadilly NG6 . . . . 160 D6
Pickard St NG18 . . . . 102 E7
Pickering Ave NG16 . . . . 143 F2
Pieris Dr NG11 . . . . 184 C1
Pierpoint Pl NG17 . . . . . . 114 F6
Pierrepont Ave NG4 . . . . 162 E1
Pierrepont Gamston Prim
Sch NG2 . . . . 186 B6
Pierrepont Rd NG2 . . . . . 174 A1
Pierson St NG24 . . . . 139 E5
Pilcher Gate NG1 . . . . . . 223 E2
Pilgrim Cl
Ranby DN22 . . . . 38 E6
Ravenshead NG15 . . . . . 116 F2
Pilgrim Ct S81 . . . . 34 F7
Pilgrim Rise DN10 . . . . 3 C1
Pilgrim Way S80 . . . . 35 F2
Pilkington Rd NG3 . . . . . 162 A1
Pilkington St 8 NG6 . . . . 160 B7
Pillared House La DN21 . . 24 D7
Pimlico Ave NG9 . . . . 171 B3
Pimlico Cl NG12 . . . . 176 E3
Pinder St NG1 . . . . 223 F2
Pine Ave
Langley Mill NG16 . . . . . 143 A3
New Ollerton NG22 . . . . . 77 D4
Pine Cl
East Leake LE12 . . . . 214 D8
Everton DN10 . . . . 11 C3
Kirkby in A NG17 . . . . 114 F6
Mansfield NG21 . . . . 103 F1
Mansfield Woodhouse NG19 88 C5
Newark-on-T NG24 . . . . . 125 B4
Newark-on-T NG24 . . . . . 140 F1
Shirebrook NG20 . . . . 72 E6
Pine Hill Cl NG5 . . . . 146 F1
Pinehurst Ave NG15 . . . . 145 C5
Pineview Cl NG18 . . . . . . 102 F2
Pinewood Ave
Arnold NG5 . . . . 148 B1
Edwinstowe NG21 . . . . . . 91 C8
Pinewood Cl
Kirkby in A NG17 . . . . 115 C6
Southwell NG25 . . . . 121 D1
Pinewood Dr NG18 . . . . . 102 F2
Pinewood Gdns NG11 . . . 195 D8
Pinewood Inf Sch NG5 . . 148 B1
Pinfold Cl
Bottesford NG13 . . . . 181 A3
Collingham NG23 . . . . . . 98 A1
Cotgrave NG12 . . . . 187 F4
Kinoulton NG12 . . . . 199 F2
Lound DN22 . . . . 20 C1
Woodborough NG14 . . . . 149 C4
Pinfold Cres NG14 . . . . . 149 C4
Pinfold Dr S81 . . . . 25 F7
Pinfold Gate LE11 . . . . . . 220 B4
Pinfold Gdns 5 LE11 . . . . 220 B4
Pinfold Jetty LE11 . . . . . . 220 C4
Pinfold La
Averham NG23 . . . . 123 E2
Balderton NG24 . . . . 140 D3
Bottesford NG13 . . . . 181 A3

Pinfold La continued
Clarborough DN22 . . . . . . 40 E8
Elston NG23 . . . . 153 D5
Harby LE14 . . . . 202 C3
Kinoulton NG12 . . . . 199 F2
Misterton DN10 . . . . 6 E2
Nottingham NG11 . . . . . . 185 B6
Shelford NG12 . . . . 164 C1
Stapleford NG9 . . . . 182 E7
Styrrup DN11 . . . . 8 D2
Pinfold Pl LE14 . . . . 202 C3
Pinfold Rd NG16 . . . . 144 C1
Pinfold The DN10 . . . . 4 B2
Pingle Cl DN21 . . . . 24 E8
Pingle Cres NG5 . . . . 160 F8
Pingle The NG10 . . . . 193 D8
Pingley Cl NG23 . . . . 138 C8
Pingley La NG23 . . . . 138 C8
Pintail Cl NG4 . . . . 175 B5
Pinxton Ct NG18 . . . . 103 B5
Pinxton Gn NG16 . . . . . . 113 F3
Pinxton La
Kirkby in A, Fulwood
NG17 . . . . 114 A7
Kirkby in A, Tichfield Park
NG17 . . . . 114 C4
South Normanton DE55 . . 113 C5
Pinxton Rd NG17 . . . . . . 114 D3
Piper Cl
Hucknall NG15 . . . . 131 B1
Long Whatton LE12 . . . . . 212 C2
Piper Dr LE12 . . . . 212 C2
Piper La S80 . . . . 61 D7
Pippin Cl
Newark-on-T NG24 . . . . . 125 B2
Nottingham NG3 . . . . 173 F7
Pitcairn Cl NG2 . . . . 173 C1
Pitch Cl NG4 . . . . 174 C8
Pithouse La LE12 . . . . . . 204 E1
Pit La DE75 . . . . 157 B6
Pitt Hill NG20 . . . . 58 F2
Pitt La DN10 . . . . 12 F3
Plains Farm Cl NG3 . . . . 162 C5
Plains Gr NG3 . . . . 162 A4
Plainspot Rd NG16 . . . . . 128 E2
Plains Rd NG3 . . . . 162 B4
Plane Cl NG6 . . . . 159 F7
Plantagenet Ct NG3 . . . . 223 F3
Plantagenet St NG3 . . . . 223 F3
Plantation Ave NG22 . . . . 66 A7
Plantation Cl NG5 . . . . . . 147 A1
Plantation Dr DN10 . . . . . 11 A1
Plantation Hill S81 . . . . . . 36 B4
Plantation La S81 . . . . . . 27 B8
Plantation Rd
East Markham NG22 . . . . 66 A6
Keyworth NG12 . . . . 197 D3
Nottingham NG8 . . . . 171 C4
Plantation Side NG7 . . . . 172 E7
Plantations The 7 NG10 193 A8
Plant La NG10 . . . . 193 A4
Plants Yd S80 . . . . 35 E2
Platt La NG12 . . . . 198 A5
Platt St NG16 . . . . 113 D2
Platts The NG24 . . . . 139 E5
Player St NG7 . . . . 222 B4
Playworld NG4 . . . . 162 F8
Plaza Gdns NG6 . . . . 160 E4
Pleasant Cl 2 LE11 . . . . . 220 A4
Pleasant Pl DE74 . . . . . . 203 D2
Pleasant Row NG7 . . . . . 172 F7
Pleasley Rd NG17 . . . . . . 101 A6
Pleasley Vale Nature Reserve
NG19 . . . . 87 D7
Plot La NG23 . . . . 98 E4
Plough Dr S81 . . . . 25 D7
Plough La
Lowdham NG14 . . . . 150 D1
Nottingham NG2 . . . . 173 E4
Ploughman Ave NG14 . . 149 A4
Ploughman Wood Nature
Reserve NG14 . . . . 149 D2
Plover Dene S81 . . . . 35 C7
Plover Wharf 3 NG2 . . . . 173 A2
Plowman Ct NG9 . . . . . . 182 D6
Plowright Ct 5 NG3 . . . . 173 D7
Plowright St 4 NG3 . . . . 173 D7
Plumb Rd NG15 . . . . 145 F7
Plummer La DE74 . . . . . . 203 C2
Plumptre Ave NG16 . . . . 143 B5
Plumptre Almshouses
NG1 . . . . 223 F1
Plumptre Cl NG16 . . . . . . 143 F1
Plumptre Pl NG1 . . . . . . 223 F2
Plumptre Sq NG1 . . . . . . 223 F2
Plumptre St NG1 . . . . . . 223 F2
Plumptre Way NG16 . . . . 143 F1
Plum Tree Ave NG19 . . . . 89 B1
Plumtree Gdns NG14 . . . 148 F7
Plumtree Rd
Bircotes DN11 . . . . 9 C6
Cotgrave NG12 . . . . 187 E3
Plumtree Sch NG12 . . . . 197 E6
Plungar Cl NG8 . . . . 172 B6
Plungar La NG13 . . . . . . 192 B2
Plungar Rd NG13 . . . . . . 191 C5
Plymouth Ave NG16 . . . . 113 C6
Poacher's La DN22 . . . . . 31 D8
Pocklington Cres NG24 . 125 D6
Pocklington Rd NG23 . . . 98 B1
Podder La NG3 . . . . 162 C6
Point The NG3 . . . . 173 D8
Pollard Dr NG18 . . . . 102 C7
Pollard's La NG25 . . . . . . 136 F7
Polly Taylor's Rd NG3 . . . . 67 E1
Polperro Way NG15 . . . . 145 D5
Pond Hills La NG5 . . . . . . 147 F1
Pond St NG17 . . . . 115 B5

Pool Cl NG16 . . . . 113 D2
Poole Mdw NG12 . . . . . . 174 F4
Popham Cl NG1 . . . . 223 F1
Popham St NG1 . . . . 223 F1
Poplar Ave
East Leake LE12 . . . . 214 D8
Kirkby in A NG17 . . . . 115 C5
Nottingham NG5 . . . . 161 A1
Sandiacre NG10 . . . . 182 A2
Poplar Cl
Bingham NG13 . . . . 178 A4
Carlton NG3 . . . . 174 D6
Sutton on T NG23 . . . . . . 96 F8
Worksop S80 . . . . 35 D1
Poplar Cres NG16 . . . . . . 159 B6
Poplar Dr
Glapwell S44 . . . . 86 B8
Pleasleyhill NG19 . . . . 87 B4
Poplar Gr
Church Warsop NG20 . . . . 74 A6
Mansfield Woodhouse NG19 89 C1
Poplar Rd DE55 . . . . 113 B7
Poplars Ave NG14 . . . . . . 164 A5
Poplars Cl NG12 . . . . 197 F4
Poplar St
Mansfield Woodhouse
NG19 . . . . 88 C3
New Ollerton NG22 . . . . . 77 D4
Nottingham NG1 . . . . 173 E4
Retford DN22 . . . . 39 F6
Poplars The
Beeston NG9 . . . . 183 F7
Nottingham NG5 . . . . 172 E8
Sutton in A NG17 . . . . 101 A3
West Bridgford NG2 . . . . 185 F7
Whitwell S80 . . . . 45 A5
Poplars Way NG18 . . . . . 116 E7
Poppy Cl NG20 . . . . 72 D3
Poppy Gdn DE55 . . . . 99 B7
Porchester Cl NG15 . . . . 146 C2
Porchester Jun Sch NG4 162 A1
Porchester Rd
Bingham NG13 . . . . 177 D4
Nottingham NG3 . . . . 162 A1
Porlock Cl 2 NG10 . . . . . 193 A8
Portage Cl NG12 . . . . 175 E2
Port Arthur Rd NG2 . . . . 174 A4
Porter Cl NG11 . . . . 195 C8
Porters Wk NG3 . . . . 174 A7
Portinscale Cl NG2 . . . . . 186 C5
Portland Coll NG18 . . . . . 116 E6
Portland Cres
Mansfield Woodhouse
NG19 . . . . 88 D3
Stapleford NG9 . . . . 182 E6
Portland Ct NG5 . . . . 161 B5
Portland Ct Mews NG19 . 88 C4
Portland Gdns NG15 . . . . 145 F7
Portland Grange NG15 . . 145 E7
Portland Hill NG7 . . . . . . 172 C1
Portland Ind Est NG17 . . 115 B7
Portland L Ctr NG3 . . . . . 173 D1
Portland Mdws DN22 . . . . 29 A6
Portland Pk Nature Reserve
NG17 . . . . 114 F3
Portland Pl
Sutton DN22 . . . . 29 A6
Worksop S80 . . . . 35 E4
Portland Prim Sch NG8 . 171 C5
Portland Rd
Beeston NG9 . . . . 182 F1
Carlton NG4 . . . . 162 C2
Eastwood NG16 . . . . 158 B8
Hucknall NG15 . . . . 146 B6
Ilkeston DE7 . . . . 157 F3
Long Eaton NG10 . . . . . . 193 B4
Nottingham NG7 . . . . 222 C3
Retford DN22 . . . . 39 D5
Selston NG16 . . . . 129 A7
Shirebrook NG20 . . . . 72 F4
West Bridgford NG2 . . . . 185 F6
Whaley Thorns NG20 . . . . 59 A2
Portland Ret Pk NG18 . . . 102 A5
Portland Row NG21 . . . . . 91 C8
Portland Sch S80 . . . . 46 F8
Portland Sq NG17 . . . . . . 100 F2
Portland St
Arnold NG5 . . . . 161 E6
Beeston NG9 . . . . 184 A4
Kirkby in A NG17 . . . . 115 A5
Mansfield NG18 . . . . 102 B6
Mansfield Woodhouse NG19 88 C3
Market Warsop NG20 . . . . 74 B4
Newark-on-T NG24 . . . . . 139 E8
New Houghton NG19 . . . . 87 A7
Sutton in A NG17 . . . . 100 F2
Worksop S80 . . . . 35 E3
Portland Terr
Gainsborough DN21 . . . . 24 D7
Meden Vale NG20 . . . . . . 60 E1
Whaley Thorns NG20 . . . . 59 A2
Portman St DN10 . . . . 9 F7
Portree Dr NG5 . . . . 146 F1
Postern St NG1 . . . . 223 D2
Post Office La
Plungar NG13 . . . . 202 F8
Redmile NG13 . . . . 192 F3
Post Office Rd NG17 . . . . 115 B5
Post Office Yd NG14 . . . . 151 D2
Posts The NG12 . . . . 189 A6
Potter La NG22 . . . . 92 D8
Potters Cl NG5 . . . . 161 A2
Potters Ct NG9 . . . . 171 D1
Potters La LE12 . . . . 214 F8
Potter St
Sutton in A NG17 . . . . 101 A4

Potter St continued
Worksop S80 . . . . 35 F2
Potters Way DE7 . . . . 170 A8
Pot Yd The NG22 . . . . 119 F6
Poulter Cl NG7 . . . . 172 D7
Poulter St NG20 . . . . 58 F1
Poulter View DN22 . . . . . . 39 F5
Poulton Dr NG2 . . . . 173 E2
Poultry NG1 . . . . 223 E2
Powell Ct NG22 . . . . 119 F5
Powell Gdns S81 . . . . 35 D7
Powtrell Pl DE7 . . . . 170 B6
Poynton St NG1 . . . . 223 D3
Poyser Cl 2 NG7 . . . . . . 161 A1
Pratt Cl NG17 . . . . 87 D1
Prebends Cl NG24 . . . . . . 138 F4
Precinct Rd NG17 . . . . . . 115 B5
Precinct The NG12 . . . . . 187 F3
Premier Rd NG7 . . . . 173 A8
Prendwick Gdns NG5 . . . 161 B8
Prest Ave NG20 . . . . 74 E8
Preston Rd
Balderton NG24 . . . . 140 E8
Rainworth NG21 . . . . 118 A8
Prestwick Cl NG8 . . . . . . 159 D2
Prestwold Ave
Mansfield NG19 . . . . 103 B8
Mansfield Woodhouse NG19 89 B1
Prestwold La LE12 . . . . . 215 C1
Prestwood Dr NG8 . . . . . 172 B7
Previn Gdns NG3 . . . . . . 173 F6
Priestgate NG22 . . . . 65 E6
Priestsic Prim Sch NG17 100 F3
Priestsic Rd NG17 . . . . . 100 E3
Primrose Ave
Farndon NG24 . . . . 139 B6
Newark-on-T NG24 . . . . . 125 B4
Selston NG16 . . . . 128 F2
Primrose Bank NG13 . . . 177 D4
Primrose Cl
7 Kirkby in A NG17 . . . . 114 F7
Nottingham NG3 . . . . 173 D7
South Normanton DE55 . . 113 B7
Primrose Cres NG4 . . . . . 174 F7
Primrose Ct NG17 . . . . . . 101 B1
Primrose La NG22 . . . . . . 78 C5
Primrose Rise NG16 . . . . 158 A8
Primrose St
Carlton NG4 . . . . 174 F7
Gainsborough DN21 . . . . 24 D7
Ilkeston DE7 . . . . 157 E3
Primrose Way
Sutton in A NG17 . . . . 100 C1
Worksop S80 . . . . 36 A6
Primula Cl NG11 . . . . 184 C2
Prince Charles Rd S81 . . . 35 D6
Prince Edward Cres
NG12 . . . . 176 A4
Prince of Wales St DN22 . 39 E6
Princes Rd LE14 . . . . 219 B6
Princess Anne Rd S81 . . . 35 E6
Princess Ave
Beeston NG9 . . . . 184 A6
Mansfield NG19 . . . . 103 A8
Market Warsop NG20 . . . . 74 C4
South Normanton DE55 . . 113 A5
Princess Cl NG4 . . . . 162 E2
Princess Diana Ct DN21 . 15 C3
Princess Dr NG10 . . . . . . 182 B4
Princess St
Eastwood NG16 . . . . 143 F3
Kirkby in A NG17 . . . . 114 D3
Long Eaton NG10 . . . . . . 193 D8
7 Loughborough LE11 . . 220 B3
Princes St NG18 . . . . 102 A5
Prince's St NG24 . . . . . . 139 F7
Princess Wlk DN22 . . . . . 15 F1
Prince St
Ilkeston DE7 . . . . 157 E4
Long Eaton NG10 . . . . . . 193 D8
Prince William Rd LE11 . 220 A6
Prince William Way
LE11 . . . . 220 A6
Prior Cl NG17 . . . . 101 B4
Prioridge NG12 . . . . 188 A2
Prior Rd NG5 . . . . 161 D6
Priors Cl NG13 . . . . 178 A5
Priors The NG14 . . . . 150 D2
Priorswell Rd S80 . . . . . . 35 F2
Priory Ave
Annesley Woodhouse
NG17 . . . . 130 B8
Ravenshead NG15 . . . . . 117 B1
Tollerton NG12 . . . . 186 C1
Priory Cir NG12 . . . . 186 C1
Priory Cl
Balderton NG24 . . . . 140 D3
Blyth S81 . . . . 18 A3
Gainsborough DN21 . . . . 24 F8
Mattersey DN10 . . . . 20 A6
Priory Cres NG4 . . . . 162 F1
Priory Ct NG4 . . . . 162 F1
Priory Ctr The S80 . . . . . . 35 E4
Priory Gr NG17 . . . . 115 D5
Priory Jun Sch 1 NG4 . . 162 F1
Priory La NG14 . . . . 151 C7
Priory Mews 7 NG7 . . . . 172 E2
Priory Pk NG14 . . . . 151 D2
Priory RC Prim Sch The
NG16 . . . . 144 B1
Priory Rd
Blidworth NG21 . . . . 118 A5
Carlton NG4 . . . . 162 F1
Eastwood NG16 . . . . 143 F1
Hucknall NG15 . . . . 145 E7

Priory Rd *continued*
  Mansfield Woodhouse NG19 **88** B3
  West Bridgford NG2 . . . . . . **186** A8
Priory Sq NG19 . . . . **88** B3
Priory St NG7 . . . . **172** E2
Pritchard Dr NG9 . . . . . . **182** E6
Private Rd
  Hucknall NG15 . . . . **145** E7
  Nottingham NG5, NG3 . . . **161** D2
  Southwell NG25 . . . . **121** E1
  Woodborough NG14 . . . . . **149** B5
Private St NG24 . . . . **140** B8
Privet Ave NG17 . . . . **115** A6
Prize CI NG11 . . . . **184** C1
Procters Dr NG23 . . . . **82** E1
Promenade NG3 . . . . **223** F3
Promenade The NG17 . . . **115** D6
Prospect CI NG17 . . . . **115** B7
Prospect Ct NG17 . . . . **99** E1
Prospect Dr
  Shirebrook NG20 . . . . **72** E3
  Worksop S81 . . . . **35** F6
Prospect Hill Inf Sch S81 . **36** A6
Prospect Hill Jun Sch
  S81 . . . . **36** A7
Prospect PI
  Nottingham NG7 . . . . **222** B1
  Sutton in A NG17 . . . . **100** E1
Prospect Prec S81 . . . . . . **36** A6
Prospect Rd
  Carlton NG4 . . . . **162** B1
  Heanor DE75 . . . . **157** A8
Prospect St
  Mansfield NG18 . . . . **102** D6
  Nottingham NG7 . . . . **222** A4
Prospect Terr
  Gainsborough DN21 . . . . . **24** D7
  Nottingham NG7 . . . . **222** A4
Providence PI 5 DE7 . . . **157** E1
Providence Rd NG16 . . . . **128** A4
Prudhoe Ct 5 NG2 . . . . . **173** D1
Pudding La LE14 . . . . **210** C5
Pulborough CI NG5 . . . . . **160** F4
Pullman Rd 4 NG2 . . . . . **173** F4
Pump Hollow La NG18 . . **103** A7
Pump Hollow Rd NG19 . . **103** A8
Pump La
  Fenton NG23 . . . . **142** E2
  Walesby NG22 . . . . **64** A2
Purbeck CI
  Long Eaton NG10 . . . . . . **193** A8
  Mansfield Woodhouse NG19 **88** C6
Purbeck Dr NG2 . . . . **185** C5
Purdy Mdw NG10 . . . . . . **193** A5
Pureland Japanese Gdn and
  Meditation Ctr NG23 . . . . **68** E5
Pyatt St NG2 . . . . **173** D1
Pye Ave NG19 . . . . **101** D7
Pye Hill Rd NG16 . . . . . . **128** A4
Pygall Ave NG11 . . . . **195** A1
Pym St NG3 . . . . **173** F6
Pym Wlk NG3 . . . . **173** E6
Python Hill Rd NG21 . . . . **104** B1

Q

Quadrangle The
  Blidworth NG21 . . . . **118** A5
  Newstead NG15 . . . . **130** D6
Quakefield Rd NG22 . . . . . **66** B6
Quaker La
  Farnsfield NG22 . . . . **119** F5
  11 Mansfield NG18 . . . . . **102** B7
Quaker Way NG18 . . . . . . **102** B7
Quantock CI NG5 . . . . . . **147** B3
Quantock Gr NG13 . . . . . **177** C4
Quantock Rd NG10 . . . . . **182** A1
Quarries Way NG17 . . . . . **114** E4
Quarry Ave NG6 . . . . **160** B6
Quarry CI NG15 . . . . **132** B8
Quarrydale Ave NG17 . . . **100** F5
Quarrydale Dr NG17 . . . . **100** F4
Quarrydale Rd NG17 . . . . **100** F4
Quarrydale Sch NG17 . . . **100** E5
Quarry DI Vw NG18 . . . . . **102** E5
Quarry Dr NG17 . . . . **115** B3
Quarry Gr S81 . . . . **35** C7
Quarry Hill NG10 . . . . . . **182** A8
Quarry La
  Linby NG15 . . . . **131** B4
  Mansfield NG18 . . . . **102** A6
Quarry Rd NG15 . . . . **132** B8
Quarry Yd NG17 . . . . **100** E2
Quartz Ave NG18 . . . . . . **102** E4
Quayside CI NG2 . . . . **173** E1
Queen Eleanor Prim Sch
  NG23 . . . . **70** E3
Queen Elizabeth Cres
  S80 . . . . **35** A4
Queen Elizabeth Rd NG9 **183** A4
Queen Elizabeth Sch The
  NG19 . . . . **88** A1
Queen Elizabeths High Sch
  DN21 . . . . **15** C3
Queen Mary's CI NG12 . . **176** D2
Queens Ave DE7 . . . . **170** A5
Queens Ave NG4 . . . . **162** C4
Queensberry St NG6 . . . . **160** E4
Queens Bower Rd NG5 . . **161** C8
Queen's Bridge Rd NG2 . **223** E1
Queensbury Ave NG2 . . . **185** C3
Queens CI S80 . . . . **45** C5
Queen's Cres DN10 . . . . . **10** A7

Queen's Ct
  Bingham NG13 . . . . **177** D5
  Clipstone NG19 . . . . **89** D3
  Newark-on-T NG24 . . . . . **125** A1
Queens Dr
  Beeston NG9 . . . . **184** A6
  Brinsley NG16 . . . . **143** E7
  Nottingham NG11 . . . . . . **185** A8
  Sandiacre NG10 . . . . **182** B4
Queens Dr NG16 . . . . . . **159** C6
Queens Dr Ind Est NG2 . **173** A1
Queensfield DN21 . . . . . . **15** B3
Queens Gr NG2 . . . . **223** E1
Queen's Head Ct NG24 . . **139** F8
Queen's Medical Ctr (Univ
  Hospl) NG7 . . . . **172** D2
Queens Rd
  Beeston NG9 . . . . **184** A6
  Carlton in L S81 . . . . **25** F7
  Hodthorpe S80 . . . . **45** C6
  Kegworth DE74 . . . . **203** D2
Queen's Rd
  Loughborough LE11 . . . . . **220** C4
  Newark-on-T NG24 . . . . . **125** A1
  Nottingham NG2 . . . . **223** F1
  Radcliffe on T NG12 . . . . . **176** A4
Queens Rd E NG9 . . . . . . **184** B7
Queens Rd N NG16 . . . . . **143** F2
Queens Rd S NG16 . . . . . **143** F1
Queens Rd W NG9 . . . . . **183** E4
Queen's Sq NG16 . . . . . . **143** F2
Queen St
  Arnold NG5 . . . . **148** A1
  Balderton NG24 . . . . **140** E3
  Bottesford NG13 . . . . **181** A2
  Collingham NG23 . . . . **98** A1
  Gainsborough DN21 . . . . . **24** D7
  Hucknall NG15 . . . . **145** F8
  Kirkby in A NG17 . . . . **115** A4
  Langley Mill NG16 . . . . . . **143** C3
  Long Eaton NG10 . . . . . . **193** E7
  3 Loughborough LE11 . . . **220** C3
  10 Mansfield NG18 . . . . . **102** B7
  Market Warsop NG20 . . . . **74** A5
  Newark-on-T NG24 . . . . . **139** E7
  Nottingham NG1 . . . . **223** E3
  Pinxton NG16 . . . . **113** C3
  Retford DN22 . . . . **39** D6
  South Normanton DE55 . . **113** A5
  Southwell NG25 . . . . **121** D1
  Sutton in A NG17 . . . . **100** F4
  Worksop S80 . . . . **35** F2
Queensway
  Gainsborough DN21 . . . . . **24** F8
  Kirkby in A NG17 . . . . **115** B2
  Mansfield Woodhouse NG19 **89** A1
  Nether Broughton LE14 . . **219** C6
  Saxilby LN1 . . . . **57** B3
  Skellingthorpe LN6 . . . . . . **71** F3
  Worksop S81 . . . . **35** F4
Queens Wlk 14 NG18 . . . **102** B7
Queen's Wlk
  Nether Langwith NG20 . . . **59** A1
  Nottingham NG2 . . . . **173** B1
Querneby Ave NG3 . . . . . **161** E2
Querneby Rd NG3 . . . . . . **161** E2
Quibell Rd NG24 . . . . **140** A5
Quibell's La NG24 . . . . . . **125** A3
Quines Hill Rd NG19 . . . . **89** A2
Quinton CI NG11 . . . . . . **185** A5
Quorn CI
  Beeston NG9 . . . . **183** E3
  Loughborough LE11 . . . . . **220** C2
Quorndon Cres NG10 . . . **193** D5
Quorn Gr NG5 . . . . **161** A3
Quorn Rd NG5 . . . . **161** A2

R

Rabbithill La NG23 . . . . **83** B6
Racecourse Rd
  Mansfield NG18 . . . . **102** E5
  Nottingham NG2 . . . . **174** A4
Rachel CI DN21 . . . . **15** C3
Radbourne Rd 9 NG2 . . . **173** F3
Radbourne St NG19 . . . . . **88** E4
Radburn Ct NG9 . . . . **170** E1
Radcliffe Gdns NG4 . . . . . **174** D8
Radcliffe Mount NG2 . . . . **173** F1
Radcliffe on Trent Inf Sch
  NG12 . . . . **176** A3
Radcliffe on Trent Jun Sch
  NG12 . . . . **175** F2
Radcliffe Rd
  Carlton NG12 . . . . **175** B1
  Cropwell Butler NG12 . . . . **189** A7
  West Bridgford NG2 . . . . . **186** D8
Radcliffe St NG2 . . . . **173** D1
Radcliffe Sta NG12 . . . . . **175** F3
Radford Bridge Rd NG8 . **172** C5
Radford Bvd NG7 . . . . . . **222** A4
Radford Cres NG4 . . . . . . **162** E2
Radford Ct NG7 . . . . **222** B3
Radford Gr La NG7 . . . . . **222** A4
Radford Prim Sch NG7 . . **222** A3
Radford St
  1 Mansfield NG18 . . . . . . **102** B6
  Worksop S80 . . . . **36** B1
Radley Rd NG22 . . . . **135** C7
Radley Sq NG6 . . . . **160** D5
Radmanthwaite Rd NG19 . **87** D3
Radmarsh Rd NG7 . . . . . **222** A1
Rad Mdws NG10 . . . . **193** C6
Radmoor Rd 7 LE11 . . . . **220** A4
Radnor Gr NG13 . . . . **177** C4
Radnor PI NG19 . . . . **87** C4

Radstock Rd NG3 . . . . . . **174** A7
Radway Dr NG11 . . . . . . **185** A5
Raeburn Dr NG9 . . . . **182** E2
Ragdale Rd NG6 . . . . **160** B8
Raglan CI NG3 . . . . **173** D7
Raglan Ct
  Beeston NG9 . . . . **172** A1
  Newark-on-T NG24 . . . . . **140** A7
Raglan Dr NG4 . . . . **163** B1
Raglan Gdns NG24 . . . . . **140** A7
Raglan Rd DN22 . . . . **40** A7
Raglan St NG16 . . . . **144** A1
Raibank Gdns NG5 . . . . . **161** E5
Railway Ave S80 . . . . **58** D8
Railway Cotts NG16 . . . . **158** F6
Railway Ct LN1 . . . . **57** A3
Railway Terr LE11 . . . . . . **220** C5
Raines Ave S81 . . . . **35** E6
Raines Pk Rd S81 . . . . **35** E7
Rainham Gdns NG11 . . . . **196** C6
Rainworth Heath Nature
  Reserve NG21 . . . . **104** A3
Rainworth L Ctr NG21 . . . **117** F8
Rainworth Wr Rd NG21 . . **103** F1
Raithby CI NG5 . . . . **161** A6
Raleigh CI
  Ilkeston DE7 . . . . **157** F3
  Nottingham NG11 . . . . . . **184** C1
Raleigh Rd NG19 . . . . . . **101** E8
Raleigh St NG7 . . . . **222** C3
Ralf CI NG2 . . . . **185** E4
Ramblers CI NG4 . . . . . . **174** E5
Ramper La LN1 . . . . **55** C7
Ramper Rd
  Letwell S81 . . . . **16** A3
  Saundby DN22 . . . . **23** D7
Rampton Gn Rd DN22 . . . **42** F1
Rampton Hospl DN22 . . . . **53** B8
Rampton La DN22 . . . . . . **42** D5
Rampton Prim Sch DN22 . **42** D1
Rampton Rd
  Laneham DN22 . . . . **54** A6
  Rampton DN22 . . . . **42** E3
Ramsdale Ave NG14 . . . . **148** D8
Ramsdale Cres NG5 . . . . **161** D2
Ramsdale Rd NG4 . . . . . . **162** E1
Ramsden Ave S81 . . . . . . **16** F2
Ramsden Cres S81 . . . . . . **25** F7
Ramsden Croft NG21 . . . . **104** A1
Ramsden Prim Sch S81 . . **26** A5
Ramsey CI
  Mansfield Woodhouse
  NG19 . . . . **89** A2
  Stapleford NG9 . . . . **170** E2
Ramsey Ct 5 NG5 . . . . . **161** B1
Ramsey Dr NG5 . . . . **161** B1
Ranby CE Prim Sch DN22 . **38** A7
Ranby House Sch DN22 . . **38** B7
Ranby Wlk NG3 . . . . **173** F6
Rancliffe Ave NG12 . . . . **197** D4
Rancliffe Farm Mews
  NG11 . . . . **196** E3
Randal Gdns 4 NG7 . . . . **172** F7
Randall CI NG24 . . . . **140** D8
Randall Way DN22 . . . . . . **29** C1
Randal St 3 NG7 . . . . . . **172** F7
Randol CI NG18 . . . . **101** D4
Ranelagh Gr NG8 . . . . . . **172** B5
Ranmere Rd NG8 . . . . . . **172** A7
Ranmoor Rd NG4 . . . . . . **162** F1
Ranmore CI NG9 . . . . **171** B2
Rannerdale CI NG2 . . . . . **186** C6
Rannoch Dr NG19 . . . . . . **101** E5
Rannoch Rise NG5 . . . . . **147** F1
Rannock Gdns NG12 . . . . **197** F3
Ranskill Gdns NG5 . . . . . **161** A8
Ranskill Prim Sch DN22 . . **19** B5
Ranskill Rd DN22 . . . . **19** E6
Ransom Dr NG3 . . . . **161** E1
Ransome CI NG24 . . . . . . **140** D8
Ransom Rd
  Mansfield NG21 . . . . **103** D3
  Nottingham NG3 . . . . **173** E8
Ransom Wood Bsns Pk
  NG21 . . . . **103** D4
Ranson Rd NG9 . . . . **183** C2
Ratcher Way NG19 . . . . . **103** B8
Ratcliffe Gate NG18 . . . . **102** C6
Ratcliffe La DE74 . . . . . . **203** C7
Ratcliffe Rd LE11 . . . . . . **220** C5
Ratcliffe St NG16 . . . . . . **143** F2
Rathgar CI NG8 . . . . **171** D4
Rathmines CI NG7 . . . . . **222** A1
Rathvale Ct NG9 . . . . **183** A4
Raven Ave NG5 . . . . **161** B4
Ravencroft La DN10 . . . . . **14** B1
Ravendale Rd DN21 . . . . . **24** E7
Ravenhill CI NG9 . . . . . . **183** B4
Ravenscourt S81 . . . . **36** A6
Ravens Ct NG5 . . . . **161** B6
Ravensdale Ave
  Long Eaton NG10 . . . . . . **182** B2
  Mansfield NG18 . . . . **102** D8
Ravensdale Dr NG8 . . . . . **171** C3
Ravensdale Rd NG18 . . . . **102** E8
Ravensdene Ct 2 NG3 . . **173** D8
Ravensfleet Rd DN21 . . . . . **7** F3
Ravenshead CE Prim Sch
  NG15 . . . . **117** A2
Ravenshill CI DN22 . . . . . **19** B4
Ravensmore Rd NG5 . . . . **161** B2
Ravenswood Rd NG5 . . . . **162** A8
Ravensworth Rd NG6 . . . **160** B8
Rawson St
  Nottingham NG7 . . . . **160** F1
  Selston NG16 . . . . **129** A6
Raylawn St NG18 . . . . . . **103** A6
Raymede CI NG5 . . . . **160** F6

Raymede Dr NG5 . . . . . . **160** E6
Raymond CI NG17 . . . . . . **114** E7
Raymond Dr NG13 . . . . . **178** A4
Raymoth La S81 . . . . **35** E7
Rayneham Rd DE7 . . . . . . **157** C4
Rayner Ct NG7 . . . . **222** B3
Raynford Ave NG9 . . . . . **183** C4
Raysmith CI NG25 . . . . . . **121** E2
Rayton La S81 . . . . **36** C3
Rayton Spur S81 . . . . **36** B3
Read Ave NG9 . . . . **184** A6
Readman Rd NG9 . . . . . . **183** A3
Rearsby CI NG8 . . . . **171** D5
Recreation Dr NG20 . . . . . **72** F2
Recreation Rd
  Annesley NG15 . . . . **130** C8
  New Houghton NG19 . . . . **86** F7
  Sandiacre NG10 . . . . **182** B6
  Shirebrook NG20 . . . . **72** E6
Recreation St
  Long Eaton NG10 . . . . . . **193** F8
  Mansfield NG18 . . . . **102** C7
  Selston NG16 . . . . **129** B6
Recreation Terr NG9 . . . . **182** D6
Recreation View NG20 . . . **72** E6
Rectors Gate DN22 . . . . . . **39** E8
Rectory Ave
  Gainsborough DN21 . . . . . **15** D1
  Nottingham NG8 . . . . **171** E4
Rectory Dr NG11 . . . . . . **185** B8
Rectory Dr The NG4 . . . . **162** F2
Rectory Gdns
  Beckingham DN10 . . . . . . **14** B1
  Kirton NG22 . . . . **78** B6
  Nottingham NG8 . . . . **171** F4
Rectory La
  Bottesford NG13 . . . . **181** B3
  Claypole NG23 . . . . **156** E7
  Gamston DN22 . . . . **50** F5
  Lea DN21 . . . . **24** F2
Rectory PI
  Barton in F NG11 . . . . . . **194** E6
  2 Loughborough LE11 . . . **220** B4
  Wymeswold LE12 . . . . . . **216** C3
Rectory Rd
  Carlton NG4 . . . . **174** E5
  Church Warsop NG20 . . . . **74** C7
  Cotgrave NG12 . . . . **187** E3
  Loughborough LE11 . . . . . **220** B5
  Retford DN22 . . . . **39** E7
  Treswell DN22 . . . . **42** B3
  West Bridgford NG2 . . . . . **185** F7
Rectory St LN5 . . . . **142** D8
Red Barn La DE55 . . . . . . **99** B3
Redbarn La DE55 . . . . **99** B3
Redbarn Way NG17 . . . . . **100** C1
Redbourne Dr NG8 . . . . . **172** C6
Redbridge Dr NG16 . . . . . **159** D3
Redcar CI
  Carlton NG4 . . . . **162** E2
  Mansfield NG18 . . . . **102** E5
Redcliffe Gdns NG3 . . . . **173** C8
Redcliffe Rd
  Mansfield NG18 . . . . **102** D6
  Nottingham NG3 . . . . **173** C8
Redcliffe St NG17 . . . . . . **101** A4
Redcroft CI NG21 . . . . **75** F2
Redfield Rd NG7 . . . . **184** B8
Redfield Way NG7 . . . . . . **184** B8
Redgate CI NG19 . . . . . . **101** E8
Redgates Ct NG14 . . . . . **148** D3
Redgate Specl Sch NG19 **101** E7
Redgate St
  Mansfield NG19 . . . . **101** E8
  Pinxton NG16 . . . . **113** D2
Redhill La DN22 . . . . **63** E8
Red Hill L Ctr NG5 . . . . . . **92** E4
Redhill L Ctr NG5 . . . . . . **147** E1
Redhill Lodge Dr NG5 . . . **147** D1
Redhill Rd NG5 . . . . **147** E1
Redhill Sch NG5 . . . . **147** E1
Red Kite CI 6 S81 . . . . . . **35** C7
Red La
  Brinsley NG16 . . . . **128** E1
  Carlton in L S81 . . . . **26** A2
  Lowdham NG14 . . . . **150** D1
Redland Ave NG4 . . . . . . **174** F8
Redland CI
  Beeston NG9 . . . . **183** C4
  Ilkeston DE7 . . . . **157** F2
Redland Dr NG9 . . . . **183** C4
Redland Gr NG4 . . . . **174** E8
Redland Rd NG19 . . . . . . **101** E8
Redlands Prim Sch S80 . . **35** D4
Red Lodge La NG13 . . . . . **166** B7
Redman CI DN21 . . . . **15** E2
Redmays Dr NG14 . . . . . . **164** B6
Redmile CE Prim Sch
  NG13 . . . . **192** F3
Redmile La NG13 . . . . . . **192** D3
Redmile Rd NG8 . . . . **160** C2
Redoubt St NG7 . . . . **222** A3
Redruth CI NG8 . . . . **171** C6
Redruth Dr NG18 . . . . . . **103** B2
Redthorn Way NG23 . . . . **156** E6
Redwing CI S81 . . . . **35** C6
Redwood NG2 . . . . **185** C6
Redwood Ave NG8 . . . . . **171** D3
Redwood Cres NG9 . . . . . **184** A5
Redwood Ct NG15 . . . . . **145** F8
Reedham Wlk 2 NG5 . . . **161** B8
Reedman Rd NG10 . . . . . **193** B4
Rees Gdns NG5 . . . . **147** A1

Rees Row DN22 . . . . **42** B1
Reform St
  Annesley Woodhouse
  NG17 . . . . **129** F8
  Sutton in A NG17 . . . . **100** F2
Regal Arts Ctr S80 . . . . . . **35** F4
Regatta Way NG2 . . . . . . **186** C8
Regency Ct NG9 . . . . **184** A7
Regents CI NG23 . . . . **112** B8
Regents Pk CI NG2 . . . . . **185** C5
Regent St
  Beeston NG9 . . . . **184** A7
  Kimberley NG16 . . . . **158** F6
  Kirkby in A NG17 . . . . **114** F4
  Langley Mill NG16 . . . . . . **143** B3
  Long Eaton NG10 . . . . . . **193** D8
  Loughborough LE11 . . . . . **220** A4
  Mansfield NG18 . . . . **102** B7
  Nottingham, New Basford
  NG7 . . . . **161** A1
  Nottingham, Standard Hill
  NG1 . . . . **223** D2
  Stapleford NG10 . . . . **182** C5
  Sutton in A NG17 . . . . **100** D2
Regina CI NG12 . . . . **175** E2
Regina Cres NG15 . . . . . **116** F1
Reg Taylor's Swan &
  Waterfowl Sanctuary
  NG25 . . . . **121** F2
Reid Gdns NG16 . . . . **159** B7
Reigate CI NG9 . . . . **183** E2
Reigate Dr NG9 . . . . **183** E2
Reigate Rd NG7 . . . . **160** F2
Reindeer St NG18 . . . . . . **102** E6
Rempstone Dr NG6 . . . . . **160** D5
Rempstone Rd
  East Leake LE12 . . . . **214** E7
  East Leake, Stanford Hills
  LE12 . . . . **214** A6
  Hoton LE12 . . . . **215** C2
  Wymeswold LE12 . . . . . . **216** A4
Renals Way NG14 . . . . . . **148** F7
Rendell Prim Sch LE11 . . **220** B5
Renfrew Ct NG19 . . . . . . **101** E5
Renfrew Dr NG8 . . . . **171** E4
Repton CI NG19 . . . . **88** E4
Repton Dr DE7 . . . . **170** B7
Repton Rd
  Nottingham NG6 . . . . **160** D6
  West Bridgford NG2 . . . . . **185** E5
Retford Coll The DN22 . . . **39** F7
Retford Gate DN22 . . . . . . **41** E7
Retford Hospl DN22 . . . . . **39** D8
Retford L Ctr DN22 . . . . . . **39** C6
Retford Little Theatre
  DN22 . . . . **39** E6
Retford Oaks High Sch
  DN22 . . . . **39** C5
Retford Rd
  Askham DN22 . . . . **52** E3
  Blyth S81 . . . . **18** B2
  Boughton NG22 . . . . **77** F7
  Mattersley DN10 . . . . **20** C6
  North Leverton w H DN22 . . **41** F8
  North Wheatley DN22 . . . . **31** C7
  Nottingham NG5 . . . . **161** A3
  Rampton DN22 . . . . **42** D1
  Ranby S81 . . . . **37** C4
  South Leverton DN22 . . . . **42** A8
  Worksop S80 . . . . **36** C2
Retford Sta DN22 . . . . **39** E5
Revelstoke Ave NG5 . . . . **146** D1
Revelstoke Way NG5 . . . . **146** E1
Revesby Gdns NG8 . . . . . **172** C7
Revesby Rd NG5 . . . . **161** F5
Revill CI
  Claypole NG23 . . . . **156** D7
  Ilkeston DE7 . . . . **157** C2
Revill Cres NG9 . . . . **182** F8
Revill Ct 13 NG17 . . . . . . **114** E7
Reydon Dr NG8 . . . . **160** D1
Reynolds Dr NG8 . . . . . . **171** F5
Rhodes Wlk NG18 . . . . . **101** E6
Rhyl Cres NG4 . . . . **162** E2
Ribblesdale S81 . . . . **36** A8
Ribblesdale Ct NG9 . . . . . **183** A4
Ribblesdale Rd
  Long Eaton NG10 . . . . . . **193** A5
  Nottingham NG5 . . . . **161** C5
Riber CI
  Annesley Woodhouse
  NG17 . . . . **115** A1
  Long Eaton NG10 . . . . . . **193** D5
Riber Cres NG5 . . . . **160** F5
Richard Bonington Prim Sch
  NG5 . . . . **147** B1
Richard Herrod Ctr NG4 **174** D8
Richards CI NG17 . . . . . . **189** A3
Richardson CI NG11 . . . . **184** C1
Richard St DN22 . . . . **40** A5
Richborough PI NG8 . . . . **171** D2
Richey CI NG5 . . . . **162** B7
Richmond Ave
  Breaston DE72 . . . . **193** A8
  Calverton NG14 . . . . **149** A8
  Eastwood NG16 . . . . **144** B2
  Ilkeston DE7 . . . . **157** F4
  Nottingham NG3 . . . . **173** F7
  Sandiacre NG10 . . . . **182** A4
Richmond CI NG24 . . . . . **140** B4
Richmond Dr
  Beeston NG9 . . . . **183** E5
  Mansfield Woodhouse
  NG19 . . . . **88** D2
  Nottingham NG3 . . . . **161** D2
  Radcliffe on T NG12 . . . . . **175** F4
Richmond Gdns NG5 . . . . **147** E1
Richmond La DN10 . . . . **9** F4

Richmond Rd
Carlton in L S81 . . . . 25 E6
Gainsborough DN21 . . . . 24 F8
Kirkby in A NG17 . . . . . . 115 D5
Retford DN22 . . . . 30 A1
West Bridgford NG2 . . . . 173 F1
Worksop S80 . . . . 36 A1
Richmond St NG18 . . . . . 102 F5
Richmond Terr NG12 . . . 175 F3
Ricket La
Blidworth NG21 . . . . 117 C5
Ravenshead NG15 . . . . . 116 F4
Ricklow Ct 🔟 NG5 . . . . . 161 A8
Rick St NG1 . . . . 223 F3
Riddell Ave S81 . . . . 16 E3
Ridding La DN10 . . . . 3 A4
Ridding Terr NG3 . . . . . . 223 E4
Ridge Cl NG17 . . . . 100 D3
Ridge La NG12 . . . . 176 A5
Ridgeway
Nottingham NG5 . . . . . . 161 A8
Shirebrook NG20 . . . . . . 72 F5
Southwell NG25 . . . . 121 D2
Worksop S81 . . . . 36 B6
Ridgeway Cl NG22 . . . . . 119 F6
Ridgeway La NG20 . . . . . 74 B3
Ridgeway St NG3 . . . . . . 173 E6
Ridgeway Terr NG20 . . . . 74 B4
Ridgeway The NG22 . . . . 120 A6
Ridgeway Wlk 🔢 NG5 . . . 161 A8
Ridgewood Dr NG15 . . . . 183 C4
Ridgewood Gr NG15 . . . . 117 A2
Ridgmont Wlk NG11 . . . . 195 D8
Ridgway Cl NG2 . . . . 186 C5
Riding La DN10 . . . . 3 A4
Ridings The
Bulcote NG14 . . . . 164 B5
Keyworth NG12 . . . . 198 A3
Mansfield Woodhouse NG19 88 F1
Ridsdale Rd NG5 . . . . 161 C5
Rifle St NG7 . . . . 222 A3
Rigg La
Blidworth NG21 . . . . 132 E7
Hucknall NG15 . . . . 132 E5
Rigley Ave 🔟 DE7 . . . . . . 157 F1
Rigley Dr NG5 . . . . 160 E7
Riley Ave NG17 . . . . 100 C3
Riley Cl NG17 . . . . 100 C3
Ring Leas NG12 . . . . 188 A2
Ringrose Cl NG24 . . . . . . 140 D8
Ringstead Cl NG2 . . . . . . 185 C5
Ringstead Wlk NG5 . . . . . 161 B8
Ringwood S81 . . . . 36 A6
Ringwood Ave NG18 . . . . 102 C4
Ringwood Cres NG8 . . . . 172 C5
Ringwood Rd NG13 . . . . . 177 C4
Rio Dr NG23 . . . . 98 A2
Ripon Rd NG3 . . . . 174 B5
Riseborough Wlk NG6 . . . 146 C1
Risegate NG12 . . . . 187 F3
Riseholme Ave NG8 . . . . 171 C3
Riseholme Rd DN21 . . . . 24 F7
Rise Park Prim Sch NG5 146 F1
Rise The NG5 . . . . 161 D3
Risley Ct DE7 . . . . 157 F3
Risley Dr NG2 . . . . 173 B2
Riste's Pl NG2 . . . . 223 F2
Ritchie Cl NG12 . . . . 188 A2
Ritson Cl NG3 . . . . 223 F4
River Cl DN22 . . . . 29 F1
Riverdale Rd NG9 . . . . . . 183 C2
Rivergreen NG11 . . . . . . 184 E3
Rivergreen Cl NG9 . . . . . 171 C2
Rivergreen Cres NG9 . . . 171 C2
River La
Misson DN10 . . . . 4 C2
Retford DN22 . . . . 39 E7
Riverleen Sch NG6 . . . . . 160 C8
River Maun Rec Ctr
NG18 . . . . 102 D8
Rivermead
Cotgrave NG12 . . . . 188 A3
Newark-on-T NG24 . . . . . 139 E6
River Rd NG4 . . . . 174 E4
Riverside
Southwell NG25 . . . . 121 F1
Whatton NG13 . . . . 179 B4
Riverside App DN21 . . . . 15 B1
Riverside Cl
Bottesford NG13 . . . . . . 181 A3
Cuckney NG20 . . . . 60 A3
Riverside Prim Sch NG2 . 173 B1
Riverside Rd
Beeston NG9 . . . . 184 A3
Newark-on-T NG24 . . . . . 139 D5
Riverside Ret Pk NG11 . 185 A8
Riverside Way
Mansfield Woodhouse
NG19 . . . . 88 D5
Nottingham NG2 . . . . . . 173 B1
Riverside Wlk NG13 . . . . 181 A3
River View
Market Warsop NG20 . . . . 74 B5
Nottingham NG2 . . . . . . 173 D1
Pye Bridge DE55 . . . . . . 128 A6
Retford DN22 . . . . 39 E3
Riverview Cotts DN10 . . . 4 C2
Riverway Gdns NG2 . . . . 173 D2
Rivington Rd NG9 . . . . . . 182 E2
Road No 1 NG4 . . . . 174 F6
Road No 2 NG4 . . . . 174 F5
Road No 3 NG4 . . . . 175 A5
Road No 4 NG4 . . . . 175 C5
Road No 5 NG4 . . . . 175 B5
Road No 7 NG4 . . . . 174 F6
Road No 8 NG4 . . . . 174 F5

Roadwood La NG23 . . . . 69 F8
Robbie Burns Rd NG5 . . . 161 C8
Robert Ave NG18 . . . . . . 101 F5
Robert Dukeson Ave
NG24 . . . . 125 B4
Robert Jones Inf Sch
NG21 . . . . 118 A5
Robert Jones Jun Sch
NG21 . . . . 118 A5
Robert Mellors Prim Sch
NG5 . . . . 161 F8
Robert Miles Jun Sch
NG13 . . . . 177 F4
Roberts Ave NG17 . . . . . 99 F2
Roberts Cl
Dunham on T NG22 . . . . . 54 A1
Kegworth DE74 . . . . 203 D1
Robert Shaw Prim Sch
NG8 . . . . 172 D6
Robert's La NG15 . . . . . . 145 E7
Roberts St
Ilkeston DE7 . . . . 170 A6
Nottingham NG2 . . . . . . 173 E4
Roberts Yd NG9 . . . . 184 A7
Robey Cl
Hucknall NG15 . . . . 131 A1
Mansfield Woodhouse NG19 89 B1
Robey Dr NG16 . . . . 143 F3
Robina Dr NG16 . . . . 158 C8
Robin Down Cl NG18 . . . . 102 C2
Robin Down La NG18 . . . . 102 C2
Robinet Rd NG9 . . . . 183 F5
Robinettes La NG16 . . . . 158 D1
Robin Gr NG15 . . . . 117 A1
Robin Hood Ave
Edwinstowe NG21 . . . . . . 91 C8
Market Warsop NG20 . . . 74 C2
Robin Hood Cl NG16 . . . . 143 F1
Robin Hood Doncaster/
Sheffield International
Airport DN10 . . . . 3 B7
Robin Hood Dr NG15 . . . . 145 E5
Robin Hood Ind Est 🔢
NG3 . . . . 173 E5
Robin Hood Jun & Inf Sch
NG5 . . . . 161 A6
Robin Hood Prim Sch
NG19 . . . . 88 B4
Robin Hood Rd
Annesley Woodhouse
NG17 . . . . 130 B8
Arnold NG5 . . . . 147 B1
Blidworth NG21 . . . . 118 B5
Robin Hood's Cave NG22 . 63 C2
Robin Hood St NG3 . . . . . 173 E5
Robin Hood Terr
Nottingham NG3 . . . . . . 223 E4
Ravenshead NG15 . . . . . 117 B3
Robin Hood Way NG2 . . . 173 C2
Robinia Ct NG2 . . . . 186 A5
Robin Mews LE11 . . . . . . 220 A3
Robins Ct NG24 . . . . 140 A8
Robinson Cl NG24 . . . . . . 140 E8
Robinson Dr S80 . . . . 35 E1
Robinson Gdns NG11 . . . . 184 C1
Robinson Rd NG3 . . . . . . 162 A2
Robin's Wood Rd NG8 . . . 172 B7
Rob Roy Ave NG7 . . . . . . 222 B1
Rochdale Ct NG18 . . . . . . 103 A5
Roche Cl NG5 . . . . 162 C4
Rochester Ave NG4 . . . . . 175 A7
Rochester Cl
Long Eaton NG10 . . . . . . 193 A7
Worksop S81 . . . . 36 A7
Rochester Ct NG6 . . . . . . 159 F6
Rochester Rd NG21 . . . . . 118 A8
Rochester Wlk NG7 . . . . . 184 A1
Rochford Ct NG12 . . . . . . 186 C3
Rock Ct
Mansfield NG18 . . . . 102 C7
Nottingham NG6 . . . . . . 160 D3
Rock Dr NG7 . . . . 222 C1
Rocket Cl NG16 . . . . 159 A7
Rockford Ct NG9 . . . . 170 E1
Rockford Rd NG5 . . . . . . 160 F3
Rock Hill NG18 . . . . 102 D6
Rock Hl Gd NG18 . . . . . . 102 D6
Rockingham Gr NG13 . . . . 177 C4
Rocklands The NG20 . . . . 72 E4
Rockley Ave
Eastwood NG16 . . . . 144 A1
Radcliffe on T NG12 . . . . 175 F4
Rockley Cl
Clipstone NG21 . . . . 90 A4
Hucknall NG15 . . . . 145 C6
Rockleys View NG14 . . . . 150 A2
Rockley Way NG20 . . . . . 72 E4
Rock St
Mansfield NG18 . . . . 102 C6
Nottingham NG6 . . . . . . 160 B8
Rock Valley NG18 . . . . . . 102 C7
Rockwood Cl NG21 . . . . . 118 A5
Rockwood Wlk NG15 . . . . 145 E6
Rodel Ct NG3 . . . . 223 F4
Roden House Bsns Ctr
NG3 . . . . 173 D5
Roden St NG3 . . . . 173 E5
Roderick Ave NG17 . . . . . 115 B1
Roderick St NG6 . . . . 160 D4
Rodery The NG18 . . . . . . 102 E5
Rodney Rd NG2 . . . . 186 A6
Rodney Way DE7 . . . . 157 F2
Rodwell Cl NG8 . . . . 172 C6
Roebuck Cl NG5 . . . . 161 B8
Roebuck Dr NG18 . . . . . . 103 B3
Roebuck Way S80 . . . . . . 48 B8

Roe Hill NG14 . . . . 149 C5
Roes La NG14 . . . . 149 A7
Roewood Cl NG17 . . . . . . 114 F7
Roewood La NG22 . . . . . . 107 F2
Roger Cl NG17 . . . . 100 F5
Roker Cl NG18 . . . . 160 A1
Rolaine Cl NG19 . . . . 88 C4
Roland Ave
Nottingham NG11 . . . . . . 185 B7
Nuthall NG16 . . . . 159 E4
Rolleston Cl NG15 . . . . . . 145 D5
Rolleston Cres NG16 . . . . 144 F1
Rolleston Dr
Arnold NG5 . . . . 162 A7
Eastwood NG16 . . . . 158 B8
Nottingham NG7 . . . . . . 222 B1
Rolleston Sta NG25 . . . . . 137 F6
Roman Bank NG19 . . . . . . 88 D3
Roman Bank La DN10 . . . . 18 E6
Roman Dr NG6 . . . . 160 E4
Romans Ct NG6 . . . . 160 E2
Romilay Cl NG9 . . . . 172 A1
Romney Ave NG8 . . . . . . 171 D2
Romsey Pl NG19 . . . . 101 D6
Rona Cl NG19 . . . . 101 E5
Rona Ct NG6 . . . . 160 E5
Ronald St NG7 . . . . 222 B3
Rookery Gdns NG5 . . . . . 161 F8
Rookery La NG17 . . . . . . 114 A8
Rookery The
Collingham NG23 . . . . . . 98 A1
🔢 Mansfield NG18 . . . . . 102 A7
Rook's La DN10 . . . . 6 E2
Rookwood Cl NG9 . . . . . . 183 E6
Rookwood Cres NG15 . . . 145 D6
Rooley Ave NG17 . . . . . . 100 C3
Rooley Dr NG17 . . . . 100 C3
Roosa Cl NG6 . . . . 159 F5
Roosevelt Ave NG10 . . . . 193 C6
Roosevelt Rd NG17 . . . . . 101 B4
Rooth St NG18 . . . . 102 B6
Ropery Rd DN21 . . . . 15 B2
Ropewalk DE74 . . . . 203 C2
Ropewalk Ind Ctr DE7 . . . 158 A1
Ropewalk The
Ilkeston DE7 . . . . 158 A1
Newark-on-T NG24 . . . . . 140 B8
Nottingham NG1 . . . . . . 223 D2
Southwell NG25 . . . . 121 E1
Ropeway The NG17 . . . . . 114 E5
Rope Wlk LE12 . . . . 205 D1
Ropsley Cres NG2 . . . . . . 186 A8
Roscoe Ave NG5 . . . . 147 E2
Roseacre NG9 . . . . 184 A5
Rose Ash La NG5 . . . . . . 161 B8
Rose Ave
Ilkeston DE7 . . . . 157 E2
Retford DN22 . . . . 40 A4
Rosebank Dr NG5 . . . . . . 148 B1
Rosebay Av NG7 . . . . 172 D8
Roseberry Ave NG2 . . . . . 173 E1
Roseberry Gdns NG15 . . . 146 C6
Roseberry St NG17 . . . . . 115 C4
Rosebery Hill NG18 . . . . . 102 C6
Rosebery St NG6 . . . . . . 160 E3
Rose Cl NG3 . . . . 173 D7
Rose Cottage Dr NG17 . . 99 F2
Rose Cotts NG14 . . . . 163 E5
Rosecroft Dr NG5 . . . . . . 161 C6
Rose Ct NG10 . . . . 182 B1
Rosedale S81 . . . . 36 A8
Rosedale Cl NG10 . . . . . . 193 B6
Rosedale Dr NG8 . . . . 171 B4
Rosedale La NG15 . . . . . . 116 F3
Rosedale Rd NG3 . . . . . . 174 C6
Rosedale Way NG19 . . . . 88 F2
Rose Farm Dr NG23 . . . . 96 F8
Rosegarth Wlk NG6 . . . . . 160 D4
Rose Gr
Beeston NG9 . . . . 184 B5
Keyworth NG12 . . . . 197 A3
Rosegrove Ave NG5 . . . . 147 F1
Rose Hill NG12 . . . . 197 E3
Rosehill Cl LN1 . . . . 57 A4
Rosehill Specl Sch NG3 173 C6
Rose La NG15 . . . . 88 C4
Rose Lea DN22 . . . . 39 D4
Roseleigh Ave NG3 . . . . . 162 D4
Rosemary Ave NG18 . . . . 102 A8
Rosemary Cl 🔢 NG8 . . . . 159 E1
Rosemary St NG18 . . . . . 102 A7
Rosemont Cl NG17 . . . . . 100 F6
Roseneath Ave NG5 . . . . 146 E1
Rosetta Rd NG7 . . . . 160 F1
Rosewall Ct NG5 . . . . 162 B7
Roseway DN21 . . . . 15 C1
Rosewood Cl
Carlton in L S81 . . . . 25 D1
Newark-on-T NG24 . . . . . 125 A4
South Normanton DE55 . . 113 B7
Rosewood Cres DE75 . . . . 143 B2
Rosewood Dr NG17 . . . . . 115 C6
Rosewood Gdns
Nottingham NG5 . . . . . . 159 F7
West Bridgford NG2 . . . . 185 C3
Rosings Ct NG17 . . . . 100 E1
Roslyn Ave NG4 . . . . 162 E2
Ross Cl
Coddington NG24 . . . . . . 126 B2
Lowdham NG14 . . . . 150 E1
Rossell Dr NG9 . . . . 182 E5
Rossendale DE7 . . . . 157 E4
Rossett Cl NG2 . . . . 186 D6
Rossington Rd NG2 . . . . . 173 F5
Ross La NG4 . . . . 163 C7
Rosslyn Dr
Hucknall NG15 . . . . 146 C8

Rosslyn Dr *continued*
Nottingham NG8 . . . . . . 160 A2
Rosslyn Pk Prim Sch
NG8 . . . . 160 B1
Rosthwaite Cl NG2 . . . . . 186 C5
Roston Cl NG18 . . . . 103 B5
Rothbury Ave NG9 . . . . . 170 D2
Rothbury Gr NG13 . . . . . . 177 C5
Rotherham Baulk S81 . . . 25 C7
Rotherham Rd NG19 . . . . 86 F8
Rothesay Ave NG7 . . . . . 222 B2
Rothley Ave NG3 . . . . . . 173 F5
Rothwell Cl
Gainsborough DN21 . . . . 24 E8
Nottingham NG11 . . . . . . 185 A4
Roughs Wood La NG15 . . 145 D4
Roulstone Cres LE12 . . . . 205 E3
Roundhill Cl NG17 . . . . . . 101 C1
Round Hill Prim Sch
NG9 . . . . 183 F7
Roundwood Rd NG5 . . . . 161 C7
Rowan Ave
Hathern LE12 . . . . 213 A2
Ravenshead NG15 . . . . . 117 A1
Stapleford NG9 . . . . 170 E2
Rowan Cl
Calverton NG14 . . . . 148 D7
Kirkby in A NG17 . . . . . . 114 F6
Mansfield NG18 . . . . 88 D1
Rowan Cres S80 . . . . 35 E1
Rowan Croft NG17 . . . . . 99 F4
Rowan Ct NG16 . . . . 159 B6
Rowan Dr
Keyworth NG12 . . . . 198 A2
Kirkby in A NG17 . . . . . . 114 F6
Nottingham NG11 . . . . . . 185 A4
Selston NG16 . . . . 128 D6
Rowan Gdns NG6 . . . . . . 159 F7
Rowans The
🔢 Gainsborough DN21 . . 15 F1
Saxilby LN1 . . . . 56 F4
Rowan Way NG24 . . . . . . 140 B5
Rowan Wlk NG3 . . . . 174 A8
Rowe Gdns NG6 . . . . 160 D6
Rowland Ave NG3 . . . . . . 162 A2
Rowland Mews NG3 . . . . . 173 E7
Rowsley Ave NG10 . . . . . 193 A5
Rowsley Ct NG17 . . . . . . 114 C8
Rowston Cl DN21 . . . . . . 15 C2
Row The NG13 . . . . 179 F6
Rowthorne La S44 . . . . . . 86 B7
Roxton Ct NG16 . . . . 158 F7
Royal Ave NG10 . . . . 182 D1
Royal Cres S81 . . . . 35 E6
Royal Ctr (Theatre Royal &
Royal Concert Hall)
NG1 . . . . 223 E3
Royal Mews NG9 . . . . 183 C3
Royal Oak Ct NG21 . . . . . 76 B2
Royal Oak Dr NG16 . . . . . 129 B7
Royal Way LE11 . . . . 220 A6
Roy Ave NG9 . . . . 184 B4
Royce Ave NG15 . . . . 145 E4
Royds Cres S80 . . . . 35 A5
Royland Rd LE11 . . . . 220 A3
Royston Cl NG2 . . . . 173 B1
Ruby Paddocks NG16 . . . . 158 F5
Ruby Wy NG15 . . . . 102 C5
Ruddington Ct 🔢 NG18 . . 103 A2
Ruddington Framework
Knitters Mus NG11 . . . . 196 C6
Ruddington La NG11 . . . . 185 B5
Ruddington Rd NG18 . . . . 103 A2
Ruddington Village Mus
NG11 . . . . 196 C7
Rudge Cl NG8 . . . . 171 F5
Rue de L'Yonne NG23 . . . 98 A2
Ruffles Ave NG5 . . . . 162 B5
Rufford Abbey NG22 . . . . 91 F6
Rufford Ave
Beeston NG9 . . . . 183 A8
Carlton NG4 . . . . 162 D2
Mansfield NG18 . . . . 102 C7
Meden Vale NG20 . . . . . . 74 F8
Newark-on-T NG24 . . . . . 139 F7
New Ollerton NG22 . . . . . 77 C4
Rainworth NG21 . . . . 104 C1
Retford DN22 . . . . 39 D3
Rufford Cl
Bilsthorpe NG22 . . . . 106 A4
Hucknall NG15 . . . . 146 C5
Sutton in A NG17 . . . . . . 100 C5
Rufford Craft Ctr NG22 . 91 F6
Rufford Ct NG21 . . . . 104 C1
Rufford Ctry Pk NG22 . . . 91 E6
Rufford Dr NG19 . . . . 88 E3
Rufford Gr NG13 . . . . 177 C4
Rufford Jun & Inf Sch
NG6 . . . . 160 A7
Rufford La
Edwinstowe NG22 . . . . . . 91 F8
Wellow NG22 . . . . 92 B8
Rufford Rd
Edwinstowe NG21 . . . . . . 91 C8
Long Eaton NG10 . . . . . . 193 B4
Nottingham NG5 . . . . . . 161 C3
Ruddington NG11 . . . . . . 196 D7
Rufford St S80 . . . . 47 B8
Rufford Way NG15 . . . . . . 186 B6
Rufford Wlk 🔢 NG6 . . . . . 160 B7
Ruffs Dr NG15 . . . . 145 E5
Rugby Cl NG5 . . . . 160 E7
Rugby Rd
Rainworth NG21 . . . . 118 A8
West Bridgford NG2 . . . . 185 C5
Rugby Terr 🔢 NG7 . . . . . . 172 F7
Rugeley Ave NG10 . . . . . 194 A7

Ruislip Cl NG16 . . . . 158 E7
Runcie Cl NG12 . . . . 187 F2
Runnymede Ct NG7 . . . . . 222 C3
Runswick Dr
Arnold NG5 . . . . 161 F8
Nottingham NG8 . . . . . . 172 A5
Runton Dr NG6 . . . . 160 F4
Rupert Cres NG24 . . . . . . 139 F7
Rupert Rd NG13 . . . . 177 D4
Rupert St DE7 . . . . 158 A1
Rushcliffe Arena NG2 . . . 185 E6
Rushcliffe Ave
Carlton NG4 . . . . 174 D8
Radcliffe on T NG12 . . . . 175 F3
Rushcliffe Ct NG6 . . . . . . 160 D6
Rushcliffe Ctry Pk NG11 196 C5
Rushcliffe Gr LE12 . . . . . . 205 E4
Rushcliffe L Ctr NG2 . . . . 185 E4
Rushcliffe Rd NG15 . . . . . 145 C5
Rushcliffe Rise NG5 . . . . 161 C5
Rushcliffe Sch NG2 . . . . . 185 F4
Rushes Sh Ctr The LE12 220 A4
Rushes The
Gotham NG11 . . . . 195 B1
🔢 Loughborough LE12 . . 220 B4
Mansfield Woodhouse
NG19 . . . . 88 D5
Rushey Cl S80 . . . . 36 B2
Rushford Dr NG8 . . . . 171 D4
Rush Leys NG10 . . . . 193 D5
Rushley View NG17 . . . . . 100 C1
Rushmere Wlk NG5 . . . . . 161 F5
Rushpool Ave NG19 . . . . . 88 D4
Rushpool Cl NG19 . . . . . . 88 F2
Rushton Gdns NG3 . . . . . 173 F7
Rushworth Ave NG2 . . . . 185 E8
Rushworth Cl NG3 . . . . . . 173 E7
Rushy Cl NG8 . . . . 171 D5
Ruskin Ave NG10 . . . . . . 193 B5
Ruskin Cl NG5 . . . . 161 D7
Ruskin Rd NG19 . . . . 87 D1
Ruskin St DN21 . . . . 24 D6
Russell Ave
Harworth DN11 . . . . 8 F4
New Balderton NG24 . . . . 140 B4
🔢 Nottingham NG8 . . . . 172 A5
Russell Cres 🔢 NG8 . . . . . 172 A5
Russell Dr NG8 . . . . 171 F5
Russell Gdns 🔢 NG9 . . . . 183 C2
Russell Pl NG1 . . . . 223 D3
Russell Rd NG7 . . . . 172 F8
Russell St
Long Eaton NG10 . . . . . . 182 D1
Loughborough LE11 . . . . 220 C4
Nottingham NG7 . . . . . . 222 C3
Sutton in A NG17 . . . . . . 100 F3
Russet Ave NG4 . . . . 174 F4
Russet Gr DN10 . . . . 10 A7
Russey Cl NG14 . . . . 150 E1
Russley Rd NG9 . . . . 183 A8
Ruth Dr NG5 . . . . 148 A1
Rutherford Ave NG18 . . . 102 E4
Ruthwell Gdns NG5 . . . . . 147 A2
Rutland NG17 . . . . 115 D6
Rutland Ave
Beeston NG9 . . . . 183 A4
Newark-on-T NG24 . . . . . 140 A6
Rutland Cl NG20 . . . . 74 A4
Rutland Cres DN11 . . . . . 8 F5
Rutland Ct DE7 . . . . 157 D1
Rutland Dr NG11 . . . . 8 F5
Rutland Gr NG10 . . . . 182 C5
Rutland House Sch NG3 173 C8
Rutland La NG13 . . . . 181 B2
Rutland Rd
Bingham NG13 . . . . 177 F5
Carlton NG4 . . . . 162 D3
Retford DN22 . . . . 40 A4
West Bridgford NG2 . . . . 186 A8
Westwood NG16 . . . . 128 C4
Rutland St
Ilkeston DE7 . . . . 157 F2
🔢 Loughborough LE11 . . 220 C3
Mansfield NG18 . . . . 102 C5
Nottingham NG1 . . . . . . 223 D2
Rutland Terr DE7 . . . . . . 157 F2
Rydal Ave NG10 . . . . 182 B2
Rydal Dr
Beeston NG9 . . . . 183 D8
Hucknall NG15 . . . . 145 F4
Worksop S81 . . . . 35 E8
Rydale Gdns DN10 . . . . . 3 A1
Rydale Rd NG5 . . . . 161 C5
Rydal Gdns NG2 . . . . 186 A5
Rydal Gr NG6 . . . . 160 E3
Ryder St NG6 . . . . 160 D4
Rye Croft DN11 . . . . 8 A4
Ryecroft St NG9 . . . . 182 F8
Ryedale Ave NG18 . . . . . 103 A5
Ryehill Cl NG2 . . . . 173 D2
Ryehill St NG2 . . . . 173 D2
Ryeholme Cl LE12 . . . . . . 205 F3
Ryeland Gdns NG2 . . . . . 173 C2
Ryemere Cl NG16 . . . . . . 143 F2
Rye St NG7 . . . . 160 F1
Rylands Cl NG9 . . . . 184 E4
Rylands Jun Sch NG9 . . . 184 A4
Ryton Cl S81 . . . . 18 B2
Ryton 🔢 NG2 . . . . 173 D1
Ryton Fields S81 . . . . 18 B2
Ryton Pk Prim Sch S80 . 35 F3
Ryton Pl NG8 . . . . 160 B1
Ryton Sq NG8 . . . . 160 B1
Ryton St S80 . . . . 35 F3

S

Sacheverall Ave NG16...113 D3
Sacred Heart Cath Prim Sch
LE11 ....220 A1
Sacred Heart RC Prim Sch
NG4..............174 D7
Saddlers Cl NG19 ..... 88 F1
Saddlers Yd NG12.....197 E7
Saddleworth Ct NG3 ..223 E4
Sadler St NG19 ....101 F8
Saffron Gdns NG2.....173 B2
St Agnes Cl NG8 ......171 D8
St Aidan's Ct NG6 .....160 E4
St Albans Cl NG10.....193 E5
St Albans Ct NG5 .....147 B2
St Albans Mews NG6 ..160 D6
St Albans Rd
  Arnold NG5 ....161 E7
  Bestwood Village NG6..146 E4
  Nottingham NG6 ....160 D7
St Albans St NG5......161 C3
St Andrew Cl NG11.....195 B1
St Andrews CE Prim Sch
NG17..............100 F6
St Andrews Cl NG6.....160 C7
St Andrew's Cl NG15 ..146 A8
St Andrews Cres NG17 ..100 F6
St Andrews Ct NG6.....160 D7
St Andrews Dr LN1......56 F4
St Andrew's Rd NG3....173 B7
St Andrew's Rise DE74 ..203 C1
St Andrews St
  Kirkby in A NG17......115 B6
  Sutton in A NG17......100 E6
St Andrew St NG18.....102 C5
St Andrews Way DN22...39 E3
St Annes CE Prim Sch
S80...............35 D2
St Annes Cl S80........35 C3
St Annes Dr S80........35 C2
St Anne's La LE12 .....213 B6
St Annes Mews S80......35 C3
St Annes View S80......35 C3
St Annes Way S80.......35 C3
St Ann's Gdns NG3.....173 E7
St Ann's Hill NG3......173 C7
St Ann's Hill Rd NG3...173 C7
St Ann's St NG1.......223 E3
St Ann's Valley NG3....173 E7
St Ann's Way
  Nottingham NG3 .....223 E4
  Shelton NG23.........168 C6
St Anns Well Inf Sch
NG3...............173 D7
St Anns Well Jun Sch
NG3...............173 F8
St Ann's Well Rd NG3 ..173 E6
St Anthony Ct NG7.....172 E2
St Augustines Cl ❸ NG7..161 A1
St Augustine's Inf Sch
S81...............36 B4
St Augustine's Jun Sch
S81...............36 B4
St Augustines RC Prim Sch
NG3...............173 C8
St Austell Dr NG11.....185 B6
St Austins Ct NG4......174 F8
St Austins Dr NG4......174 F8
St Bartholomew's Rd
NG3...............173 F7
St Botolphs Cl LN1......57 B5
St Botolphs Gate LN1 ...57 A5
St Catherines Ct NG24...139 E7
St Catherines St NG12...175 E2
St Catherine St NG18...102 C5
St Cecilia Gdns NG3....223 F4
St Chad's Cl NG18.....102 C3
St Chad's Rd NG3......173 E5
St Christopher St ❾
NG2...............173 F4
St Clare's Ave NG14 ...140 A6
St Cuthbert's Rd ⓫ NG3..173 E5
St Cuthbert St S80......35 F1
St David's Cl S81.......36 A6
St Edmund Campion Prim
Sch NG2............186 A6
St Edmund's Ave NG19 ..88 C3
St Edmunds CE Prim Sch
NG19...............88 C3
St Edwards RC Prim Sch
NG3...............173 F7
St Edwin's Dr NG21......76 A2
St Ervan Rd NG11......185 B6
St Francis Hospl NG5 ..161 B5
St George's Ct NG15...146 A8
St George's Dr NG2 ....173 B2
St George's Ms LN1......56 F4
St Georges Priory NG2...173 C2
St Giles Specl Sch DN22...39 C8
St Giles Way NG12 .....189 A4
St Giles' Way NG24.....140 E4
St Helens Ave NG16.....113 C3
St Helen's Cres
  Burton Joyce NG14 ...163 F4
  Trowell NG9.........170 C4
St Helen's Dr NG16.....128 D7
St Helen's Gr NG14.....163 E3
St Helen's La NG22.....120 F2
St Helen's St
  Retford DN22.........40 B4
  West Bridgford NG2 ..185 F6
St Helen's St NG7......222 C3

St James Ave DE7......170 A7
St James Ct NG10......182 B3
St James' Dr NG16.....143 D8
St James's Ct NG15 ...146 A8
St James's St
  Nottingham NG1 .....223 D2
  Stapleford NG9 ......182 C6
St James's Terr NG9 ..182 D6
St James's Terr NG1 ..223 D2
St John Baptist CE Prim Sch
NG4...............174 E6
St John's Ave NG17....115 B4
St Johns CE Prim Sch
  Stapleford NG9 ......182 E7
  Worksop S81..........35 E7
St John's Cl NG16.....128 D1
St John's Cres NG15...146 C5
St John's Ct NG4......174 D7
St Johns Ctr NG18.....102 A7
St John's Dr DN22.......30 D4
St John's Pl ❾ NG18 ...102 A7
St John's Rd
  Ilkeston DE7.........170 A7
  Ruddington NG11.....196 C7
St John's St NG10.....193 D7
St John St
  Mansfield NG18.......102 B7
  Retford DN22.........39 F7
St John's Terr DN21......24 D7
St Josephs Prim Sch
DN22..............39 D7
St Joseph's RC Prim Sch
NG22...............77 E5
St Josephs Sch NG1 ..223 D3
St Jude's Ave NG3 ....161 E2
St Judes Way NG11....104 A1
St Laurence CE Prim Sch
NG10..............193 E6
St Laurence Ct NG10 ..193 E6
St Lawrence Bvd NG12..175 E2
St Leonard's DN11 ......8 A7
St Leonard's Ct NG24...124 F1
St Leonard's Dr NG8 ..171 F4
St Leonards Way NG19 ..103 B8
St Leven Cl NG8 ......171 D8
St Luke's CE Prim Sch
S81................34 F8
St Luke's Cl NG2 .....186 B5
St Luke's St ❻ NG3 ...173 E5
St Lukes Way NG22 .....53 A8
St Luke's Way NG14 ...175 F8
St Margaret Clitherow Cath
Prim Sch NG8 ......161 C8
St Margarets Ave NG8 ..172 C8
St Margaret St NG18 ..102 C5
St Mark's Cl S81.......35 D8
St Mark's La NG24.....139 F8
St Mark's Pl NG24.....139 F8
St Marks St NG3 .....223 F3
St Martin's Ave DN10...9 F7
St Martins Cl S81......18 B2
St Martin's Cl
  Firbeck S81 ....16 A6
  Nottingham NG8 .....171 E8
St Martins Rd DN22.....42 C8
St Martin's Rd NG8....171 E8
St Martin's Wlk S80.....45 C6
St Mary & Martin Prim Sch
of S81..............18 B2
St Mary's Ave NG4 ....162 E2
St Marys Cath Prim Sch
NG7...............172 E4
St Mary's CE Prim Sch
  Edwinstowe NG21.....76 A3
  Nottingham NG6 .....160 C8
  Tickhill DN11 ....8 A7
St Mary's Church NG1 ..223 F2
St Marys Cl NG9 ......183 D1
St Mary's Cl
  Arnold NG5 ....147 F1
  Bottesford NG13.....181 B3
  ❺ Loughborough LE11 ..220 A4
  Lowdham NG14.......150 D2
St Mary's Cres
  East Leake LE12 .....205 F3
  Ruddington NG11.....196 C7
  Tickhill DN11 ....8 A7
St Mary's Ct NG17.....100 D4
St Mary's Dr NG21......76 A2
St Mary's Gate
  Nottingham NG1 .....223 F2
  Tickhill DN11 ....8 A7
St Mary's Gdns NG24...139 F5
St Mary's La NG13.....181 B2
St Mary's Mews DN11 ...8 A7
St Mary's Pl NG1......223 F2
St Marys Prim Sch ⓭
LE11 ....220 A4
St Mary's Prim Sch
NG17..............100 C3
St Marys Rd NG13.....177 F5
St Mary's Rd
  Sutton in A NG17......100 D3
  Tickhill DN11 ....8 A7
St Mary's Way NG15...146 A8
St Mary's Wlk NG16 ...128 B3
St Matthews CE Prim Sch
NG23...............81 E7
St Matthias Rd NG3....173 E6
St Mawes Ave NG11....185 B6
St Mellion Way ❸ NG17..114 E7
St Michaels Ave NG8 ..171 D8
St Michael's Ave NG4...162 E2
St Michael's Cl NG21 ..120 F1
St Michael's Gn DN22...39 D8
St Michael's Sq NG9....183 B8
St Michael's St NG17 ..101 A3

St Michael's View NG15 ..131 B1
St Nicholas Cl NG5.....161 E7
St Nicholas St NG1....223 E2
St Patricks Cath Prim Sch
NG11..............185 B8
St Patricks RC Prim Sch
NG18..............103 A5
St Patrick's Rd
  Hucknall NG15.......145 F7
  Nuthall NG16........159 C6
St Paul's Ave NG7.....172 F7
St Paul's Rd
  Gainsborough DN21 ...15 B3
  Worksop S80..........36 A2
St Paul's St ❶ NG8....172 D5
St Paul's Terr NG7.....172 F7
St Peters Ave LE12.....213 A1
St Peter's Ave NG20 ...74 B6
St Peters CE Jun Sch
NG11..............196 D8
St Peters CE Prim Sch
  East Bridgford NG13...165 C3
  Farndon NG24.......139 A5
  Gringley on the Hill DN10..12 E2
  Mansfield NG18.......103 A2
St Peter's Church Wlk
NG1...............223 E2
St Peters Cl
  East Stockwith DN21....7 E2
  Farndon NG24.......138 F4
  New Ollerton NG22.....77 B4
St Peter's Cres NG11...196 C7
St Peters Dr NG21.....104 A1
St Peter's Gate NG1 ..223 E2
St Peter's La DN22......21 D5
St Peter's Ret Pk NG18 ..102 B6
St Peter's Sq NG1.....223 E2
St Peter's St NG7.....222 A3
St Peter's Way NG18 ..102 C6
St Philip Neri RC Prim Sch
NG19..............102 A8
St Saviour's Cl DN22....40 A8
St Saviour's Gdns NG2...173 D2
St Stephen's Ave ❼ NG2..173 F4
St Stephen's Rd
  Nottingham NG2 .....173 F4
  Retford DN22.........40 B4
St Swithuns CE Prim Sch ❶
DN22..............39 F7
St Teresas RC Prim Sch
NG8...............172 A8
St Thomas' Ave NG17...115 B4
St Thomas Dr NG13....179 A5
St Vincent Cl NG10....193 E6
St Wilfreds Cl NG23....110 F2
St Wilfrids Dr NG17....114 D5
St Wilfrids Prim Sch
NG14..............148 E7
St Wilfrid's Sq NG14...148 F7
Salamander Cl NG4....162 D2
Salcey Dr NG9 ....170 D2
Salcombe Cir NG5......147 D1
Salcombe Cl NG16.....144 C1
Salcombe Cres NG11...196 D8
Salcombe Dr NG5......147 D1
Salcombe Gr DN10......9 F8
Salcombe Rd NG5......160 F3
Salford Gdns NG3......223 F3
Salisbury Ave LE12.....205 F1
Salisbury Cl
  Mansfield Woodhouse
  NG19...............88 D4
  Morton DN21.........15 B5
Salisbury Rd
  Mansfield NG19.......101 E8
  Newark-on-T NG24...139 F6
Salisbury Sq NG7......222 A2
Salisbury St
  Beeston NG9.........184 B7
  Gainsborough DN21 ...15 C2
  Long Eaton NG10.....193 E7
  Loughborough LE11...220 C4
  Nottingham NG7 .....222 A2
Sallie Bank La LN1......55 B4
Salmon Cl NG6........159 F7
Salmon La NG17.......129 D7
Salop St NG5..........161 D7
Saltburn Rd NG8......172 A6
Salterford Ave NG14...148 F8
Salterford House Sch
NG14..............133 D5
Salterford La NG14....133 D5
Salterford Rd NG15....145 E5
Saltford Cl NG4.......162 F2
Salt Hill S81...........16 B5
Salthouse Ct NG9......184 A7
Salthouse La NG9......184 A8
Saltney Way NG11.....185 A3
Salvin Cl NG12........189 A4
Sampson's La NG19.....87 B3
Sampson St NG17......130 A8
Samson Cl NG11.......196 B8
Samuel Barlow Prim Sch
NG21...............90 A3
Samuel Cl NG19.......101 F8
Samuel Way NG18.....102 C8
Sandale Cl NG2.......186 C6
Sandalwood Cl NG18 ..103 B4
Sandalwood Dr NG17 ..115 C6
Sandays Cl NG2.......173 C1
Sandbeck Ct DN10......10 A8
Sandby Ct NG9........183 C5
Sanders Ave NG18.....102 D6
Sanders Rd NG23.......97 F7
Sanderson Dr NG3.....162 D6
Sanderson's Bank DN9...2 B3
Sandfield Ave NG15....132 B8
Sandfield Cl NG18.....103 B4

Sandfield Ctr NG7.....222 B2
Sandfield La NG22......78 B6
Sandfield Rd
  Annesley Woodhouse
  NG17..............129 F8
  Arnold NG5 ....161 F5
  Beeston NG9.........182 E2
  Nottingham NG7 .....222 B2
Sandfield Way NG24...139 D5
Sandford Ave NG10....193 E7
Sandford Rd NG3......162 A3
Sandgate NG9 ....171 D1
Sandgate Ave NG19.....88 D4
Sandgate Rd NG19......88 D4
Sandhill Rd
  Farndon NG24.......139 A5
  Selston NG16........129 B3
Sandhills Cl NG24.....124 E1
Sandhills Pk NG24.....124 E1
Sandhill St S80........35 E3
Sandholes The NG22...119 E6
Sandhurst Ave NG18 ..102 C4
Sandhurst Dr
  Beeston NG9.........183 C2
  Ruddington NG11.....196 B6
Sandhurst Rd NG6.....146 C1
Sandiacre Rd NG9 ....182 C6
Sand La
  Besthorpe NG23.......97 F7
  Broadholme NG23.....70 E8
  Spalford NG23........83 A7
  Torksey LN1..........44 C2
Sandmartins S81........35 C7
Sandmartins Cl NG18 ..102 C5
Sandon St NG7........161 A1
Sandown Rd
  Beeston NG9.........182 F2
  Mansfield NG18.......103 B4
  Sutton in A NG17.....101 B3
Sandpiper Cl NG13.....177 F3
Sandpiper Way NG7....222 A2
Sand Pit La LE14......211 C3
Sandringham Ave NG2 ..185 E8
Sandringham Cres
  Nottingham NG8 .....171 C5
  Worksop S81..........35 E6
Sandringham Ct
  Harworth DN11 ....9 A5
  Mansfield Woodhouse NG19 ..88 B6
Sandringham Dr
  Beeston NG9.........171 C1
  Mansfield Woodhouse NG19 ..88 B6
Sandringham Pl NG15 ..146 B8
Sandringham Rd
  Mansfield Woodhouse
  NG19...............88 E5
  ❷ Nottingham NG2...173 F4
  Retford DN22.........29 D1
  Sandiacre NG10......182 B3
Sandrock Rd DN11......8 F5
Sands Cl NG4.........174 E5
Sandsfield La DN21.....24 D6
Sands The LE14......211 D3
Sandstone Pl NG18....102 E5
Sandwell Cl NG10.....193 A6
Sandwich Cl ❺ NG17...114 E7
Sandwood Cl DE55.....99 A3
Sandycliffe Cl NG19.....88 F1
Sandyford Cl NG6.....160 C3
Sandy La
  Beeston NG9.........171 D1
  Carlton NG12........175 B2
  Edwinstowe NG21.....91 B8
  Gamston DN22.......50 F4
  Hucknall NG15.......146 A7
  Mansfield NG18.......102 D7
  Market Warsop NG20 ..74 B5
  Oxton NG25..........134 C3
  Ravenshead NG15.....117 B3
  Worksop S80..........35 D4
Sandymount DN11......9 A5
Sandymount E DN11.....9 A4
Sandymount W DN11....9 A4
Sanger Cl NG11.......195 C8
Sanger Gdns NG11....195 C8
Sankey Dr NG6........160 A7
Santon Cl NG19........89 A2
Santon Rd NG19........89 A2
Sapele Cl NG4.........163 A2
Sapling Cl NG24.......140 C5
Sapphire Cl NG21......104 C1
Sapphire Dr NG17.....115 C4
Sapphire St NG18.....102 C5
Saracen Cl DN21.......24 F6
Saracen La DN10.......9 F2
Saracen's Head Yd NG24 ..139 F4
Sargent Gdns ❶ NG3...173 F6
Sartfield Rd NG19......89 B2
Saskatoon Cl NG12....175 E2
Saucemere Dr NG24...139 F6
Saucers The NG13.....178 E7
Saunby Cl NG5........162 B7
Saundby Ave NG19......87 D1
Saundby Rd DN22......23 D4
Savage's Rd NG11.....196 C8
Savages Row NG11....196 C8
Saversick La NG25....136 A8
Savile Rd NG22.......105 F6
Savile St DN22........39 E6
Saville Cl NG9........182 B8
Saville House Sch NG19...88 B3
Saville Rd
  Arnold NG5 ....161 F5
  Sutton in A NG17.....100 F6
Saville St NG21.......118 B5
Saville Way NG20......74 A4
Sawley Dr NG18.......103 B4

Sawley Jun & Inf Sch
NG10..............193 A5
Saw Pit Ind Est DE55...99 C6
Saw Pit La DE55.......99 B5
Sawyers Cl NG24......140 B8
Saxby Dr NG18........103 B4
Saxelby Gdns NG6....160 B8
Saxilby Rd
  Saxilby LN1...........57 A1
  Skellingthorpe LN6....71 F8
Saxilby Sta LN1........57 A3
Saxondale Dr
  Nottingham NG6 .....160 E5
  Radcliffe on T NG12...176 D3
Saxon Gn NG7........222 A1
Saxon Way
  Cotgrave NG12.......188 A1
  Harworth DN11 ....8 F4
Saxton Cl
  Beeston NG9.........184 B6
  Worksop S80..........35 D2
Scafell Way NG11.....195 D7
Scalby Cl NG16.......143 D2
Scalford Dr NG8......172 C4
Scampton Rd S81.......35 D8
Scampton Way DN21....24 F7
Scarborough Rd NG22...105 F6
Scarborough St NG3 ..223 F3
Scarbrough Cl DN11 ...8 A7
Scarcliffe Ct NG17....100 F3
Scarcliffe La NG20......72 C7
Scarcliffe St NG18....102 D6
Scarcliffe Terr NG20 ...59 A2
Scarfell Cl NG2.......186 C5
Scarf Wlk NG2........185 B7
Scargill Ave NG16.....144 B1
Scargill Cl NG16......144 B1
Scargill Wlk NG16.....143 F3
Scarle La LN6..........84 C3
Scarrington Ct ❶ NG18 ..103 A2
Scarrington Rd NG2....173 F1
Sceptre St NG5........161 C2
School Ave NG15......145 D4
School Cl
  Newton DE55.........99 B3
  Nottingham NG2 .....173 D1
School Gn NG12.......205 E1
School Hill NG15......130 B8
School House La DN10...13 F6
School La
  Beckingham LN5 .....142 D8
  Beeston NG9.........183 C4
  Bingham NG13.......177 E5
  Caunton NG23.......109 B4
  Claypole NG23.......156 E7
  Colston Bassett NG12 ..200 D7
  Cuckney NG20........60 A3
  Eakring NG22.........92 E1
  East Stoke NG23.....153 C8
  Farndon NG24.......139 A4
  Halam NG22.........121 A3
  Harby LE14..........202 A3
  Kirklington NG22.....120 F7
  Kneesall NG22........93 F5
  Long Clawson LE14 ..211 C3
  Mansfield Woodhouse NG19 ..88 C3
  North Scarle LN6......83 D2
  Norwell NG23........110 A8
  Ollerton NG22.........77 B3
  Rempstone LE12.....215 D5
  South Normanton DE55...113 B4
  Whatton NG13.......179 B3
School Rd
  Langold S81..........16 E3
  Selston NG16........129 A7
School St
  Kirkby in A NG17.....115 B5
  Loughborough LE11...220 B4
School View NG13.....181 A2
School Wlk
  Bawtry DN10.........10 A7
  Bestwood Village NG6..146 E4
School Woods Cl DE75 ..157 B6
Schrimshire's Rd DN22...32 A1
Science Rd NG7.......172 D1
Scofton Cl S81..........35 C8
Scotholme Ave ❼ NG7 ..172 F8
Scotholme Prim Sch
NG7...............172 F8
Scot La DN10..........10 A7
Scotland Bank NG12 ..187 F3
Scotland Rd NG5......160 F3
Scotswood Rd NG19.....88 B6
Scott Ave NG9.........184 A5
Scott Cl
  Claypole NG23.......156 D7
  Nottingham NG6 .....159 F5
  Worksop S81..........36 C4
Scotton Sq DN22.......29 D1
Scott St DN21..........15 C1
Scotts Way NG17......115 B1
Scratta La S80.........34 C2
Scrimshire La NG12....187 E3
Script Dr NG6........160 E4
Scrivelsby Gdns NG9...183 D1
Scrooby Rd
  Bircotes DN11 ....9 C4
  Harworth DN11 ....8 F3
Seaburn Rd NG9......182 E2
Seaford Ave NG8.......172 B5
Seaford Way DE7......157 F5
Seaforth Sq NG19.....101 D5
Seagrave Ave NG7.....115 B1
Seagrave Prim Sch NG8 ..159 D2
Seagrave Rd NG8......159 D1
Seamer Rd NG16......158 F7
Searby Rd NG17.......101 C1
Searwood Ave NG17 ..114 E7

Seatallen Cl NG2.........186 C6
Seathwaite Cl NG2........186 D4
Seatoller Cl NG2..........186 C5
Seaton Cres NG8..........160 A1
Second Ave
  Beeston NG9 ....184 C6
  Carlton, Gedling NG4...162 F1
  Carlton, Thorneywood
  NG4.....................174 C8
  Clipstone NG21 ....90 A3
  Edwinstowe NG21 ....76 A2
  Mansfield NG21..........103 F2
  Mansfield Woodhouse NG19 89 A1
  Nottingham NG6 ....160 B7
Sedgebrook Cl NG6.......160 C3
Sedgebrook St NG19......88 E3
Sedgeley Rd NG12.........186 D1
Sedgewood Gr NG11......184 E3
Sedgley Ave NG2..........173 F5
Sedgmere DN22............39 C4
Sedgwick St
  Langley Mill NG16.......143 B3
  Westwood NG16..........128 B3
Sedley Ave NG16..........159 C6
Seely Ave NG14...........148 E8
Seely Jun Sch NG5........161 C3
Seely Rd NG7.............222 C3
Sefton Ave NG9...........182 E8
Sefton Dr NG3............161 D2
Selassie Ct NG8..........159 D2
Selbourne Ct 4 LE11.....220 C4
Selbourne St LE11........220 C4
Selby Cl NG9.............182 E3
Selby La NG12............197 F2
Selby Rd
  Styrrup DN11............8 E2
  West Bridgford NG2.....185 F5
Selhurst Ct NG7...........172 F7
Selhurst St 5 NG7.......172 F7
Selkirk Way 13 NG5......161 B1
Sellars Ave NG11.........196 C6
Seller's Wood Dr NG6....160 A7
Seller's Wood Dr W NG6. 159 F8
Sellers Wood Nature Reserve
  NG6....................159 E7
Selly Church Prim Sch
  NG5....................132 E2
Selsey Ct DN22............29 E1
Selside Ct NG9...........183 A4
Selston Bagthorpe Prim Sch
  NG16...................129 A4
Selston CE Inf Sch NG16 128 E6
Selston Dr NG8...........172 C3
Selston L Ctr NG16.......128 E7
Selston Rd NG16..........128 B5
Selwyn Cl NG6...........160 E5
Selwyn St NG18..........102 E5
Sennen Ct DN22...........29 E1
Serif Cl NG5.............161 B1
Serlby Rd NG16...........144 A3
Serlby Rise NG3..........173 F6
Serpentine Cl NG12.......176 D2
Seven Hills NG24.........125 A3
Seven Oaks Cres NG9 ....171 C1
Seven Oaks Rd DE7.......170 A1
Seventh Ave
  Beeston NG9............184 C5
  Clipstone NG21 ....89 E2
  Mansfield NG19..........103 A8
Severals NG9.............182 F7
Severn St NG6............160 B7
Seward St 2 LE11........220 A3
Seymour Rd
  Eastwood NG16..........143 F1
  Hucknall NG15...........145 E6
  West Bridgford NG2.....186 B8
Seymour St NG3..........173 E5
SGCS Bsns Pk NG11......184 A5
Shackleton Cl NG8........159 D2
Shacklock Cl NG5.........147 A2
Shadwell Gr NG12.........175 E3
Shady La NG9.............183 D2
Shaftesbury Ave
  Burton Joyce NG14......164 A5
  Long Eaton NG10........193 B4
  Mansfield NG19...........87 E2
  Radcliffe on T NG12.....176 E3
  Sandiacre NG10.........182 A5
Shaftesbury St 4 NG7...161 A1
Shaftesbury Way NG23....98 A1
Shakespeare Ave NG19....88 B4
Shakespeare Cl NG4 .....174 E5
Shakespeare Rd NG16.....158 C5
Shakespeare St
  Gainsborough DN21.......24 D6
  Long Eaton NG10........182 D1
  Loughborough LE11......220 B4
  New Balderton NG24.....140 B6
  Nottingham NG1 ....223 E3
  Worksop S81..............36 B4
Shakespeare Villas NG1 . 223 E3
Shaldon Cl NG5...........146 F1
Shale La NG14............152 A8
Shandwick Cl NG5.........148 B1
Shanklin Dr NG9..........182 D7
Shanwell Cl NG8..........159 D2
Shardlow Way NG18.......103 B4
Sharnford Way NG9.......171 B3
Sharp Cl NG10............193 C6
Sharpes Wy NG5..........147 B5
Sharphill Rd NG12........186 B4
Sharpley Dr LE12.........205 F3
Sharrard Cl NG24.........129 A2
Sharrat Ct 12 NG18.......103 A2
Shaw Cres NG17..........145 E4
Shaw Croft NG17.........100 F5
Shaw Rd DN10............12 F4
Shaw St E DE7...........170 A6

Shaw St W DE7 ....170 A6
Shaw St
  Mansfield NG18..........102 E7
  Ruddington NG11........196 C6
  Worksop S80.............35 E3
Sheaf Pl S81..............35 E7
Shearing Cl NG4..........163 A1
Shearing Hill NG4.........163 A1
Sheepbridge La NG18.....101 F5
Sheepfold La NG11........196 C6
Sheepwalk La NG15.......116 F2
Sheepwash La
  Sutton in A NG17.......101 B2
  Tickhill DN11............8 E8
Sheet Stores Ind Est
  NG10...................193 D5
Sheffield Rd S81..........18 A3
Shelby Cl NG7............222 A2
Sheldon Cl NG10..........182 B3
Sheldrake Rd NG24.......140 D8
Shelford Ave NG17........114 D6
Shelford Cl
  Beeston NG9............183 D4
  Radcliffe on T NG12.....176 A4
Shelford Cres NG14.......164 A5
Shelford Dr NG13.........177 D4
Shelford Hill
  Mansfield NG19..........101 E6
  Radcliffe on T NG12.....176 C7
Shelford Rd
  Carlton NG4............162 D3
  Radcliffe on T NG12.....176 A5
Shelford Rise NG3........174 A5
Shellburne Cl NG5........160 E8
Shelley Ave
  Mansfield Woodhouse
  NG19...................88 B4
  Nottingham NG11.......184 E3
Shelley Cl
  Balderton NG24.........140 D3
  Hucknall NG15...........145 D6
  Nuthall NG16............159 B6
Shelley Rd NG5...........161 D7
Shelley St S80............36 A3
Shelthorpe La LE11.......220 B1
Shelthorpe Prim Sch
  LE11...................220 C1
Shelthorpe Rd LE11.......220 B1
Shelton Ave
  Hucknall NG15...........146 D4
  Newark-on-T NG24 .....139 E5
Shelton Cl NG19...........87 E1
Shelton Gdns NG11.......196 B7
Shelton Rd NG18..........103 A2
Shelton St NG3...........223 F4
Shenfield Gdns NG5.......146 D1
Shepard Cl NG6...........159 F6
Shepherd's Ave S81........36 A5
Shepherds Cl NG6........172 A7
Shepherd's Cl LE12.......213 C5
Shepherds Oak NG17.....100 F6
Shepherd Specl Sch
  NG8....................171 F8
Shepherds Way NG11......101 B2
Shepherds Wood Dr
  NG8....................172 C7
Shepherd Wlk DE74......203 C1
Shepshed Rd LE12........212 F1
Shepton Cl DE7...........157 D3
Shepton Cres NG8........160 B1
Sheraton Dr NG8.........171 E3
Sherborne Rd
  Nottingham NG8.........160 A1
  West Bridgford NG2.....185 F5
Sherbrook Ave NG5.......161 D6
Sherbrook Cl NG14.......148 E8
Sherbrooke Rd NG5.......161 B1
Sherbrook Rd NG5........161 D6
Sherbrook Terr NG5.......161 D6
Sheridan Cl NG24.........140 D5
Sheridan Ct NG9..........170 F1
Sheridan Wy
  Hucknall NG15...........146 A5
  Nottingham NG5.........161 A3
Sheriff's Lodge The NG1. 223 F1
Sheriffs Way NG2.........173 C2
Sheringham Cl NG5.......161 F6
Sheringham Dr NG18.....102 C5
Sherman Dr NG9..........183 C2
Sherriff's Lea NG9........182 E2
Sherrington Cl NG11......195 C8
Sherview Ave NG18.......103 A7
Sherwin Cl NG3..........223 E4
Sherwin Gr NG7..........222 A1
Sherwin Rd
  Nottingham NG7.........222 A1
  Stapleford NG9..........170 F1
Sherwin Wlk NG3.........223 E4
Sherwood Ave
  Blidworth NG21.........118 C5
  Calverton NG14.........148 D8
  Edwinstowe NG21........76 A2
  Newark-on-T NG24 .....140 A8
  5 Nottingham NG5.....161 D3
  Pinxton NG16...........113 D3
  Shirebrook NG20.........72 E4
Sherwood Cl NG18........102 E7
Sherwood Cres S81.........18 A2
Sherwood Day Hospl
  NG5....................161 B4
Sherwood Dene 8 NG17 114 E1
Sherwood Dr
  New Ollerton NG22.......77 C4
  Shirebrook NG20.........72 E3
Sherwood Energy Village
  NG22...................77 C3
Sherwood Forest Art & Craft
  Ctr NG21................76 A3

Sherwood Forest Ctry Pk
  NG22....................76 A4
Sherwood Forest Farm Pk
  NG20....................89 F7
Sherwood Forest Fun Pk
  NG22....................76 B4
Sherwood Gr
  Bingham NG13...........177 D4
  Calverton NG14.........148 F8
Sherwood Hall Gdns
  NG18...................102 F8
Sherwood Hall Rd NG18 .102 E7
Sherwood Hall Sch & Sixth
  Form NG18..............102 F7
Sherwood Heath Nature
  Reserve NG22............76 A4
Sherwood Jun Sch NG20 . 74 B3
Sherwood Lodge Dr
  NG5....................132 C2
Sherwood Pines Forest Pk
  NG21....................90 E3
Sherwood Pk NG15........129 F6
Sherwood Pl
  Annesley Woodhouse
  NG17...................115 A1
  Clipstone NG21 ....90 B4
Sherwood Rd
  Harworth DN11..........8 F5
  Rainworth NG21.........104 B1
  Retford DN22.............39 E3
  Sutton in A NG17.......100 C1
  Worksop S80.............35 F4
Sherwood Rise
  Annesley Woodhouse
  NG17...................115 A1
  Eastwood NG16.........143 F1
  Mansfield Woodhouse NG19 88 A2
  Nottingham NG7 ....173 B8
Sherwood St
  Annesley Woodhouse
  NG17...................130 A8
  Hucknall NG15..........146 C6
  Huthwaite NG17.........99 F3
  Kirkby in A NG17.......115 B5
  10 Mansfield NG18......102 B6
  Mansfield Woodhouse NG19 88 B2
  Market Warsop NG20.....74 B3
  Newton DE55.............99 B4
Sherwood Swimming Baths
  NG19....................88 B1
Sherwood Vale NG5.......161 E3
Sherwood Way NG16......129 B7
Sherwood Wlk NG15......131 A2
Shetland Cl NG19..........88 F1
Shilling Way NG10........193 A7
Shilo Way NG16...........158 B4
Shining Cliff Ct DN10......9 F8
Shipley Ct DE7...........157 D1
Shipley Ctry Pk DE75....157 A4
Shipley Rd NG8...........159 F2
Shipley Rise NG4.........174 E2
Shipstone St
  Ilkeston DE7.............170 B6
  3 Nottingham NG7......172 F8
Shipstones Yd NG6.......160 C8
Shirburn Ave NG18........102 C8
Shirebrook Bsns Pk NG20 72 F2
Shirebrook CE NG6.......160 C3
Shirebrook Sta NG20.......73 A4
Shire Cl S81..............26 A7
Shire La NG23, NG24....156 B7
Shireoaks Comm S81 .....34 F7
Shireoaks Ct 2 NG18....103 A2
Shireoaks Rd S80.........35 B5
Shireoaks Row S81........34 E7
Shireoaks Sta S81.........34 E7
Shireoak Triangle Bsns Pk
  S81....................35 A7
Shires The
  Mansfield Woodhouse
  NG19....................88 F1
  Sutton in A NG17.......100 D1
Shirland Dr NG18.........103 B4
Shirley Dr NG5...........162 B7
Shirley Rd NG3...........173 C8
Shirley St NG10...........193 A4
Shoreswood Cl 1 NG5 ..161 B8
Shortcross Ave NG3.......161 F4
Short Hill NG1...........223 F2
Short St
  Market Warsop NG20.....74 B4
  Sutton in A NG17.......101 A3
Short Wheatley La NG23 .112 B5
Shortwood Ave NG15.....145 F5
Shortwood Cl NG1.......223 F1
Shortwood La NG22.......93 C8
Shorwell Rd NG3.........174 C7
Shotton Dr NG5..........148 A8
Shoulder of Mutton Hill
  NG17...................115 B1
Shrewsbury Rd
  Bircotes DN11...........9 B4
  Nottingham NG2.........174 A4
  Worksop S80.............36 B2
Shrewsbury View DN22....29 C1
Shrimpton Ct NG11.......196 D6
Shropshire Ave NG16.....128 C4
Sibcy La NG24...........140 D3
Sibson Dr DE74...........203 B2
Sibson Wlk NG5...........147 F2
Sibthorpe St NG18........102 A5
Siddalls Dr NG17.........100 B3
Side La NG20.............106 E8
Side Ley DE74............203 C3
Side Row NG24...........140 B8
Sidings Rd NG17..........115 C7
Sidings The
  Aslockton NG13..........179 A4

Sidings The continued
  Kimberley NG16.........159 A6
  Saxilby LN1..............57 A3
Sidlaw Rise NG5..........147 B2
Sidmouth Cl NG12........197 E4
Sidney Rd NG9...........183 E7
Sidney St
  Kimberley NG16.........158 F6
  Long Eaton NG10........193 D6
Sidsaph Hill DN10.........14 A5
Siena Gdn NG19...........89 A2
Sikorski Cl NG24..........124 F1
Silbury Cl NG11...........195 D7
Silk Holme DE55..........113 B4
Silk St NG17.............100 E1
Silver Birch Cl NG6.......160 B8
Silverdale NG9............182 E5
Silverdale Ave NG19.......88 B4
Silverdale Cl DN22........29 C1
Silverdale Rd NG7........160 F2
Silver Hill Cl NG8.........159 D2
Silverhill Cotts NG17.....100 A8
Silverhill La NG17..........99 F8
Silverhow Cl NG2.........186 C6
Silver St
  Gainsborough DN21......24 C8
  Grassthorpe NG23.......81 F4
  North Clifton NG23......68 E5
  Retford DN22.............39 D5
Silverwood Ave NG15.....117 A1
Silverwood Rd
  Beeston NG9............183 D6
  Bottesford NG13........181 A2
Silvey Ave NG25..........121 D2
Sime St S80...............35 E4
Simkin Ave NG3..........162 A1
Simon Cl DN22............42 B1
Simone Gdns NG7.........184 E1
Simons Ct NG9...........171 D1
Simpson Cl NG24.........140 E3
Simpson Rd NG19.........101 D7
Singleton Ave NG18.......102 E8
Sir Edmund Hillary Prim Sch
  S81....................36 A4
Sir John Sherbrooke Jun Sch
  NG14...................148 E8
Siskin Cl S81.............35 C7
Sisley Ave NG9...........182 E6
Sitwell Cl NG9............36 B4
Sitwell Rd S81............36 C4
Six Hills La LE14.........219 A2
Sixth Ave
  Beeston NG9............184 D6
  Clipstone NG21 ....89 E3
  Edwinstowe NG21........76 A1
  Mansfield NG19..........103 A8
Skeavington's La DE7 ....157 E5
Skegby La NG17, NG19...101 C6
Skegby Mount NG19......101 E5
Skegby Rd
  Annesley Woodhouse
  NG17...................129 F8
  Huthwaite NG17.........100 A3
  Normanton on T NG23....81 C7
  Sutton in A NG17.......101 A4
Skelwith Cl NG2..........186 C5
Skerry Hill NG18..........102 E7
Skerry La NG13...........181 F1
Sketchley Ct 2 NG6.....160 A7
Sketchley St NG3.........173 F6
Skiddaw Cl NG2..........186 D5
Skipton Cir NG3..........174 A5
Skipton Cl DE7...........157 D3
Skirbeck Dr LN1..........57 A3
Skithorne Rise NG14.....164 D8
Skylark Cl NG13..........177 F3
Skylark Dr NG6...........160 D4
Skylarks Nature Reserve
  NG12...................175 A3
Slack's La NG13..........152 B2
Slack Wlk S80............35 E1
Slade Cl DE55............113 B4
Slade Rd NG9............183 B5
Slaidburn Ave NG11......185 A5
Slake La NG24...........124 E6
Slant La NG19............88 B4
Slater St NG17...........100 F4
Slaughter House La
  NG24...................124 F1
Sleaford Rd
  Beckingham LN5........142 D8
  Coddington NG24.......126 D2
  Newark-on-T NG24.....125 A1
Sleights La NG16.........113 C2
Sloan Dr NG9............171 B3
Sloane Ct NG11..........185 C3
Slowthorne Gdns 2
  NG5....................161 D8
Smalley Cl NG16.........129 A1
Small Farm Ctr NG13....202 E7
Small Gate NG19..........88 E6
Small's Croft NG14.......149 C6
Smeath La DN22...........30 C4
Smeath Rd
  Retford DN22............30 A3
  Selston NG16...........129 A2
Smedley Ave DE7.........170 A7
Smedley Cl NG8..........160 B2
Smedley's Ave NG10......182 B5
Smeeton St DE75.........143 B1
Smite Cl NG13...........179 A4
Smite La NG13...........179 E7
Smith Dr NG16...........143 A3
Smithfield Ave NG9.......170 A7
Smiths Cl NG12...........189 A4
Smithson Cl NG24........140 C4
Smithson Dr NG8.........171 B4
Smith Sq DN11...........8 F4

Smith St
  Mansfield NG18..........102 E6
  Newark-on-T NG24 .....140 A8
Smithurst Rd NG16.......158 B7
Smithy Cl NG11...........184 D2
Smithy Cres NG5.........161 F8
Smithy La LE12..........212 A2
Smithy Row NG1.........223 E2
Smithy View NG14.......148 E2
Snaefell Ave NG19.........89 A2
Snape La DN11...........9 A2
Snape Nook Ct NG6......159 F7
Snape Wood Prim Sch
  NG6....................160 A7
Snape Wood Rd NG6.....159 F7
Snead Ct NG5............147 A1
Sneinton Bvd NG2........174 A4
Sneinton CE Prim Sch
  NG2....................173 F5
Sneinton Dale NG2.......174 A5
Sneinton Hermitage
  NG2....................173 E3
Sneinton Hollows NG2 ...173 F4
Sneinton Rd NG2.........173 E4
Snell Cl NG23.............81 E1
Snipe Pk Rd DN11.........9 B4
Snowdon Cl 2 NG5......147 B1
Snowdon Rd NG23........112 A8
Soarbank Cl NG16........158 E7
Soar La
  Normanton on S LE12...213 D3
  Sutton Bonington LE12..212 F8
Sobers Gdns NG5.........162 B6
Softwood Cl NG6..........159 F7
Soloman Pk NG16.........158 B2
Soloman Rd NG16........158 B2
Solway Cl NG9............183 E5
Somerby Ct NG9..........171 B3
Somerby Rd DN21.........15 F1
Somerleyton Dr DE7......170 A4
Somersall St NG19........101 E8
Somersby Ct NG18........103 B5
Somersby Rd NG5.........162 A5
Somerset Cl NG10........194 A8
Somerton Ave NG11......185 A4
Somerton Rd S81..........35 C8
Songthrush Ave NG6.....160 D4
Sookholme Cl NG20.......72 F3
Sookholme La NG20.......73 E3
Sookholme Rd
  Market Warsop NG20.....73 E1
  Shirebrook NG20.........72 F3
Sophie Rd NG7...........222 B4
Sorrel Dr NG13...........177 C4
Soss La DN10.............7 B2
Sotheby Ave NG17.......101 C1
Soudan Dr NG2...........173 B1
Sough Rd DE55...........113 B7
Southampton St NG3.....173 E6
South Ave
  Bawtry DN10............10 A8
  Radcliffe on T NG12.....176 B3
  Rainworth NG21........104 A1
  Shirebrook NG20.........72 F3
  Worksop S80.............36 B1
Southbreck Rise S80.......36 B1
Southchurch Dr NG7......184 F2
Southcliffe Rd NG4.......174 D7
South Cres
  Bottesford NG13........181 A1
  Clipstone NG21 ....90 A3
South Croft NG22.........51 F2
Southdale Dr NG4.........174 D7
Southdale Rd NG4........174 D7
Southdene S81.............36 A6
South Devon Ave NG3....162 B2
South Dr NG22............105 F7
South End NG23...........111 F7
Southend Ave NG24.......139 F7
Southern Wood S80........46 E8
Southey St NG7..........222 C4
Southfall Cl DN22..........19 B5
Southfield NG24..........140 E3
Southfield Dr DE55........113 C5
Southfield Ind Est S80 ....45 A4
Southfield La S80..........45 A4
Southfield Rd NG18.......172 D6
Southfields NG10..........193 B7
Southfields Ave NG16.....113 D4
Southfields Rise DN22.....42 C8
Southgate DN22...........39 E3
Southgate Rd NG20.......74 C5
Southglade Food Pk
  NG5....................160 E6
Southglade Jun & Inf Sch
  NG5....................161 A7
Southglade L Ctr NG5....160 F7
Southglade Rd NG5.......160 F6
Southgore La DN22........42 D8
Southgreen Cl NG18......102 E2
Southgreen Hill NG18.....102 E2
South La NG23............81 E5
Southlands Ave DN21......15 B4
Southlands Dr DN21......15 B4
Southlands Gdns DN21....15 B4
Southlea Rd NG4.........174 D7
Southmoor La LN1.........69 B7
Southmoor Rd S80........35 F2
South Moor Rd DN10......13 F6
South Nottingham Coll
  NG11...................185 A1
Southolme DN21..........24 D8

South Par
Bawtry DN10 . . . . **10** A6
Gainsborough DN21 . . . **24** F7
Nottingham NG1 . . . . **223** E2
Saxilby LN1 . . . . **57** A4
Worksop S81 . . . . **36** A4
Southpark Ave NG18 . . . **102** F2
Southport Terr 4 NG7 . **172** E7
South Rd
Beeston NG9 . . . . **184** B4
Nottingham, Dunkirk NG7 . **172** D2
Nottingham, The Park NG7 **222** C1
West Bridgford NG2 . . . . **185** E6
South Ridge Dr NG18 . . **102** D3
South Scarle La LN6 . . . . **83** D1
South Scarle Rd NG23 . . **98** B2
South Sherwood St NG1 . **223** E3
Southside NG5 . . . . **162** C7
South Snape Cl NG6 . . . **159** F7
South St
Bole DN22 . . . . **23** E2
Eastwood, Bailey Grove
NG16 . . . . **143** E2
Eastwood, Giltbrook NG16 **158** C8
Hucknall NG15 . . . . **146** A7
Long Eaton NG10 . . . . . . **193** E7
Loughborough LE11 . . . . **220** B3
Morton DN21 . . . . **15** B4
Normanton on T NG23 . . **81** E6
Retford DN22 . . . . **39** F6
South Normanton DE55 . **113** B6
South View
Austerfield DN10 . . . . **3** C1
Whitwell S80 . . . . **45** A5
Worksop S81 . . . . **35** F5
South View Dr DN22 . . . . **30** D3
Southview Gdns NG15 . . **117** A2
South View Rd NG4 . . . . **162** D1
Southwark Prim Sch
NG6 . . . . **160** E3
Southwark St NG6 . . . . . **160** E3
Southwell Cl
East Leake LE12 . . . . **205** E1
Kirkby in A NG17 . . . . . . **115** A6
Worksop S80 . . . . **36** A2
Southwell La NG17 . . . . . **114** F6
Southwell La Ind Est
NG17 . . . . **115** A7
Southwell L Ctr NG25 . . **136** D7
Southwell Minster NG25. **136** E8
Southwell Rd
Farnsfield NG22 . . . . **120** A5
Kirklington NG22 . . . . . . **120** F7
Lowdham NG14 . . . . **150** F2
Nottingham NG1 . . . . **223** F2
Oxton NG25 . . . . **134** D4
Thurgarton NG14 . . . . . . **151** D8
Southwell Rd E
Mansfield NG21 . . . . **103** E2
Rainworth NG21 . . . . **118** B8
Southwell Rd W NG18 . . **102** E5
Southwell Rise NG16 . . . **158** B7
South Wilford Endowed Prim
Sch NG11 . . . . **185** B7
Southwold Dr NG8 . . . . . **172** C5
Southwold Prim Sch
NG8 . . . . **172** D5
South Wolds Com Sch
NG12 . . . . **197** E3
Southwood Ave NG17 . . **100** D4
South Yorkshire Aviation
Mus S81 . . . . **16** B7
Sovereign Gr NG10 . . . . **193** B7
Sowter Ave NG17 . . . . . . **100** E4
Spa Cl NG17 . . . . **114** F8
Spafford Cl DN21 . . . . . . **44** D8
Spa La NG13 . . . . **180** B7
Spalding Rd NG3 . . . . . . **173** F5
Spalford La LN6 . . . . **83** D4
Spalford Rd LN6 . . . . **83** E5
Spalford Warren Nature
Reserve LN6. . . . . **83** A5
Spang La NG17 . . . . **99** F4
Spaniel Row NG1 . . . . . . **223** E2
Spa Ponds Nature Reserve
NG19. . . . . **89** C4
Spa Rd DN22 . . . . **39** F6
Sparken Cl S80 . . . . **46** E8
Sparken Dale S80. . . . . . **46** E8
Sparrow Cl DE7. . . . . **170** A4
Sparrow Hill 6 LE11 . . . **220** B4
Sparrow La NG23 . . . . . . **68** B1
Spean Ct 4 NG8 . . . . . . **172** A5
Spean Dr NG8 . . . . **172** B7
Speeds Pingle 1 LE11 . . **220** A4
Speedwell La NG16 . . . . **158** E6
Speedwell Pl S80 . . . . . . **35** E4
Spencer Ave
Arnold NG3 . . . . **162** C5
Sandiacre NG10 . . . . **182** B6
Spencer Cl NG11 . . . . . . **196** B7
Spencer Cres NG9 . . . . . **182** F8
Spencer Dr NG16 . . . . . . **159** C6
Spencer St NG18 . . . . . . **102** A6
Sperry Cl NG16 . . . . **128** F6
Spey Cl NG15 . . . . **145** D3
Spicer Cl NG3 . . . . **183** C2
Spicers Ct DN22 . . . . **39** F6
Spindle Gdns NG6 . . . . . **160** A7
Spindle View NG14. . . . . **165** A5
Spinney Cl
Cotgrave NG12 . . . . **187** F2
Kirkby in A NG17 . . . . . . **114** E6
Mansfield Woodhouse NG19 **88** E6
Newark-on-T NG24 . . . . . **139** E6

Spinney Cl *continued*
West Bridgford NG2 . . . . . **186** C4
Spinney Cres NG9. . . . . . **182** F3
Spinney Dr NG10. . . . . . . **182** C2
Spinneymead DN22 . . . . **19** B5
Spinney Rd
Bingham NG13. . . . . **177** D4
Keyworth NG12 . . . . **197** E3
Long Eaton NG10. . . . . . . **182** C2
Spinney Rise NG9. . . . . . **182** E3
Spinney The
Arnold NG5 . . . . **161** A4
Bestwood Village NG6. . . **146** E5
Bulcote NG14. . . . . **164** B5
Elston NG23. . . . . **153** D5
Farnsfield NG22. . . . . **119** E6
Mansfield NG18. . . . . **116** D7
Shirebrook NG20. . . . . . . **72** D3
Winthorpe NG24 . . . . **125** C5
Spinney Way NG11. . . . . **185** A4
Spinningdale NG5 . . . . . . **162** B8
Spire Cl NG17. . . . . **129** E8
Spire View NG13. . . . . . . **181** B3
Spitalfields S81. . . . . **18** B2
Spital Hill
Gainsborough DN21 . . . . . **15** D1
Retford DN22. . . . . **39** F7
Spital Rd S81. . . . . **18** B1
Spital Terr DN21 . . . . **15** D1
Spondon St NG5. . . . . . . **161** C2
Sporton Cl DE55 . . . . **113** A7
Sporton La DE55 . . . . **113** B7
Spotlight Gall (Town Hall)
NG24. . . . . **139** F8
Spray Cl NG4 . . . . **174** E5
Spridgeon Cl NG10. . . . . . **182** B2
Spright Cl NG24. . . . . **125** C6
Spring Cl NG16 . . . . **159** A7
Spring Ct NG22 . . . . **119** E7
Spring Dale Gdns NG9 . . **170** D3
Springdale La NG13 . . . . **165** E2
Spring Dr NG24 . . . . **140** F2
Springfield DE74. . . . . . . **203** B1
Springfield Ave
Eastwood NG16 . . . . **144** A2
Long Eaton NG10 . . . . . . **193** F8
Sandiacre NG10 . . . . **182** B3
Shirebrook NG20. . . . . . . **72** E5
Springfield Cl
Cropwell Bishop NG12. . . **189** B4
Gainsborough DN21 . . . . **24** E8
Mansfield NG18. . . . . **103** A5
Springfield Ct NG9. . . . . . **170** E1
Springfield Dr NG6. . . . . . **159** F6
Springfield Gdn DE7. . . . **157** F2
Springfield Prim Sch
NG6. . . . . **146** C1
Springfield Rd
Arnold NG5 . . . . **147** E1
Hucknall NG15. . . . . **145** D6
Retford DN22. . . . . **39** F8
Southwell NG25. . . . . **121** D2
Springfield Ret Pk NG6 . . **160** C8
Springfields NG2 . . . . **185** D6
Springfield St NG7. . . . . . **160** F1
Springfield Way NG17. . . **115** D6
Spring Gdns
Bawtry DN10 . . . . **10** A8
Gainsborough DN21 . . . . **24** D8
Newark-on-T NG24 . . . . . **139** E7
Spring Gdn Terr DE7. . . . **157** F2
Spring Gn NG11. . . . . **195** E7
Springhead Ct NG6 . . . . . **160** A6
Spring Hill
Kimberley NG16. . . . . **158** F5
Mansfield Woodhouse NG19 **88** B3
Southwell NG25. . . . . **136** F7
Whitwell S80 . . . . **45** A6
Springhill Cl NG6 . . . . . . **146** B1
Spring La
Arnold NG3 . . . . **162** E6
Balderton NG24 . . . . **140** F2
Elmton NG20. . . . . **58** A7
Farnsfield NG22. . . . . **119** E7
Flintham NG13. . . . . **166** F7
Lambley NG4 . . . . **163** B6
Long Whatton LE12 . . . . . **212** C2
Shireoaks S80. . . . . **34** F5
Sturton le S DN22 . . . . . . **32** D4
Springland Farm Cotts
NG16 . . . . **159** D6
Spring Mdw NG12. . . . . . **188** A3
Spring Moor NG2 . . . . . . **174** D5
Spring Rd
Nottingham NG6 . . . . **160** C7
Sutton in A NG17 . . . . . . **100** E2
Springs Rd DN10. . . . . . . **4** D6
Spring St
Hucknall NG15. . . . . **146** A7
Whitwell S80 . . . . **45** A6
Spring Street Prim Sch
NG15. . . . . **146** A7
Spring Terr NG16 . . . . . . **159** D5
Spring The NG10. . . . . . . **193** D5
Springthorpe Rd DN21 . . **24** F8
Springwell St NG17 . . . . **99** F2
Spring Wlk S80 . . . . **35** E1
Springwood Gdns NG5 . . **161** F3
Springwood View Cl
NG17. . . . . **100** C3
Spruce Ave NG16 . . . . . . **128** D6
Spruce Ct S80 . . . . **35** B2
Spruce Gdns NG6 . . . . . . **160** A7
Spruce Gr
Hucknall NG15. . . . . **146** B4
Kirkby in A NG17 . . . . . . **115** C6
Sprydon Wlk NG11. . . . . . **195** F7
Spur Cres S80 . . . . **47** B8

Squares Dr NG6 . . . . **147** B5
Square The
Beeston NG9 . . . . **183** F6
Bestwood Village NG6. . . **146** E4
Bottesford NG13 . . . . **181** A3
Costock LE12 . . . . **206** C1
Gotham NG11 . . . . **195** B1
Keyworth NG12 . . . . **197** E2
Nottingham NG8 . . . . **171** E4
Rainworth NG21 . . . . **104** B1
Retford DN22. . . . . **39** E7
Squires Ave NG6 . . . . **160** B8
Squires Cl NG12 . . . . **189** B4
Squires Croft NG21 . . . . . **90** C5
Squires La NG17 . . . . **90** B6
Squires Way NG2 . . . . . . **185** D6
Squirrel Way 3 LE11. . . . **220** A2
Stable Cl
East Bridgford NG13 . . . . **165** D3
Worksop S81 . . . . **36** A7
Stacey Ave NG5 . . . . **160** F8
Stacey Rd NG19 . . . . **87** D2
Stadium Cl S81 . . . . **35** C6
Stadium Ind Pk NG10 . . . **193** F8
Stafford Ave
New Balderton NG24. . . . **140** C4
Nottingham NG6 . . . . **160** B6
Stafford Ct NG6 . . . . **159** F5
Staffords Acre DE74. . . . **203** C2
Stafford St
Long Eaton NG10 . . . . . . **193** F8
Mansfield NG19 . . . . **101** F8
Stagsden Cres NG8 . . . . **171** C5
Staindale Dr NG8 . . . . . . **160** D1
Stainforth St NG19 . . . . . **88** C2
Stainmore Gr NG13 . . . . **177** C4
Stainsborough Rd NG15 . **145** C6
Stainsby Mill S44 . . . . . . **85** D7
Stainsby Dr NG18 . . . . . . **103** A7
Stainsby Gr NG17 . . . . . . **99** F2
Stamford Cl NG10. . . . . . **193** E4
Stamford Ct 4 NG5. . . . . **161** B8
Stamford Rd NG2 . . . . . . **186** A6
Stamford St
Awsworth NG16. . . . . **158** C4
Eastwood NG16 . . . . **144** C1
2 Ilkeston DE7. . . . . **157** E1
Stamper Cres NG17 . . . . **100** F6
Stanage Ct NG18. . . . . . . **103** B5
Stancliffe Ave NG6 . . . . . **160** C7
Standard Hill NG1. . . . . . **223** D2
Standhill Ave NG4 . . . . . . **174** B8
Standhill Inf Sch NG4 . . . **174** B7
Standhill Rd NG4 . . . . . . **174** B8
Stanesby Rise NG7. . . . . **184** E1
Stanford Gdns NG12 . . . . **175** F4
Stanford Hill 1 LE11. . . . **220** B6
Stanford La LE12. . . . . . . **220** D7
Stanford Rd LE12 . . . . . . **213** F1
Stanford St NG1 . . . . **223** E2
Stanhome Dr NG2. . . . . . **185** D4
Stanhome Sq NG2 . . . . . **185** D4
Stanhope Ave
Newark-on-T NG24 . . . . . **125** C3
Nottingham NG5 . . . . **161** B1
Stanhope Cl NG22. . . . . . **64** A2
Stanhope Cres
Arnold NG5 . . . . **161** E8
Stoke Bardolph NG14 . . . **175** F7
Stanhope Prim Sch NG4 **162** D3
Stanhope Rd
Arnold NG5 . . . . **161** E8
Carlton NG4 . . . . **162** D3
Stanhope St
Ilkeston DE7 . . . . **170** A6
Long Eaton NG10. . . . . . . **193** D8
Nottingham NG1 . . . . **223** F2
Stanhope Way NG13. . . . **177** C4
Staniland Cl 3 NG9. . . . . **183** C2
Stanley Ave 5 NG7 . . . . . **173** A8
Stanley Cl NG15. . . . . **117** A3
Stanley Dr NG9 . . . . **171** A1
Stanley La NG17 . . . . **85** D2
Stanley Pl NG1. . . . . **223** D3
Stanley Rd
Mansfield NG18. . . . . **102** B4
Mansfield Woodhouse NG19 **89** B1
Nottingham, Hyson Green
NG7. . . . . **173** A8
Nottingham, Portchester
NG3. . . . . **162** A1
West Bridgford NG2 . . . . **185** F6
Stanley St
Gainsborough DN21 . . . . **24** D6
Long Eaton NG10 . . . . . . **193** E7
Loughborough LE11. . . . . **220** B2
Newark-on-T NG24 . . . . . **125** B1
Retford DN22. . . . . **40** A4
Worksop S81 . . . . **35** E5
Stanley Terr NG24 . . . . . . **140** B8
Stanmore Cl NG8 . . . . . . **159** E3
Stanmore Gdns NG5 . . . . **161** F6
Stannier Wy NG16 . . . . . **159** A7
Stansfield St NG7 . . . . . . **222** A3
Stanstead Ave
Nottingham NG5 . . . . **146** D1
Tollerton NG12 . . . . **186** D1
Stanstead Prim Sch NG5 **160** E8
Stanthorne Cl NG11. . . . . **185** A4
Stanton Cres NG17 . . . . . **100** D3
Stanton Gate DE7. . . . . . **170** C1
Stanton La NG12 . . . . **198** B2
Stanton Pl
Mansfield NG18. . . . . **102** A7
New Houghton NG19 . . . . **86** F7
Stanton Rd NG10. . . . . . . **182** A7
Stanton St NG19 . . . . **86** F7
Stanton Vale Sch NG10 . **193** C7

Stanway Cl NG3. . . . . **174** C6
Stanwick Cl NG8 . . . . **171** E8
Stapleford La
Beeston NG9 . . . . **182** F3
Coddington NG24. . . . . . . **126** D3
Stapleford Rd NG9 . . . . . **170** D3
Staplehurst Dr NG5 . . . . . **161** A4
Staple La NG24 . . . . **140** C2
Staples St NG3. . . . . **161** E2
Stapleton Rd DE7. . . . . . . **157** E4
Starch Cl LE12. . . . . **205** E1
Starch La NG10 . . . . **182** C7
Starr Ave NG17 . . . . **100** F3
Starth Wood Rd NG15. . . **145** D4
Statham Ct S81 . . . . **36** B5
Stathern La LE14. . . . . . . **202** B2
Stathern Rd LE14 . . . . . . **202** C3
Stathern Wlk NG5. . . . . . **161** B7
Station Ave
Carlton NG4. . . . . **163** A1
Ranskill DN22 . . . . **19** B5
Station Cl NG23. . . . . **112** B7
Station Ct 3 DE7. . . . . . . **157** E1
Station Hill NG19 . . . . . . **88** B3
Station La
Edwinstowe NG21 . . . . . . **76** B1
Farnsfield NG22. . . . . **119** E7
Ironville NG16. . . . . **128** A3
Old Dalby LE14 . . . . **218** F4
Station Rd
Awsworth NG16. . . . . **158** C5
Barnby Moor DN22 . . . . . **28** E5
Bawtry DN10 . . . . **10** A7
Beckingham DN10 . . . . . . **23** C8
Beeston NG9 . . . . **184** A5
Bleasby NG14 . . . . **151** F8
Bottesford NG13 . . . . **181** C3
Burton Joyce NG14 . . . . . **163** F3
Carlton NG4. . . . . **174** F7
Clipstone NG21 . . . . **89** E2
Collingham NG23. . . . . . . **112** A8
East Leake LE12 . . . . **205** D1
Edingley NG22 . . . . **120** E5
Fiskerton NG25, NG23. . . **137** E4
Harby NG23 . . . . **70** E3
Heanor NG16. . . . . **143** A2
Hucknall NG15. . . . . **146** B7
Ilkeston DE7 . . . . **157** F1
Kegworth DE74 . . . . **203** F2
Keyworth NG12 . . . . **197** E6
Kimberley NG16. . . . . **158** F6
Kingston-on-S LE12 . . . . **204** A3
Langley Mill NG16 . . . . . . **143** B2
Long Eaton NG10. . . . . . . **193** F8
Lowdham NG14 . . . . **150** E1
Mansfield NG18. . . . . **102** B6
Misson DN10 . . . . **4** B3
Newstead NG15. . . . . **130** E6
Nottingham NG6 . . . . **160** C6
Ollerton NG22 . . . . **77** A3
Rainworth NG21 . . . . **118** A8
Ranskill DN22 . . . . **19** B4
Retford DN22. . . . . **39** E5
Rolleston NG23 . . . . **138** A6
Sandiacre NG10 . . . . **182** C5
Scrooby DN10 . . . . **10** A2
Selston NG16. . . . . **113** E1
Shirebrook NG20 . . . . **72** E6
South Leverton DN22 . . . **42** D8
Southwell NG25. . . . . **121** F1
Sturton le S DN22 . . . . . . **32** C6
Sutton in A NG17 . . . . . . **101** B1
Sutton on T NG23. . . . . . **96** E8
Thurgarton NG14. . . . . . . **151** D6
Torksey LN1. . . . . **44** B3
Upper Broughton LE14 . . **218** C8
Walkeringham DN10 . . . . **14** A5
Whitwell S80 . . . . **45** A5
Widmerpool NG12 . . . . . . **208** E6
Station St
Bingham NG13. . . . . **177** F5
Cossall DE7 . . . . **158** A2
Kirkby in A NG17 . . . . . . **115** A5
Long Eaton NG10 . . . . . . **193** E7
6 Mansfield NG18 . . . . . **102** B6
Mansfield Woodhouse NG19 **88** B3
Misterton DN10 . . . . **7** A2
Nottingham NG2 . . . . **223** F1
Sutton in A NG17. . . . . . . **100** F2
Station Terr
Hucknall NG15. . . . . **146** B7
Radcliffe on T NG12. . . . . **175** F3
Station View NG20. . . . . . **72** E3
Station Yd NG17 . . . . **100** F7
Staunton Dr NG5. . . . . . . **161** C4
Staunton Hall NG13 . . . . **169** B3
Staunton Rd NG24 . . . . . **139** F5
Staveley Ct
Farndon NG24 . . . . **139** A4
1 Loughborough LE11 . . **220** B5
Stavely Wy NG2. . . . . **186** C7
Staverton Rd NG8. . . . . . **171** E7
Staythorpe Rd
Averham NG23. . . . . **123** E1
Rolleston NG23 . . . . **138** C7
Steadfold Cl NG6 . . . . . . **160** B6
Steads Cl NG4 . . . . **174** F7
Steedman Ave NG3 . . . . **162** A4
Steeles Dr NG24 . . . . **140** E3
Steeles Way NG4 . . . . . . **163** B7
Steeple Row 3 LE11. . . . **220** B4
Steeples The NG17. . . . . **129** E8
Steetley La
Rhodesia S80. . . . . **35** A4
Whitwell S80 . . . . **34** E4
Steinbeck Rd NG4 . . . . . . **174** C7
Stella Ave NG12. . . . . **197** D8
Stella Gr NG12. . . . . **197** D8

Stella St NG18 . . . . **102** B5
Stenton Cl NG25. . . . . **121** E2
Stepnall Hts NG22 . . . . . **77** E6
Stepney Ct NG8 . . . . **159** F1
Sterling Cl S81 . . . . **35** E8
Sterling Dr NG24. . . . . . . **125** E1
Sterndale Rd NG10. . . . . **193** B6
Sternthorpe Cl NG23 . . . . **81** E1
Steven Cl NG9 . . . . **182** F4
Stevenholme Cres NG5. . **161** A6
Stevenson Cres NG17 . . . **100** E2
Stevenson Gdns NG11. . . **196** D6
Stevenson Jun Sch NG9. **182** F8
Stevenson Rd S81. . . . . . **36** B4
Stevens Rd NG10. . . . . . . **182** A5
Stewart Cl S81. . . . . **25** E6
Stewarton Cl NG5. . . . . . **148** B1
Stewart Rd S81 . . . . **25** E6
Stiles Rd NG5. . . . . **162** C6
Stillwell Gdns S81 . . . . . . **35** E7
Stinsford Cl 6 NG5 . . . . . **161** C6
Stinting La NG19. . . . . . . **88** E2
Stirling Ave
Bawtry DN10. . . . . **10** A8
Mansfield NG19 . . . . **101** E5
Stirling Cl DN21 . . . . **15** E2
Stirling Dr
Carlton in L S81. . . . . **25** E6
Newark-on-T NG24 . . . . . **125** E2
Stirling Gdns NG9. . . . . . **183** B2
Stirling Gr
Kimberley NG16. . . . . **158** E7
Nottingham NG11 . . . . . . **195** F8
Stirling Rd DN22 . . . . **39** D5
Stockdale Cl NG5 . . . . . . **147** A3
Stockgill Cl NG2 . . . . **186** C6
Stockhill Cir NG8 . . . . **160** C2
Stockhill La NG6 . . . . **160** C3
Stocking La
Askham DN22 . . . . **51** E3
East Leake LE12 . . . . **205** D4
Stocks Fold
East Markham NG22 . . . . **65** F7
Tuxford NG22. . . . . **66** F7
Stocks Rd NG16 . . . . **158** E7
Stockton St 4 NG6 . . . . . **160** B7
Stock Well NG6. . . . . **160** B6
Stockwell Gate 8 NG18. **102** B7
Stockwell La NG12 . . . . . **189** B4
Stockwell The LE12 . . . . **216** C3
Stockwith Rd DN10 . . . . . **14** B8
Stodman Mews NG24 . . . **139** F8
Stodman St NG24. . . . . . **139** E4
Stoke Ave NG24. . . . . **139** E4
Stoke Ferry La NG12 . . . . **164** A1
Stoke La
Burton Joyce NG14 . . . . . **163** F2
Stoke Bardolph NG14 . . . **175** D8
Stokes Ind Est NG18. . . . **101** E4
Stolle Cl NG5 . . . . **162** C7
Stoneacre NG5 . . . . **161** B8
Stonebridge City Farm
NG3. . . . . **173** E5
Stonebridge Ct Ind Est 9
NG3. . . . . **173** E5
Stonebridge Dr LE12 . . . **205** F2
Stonebridge La NG20. . . . **74** A4
Stonebridge Rd NG20 . . . **74** A4
Stone Bridge Rd NG3 . . . **173** E5
Stonechurch View NG15. **130** B4
Stone Cres NG19 . . . . . . **101** D7
Stone Cross La NG18. . . **102** B8
Stonehaven Cl NG5 . . . . **148** B1
Stonehill Cl DN22 . . . . . . **19** B5
Stonehills DE74. . . . . **203** C2
Stonehurst La LE12 . . . . **213** D3
Stone La DN22. . . . . **31** D8
Stoneleigh Cl NG9 . . . . . **183** C5
Stone Leigh Cl NG18 . . . **102** E5
Stoneleigh St NG7 . . . . . **222** D3
Stonemasons Mews
NG17. . . . . **115** B5
Stone Mdws NG10 . . . . . **193** F6
Stone Mill Grange NG20. **74** C6
Stonepit Cl NG3. . . . . **161** F1
Stoney Bank NG14 . . . . . **150** D2
Stoneycroft Rd NG6. . . . . **160** E5
Stoneyford Rd NG17 . . . . **100** E4
Stoney Houghton Gdns
NG6 . . . . **159** F3
Stoney La
Brinsley NG16. . . . . **143** D6
Selston NG16. . . . . **128** E7
Trowell NG9 . . . . **170** B5
Stoney St
Beeston NG9 . . . . **183** F7
Nottingham NG1 . . . . **223** F2
Sutton in A NG17. . . . . . . **101** A7
Stonish Hill NG22 . . . . . . **92** C1
Stoppard Cl DE7. . . . . **157** D2
Storcroft Rd DN22 . . . . . . **40** A5
Storey Ave NG4. . . . . **162** E2
Stormont Cl DE55. . . . . . **113** B4
Stornoway Cl NG9 . . . . . **184** B5
Storth Ave NG15. . . . . . . **146** A6
Storthfield Way DE55 . . . **113** B4
Storth La DE55. . . . . **113** B4
Stort Sq NG19 . . . . **88** D2
Story Gdns NG15. . . . . . . **146** C5
Stotfield Rd NG8. . . . . **171** B5
Stourdale Cl NG10 . . . . . **193** A6
Stow Ct NG19. . . . . **88** E3
Stowe Ave NG2 . . . . **185** D5
Stow Pk Rd DN21 . . . . . . **44** D8
Strafford St DN21 . . . . . . **24** D6
Straight Mile DN22. . . . . . **38** D6
Strand The NG9. . . . . **183** D1
Stranraer Cl NG19 . . . . . . **88** C6

Stratford Cl NG4 174 F5
Stratford Cres DN22 39 D6
Stratford Rd NG2 185 F7
Stratford St DE7 157 F4
Strathavon Rd S81 25 F6
Strathglen Cl NG16 158 E7
Strathmore Cl NG15 145 E5
Strathmore Ct DN11 9 A5
Strathmore Dr S81 25 F6
Strathmore Rd NG5 148 B1
Strawberry Bank NG17 99 E4
Strawberry Hall La NG24 125 B2
Strawberry Rd DN22 40 A6
Strawberry Way NG19 103 B8
Straw's La NG13 165 D3
Street La Rd DN22 42 E8
Strelley La NG8 171 B7
Strelley Rd NG8 159 E1
Strelley St NG6 160 B7
Striding Edge Cl NG10 182 B2
Stripe Rd DN11 8 E8
Stripes View NG14 148 F6
Strome Cl 8 NG2 173 B2
Strome Ct 1 NG2 173 C2
Stroud Ct NG13 181 B3
Stroud's Cl LE14 211 F8
Stuart Ave
Mansfield NG18 102 F8
New Ollerton NG22 77 D6
Stuart Cl NG5 162 B8
Stuart St
Mansfield NG18 102 E7
Sutton in A NG17 100 E1
Stubbing La S80 35 D3
Stubbins La NG25 136 C5
Stubbins Wood NG20 72 E6
Stubbins Wood La NG20 72 E5
Stubbin Wood Spec Sch NG20 72 E6
Stubton Rd NG23 156 F6
Studland Cl NG19 88 D6
Studland Way NG2 185 C5
Sturgate Wlk DN21 24 F7
Sturgeon Ave NG11 184 F4
Sturton CE Prim Sch DN22 32 D4
Sturton Rd
Bole DN22 23 D2
North Leverton w H DN22 32 D1
Saxilby LN1 57 A7
South Wheatley DN22 31 E7
Sturton St NG7 173 A8
Styring St NG9 183 F6
Styrrup La DN11 8 B1
Styrrup Rd DN11 8 E3
Sudbury Ave
Ilkeston DE7 170 A7
Sandiacre NG10 182 B6
Sudbury Ct NG18 103 B5
Sudbury Dr NG17 99 F2
Sudbury Mews NG16 143 E1
Suez St NG7 160 F1
Suff La NG16 113 C3
Suffolk Ave
Beeston NG9 184 C4
Bircotes DN11 9 D4
Hucknall NG15 145 C5
Suffolk Gr DN11 9 C4
Suffolk Rd DN11 9 C4
Sulby Cl NG19 89 B2
Sullivan Cl NG3 174 A6
Sumburgh Rd NG11 185 A1
Summercourt Dr NG15 116 F3
Summerfield Rd 11 NG17 114 E7
Summerfields Way DE7 157 D3
Summerfields Way S DE7 157 D2
Summergangs La DN21 24 D5
Summer Hill DN21 15 E1
Summer Leys La NG2 223 F1
Summer's Rd NG24 125 A2
Summer Way NG12 175 E4
Summerwood La NG11 195 E7
Summit Cl NG17 115 A6
Summit Dr NG20 72 E4
Sunbeam St NG13 179 B4
Sunbourne Ct NG7 222 C4
Sunbury Gdns NG5 148 A1
Sunderland Gr NG8 159 D2
Sunderland Pl DN11 8 B7
Sunderland St DN11 8 B7
Sundown Adventureland DN22 42 E3
Sundridge Pk Cl NG2 185 C5
Sunfield Ave S81 36 A4
Sunflower Cl NG20 72 D3
Sunlea Cres NG9 182 F5
Sunnindale Dr NG12 186 E1
Sunningdale DN22 39 D2
Sunningdale Cl 4 NG17 114 E7
Sunningdale Dr NG14 149 C5
Sunningdale Rd NG6 160 E6
Sunninghill Dr NG11 184 E3
Sunninghill Rise NG5 148 A1
Sunny Bank
Mansfield NG18 102 C3
Newton DE55 99 A5
Worksop S81 36 A4
Sunnydale Rd NG3 174 B6
Sunnymede S81 36 A6
Sunnyside
Farnsfield NG22 119 F5
Whitwell S80 45 A6
Worksop S81 35 F6
Sunnyside Prim Sch NG9 183 B6
Sunnyside Rd NG9 183 C6
Sunridge Ct NG3 173 C8
Sunrise Ave NG5 160 F5
Sunrise Hill Nature Reserve NG5 161 A6
Superbowl 2000 NG18 102 B7
Surbiton Sq NG8 160 B3
Surfleet Cl NG8 171 C3
Surgery La NG21 118 A4
Surgey's La NG5 148 A2
Surrey Dr NG19 101 F8
Susan Cl NG15 131 B1
Susan Dr NG6 160 D4
Sussex Way NG10 182 B5
Sutherland Cl S81 25 F8
Sutherland Dr NG2 186 A4
Sutherland House Prim Sch NG3 174 B7
Sutherland House Sec Sch NG3 161 C1
Sutherland Rd NG3 174 B7
Suthers Rd DE74 203 C2
Sutton Ave NG24 139 E5
Sutton Bonington Prim Sch LE12 213 B6
Sutton Bonington Spinney & Mdws Nature Reserve LE12 213 A7
Sutton Cl
Sutton Bonington LE12 213 C5
Sutton in A NG17 101 A6
Sutton Ct NG16 143 F2
Sutton Ctr Com Coll NG17 100 F2
Sutton Cum Lound CE Prim Sch DN22 29 A6
Sutton Gdns NG11 196 C6
Sutton La
Granby NG13 191 D6
Retford DN22 29 A1
Sutton L Ctr NG17 100 F2
Sutton Mid La NG17 114 F6
Sutton on Trent Prim Sch NG23 97 A8
Sutton Parkway Sta NG17 115 B8
Sutton Passeys Cres NG8 172 B3
Sutton Pool Complex NG17 100 E2
Sutton Rd
Arnold NG5 147 F2
Beckingham LN5 142 E6
Huthwaite NG17 99 F3
Kegworth DE74 203 C1
Kirkby in A NG17 114 E6
Mansfield NG18 101 E5
Sutton in A NG17 100 A3
Sutton Road Prim Sch NG18 101 F6
Swab's La
Cropwell Bishop NG12 188 F1
Owthorpe NG12 199 F8
Swain's Ave NG3 174 A6
Swaledale S81 36 A7
Swaledale Cl NG8 160 C1
Swales Cl DN22 39 C8
Swallow Cl
Mansfield NG18 103 B4
Nottingham NG6 160 D3
Swallow Ct DN10 7 A2
Swallow Dr
Bingham NG13 177 F3
Claypole NG23 156 D7
Swallow Gdns NG4 162 B1
Swallow Gr S81 35 D7
Swallows Dr LE14 202 F3
Swallow Wlk LE12 213 A1
Swan Ct
Sutton Bonington LE12 213 B6
Worksop S81 35 C7
Swan La NG19 88 B3
Swan Mdw NG4 174 F4
Swann Yd NG17 99 F3
Swansdowne Dr NG7 184 F2
Swanson Ave NG17 99 F3
Swans Quay DN22 39 F5
Swan St
Bawtry DN10 10 A6
Loughborough LE11 220 B4
Swanwick Ave NG20 72 F3
Sweeney Ct 3 NG5 161 A8
Sweet Leys Dr LE12 205 E3
Sweet Leys Rd 7 NG2 173 C1
Swenson Ave NG7 222 A1
Swift Ct NG16 143 F2
Swift's Cl LE12 216 C3
Swifts Vw NG17 114 F1
Swigert Cl NG6 159 F5
Swildon Wlk NG5 160 F8
Swinburne Cl NG24 140 D5
Swinburne St 3 NG3 173 F6
Swinburne Way NG5 161 D7
Swinderby Cl
Gateford S81 35 C8
Newark-on-T NG24 125 D1
Swinderby Rd
Collingham NG23 112 B8
Eagle LN6 84 D1
North Scarle LN6 83 E2
Swindon Cl NG16 158 B7
Swinecote Rd NG21 76 B4
Swiney Way NG9 183 A2
Swinfen Broun NG18 102 C3
Swingate NG16 159 A5
Swinnow Rd DN11 9 C4
Swinscoe Gdns NG5 160 F8
Swinstead Cl NG8 171 F6
Swinton Copse NG22 77 E6
Swinton Rise NG15 117 A2
Swish La NG22 105 F8
Swithland Dr NG2 185 E4
Swynford Cl LN1 55 B4
Sycamore Ave
Glapwell S44 86 B8
Kirkby in A NG17 114 E6
Sycamore Cl
Bingham NG13 178 A4
Hucknall NG15 145 E5
Newark-on-T NG24 139 D3
Pinxton NG16 113 D3
Radcliffe on T NG12 175 F2
Rainworth NG21 104 B1
Selston NG16 128 D7
Worksop S80 35 E1
Sycamore Cres
Bawtry DN10 9 F7
Sandiacre NG10 182 A7
Sycamore Ct NG9 184 A7
Sycamore Dr
Gainsborough DN21 15 E2
Ilkeston DE7 170 B7
Sycamore Gr NG18 102 F5
Sycamore Jun & Inf Sch NG3 223 F4
Sycamore La NG14 152 B7
Sycamore Millennium Ctr NG3 173 D8
Sycamore Pl 2 NG3 173 C8
Sycamore Rd
Awsworth NG16 158 C5
Carlton in L S81 25 E7
East Leake LE12 214 D8
Long Eaton NG10 193 C5
Mansfield Woodhouse NG19 88 C5
New Ollerton NG22 77 D4
Sycamore Rise NG6 160 C4
Sycamore St NG20 74 A6
Sycamores The
Eastwood NG16 143 E1
South Normanton DE55 113 A5
Sydenham Ct 6 NG7 172 E2
Syderstone Wlk NG5 161 F6
Sydney Cl NG19 88 C6
Sydney Gr NG12 175 E3
Sydney Rd NG8 172 B5
Sydney St NG24 125 A1
Sydney Terr NG24 140 A7
Syerston Rd NG18 103 A2
Syerston Wy NG24 125 D1
Syke Rd NG5 160 F8
Sykes La
Balderton NG24 140 D3
Saxilby LN1 56 E5
Saxilby LN1 56 F4
Sylvan Cres NG17 101 A5
Sylvester St NG18 101 F6
Synge Cl NG11 195 C8
Sywell Cl NG17 100 F5

T

Taft Ave NG10 182 B6
Taft Leys Rd LE12 205 F2
Talbot Ct NG12 175 E3
Talbot Dr NG9 170 D2
Talbot Rd
Bircotes DN11 9 B4
Worksop S80 36 A2
Talbot St
Mansfield NG18 102 B4
Nottingham NG1 223 D3
Pinxton NG16 113 C2
Tales of Robin Hood The NG1 223 E2
Tall Gables NG22 54 C1
Tamarix Cl NG4 163 A2
Tambling Cl NG5 162 B6
Tame Cl NG11 184 E4
Tamworth Gr NG7 184 F2
Tamworth Rd NG10 193 C5
Tanglewood LN6 84 D3
Tangmere Cres NG8 159 E1
Tanner's La LE12 213 A1
Tannery Wharf NG24 139 E8
Tanwood Rd NG9 183 B1
Tanyard NG22 79 E6
Tapton Pk 3 NG18 103 B7
Tarbert Cl NG2 173 B2
Target St NG7 222 A3
Tarn Cl NG16 143 B4
Tatham's La DE7 157 E2
Tatmarsh LE11 220 B5
Tattersall Wlk NG19 88 E4
Tattershall Dr
Beeston NG9 184 B7
Nottingham NG7 222 C2
Taunton Rd NG2 185 F6
Taupo Dr NG15 145 D5
Tavern Ave NG8 160 C2
Tavistock Ave NG3 161 C1
Tavistock Cl NG15 145 D5
Tavistock Dr NG3 161 C1
Tavistock Rd NG2 185 F6
Taylor Cl NG2 174 A4
Taylor Cres
Stapleford NG9 182 E8
Sutton in A NG17 100 F1
Taylor's Cl NG18 102 E8
Taylors Croft NG14 149 C4
Taylor St DE7 157 F1
Teague Pl S80 35 D3
Teak Cl NG3 173 D7
Teal Ave NG18 103 B4
Tealby Cl NG6 159 F7
Tealby Wlk NG19 88 E4
Teal Cl
Carlton NG4 175 B6
Shirebrook NG20 72 D3
Teal Ct S81 35 D7
Teal Wharf 4 NG2 173 A2
Teasels The NG13 177 D3
Technology Dr NG9 184 A5
Tedburn Dr NG18 103 A2
Teddy's Farm Pk LN5 142 E8
Teesbrook Dr NG8 171 B4
Teesdale Ct NG9 183 A4
Teesdale Rd
Long Eaton NG10 193 A6
Nottingham NG5 161 B2
Teignmouth Ave NG18 102 F6
Telford Dr
Eastwood NG16 144 B3
Newark-on-T NG24 125 C3
Temperance La NG23 111 F8
Templar Rd NG9 184 B6
Temple Cres NG16 159 D4
Temple Dr NG16 159 E4
Templemans Way NG25 136 F8
Templemen Cl NG11 196 B7
Templeoak Dr NG8 171 D3
Tenbury Cres NG8 160 C1
Tenby Gr S80 36 A2
Tene Cl NG5 147 F2
Tenman La NG13 166 A2
Tennis Ct Ind Est NG2 174 A3
Tennis Dr NG7 222 C2
Tennis Mews NG7 222 C2
Tennyson Ave
Carlton NG4 162 F1
Mansfield Woodhouse NG19 88 C2
Tennyson Ct NG15 145 D6
Tennyson Dr
Beeston NG9 183 D2
Worksop S81 36 C4
Tennyson Rd
Arnold NG5 161 E4
Balderton NG24 140 D4
Tennyson Sq NG16 158 C4
Tennyson St
Gainsborough DN21 15 D1
Ilkeston DE7 157 E3
Kirkby in A NG17 115 B4
10 Mansfield NG18 102 A7
Nottingham NG7 222 C4
Tenter Cl
Long Eaton NG10 193 D5
Nottingham NG5 160 F8
Sutton Forest Side NG17 101 A3
Tenter La NG18 102 A5
Tenters La NG22 92 E1
Tenzing Wlk NG24 140 E4
Terrace La NG19 86 F5
Terrace Rd NG18 102 C8
Terrace St NG7 172 F7
Terrian Cres NG2 185 F7
Terry Ave NG24 125 B3
Terton Rd NG5 160 F8
Tetford Wlk NG19 88 E4
Tetney Wlk NG8 172 A6
Tettenbury Rd NG5 160 F3
Teversal Ave
Nottingham NG7 222 B2
Pleasleyhill NG19 87 B4
Teversal Pastures Nature Reserve NG17 100 E8
Teversal Visitor Ctr NG17 100 B7
Tevery Cl NG9 182 E8
Teviot Rd NG5 160 F5
Tewkesbury Ave NG19 88 D4
Tewkesbury Cl NG2 186 A6
Tewkesbury Dr
Kimberley NG16 158 E7
Nottingham NG6 160 E4
Tewkesbury Rd NG10 193 E4
Thackeray Cl S81 36 B4
Thackeray's La NG5 161 E5
Thackerey St NG7 222 B3
Thales Dr NG5 162 C7
Thames St NG6 160 B7
Thane Rd NG9 184 E6
Thaxted Cl NG8 171 D6
Theaker Ave DN21 15 F1
Theaker La DN10 10 D5
Theatre Sq NG1 223 D3
Thelda Ave NG12 197 E3
Theresa Ct NG24 140 D4
Thetford Cl NG5 162 A6
Thickley Cl NG20 72 F4
Thievesdale Ave S81 35 F7
Thievesdale Cl S81 36 A7
Third Ave
Beeston NG9 184 C6
Carlton, Gedling NG4 162 F1
Carlton, Thorneywood NG4 174 B8
Clipstone NG21 89 F3
Edwinstowe NG21 76 A1
Mansfield NG21 103 F2
Mansfield Woodhouse NG19 89 A1
Nottingham NG6 160 B7
Thirlbeck NG12 188 A1
Thirlmere NG2 186 D5
Thirlmere Cl
Long Eaton NG10 182 B2
Nottingham NG3 173 F7
Thirlmere Rd NG10 182 B2
Thirston Cl NG6 159 F7
Thistle Bank
East Leake LE12 205 E3
Mansfield Woodhouse NG19 88 F4
Thistle Cl NG16 158 B8
Thistledown Rd NG11 195 E7
Thistle Gn Cl DE75 143 B1
Thistle Rd DE7 170 A4
Thomas Ave NG12 176 C3
Thomas Cl NG3 223 F4
Thomas Parkyn Cl NG11 206 E7
Thomas Rd
Kegworth DE74 203 C1
Newark-on-T NG24 140 F2
Thomas St DN22 39 F5
Thompson Ave DN11 8 F4
Thompson Cl
Beeston NG9 183 C3
East Leake LE12 205 E2
Thompson Cres NG17 100 F1
Thompson Gdns NG5 147 A1
Thompson St NG16 143 B3
Thonock Dr LN1 56 F4
Thonock Hill DN21 15 D3
Thonock Rd DN21 15 E5
Thoresby Ave
Carlton NG4 162 D2
Edwinstowe NG21 76 A2
Kirkby in A NG17 115 D4
Newark-on-T NG24 140 A6
Nottingham NG2 173 F3
Shirebrook NG20 72 E4
Thoresby Cl
Harworth DN11 9 B5
Meden Vale NG20 74 D8
Radcliffe on T NG12 176 A4
Thoresby Cres NG17 100 C6
Thoresby Ct NG3 173 D8
Thoresby Dale NG15 146 B7
Thoresby Gall (Pierrepont Art Gall) NG22 62 D3
Thoresby Glade NG22 106 A5
Thoresby Rd
Beeston NG9 171 C2
Bingham NG13 177 C4
Long Eaton NG10 193 C6
Mansfield NG21 103 F1
Mansfield Woodhouse NG19 88 A3
Thoresby St
3 Mansfield NG18 102 A7
10 Nottingham NG2 173 E4
Sutton in A NG17 101 A4
Thoresby Way DN22 39 E3
Thor Gdns NG5 146 F2
Thorn Ave NG19 87 F1
Thorn Bank DN9 2 C8
Thornbury Dr NG19 101 D8
Thornbury Hill La S81 16 D8
Thornbury Way NG5 160 F7
Thorncliffe Rd NG3 173 C8
Thorncliffe Rise NG3 173 C8
Thorndale Rd
Calverton NG14 148 F7
Nottingham NG6 160 C2
Thorndike Cl NG9 184 B4
Thorndike Way DN21 24 E7
Thorn Dr NG16 158 B8
Thorner Cl NG6 160 E5
Thorne Rd DN10 10 B8
Thorney Abbey Rd NG21 118 B5
Thorney Ct 8 NG18 103 A2
Thorney Hill NG3 173 F7
Thorneywood Ave NG17 129 E8
Thorneywood Mount NG3 173 F7
Thorneywood Rd NG10 193 F8
Thorn Gr NG15 146 B4
Thornham Cres NG17 129 F8
Thornhill Cl NG9 171 B2
Thornhill Dr
Boughton NG22 77 E5
South Normanton DE55 113 B6
Thornhill La DN22 33 C2
Thornhill Rd DN11 8 E4
Thornley St 7 NG7 172 E7
Thornthwaite Cl NG2 186 C6
Thornton Ave NG5 147 D1
Thornton Cl
Mansfield NG18 103 B5
Nottingham NG8 171 E4
Thornton Dale S81 36 B7
Thornton Rd NG23 112 A8
Thorntons Cl NG12 188 A2
Thornton St
Gainsborough DN21 24 D7
Sutton in A NG17 100 F1
Thorn Tree Gdns NG16 143 F4
Thorold Cl NG7 184 E2
Thoroton Ave NG24 140 D3
Thoroton St NG7 222 C3
Thoroughfare La NG23 125 D7
Thorpe Cl
Coddington NG24 126 B2
Newark-on-T NG24 139 E4
18 Nottingham NG5 161 A8
Stapleford NG9 182 D7
Thorpe Cres NG3 162 A1
Thorpe La
Eagle LN6 84 E2
Shireoaks S80 34 C6
Thorpelands Ave NG19 88 E1
Thorpe Lea NG14 165 A5
Thorpe Leys NG10 193 D5
Thorpe Rd
Eastwood NG16 143 F4
Mansfield NG18 103 A2
Mattersey DN10 20 B8
Thorpe St
Askham DN22 52 C7
Ilkeston DE7 157 E3
Thrapston Ave NG5 147 F2
Three Leys La DN22 32 D3

Three Tuns Rd NG16 . . . . 144 A2
Threlkeld Cl NG2 . . . . 186 C6
Thrumpton Ave NG10 . . . . 194 A7
Thrumpton Cl DN22 . . . . 39 F4
Thrumpton Dr NG2 . . . . . . 173 B1
Thrumpton Hall NG11 . . . . 194 B3
Thrumpton La DN22 . . . . . . 39 F5
Thrumpton Prim Sch
DN22 . . . . 39 F4
Thurcaton Way DE55 . . . . . 99 A3
Thurgarton Ave **8** NG2 . 173 F4
Thurgarton La NG14 . . . . . 151 E3
Thurgarton St NG2 . . . . . . 173 F4
Thurgarton Sta NG14 . . . . 151 D6
Thurland St NG1 . . . . 223 E2
Thurlby Cl NG12 . . . . 189 A4
Thurlby Ct NG19 . . . . 88 E4
Thurlby La
Stanton-on-t-W NG12 . . . . 198 C1
Widmerpool NG12 . . . . 208 D8
Thurlby Rd DN21 . . . . 24 F8
Thurlestone Dr NG3 . . . . . 162 C6
Thurley Wlk NG18 . . . . . . 103 B4
Thurloe Ct NG11 . . . . 185 C3
Thurman Dr NG12 . . . . 187 F3
Thurman St
Ilkeston DE7 . . . . 170 A6
Nottingham NG7 . . . . 222 B4
Thursby Rd NG11 . . . . 184 E3
Thymus Wlk NG11 . . . . . . 184 C1
Thyra Ct NG3 . . . . 161 E1
Thyra Gr
Beeston NG9 . . . . 184 A6
Nottingham NG3 . . . . 161 D1
Tibshelf Rd NG17 . . . . 100 A7
Tibshelf Schs DE55 . . . . . . 99 A7
Tickhill Castle DN11 . . . . 8 A6
Tickhill Rd
Bawtry DN10 . . . . 9 F7
Harworth DN11 . . . . 8 E5
Tideswell Cl NG15 . . . . . . 117 A3
Tideswell Ct NG18 . . . . . . 102 D7
Tidworth Cl NG8 . . . . 172 A6
Tilberthwaite Cl NG2 . . . . 186 C6
Tilbury Rise NG8 . . . . 160 B3
Tilford Gdns NG9 . . . . 182 E6
Till Bridge La DN21 . . . . . . 44 F7
Tiln Ct DN22 . . . . 29 F1
Tiln La DN22 . . . . 29 F3
Tilstock Ct NG16 . . . . 159 A8
Timothy Rd NG22 . . . . 79 C3
Tindale Bank Rd DN10 . . . . . 6 C7
Tinker La DN22 . . . . 27 F6
Tinker's La NG23 . . . . 97 F8
Tinkers Way NG7 . . . . 223 D1
Tinsley Cl NG23 . . . . 156 E6
Tinsley Rd NG16 . . . . 143 D1
Tintagel Gn NG7 . . . . 184 E1
Tintern Dr NG8 . . . . 160 E2
Tippett Ct NG3 . . . . 173 F6
Tippings La NG22 . . . . 119 F5
Tip Tree Cl NG16 . . . . 158 F7
Tiree Cl NG9 . . . . 170 D2
Tishbite St **7** NG6 . . . . . 160 B7
Tissington Ave NG20 . . . . . 74 C7
Tissington Cl **3** NG7 . . . 173 A8
Tissington Rd NG7 . . . . . . 173 A8
Titchfield Ave
Mansfield Woodhouse
NG19 . . . . 88 D3
Sutton in A NG17 . . . . 100 E2
Titchfield St
Hucknall NG15 . . . . 146 A7
Mansfield NG18 . . . . 102 A8
Market Warsop NG20 . . . . . 74 B3
Titchfield Terr NG15 . . . . . 146 B7
Tithby Ct **10** NG18 . . . . . 103 A2
Tithby Dr NG5 . . . . 161 D4
Tithby Rd
Bingham NG13 . . . . 177 E2
Cropwell Butler NG12 . . . . 189 C6
Tithe Barn Ct NG24 . . . . . 125 A1
Tithe Gdns **2** NG5 . . . . . 147 A1
Tithe La NG14 . . . . 148 F7
Tithes La DN11 . . . . 8 A7
Tiverton Cl
Hucknall NG15 . . . . 145 D5
Nottingham NG8 . . . . 160 B2
Toad La
Elston NG23 . . . . 153 E4
Epperstone NG14 . . . . 150 A5
Laxton NG22 . . . . 79 B2
Tobias Cl NG5 . . . . 160 F8
Todd Cl NG11 . . . . 195 C8
Todd Ct NG11 . . . . 195 C8
Toft Cl NG12 . . . . 187 E2
Toft Rd NG9 . . . . 183 A3
Tokenhouse Yd NG1 . . . . . 223 E2
Toll Bar Ave NG13 . . . . . . 181 A3
Tollerton Gn NG6 . . . . 160 D5
Tollerton La NG12 . . . . . . 186 E5
Tollerton Prim Sch
NG12 . . . . 186 E1
Tollhouse Hill NG1 . . . . . . 223 D3
Tolney La NG24 . . . . 139 E7
Tom Blower Cl NG8 . . . . . 172 A5
Tomlinson Ave NG11 . . . . 195 A1
Tom Otter's La NG23 . . . . . 70 E8
Tom Wass Rd NG17 . . . . . 114 E8
Tonbridge Mount NG8 . . . 171 D2
Tooley St DN21 . . . . 24 D7
Toot Hill Comp Sch
NG13 . . . . 177 E4
Toothill La NG18 . . . . 102 C7

Toothill Rd
Loughborough LE11 . . . . . 220 B5
7 Mansfield NG18 . . . . . 102 B7
Topaz Gr NG18 . . . . 102 C5
Top Gn LE14 . . . . 210 A1
Top La NG19 . . . . 87 A1
Topliff Rd NG9 . . . . 183 C2
Top Pasture La DN22 . . . . . 31 E8
Top Rd
Blidworth NG21 . . . . 118 A2
Misson DN10 . . . . 4 D3
Ruddington NG11 . . . . 196 C6
Thorney NG23 . . . . 69 F5
Top Row
Newark-on-T NG24 . . . . . . 140 C8
Westwood NG16 . . . . 128 A5
Top Sandy La NG20 . . . . . . 74 C3
Top St
Askham NG22 . . . . 51 F2
Bawtry DN10 . . . . 10 A7
East Drayton DN22 . . . . . . 53 B3
Elston NG23 . . . . 153 D4
North Wheatley DN22 . . . . 31 D8
Rainworth NG21 . . . . 104 B1
Topyard La DN22 . . . . 30 D6
Torbay Cres NG5 . . . . 161 B5
Torkard Dr NG5 . . . . 160 F8
Torksey Avc LN1 . . . . 56 F4
Torksey Ferry Rd DN22 . . . 43 C2
Torksey Mews DN22 . . . . . 39 D2
Torksey St DN22 . . . . 43 A2
Torksey Wlk NG19 . . . . 88 E4
Tor La NG22 . . . . 77 A3
Torr St DN21 . . . . 24 D8
Torvill Dr NG8 . . . . 171 E5
Toston Dr NG8 . . . . 172 C4
Totland Dr NG8 . . . . 160 D2
Totland Rd NG9 . . . . 171 C2
Totlcy Cl NG6 . . . . 146 C2
Totnes Cl NG15 . . . . 145 D6
Totnes Rd NG3 . . . . 174 B5
Toton Banks Road Inf Sch
NG9 . . . . 182 F2
Toton Cl NG6 . . . . 160 D5
Toton La NG9 . . . . 182 E6
Tottle Gdns **2** NG7 . . . . 172 D6
Tottle Rd NG11 . . . . 185 A8
Tow Ct NG24 . . . . 139 A4
Tower Cres NG16 . . . . 159 A4
Tower St DN21 . . . . 15 D1
Towe's Mount NG4 . . . . . . 174 E7
Towle St NG10 . . . . 193 A4
Towlsons Croft NG6 . . . . . 160 D3
Town End La NG23 . . . . . . 167 B8
Town La DE55 . . . . 99 B3
Towngate DN10 . . . . 10 A7
Townroe Dr NG19 . . . . . . 101 D7
Townsend Ct NG5 . . . . . . 147 A1
Townside Cl NG10 . . . . . . 193 B4
Townside La DN22 . . . . 42 D3
Townside Rd DN22 . . . . . . 32 D1
Town St
Askham NG22 . . . . 52 A3
Beeston NG9 . . . . 183 B8
Claypole NG23 . . . . 156 D7
Clayworth DN22 . . . . 21 D5
Cottam DN22 . . . . 43 D5
Grassthorpe NG23 . . . . 81 F4
Hawksworth NG13 . . . . . . 167 C3
Lound DN22 . . . . 20 C1
Pinxton NG16 . . . . 113 E3
Sandiacre NG10 . . . . 182 B6
South Leverton DN22 . . . . 42 C7
Sutton DN22 . . . . 28 F6
Treswell DN22 . . . . 42 B3
Town View NG16 . . . . 158 F7
Towpath Cl LE11 . . . . 220 C5
Towson Ave NG16 . . . . . . 143 C2
Towson Field LE12 . . . . . . 205 E2
Towyn Ct **8** NG5 . . . . . . 161 A7
Tracy Cl NG7 . . . . 171 D1
Trafalgar Cl NG7 . . . . 222 B4
Trafalgar Rd
Beeston NG9 . . . . 184 A4
Long Eaton NG10 . . . . 193 D6
Trafalgar Sq
Long Eaton NG10 . . . . 193 E7
Sutton on T NG23 . . . . 97 A8
Traffic St NG2 . . . . 223 E1
Trafford Gdns **1** NG8 . . . 172 D7
Tranby Gdns NG8 . . . . 171 F4
Tranker La S81 . . . . 35 A6
Travell's Hill LE12 . . . . . . 214 A7
Travers Rd NG10 . . . . 182 A6
Treegarth Sq NG5 . . . . . . 147 B1
Tree View Ct NG5 . . . . 147 C1
Trefan Gdns NG5 . . . . 161 A7
Trelawn Cl **1** NG5 . . . . . 161 D2
Tremayne Rd NG8 . . . . . . 171 C6
Trenchard Cl NG13 . . . . . 177 C8
Trenchham Gdns NG14 . . 163 D3
Trent Ave NG11 . . . . 196 C8
Trent Bridge
(Nottinghamshire Cty CC)
NG2 . . . . 173 E1
Trent Bsns Ctr NG10 . . . . 182 C1
Trent Bvd NG2 . . . . 174 A1
Trent Cl NG23 . . . . 110 F2
Trent Coll NG10 . . . . 193 C8
Trent Cres NG9 . . . . 183 E3
Trent Dr NG15 . . . . 145 D3
Trent Gdns NG14 . . . . 164 A4
Trentham Dr NG8 . . . . 172 C7
Trentham Gdns NG8 . . . . 172 C7

Trent La
Besthorpe NG23 . . . . 97 E6
Burton Joyce NG14 . . . . . 164 C4
East Bridgford NG13 . . . . 165 B4
Girton NG23 . . . . 82 E2
Kelham NG23 . . . . 124 B5
Long Eaton NG10 . . . . 193 F5
Newark-on-T NG24 . . . . . . 125 A2
North Clifton NG23 . . . . . . 68 E5
Nottingham NG2 . . . . 174 A3
South Clifton NG23 . . . . . . 68 D1
Trenton Cl NG9 . . . . 171 A1
Trenton Dr NG10 . . . . 194 A8
Trent Port Rd DN21 . . . . . . 44 B8
Trent Rd
Beeston NG9 . . . . 184 B4
Nottingham NG2 . . . . 173 F4
Wellow NG22 . . . . 78 A4
Trentside NG14 . . . . 165 A4
Trentside N NG2 . . . . 173 E1
Trent S Ind Pk NG2 . . . . . 174 A3
Trent St
Gainsborough DN21 . . . . . 24 D7
Long Eaton NG10 . . . . 193 E8
Nottingham NG1 . . . . 223 E1
Retford DN22 . . . . 40 A6
Worksop S80 . . . . 35 E4
Trent Vale Inf Sch NG9 . . 184 B4
Trent Vale Rd NG9 . . . . . . 184 A4
Trent Valley View NG3 . . . 162 A1
Trcnt Vicw DN22 . . . . 44 C8
Trentview Ct NG2 . . . . 173 F2
Trent View Gdns NG12 . . . 176 A5
Trent Way NG24 . . . . 125 B2
Trent Wlk NG19 . . . . 88 E4
Tressall Cl DE7 . . . . 170 A8
Treswell Ct **9** NG18 . . . . 103 A2
Treswell Rd
Rampton DN22 . . . . 42 F2
South Leverton DN22 . . . . 42 C5
Treswell Wood Nature
Rcscrvc DN22 . . . . 41 E4
Trevelyan Rd NG2 . . . . 173 F1
Trevino Gdns **10** NG5 . . 147 A1
Trevone Ave NG9 . . . . 182 E6
Trevor Rd
Beeston NG9 . . . . 183 F5
West Bridgford NG2 . . . . . 186 A6
Trevose Gdns NG5 . . . . . . 161 D3
Treyford Cl NG11 . . . . 185 A4
Triangle The DE7 . . . . 170 A6
Tricornia Dr NG6 . . . . 160 B4
Tring Vale NG5 . . . . 161 A4
Trinity Ave NG7 . . . . 222 B1
Trinity Cl DE7 . . . . 157 E3
Trinity Cres
East Markham NG22 . . . . . 66 B7
Lambley NG4 . . . . 163 C7
Wymeswold LE12 . . . . 216 B3
Trinity Rd
Newark-on-T NG24 . . . . . . 140 A4
Retford DN22 . . . . 29 D1
Southwell NG25 . . . . 136 C8
Trinity Sch The NG8 . . . . . 172 A4
Trinity Sq NG1 . . . . 223 E3
Trinity St
Gainsborough DN21 . . . . . 24 D7
Loughborough LE11 . . . . . 220 C3
Trinity Wlk NG1 . . . . 223 E3
Trinstead Way NG5 . . . . . 161 C7
Triumph Cl NG22 . . . . 106 F8
Triumph Rd
Eakring NG22 . . . . 106 E8
Nottingham NG7 . . . . 172 D4
Trivett Sq NG1 . . . . 223 F2
Troon Cl NG16 . . . . 158 E7
Trough La NG16 . . . . 158 F8
Trough Rd NG16 . . . . 159 A8
Troutbeck NG12 . . . . 188 A3
Troutbeck Cres NG9 . . . . 183 C8
Trowell Ave
Ilkeston DE7 . . . . 170 A5
Nottingham NG8 . . . . 171 B5
Trowell CE Prim Sch
NG9 . . . . 170 D4
Trowell Ct **7** NG18 . . . . . 103 A2
Trowell Gr
Long Eaton NG10 . . . . 182 C1
Stapleford NG9 . . . . 170 E3
Trowell La LE12 . . . . 213 E7
Trowell Pk Dr NG9 . . . . . . 170 D2
Trowell Rd
Nottingham NG8 . . . . 171 D5
Stapleford NG9 . . . . 170 D2
True Lovers Wlk **1** LE11 220 A3
Trueman Ct S81 . . . . 36 B5
Trueman Gdns NG5 . . . . . 162 B6
Trueman St DE7 . . . . 157 F4
Truman Cl NG3 . . . . 223 F4
Truman Dr NG15 . . . . 146 A6
Truman's Rd NG2 . . . . 173 D1
Truman St
Cossall DE7 . . . . 158 A1
Kimberley NG16 . . . . 158 D7
Truro Cl LE12 . . . . 205 E1
Truro Cres NG7 . . . . 172 E7
Trusley Wlk NG19 . . . . 88 E4
Tryst The NG24 . . . . 125 A2
Tuckers Cl LE11 . . . . 220 C2
Tudor Ave NG18 . . . . 102 F8
Tudor Cl
Carlton NG4 . . . . 174 E5
Long Eaton NG10 . . . . 182 E1
Newark-on-T NG24 . . . . . . 140 B8
Tudor Cres NG21 . . . . 118 A8
Tudor Ct
Arnold NG5 . . . . 162 B5
Hucknall NG15 . . . . 145 C5

Tudor Dr
Mansfield NG18 . . . . 102 C4
Morton DN21 . . . . 15 B4
Tudor Gr NG1 . . . . 223 D4
Tudor Rd NG2 . . . . 185 F7
Tudor Sq NG2 . . . . 185 F7
Tudor St NG17 . . . . 100 E1
Tudsbury Terr NG17 . . . . . 101 A3
Tudwal Cl NG5 . . . . 161 A7
Tudwal Wlk **2** NG5 . . . . 161 A7
Tulip Ave NG3 . . . . 173 D7
Tullp Rd NG16 . . . . 158 B4
Tunnel Rd
Nottingham NG7 . . . . 222 C2
Retford DN22 . . . . 39 E5
Tunstall Cres NG8 . . . . . . 160 A1
Tunstall Dr NG5 . . . . 160 F4
Tunstall Rd NG5 . . . . 161 F4
Turnberry S81 . . . . 36 B5
Turnberry Ave **6** NG6 . . 114 E7
Turnberry Cl
Beeston NG9 . . . . 183 C6
Ilkeston DE7 . . . . 157 C2
Turnberry Ct NG12 . . . . . . 186 C3
Turnberry Rd NG6 . . . . . . 160 D6
Turner Ave
Langley Mill NG16 . . . . . . 143 A3
Loughborough LE11 . . . . . 220 A2
Turner Cl NG9 . . . . 182 E6
Turner Dr
Eastwood NG16 . . . . 158 B7
Worksop S81 . . . . 35 F4
Turner Rd
Long Eaton NG10 . . . . 193 C4
Worksop S81 . . . . 35 E4
Turners Croft DN22 . . . . . . 42 C8
Turner St NG15 . . . . 146 A7
Turneys Ct NG2 . . . . 173 E1
Turney St NG2 . . . . 173 D1
Turnley Rd DE55 . . . . 113 C6
Turnpike La NG9 . . . . 184 A8
Turnstone Crcs NG18 . . . 103 C4
Turnstone Wharf **1** NG7 172 F2
Turpin Ave NG4 . . . . 162 D3
Turpin Cl DN21 . . . . 15 F1
Turton Cl NG16 . . . . 143 A3
Turvey La LE12 . . . . 212 D2
Tuxford Ave NG20 . . . . 74 E8
Tuxford Ct **6** NG18 . . . . 103 A2
Tuxford Prim Sch NG22 . . 65 E2
Tuxford Rd
Boughton NG22 . . . . 77 E5
East Markham NG22 . . . . . 65 F5
Egmanton NG22 . . . . 79 E7
Normanton on T NG23 . . . 81 D6
Walesby NG22 . . . . 64 C2
Tuxford Sch NG22 . . . . 66 A3
Tuxford Windmill NG22 . . . 65 E4
Tuxford Wlk NG3 . . . . 173 F6
Twells Cl NG3 . . . . 173 F7
Twentylands Dr LE12 . . . . 205 D1
Twin Oaks Dr NG17 . . . . . 100 C1
Twinyards Cl NG17 . . . . . . 100 C1
Twitchell The
Beeston NG9 . . . . 183 E4
Newark-on-T NG24 . . . . . . 139 E5
Sutton in A NG17 . . . . 100 F1
Two Acres S81 . . . . 18 B2
Twycross Rd NG5 . . . . 161 B7
Twyford Gdns NG11 . . . . . 184 E4
Twyford La DN22 . . . . 50 C3
Tyburn Cl NG5 . . . . 147 A1
Tylden Rd S80 . . . . 35 B5
Tylden Way S80 . . . . 35 A5
Tynedale Cl
Long Eaton NG10 . . . . 193 A6
Nottingham NG8 . . . . 160 D1
Tyne Gdns NG15 . . . . 145 D3

U

Ulldale Ct NG9 . . . . 183 B4
Ullscarf Cl NG2 . . . . 186 C5
Ullswater Cl NG2 . . . . 162 F2
Ullswater Cres NG9 . . . . . 183 D8
Ullswater Dr NG15 . . . . . . 145 F7
Ulster Rd DN21 . . . . 15 D2
Underwood Ave DN22 . . . . 19 B3
Underwood CE Prim Sch
NG16 . . . . 128 F1
Underwood Gdns S80 . . . . 35 C3
Union Cl NG15 . . . . 131 A2
Union Rd NG3 . . . . 223 F3
Union St
Beeston NG9 . . . . 184 A6
Bingham NG13 . . . . 177 E4
Long Eaton NG10 . . . . 193 E8
Loughborough LE11 . . . . . 220 A4
Mansfield NG18 . . . . 102 A7
Retford DN22 . . . . 39 F7
Selston NG16 . . . . 129 A4
Sutton in A NG17 . . . . 100 F2
Unity Cres NG3 . . . . 162 C2
Unity Prim Sch NG7 . . . . . 222 C4
Unity Rd NG17 . . . . 115 B7
University Bvd NG7 . . . . . 184 C8
University of Nottingham
NG7 . . . . 172 D2
University of Nottingham
Department of Ag
Economics LE12 . . . . . . 213 B8
Unwin Rd NG17 . . . . 101 B3
Unwin St NG17 . . . . 100 A3
Uplands Ct NG8 . . . . 171 F6
Upminster Dr
Arnold NG5 . . . . 147 F1
Nuthall NG16 . . . . 159 D3

Upper Canaan NG11 . . . . 196 D8
Upper Coll St NG1 . . . . . . 223 D3
Upper Dunstead Rd
NG16 . . . . 143 B4
Upper Eldon St NG2 . . . . 173 E4
Upper Mexborough Rd
NG16 . . . . 129 A7
Upper Orch St NG9 . . . . . 182 E7
Upper Parliament St
NG1 . . . . 223 E3
Upper Row NG22 . . . . 54 B2
Upper Wellington St
NG10 . . . . 182 C1
Uppingham Cres NG2 . . . 185 D5
Uppingham Gdns NG2 . . 173 D2
Upton Cl DE75 . . . . 143 A1
Upton Dr NG5 . . . . 161 D5
Upton Hall Time Mus
NG25 . . . . 122 E1
Upton Hill NG22 . . . . 52 A4
Upton Mount NG19 . . . . . . 87 E1
Upton Rd
Askham NG22 . . . . 52 A4
Southwell NG25 . . . . 122 A1
Upton Wlk DN21 . . . . 24 F7
Urban Rd NG17 . . . . 115 A5
Utile Gdns **3** NG6 . . . . . 160 A7

V

Vale Ave NG20 . . . . 74 A4
Vale Cl
Aslockton NG13 . . . . 179 A4
Eastwood NG16 . . . . 144 B2
Mansfield NG18 . . . . 102 E4
Vale Cres N NG8 . . . . 172 D6
Vale Cres S NG8 . . . . 172 D6
Vale Dr NG20 . . . . 72 F2
Vale Gdns NG4 . . . . 174 D5
Valentine Ave NG16 . . . . . 128 E7
Vale Rd
Carlton NG4 . . . . 174 E5
Mansfield Woodhouse NG19 88 B4
Valeside Gdns NG4 . . . . . 174 E5
Vale The DE7 . . . . 157 E3
Valetta Rd NG5 . . . . 162 B7
Vale View NG23 . . . . 156 D1
Vallance St NG19 . . . . 88 B4
Valley App NG22 . . . . 105 F7
Valley Comp Sch S81 . . . . 35 E5
Valley Dr NG16 . . . . 144 B1
Valley Farm Ct **16** NG5 . 161 A8
Valley Gdns NG2 . . . . 186 C5
Valley La NG23 . . . . 169 D8
Valley Prospect NG24 . . . 139 D5
Valley Rd
Beeston NG9 . . . . 183 B5
Bilsthorpe NG22 . . . . 105 F7
Carlton NG4 . . . . 162 B3
Kimberley NG16 . . . . 158 D7
Nottingham NG5 . . . . 161 B4
Radcliffe on T NG12 . . . . . 176 A5
Shirebrook NG20 . . . . 72 E5
West Bridgford NG2 . . . . . 186 B5
Worksop S81 . . . . 35 E6
Valley View NG24 . . . . 126 A1
Valley Vw NG18 . . . . 102 E4
Valmont Ave NG18 . . . . . . 103 A6
Valmont Rd
Beeston NG9 . . . . 183 A7
Nottingham NG5 . . . . 161 A3
Vancouver Ave NG12 . . . . 175 E2
Vanessa Dr DN21 . . . . 15 C3
Vanguard Rd NG10 . . . . . 193 D5
Varden Ave NG9 . . . . 172 A1
Varney Rd NG11 . . . . 184 F3
Vaughan Ave
Bottesford NG13 . . . . 181 C2
Hucknall NG15 . . . . 131 C1
Vaughan Pl NG20 . . . . 72 E6
Vaughan Rd NG9 . . . . 183 A4
Vedonis Pk NG15 . . . . 146 A5
Vellus Ct NG17 . . . . 101 B2
Ventnor Rise NG5 . . . . . . 160 F4
Ventura Dr NG5 . . . . 146 C1
Venus Cl NG6 . . . . 160 E5
Vera Cres NG21 . . . . 118 B8
Verbena Cl **3** NG3 . . . . 173 D7
Verder Gr NG5 . . . . 160 E8
Vere Ave NG17 . . . . 100 E5
Vere St NG6 . . . . 160 B7
Verne Cl NG4 . . . . 174 C7
Verney St NG19 . . . . 86 F7
Verney Way NG19 . . . . 86 F7
Vernon Ave
Beeston NG9 . . . . 183 F6
Carlton NG4 . . . . 162 F1
Newark-on-T NG24 . . . . . . 140 B8
Nottingham, Old Basford
NG6 . . . . 160 E3
Nottingham, Wilford NG11 185 B8
Ravenshead NG15 . . . . . . 116 F1
Retford DN22 . . . . 40 A4
Vernon Cres NG15 . . . . . . 117 A1
Vernon Ct
Nuthall NG16 . . . . 159 F3
Shirebrook NG20 . . . . 73 A4
Vernon Dr NG16 . . . . 159 F3
Vernon Pk Dr NG6 . . . . . . 160 E3
Vernon Pk Trad Est NG5 . 160 E3
Vernon Rd
Kirkby in A NG17 . . . . 114 F7
Nottingham NG6 . . . . 160 E3
Vernon St
Ilkeston DE7 . . . . 157 F4
Newark-on-T NG24 . . . . . . 140 B8
Nottingham NG1 . . . . 223 D3

Vernon St *continued*
Shirebrook NG20 73 A4
Verona Ave NG4 174 F6
Verona Ct NG18 103 A3
Veronica Dr
Carlton NG4 162 D1
Eastwood NG16 158 C8
Veronica Wlk NG11 184 C1
Veronne Dr NG17 101 A6
Versailles Gd NG15 146 A5
Vesper Ct NG18 102 F8
Vessey Cl NG24 140 C4
Vessey Rd S81 35 E7
Vexation La NG22 91 E7
Vicarage Ave DE7 157 D4
Vicarage Cl
Collingham NG23 98 A1
Nottingham, Old Basford NG5 160 F3
Nottingham, St Ann's NG3 223 E4
Shirebrook NG20 72 E3
Vicarage Ct NG17 100 E7
Vicarage Dr
Burton Joyce NG14 163 E4
Clarborough DN22 30 D5
Vicarage Gn NG12 186 B3
Vicarage La
Beckingham DN10 14 C2
Farnsfield NG22 119 E6
Kneeton NG13 151 F1
North Muskham NG23 110 D4
Radcliffe on T NG12 175 E3
Ruddington NG11 196 C7
Vicarage Rd NG25 136 C8
Vicarage St
Beeston NG9 183 E6
Ilkeston DE7 157 D4
Vicarage Way NG17 129 F8
Vicar La
Misson DN10 4 C3
Tibshelf DE55 99 A6
Vicars Ct NG21 89 E2
Vicar's La DN22 43 A2
Vicar's Wlk S80 35 F2
Vicar Water Ctry Pk NG21 89 E1
Vicar Way NG18 103 B7
Vickers St
Market Warsop NG20 74 B4
Nottingham NG3 173 D8
Vickers Way NG22 105 F7
Victor Cres NG10 182 C4
Victoria Ave
Lowdham NG14 150 E1
5 Nottingham NG2 173 F4
Victoria Cl
Boughton NG22 77 E5
Gainsborough DN21 24 F6
Victoria Cres NG5 161 D2
Victoria Ct
Ilkeston DE7 157 E1
Mansfield NG18 102 A5
Victoria Emb NG2 185 D8
Victoria Gdns
Newark-on-T NG24 140 A8
Watnall NG16 145 A1
Victoria Gr NG15 131 B1
Victoria L Ctr NG1 223 F3
Victoria Pk NG4 175 B6
Victoria Pk L Ctr DE7 157 E2
Victoria Pk Way NG4 175 B6
Victoria Rd
Bingham NG13 178 A5
Bunny NG11 196 E1
Carlton NG4 175 A6
Kirkby in A NG17 114 F5
Nottingham NG5 161 B3
Pinxton NG16 113 D3
Retford DN22 39 E6
Sandiacre NG10 182 B5
Selston NG16 129 A7
West Bridgford NG2 185 E7
Worksop S80 35 F2
Victoria Ret Pk NG4 175 B6
Victoria Sh Ctr NG1 223 E3
Victoria Sq S80 35 F3
Victoria St
Carlton NG4 162 F1
Hucknall NG15 146 A8
Ilkeston DE7 157 F3
Kimberley NG16 159 A6
Langley Mill NG16 143 C3
Long Eaton NG10 193 B5
Loughborough LE11 220 B3
Market Warsop NG20 74 A5
Newark-on-T NG24 139 E7
Nottingham NG1 223 E2
Radcliffe on T NG12 175 F3
Selston NG16 129 A7
Shirebrook NG20 72 F4
South Normanton DE55 113 A6
Stanton Hill NG17 100 C6
Stapleford NG9 182 D7
Sutton in A NG17 100 E2
Victoria Terr DE55 99 B7
Victor Terr 6 NG5 161 C2
Victory Cl
Kirkby in Ashfield NG17 115 B6
Long Eaton NG10 193 D5
Mansfield Woodhouse NG19 89 A1
Victory Dr NG19 88 F1
Victory Rd NG9 184 A4
Village Cl
Farndon NG24 139 B5
West Bridgford NG12 186 B3
Village Farm Cl LE12 204 F1
Village Rd
Normanton on S LE12 213 D2
Nottingham NG11 184 D2
Village St
Owthorpe NG12 199 E7
West Bridgford NG12 186 B3
Village Way NG24 139 A5
Villa Rd
Keyworth NG12 197 F4
Nottingham NG3 173 C7
Villa St NG9 183 F7
Villas The NG20 59 A3
Villiers Rd
Arnold NG5 161 D4
Mansfield NG18 102 E7
West Bridgford NG2 186 A6
Vina Cooke Mus of Dolls & Bygone Childhood NG23 110 F7
Vincent Ave NG9 183 F5
Vincent Gdns 8 NG7 172 E7
Vine Cl NG13 181 A1
Vine Cres NG10 182 B6
Vine Farm Cl NG12 187 E3
Vine Rd DN11 8 C7
Vines Cross NG8 171 E2
Vine Terr NG15 146 B7
Vine Tree Terr LE12 215 C1
Vine Way NG24 140 B8
Violet Ave NG16 144 B1
Violet Cl
Nottingham NG6 160 D3
Shirebrook NG20 72 D3
Violet Hill NG18 103 A8
Violet Rd
Carlton NG4 162 D1
West Bridgford NG2 186 A8
Vista The NG9 182 E5
Vivian Ave NG5 173 B8
Vixen Cl NG24 139 F4
Viyella Gd NG15 146 A5
Voce Ct S81 36 B6
Vulcan Cl NG6 160 E4
Vulcan Pl S80 35 F3
Vyse Dr NG10 193 C6

W

Waddington Dr NG2 185 D4
Wade Ave DE7 170 A7
Wade Cl NG18 102 C3
Wades Ave NG7 172 E8
Wadham Rd NG5 161 E5
Wadhurst Gdns NG3 223 F4
Wadhurst Gr NG8 171 D2
Wadnal La NG23 80 F3
Wadsworth Rd NG9 182 F8
Wagstaff La NG16 128 B4
Wain Ct S81 36 B7
Waingrove NG11 185 A3
Wainwright Ave NG19 101 D8
Wakefield Ave NG12 176 A4
Wakefield Croft DE7 157 C3
Wakeling Cl NG25 136 E8
Walbrook Cl NG8 160 A3
Walcote Dr NG2 185 C4
Walcot Gn NG11 184 D1
Waldeck Rd NG5 161 B1
Waldemar Gr NG9 184 A6
Waldron Cl 1 NG2 173 D2
Walesby CE Prim Sch NG22 64 A2
Walesby Ct 1 NG18 103 A3
Walesby Dr NG17 115 D5
Walesby La NG22 77 C5
Walford Cl NG13 181 A2
Walgrave Wlk 12 NG5 161 A7
Walkden St NG18 102 B7
Walker Cl
Newark-on-T NG24 140 A7
New Ollerton NG22 77 C5
Walker Gr NG9 182 E6
Walkeringham Prim Sch DN10 13 F6
Walkeringham Rd
Beckingham DN10 14 B2
Gringley on t H DN10 13 A3
Walkerith Rd
Morton DN21 15 A5
Walkerith DN10 14 D8
Walkers Ave NG16 143 E6
Walkers Cl
Bingham NG13 177 E4
Mansfield Woodhouse NG19 89 B1
Walker Sq NG5 160 E3
Walker St
Eastwood NG16 144 A3
Nottingham NG2 173 E4
Walkers Yd NG12 175 F3
Walk Mill Dr NG15 131 B1
Walks of Life Heritage Ctr NG22 66 A3
Walk The DN21 24 F7
Wallace Ave NG4 174 F7
Wallace Rd LE11 220 A2
Wallace St NG11 195 B2
Wallan St NG7 222 A4
Wallet St NG4 175 A7
Wallett Ave NG9 183 F8
Wallingbrook Rise S80 35 B3
Wallingwells La S81 25 A6
Wallis Rd NG18 102 C7
Wallis St NG6 160 E4
Wall St DN21 24 D7
Walnut Ave
Shireoaks S81 34 F7
Tickhill DN11 8 B7
Walnut Cl
Aslockton NG13 178 F5
Ilkeston DE7 170 A7
Walnut Dr
Beeston NG9 183 B8
Calverton NG14 148 F8
Walnut Gr
Cotgrave NG12 187 F3
East Bridgford NG13 165 C2
Radcliffe on T NG12 175 F3
Walnut Paddock LE14 202 B3
Walnut Rd NG13 181 A2
Walnut Tree Cres NG19 89 D2
Walnut Tree Gdns NG6 159 F7
Walnut Tree La NG13 165 C2
Walsham Cl NG9 183 C2
Walsingham Rd NG5 162 B5
Walter Halls Prim Sch NG3 161 E2
Walter's Cl NG24 139 A5
Walters Cres NG16 128 D6
Walter St NG7 222 C4
Waltham Cl
Balderton NG24 140 D3
West Bridgford NG2 186 B6
Waltham La
Harby LE14 202 B1
Long Clawson LE14 211 E2
Waltham Rd NG15 117 A2
Walton Ave NG3 173 F5
Walton Cl NG19 103 B8
Walton Cres NG4 174 E7
Walton Dr
Keyworth NG12 197 F3
Sutton in A NG17 114 D8
Walton Rd NG5 148 A1
Walton's La NG23 110 E3
Walton St
Long Eaton NG10 182 D1
Sutton in A NG17 101 A3
Wands Cl NG25 136 D8
Wansbeck Cl NG7 222 C3
Wansford Ave NG5 147 F1
Wanstead Way NG5 146 E1
Wapping La DN21 44 C8
Warburton St NG24 125 A1
Ward Ave
Hucknall NG15 130 F1
Nottingham NG5 162 A3
Wardle Gr NG5 162 A8
Wardlow Rd DE7 157 E3
Ward Pl NG18 101 E6
Ward Rd NG21 89 F4
Ward's End LE11 220 B3
Ward St 2 NG7 172 F8
Wareham Cl
Nottingham NG8 160 A3
West Bridgford NG2 185 C5
Warkton Cl NG9 183 C5
Warnadene Rd NG17 114 E8
Warner Pl LE11 220 C4
Warners La 9 LE11 220 B4
Warner St NG7 222 A3
Warrands Cl NG25 136 C8
Warren Ave
Annesley NG15 130 C8
Nottingham NG5 161 A2
Stapleford NG9 182 D7
Warren Ave Extension NG9 182 D7
Warren Cl
Gainsborough DN21 15 B2
2 Sutton in Ashfield NG17 100 A2
Warren Ct NG9 182 D7
Warrender Cl NG9 171 C1
Warrener Gr NG5 160 E8
Warrenhill Cl NG5 161 C7
Warren La
Kegworth DE74 193 B2
Long Eaton DE74 203 B7
Warren Prim Sch NG5 147 A2
Warren Rd
Annesley Woodhouse NG17 115 B1
Hucknall NG15 145 D5
Warren The NG12 187 F2
Warren Way NG19 103 C8
Warrington Rd NG6 160 C7
Warser Gate NG1 223 F2
Warsop Cl NG8 159 D2
Warsop La NG21 117 F7
Warsop Rd NG19 88 D3
Warton Ave NG3 173 F8
Warwick Ave
Arnold NG5 161 E5
Beeston NG9 183 F7
Carlton in L S81 25 F6
Warwick Cl
Kirkby in A NG17 115 D5
Saxilby LN1 57 A4
Warwick Dr
Mansfield NG18 102 E7
Shipley DE7 157 C3
Warwick Gdns NG12 187 F1
Warwick Rd
Balderton NG24 140 D4
Long Eaton NG10 194 A7
Nottingham NG3 161 D2
Wasdale Cl NG2 186 C5
Washdyke La NG15 145 F8
Washington Dr
Mansfield NG18 101 F5
Stapleford NG9 170 F1
Washington St DN21 24 D6
Wash Pit La NG12 200 D8
Wasnidge Cl NG3 223 F3
Wasnidge Wlk NG3 223 F4
Watchwood Gr NG14 148 F8
Watcombe Cir NG5 161 B1
Watcombe Rd NG5 161 C1
Watendlath Cl NG2 186 C5
Waterdown Rd NG11 184 D1
Waterford St NG6 160 E3
Waterfront Ctry Pk DN10 7 C2
Waterfurrows La NG12 164 D1
Waterhouse La NG4 163 A2
Water La
Carlton in L S81 26 A6
Long Clawson LE14 211 E4
Mansfield NG19 87 B3
Newark-on-T NG24 124 F1
Oxton NG25 134 B3
Radcliffe on T NG12 175 E3
Retford DN22 39 F8
Shelford NG12 164 D1
South Normanton DE55 113 B6
Tickhill DN11 8 A6
Waterloo Cl DE55 113 C8
Waterloo Cres NG7 222 C4
Waterloo La NG9 170 F6
Waterloo Prom NG7 222 C4
Waterloo Rd
Beeston NG9 184 A5
Hucknall NG15 131 A2
Nottingham NG7 222 C4
Water Mdws S80 35 D1
Water Mdws Swimming Complex NG18 102 C6
Watermeadow Cl NG19 88 D6
Watermeadows The NG10 193 B8
Water Orton Cl NG9 182 E3
Waterside Cl
2 Loughborough LE11 220 B5
Sandiacre NG10 182 B3
West Bridgford NG2 186 C6
Waterside Gdns NG7 172 E1
Waterslack Rd DN11 9 B4
Waterson Ave NG18 102 F3
Waterson Cl NG18 103 A4
Waterson Oaks NG18 102 F4
Waterway St W NG2 173 C2
Waterway St 3 NG2 173 D2
Waterway The NG10 182 C4
Waterworks St DN21 24 D6
Watford Rd NG8 160 B2
Watkins La DN22 32 D6
Watkin St NG3 223 E4
Watnall Cres NG19 101 E7
Watnall Rd
Hucknall NG15 145 E4
Nuthall NG16 159 C6
Watson Ave
Mansfield NG18 102 C7
Nottingham NG3 174 B6
Watson Rd
Ilkeston DE7 157 C2
Worksop S80 35 F2
Watson's La LE14 202 B3
Watson St NG20 74 B4
Wavell Cl S81 35 D7
Wavell Cres DN10 11 A1
Waveney Cl NG5 162 A6
Waverley Ave
Beeston NG9 184 A5
Carlton NG4 163 A1
Waverley House PNEU Sch NG7 222 C4
Waverley Pl S80 47 A8
Waverley Rd NG18 102 B4
Waverley St
Long Eaton NG10 193 E8
Nottingham NG7 223 D4
Tibshelf DE55 99 A7
Waverley Terr NG1 223 D3
Waverley Way S80 47 A8
Waverly Cl NG17 115 D5
Wayford Wlk 6 NG6 160 B8
Wayne Cl NG7 184 E1
Weardale Rd NG5 161 B2
Wearmouth Gdns 5 NG5 147 A1
Weaver Cl LE11 220 B1
Weavers Cl LE12 205 F3
Weaver's La NG15, NG16 129 F3
Weavers The NG24 139 C6
Weaverthorpe Rd NG5 162 A5
Webb Rd NG8 172 B7
Webster Ave NG16 143 F1
Webster Cl NG21 104 B1
Weedon Cl NG3 174 A6
Weekday Cross NG1 223 E2
Weetman Ave NG20 74 B6
Weetman Gdns 12 NG5 161 A8
Weighbridge Rd NG18 102 C6
Weightman Dr NG16 158 B7
Welbeck Ave
Carlton NG4 162 D2
Newark-on-T NG24 125 A1
Welbeck Cl
Nottingham NG3 223 E4
Sutton in A NG17 100 F5
Welbeck Dr NG21 75 F2
Welbeck Gdns
Beeston NG9 182 F3
Nottingham NG3 162 A4
Welbeck Gr NG13 177 C4
Welbeck Pl NG22 66 A3
Welbeck Prim Sch NG2 173 C2
Welbeck Rd
Harworth DN11 9 A5
Long Eaton NG10 182 C3
Mansfield Woodhouse NG19 88 C3
Radcliffe on T NG12 176 A4
Retford DN22 39 E4
West Bridgford NG2 185 E8
Welbeck Sq NG17 100 C6
Welbeck St
Creswell S80 58 E8
Kirkby in A NG17 115 C5
Mansfield NG18 102 A7
Market Warsop NG20 74 B4
Sutton in A NG17 100 F2
Whitwell S80 45 A6
Worksop S80 35 F4
Welbeck Wlk NG3 223 E4
Welby Ave NG7 222 B2
Welch Ave NG9 182 E8
Weldbank Cl NG9 183 B4
Welfare Cl NG20 72 E3
Welfitt Gr NG20 59 B2
Welham Cres NG5 162 A7
Welham Gr DN22 40 A8
Welham Rd DN22 40 A8
Welland Cl
Newark-on-T NG24 125 B2
Worksop S81 35 E7
Wellcroft Cl NG18 101 F5
Wellesley Cl S81 35 D8
Wellesley Cres NG8 159 D2
Well Fen La NG23 156 D7
Wellin Cl NG12 186 B3
Wellin Ct NG12 186 B3
Wellington Cir NG1 223 D2
Wellington Cl NG20 74 B3
Wellington Cres NG2 185 F7
Wellington Gr DN10 9 F8
Wellington Pl NG16 143 F2
Wellington Rd
Burton Joyce NG14 164 A5
1 Newark-on-T NG24 140 A8
Wellington Sq
Nottingham NG7 222 C3
Retford DN22 39 F7
Wellington St
Eastwood NG16 143 F3
Gainsborough DN21 24 D7
Long Eaton NG10 182 C2
Loughborough LE11 220 C3
Nottingham NG3 223 E4
Retford DN22 39 F7
Stapleford NG9 182 C6
Wellington Terr NG7 222 C3
Wellington Villas NG7 222 C3
Wellin La NG12 186 B3
Well La LE14 210 A1
Wellow Cl NG17, NG19 101 D8
Wellow Gn NG22 77 D2
Wellow House Sch NG22 77 D1
Wellow Rd
Eakring NG22 92 E2
Wellow NG22 77 C2
Wells Cl NG19 88 D4
Wells Gdns NG3 173 F8
Wells La DN22 43 D5
Wellspring Dale NG9 182 E5
Wells Rd Ctr Hospl NG3 161 F2
Wells Rd The NG3 161 F1
Welshcroft Cl NG17 115 A6
Welstead Ave NG8 160 B2
Welton Gdns NG6 160 A8
Welwyn Ave NG19 88 E4
Welwyn Rd NG8 171 E5
Wembley Gdns NG9 171 B2
Wembley Rd
Arnold NG5 162 B5
Langold S81 16 F3
Wembley St DN21 24 D8
Wemyss Gdns NG8 172 D3
Wendling Gdns NG5 161 B8
Wendover Dr NG8 160 B2
Wenham La NG17 99 F4
Wenlock Cl NG16 158 C8
Wenlock Dr NG2 185 F5
Wensleydale S81 36 B7
Wensleydale Cl
Mansfield NG19 88 E1
Nottingham NG8 160 D1
Wensleydale Rd NG10 193 B6
Wensley Rd NG5 161 E5
Wensor Ave NG9 183 F8
Wentbridge Dr NG18 103 A4
Wentworth Cl NG19 88 F2
Wentworth Cnr NG24 139 E5
Wentworth Croft DE75 143 A3
Wentworth Ct NG16 158 E6
Wentworth Gn DN22 39 D3
Wentworth Rd
Beeston NG9 183 C6
Kirkby in A NG17 114 E7
Nottingham NG5 161 B2
Wentworth St DE7 158 A2
Wentworth Way NG12 186 C3
Wesleyan Chapel Wlk NG9 182 D7
Wesley Cl
Balderton NG24 140 D4
Hathern LE12 213 A1
Wesley Gr 10 NG5 161 B1
Wesley Pl NG9 182 E8
Wesley Rd DN22 39 F7
Wesley St
Annesley Woodhouse NG17 130 A8
Ilkeston DE7 157 E4
Langley Mill NG16 143 C3
12 Nottingham NG5 161 B1
Wesley Way NG11 196 D6
Wessex Cl S81 36 A6
Wessex Rd S81 36 A6
West Ave
Kirkby in A NG17 115 C4

West Ave continued
Sandiacre NG10. . . . . . . .182 A6
Stapleford NG9. . . . . . . .182 E8
West Bridgford NG2. . . .185 E7
West Bank LN1. . . . . 56 F2
West Bank Ave NG18. . . .102 B8
West Bank Lea NG19. . . . 88 B1
West Bank Link NG19. . . . 88 B1
West Bank Mews DE74. .203 C2
West Bank Wynd NG18. .102 B8
Westbourne Cl
Retford DN22. . . . . 40 A6
Sutton in A NG17. . . . . .100 D3
Westbourne Rd
Selston NG16. . . . . .129 A2
Sutton in A NG17. . . . . .100 D3
Westbourne View NG17 .100 D3
Westbrecks La DN22. . . . 43 A5
West Bridgford Inf Sch
NG2. . . . . .185 E7
West Bridgford Jun Sch
NG2. . . . . .185 F6
West Bridgford Sch The
NG2. . . . . .185 D5
Westbrook Ave NG15. . . .116 F3
West Brook La NG23. . . .112 A6
West Burton Meadow Nature
Reserve DN22 . . . . .32 D7
West Burton Medieval
Village of DN22 . . . . .32 F7
Westbury Cl NG5. . . . . . .183 C4
Westbury Rd NG5. . . . . . .161 A3
Westbury Sch NG8. . . . . .171 E8
Westby La NG16. . . . . . . .158 D3
West Carr Rd DN22. . . . . 39 D6
West Cl NG12. . . . . .197 E2
Westcliffe Ave
Carlton NG4. . . . . .162 D3
Radcliffe on T NG12. . . .176 A4
West Cres
Beeston NG9. . . . . .184 B4
Kirkby in A NG17. . . . . .115 C4
Westcroft Dr LN1. . . . . . . 57 A5
Westcross Ave NG9. . . . . .182 E8
West Ct DN22. . . . . 39 D7
Westdale Ave NG17. . . . .101 A5
Westdale Cl NG16. . . . . . .193 A5
Westdale Cres NG4. . . . . .162 E1
Westdale Inf Sch NG3. . .162 C3
Westdale Jun Sch NG3. . .162 B3
Westdale La E NG4. . . . . .162 E1
Westdale La W NG3. . . . . .162 A3
Westdale Rd
Mansfield NG19. . . . . 88 B1
Westwood NG16 . . . . . . .128 C4
West Dr NG21 . . . . 76 A2
West End
Beeston NG9. . . . . .183 F5
Calverton NG14. . . . . . . .148 C7
Farndon NG24 . . . . .138 F4
Long Clawson LE14 . . . . .211 C3
Long Whatton LE12 . . . . .212 A4
Pinxton NG16. . . . . .113 C4
Sutton in A NG17. . . . . .100 E2
West End Arc NG1. . . . . . .223 D2
West End Cl NG13. . . . . . .181 A2
West End St NG9. . . . . . . .182 C5
Westerdale S81. . . . . 36 A8
Westerfield Way NG11. . .185 A5
Westerham Cl NG8. . . . . .171 D7
Westerham Rd NG11. . . . .196 B6
Westerlands NG9 . . . . . . .182 F6
Western Ave
Bingham NG13. . . . . . . .177 D5
Kirkby in A NG17. . . . . .115 B3
Mansfield NG18. . . . . . . .101 F5
Saxilby LN1 . . . . 56 F4
Western Bvd NG8. . . . . . .172 D8
Western Fields NG11. . . .196 B6
Western Gdns NG8. . . . . .172 D8
Western St NG1. . . . . .223 F3
Western Terr NG7 . . . . . . .222 C2
Western Wlk DN10. . . . . . 10 A8
Westfield Cl
Mansfield NG19. . . . . . . .101 F8
Sutton in A NG17. . . . . .100 E2
Westfield Dr
Ilkeston DE7. . . . . .157 D2
Mansfield NG19. . . . . . . .101 E8
Worksop S81. . . . . 36 A5
Westfield La
Collingham NG23. . . . . . .111 E8
Mansfield NG18, NG19 . . .101 E8
Woodborough NG14 . . . . .149 A4
Westfield Rd
Annesley Woodhouse
NG17. . . . . .115 B1
Bingham NG13. . . . . . . .177 D4
Retford DN22. . . . . 39 D6
Westfield Way NG24 . . . . .139 A4
West Furlong
Cotgrave NG12 . . . . .188 A2
Retford DN22. . . . . 39 D8
Westgate
Southwell NG25. . . . . . . .136 D8
Worksop S80. . . . . 35 E2
West Gate
Long Eaton NG10. . . . . . .193 E7
[1] Mansfield NG18 . . . . .102 B7
Tickhill DN11. . . . . 8 A6
Westgate Ms NG25. . . . . .136 D8
Westgate St NG3. . . . . . .173 E6
Westgate View S80. . . . . . 35 E2

Westglade Jun & Inf Sch
NG5. . . . . .160 F8
West Gr Rd DN22 . . . . 39 F5
Westhay Ct NG8 . . . . .172 C5
West Hill
Mansfield NG18. . . . . . . .102 A8
Sutton in A NG17. . . . . .100 D6
West Hill Ave NG18. . . . . .102 B7
West Hill Pk NG19 . . . . 88 B3
West Hill Rd DN22 . . . . . . 39 D3
West Hill Wy NG18. . . . . .102 B7
Westholme Gdns NG8. . . .172 C6
Westhorpe NG25. . . . . . . .136 C8
Westhorpe Ave NG3. . . . .173 F5
Westhorpe Dr NG10. . . . . .193 C8
Westhorpe Mkt Pl NG25 .136 C8
West La
Edwinstowe NG21. . . . . . . 76 A2
Girton NG23. . . . . 82 E1
Westland Ave NG15 . . . . .145 D4
Westland Dr NG16 . . . . . .113 C3
West Leake La NG11 . . . . .204 D5
West Leake Rd LE12. . . . .205 C1
Westleigh NG19. . . . . 88 D6
Westleigh Rd NG8 . . . . . .159 E2
Westminster Ave
Kirkby in A NG17. . . . . .115 C5
Stapleford NG10. . . . . . .182 C5
Westminster Cl
Morton DN21. . . . . 15 B5
Nottingham NG3. . . . . . .173 E7
Worksop S81. . . . . 36 A7
Westminster Dr NG12 . . .176 E3
West Moor NG2. . . . . .174 D4
Westmoore Cl NG3. . . . . .162 A3
Westmoor La LN1. . . . . . . 55 D3
West Moor Rd DN10. . . . . 13 E6
Westmoreland Ct [8]
NG5. . . . . .161 B1
Westmorland Ct DN11. . . . 9 D4
Westmorland Dr S81. . . . . 25 F8
Westmorland Way NG16. .128 B3
West Nottinghamshire Coll
NG18. . . . . .102 C2
Weston Ave NG7. . . . . . . .173 A7
Weston Cl
Arnold NG5. . . . . .161 E4
Sutton in A NG17. . . . . .115 C8
Weston La NG23. . . . . 81 D5
Weston Rd NG2,NG23. . . . 80 A6
Weston St DE75. . . . . . . .157 A8
West Pk L Ctr DE72. . . . . .193 B7
West Pk Pl DN22. . . . . 39 D6
Westray Cl NG9. . . . . .171 B3
West St
Arnold NG5. . . . . .161 E7
Harworth DN11. . . . . 9 A5
Hucknall NG15. . . . . . . .146 A4
Kimberley NG16. . . . . . . .159 A4
Langley Mill NG16 . . . . .143 B3
Misson DN10. . . . . 4 B2
Morton DN21. . . . . 15 B4
Nottingham NG2. . . . . . .173 A4
Retford DN22. . . . . 39 E6
Warsop Vale NG20 . . . . . . 73 D4
Whaley Thorns NG20. . . . 59 A3
Worksop S80. . . . . 35 E2
West Terr
Hucknall NG15. . . . . . . .146 A7
[6] Ilkeston DE7. . . . . . .157 F1
West Thorpe LE12 . . . . . .217 C7
West View
Carlton in L S81. . . . . . . 25 F8
West Bridgford NG2 . . . .185 D5
Westview Ct NG4 . . . . . . .174 F8
West View Rd NG4 . . . . . .174 F8
Westville Dr NG15 . . . . . .145 E4
Westville Gdns NG3 . . . . .173 D7
Westward Ave NG9 . . . . . .184 A5
Westway
Cotgrave NG12 . . . . .187 F2
Worksop S81. . . . . 36 A7
West Wells La DN10. . . . . 12 E2
Westwick Rd NG8 . . . . . . .171 C5
Westwick St DE7. . . . . . . .170 A6
West Wlk
[1] Nottingham NG1. . . . .173 E4
Retford DN22. . . . . 39 C8
Westwood Dr S80. . . . . . . 35 B3
West Wood Est DN10. . . . . 9 F6
Westwood Inf Sch NG16 .128 C4
Westwood Rd
Bircotes DN10. . . . . 9 F6
Nottingham NG2. . . . . . .173 F4
Wetherby Cl
Kimberley NG16. . . . . . . .158 E7
Nottingham NG8 . . . . . . .160 B1
Wetherlam Cl NG2. . . . . .173 C2
Wetlands Waterfowl Reserve
DN22. . . . . 29 D7
Wetsyke La NG24. . . . . . .140 E4
Whaddon Ct LE11. . . . . . .220 C1
Whaley Bridge Cl NG18. .103 C5
Whaley Comm S44. . . . . . 58 D4
Whaley Rd NG20 . . . . 58 E2
Whaley Thorns Heritage Ctr
NG20. . . . . 59 A3
Whaley Thorns Prim Sch
NG20. . . . . 59 A3
Wharfdale Gdns NG18. . .103 A5
Wharfdale Rd NG10. . . . . .193 A6
Wharfedale
Nottingham NG8 . . . . . . .171 B3
Worksop S81. . . . . 36 A7
Wharf La NG12. . . . . .175 E3
Wharf Rd
[9] Mansfield NG18. . . . .102 B6
Misterton DN10. . . . . 6 F1

Wharf Rd continued
Nottingham NG7. . . . . . .223 D1
Pinxton NG16. . . . . .113 D2
Retford DN22. . . . . 39 E6
Stanton Hill NG17. . . . . .100 C6
Wharf St DN10. . . . . 10 A7
Wharmby Ave NG19. . . . . 87 D3
Wharncliffe Rd
[7] Ilkeston DE7. . . . . . .157 E1
Loughborough LE11. . . . .220 C3
Retford DN22. . . . . 39 E4
Wharton St DN22. . . . . . . 40 A6
Whatten Gdns LE12. . . . .212 E5
Whatton Ct [2] NG18. . . .103 A3
Whatton Rd
Hathern LE12. . . . . .212 D4
Kegworth DE74. . . . . . . .203 C1
Whatton Rise NG5. . . . . . .161 B4
Wheatacre Rd NG7. . . . . .184 F1
Wheat Cl NG8 . . . . .171 D5
Wheat Croft S81. . . . . 36 B7
Wheatcroft View NG11. . .185 C3
Wheatfield Cres NG19. . . . 88 E5
Wheatfield Dr DN11. . . . . . 8 B8
Wheatfields Rd NG3. . . . .174 A7
Wheatfield Way NG17. . . .100 E7
Wheatgrass Hill NG25,
NG23. . . . . .122 D4
Wheatgrass Rd NG9. . . . .183 B5
Wheatland Dr LE11. . . . . .220 C2
Wheatley Ave NG17. . . . . .114 F5
Wheatley Cl
Mansfield Woodhouse
NG19. . . . . 88 F1
Ruddington NG11. . . . . . .196 C5
Wheatley Dr NG4. . . . . . .174 C7
Wheatley Gr NG9. . . . . . .183 F4
Wheatley La NG23. . . . . . .112 B4
Wheatley Rd
Clayworth DN22 . . . . 21 F3
Sturton le S DN22 . . . . . . 32 B6
Wheatsheaf Av [3] NG24. .125 B4
Wheatsheaf Ct NG14 . . . .163 F4
Wheeldale Cl NG8 . . . . . .171 B4
Wheeler Ave NG16 . . . . . .144 B1
Wheeler Gate
Nottingham NG1. . . . . . .223 E2
Selston NG16. . . . . .129 A2
Wheldon Ave NG4 . . . . . . .162 C2
Wheldon Sch The NG4 . . .162 C1
Whernside Rd NG5. . . . . .161 F5
Whetstone Cl NG8. . . . . . .159 D3
Whickham Ct [4] NG2. . . .173 D1
Whilton Cl NG17. . . . . . . .101 B5
Whimpton Medieval Village
of NG22 . . . . 67 E8
Whimsey Pk NG4 . . . . . . .174 E6
Whinbush La NG14. . . . . .133 D4
Whinfell Cl NG7. . . . . . . .184 F2
Whinlatter Dr NG2. . . . . .186 C6
Whinleys Rd DN22 . . . . . . 31 A2
Whinney Bank NG19. . . . . 88 D4
Whinney Hill NG19. . . . . . 88 D4
Whinney La NG22. . . . . . . 77 D5
Whinney Moor Cl DN22. . . 39 F5
Whinney Moor La DN22 . . 39 F5
Whinney Moor Way DN22 39 F5
Whiston Cl NG5. . . . . .161 A6
Whitaker Cl DN22. . . . . . . 29 C1
Whitbread St NG7. . . . . . .172 F8
Whitburn Rd NG9 . . . . . . .182 E3
Whitby Cl NG8 . . . . .171 B4
Whitby Cres NG5. . . . . . . .162 A5
Whitby Rd
Eastwood NG16. . . . . . . .144 A3
Harworth DN11. . . . . 9 A5
Whitchurch Cl NG5 . . . . . .160 F8
Whitcombe Ct DN22. . . . . 39 C4
Whitcombe Gdns [11]
NG5. . . . . .147 A1
White Ave S81. . . . . 16 E3
Whitebeam Gdns NG6. . . .159 F7
Whitechapel St NG6 . . . . .160 D2
White Furrows NG12 . . . . .187 E2
Whitegate LE11. . . . . .220 C5
Whitegate Prim Sch
NG11. . . . . .184 D1
Whitegates Further Ed Unit
S80 . . . . 35 F1
Whitegates Way NG17. . . . 99 E2
Whitegate Vale NG11 . . . .184 C1
Whitehall Ct DN22 . . . . . . 39 E6
Whitehall Gdns DN22. . . . 39 F6
Whitehall Rd DN22. . . . . . 39 F6
White Hart La NG23. . . . . .112 A8
White Hart St NG18. . . . . .102 B6
White Hart Yd S80. . . . . . . 35 E1
Whitehead Cl DE7 . . . . . . .157 D2
Whitehead Dr NG16 . . . . .143 D8
Whitehead La NG17. . . . . .100 F6
Whitehouse Ave LE11. . . .220 C2
White House Rd DN11. . . . . 9 C4
Whitehouses Rd DN22. . . . 40 A4
Whitelands NG12 . . . . . . .188 A2
White Lodge Gdns NG8. . .171 D3
Whitely Cl NG9 . . . . .182 E7
Whitemoor Ave [5] NG8. . .172 D8
Whitemoor Ct NG8. . . . . . .172 D8
Whitemoor La NG23. . . . . .112 A4
Whitemoor Prim Sch
NG8. . . . . .160 D1
Whitemoor Rd NG6. . . . . .160 D2
Whitemoss Cl NG8. . . . . . .171 E3
White Post Farm Ctr The
NG22. . . . . .119 B7
White Rd NG5. . . . . .160 E3
White's Ave NG4 . . . . .174 B6

Whitestone Cl NG18. . . . .103 A3
Whitestub La NG22. . . . . .106 F5
Whites Wood La DN21. . . . 24 E8
White's Wood La [5] DN21 24 F8
Whitewater Cl NG22 . . . . . 77 C5
Whitewater La NG22. . . . . 63 B1
Whitewater Rd NG22. . . . . 77 C5
Whitewates La S81. . . . . . 18 A5
Whitfield Cl NG11. . . . . . .185 B6
Whitfield St NG24. . . . . . .140 A7
Whiting Ave NG9. . . . . . . .182 F2
Whitney Cl NG19. . . . . 89 A1
Whitsun Dale S81. . . . . . . 36 B8
Whittaker Rd
Beeston NG9. . . . . .183 A3
Rainworth NG21. . . . . . .118 A8
Whittier Rd NG2. . . . . . . .174 A3
Whittingham Cl NG3. . . . .162 A3
Whittingham Rd NG3. . . . .162 A3
Whittle Cl NG24. . . . . .125 C2
Whitton Cl
[4] Beeston NG9. . . . . . .183 C2
[3] Nottingham NG5. . . . .147 B1
Ranskill DN22. . . . . 19 B4
Whitwell Cl NG8 . . . . .159 E1
Whitwell Prim Sch S80. . . 45 A5
Whitwell Rd
Nottingham NG8. . . . . . .159 E1
Thorpe Salvin S80 . . . . . . 34 A4
Whitwell Sta S80. . . . . 45 A5
Whitworth Dr
Carlton NG4. . . . . .163 C2
Radcliffe on T NG12. . . .175 F2
Whitworth Rise NG5. . . . .160 F8
Whomsley Cl NG24. . . . . .140 D8
Whyburn La NG15. . . . . . .145 D7
Whyburn Prim Sch NG15 145 C5
Whyburn St NG15. . . . . . .146 C5
Whyston Ct NG15. . . . . . .145 C5
Wibberley Dr NG11. . . . . .196 B7
Wichnor Cl NG11. . . . . . . .184 E4
Wickens Wlk NG3. . . . . . .173 E6
Wickerwood Dr NG17 . . . .114 E6
Wicket Gr NG7. . . . . .222 A2
Wickstead Cl NG5. . . . . . .161 F3
Widdowson Cl NG6. . . . . .159 F8
Widecombe La NG11. . . . .195 D8
Wide La
Hathern LE12. . . . . .213 A1
Wymeswold LE12. . . . . . .217 C3
Wide St LE12 . . . . .213 A1
Widmerpool La LE12. . . . .217 D8
Widmerpool Rd NG12. . . .207 E3
Widmerpool St NG16. . . . .113 C2
Wighay Rd NG15 . . . . . . .131 A2
Wigley Cl NG3. . . . . .173 E6
Wigman Rd NG8 . . . . .171 E7
Wigsley Rd
Harby NG23. . . . . 70 C2
North Scarle LN6. . . . . . . 83 D5
Wigthorpe La S81. . . . . . . 26 A4
Wigwam Gr NG15 . . . . . . .146 C7
Wigwam La NG15 . . . . . . .146 C7
Wilberforce Rd NG19. . . . . 87 D2
Wilcox Ave NG19. . . . . 88 B5
Wilcox Dr NG16. . . . . .129 A1
Wilde Cres NG16. . . . . . . .129 A6
Wilden Cres NG7 . . . . .184 E4
Wildflower Gr NG17. . . . . .100 D1
Wild Hill NG17. . . . . 99 E7
Wildman St NG7 . . . . .222 C4
Wildman Villas DN10. . . . . 14 B1
Wilford Cl NG24 . . . . .140 B8
Wilford Cres NG16 . . . . . .196 C8
Wilford Cres E NG2 . . . . . .173 D1
Wilford Cres W NG2. . . . . .173 C1
Wilford Gr
Nottingham NG2. . . . . . .173 C1
West Bridgford NG2 . . . .185 D8
Wilford La NG2. . . . . .185 C7
Wilford Rd
Mansfield NG18. . . . . . . .103 A3
Nottingham NG2. . . . . . .223 E1
West Bridgford NG11 . . . .185 C2
Wilford Sports Complex
NG2. . . . . .185 D6
Wilford St NG2. . . . . .223 E1
Wilfred Ave NG24. . . . . . .140 C4
Wilfrid Gr NG2. . . . . .185 E3
Wilhallow La NG16. . . . . . .128 E2
Wilkins Gdns NG11. . . . . .184 C1
Wilkinson Ave NG9. . . . . .183 F6
Wilkinson Cl NG19. . . . . . . 87 A5
Wilkinson St NG7. . . . . . . .172 E8
Willand Ct DN22. . . . . 29 E1
Willaston Cl NG6. . . . . . . .160 C4
Willbert Rd NG5. . . . . . . .148 A1
Willerby Rd NG5. . . . . . . .162 A5
Willersley Dr NG2. . . . . . .173 C2
Willesden Gn NG16 . . . . . .159 D3
Willetts Ct NG17. . . . . . . .100 F1
Willey La NG16. . . . . .144 A8
William Ave NG16. . . . . . .143 F2
William Booth Birthplace
Mus NG2 . . . . .173 E4
William Booth Inf Sch
NG2. . . . . .173 E4
William Booth Rd NG2. . .174 A4
William Bradford Cl DN10 . 3 C1
William Cl NG4 . . . . .175 B8
William & Henry Mews
LN6. . . . . 84 D3
William Lilley Inf Sch
NG9. . . . . .182 D6
William Old Ct [3] NG8. . .172 A5
William Rd
Stapleford NG9 . . . . .182 D7
West Bridgford NG2 . . . .185 E7

William Sharp Sch NG8 .171 C7
Williams La NG24. . . . . . .140 E2
Williamson St NG19. . . . . .101 E7
Williams Rd NG9. . . . . . . .183 B3
Williams St S81. . . . . 16 E3
William St
Hucknall NG15. . . . . . . .146 A7
Long Eaton NG10. . . . . . .182 C2
Loughborough LE11. . . . .220 A3
Newark-on-T NG24 . . . . .140 A8
Saxilby LN1 . . . . 57 A3
Willingham Rd DN21. . . . . 24 F2
Willis Rd NG24. . . . . .139 F6
Willoughby Ave
Long Eaton NG10. . . . . . .182 C3
Nottingham NG7. . . . . . .222 B2
Willoughby Chase DN21. . 24 E5
Willoughby Cl NG7. . . . . . .184 B8
Willoughby Ct
[11] Mansfield NG18. . . . .103 A2
Norwell NG23 . . . . .110 A8
Nottingham NG7 . . . . . . .222 B1
Willoughby Prim Sch
LE14 . . . . .217 B7
Willoughby Rd
West Bridgford NG2 . . . .185 F6
Widmerpool NG12 . . . . . .208 C3
Willoughby St
Beeston NG9. . . . . .184 A6
Cossall DE7 . . . . .158 A2
Gainsborough DN21 . . . . . 24 D5
Nottingham NG7. . . . . . .222 B1
Willoughby Way NG22 . . . . 64 B2
Willow Ave
Carlton in L S81. . . . . . . 25 C7
Carlton NG4. . . . . .175 A6
Hucknall NG15. . . . . . . .145 D4
Kirkby in A NG17. . . . . .114 C6
Long Eaton NG10. . . . . . .182 C2
Mansfield Woodhouse NG19 89 A1
Misterton DN10. . . . . 6 F2
Shirebrook NG20. . . . . . . 72 D5
Stapleford NG9. . . . . . . .182 D6
Willowbridge Cl DN22. . . . 39 E6
Willowbridge La NG17 . . . .100 C3
Willow Brook NG12 . . . . . .198 A2
Willowbrook Ct [6] NG2. .173 C1
Willow Brook Prim Sch
NG12. . . . . .198 A2
Willow Cl
Burton Joyce NG14. . . . . .163 F5
East Leake LE12 . . . . . . .214 C2
Gainsborough DN21 . . . . . 15 B3
Radcliffe on T NG12. . . .175 F2
Saxilby LN1 . . . . 57 B3
Selston NG16. . . . . .129 B7
South Normanton DE55. . .113 A5
Worksop S80. . . . . 35 E1
Willow Cres
Carlton NG4. . . . . .163 A2
Lambley NG4. . . . . .163 C6
Sutton in A NG17. . . . . .100 D3
Willow Ct NG16. . . . . .129 A1
Willowdene NG12. . . . . . . .188 A3
Willow Dr
Annesley Woodhouse
NG15. . . . . .129 F6
North Muskham NG23. . . .110 C2
Willow Farm Prim Sch
NG4. . . . . .163 A2
Willow Gd NG17 . . . . .101 B2
Willow Hill Cl NG6 . . . . . .160 A6
Willow Holt
Lowdham NG14 . . . . .150 E1
Retford DN22. . . . . 39 E3
Willow La
Carlton NG4. . . . . .163 A2
Langar NG13 . . . . .190 C2
Willow Pool La LE12 . . . . .213 C5
Willow Rd
Bingham NG13. . . . . . . .178 A4
Carlton NG4. . . . . .175 A6
New Balderton NG24. . . . .140 C5
Nottingham NG7 . . . . . . .172 E2
West Bridgford NG2 . . . .185 E3
Willow Rise NG10. . . . . . . .182 B5
Willows The
Farndon NG24 . . . . .139 A4
Nottingham NG8 . . . . . . .172 A7
Pleasley NG19. . . . . 87 A6
Willow Tree Cl NG19 . . . . . 89 D2
Willow Wong NG14. . . . . . .163 F5
Will Scarlet Cl NG21 . . . . .118 A4
Willwell Dr NG2 . . . . .185 C3
Wilmington Ct LE11. . . . . .220 C2
Wilmington Gdns NG5. . . .161 C3
Wilmore Way NG19 . . . . . .101 C5
Wilmot La NG9 . . . . .183 F5
Wilmot St
Ilkeston DE7. . . . . .157 E1
Long Eaton NG10. . . . . . .193 A4
Wilne Ave NG10. . . . . .193 A4
Wilne Rd NG10. . . . . .193 A4
Wilsic Rd DN11. . . . . 8 A8
Wilson Ave NG17. . . . . . . .114 F5
Wilson Cl
Arnold NG5. . . . . .162 B5
Mattersey DN10 . . . . 20 A8
Wilson Rd NG16 . . . . .143 F1
Wilson's La NG25 . . . . . . .137 E4
Wilson St
Gainsborough DN21 . . . . . 15 B1
Newark-on-T NG24 . . . . .124 F1
Pinxton NG16. . . . . .113 D3
Radmanthwaite NG19 . . . . 87 D2
Wilsthorpe Com Sch
NG10. . . . . .182 B1
Wilsthorpe Rd DE72. . . . . .193 A4

Wilton Ave LE11 . . . . 220 C1
Wilton Pl DE7 . . . . 157 F1
Wilton Rd NG7 . . . . 222 A4
Wilton St
  5 Ilkeston DE7 . . . . . . 157 F1
  Nottingham NG6 . . . . . . 160 E4
Wilton Terr NG6 . . . . 160 E4
Wiltshire Ave NG16 . . . . . 159 E3
Wilwell Farm Cutting Nature
  Reserve NG11 . . . . 185 B2
Wimbishthorpe Cl NG13 . 181 A3
Wimbledon Dr NG16 . . . . 159 E3
Wimbledon Rd NG5 . . . . . 161 A3
Wimborne Cl NG2 . . . . . . 185 C5
Wimbourne Rd NG7 . . . . 222 B4
Wimpole Rd NG9 . . . . 171 D1
Winborne Cl NG19 . . . . . . 101 D6
Winchester Ave NG9 . . . . 183 E7
Winchester Cl
  East Leake LE12 . . . . . . 205 E3
  Mansfield NG18 . . . . 103 E3
  Worksop S81 . . . . 36 A7
Winchester Cres DE7 . . . . 170 A8
Winchester Ct NG5 . . . . . 161 E3
Winchester Dr NG19 . . . . . 88 D4
Winchester St NG5 . . . . . . 161 D2
Winchester Terr **7** NG5 . 161 C3
Winchilsea Ave NG24 . . . . 140 A7
Windermere Ave DN11 . . . . 8 E4
Windermere Cl
  Carlton NG4 . . . . 162 F2
  West Bridgford NG2 . . . . 186 C6
  Worksop S81 . . . . 35 E8
Windermere Gdns NG10 . 182 B2
Windermere Rd
  Beeston NG9 . . . . 183 D8
  Hucknall NG15 . . . . 145 F4
  Long Eaton NG10 . . . . . . 182 A2
  Nottingham NG7 . . . . . . 173 A8
Windley Dr DE7 . . . . 157 D3
Windmill Ave NG15 . . . . . 146 A6
Windmill Cl NG3 . . . . 173 F5
Windmill Ct NG12 . . . . . . 197 F2
Windmill Gr NG15 . . . . . . 146 A6
Windmill Hill NG25 . . . . . 134 C5
Windmill La
  Mansfield NG18 . . . . 102 C8
  Nottingham NG2 . . . . . . 173 F5
  Worksop S80 . . . . 47 B7
Windmill Rd LE11 . . . . . . 220 D3
Windmill View NG2 . . . . . 174 A4
Windmill Way DE74 . . . . 203 B2
Windrush Cl NG9 . . . . 171 D1
Windsmoor Rd NG16 . . . 143 D8
Windsor Ave
  Newark-on-T NG24 . . . . 139 E6
  Sutton in A NG17 . . . . . . 100 B3
Windsor Cl
  Collingham NG23 . . . . . . 112 A8
  Gringley on t H DN10 . . . . 12 E2
  Hucknall NG15 . . . . 146 B8
  Trowell NG9 . . . . 170 A5
Windsor Cres
  Arnold NG5 . . . . 162 B5
  Stapleford NG9 . . . . 182 E7
Windsor Ct
  Bingham NG13 . . . . 177 C4
  Harworth DN11 . . . . 9 B5
  Sandiacre NG10 . . . . 182 B4
Windsor Dr NG20 . . . . 74 A4
Windsor Gdns
  Carlton in L S81 . . . . 25 E6
  Mansfield NG18 . . . . 102 D5
Windsor Rd
  Carlton in L S81 . . . . 25 E6
  Clipstone NG19 . . . . 89 D3
  Mansfield NG18 . . . . 102 D5
  Newark-on-T NG24 . . . . 139 F6
  Retford DN22 . . . . 29 C1
  Selston NG16 . . . . 129 A8
  Worksop S81 . . . . 35 D7
Windsor St
  Beeston NG9 . . . . 184 A6
  Stapleford NG9 . . . . 182 E7
Windyridge DN10 . . . . 11 C3
Windy Ridge NG20 . . . . . . 74 C3
Wing Alley NG1 . . . . 223 F2
Wingate Cl NG8 . . . . 171 F6
Wingbourne Wlk NG6 . . . 146 C1
Wingfield Ave S81 . . . . 36 A6
Wingfield Dr
  Beeston NG9 . . . . 172 A1
  Ilkeston DE7 . . . . 157 D3
Wingfield Rd NG18 . . . . . 103 A4
Wings Dr NG15 . . . . 145 D3
Winifred Cres NG14 . . . . . 163 F4
Winifred St
  Hucknall NG15 . . . . 146 B6
  Rhodesia S80 . . . . 35 A4
Winkburn La NG22 . . . . . 121 E2
Winkburn Rd NG19 . . . . . 101 F7
Winnery Cl DN11 . . . . 8 A8
Winrow Gdns NG6 . . . . . 160 C3
Winscale Ave NG5 . . . . . . 161 A8
Winscale Gdns **15** NG5 . 161 A8
Winscombe Mount NG11 195 E7
Winsford Cl NG2 . . . . 160 B2
Winstanley Dr NG24 . . . . 140 E8
Winster Ave
  Carlton NG4 . . . . 162 D1
  Ravenshead NG15 . . . . . 117 B3
Winster Cl NG9 . . . . 171 F1
Winster Gr S81 . . . . 35 F8
Winster Way NG18 . . . . . 103 E1
Winston Cl
  Arnold NG3 . . . . 162 C5
  Stapleford NG9 . . . . 182 E8
Winston Ct NG24 . . . . 139 E5

Winston Dr NG23 . . . . . . 153 E4
Winston Gn DN10 . . . . 19 F8
Winston Gr NG22 . . . . 30 A1
Winterbank Cl NG17 . . . . 100 D1
Winterbeck Cl NG13 . . . . 181 A3
Winterbourne Dr NG9 . . . 170 E1
Winterdale Cl NG24 . . . . 125 D1
Wintern Ct DN21 . . . . 24 D6
Winterton Cl NG5 . . . . . . 161 F6
Winterton Rise NG5 . . . . . 161 B7
Winthorpe Prim Sch
  NG24 . . . . 125 D7
Winthorpe Rd
  Arnold NG5 . . . . 162 A7
  Gateford S81 . . . . 35 C8
  Newark-on-T NG24 . . . . 125 B3
Winthorpe St NG19 . . . . 101 D6
Wintringham Cres NG5 . 162 A5
Wire La DE55 . . . . 99 B3
Wisa Terr NG5 . . . . 161 D2
Wiseton Rd DN22 . . . . 21 C6
Wishford Ave NG7 . . . . . 222 A1
Wisley Cl NG11 . . . . 185 C3
Wistow Cl NG8 . . . . 172 E8
Witch La NG23 . . . . 96 F8
Witham Cl NG24 . . . . 125 B2
Withern Rd NG8 . . . . 159 F1
Withorn Mews NG19 . . . 101 E7
Witney Cl NG5 . . . . 160 E7
Wittering Cl NG10 . . . . . . 193 E5
Wiverton Rd
  Bingham NG13 . . . . 177 E4
  Nottingham NG7 . . . . . . 173 A8
Woburn Ave NG17 . . . . . 115 C5
Woburn Cl NG2 . . . . 186 C4
Woburn Croft NG10 . . . . 182 A4
Woburn Gr DN22 . . . . 39 E3
Woburn La NG19 . . . . 87 C4
Woburn Pl NG19 . . . . 87 C4
Woburn Rd NG19 . . . . 87 C4
Woburn Rise NG5 . . . . . . 162 B5
Wodehouse Ave NG11 . . . 195 B2
Wolds Dr NG12 . . . . 197 F3
Wolds Rise NG12 . . . . 197 F3
Wolfit Ave NG24 . . . . 140 E5
Wollacombe Cl NG3 . . . . 162 D5
Wollaton Ave NG4 . . . . . 162 E2
Wollaton Cl NG18 . . . . . . 103 B7
Wollaton Cres NG9 . . . . . 183 E8
Wollaton Ct NG6 . . . . 160 E6
Wollaton Hall NG8 . . . . . 172 A3
Wollaton Hall Dr NG8 . . 172 D3
Wollaton Paddocks NG8 . 171 C4
Wollaton Pk NG8 . . . . 171 F3
Wollaton Rd
  Beeston NG9 . . . . 183 E7
  Kirkby in A NG17 . . . . . . 115 C5
  Nottingham NG8 . . . . . . 172 D5
Wollaton Rise NG8 . . . . . 171 E2
Wollaton St NG1 . . . . 223 D3
Wollaton Vale NG8 . . . . . 171 E2
Wolseley Ave NG17 . . . . . 100 F3
Wolsey Ave NG7 . . . . 222 B3
Wolsey Dr NG17 . . . . 115 B7
Wolsey Way **2** LE11 . . . . 220 C4
Wonderland Pleasure Pk
  NG22 . . . . 119 B7
Wong La DN11 . . . . 8 A8
Wood Ave
  Creswell S80 . . . . 58 C8
  Sandiacre NG10 . . . . 182 A5
Woodbank Dr NG8 . . . . . 171 D2
Woodbeck Rise DN22 . . . . 39 E8
Woodborough La NG5 . . . 148 C3
Woodborough Rd
  Mansfield NG19 . . . . 87 E1
  Nottingham NG3, NG1 . . 161 E2
Woodbridge Ave NG11 . . 184 E2
Woodbridge Cl DE75 . . . . 143 B1
Woodchurch Rd NG5 . . . . 147 B1
Wood Cl NG18 . . . . 102 F8
Woodcoates Rd NG22 . . . . 67 B5
Wooden Beck Hill DN10 . . 13 C4
Wood End Dr NG15 . . . . . 117 A2
Woodfield Rd
  Gainsborough DN21 . . . . . 15 F1
  Nottingham NG8 . . . . . . 159 E1
  Pinxton NG16 . . . . 113 D4
Woodford Cl NG5 . . . . . . 146 E1
Woodford Rd
  Arnold NG5 . . . . 162 A5
  Hucknall NG15 . . . . 146 B6
Wood Gate LE11 . . . . 220 B3
Woodgate Cl NG12 . . . . . 187 E3
Woodgate Ct NG7 . . . . . . 222 C3
Woodgate La
  Beckingham LN5 . . . . . . 142 E8
  Cotgrave NG12 . . . . 187 D3
Woodgate Rd LE12 . . . . . 214 C8
Wood Gr NG14 . . . . 148 F8
Woodhall Cl
  2 Kirkby in A NG17 . . . . 114 E7
  Mansfield NG18 . . . . 102 F8
Woodhall Cres LN1 . . . . . . 56 F4
Woodhall Gdns NG18 . . . 102 F8
Woodhall La DN22 . . . . 39 D2
Woodhall Rd NG8 . . . . . . 172 B5
Woodhead Cl NG21 . . . . . 76 B1
Woodhedge Dr NG3 . . . . 174 A8
Wood Hill LE14 . . . . 218 E3
Woodhill Ave DN21 . . . . . 15 F1
Woodhill Rd NG23 . . . . . . 98 A1
Woodhouse La
  Carlton in L S81 . . . . 26 A7
  Sutton in A NG17 . . . . . . 101 A7

Woodhouse Pl NG22 . . . . . 66 A2
Woodhouse Rd NG18 . . . . 102 B8
Woodhouse St NG3 . . . . . 173 F5
Woodhouse Way NG16 . . 159 D3
Wood La
  Barkestone-le-V NG13 . . 192 C1
  Beckingham DN10 . . . . . . 23 B8
  Carlton NG4 . . . . 163 A2
  Creswell S80 . . . . 58 B8
  Egmanton NG22 . . . . 79 F5
  Gringley on t H DN10 . . . . 12 E3
  Grove DN22 . . . . 41 E4
  Hucknall NG15 . . . . 145 F7
  Kersall NG22 . . . . 94 A1
  Kingston-on-S NG11 . . . . 204 F7
  Market Warsop NG20 . . . . 73 F7
  North Wheatley DN22 . . . . 22 D1
  Shirebrook NG19 . . . . 72 E1
  South Scarle NG23 . . . . . . 98 E6
Woodland Ave
  Gainsborough DN21 . . . . . 15 B3
  Huthwaite NG17 . . . . 99 E4
  Ilkeston DE7 . . . . 157 D4
  Worksop S80 . . . . 36 B1
Woodland Cl
  Clipstone NG21 . . . . 90 B4
  Cotgrave NG12 . . . . 187 F2
  Farnsfield NG22 . . . . 120 A6
  Radcliffe on T NG12 . . . . 176 B3
Woodland Cres NG18 . . . 102 F4
Woodland Dr
  Mansfield NG18 . . . . 102 F4
  Nottingham NG3 . . . . . . 161 D2
  Nuthall NG16 . . . . 159 F4
  Southwell NG25 . . . . 121 D1
  Worksop S81 . . . . 35 E6
Woodland Gr
  Arnold NG5 . . . . 161 D4
  Beeston NG9 . . . . 183 D5
  Carlton NG4 . . . . 174 F6
  Mansfield Woodhouse NG19 88 C4
  Market Warsop NG20 . . . . 74 B4
Woodland Rd
  Mansfield NG18 . . . . 102 F8
  West Bridgford NG2 . . . . 173 F1
Woodland Rise NG15 . . . 117 A2
Woodlands NG12 . . . . 125 D7
Woodlands Cl
  Newark-on-T NG24 . . . . 139 E6
  Wymeswold LE12 . . . . . . 216 C3
Woodlands Dr LE11 . . . . . 220 A2
Woodlands Farm Cl
  NG15 . . . . 145 D4
Woodlands Gr NG15 . . . . 145 D4
Woodlands Sch NG8 . . . . 172 A8
Woodlands The
  Blyth S81 . . . . 18 B6
  Mansfield NG18 . . . . 88 B1
  Nottingham NG6 . . . . . . 160 D5
  Whaley Thorns NG20 . . . . 59 A3
Woodlands Way NG17 . . . 100 C1
Woodland View
  Southwell NG25 . . . . 136 D8
  Whaley Thorns NG20 . . . . 59 A3
Woodland Way NG16 . . . . 143 E2
Woodland Wlk NG17 . . . . 115 D5
Woodlane Gdns NG3 . . . . 173 F7
Woodleigh NG12 . . . . 197 E2
Woodley Sq NG6 . . . . 146 C2
Woodley St NG11 . . . . . . 196 C7
Wood Link NG6 . . . . 159 E7
Wood Nook Cl NG16 . . . . 128 F6
Woodpecker Cl NG13 . . . 177 F3
Woodpecker Dr NG21 . . . 118 B8
Woodrow Av NG5 . . . . . . 172 A8
Woodruff La NG22 . . . . . 106 A5
Woodsend NG14 . . . . 163 F4
Woodsetts La S81 . . . . 25 A1
Woodsford Gr NG7 . . . . . 184 E2
Woods Foundation CE Prim
  Sch NG14 . . . . 149 B4
Woods Hill NG17 . . . . 100 E2
Woodside
  Eastwood NG16 . . . . 143 E3
  Farnsfield NG22 . . . . 120 A6
  Retford DN22 . . . . 39 C8
  Sutton in A NG17 . . . . . . 100 E1
Woodside Ave
  Mansfield NG18 . . . . 102 D3
  Nuthall NG16 . . . . 159 B5
  Radcliffe on T NG12 . . . . 176 B3
Woodside Cres
  Ilkeston DE7 . . . . 157 D5
  Long Eaton NG10 . . . . . . 193 A6
Woodside Dr NG5 . . . . . . 161 D8
Woodside Rd
  Beeston, Chilwell NG9 . . . 183 A5
  Beeston NG9 . . . . 183 F8
  Burton Joyce NG14 . . . . 163 D3
  Radcliffe on T NG12 . . . . 176 B3
  Ravenshead NG15 . . . . . 116 F3
  Sandiacre NG10 . . . . 182 B5
  Shirebrook NG20 . . . . 72 E5
  Shireoaks S81 . . . . 34 F7
Woodside View DN11 . . . . . 9 B4
Woods La NG14 . . . . 148 E2
Wood's La NG23 . . . . 153 A1
Wood St
  Arnold NG5 . . . . 161 F8
  Eastwood NG16 . . . . 143 F3
  Ilkeston DE7 . . . . 157 F1
  Mansfield NG18 . . . . 102 B5
  Market Warsop NG20 . . . . 74 B5
  Newark-on-T NG24 . . . . 140 B8
  Nottingham NG7 . . . . . . 222 C3
Woods Terr DN21 . . . . 15 C2
Woodstock Ave NG7 . . . . 222 A4

Woodstock Cl NG24 . . . . 140 C8
Woodstock Rd NG9 . . . . . 182 F3
Woodstock St NG15 . . . . . 146 B6
Woodston Wlk NG5 . . . . . 148 A2
Woodthorpe Ave
  Arnold NG5 . . . . 161 E4
  Loughborough LE11 . . . . 220 B1
Woodthorpe Ct NG5 . . . . 161 E3
Woodthorpe Dr NG3 . . . . 161 E4
Woodthorpe Gdns NG5 . . 161 F3
Woodthorpe Rd
  Loughborough LE11 . . . . 220 B1
  Nottingham NG3 . . . . . . 161 F3
Woodview NG12 . . . . 188 A2
Wood View NG2 . . . . 186 B4
Woodview Bsns Ctr **15**
  NG5 . . . . 147 A1
Woodview Ct NG4 . . . . . . 174 C5
Woodview Gdns NG19 . . . 89 C2
Woodville Cl NG9 . . . . . . 183 C6
Woodville Dr NG5 . . . . . . 161 C3
Woodville Rd **2** NG5 . . . 161 C2
Woodward St NG2 . . . . . 173 D1
Woodwards The NG24 . . . 140 C6
Woodyard La NG8 . . . . . . 172 A5
Wooliscroft Way DE7 . . . 157 C6
Woollaton St NG15 . . . . . 146 B7
Woolmer Rd NG2 . . . . . . 173 C1
Woolpack La NG1 . . . . . . 223 F2
Woolpack St DN22 . . . . . . 39 F7
Woolsington Cl NG8 . . . . 159 D2
Woolsthorpe Cl **2** NG8 . . 172 A6
Wootton Cl
  East Leake LE12 . . . . . . 205 E2
  Nottingham NG8 . . . . . . 171 D7
Worcester Ave NG19 . . . . 88 C6
Worcester Cl
  Lowdham NG14 . . . . 150 E1
  Worksop S81 . . . . 36 A7
Worcester Gdns NG5 . . . . 161 E5
Worcester Mews NG19 . . 88 C6
Worcester Rd NG5 . . . . . . 161 E5
Wordsworth Ave
  Hucknall NG15 . . . . 145 D6
  Mansfield Woodhouse NG19 88 B4
  Sutton in A NG17 . . . . . . 100 B3
Wordsworth Dr NG24 . . . 140 D5
Wordsworth Rd
  Arnold NG5 . . . . 161 D7
  Awsworth NG16 . . . . 158 C4
  Nottingham NG7 . . . . . . 222 A4
  West Bridgford NG2 . . . . 185 E6
Workhouse The NG25 . . . 122 A1
Worksop Coll S80 . . . . 47 B7
Worksop L Ctr S81 . . . . . . 35 E6
Worksop Mus S80 . . . . 35 F2
Worksop Priory CE Prim Sch
  S80 . . . . 35 F1
Worksop Rd
  Babworth DN22 . . . . 49 C7
  Blyth S81 . . . . 18 A2
  Cuckney NG20 . . . . 60 A4
  Edwinstowe NG21, NG22 . . 76 D5
  Nottingham NG3 . . . . . . 173 F5
  Whitwell S80 . . . . 45 A7
  Woodsetts S81 . . . . 25 A2
Worksop Sta S80 . . . . 35 F4
Worrall Ave
  Arnold NG5 . . . . 161 F7
  Long Eaton NG10 . . . . . . 182 F1
Worsborough Cl NG8 . . . 101 E5
Worth St NG4 . . . . 174 E8
Wortley Ave NG9 . . . . 170 D3
Wortley Cl DE7 . . . . 170 A8
Wortley Hall Cl NG7 . . . . 172 C2
Worwood Dr NG2 . . . . . . 185 C4
Wossock La LE12 . . . . . . 204 F3
Woulds Field NG12 . . . . . 187 F1
Wray Cl NG3 . . . . 173 E5
Wren Ct
  Long Eaton NG10 . . . . . . 193 A4
  Worksop S81 . . . . 35 C7
Wrenthorpe Vale NG11 . . 195 E8
Wrightson Cl NG17 . . . . . 101 B3
Wrights Orch NG12 . . . . 197 E2
Wright St
  Carlton NG4 . . . . 175 A7
  Newark-on-T NG24 . . . . 140 B8
Wright Wilson St DN22 . . . 39 F6
Wroot Rd DN9 . . . . 1 B6
Wroughton Cl NG16 . . . . 144 A2
Wroxham Dr NG8 . . . . . . 171 D2
Wycar Rd NG24 . . . . 102 A4
Wychwood Dr NG9 . . . . . 170 D4
Wychwood Rd NG13 . . . . 177 C4
Wycliffe Gr NG3 . . . . 161 E2
Wycliffe St NG7 . . . . 160 F1
Wycombe Cl NG11 . . . . . 195 D8
Wye Gdns NG7 . . . . 172 D6
Wyggeston Rd NG13 . . . . 181 B2
Wykeham Rd NG5 . . . . . . 162 A5
Wyke La NG24 . . . . 138 F5
Wykes Ave NG4 . . . . 162 F2
Wymeswold CE Sch
  LE12 . . . . 216 C3
Wymeswold Ind Est
  LE12 . . . . 216 A1
Wymeswold Meadows Nature
  Reserve LE12 . . . . 216 E3
Wymeswold Rd
  Hoton LE12 . . . . 215 E2
  Rempstone LE12 . . . . . . 215 E5
  Wysall NG12 . . . . 207 C2
Wymondham Cl NG5 . . . . 162 A6
Wynbreck Dr NG12 . . . . . 197 F3
Wyndale Dr NG18 . . . . . . 103 A5
Wyndham Ct NG9 . . . . . . 183 B4

Wyndham Mews NG3 . . . 173 B7
Wyndings The NG5 . . . . . 161 F4
Wynhill Ct NG13 . . . . 177 C5
Wynlea Dr S81 . . . . 16 F6
Wynndale Prim Sch
  NG18 . . . . 103 A5
Wynward Cl DE7 . . . . 157 C3
Wynwood Cl NG9 . . . . . . 183 B2
Wynwood Rd NG9 . . . . . . 183 B1
Wyrale Dr NG8 . . . . 159 E1
Wysall Cl NG19 . . . . 87 E1
Wysall La
  Keyworth NG12 . . . . 207 D7
  Wymeswold LE12 . . . . . . 216 D5
Wysall Rd
  Costock LE12 . . . . 206 C1
  Keyworth NG12 . . . . 197 B1
  Rempstone LE12 . . . . . . 215 F6
  Widmerpool LE12 . . . . . . 208 B4
  Wysall NG12 . . . . 207 A2
Wyton Cl NG5 . . . . 161 A5
Wyvelle Cres DE74 . . . . . 203 C3
Wyvern Ave NG10 . . . . . . 193 D6
Wyvern Cl NG16 . . . . 158 A8
Wyville Cl NG7 . . . . 222 A3

Y

Yalding Dr NG8 . . . . 171 C4
Yalding Gdns NG8 . . . . . . 171 C4
Yarwell Cl NG3 . . . . 174 C7
Yatesbury Cres NG8 . . . . 171 E8
Yates Gdns **2** NG5 . . . . . 161 A8
Yellowhammer Dr S81 . . . 35 D7
Yeoman Ave NG6 . . . . . . 146 F4
Yeoman Cl S80 . . . . 36 A1
Yeoman Park Specl Sch
  NG19 . . . . 88 C4
Yeomans Ct NG7 . . . . 222 C2
Yeovil Ct **3** NG18 . . . . . 103 A2
Yew Barrow Cl NG2 . . . . . 186 C5
Yew Cl
  East Leake LE12 . . . . . . 214 D8
  Nottingham NG5 . . . . . . 161 D2
Yewdale Cl
  Nottingham NG11 . . . . . 195 D8
  West Bridgford NG2 . . . . 186 C5
Yew Tree Ave
  5 Kirkby in A NG17 . . . . 114 F6
  Nottingham NG5 . . . . . . 161 C1
Yew Tree Cl
  New Ollerton NG22 . . . . . . 77 C5
  Radcliffe on T NG12 . . . . 175 D3
Yew Tree Dr
  Bawtry DN10 . . . . 9 F7
  Huthwaite NG17 . . . . 99 F2
  Shirebrook NG20 . . . . 72 D5
Yew Tree La
  Carlton NG4 . . . . 163 A2
  Nottingham NG11 . . . . . 184 C2
Yew Tree Rd
  Elkesley DN22 . . . . 50 B4
  Hucknall NG15 . . . . 146 B4
  New Ollerton NG22 . . . . . . 77 C5
Yew Tree Way NG24 . . . . 125 F2
Yonge Cl NG12 . . . . 175 E2
York Ave
  Beeston NG9 . . . . 183 F4
  Sandiacre NG10 . . . . 182 A5
  Westwood NG16 . . . . 128 B4
York Cl
  Carlton NG4 . . . . 162 F2
  East Leake LE12 . . . . . . 205 C4
York Dr NG8 . . . . 159 D2
Yorke St
  Hucknall NG15 . . . . 146 A7
  Mansfield Woodhouse NG19 88 B2
York Pl S81 . . . . 34 F7
York Rd
  Harworth DN11 . . . . 9 A4
  Long Eaton NG10 . . . . . . 182 D1
  Loughborough LE11 . . . . 220 A3
  Shirebrook NG20 . . . . 72 E3
  Tickhill DN11 . . . . 8 B7
York St
  Carlton NG4 . . . . 175 A7
  East Markham NG22 . . . . . 65 F7
  Mansfield NG18 . . . . 102 A5
  Nottingham NG1 . . . . . . 223 E4
  Sutton in A NG17 . . . . . . 100 E3
York Terr
  Market Warsop NG20 . . . . 74 B4
  Misterton DN10 . . . . 7 A2
  Pinxton NG16 . . . . 113 C1
Young Cl NG6 . . . . 159 F5
Young Cres NG17 . . . . . . 101 B2
Youngs Av NG24 . . . . 140 E2
Youngs Cl NG24 . . . . 125 E2
Yvonne Cres NG4 . . . . . . 174 F7

Z

Zouch Rd LE12 . . . . 213 A3
Zulla Rd NG3 . . . . 173 C8
Zulu Rd NG7 . . . . 160 F2

PHILIP'S MAPS

the Gold Standard for drivers

◆ **Philip's street atlases cover all of England, Wales, Northern Ireland and much of Scotland**

◆ Every named street is shown, including alleys, lanes and walkways

◆ Thousands of additional features marked: stations, public buildings, car parks, places of interest

◆ Route-planning maps to get you close to your destination

◆ Postcodes on the maps and in the index

◆ Widely used by the emergency services, transport companies and local authorities

For national mapping, choose **Philip's Navigator Britain** the most detailed road atlas available of England, Wales and Scotland. Hailed by Auto Express as 'the ultimate road atlas', Navigator shows every road and lane in Britain.

Street atlases currently available

England

Bedfordshire and Luton	Surrey
Berkshire	East Sussex
Birmingham and West Midlands	West Sussex
	Tyne and Wear
Bristol and Bath	Warwickshire and Coventry
Buckinghamshire and Milton Keynes	Wiltshire and Swindon
	Worcestershire
Cambridgeshire and Peterborough	East Yorkshire Northern Lincolnshire
Cheshire	North Yorkshire
Cornwall	South Yorkshire
Cumbria	West Yorkshire
Derbyshire	
Devon	**Wales**
Dorset	Anglesey, Conwy and Gwynedd
County Durham and Teesside	Cardiff, Swansea and The Valleys
Essex	Carmarthenshire, Pembrokeshire and Swansea
North Essex	
South Essex	
Gloucestershire and Bristol	Ceredigion and South Gwynedd
Hampshire	Denbighshire, Flintshire, Wrexham
North Hampshire	
South Hampshire	Herefordshire Monmouthshire
Herefordshire Monmouthshire	Powys
Hertfordshire	
Isle of Wight	**Scotland**
Kent	Aberdeenshire
East Kent	Ayrshire
West Kent	Dumfries and Galloway
Lancashire	Edinburgh and East Central Scotland
Leicestershire and Rutland	Fife and Tayside
Lincolnshire	Glasgow and West Central Scotland
Liverpool and Merseyside	Inverness and Moray
London	Lanarkshire
Greater Manchester	Scottish Borders
Norfolk	
Northamptonshire	**Northern Ireland**
Northumberland	County Antrim and County Londonderry
Nottinghamshire	
Oxfordshire	County Armagh and County Down
Shropshire	
Somerset	Belfast
Staffordshire	County Tyrone and County Fermanagh
Suffolk	

Philip's maps and atlases are available from bookshops, motorway services and petrol stations.

For further details visit
www.philips-maps.co.uk